Not For Tourists™ Guide to **LONDON**

**Get more on
notfortourists.com**

Keep connected with:

**Twitter:
twitter/notfortourists**

**Facebook:
facebook/notfortourists**

**iPhone App:
nftiphone.com**

www.notfortourists.com

Not For Tourists Inc

Published and designed by:
Not For Tourists, Inc.
NFT.—Not For Tourists. Guide to LONDON
www.notfortourists.com

NEW YORK STAFF
Publisher
Jane Pirone

Information Design
Jane Pirone
Rob Tallia
Scot Covey

Managing Editors
Rob Tallia
Craig Nelson

Production Manager
Aaron Schielke

Database Manager
Michael Dale

Cartography
Jonathan Levy
Nick Trotter

Research
Michael Dale
Susan Lee
Keely B. Hild
Zachary Wilson
John-Paul Anthony

Graphic Design & Production
Annika Koski
Aaron Schielke
Sarah Wyman

Sales & Marketing
Sarah Hocevar
Michael Salerno
Elina Salnikova
Cathy Vu

Information Systems Manager
Juan Molinari

Proofreader
Scott Sendrow

Director
Stuart Farr

LONDON STAFF
City Editor: Michael Kasparis
Restaurant Editor:
Julia Dennison
Shopping Editor:
Claire Storrow
Nightlife Editor:
Michael Kasparis
Parks Editor: Anne Seymour
Sports Editor:
Michael Kasparis
University Editor: Kate Atwell
Transport Editor:
Michael Kasparis
General Information Editor:
Julia Dennison
Arts Editor: Anne Seymour
Neighborhood Writer:
Niklas Vestberg

Maps derived from digital data © Collins Bartholomew Limited 2009.

Printed in China
ISBN# 978-0-9795339-7-6 $18.99 US / £9.99 UK
Copyright © 2010 by Not For Tourists, Inc.
3rd Edition

Every effort has been made to ensure that the information in this book is as up-to-date as possible at press time. However, many details are liable to change—as we have learned. The publishers cannot accept responsibility for any consequences arising from the use of this book.

Not For Tourists does not solicit individuals, organizations, or businesses for listings inclusion in our guides, nor do we accept payment for inclusion into the editorial portion of our book; the advertising sections, however, are exempt from this policy. We always welcome communications from anyone regarding ANYTHING having to do with our books; please visit us on our website at www.notfortourists.com for appropriate contact information.

Dear NFT User,

By the time you read this, dear reader, we Londoners could be buried under buildings collapsed from over-crowding, chained to trees in the Lea Valley to halt the 2012 Olympic bulldozers' greedy onward march, or simply be in a permanent state of ecstasy induced by our heroes' triumph in the World Cup. If we're being realistic, however, the overwhelming likelihood is that we'll be caught in an awful post-election lull, as whomever manages to worm their way into Downing Street will have such a small mandate they'll be powerless to do anything. We'll probably be looking for another England manager after crashing out disastrously in the first round in South Africa and, well, we'll just build some shiny new apartment blocks for our burgeoning urban spillage.

But before we hit the brick wall of fate, let's slow down and have a peek at the past. 2010 saw some major wound-licking in almost all aspects of London life. For a while there the sun was almost obscured by jumping stockbrokers. Then the news was bursting with stories of infrastructure meltdown, or freeze-up, or whatever, when London and all the other cities-in-the-UK-which-we-can't-name-off-the-top-of-our-heads literally froze. We built snowmen who caught swine-flu. We couldn't get to work. So we had fun instead! Yes, we are now in the depths of sunshine-filled economic recovery, our city has burst open like a ripe pomegranate, spilling forth succulent seeds of well, you get the picture. We've shopped, bopped, slopped, glugged, groped and sloped more than ever before, and we've discovered more of London than we thought possible.

In between engaging in these nefarious activities we've used our downtime well. Like pallid scribes in the basement corners of John Soane's house, we've hammered out a year's living into these very pages. All those shops we've ruined ourselves in, those gigs in new places we've got crushed in, all that food we can't pronounce—it's all been crammed (in an orderly, beautifully designed fashion) into your NFT Guide to London!

Yeah yeah, we can hear you there in the back, saying that no-one's perfect. And while you are wrong in this respect we'll play humble for the moment. Yes, we've managed to find aspects to improve in your latest NFT. New blurbs, updated and vastly expanded listings (we now have nearly 5,500 listings for you to peruse), new overviews and bettered maps. And yes, there are now quite a few independent coffee shop listings spattered around the map. Okay, so we're not that good at humble.

There's other ways to digest London's bounty too. 2009 saw the launch of our London iPhone App—an interactive, utterly indispensable lifetime partner for whenever times are hard or boring. Online at www.notfortourists.com you can delve deeper into our world with constantly updated reviews and bloggings for both London and some other two-bit towns you could go to if you ever—gasp—decided to leave the Big Smoke.

But you aren't going anywhere really, are you? No, for now you're snuggled in the warm embrace of your city with NFT at your side. You're enjoying the best years of your life and we're here to tell you how.

"London, giddy London—home of the brash, outrageous and free" (Morrissey)

All the best,

Michael, Jane, Rob & Craig

Underground Map and Bus Map
foldout, last page

Map 1 · **Marylebone (West)**

Road A501

Marylebone Road

A501

Marylebone

Edgware Road

Chapel Street

A501

Walmer Street

Circus M

Salisbury Pl

Bickenhall Street

76

Wyndham Street

Knox

Thornton Place

Street

Place

Homer Street

Cabbell Street

Edgware Road A5

Old Marylebone Road A501

Harcourt Street

Siddons Pl

York Street

York STREET

A41

Gloucester Place A41

Spring MS

Montagu Mansions

Durw

Bakerloo

MS

Watsons M

Crawford

Durweston Street

Upper Montagu

Junct Mews

Crawford Street

Street

Mews

Clay Street

Montagu Row

Marylebone A41

Shorbck

ssex Gardens A4209

Crawford Place

Homer Row

Stourman Street

Beverston Street

Wyndham M

Montagu Place

MS N

Dorset Street

Blandford

Quadrangle

Brendon Street

Cato Street

Molyneux Street

Bryanston Place

Montagu Place

Rodmanton

Quadrangle

Norfolk Cres/Burwood Pl

A

31

Harrowby Street

Bryanston Mews West

Bryanston Square

Montagu Square

Montagu Square

Gloucester Place A41

St.

Carlton St

Blandford

Cambridge Sq

Castlereagh St

Bryanston Square

Montagu Mews W

George Street

George Street

Norfolk Crescent

Brown Street

Seymour Place

Bryanston Mews E

Montagu Mews S

Park West Pl

Nutford Place

MARYLEBONE

Portman Close

rk Cres

Kendal Street

Park Street

Forset Street

George Street

Portman Close

Baker Street A41

Robe

Titchborne Row

Oxford Square

Kendal Street

Place

Clenston Mews

Montagu

Montagu Mews S

Portman Close

Baker

Porchester Place

Portsea Place

Stourcliffe Street

Wythburn Pl

Brunswick MS

Fitzha

Connaught Street

Portsea M

Upper Berkeley Street

Hampden

New Quebec St

Portman Square A41

Seymour

aught Close

St.Georges

Archery Close

Gurney Street

Great Cumberland Place

Quebec MS

Berkeley Mews

M

Albion Dr

Halls

Great

New Quebec St

Portman Square

Albion St

Georges Fields

Cumberland

Portman Square A41

Portman Square

Albion M.

Frederick

Seymour Street

Place

Albion Close

Cl

Bryanston

Quebec Street

Portman Mews South

Orchard Street

Edw

Bayswater Road A402

Connaught Place

Street

Bryanston Street

Portman

Granville

The (North Carriage Drive) Ring

Marble Arch A402

Great Cumberland

Street

Oxford Street A40

North Audley Street

Marble Arch

Tyburn Way

Marble Arch

Cumberland Gate A40

North Row

North Row

Speakers Corner

Park Lane A4202

Green

Street

Red Pl

North Audley Street

B

PAGE
342

Dunraven Street

Lees

PL

Providen

Hyde Park

Woods Mews

Park Street

Upper Brook Street

Gro

Park Lane A4202

Street

Blackburne's Mews

Brook Gate

A4202

Culross Street

9

Grosvenor Gate

Upper Grosvenor Street

Grosvenor

| 0.25 mile | 0.25 km |

Where the mullah meets the hookah, a stroll down Edgware Road is soundtracked by gurgling shisha pipes and bangin' Arabic pop music. To the east, ostentatiously bejewelled madams patrol Montague Square. They'd turn their noses up at a shawarma at Beirut Express on the way to the Sequoia Ruby Lo, and probably wouldn't deign to shop at Maroush Deli. Good, more for the rest of us.

Map 1

£ Banks

Abbey • 388 Edgware Rd
Barclays • 9 Portman St
Barclays • 93 Baker St
Barclays • 127 Edgware Rd
Halifax • 200 Edgware Rd
Halifax • 20 N Audley St
Lloyds • 195 Edgware Rd
NatWest • 508 Edgware Rd
NatWest • 81 Edgware Rd
NatWest • 69 Baker St
NatWest • 1 Portman Sq

Cinemas

Odeon Marble Arch • 10 Edgware Rd
Everyman Baker Street • 96 Baker St

Coffee

Apostrophe • 19 Baker St
Bagel Factory • 39 Paddington St
Caffe Nero • 184 Edgware Rd
Eat. • 400 Oxford St
Eat. • 114 Baker St
Kings Café • 177 Edgware Rd
Pret A Manger • 556 Oxford St
Starbucks • 29 N Audley St
Starbucks • 34 Edgware Rd

Landmarks

Marble Arch • Oxford St & Park Ln
Speakers' Corner • Cumberland Gate & Park Ln

Nightlife

Duke of York • 45 Harrowby St
Sequoia Ruby Lounge • 23 Orchard St

Post Offices

• **Baker St** • 111 Baker St
• **Edgware Rd** • 354 Edgware Rd

Restaurants

• **Beirut Express** • 112 Edgware Rd
• **Locanda Locatelli** • 8 Seymour St
• **Maroush IV** • 68 Edgware Rd
• **Nippon Tuk** • 225 Edgware Rd

Shopping

• **Maroush Deli** • 45 Edgware Rd
• **Phil Parker** • 106 Crawford St
• **Primark** • 499 Oxford St
• **Spymaster** • 3 Portman Sq
• **Totally Swedish** • 32 Crawford St

Supermarkets

• **Sainsbury's** • 55 Bryanston St

Map 2

Granted the plush boutiques and old moneyisms of Marylebone are far removed from most Londoners' lives but that's not to say you can't go window shopping, and with VV Rouleaux and the Button Queen nearby, you could even craft your own outfit. Don't forget to stop in at Claridge's to tell Gordon Ramsay to f*** off, then sedate yourself in the beautiful book haven that is Daunt.

£ Banks

Abbey • 14 Hanover Sq
Abbey • 27 Marylebone High St
Barclays • 8 Hanover St
Barclays • 5 Marylebone High St
Halifax • 5 Hanover St
Halifax • 116 Marylebone High St
HSBC • 90 Baker St
HSBC • 19 St George St
HSBC • 431 Oxford St
HSBC • 19 Marylebone High St
Lloyds • 399 Oxford St
Lloyds • 10 Hanover St
NatWest • 1 Cavendish Sq
NatWest • 10 Marylebone High St
Royal Bank of Scotland • 97 New Bond St
Royal Bank of Scotland • 28 Cavendish Sq

☕ Coffee

Apostrophe • 23 Barrett St
Caffe Nero • 273 Regent St
Caffe Nero • Marylebone Rd
Coffee Republic • 2 S Molton St
Costa • 69 Wigmore St
Eat. • 9 Avery Row
Eat. • 319 Regent St
Eat. • 25 Hanover Sq
Eat. • 92 Wimpole St
Eat. • 214 Oxford St
Paul Rothe & Son • 35 Marylebone Ln
Pret A Manger • 31 Cavendish
Pret A Manger • 1 Tenterden St
Pret A Manger • 18 Hanover St
Starbucks • 22 Princes St
Starbucks • 14 James St
Starbucks • 63 S Molton St

O Landmarks

Hertford House • Manchester Sq & Hinde St
Jimi Hendrix Memorial Blue Plaque • 23 Brook St

📖 Libraries

Royal College of Nursing Library • 20 Cavendish Sq

Y Nightlife

Claridge's Bar • 55 Brook St
Inn 1888 • 21 Devonshire St

Moors Bar • 57 Paddington St
The Phoenix • 37 Cavendish Sq

✉ Post Offices

Marylebone • 24 Thayer St

🍽 Restaurants

Comptoir Libanais • 65 Wigmore St
Diwan • 31 Thayer St
The Golden Hind • 73 Marylebone Ln
Galvin Bistrot de Luxe • 66 Baker St
Gordon Ramsay at Claridge's • Brook St
Hush Brasserie • 8 Lancashire Ct
La Galette • 56 Paddington St
No. 5 Cavendish Square • 5 Cavendish Sq
Patisserie Valerie • 105 Marylebone High St
The Providores • 109 Marylebone High St
Sakura • 9 Hanover St

🛍 Shopping

Browns South Molton Street • 24 S Molton St
The Button Queen • 76 Marylebone Ln
Content Beauty/Wellbeing • 14 Bulstrode Street
Daunt Books • 83 Marylebone High St
Divertimenti • 33 Marylebone High St
Duffer of St George • 268 Oxford St
Fenwick • 63 New Bond St
French Sole • 61 Marylebone Ln
Gray's Antique Market • 58 Davies St
John Lewis • 278 Oxford St
La Fromagerie • 2 Moxon St
Marimekko • 16 St Christopher's Pl
Monocle • 2 George St
Niketown • 236 Oxford St
Noa Noa • 14 Gees Ct
Paul Smith • 38 Marylebone High St
Paul Smith Sale Shop • 23 Avery Row
Romanian Charity Shop • 18 Fitzhardinge St
Selfridges & Co • 400 Oxford St
Skandium • 86 Marylebone High St
VV Rouleaux • 102 Marylebone Ln
The Widescreen Center • 47 Dorset St
Zara • 242 Oxford St

🛒 Supermarkets

Marks & Spencer • Bond St Station
Waitrose • 98 Marylebone High St

Map 3

...ke Sisyphus rolling his boulder up the hill, so can the traipse between Oxford ...ircus and Tottenham Court Road feel like a hellish condemnation. Sweeten your ...enom for the area with a cream puff at Beard Papa's and a visit to Pollock's Toy ...useum. Watch admen pissing their expense accounts up the wall at the Charlotte ...reet Hotel bar, making sure you're nearby for last orders. Then roll to Bradley's ...r after-hours seediness.

£ Banks

- **Abbey •** 165 Oxford St
- **Barclays •** 15 Great Portland St
- **Barclays •** 190 Tottenham Ct Rd
- **Halifax •** 60 Oxford St
- **Halifax •** 110 Tottenham Ct Rd
- **HSBC •** 39 Tottenham Ct Rd
- **HSBC •** 117 Great Portland St
- **HSBC •** 156 Tottenham Ct Rd
- **HSBC •** 196 Oxford St
- **Lloyds •** 190 Great Portland St
- **Lloyds •** 88 Tottenham Ct Rd
- **Lloyds •** 32 Oxford St
- **NatWest •** 125 Great Portland St
- **Royal Bank of Scotland •**
  171 Tottenham Ct Rd

Cinemas

- **Odeon Tottenham Court •**
  30 Tottenham Ct Rd

Coffee

- **Apostrophe •** 40 Great Castle St
- **Apostrophe •** 216 Tottenham Court Rd
- **BB's Coffee and Muffins •** 120 Oxford St
- **Caffe Nero •** 79 Tottenham Ct Rd
- **Caffe Nero •** 187 Tottenham Ct Rd
- **Caffe Nero •** 2 Charlotte St
- **Caffe Nero •** 48 Oxford St
- **Coffee Republic •** 99 Tottenham Ct Rd
- **Eat. •** 44 Goodge St
- **Eat. •** 68 Oxford St
- **Eat. •** 94 Tottenham Ct Rd
- **Kaffeine •** 66 Great Titchfield St
- **Lantana •** 13 Charlotte Pl
- **Pret A Manger •** 298 Regent St
- **Starbucks •** 203 Oxford St
- **Starbucks •** 51 Goodge St

Landmarks

- **BT Tower •** 60 Cleveland St
- **Charlotte Street •** Charlotte St
- **Middlesex Hospital •**
  Mortimer St & Cleveland St
- **Pollock's Toy Museum •** 1 Scala St
- **Sinner Winner Man •** 216 Oxford St
- **Tottenham Court Road •**
  Tottenham Ct Rd

Libraries

- **RIBA British Architectural Library •**
  66 Portland Pl
- **Institute of Contemporary History and
  Wiener Library •** 4 Devonshire St
- **Royal Institute of British Architects •**
  66 Portland Pl

Nightlife

- **100 Club •** 100 Oxford St
- **The Albany •** 240 Great Portland St
- **Bourne & Hollingsworth •**
  28 Rathbone Pl
- **Bradleys Spanish Bar •** 42 Hanway St
- **Bricklayers Arms •** 31 Gresse St
- **Charlotte Street Hotel •** 15 Charlotte St
- **The Cock •** 27 Great Portland St
- **The Fitzroy Tavern •** 16 Charlotte St
- **The Jerusalem Tavern •** 55 Britton St
- **Market Place •** 11 Market Pl
- **Northumberland Arms •** 43 Goodge St
- **Punk •** 14 Soho St
- **The Rising Sun •** 46 Tottenham Ct Rd
- **The Roxy •** 3 Rathbone Pl
- **The Social •** 5 Little Portland St
- **The Yorkshire Grey •** 46 Langham St

Post Offices

- **Great Portland St •** 55 Great Portland St
- **Newman St •** 19 Newman St
- **Oxford Street •** 120 Oxford St

Restaurants

- **Archipelago •** 110 Whitfield St
- **Ask •** 48 Grafton Way
- **Beard Papa •** 143 Oxford St
- **Carluccio's •** 8 Market Pl
- **Chutney & Lager •** 43 Great Titchfield St
- **Crazy Bear •** 26 Whitfield St
- **Eagle Bar Diner •** 3 Rathbone Pl
- **Elena's L'Etoile •** 30 Charlotte St
- **Govinda's •** 9 Soho St
- **Icco Pizza •** 46 Goodge St
- **Latium •** 21 Berners St
- **Market Place •** 11 Market Pl
- **Navarro's •** 67 Charlotte St
- **Ragam •** 57 Cleveland St
- **Rasa Express •** 5 Rathbone St
- **Roka •** 37 Charlotte St
- **Salt Yard •** 54 Goodge St
- **Sardo •** 45 Grafton Way
- **Squat & Gobble •** 69 Charlotte St
- **Stef's •** 3 Berners St
- **Thai Metro •** 36 Charlotte St

Shopping

- **Computer Exchange •** 32 Rathbone Pl
- **Chess & Bridge •** 369 Euston Rd
- **Harmony •** 103 Oxford St
- **Hobgoblin Shop •** 24 Rathbone Pl
- **Mango •** 225 Oxford St
- **Maplin •** 218 Tottenham Ct Rd
- **Paperchase •** 213 Tottenham Ct Rd
- **R.D. Franks •** 5 Winsley St
- **Scandinavian Kitchen •**
  61 Great Titchfield St
- **Stargreen Box Office •** 20 Argyll St
- **Topshop •** 36 Great Castle Street
- **Topshop •** 216 Oxford St
- **Urban Outfitters •** 200 Oxford St

Supermarkets

- **Marks & Spencer •** 55 Tottenham Ct Rd
- **Sainsbury's •** 35 Mortimer St
- **Sainsbury's •** 17 Tottenham Ct Rd
- **Sainsbury's •** 145 Tottenham Ct Rd
- **Tesco •** 10 Goodge St

Map 4

bloomsbury offers a chaotic throng of academics, belligerent tourists and scientologists. The Virginia Woolf Effect is in its leafy squares, UCL, and the British Museum (blue plaques galore!). Go posh bowling (All Star Lanes), booze at a victoria gin palace (Princess Louise) and marvel at Britain's colonial loot at the British Museum. Should the heavens open, head to James Smith & Sons for a delightful range of brollies.

Banks

Barclays • 58 Southampton Row
Barclays • 73 Russell Sq
Co-Operative • 64 Southampton Row
HSBC • 210 High Holborn
HSBC • 1 Woburn Pl
Lloyds • Southampton Row
Royal Bank of Scotland • High Holborn

Cinemas

Horse Hospital • 30 Colonnade
Odeon Tottenham Court • 30 Tottenham Ct Rd

Coffee

Café Deco • 43 Store St
Costa • 44 New Oxford St
Costa • 82 Gower St
London Review Cake Shop • 14 Bury Pl
Pret A Manger • 40 Bernard St
Pret A Manger • 23 Southampton Row
Pret A Manger • 44 New Oxford St
Pret A Manger • 102 Southampton Row
Ruskins Cafe • 41 Museum St
Starbucks • 124 Southampton Row
Starbucks • 112 New Oxford
Starbucks • 425 Oxford St

Emergency Rooms

University College Hospital • 235 Euston Rd

Landmarks

The British Museum • Great Russell St & Museum St
Centre Point • 101 New Oxford St
Kingsway Tram Tunnel • Theobalds Rd & Southampton Row
Senate House • Malet St & Torrington Sq
Tavistock Square • Tavistock Sq

Libraries

Anthropology Library • Great Russell St
Birkbeck College Library • Malet St
German Historical Institute Library London •
17 Bloomsbury Sq
Institute of Advanced Legal Studies Library •
17 Russell Square
University of London, Senate House Library •
Malet St

Nightlife

All Star Lanes • Victoria House, Bloomsbury Pl
Bloomsbury Bowling Lanes • Bedford Way
The Fly • 36 New Oxford
Marquis of Cornwallis • 31 Marchmont St
Old Crown • 33 New Oxford St
The Plough • 27 Museum St
Point 101 • 101 New Oxford St
The Princess Louise • 208 High Holborn
ULU • 1 Malet St

Post Offices

Marchmont St • 33 Marchmont St
Russell Square • 9 Russell Sq

Restaurants

Alara • 58 Marchmont St
Bi Won • 24 Coptic St
Savoir Faire • 42 New Oxford St

Shopping

Blade Rubber Stamps Ltd • 12 Bury Pl
British Museum shop • Great Russell St
Cinema Bookshop • 13 Great Russell St
Gosh! Comics • 39 Great Russell St
James Smith & Sons • 53 New Oxford St
London Review Bookshop • 14 Bury Pl
Maplin • 218 Tottenham Ct Rd
Paperchase • 213 Tottenham Ct Rd
Shepherds Bookbinders • 76 Southampton Row
York Cameras • 18 Bury Pl

Supermarkets

Waitrose • Brunswick Sq

Map 5

gog with students, this tract of Bloomsbury is a bustling cultural playground. he brilliant Renoir Cinema resides in the belly of the Brunswick Centre, a Brutalist asterpiece with some posh shops thrown in for good measure. For contrast, stroll ver to Lamb's Conduit Street and enjoy some boutique shopping. Indulge in a it-down cream tea at Bea's or fill up on pizza slices at Malletti.

💷 Banks

Lloyds • 344 Gray's Inn Rd

🎭 Cinemas

Renoir Cinema • 1 Brunswick Sq

☕ Coffee

Pret A Manger • 15 Theobald's Rd
Starbucks • 57 Theobald's Rd
T-HQ • 55 Gray's Inn Rd

🏛 Landmarks

The Dickens House Museum • 48 Doughty St
Gray's Inn Field • Theobald's Rd
Doughty Street • Doughty St & Guilford St

📖 Libraries

Holborn Library • 32 Theobald's Rd
Royal National Institute of the Blind
  Research Library • 105 Judd St
St Pancras Library • Argyle St

🍸 Nightlife

06 St Chad's Place • 6 St Chad's Pl
The Blue Lion • 133 Gray's Inn Rd
Calthorpe Arms • 252 Gray's Inn Rd
Duke of York • 156 Clerkenwell Rd
King's Cross Social Club • 2 Brittania Street
Monto Water Rats • 328 Gray's Inn Rd
The Perseverance • 63 Lamb's Conduit St
Smithy's • 15 Leeke St

✉ Post Offices

• Mount Pleasant • Farringdon Rd & Rosebery Ave

🍴 Restaurants

• Acorn House • 69 Swinton St
• Aki Bistro • 182 Gray's Inn Rd
• Beas of Bloomsbury • 44 Theobald's Rd
• Bread and Butter Sandwich Bar • 100 Judd St
• Ciao Bella • 86 Lamb's Conduit St
• Cigala • 54 Lamb's Conduit St
• The Food Bazaar • 59 Gray's Inn Rd
• Fryer's Delight • 19 Theobald's Rd
• Konstam • 2 Acton St
• La Provence • 63 Gray's Inn Rd
• Malletti • 174 Clerkenwell Rd
• Mary Ward Centre • 42 Queen Sq
• Paolina Thai Snack Bar • 181 King's Cross Rd
• The Perseverance • 63 Lamb's Conduit St
• Swintons • 61 Swinton St
• Thai Candle • 38 Lamb's Conduit St

🛍 Shopping

• Bibas Hair and Beauty • 72 Marchmont St
• Brunswick Centre • Hunter St
• The Flash Centre • 68 Marchmont St
• Folk • 49 Lamb's Conduit St
• International Magic • 89 Clerkenwell Rd
• Joy • Brunswick Centre
• Magma Concept Store • 117 Clerkenwell Rd
• Something • 58 Lamb's Conduit St

Clerkenwell is London's own little village where one can get lost in the maze-like alleyways. At its heart is Clerkenwell Green, an old-time square that pops up in Dickens, but most of the action takes place around Exmouth Market nowadays. Sup up a pint on the pavement at the packed out Wilmington Arms, play some babyfoot at KICK!, then get inked with your new-found random drinking buddy at either London Tattoo or The Family Business.

Libraries

Finsbury Library • 245 St John St
Marx Memorial Library • 37 Clerkenwell Green

Nightlife

Bandstand Busking • Northampton Square
The Betsey Trotwood • 56 Farringdon Rd
The Boadicea • 292 St John St
Café Kick • 43 Exmouth Market
Cicada • 132 St John St
Dollar Grills and Martinis • 2 Exmouth Market
The Dovetail • 9 Jerusalem Passage
Filthy McNasty's • 68 Amwell St
The Harlequin • 27 Arlington Way
Old Red Lion • 418 St John St
The Slaughtered Lamb • 34 Great Sutton St
The Three Kings • 7 Clerkenwell Close
Wilmington Arms • 69 Rosebery Ave

Restaurants

Bada Bing! • 120 St John St
Clarks Pie and Mash • 46 Exmouth Market
Dans Le Noir • 30 Clerkenwell Green
The Eagle • 159 Farringdon Rd
Little Bay • 171 Farringdon Rd
Moro • 34 Exmouth Market
The Quality Chop House • 94 Farringdon Rd
Sandwichman • 23 Easton St

Shopping

• The Black Tulip • 28 Exmouth Market
• Bobbin Bicycles • 397 St John St
• Covet • 21 Arlington Way
• EC One Jewellery • 41 Exmouth Market
• The Family Business Tattoo Shop • 58 Exmouth Market
• London Tattoo • 332 Goswell Rd
• M and R Meats • 399 St John St
• Metro Imaging Ltd • 32 Great Sutton St
• Timorous Beasties • 46 Amwell St
• Wyvern Bindery • 56 Clerkenwell Rd

Supermarkets

• Waitrose • Aylesbury St & St John St

Barbican / City Road (South)

Map 7

ou may feel like an extra from Blade Runner weaving through the towering oncrete, but this busy area is ringing with history. The Nazis flattened the place, aving St Giles' Cripplegate Church standing alone in the Barbican's shadow. t the estate's lake and events are a cultural oasis, while Ironmonger Row Baths ovide manna for weary souls. Pick up a soup at NUSA and find stillness in St uke's Gardens.

Banks

Barclays • 128 Moorgate
HSBC • 74 Goswell Rd
Lloyds • 69 St

Cinemas

Barbican Centre Cinema • Silk St & Whitecross St

Coffee

Caffe Nero • 40 City Rd
Coffee Republic • City Rd
Costa • 68 Goswell Rd
Costa • Ropemaker St
Eat. • 143 Moorgate
Pitch 42 • Whitecross St Market
Popular Cafe • 85 Lever St
Pret A Manger • 9 Goswell Rd
Pret A Manger • Ropemaker St

Landmarks

Barbican Centre • Silk St & Whitecross St
Bunhill Fields • 38 City Rd
Church of St Bartholomew the Great • 6 Kinghorn St
LSO St Luke's • 161 Old St
St. Giles • Fore St & Wood St

Libraries

Barbican Library • Silk St
Wandsworth Town Library • 11 Garrett St

Post Offices

Old Street • 205 Old St

Restaurants

• **Bavarian Beerhouse** • 190 City Rd
• **Carnevale** • 135 Whitecross St
• **De Santis** • 11 Old St
• **NUSA Kitchen** • 9 Old St

Shopping

• **Bread & Honey** • 205 Whitecross St

Supermarkets

• **Waitrose** • Whitecross St

Liverpool Street / Broadgate

Map 8

grimy maw that spews trendos onto Bishopsgate, Liverpool Street is the gateway
the nowness of Brick Lane and Shoreditch. Its arse-end lets out suits and money
to the borders of the City. Avoid a 'flash-mob' in the Light after a grease-up in
amascu Bite, but c'mon, you know you're really on your way to an all night rave
Stokey so cut the crap and get on the 149.

£ Banks

- **Abbey** • 59 London Wall
- **Abbey** • 224 Bishopsgate
- **Barclays** • 128 Moorgate
- **Halifax** • 136 Bishopsgate
- **HSBC** • 1 South Pl
- **Lloyds** • 109 Finsbury Pavement
- **NatWest** • 94 Moorgate

Coffee

- **AMT** • Liverpool St & Broadgate Circle
- **Benugo** • 82 City Rd
- **Caffe Nero** • 2 Bishopsgate
- **Caffe Nero** • 40 City Rd
- **Caffe Nero** • 75 London Wall
- **Costa** • 1 Ropemaker St
- **Costa** • 18 Liverpool St
- **Eat.** • 1 City Rd
- **Eat.** • 143 Moorgate
- **Eat.** • 176 Bishopsgate
- **Eat.** • 34 Broadgate Circle
- **Eat.** • 62 London Wall
- **Eat.** • 80 Old Broad St
- **Fab Food Patisserie** • 26 Curtain Rd
- **Starbucks** • Liverpool St Station
- **Starbucks** • 8 Charterhouse Buildings
- **Starbucks** • 28 Broadgate Circle

Landmarks

- **Fulcrum at Broadgate** • Broadgate

Libraries

- **Bishopsgate Library** • 230 Bishopsgate

Nightlife

- **The Light** • 233 Shoreditch High St
- **Lounge Bohemia** • 1 Great Eastern St
- **The Red Lion** • 1 Eldon St
- **Sosho** • 2 Tabernacle Street

Restaurants

- **Damascu Bite Kebab** • 21 Shoreditch High St
- **Eyre Brothers** • 70 Leonard St
- **Gaucho Broadgate** • 5 Finsbury Ave
- **Ponti's Caffe** • 176 Bishopsgate

Supermarkets

- **Tesco** • 158 Bishopsgate

Map 9

Monopoly you can buy both Mayfair and Park Lane, build hotels, and end up ally screwing everyone else. In reality you may struggle to afford a t-shirt here at if you can, try APC or Marc Jacobs. Still got change? Then empty the rest of ur pockets at the Ritz for afternoon tea. Stake out Mahiki to freak out some minor als or test security at the Palace to freak out some major ones.

Banks

- **Barclays** • 11 Bruton St
- **Halifax** • 51 Berkeley St
- **HSBC** • 18 Curzon St
- **HSBC** • 79 Piccadilly
- **Lloyds** • 14 Berkeley Sq
- **Lloyds** • 50 Grosvenor St
- **NatWest** • 4 Berkeley Sq
- **NatWest** • 94 Moorgate
- **Royal Bank of Scotland** • 43 Curzon St
- **Royal Bank of Scotland** • 24 Grosvenor Pl

Cinemas

- **Curzon Mayfair** • 38 Curzon St

Coffee

- **Apostrophe** • 10 Grosvenor St
- **Caffe Nero** • 50 Curzon St
- **Caffe Nero** • 70 Piccadilly
- **Costa** • 9 Eldon St
- **Eat.** • 8 Berkeley Sq
- **Eat.** • 55 Stratton St
- **Starbucks** • 52 Berkeley St
- **Starbucks** • 84 Piccadilly

Landmarks

- **50 Berkeley Square** • 50 Berkeley Sq
- **Apsley House** • 149 Piccadilly
- **Buckingham Palace** • The Mall
- **Down Street Station** • Down St & Piccadily

Libraries

- **Mayfair Library** • 25 South Audley St
- **Royal Society of Chemistry Library and Information Centre** • Piccadilly

Nightlife

- **1707 Wine Bar** • 181 Piccadilly
- **bbar** • 43 Buckingham Palace Rd
- **Funky Buddah** • 15 Berkeley St
- **Mahiki** • 1 Dover St
- **Shepherd's Tavern** • 50 Hertford St

Post Offices

- **Albemarle St** • 44 Albemarle St
- **Mayfair** • 32 Grosvenor St

Restaurants

- **Alain Ducasse at The Dorchester** • Park Ln
- **El Pirata of Mayfair** • 5 Down St
- **The English Tea Room at Browns** • Albemarle St
- **Galvin at Windows** • 28th Floor, Hilton Park Lane
- **Kiplings** • 2 Hill St
- **L'Autre** • 5 Shepherd St
- **Nobu** • 19 Old Park Ln
- **The Ritz** • 150 Piccadilly
- **Theo Randall at the InterContinental** • 1 Hamilton Pl
- **The Wolseley** • 160 Piccadilly

Shopping

- **APC** • 35 Dover St
- **Diane Von Furstenberg** • 25 Bruton St
- **Dover Street Market** • 17 Dover St
- **Green Valley** • Berkeley St
- **Marc Jacobs** • 24 Mount St
- **Matthew Williamson** • 28 Bruton St
- **Stella McCartney** • 30 Bruton St

Supermarkets

- **Marks & Spencer** • 78 Piccadilly
- **Sainsbury's** • 38 Stratton St

Map 10

rget visions of Austin Powers "yeah baby" grooviness, Carnaby Street is a slick udy in consumerism with all major streetwear labels present, but the grand dame department stores, Liberty, retains top marks for a unique shopping experience. ve a coffee in Sacred if you can find a seat or else retreat to the John Snow r a cheeky pint. The real John Snow can occasionally be spotted in Flat White Map 11).

Banks

- bbey • 34 Piccadilly
- arclays • 48 Regent St
- HSBC • 133 Regent St
- loyds • 39 Picadilly
- atWest • 208 Piccadilly Circus
- atWest • 250 Regent St
- oyal Bank of Scotland • 60 Conduit St

Coffee

- affe Nero • 62 Brewer St
- affe Nero • 26 Piccadilly
- affe Nero • 225 Regent St
- osta • 11 Argyll St
- at. • 19 Golden Sq
- at. • 8 Vigo St
- ernandez & Wells • 73 Beak St
- Pret A Manger • 298 Regent St
- Pret A Manger • 27 Great Marlborough
- Sacred Cafe • 13 Ganton St
- Starbucks • 16 Lexington St
- Starbucks • 171 Picadilly

Landmarks

- Burlington Arcade • Burlington Arcade & Piccadilly
- Carnaby Street • Carnaby St
- Kingly Court • Kingly St & Foubert's Pl
- Statue of Eros • Piccadilly Circus

Nightlife

- 22 Below • 22 Great Marlborough St
- 5th View • 203 Piccadilly
- Ain't Nothing But The Blues Bar • 20 Kingly St
- Beyond Retro • 58 Great Marlborough St
- Cheers Bar • 72 Regent St
- Courthouse Bar • 19 Great Marlborough St
- John Snow • 39 Broadwick St
- Milk & Honey • 61 Poland St
- The Pigalle Club • 215 Piccadilly
- Red • 5 Kingly St
- Strawberry Moons • 15 Heddon St

Restaurants

- Atlantic Bar & Grill • 20 Glasshouse St
- Bob Bob Ricard • 1 Upper James St
- Cecconi's • 5 Burlington Gardens
- Cha Cha Moon • 15 Ganton St
- Chowki • 2 Denman St
- Dehesa • 25 Ganton St
- Fernandez and Wells Coffee Bar • 73 Beak St
- Kulu Kulu • 76 Brewer St
- Le Pain Quotidien • 18 Great Marlborough St
- Mildred's • 45 Lexington St
- Mosaico • 13 Albermale St
- Nordic Bakery • 14 Golden Sq
- The Photographers' Gallery • 16 Ramillies St
- Ping Pong • 45 Great Marlborough St
- Pure California • 39 Beak St
- Sartoria • 20 Saville Row
- Sketch • 9 Conduit St
- Taro • 61 Brewer St
- Ten Ten Tei • 56 Brewer St
- Tentazioni Restaurant • 2 Mill St
- Thanks for Franks • 26 Fouberts Pl
- Tibits • 12 Heddon St
- Toku @ The Japan Centre • 212 Piccadilly
- Wagamama • 10 Lexington St
- Wild Honey • 12 St George St
- Yauatcha • 15 Broadwick St
- Yoshino • 3 Piccadilly Pl

Shopping

- Abercrombie & Fitch • 7 Burlington Gardens
- Anthropologie • 158 Regent St
- American Apparel • 3 Carnaby St
- Apple Store • 235 Regent Street
- Arigato • 48 Brewer St
- b store • 24 Savile Row
- Banana Republic • 224 Regent St
- Behave • 48 Lexington Sreet
- Beyond Retro Soho • 58 Great Marlborough St
- The Black Pearl • 10 Kingly Ct
- Burlington Arcade • Burlington Arcade
- Cos • 222 Regent St
- The European Bookshop • 5 Warwick St
- Fortnum and Mason • 181 Piccadilly
- Freggo • 27 Swallow St
- Georgina Goodman • 44 Old Bond St
- Hamley's • 188 Regent St
- Hatchard's • 187 Piccadilly
- Hoss Intropia • 211 Regent St
- Lazy Oaf • 19 Fouberts Place
- Liberty • 214 Regent St
- Lillywhites • 24 Lower Regent St
- Lucky Voice • 52 Poland St
- Mrs Kibble's Olde Sweet Shoppe • 57 Brewer St
- Muji • 41 Carnaby St
- Phonica • 51 Poland St
- Playlounge • 19 Beak St
- Richard James • 29 Savile Row
- Rigby & Peller • 22 Conduit St
- SKK (Lighting) • 34 Lexington St
- Twinkled • 1 Kingly Ct
- Twosee • 21 Fouberts
- The Vintage Magazine Shop • 39 Brewer St
- Whole Foods Market • 69 Brewer St

Supermarkets

- Fresh & Wild • 73 Brewer St
- Whole Foods Market • 69 Brewer St

Map 1

y day the turning out of London's new favourite caffeine kick—the flat white courtesy of the Aussies—is relentless at LJ and Milk Bar. All the better to fuel the ight's activities: this is still the heart of the red light district, but it's no longer a sordid affair. Berwick Street is still loved for its record shops and market, and ncredible Gaga-esque latex dresses can be found in Paradiso.

£ Banks

- **HSBC** • 17 Gerrard St
- **NatWest** • 20 Dean St

Cinemas

- **Cineworld Shaftesbury Avenue** • 13 Coventry St
- **Curzon Soho** • 99 Shaftesbury Ave
- **Empire Leicester Square** • 5 Leicester Square
- **Prince Charles Cinema** • 7 Leicester Pl

Coffee

- **Coffee Republic** • 7 Coventry St
- **Coffee Republic** • 38 Berwick St
- **Costa** • 62 Shaftesbury Ave
- **Fernandez & Wells Espresso Bar** • 16 St Anne's Ct
- **LJ Coffee House** • 3 Winnett St
- **Milk Bar** • 3 Bateman St
- **Prince Charles Cinema** • 7 Leicester Pl
- **Starbucks** • 60 Wardour St

O Landmarks

- **Huge Tree In Pub (Waxy O'Connor's)** • 14 Rupert St
- **Berwick Street Market** • Berwick St & Rupert St
- **John Snow Water Pump** • Broadwick Street

Nightlife

- **Blue Posts** • 22 Berwick St
- **The Blue Posts** • 28 Rupert St
- **Candy Bar** • 4 Carlisle St
- **The Comedy Store** • 1 Oxendon St
- **De Hems** • 11 Macclesfield St
- **The Endurance** • 90 Berwick St
- **Freedom** • 66 Wardour St
- **The French House** • 49 Dean St
- **LVPO** • 50 Dean St
- **Madame Jojo's** • 8 Brewer St
- **Shadow Lounge** • 5 Brewer St
- **Village** • 81 Wardour St

Restaurants

- **Balans** • 60 Old Compton St
- **Bar Bruno** • 101 Wardour St
- **Beetroot** • 92 Berwick St
- **Bocca di Lupo** • 12 Archer St
- **Busaba Eathai** • 110 Wardour St
- **Cafe Espana** • 63 Old Compton St
- **Grace** • 42 Great Windmill St
- **Hummus Bros** • 88 Wardour St
- **Imli** • 167 Wardour St
- **Italian Graffiti** • 163 Wardour St
- **Leong's Legends** • 4 Macclesfield St
- **Jerk City** • 189 Wardour St
- **Melati** • 30 Peter St
- **Malletti** • 26 Noel St
- **Maoz** • 43 Old Compton St
- **Paul** • 49 Old Compton St
- **Pizza Express Jazz Club** • 10 Dean St
- **Randall & Aubin** • 16 Brewer St
- **Red Veg** • 95 Dean St
- **Snog** • 9 Brewer St
- **Soho Thai** • 27 St. Annes Ct
- **St Moritz** • 161 Wardour St
- **Won Kei** • 41 Wardour St
- **Yoshino Delicatessen** • 59 Shaftesbury Ave

Shopping

- **Algerian Coffee Store** • 52 Old Compton St
- **American Retro** • 35 Old Compton St
- **Bang Bang** • 9 Berwick St
- **Calumet Trading** • 175 Wardour St
- **Chappel of Bond Street** • 152 Wardour St
- **Cheapo Cheapo Records** • 53 Rupert St
- **Cowling & Wilcox** • 26 Broadwick St
- **Gerry's** • 74 Old Compton St
- **I Camisa & Son** • 61 Old Compton St
- **Paradiso Boudoir** • 60 Dean St
- **Revival Records** • 30 Berwick St
- **Sister Ray** • 34 Berwick St
- **Snog** • 9 Brewer St
- **Sounds of the Universe** • 7 Broadwick St
- **Vinyl Junkies** • 94 Berwick St

Map 1

...can be difficult containing one's enthusiasm for London while listening to music
at classic club Ronnie Scott's, or gorging on pastries at Maison Bertaux. Between
another blast of poppers at G-A-Y and shredding on Denmark Street you might
notice that greedy landlordism has forced many independent businesses to shut
down (bye bye Shipley's Books). Hopefully the recession will curb the tide of
development...

Banks

- **Barclays** • 27 Soho Sq
- **Barclays** • 25 Charing Cross
- **HSBC** • 138 Shaftesbury Ave
- **Royal Bank of Scotland** • 49 Charing Cross Rd

Cinemas

- **Vue West End Cinema** • 3 Cranbourn St

Coffee

- **Caffe Nero** • 32 Cranbourn St
- **Caffe Nero** • 43 Frith St
- **Caffe Nero** • 155 Charing Cross Rd
- **Eat.** • 16 Soho Sq
- **Eat.** • 155 Charing Cross Rd
- **First Out Cafe Bar** • 52 St Giles High St
- **Foyles** • 113 Charing Cross Rd
- **Maison Bertaux** • 28 Greek St

Landmarks

- **Denmark Street** • Denmark St
- **FA Headquarters** • 25 Soho Sq
- **Old Compton Street** • Old Compton St
- **The Phoenix Garden** • 21 Stacey St
- **Soho Square** • Soho Sq

Nightlife

- **12 Bar Club** • 22 Denmark St
- **Cafe Boheme** • 13 Old Compton St
- **The Borderline** • 16 Manette St
- **Comptons** • 53 Old Compton St
- **Crobar** • 17 Manette St
- **G-A-Y Bar** • 30 Old Compton St
- **G-A-Y Late** • 5 Goslett Yard
- **Garlic & Shots** • 14 Frith St
- **Green Carnation** • 5 Greek St
- **Jazz After Dark** • 9 Greek St
- **Karaoke Box** • 18 Frith St
- **Ku Bar** • 30 Lisle St
- **Lab 12** • Old Compton St
- **Montagu Pyke** • 105 Charing Cross Rd
- **Ronnie Scott's Jazz Club** • 47 Frith St
- **The Royal George** • 133 Charing Cross Rd
- **The Toucan** • 19 Carlisle St

Restaurants

- **Abeno Too** • 17 Great Newport St
- **Arbutus** • 63 Frith St
- **Assa** • 53 St Giles High St
- **Bar Italia** • 22 Frith St
- **Barrafina** • 54 Frith St
- **Bincho Soho** • 16 Old Compton St
- **Boheme Kitchen and Bar** • 19 Old Compton St
- **Café Emm** • 17 Frith St
- **Chinese Experience** • 118 Shaftesbury Ave
- **Corean Chilli** • 51 Charing Cross Rd
- **Ed's Easy Diner** • 12 Moor St
- **Friendly Inn** • 47 Gerrard St
- **Gaby's** • 30 Charing Cross Rd
- **Garlic & Shots** • 14 Frith St
- **Gay Hussar** • 2 Greek St
- **Haozhan** • 8 Gerrard St
- **Kettners** • 29 Romilly St
- **La Porchetta Pollo Bar** • 20 Old Compton St
- **Le Beaujolais** • 25 Litchfield St
- **Maison Bertaux** • 27 Greek St
- **Malaysia Kopi Tiam** • 67 Charing Cross Rd
- **New World** • 1 Gerrard Pl
- **Stockpot** • 18 Old Compton St
- **Taro** • 10 Old Compton St

Shopping

- **Angels** • 119 Shaftesbury Ave
- **Fopp** • 1 Earlham St
- **Forbidden Planet** • 179 Shaftesbury Ave
- **Harmony** • 167 Charing Cross Rd
- **Julienne & Porselli** • 9 West St
- **Kokon to Zai** • 57 Greek St
- **Macaris** • 92 Charing Cross Rd
- **Magma** • 8 Earlham St
- **Maison Bertaux** • 27 Greek St
- **Ray's Jazz** • 113 Charing Cross Rd
- **Rockers** • 5 Denmark St
- **Turnkey** • 114 Charing Cross Rd
- **Wunjo Guitars** • 20 Denmark St

31

Covent Garden

Map 13

Covent Garden is a shopper's delight, especially on Endell Street and Neal Street. However, such activity will not offer a respite from the Piazza and its hordes of spatially unaware folk. Stop for fish and chips at Rock & Sole Plaice followed by gelato at Scoop. Come the evening, sip cocktails at Freud or convene with the ghost of Bernard Shaw at the Lamb & Flag.

£ Banks

- **Abbey** • 36 King St

Coffee

- **AMT** • 14 Neal St
- **Bagel Factory** • 18 Endell St
- **Café Metro** • 33 Catherine St
- **Caffe Nero** • 30 Monmouth St
- **Caffe Nero** • 83 Long Acre
- **Coffee, Cake & Kink** • 61 Endell St
- **Pret A Manger** • 65 Long Acre
- **Starbucks** • 10 Russell St
- **Starbucks** • 55 Long Acre

Landmarks

- **Oasis Lido** • 32 Endell St
- **Seven Dials** • Upper St Martin's Ln & Earlham St

Nightlife

- **AKA** • 18 W Central St
- **Bunker** • 41 Earlham St
- **The Cross Keys** • 31 Endell St
- **The End** • 18 W Central St
- **Freud** • 198 Shaftesbury Ave
- **Guanabara** • Parker St
- **Lamb & Flag** • 33 Rose St
- **Octave** • 27 Endell St
- **Poetry Society Cafe** • 22 Betterton St

Post Offices

- **High Holborn** • 181 High Holborn

Restaurants

- **Battersea Pie Station** • Covent Garden Piazza
- **Belgo Centraal** • 29 Shelton St
- **Café Mode** • 57 Endell St
- **Candy Cakes** • 36 Monmouth St
- **Food for Thought** • 31 Neal St
- **Great Queen Street** • 32 Great Queen St
- **Kulu Kulu** • 51 Shelton St
- **Mon Plaisir** • 21 Monmouth St
- **The Punjab** • 80 Neal St
- **Rock & Sole Plaice** • 47 Endell St
- **Sarastro** • 126 Drury Ln
- **Souk Medina** • 1 Shorts Gardens

Shopping

- **Artbox** • 29 Earlham St
- **The Astrology Shop** • 78 Neal St
- **The Bead Shop** • 21 Tower St
- **Ben's Cookies** • 13 The Piazza
- **Blackout II** • 51 Endell St
- **Cath Kidston** • 28 Shelton St
- **Coco de Mer** • 23 Monmouth St
- **Cyber Candy** • 3 Garrick St
- **David and Goliath** • 4 The Market Pl
- **Hope and Greenwood** • 1 Russell St
- **Kiehls** • 29 Monmouth St
- **Koh Samui** • 65 Monmouth St
- **Libidex at Liberation** • 49 Shelton St
- **The Loft** • 35 Monmouth St
- **London Graphic Centre** • 16 Shelton St
- **Miss Lala's Boudoir** • 18 Monmouth St
- **Neal's Yard Dairy** • 17 Shorts Gardens
- **Nigel Hall** • 18 Floral St
- **Octopus** • 54 Neal St
- **Orla Kiely** • 31 Monmouth St
- **Poetry Cafe** • 22 Betterton St
- **Pop Boutique** • 6 Monmouth St
- **Rokit** • 42 Shelton St
- **Rossopomodoro** • 50 Monmouth Street
- **Scoop** • 40 Shorts Gardens
- **Screenface** • 48 Monmouth St
- **Slam City Skates** • 16 Neal's Yard
- **Stanford's** • 12 Long Acre
- **Superdry** • 24 Earlham St (Thomas Neal Centre)
- **Tabio** • 66 Neal St
- **Urban Outfitters** • 42 Earlham St

Supermarkets

- **Sainsbury's** • 129 Kingsway

Holborn / Temple

An essential cog in London's machine, this area is resplendent with curios (Old Curiosity Shop, Sweeney Todd's), public squares full of depressed lawyers and legions of serious-looking people being integrated into The System. The ghosts of Londons past hover around Temple and the Strand, where you'll also find Aldwych film for brunch and a flick. 50 types of vodka-shaped escapism can be found at Na Zdrowie.

Map 14

Banks

- Abbey • 10 Leather Ln
- Abbey • 306 High Holborn
- Barclays • 99 Hatton Garden
- Barclays • 147 Holborn
- Barclays • 19 Fleet St
- HSBC • 31 High Holborn
- Lloyds • 6 Holborn Circus
- Lloyds • 296 High Holborn
- NatWest • 65 Aldwych
- NatWest • 214 High Holborn
- NatWest • 332 High Holborn
- NatWest • King's College Student Union-Macadam Bldg
- Royal Bank of Scotland • 1 Fleet St

Cinemas

- Aldwych Film • 1 Aldwych

Coffee

- Caffe Nero • 333 High Holborn
- Costa • 15 Chichester Rents
- Eat. • 105 Kingsway
- Eat. • 239 High Holborn
- Eat. • 34 High Holborn
- Eat. • 7 Kingsway
- Eat. • 77 Chancery Lane
- Eat. • 78 Hatton Garden
- Pret A Manger • 10 Leather Ln
- Pret A Manger • 240 High Holborn
- Pret A Manger • 29 Kingsway
- Starbucks • 10 Kingsway
- Starbucks • 28 Chancery Ln
- Starbucks • 99 Kingsway

Landmarks

- Aldwych Tube Station • Strand & Surrey St
- BBC Bush House • Aldwych & Kingsway
- Hatton Garden • Hatton Garden
- Inner Temple Garden • Inner Temple
- Lincoln's Inn Fields • High Holborn & Chancery Ln
- The Old Curiosity Shop • 13 Portsmouth St
- Royal Courts of Justice • Strand & Bell Yard
- Sir John Soane's Museum • 13 Lincoln's Inn Fields
- Site of Sweeney Todd's Barber Shop • 186 Fleet St
- Somerset House • Somerset House Trust, The Strand

Libraries

- British Library of Political and Economic Science • 10 Portugal Street

Nightlife

- Cittie of Yorke • 22 High Holborn
- The Enterprise • 38 Red Lion St
- The Lamb • 92 Lamb's Conduit St
- Na Zdrowie The Polish Bar • 11 Little Turnstile
- The Seven Stars • 53 Carey St
- Temple Bar • Temple Pl
- Tutu's • Surrey St
- Volupte • 9 Norwich St

Post Offices

- Aldwych • 95 Aldwych
- Grays Inn • 19 High Holborn
- Holborn Circus • 124 High Holborn

Restaurants

- Asadal • 227 High Holborn
- Casanova's Treats • 13 Lamb's Conduit Passage
- Indigo @ OneAldwych • 1 Aldwych

Shopping

- Konditor & Cook • 46 Gray's Inn Rd
- Topshop • 60 The Strand

Supermarkets

- Sainsbury's • 129 Kingsway
- Sainsbury's • 60 Fetter Ln
- Sainsbury's • 71 High Holborn

35

e choices for eating out and drinking in this quarter are myriad, but we commend getting your chops around a side of cow. Choose from Smithfield r & Grill, Smith's or Gaucho. Still hungry after that? Mosey on to Vivat Bacchus to plore their Cheese Room and quaff red wine. Then stay up all night at Fabric and me down in the rather brilliant Postman's Park.

Banks

- Abbey • 11 Ludgate Hill
- Barclays • 89 Charterhouse St
- Barclays • 81 Fleet St
- Halifax • 71 Fleet St
- HSBC • 165 Fleet St
- HSBC • 1 St Paul's Churchyard
- Lloyds • 33 Ludgate Hill
- NatWest • 156 Fleet St
- Royal Bank of Scotland • 9 Paternoster Row
- Royal Bank of Scotland • 36 New Bridge St

Coffee

- Apostrophe • 3 St Bride St
- Apostrophe • 10 St Pauls Churchyard
- Bagel Factory • 54 Cowcross St
- Café Deco • Charterhouse St & E Poultry Ave
- Caffe Nero • Shoe Lane
- Caffe Nero • 118 Newgate St
- Caffe Nero • Paternoster Sq
- Costa • 13 New Bridge St
- Costa • 46 Cowcross St
- Dose • 69 Long Ln
- Eat. • 88 Cowcross St
- Farm Collective • 91 Cowcross St
- Meze Meze • 95 Turnmill St
- Pret A Manger • 101 Turnmill St
- Pret A Manger • 5 St John's Sq
- Pret A Manger • 19 Ludgate Hill
- Pret A Manger • 10 Paternoster Sq
- Pret A Manger • 101 New Bridge St
- Pret A Manger • 143 Fleet St
- Starbucks • 1 Paternoster Sq
- Starbucks • 32 Fleet St
- Starbucks • 3 Fleet Pl
- Starbucks • 30 New Bridge St
- Starbucks • 50 Cowcross St
- Starbucks • 55 Ludgate Hill
- Starbucks • 150 Fleet St

Landmarks

- Daily Express Building • 121 Fleet St
- Millennium Bridge • Millennium Bridge
- Postman's Park • King Edward St & Little Britain

Libraries

- Shoe Lane Library • Little New St
- Society of Genealogists Library •
  14 Charterhouse Buildings [Goswell Road]

Nightlife

- Corney & Barrow • 10 Paternoster Sq
- The Deux Beers • 3 Hatton Wall
- Fabric • 77 Charterhouse St
- Fox and Anchor • 115 Charterhouse St
- The Hat and Tun • 3 Hatton Wall
- Smithfield Bar & Grill • 2 W Smithfield
- Ye Old Mitre • 1 Ely Ct
- Ye Olde Cheshire Cheese • 154 Fleet St
- Ye Olde London • 42 Ludgate Hill

Post Offices

- Farringdon Road • 89 Farringdon Rd

Restaurants

- Beppe's • 23 West Smithfield
- The Bleeding Heart • Bleeding Heart Yard, off Greville St
- Cafe du Marche • 22 Charterhouse Sq
- Gaucho Smithfield • 93 Charterhouse St
- Hix Oyster And Chop House • 36 Cowcross St
- Kurz + Lang • 1 St John St
- The Larder • 91 St John St
- Pho • 86 St John St
- Portal • 88 St John St
- Smiths of Smithfield • 67 Charterhouse St
- St Germain • 89 Turnmill St
- St John's Smithfield • 26 St John St
- Tinseltown • 44 St. John St
- Vivat Bacchus • 47 Farringdon St
- Yo! Sushi • 5 St Paul's

Shopping

- Pure Groove Records • 6 West Smithfield

Supermarkets

- Marks & Spencer • Ave Maria Lane
- Sainsbury's • 23 Farringdon Rd

Map 16 · **Square Mile (West)**

N

St. A1
St.
1
Markwell Sq
2
Great Guns

London Wall A1211
7

Mont. St
King Edward
Little Britain
Postman's Park
Angel St

St. Martins-le-Grand
Aldersgate St
Gresham Street
Noble Street
Oat La
Staining Ln
Wood Street
Love La
Aldermanbury
Alder.
Square
Addle

Basinghall Av
Horse Yd
White
Coleman St
Moorgate
Tele
Arm
Gre

A

Newgate St A40
St.Paul's
Foster Lane
Carey Lane
Gutter Lane
Gold. St
Gresham Street
Milk Street
Mumford Ct
Russia Ct
Russia St
Mitre Ct
Lawrence La
King Street
Wood Street
The Guildhall
Street
Fred. Pl
Ironmonger La
Old Jewry
Dove Ct
Grocers' Hall Ct
Kings
Lothb
Princes Street

2

15

St. Paul's Cathedral
St. Paul's Chyd
New Change
Festival Gardens
St. Paul's Churchyard
Carter Lane
Knightrider St
Godliman St
Queen Victoria Street
Castle Baynard St
Ben.
Lambeth Hill

2 3 £
Cheapside
St. Mary le Bow Church
£
Poultry
Bread St
Queen St
Well Ct
Pancras La
Bucklersbury
Watbrook
£

B

Distaff La
Cannon
Friday St
Watling Street
Watling Ct
Bread Street
Queen Victoria Street
Greater Trinity La
Cleary Garden
Huggin Ct
Lambeth Hill
2
Mansion House
St. Thomas Apostle
Garlick Hill
Skinners La
Cannon Street
Queen St
Tower Royal
Cloak La
College Hill
College Street
College Street Park
Temple of Mithras
17
Dowgate
Ox
Monu
Mon

£

Upper
White
Lion
Hill
Upper Thames Street
Thames Street A3211
High Timber Street
Trig La
Broken Wf
Gardners La
Stew La
Queenhithe
Kennet Wharf La
Southwark Bridge
Bell Wharf Ln
Cousin Lane

0.25 mile
0.25 km

River Thames

...ah, the City, that faceless square mile at which we direct such disgust and ...ehemence for the state we're in. Despite meltdowns and protests, the world ...ontinues to turn, stocks are traded, and bonuses return. This place has always ...een empty at the weekends so you can enjoy the caryatids and Doric columns ... peace. And of course take in the duomo at San Paulo (so much more romantic ...n't you think?)

£ Banks

Barclays • 1 King St
Halifax • 134 Cheapside
HSBC • 60 Queen Victoria St
Lloyds • 70 Cheapside

Coffee

Coffee Republic • 32 Coleman St
Costa • 9 Bow Ln
Costa • 99 Gresham St
Eat. • 15 Basinghall St
Eat. • 88 Wood St
Eat. • 143 Cheapside
Fab Food Patisserie • 19 Watling St
Fresco Café Bar • 21 Masons Ave
Pret A Manger • 30 Gresham St
Starbucks • 1 Poultry
Starbucks • 143 Cheapside

Landmarks

The Guildhall • Gresham St & Basinghall St
St Mary le Bow Church • Cheapside & Bow Ln
St. Paul's Cathedral • St. Paul's Church Yard & Cannon St
Temple of Mithras • Queen Victoria St & Queen St

✉ Post Offices

Southwark • 136 Southwark Bridge Rd

📖 Libraries

• City Business Library • Aldermanbury Square
• Guildhall Library • Aldermanbury

▼ Nightlife

• Hatchet • 28 Garlick Hill
• The Mansion House • 44 Cannon Street
• The Samuel Pepys • 48 Upper Thames Street
• Ye Olde Watling • 29 Watling Street

Restaurants

• Sweetings • 39 Queen Victoria St

Shopping

• Church's Shoes • 90 Cheapside
• Manucci • 5 Cheapside
• Space NK Apothecary • 145 Cheapside

Supermarkets

• Marks & Spencer • Cannon St Station

...ndon's most Jekyll-and-Hyde-like hood. By day, the Banking district throbs ...th suits losing fortunes. They still dig steaks at Gaucho City though perhaps the ...chelin-starred Rhodes 24 is out of their price range now. Well, probably not. ...e Counting House is for after-work beers while the possibility of shopping at ...e Royal Exchange is laughable, but who says you have to buy? By night, well, ...t don't go there.

Banks

- ...bbey • 48 Moorgate
- ...bbey • 51 Gracechurch St
- ...arclays • 29 Wormwood St
- ...o-Operative • 80 Cornhill
- ...alifax • 33 Old Broad St
- ...alifax • 58 Moorgate
- ...SBC • 95 Gracechurch St
- ...SBC • 100 Old Broad St
- ...oyds • 34 Moorgate
- ...oyds • 39 Threadneedle St
- ...atWest • 1 Prince's St
- ...atWest • 15 Bishopsgate
- ...oyal Bank of Scotland • 62 Threadneedle St

Coffee

- ...agel Factory • 59 Moorgate
- ...affè Nero • 22 Wormwood Stree
- ...at. • 54 Cornhill
- ...at. • 123 Cannon St
- ...i Bagel • 27 Throgmorton St
- ...ret A Manger • 43 King William St
- ...tarbucks • 5 Camomile St
- ...tarbucks • 13 Old Broad St
- ...tarbucks • 48 Gracechurch St
- ...tarbucks • 74 Cornhill
- ...tarbucks • 90 Old Broad St

Landmarks

- ...ank of England • Threadneedle St & Prince's St
- ...ondon Stone • 111 Cannon St
- ...hreadneedle Street • Threadneedle St

Nightlife

- **The Counting House** • 50 Cornhill
- **Grand Cafe & Bar** • The Ctyard, Royal Exchange

Post Offices

- **Moorgate** • 53 Moorgate

Restaurants

- **Gaucho City** • 1 Bell Inn Yard
- **The Mercer** • 34 Threadneedle St
- **Nusa Kitchen** • 2 Adams Ct
- **Rhodes 24** • 25 Old Broad St
- **Wasabi** • 52 Old Broad St

Shopping

- **Paul A Young Fine Chocolates** • 20 Royal Exchange
- **Pretty Ballerinas** • Royal Exchange • Threadneedle St
- **Sweatshop (City branch - at Cannon's Gym)** • Cousin Lane

Supermarkets

- **Marks & Spencer** • Cannon St Station
- **Sainsbury's** • 10 Lombard St

Map 1

ough on the fringe of the financial cesspit, Aldgate is brilliant to walk and gawp ound in. A. Gold's British deli (Yes…ça exist!) is fabulous, as is the atmospheric eighbourhood around Petticoat Lane, where Jack The Ripper used to stalk ozzers. After stodge at Jeff's head South, pass the Erotic Gherkin (ahem), and go ege the London Wall alongside the tourists. Alternatively go become one yourself Pudding Lane.

Banks

Barclays • 114 Fenchurch St
Barclays • 99 Commercial St
HSBC • 20 Eastcheap
HSBC • 60 Fenchurch St
Lloyds • 72 Fenchurch St
Lloyds • 113 Leadenhall St
NatWest • 116 Fenchurch St
NatWest • 2 Eastcheap
Royal Bank of Scotland • 5 Great Tower St
Royal Bank of Scotland • 54 Lime St

Coffee

Cafe Cotto • 12 Mitre St
Caffe Nero • 1 Fenchurch Pl [Coopers Row]
Caffe Nero • 23 Eastcheap
Caffe Nero • 88 Leadenhall St
Eat. • 28 Brushfield St
Eat. • 84 Aldgate High St
Eat. • 2 Eastcheap
Eat. • 155 Fenchurch St
Eat. • 26 Leadenhall St
Eat. • 122 Minories
Eat. • 48 Mark Ln
Eat. • 2 Tower Hill
Eat. • 33 St Mary Axe
Market Coffee House • 52 Brushfield St
Pret A Manger • 3 Cutler St
Starbucks • 8 Brushfield St
Starbucks • 14 New St
Starbucks • 20 Eastcheap
Starbucks • 48 Minories
Starbucks • 66 St Mary Axe

Landmarks

The Gherkin • 30 St Mary Axe
Jewish Soup Kitchen • Brune St & Tenter Ground
The Lloyds Building • 1 Lime St
Leadenhall Market • Leadenhall Market
London Wall • Cooper's Row & Trinity Sq
The Monument • Monument St & Fish St Hill
Pudding Lane • Pudding Lane
Royal Raven Lodgings •
Wakefield Tower (Tower of London)
Thames Clipper • Tower Pier
Tower 42 (Natwest Tower) • 25 Old Broad St
Tower of London • The Tower of London

Libraries

• Camomile Street • 15 Camomile St
• The Women's Library • 25 Old Castle St

Nightlife

• Dion City • 52 Leadenhall St
• Kenza • 10 Devonshire Sq
• Mary Janes • 124 Minories
• The Minories • 64 Minories
• Pepys Bar at the Novotel Hotel • 10 Pepys St
• Prism • 147 Leadenhall St
• Revolution • 140 Leadenhall St
• T Bar 18 • Houndsditch

Post Offices

• The City of London BO • 12 Eastcheap

Restaurants

• Jeff's Cafe • 14 Brune St
• S & M Cafe • 48 Brushfield St

Shopping

• A. Gold • 42 Brushfield St
• Montezuma's • 51 Brushfield St
• Petticoat Lane Market • Middlesex St
• Precious • 16 Artillery Passage
• Sweaty Betty • 5 Rood Lane

Supermarkets

• Sainsbury's • 45 Fenchurch St

Map 19

gg and Range Rover fetishists are in a constant state of climax around here. It
...ure is pretty when the sun isn't being blocked by expensively coiffured bouffants,
...out one suspects the plummy accents and tasteless richness would dent anyone's
...nthusiasm for chic dog clothes (Mungo & Maud) or curry (Amaya). Victoria's
...ed Cross Charity shop provides opportunities for us to pick over upper class
...eftovers.

£ Banks

Barclays • 8 W Halkin St
HSBC • 19 Grosvenor Pl
HSBC • 13 Sloane Sq
NatWest • 141 Ebury St
NatWest • 2 Sloane Gardens

☕ Coffee

Starbucks • 53 Pimlico Rd
Tomtom Coffee House • 114 Ebury St

📖 Libraries

Instituto Cervantes • 102 Eaton Square
Victoria Library • 160 Buckingham Palace Rd
Westminster Music Library • 160 Buckingham Palace Rd

Y Nightlife

The Blue Bar • The Berkeley Hotel • Wilton Pl
Nag's Head • 53 Kinnerton St
The Plumber's Arms • 14 Lower Belgrave St
Wilton Arms • 71 Kinnerton St

🍴 Restaurants

Amaya • Halkin Arcade, Motcomb St
Boisdale, Victoria • 15 Eccleston St
Noura • 12 William St
One-O-One • 101 Knightsbridge
Yo! Sushi • 102 Knightsbridge

🛍 Shopping

British Red Cross Victoria • 85 Ebury St
Moyses Flowers • Peter Jones - Sloane Sq
Mungo & Maud • 79 Elizabeth St
Peter Jones • Sloan Sq

🛒 Supermarkets

Waitrose • 27 Motcomb St

ince the Tower of London closed for business, prisoners have been routinely ortured at weekends in Victoria Station. Surrounding the transit hubs is a dignified hood Churchill and Mozart called home. Do a late-night tramp photoshoot on the teps of the magnificent houses of Lupus Street (with a camera from Grays) before eading to the Cask & Glass for a knees-up with your new pals.

£ Banks

Barclays • 1 Churton St
Halifax • 62 Victoria St
HSBC • 89 Buckingham Palace Rd
HSBC • 166 Vauxhall Bridge Rd
Lloyds • 98 Victoria St
NatWest • 169 Victoria St

Coffee

Bagel Factory • Victoria Station
Bagel Factory • Victoria Place Shopping Centre • Buckingham Palace Rd
Caffe Nero • 31 Warwick Way
Costa • 3 Cardinal Walk
Costa • 115 Buckingham Palace Rd
Eat. • Cardinal Pl
Pret A Manger • 12 Victoria St
Pret A Manger • 173 Victoria St
Pret A Manger • Unit 36B • Victoria Station
Pret A Manger • 92 Buckingham Palace Rd
Starbucks • 137 Victoria St
Starbucks • Buckingham Palace Rd & Lower Belgrave St

Post Offices

Vauxhall Bridge Road • 167 Vauxhall Bridge Rd

Landmarks

• **Little Ben** • Victoria St & Vauxhall Bridge Rd
• **Westminster Cathedral** • 42 Francis St

Nightlife

• **The Cardinal** • 23 Francis St
• **Cask & Glass** • 39 Palace St

Restaurants

• **Grumbles** • 35 Churton St

Shopping

• **Grays of Westminster** • 40 Churton St
• **La Bella Sicilia** • 23 Warwick Way
• **Rippon Cheese Stores** • 26 Upper Tachbrook St
• **Runners Need** • 24 Palace Street
• **Topshop** • 18 Victoria St

Supermarkets

• **Marks & Spencer** • Victoria Mainline Station

Hugging the curve of the Thames, this princely patch of Pimlico combines the stately Tate with imposing embankment architecture and ancient houses. Check out the old-money splendour of Vincent Street before grabbing lunch at the Regency, a true gem of a caf. Much fun can be had by pretending you acutally live around here, so in this spirit head to the Morpeth as your local.

Map 2

 Banks
NatWest • 27 Horseferry Rd

 Coffee
Starbucks • 35 Horseferry Rd

 Landmarks
Millbank Tower • 21 Millbank
The Shard Building Site • 32 Vauxhall Bridge Rd

Libraries
Pimlico Library • Rampayne St
Royal Horticultural Society Library • 80 Vincent Sq

 Nightlife
• **Morpeth Arms** • 58 Millbank

 Restaurants
• **The Regency Cafe** • 17 Regency St
• **Vincent Rooms** • 76 Vincent Square

 Shopping
• **Black Rose** • 112 Belgrave Rd

he long shadow of government falls over these parts, beautiful as they are.
otestors and wannabe Guy Fawkeses head to Parliament Square, where they
an harangue whichever bunch of jokers are esconced in the Houses of Parliament.
et away from tourists at the tiny St Stephen's Tavern, or grab a classy cocktail at
e Cinnamon Club. If you must shop head to Victoria Street.

Banks

Abbey • 115 Victoria St
Barclays • 13 Artillery Row
Barclays • 2 Victoria St
HSBC • 8 Victoria St
Lloyds • 1 Butler Pl
Lloyds • 4 Dean Stanley St
NatWest • 57 Victoria St
Royal Bank of Scotland • 119 Victoria St

Coffee

Caffe Nero • 1 Bridge St
Caffe Nero • 105 Victoria St
Eat. • 3 Strutton Ground
Fresco Cafe Bar • 11 Tothill St
Pret A Manger • 75 Victoria St
Pret A Manger • 49 Tothill St
Puccino's • 6 Victoria St
Starbucks • 27 Victoria St

Landmarks

Big Ben • House of Commons
Field of Remembrance • Victoria St & Dean's Yard
New Scotland Yard Sign • 8 Broadway
Smith Square • Smith Sq
UK Parliament • Victoria St & Abingdon St
Westminster Tube Station •
Bridge St & Victoria Embankment

Libraries

• **St James's Library** • 62 Victoria St

Nightlife

• **The Albert** • 52 Victoria St
• **The Cinnamon Club** • 30 Great Smith St
• **The Speaker** • 46 Great Peter Street
• **Two Chairmen** • 39 Dartmouth St
• **St Stephen's Tavern** • 10 Bridge Street

Shopping

• **Haelen Centre** • 41 Broadway
• **National Map Centre** • 22 Caxton St

Map 23

Dignified, decadent, exclusive, Pall Mall and St. James's Street are where the aristobrats come out to play. With stuffy gentlemen's clubs, bespoke tailors and the stale scent of a cigar-fuelled colonialist past pervading you'll want to sweeten up with a macaroon at Laduree. Giro the Nazi dog observes the liberals who get culture fixes at the ICA, but he can't come for scraps at Inn The Park.

£ Banks

- **Barclays** • 31 St James's St
- **HSBC** • 69 Pall Mall
- **Lloyds** • 7 Pall Mall
- **Lloyds** • 8 Waterloo Pl
- **Royal Bank of Scotland** • 48 Haymarket

Cinemas

- **Apollo Cinema Piccadilly Circus** • 19 Lower Regent St
- **Cineworld Haymarket** • 63 Haymarket
- **ICA Cinema** • The Mall & Horse Guards Rd
- **Odeon Leicester Square** • 24 Leicester Sq
- **Odeon Panton Street** • 11 Panton St
- **Odeon West End Cinema** • 40 Leicester Sq

Coffee

- **Apostrophe** • 16 Regent St
- **Caffe Nero** • 35 Jermyn St
- **Coffee Republic** • 63 Haymarket
- **Eat.** • 18 Regent St
- **Eat.** • 3 Duke of York St
- **Eat.** • 9 Crown Passage
- **ICA Cafe** • The Mall
- **Pret A Manger** • 8 King St

O Landmarks

- **Economist Plaza** • 25 St James's St
- **Giro the Nazi Dog** • 9 Carlton House Terrace
- **Leicester Square** • Leicester Sq
- **TKTS** • Leicester Square & St Martin's St

Libraries

- **London Library** • 14 St James's Sq
- **Westminster Reference Library** • 35 St Martin's St

Nightlife

- **Aura** • 48 St James's St
- **ICA** • The Mall
- **The Sports Cafe** • 80 Haymarket

Restaurants

- **Inn The Park** • St James' Park
- **Laduree** • 71 Burlington Arcade
- **Stockpot** • 38 Panton St
- **The Wolsey** • 160 Piccadilly

Shopping

- **Partridges Deli** • 2 Duke of York St
- **National Map Centre** • 22-24 Caxton St
- **Richard Caplan** • 25 Bury St

Map 24 · Trafalgar Square / The Strand

N

Long Acre

Monmouth

West Street

Moor St

Tower Court

Shelton Street

Langley Street

Neal's Yard

Shorts Gardens

B402

Earlham Street

B401

Russell Street

Catherine Street

Aldwych

Floral Street

Wellington Street B401

Exeter Street

Montreal Place

12

13

14

Itchfield Street

Charing Cross Road A401

Great Newport St

Upper St. Martin's Lane

B404

Garrick Street

Rose Street

King Street

Bedfordbury

Henrietta Street

Tavistock Street

Burleigh Street

Lancaster Place A301

1

2

Dolphin Yard

Gerrard Place

Newport Pl

Little Newport St

New Row

The Actors Church

Maiden Lane

Southampton St

Savoy Court

Savoy Way

Savoy Hill

Savoy Steps

Savoy Buildings

Lisle Street

Leicester Square

Cranbourn St

St. Martin's Lane B404

Jane Austen Residence

Bedford Court

Chandos Place

Adam St

Strand

Strand

Right-hand Drive Street

3 £

4 £

Sewer Lamp

Leicester Square

Charing Cross Rd

William IV Street

Adelaide St

Durham House St

Robert St

John Adam Street

Cleopatra's Needle

A

Whitcomb Street

Orange Street

St. Martin's Street

Irving Street

St. Martin's Place

Eleanor Cross

£

£

York Buildings

Rhodesia Terrace

Lower Robert St

Victoria Embankment Gardens

Suffolk Street

Suffolk Pl

National Gallery & National Portrait Gallery

PAGE 482

St. Martin-in-the-Fields

Duncannon St

Strand A4

2 £

2 £

2

John Adam Street

Buckingham Street

Pall Mall East

Cockspur Street

Trafalgar Square

Trafalgar Square A4

Corner House Street

Hungerford Lane

Villiers Street

Charing Cross Station

PAGE 410

Embankment

Warwick Ho

Cockspur Court

Spring Gardens

Northumberland Ave

Craven Street

Embankment Place

House Terrace

The Mall

Horse Guards Rd

Northumberland Avenue

River Thames

Top Secret Tunnels

Craigs Ct

Great Scotland Yard

Whitehall Place

Victoria Embankment Gardens

Victoria Embankment

The Banqueting House

Whitehall A3212

Whitehall Court

23

B

St. James's Park

Whitehall Gdns

Horse Guards Avenue

Victoria Embankment Gardens

10 Downing St

Downing Street

Richmond Terrace

King Charles Street

Parliament Street A3212

Derby Gate

Canon Row

Westminster

A3211

22

0.25 mile

0.25 km

Trafalgar Square / The Strand

he hawkers came and removed the flying rats and lo! the Square was clean and isible. This ain't Mary Poppins—don't feed the birds you dirty tourists. Instead go o Terroirs and pretend you know a lot about wine. Eat at Wahaca, one of London's ew good Mexicans, then walk it off on Waterloo Bridge and watch the sun set over he Thames. Aah. That's why you love London.

Map 24

£ Banks

Abbey • 406 Strand
Barclays • 366 Strand
HSBC • 455 Strand
Lloyds • 48 Strand
Lloyds • 222 Strand
NatWest • 38 Strand
NatWest • 34 Henrietta St
NatWest • 217 Strand

☕ Coffee

Apostrophe • 215 Strand
Café Express • 372 Strand
Caffe Nero • 10 Bedford St
Caffe Nero • 181 Strand
Caffe Nero • 125 Strand
Caffe Nero • 36 St Martin's Ln
Caffe Nero • 29 Southampton St
Coffee Republic • 79 Strand
Costa • 17 Embankment Pl
Eat. • 41 Bedford St
Eat. • 39 Villiers St
Great American Bagel Factory • 45 Villiers St
Pret A Manger • 135 Strand
Pret A Manger • 421 Strand
Pret A Manger • 7 St Martin's Ln
Scott's Sandwich Bar • 10 New Row
Starbucks • 355 Strand
Starbucks • 442 Strand
Starbucks • 14 Villiers St
Starbucks • 1 Villiers St

○ Landmarks

10 Downing Street • 10 Downing St
The Actors' Church • 29 Bedford St
The Banqueting House • Whitehall & Horse Guards Ave
Cleopatra's Needle • Embankment
Eleanor Cross • Charing Cross Station, The Strand
Jane Austen Residence • 10 Henrietta St
Right-hand Drive Street • Savoy Ct
Sewer Lamp • Carting Lane & Strand
St Martin-in-the-Fields • St Martin's Pl & Duncannon St
Top Secret Tunnels • 6 Craig's Ct
Trafalgar Square • Trafalgar Sqaure

📖 Libraries

Charing Cross Library • 4 Charing Cross Rd
Royal United Services Institute Library • Whitehall

🍸 Nightlife

• **Asia de Cuba** • 45 St. Martin's Lane
• **The Chandos** • 29 St Martins Lane
• **The Coal Hole** • 91 Strand
• **Covent Garden Comedy Club** • The Arches, Off Villiers St
• **Gordon's Wine Bar** • 47 Villiers St
• **Heaven** • Under the Arches, off Villiers St
• **Maple Leaf** • 41 Maiden Ln
• **Punch & Judy** • The Covent Garden Piazza
• **Retro Bar** • 2 George Ct
• **Roadhouse** • 35 The Piazza
• **The Sherlock Holmes** • 10 Northumberland St
• **The Ship and Shovell** • 1 Craven Passage
• **Zoo Bar & Club** • 13 Bear St

✉ Post Offices

• **Trafalgar Square** • 24 William IV St

🍽 Restaurants

• **Bistro 1** • 33 Southampton St
• **Cafe in the Crypt** • 6 St Martin's Pl
• **Covent Garden Market Cafe** • Covent Garden
• **Farmer Brown** • 4 New Row
• **Gourmet Burger Kitchen** • 13 Maiden Ln
• **India Club** •
  143 Strand (Second floor, Strand Continental Hotel)
• **J Sheekey** • 28 St Martins Ct
• **RS Hispaniola** • Victoria Embankment
• **Rules** • 35 Maiden Ln
• **Scott's Sandwich Bar** • 10 New Row
• **Thai Pot** • 1 Bedfordbury
• **Wahaca** • 66 Chandos Pl

🛍 Shopping

• **Austin Kaye** • 425 The Strand
• **Australia Shop** • 27 Maiden Ln
• **Gelato Mio** • 45 Villiers St
• **The Italian Bookshop** • 5 Cecil Ct
• **London Camera Exchange** • 98 Strand
• **Motor Books** • 13 Cecil Ct
• **Rohan** • 10 Henrietta St
• **Stanley Gibbons** • 399 Strand

🛒 Supermarkets

• **Marks & Spencer** • Charing Cross Station

Map 25

he "new Notting Hill" label weighs heavily on the Kensals. They look east for nspiration, ignoring the Harlesden yardies at their backs. Thai Rice serves eastern ood, while Portobello's Mexican spice shack Santo slings some of the best Mexican n the city and grooves to the Latino cool with regular DJ sets. Prepare for Carnival by visiting What Katie Did for exhibitionist outfits, while Trellick Tower is perfect for eal—"I mean it, I'll jump"—attention-seekers.

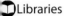 Landmarks

Trellick Tower • 5 Golborne Rd

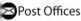 Libraries

Kensal Library • 20 Golborne Rd
Queen's Park Library • 666 Harrow Rd

Post Offices

Maida Hill • 377 Harrow Rd
Portobello Road • 325 Portobello Rd

Restaurants

• **Santo** • 299 Portobello Rd
• **Thai Rice** • 303 Portobello Rd

Shopping

• **Constructive Lives** • 312 Portobello Rd
• **Honest Jon's** • 278 Portobello Rd
• **Rellik** • 8 Golborne Rd
• **What Katie Did** • 281 Portobello Rd

Supermarkets

• **Iceland** • 512 Harrow Rd

not as posh as Maida Vale or as cool as Ladbroke Grove, Maida Hill is slightly grubby to the south, not helped by the distinctly unlovely Harrow Road. Things get more upmarket heading north, but the beating heart of the hill can be found Saturdays around Harrow Road's new market. Hang out at cosy yet lively Victorian pub The Skiddaw for a round of Aspalls and a board game or two.

£ **Banks**

Royal Bank of Scotland · 2 Elgin ave

🍸 **Nightlife**

The Skiddaw · 46 Chippenham Rd

✉ **Post Offices**

Kilburn Park · 5 Chippenham Gardens

Map 2

61

Map 2

u don't come to Maida Vale for the nightlife, end of story. Though pretty, canal-side
alks are a different matter. Away from 'Little Venice' are endless rows of identical-looking
dwardian mansion blocks on peaceful, tree-lined avenues. It's clean, peaceful, and nice
ranslation: quite dull).Locals frequent the cafés and eateries around the Maida Vale tube
ation and on Clifton Road. Head to The Robert Browning for cheap Sam Smith's beer by
roasting fire or the E Bar for basement schmoozing and Spanish tapas.

Banks

Abbey • 131 Kilburn Park Rd
Barclays • 320 Elgin ave
NatWest • 298 Elgin ave

Coffee

Starbucks • 168 Randolf Ave

Libraries

Maida Vale Library • Sutherland Ave

Nightlife

The Bridge House • 13 Westbourne Terrace Rd
E Bar • 2 Warrington Crescent
The Robert Browning • 15 Clifton Rd
The Warwick Castle • 6 Warwick Pl
The Waterway • 54 Formosa St

Map 28

ook at that Westway and tell us you can't hear the opening chords of "London Calling." Maybe Rudie didn't fail but he moved up and moved out. This is the quiet, eafy Notting Hill of gated gardens away from the Hugh Grant-hungry tourists couring Portobello Road. Head to Clarendon Cross or Portland Road for food and tuff. Grab a bite at Julie's or wander down to Holland Park Avenue for organic eats at Jeroboams Deli.

 # £ Banks
Barclays • 137 Ladbroke Grove

Coffee
Starbucks • 76 Holland Park Ave

Nightlife
Julie's Bar • 135 Portland Rd

Shopping
Cowshed • 119 Portland Rd
The Cross • 141 Portland Rd
Gelato Mio • 138 Holland Park Ave
Jeroboams • 96 Holland Park Ave
Virginia • 98 Portland Road

Map 29 · **Notting Hill Gate**

N

**WESTBOURNE
GREEN**

25

26

30

28

Portobello
Road Market

**NOTTING
HILL**

Westbourne Grove A4206

**Ladbroke
Square Gardens**

**Notting
Hill Gate**

Notting Hill Gate A402

34

35

PAGE
342

KENSINGTON

**Kensington
Gardens**

0.25 mile

0.25 km

is hard to believe that until relatively recently this now home of the mega-rich was ensington's rough bad-boy slum. Traces of the Gate's multicultural past are in the rinkles of the old eccentrics in the Uxbridge Arms, the lively Portobello Market, and he buzz of the summer Carnival. Pig out on some of London's best fish n' chips at Costas to feel old and bitter, go scowl at skinny jeans-clad teenagers in the Notting Hill Arts lub. Don't forget The Electric Cinema for movie-going in style.

Map 29

£ Banks

- Abbey • 174 Portobello Rd
- Abbey • 88 Notting Hill Gate
- Barclays • 35 Notting Hill Gate
- HSBC • 152 Portobello Rd
- HSBC • 25 Notting Hill Gate
- Lloyds • 50 Notting Hill Gate
- NatWest • 46 Notting Hill Gate
- Royal Bank of Scotland • 78 Notting Hill Gate

Cinemas

- The Electric Cinema • 191 Portobello Rd
- Gate Picturehouse • 87 Notting Hill Gate
- Notting Hill Coronet • 103 Notting Hill Gate

Coffee

- Apostrophe • 138 Notting Hill Gate
- Caffe Nero • 113 Westbourne Grove
- Caffe Nero • 53 Notting Hill Gate
- Caffe Nero • 168 Portobello Rd
- Coffee Republic • 214 Portobello Rd
- Eat. • 68 Notting Hill Gate
- Pret A Manger • 65 Notting Hill Gate
- Starbucks • 96 Westbourne Grove
- Starbucks • 227 Portobello Rd
- Starbucks • 26 Pembridge Rd
- Starbucks • 140 Notting Hill Gate
- Starbucks • 64 Notting Hill Gate

Landmarks

- Portobello Road Market • 223 Portobello Rd

Libraries

- North Kensington Library • 108 Ladbroke Grove
- Notting Hill Gate Library • 1 Pembridge Sq

Nightlife

- Mau Mau • 265 Portobello Rd
- Montgomery Place • 31 Kensington Park Rd
- Notting Hill Arts Club • 21 Notting Hill Gate
- Sun in Splendour • 7 Portobello Rd
- Trailer Happiness • 177 Portobello Rd
- Uxbridge Arms • 13 Uxbridge St
- Windsor Castle • 114 Campden Hill Rd

Post Offices

- Kensington Church St • 190 Kensington Church St
- Ladbroke Grove • 116 Ladbroke Grove

Restaurants

- Beach Blanket Babylon • 45 Ledbury Rd
- Cafe Diana • 5 Wellington Terrace
- Costas • 14 Hillgate St
- Crazy Homies • 125 Westbourne Park Rd
- The Electric Brasserie • 191 Portobello Rd
- Eve's Market Cafe • 222 Portobello Rd
- Geales • 2 Farmer St
- Lucky 7 • 127 Westbourne Park Rd
- Manzara • 24 Pembridge Rd
- Osteria Basilico • 29 Kensington Park Rd
- Taqueria • 139 Westbourne Grove

Shopping

- & Clarke's Bread • 124 Kensington Church St
- Bodas • 38 Ledbury Rd
- Diane von Furstenberg • 83 Ledbury Rd
- The Grocer on Elgin • 6 Elgin Crescent
- The Hummingbird Bakery • 133 Portobello Rd
- James Knight of Mayfair • 67 Notting Hill Gate
- Melt • 59 Ledbury Rd
- Mr Christian's Delicatessen • 11 Elgin Crescent
- Music & Video Exchange • 38 Notting Hill Gate
- Negozio Classica • 283 Westbourne Grove
- Portobello Road Market • Portobello Rd
- R Garcia and Sons • 248 Portobello Rd
- Retro Man • 34 Pembridge Rd
- Retro Woman • 32 Pembridge Rd
- Rough Trade Talbot West • 130 Talbot Rd
- Travel Bookshop • 13 Blenheim Crescent

Map 30

London's unofficial 'Little Beirut' seems to attract both camera-clad tourists (who have strayed too far from Hyde Park) as well as Londoners (who look for food gems on Westbourne Grove). While the place is bustling, beware of the overpriced, and frankly s***, tourist traps on Queensway. Instead, chill out with a shisha at Berdees, and then get adventurous and try your hand at 1950s-style bowling at All Star Lanes. Alternatively, do it like the Victorians did and get a rub down at Porchester Gate Spa.

Banks

- **Barclays** • 93 Queensway
- **Halifax** • 23 Whiteleys Of Bayswater
- **HSBC** • 43 Queensway
- **Lloyds** • 30 Westbourne Grove
- **NatWest** • 16 Westbourne Grove

Cinemas

- **Odeon Whiteleys** • Queensway & Porchester Gardens

Coffee

- **Pret A Manger** • 127 Queensway
- **Starbucks** • 49 Queensway

Libraries

- **Paddington Library** • Porchester Rd

Nightlife

- **The Cow** • 89 Westbourne Park Rd

Post Offices

- **Harrow Rd** • 272 Harrow Rd
- **Queensway** • 118 Queensway

Restaurants

- **Berdees Coffee Shop** • 84 Bishop's Bridge Rd
- **The Cow** • 89 Westbourne Park Rd
- **Kiasu** • 48 Queensway
- **Royal China** • 13 Queensway
- **Tiroler Hut** • 27 Westbourne Grove

Shopping

- **Al Saqi Books** • 26 Westbourne Grove
- **Planet Organic** • 42 Westbourne Grove
- **Porchester Gate Spa** • Queensway & Porchester Rd
- **Whiteleys Shopping Centre** • Queensway

Supermarkets

- **Sainsbury's** • 88 Westbourne Grove
- **Waitrose** • 38 Porchester Sq

Paddington Bear may not seem so cuddly if he were one of today's commuters hanging around Paddington Station. This area can seem like zombie land, a mass of tired-looking, harassed faces grabbing food from one of the endless chain eateries. It's not all bad news though. Evening boredom can be banished by listening to famous war correspondents' exotic tales over a meal at the Frontline Club. For all other woes, solve it with caffeine at Markus Coffee Company.

Map 3

Banks
- **Barclays** • 17 Spring St
- **HSBC** • 2 Craven Rd
- **NatWest** • 26 Spring St

Cinemas
- **Frontline Club** • 13 Norfolk Pl

Coffee
- **Caffe Nero** • 14 Spring St
- **Caffe Nero** • Paddington Station
- **Costa** • 254 Edgware Rd
- **Pat.** • Paddington Station
- **Markus Coffee Company** • 13 Connaught St
- **Pret A Manger** • 9 Sheldon Sq
- **Serpentine Bar & Kitchen** • Serpentine Rd

Emergency Rooms
- **St Mary's Hospital** • Praed St & Winsland St

Landmarks
- **Paddington Bear Statue** • Paddington Station
- **Tony Blair's House** • Connaught Square & Seymour St
- **Westway Flyover** •

Nightlife
- **Frontline Club** • 13 • Norfolk Pl
- **The Royal Exchange** • 26 Sale Pl

Post Offices
- **Edgware Rd** • 354 Edgware Rd
- **Paddington** • 4 Praed St

Restaurants
- **Bonne Bouche** • 129 Praed St
- **Comptoir Libanais** • 26 London St
- **Mandalay** • 444 Edgware Rd

Supermarkets
- **Sainsbury's** • Paddington Station
- **Sainsbury's** • 12 Sheldon Sq

n't be scared. This part of town won't bite…much. Things may look a bit drab, and deed you wouldn't want to spend your Friday nights in many of the pubs here, but Uxbridge Road looks truly can be deceiving. While it's nothing special from the tside, Esarn Kheaw will blow your head off with authentic Thai green curry and ave you begging for more. To bring you back down to earth, The Queen Adelaide is e place to have a laid-back beer. Just forget about the shotgun under the counter.

Nightlife

Bush Hall • 310 Uxbridge Rd
The Goldhawk • 122 Goldhawk Rd
The Queen Adelaide • 412 Uxbridge Rd
White Horse • 31 Uxbridge Rd

Restaurants

Abu Zaad • 29 Uxbridge Rd
Esarn Kheaw • 314 Uxbridge Road
Vine Leaves Taverna • 71 Uxbridge Rd

Shopping

Nut Case • 352 Uxbridge Rd

Map 3

he Bush' has had a bit of a face-lift over the past few years. Once the former grime ab of West London, it now sports one of Europe's biggest shopping centres, Westfield, d with it comes more traffic and more chain shops. Fear not though, for Shepherds ash Market still keeps the place decidedly unpretentious, while the Empire continues attract the best up-and-coming bands. Hang out with the BBC kids at The Albertine d grab a bonza pie from the Bush's very own Aussie pie shop, Jumbucks.

Banks

Abbey • 23 Shepherd's Bush Green
Barclays • 74 Shepherd's Bush Green
HSBC • 16 Shepherd's Bush Green
NatWest • 25 Shepherd's Bush Green

Cinemas

Vue Shepherds Bush • Shepherds Bush Green & Rockley Rd

Coffee

BB's Coffee & Muffins •
Richmond Way & Charecroft Way
BB's Coffee & Muffins •
2117 Westfield London Shopping Center
Costa • 72 Uxbridge Rd
Starbucks • 62 Uxbridge Rd

Landmarks

BBC Television Centre • Wood Ln & Ring Rd

Libraries

Shepherds Bush Library • 6 Wood Ln

Nightlife

• Albertine • 1 Wood Lane
• The Defectors Weld • 170 Uxbridge Rd
• Ginglik • 1 Shepherd's Bush Green
• Shepherd's Bush Empire • Shepherd's Bush Green

Post Offices

• Shepherds Bush Road • 146 Shepherd's Bush Rd

Restaurants

• Jasmine • 16 Goldhawk Rd
• Jumbucks • 24 Shepherd's Bush Green
• Le Cinnamon • 158 Shepherd's Bush Rd
• Popeseye • 108 Blythe Rd

Shopping

• Westfield Centre • Ariel Way

Supermarkets

• Sainsbury's • 164 Uxbridge Rd

West Kensington / Olympia

West Ken is a Jekyll-and-Hyde kind of place. The calm, village atmosphere around Holland Park soon gives way to an 'in your face' cluster of kebab shops and grime once you go south of High Street Kensington. While the hoards head to Hyde Park, Holland Park is its unloved—yet more intimate—cousin. Kyoto Garden will draw you in for hours. Down the road, Olympia Exhibition Centre gets that middle class blood boiling—Erotica Show anyone? Near the tube, Café Continente is the place to go for a caffeine fix and a stack of blueberry pancakes.

£ Banks

Barclays • 137 N End Rd

Coffee

Cafe Continente • 62 N End Rd

Landmarks

Kyoto Garden (Holland Park) • 100 Holland Park Ave

Libraries

Barons Court • North End Crescent

Nightlife

The Cumberland Arms • 29 N End Rd
Famous 3 Kings • 171 North End Road
Plum Bar • 380 Kensington High St

Post Offices

Olympia • 8 North End Road

Restaurants

The Belvedere Restaurant • Abbotsbury Road

Shopping

Homebase • 195 Warwick Rd

Map 34

Kensington is the London of Disney fantasy--grand old homes and tea at 3pm. It's the kind of place where a gentile mews cottage will set you a back a cool mill, but if you live here you'll still have some change left over for an SUV and a box of organic veg. You're not going to score any cool points for hanging out here but there's nothing better than frisbee and a picnic (from Whole Foods of course) in Hyde Park on those treasured London summer days. If you've got the cash to splash, High Street Ken has the goods but instead take a detour to the Builders Arms for a not-so-posh pint.

£ Banks

- **Abbey** • 144 Kensington High St
- **Barclays** • 208 Kensington High St
- **Halifax** • 180 Kensington High St
- **HSBC** • 92 Kensington High St
- **Lloyds** • 112 Kensington High St
- **NatWest** • 55 Kensington High St
- **Royal Bank of Scotland** • 175 Kensington High St

Cinemas

- **Odeon Kensington** • Kensington High St & Edwards Sq

Coffee

- **Caffe Nero** • 160 Kensington High St
- **Caffe Nero** • 1 Wrights Ln
- **Costa** • 149 Cromwell Rd
- **Pret A Manger** • 149 Kensington High St
- **Pret A Manger** • 123 Kensington High St
- **Starbucks** • 25 Kensington High St
- **Starbucks** • 197 Kensington High St

Landmarks

- **Kensington Palace Gardens** • Kensington Palace Gardens

Libraries

- **Kensington Central Library** • Phillimore Walk

Nightlife

- **Builders Arms** • 1 Kensington Ct Pl

Post Offices

- **Kensington High St** • 257 Kensington High St

Restaurants

- **Byron** • 222 Kensington High St
- **Clarke's** • 124 Kensington Church St
- **Kensington Roof Gardens** • 99 Kensington High St
- **Maggie Jones's** • 6 Old Court Pl
- **Zaika** • 1 Kensington High St

Shopping

- **Ben's Cookies** • 12 Kensington High St
- **Buttercup Cake Shop** • 16 St Albans Grove
- **Notting Hill Housing Trust** • 57 Kensington Church St
- **Trailfinders** • 194 Kensington High St
- **Urban Outfitters** • 36 Kensington High St
- **Whole Foods Market** • 63 Kensington High St

Supermarkets

- **Sainsbury's** • 162 Earl's Ct Rd
- **Tesco** • 100 W Cromwell Rd
- **Waitrose** • 243 Kensington High St

Once known as Albertopolis, this place started out as Prince Albert's playground of learning. These days the museums are the carrot that draws the tourists westwards from the buzzing centre. Free entry to museums means more money for treats, and if it's treats you're after, the frozen yoghurt at Snog or crepes at Cafe Crepe will keep you happy. We suggest slaking your thirst for a good night out in a different babe.

£ Banks
Barclays • 114 Gloucester Rd
HSBC • 95 Gloucester Rd
NatWest • 18 Cromwell Pl

Cinemas
Cine Lumiere • 17 Queensberry Pl

Coffee
Café Deco • 62 Gloucester Rd
Pret A Manger • 99 Gloucester Rd
Pret A Manger • 15 Old Brompton Rd
Starbucks • 17 Gloucester Rd
Starbucks • 83 Gloucester Rd

Landmarks
• **Albert Memorial** • Kensington Gardens
• **Royal Albert Hall** • Kensington Gore

Libraries
• **French Institute Library** • 17 Queensberry Pl
• **National Art Library** • Cromwell Rd
• **Natural History Museum** • Cromwell Rd

Nightlife
• **Boujis** • 43 Thurloe St

Post Offices
• **Gloucester Road** • 118 Gloucester Rd
• **South Kensington Station** • 41 Old Brompton St

Restaurants
• **Cafe Creperie** • 2 Exhibition Rd
• **Caffe Forum** • 145 Gloucester Rd
• **Da Mario** • 15 Gloucester Rd
• **Jakob's** • 20 Gloucester Rd
• **The Kensington Creperie** • 2 Exhibition Rd
• **Little Japan** • 32 Thurloe St
• **Oddono's** • 14 Bute St
• **Pasha** • 1 Gloucester Rd

Shopping
• **Partridges Deli** • 17 Gloucester Rd
• **Snog** • 32 Thurloe Pl

Supermarkets
• **Sainsbury's** • 158 Cromwell Rd
• **Waitrose** • 128 Gloucester Rd

Map 3

Move on over Z List celebrity, only the truly rich shop here! While you can't move for fur or tourists, Knightsbridge is still a great place to shop. Window shop that is. Harrods and Harvey Nics are the big boys here and if you're after £40 soap you are in the right place. For the rest of us there's the Victoria & Albert Museum - free entry, brilliant cafe to escape the crowds, and multiple naked male sculptures to ogle.

£ Banks

Barclays • 137 Brompton Rd
Halifax • 110 Brompton Rd
HSBC • 237 Brompton Rd
HSBC • 202 Sloane St
Lloyds • 9 Brompton Rd
NatWest • 186 Brompton Rd
NatWest • 185 Sloane St

Coffee

Bagel Factory • 102 Brompton Rd
Caffe Nero • 124 Brompton Rd
Costa • 197 Brompton Rd
Eat. • 106 Brompton Rd
Pret A Manger • 132 Brompton Rd
Starbucks • 44 Brompton Rd

Landmarks

Holy Trinity Brompton • Brompton Rd & Knightsbridge
Victoria & Albert Museum • Cromwell Rd & Thurloe Pl

Libraries

Goethe-Institut Library • 50 Princes Gate

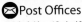 Post Offices

• **Knightsbridge** • 6 Raphael St

Restaurants

• **Zuma** • 5 Raphael St

Shopping

• **Burberry** • 2 Brompton Road
• **Divertimenti** • 227 Brompton Rd
• **Harrods** • 87 Brompton Rd
• **Harvey Nichols** • 109 Knightsbridge
• **Rigby & Peller** • 2 Hans Rd
• **Skandium** • 247 Brompton Rd
• **Space NK Apothecary** • 307 Brompton Rd

Supermarkets

• **Marks & Spencer** • 179 Brompton Rd
• **Sainsbury's** • 112 Brompton Rd

ean, green, and thankfully not so mean, Chiswick's leafy, cosmopolitan pavement dining s the epitome of what makes West London, well, West London. Chiswick's tranquil, leafy illage feel is perhaps what draws families with stacks of laid-back pavement dining on he High Road. Hit Turnham Green Terrace for boutique shopping, and on sunny days it's ce cream from Foubert's and an afternoon chilling out on Acton Green. Off the High Road he Devonshire is a more affordable Gordon Ramsay venture but the High Road Brasserie till remains the place to be seen.

 Banks

Halifax • 91 King St
Lloyds • 308 Chiswick High Rd

 Coffee

Carluccio's • 342 Chiswick High Rd
Starbucks • 280 Chiswick High Rd

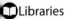 Libraries

Chiswick Library • Duke's Ave

Nightlife

Carvosso's • 210 Chiswick High Rd
George IV • 185 Chiswick High Rd
The Packhorse & Talbot • 145 Chiswick High Rd

Post Offices

• **Chiswick High Road** • 110 Chiswick High Rd

Restaurants

• **Boys Authentic Thai** • 95 Chiswick High Rd
• **Chris' Fish and Chips** • 19 Turnham Green Terrace
• **The Devonshire** • 126 Devonshire Rd
• **Fish Hook** • 6 Elliot Rd
• **Foubert's** • 2 Turnham Green Terrace
• **Franco Manca** • 144 Chiswick High Rd
• **High Road Brasserie** • 162 Chiswick High Rd
• **La Trompette** • 5 Devonshire Rd
• **Maison Blanc** • 26 Turnham Green Terrace
• **Kalamari** • 4 Chiswick High Rd
• **Turnham Green Cafe** • 57 Turnham Green Terrace
• **Zizzi** • 231 Chiswick High Rd

Shopping

• **As Nature Intended** • 201 Chiswick High Rd
• **The Bread Shop** • 296 Chiswick Rd
• **Eco-Age** • 213 Chiswick High Rd
• **Mortimer & Bennett** • 33 Turnham Green Terrace
• **Outsider Tart** • 83 Chiswick High Rd
• **Oxfam Books** • 90 Chiswick High Rd
• **Theobroma Cacao** • 43 Turnham Green Terrace
• **Something Nice** • 40 Turnham Green Terrace
• **Wheelers Garden Centre** • Turnham Green Terrace

Wedged between Chiswick and Hammersmith, with the actual brook now a sewer, there's not much more to Stamford Brook than a tube station and some very expensive houses. However there are a few gems. On King Street, Tosa serves up some authentic Japanese yakitori while thirsty Brookites head to The Carpenter's Arms for oysters and a Guinness in the garden.

Map 3

£ Banks

HSBC • 2 Chiswick High Rd

Coffee

Cafe Ginkgo • 243 Ravenscourt Park

Nightlife

The Raven • 375 Goldhawk Rd

Restaurants

Carpenter's Arms • 89 Black Lion Ln
Tosa • 332 Kings St

Supermarkets

Sainsbury's • 120 Chiswick High Rd
Tesco • 327 King St

Shopping

Mac's Cameras • 262 Kings St
Thai Smile • 287 King

Far enough out on the tube to scare the tourists, this area is a haven for locals who want it all on their doorstep. International flavours? Please, it's like a Benetton ad here: try Lowiczanka, Sagar, or Blah Blah Blah. Pretty Thames walk? Check!—along with The Dove, one of the city's most picturesque pubs. Bushwacker Whole Foods s like the local corner shop. Life's good in these parts.

£ Banks

- **Barclays** • 75 King St

Cinemas

- **Cineworld Hammersmith** • 207 King St

Coffee

- **Caffe Nero** • 1 King St
- **Coffee Republic** • 207 King St
- **Starbucks** • 38 King St

Nightlife

- **The Dove** • 19 Upper Mall
- **Ruby Grand** • 227 King St

Post Offices

- **King St** • 168 King St

Restaurants

- **Blah Blah Blah** • 78 Goldhawk Rd
- **Lowiczanka Polish Cultural Centre** • 238 King Street
- **Mahdi** • 215 King St
- **Sagar** • 157 King St

Shopping

- **Bushwacker Wholefoods** • 132 King St

Supermarkets

- **Iceland** • 111 King St
- **Tesco** • 327 King St

Map 4

…o the shops and pubs on offer are all pretty drab, but Hammersmith has three great venues for the more culturally inclined. Check out The Apollo for mainstream …ands and big-name comedians, The Lyric for the latest in modern theatre, and The …iverside for an awesome selection of foreign/art house films. London's vegetarians …lock to The Gate, with its seriously original and inventive menu.

£ Banks

HSBC • 1 Beadon Rd
Lloyds • 21 King St

Cinemas

Riverside Studios • Crisp Rd & Queen Caroline St

Coffee

Cafe Brera • Hammersmith Foyer & Roof Garden
Cafe Brera • King St & Angel Walk
Costa • Butterwick
Pret A Manger • Butterwick
Starbucks • 200 Hammersmith Rd

Emergency Rooms

Charing Cross Hospital •
Fulham Palace Rd & St Dunstan's Rd

Libraries

Hammersmith Library • Shepherds Bush Rd

Nightlife

• **Brook Green Hotel** • 170 Shepherd's Bush Rd
• **The Distillers** • 64 Fulham Palace Rd
• **Hammersmith Apollo** • 45 Queen Caroline St
• **Lyric Hammersmith** • King St

Post Offices

• **Hammersmith** • 16 King's Mall

Restaurants

• **The Gate** • 51 Queen Caroline St

Supermarkets

• **Tesco** • 180 Shepherd's Bush Rd
• **Tesco** • 13 Broadway Ctr

Map 4

arons Court doesn't have a scene as such, but it is elegantly lovely. Ignore North End oad—a fried chicken blot among Edwardian mansions—and instead get lost in Lille oad's antique stores. Curtains Up offers intimate theatre in the pub vaults. If you eed a change from polished chic, seek the Colton Arms for a jug-pint in its cottage yle garden.

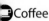 Banks

Abbey • 421 N End Rd
Lloyds • 417 N End Rd

Coffee

Café La Cigale • 353 N End Rd
Costa • 431 North End Rd

Landmarks

Empress State Buidling • Lillie Rd & North End Rd

Nightlife

Colton Arms • 187 Greyhound Road
The Curtains Up • 28 Comeragh Rd
The Fu'ham Mitre • 81 Dawes Rd
Queen's Arms • 171 Greyhound Rd

Post Offices

Dawes Road • 108 Dawes Rd
Olympia • 8 North End Road

Restaurants

• Best Mangal • 104 N End Rd
• Bombay Bicycle Club • 352 N End Rd
• Ta Krai • 100 North End Rd

Shopping

• Curious Science • 319 Lillie Road

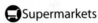 Supermarkets

• Co-Op • 88 N End Rd
• Iceland • 290 North End Rd
• Sainsbury's • 342 N End Rd

Map 43 · West Brompton / Fulham Broadway / Earl's Court

lively mix of Aussies, Saffas, rich kids, and sweaty Chelsea fans occupy these neighbourhoods. Fulham Broadway is the focus of the action offering heaving bars and clubs. Earl's Court is slightly more sedate while West Brompton is positively sleepy in comparison. On Brompton Road '60s boho café The Troubadour is still a happening spot for live music and a coffee while Vingt Quatre is a 24-hour institution serving fry-ups to clubbers in the early hours.

Banks

• Barclays • 191 Earl's Ct Rd
• Barclays • 20 Fulham Broadway
• HSBC • 315 Fulham Rd
• Lloyds • 179 Earl's Ct Rd

Cinemas

• Cineworld Fulham Road • 142 Fulham Rd
• Vue Fulham • Fulham Rd & Cedarne Rd

Coffee

• Caffe Nero • 480 Fulham Rd
• Caffe Nero • 174 Fulham Rd
• Coffee Republic • 142 Fulham Rd
• Pret A Manger • Fulham Broadway Retail Centre
• Starbucks • 259 Old Brompton Rd
• Starbucks • 186 Earl's Ct Rd
• The Troubadour • 263 Old Brompton Rd

Landmarks

• Stamford Bridge • Fulham Road & Moore Park Rd

Libraries

• Brompton Library • 210 Old Brompton Rd
• Institute of Cancer Research Library • 237 Fulham Rd

Post Offices

• Earls Court • 185 Earl's Court Rd
• Fulham Road • 369 Fulham Rd

Restaurants

• The Blue Elephant • 4 Fulham Broadway
• Bodean's • 4 Broadway Chambers
• Chutney Mary • 535 King's Rd
• Vingt Quatre • 325 Fulham Rd
• Yo! Sushi • Fulham Road

Shopping

• Fulham Broadway Centre • Fulham Road

Supermarkets

• Sainsbury's • Fulham Rd
• Tesco • 459 Fulham Rd
• Waitrose • 380 North End Rd

Map 44

his area drips old money, 4x4s, and people who own rather large things, like, say, evon. The only way to do Chelsea is to be seen doing it—and if you're paying all at money at least make it worthwhile. Drink one of Eight Over Eight's innovative ocktails, taste Michelin-starred food at Aubergine, and blow a week's wage on a esigner sock from The Shop At Bluebird.

Banks

Barclays • 348 King's Rd

Coffee

Starbucks • 388 King's Rd

Emergency Rooms

Chelsea and Westminster Hospital • 369 Fulham Rd

Nightlife

Brinkley's • 47 Hollywood Rd
The Drayton Arms • 153 Old Brompton Rd
The Duke of Clarence • 148 Old Brompton Rd
Rumi • 531 King's Rd

Restaurants

Aubergine • 11 Park Walk
Eight Over Eight • 392 King's Rd
The Bluebird • 350 King's Rd

Shopping

Furniture Cave • 533 Kings Rd
Richer Sounds • 258 Fulham Rd
The Shop At Bluebird • 350 King's Rd

Supermarkets

Sainsbury's • 295 Fulham Rd

Map 4

...elsea East is what Hollywood thinks all of London is like, full of dapper English chaps
...d potential princesses (who, incidentally, donate their clothes to the Red Cross shop;
...mmage here for London's best bargains!) King's Road buzzes as it did when it spawned
...e Swinging '60s, and foodies are spoiled around Cale Street. Tom's Kitchen is your place
... Sloaney eating without the Sloaney allowance. For a cheaper and sweeter taste of the
...ea get to The Hummingbird Bakery for addictive oh-so-good cupcakes.

£ Banks

- **Abbey** • 90 Old Brompton Rd
- **Barclays** • 108 Queen's Gate
- **HSBC** • 1 Sydney Pl
- **Lloyds** • 67 Old Brompton Rd
- **NatWest** • 224 King's Rd
- **Royal Bank of Scotland** • 29 Old Brompton Rd

Cinemas

- **Curzon Chelsea** • 206 King's Rd
- **Cineworld Chelsea** • 279 King's Rd

Coffee

- **Cafe de la Paix** • 159 King's Rd
- **Caffe Nero** • 115 King's Rd
- **Caffe Nero** • 201 King's Rd
- **Caffe Nero** • 66 Old Brompton Rd
- **Starbucks** • 123 King's Rd
- **Starbucks** • 72 Old Brompton Rd

Libraries

- **Chelsea Library** • King's Rd

Post Offices

- **Elm Park** • 66 Elm Park Rd

Nightlife

- **The Anglesea Arms** • 15 Selwood Terrace
- **Apartment 195** • 195 Kings Rd
- **Chelsea Potter** • 119 Kings Rd
- **The Pig's Ear** • 35 Old Church St

Restaurants

- **Chelsea Kitchen** • 451 Fulham Rd
- **Four o nine** • 409 Clapham Rd
- **Le Columbier** • 145 Dovehouse St
- **The Hummingbird Bakery** • 47 Old Brompton Rd
- **Made In Italy** • 249 King's Rd
- **My Old Dutch Pancake House** • 221 King's Rd
- **The Pig's Ear** • 35 Old Church St
- **Sushinho** • 312 King's Rd
- **Tom's Kitchen** • 27 Cale St
- **Tom's Place** • 1 Cale St

Shopping

- **British Red Cross Chelsea** • 69 Old Church St
- **Frock Me! Vintage Fashion Fair** •
  Chelsea Town Hall, Kings Rd
- **Kate Kuba** • 24 Duke of York Sq
- **Nomad Books** • 781 Fulham Rd
- **Sweaty Betty** • 125 King's Rd

Supermarkets

- **Waitrose** • 196 King's Rd

Map 46

You've got to love a place that spawns an adjective. If you've never met any 'Sloaney' types and are curious as to why the whole of London gets so riled about them, take a walk along the King's Road and observe. Peter Jones stands tall over the square and offers everything you didn't know you wanted. This rather beautiful nabe also hosts some bank-breaking eateries, such as Gordon Ramsay and Bibendum, as well as its fare share of cultural fare— the Saatchi Gallery being the finest example.

Banks

- Abbey • 138 King's Rd
- Barclays • 30 Sloane Sq
- Lloyds • 33 King's Rd

Coffee

- Eat. • 82 King's Rd
- Pret A Manger • 80 King's Rd
- Starbucks • 65 Sloane Ave
- Starbucks • 128 King's Rd

Landmarks

- Saatchi Gallery • Duke of York HQ, King's Rd

Post Offices

- Kings Walk • 122 King's Rd

Restaurants

- **The Admiral Codrington** • 17 Mossop St
- **Bibendum Restaurant & Oyster Bar** • 81 Fulham Rd
- **Blushes Cafe** • 52 King's Rd
- **Foxtrot Oscar** • 79 Royal Hospital Rd
- **Restaurant Gordon Ramsay** • 68 Royal Hospital Rd
- **Le Cercle** • 1 Wilbraham Pl
- **Tom Aikens** • 43 Elystan St

Shopping

- **Fresh Line** • 55 King's Rd
- **Partridges** • 2 Duke of York Sq
- **Peter Jones** • Sloane Sq
- **Rigby & Peller** • 13 Kings Rd
- **Space NK Apothecary** • 307 King's Rd

Supermarkets

- **Sainsbury's** • 75 Sloane Ave

This area is an estate agent's wet dream. Leafy, well-heeled, on the river, and made for families. Catch the great English game at Craven Cottage before making the most of the riverside and grabbing a pint at The Crabtree Tavern. Now that you're tipsy, head to The River Café where you'll feel less pained shelling out for top-notch, dead-posh grub.

Map 4

Coffee

Starbucks • 220 Fulham Palace Rd

Nightlife

The Crabtree Tavern • Rainville Rd

Post Offices

Fulham Palace Road • 185 Fulham Palace Rd

Restaurants

The River Café • Thames Wharf, Rainville Rd

Supermarkets

Sainsbury's • 179 Fulham Palace Rd

expensive home to rivals Fulham and Chelsea FC with a strong possibility of encountering some Chanel-clad WAGS. Fulham Road is where the good stuff is, but mostly on Map 43. Be a dreamer and stare out at The Thames in Fulham Palace Gardens or next time you're at the tube station soak up some WWII history and look at for The Putney Bridge Tube Pill Box.

Banks

HSBC • 593 Fulham

Coffee

Caffe Nero • 717 Fulham Rd
Local Hero • 640 Fulham Rd
Starbucks • 809 Fulham Rd
Tinto Coffee • 411 Fulham Palace Rd

Landmarks

Putney Bridge Tube Pill Box • Putney Bridge Station

Libraries

Fulham Library • 598 Fulham Rd

Nightlife

Wheatsheaf • 582 Fulham Rd

Post Offices

• **Fulham** • 815 Fulham Rd

Restaurants

• **Drawing Room Cafe** • Bishop's Ave
• **Fisher's Chips** • 19 Fulham High St

Shopping

• **Hurlingham Books** • 91 Fulham High St

you know you're in a classy neighbourhood when the kebab house (Kebab Kid) gets people travelling across London. Things here aren't cheap and you may be unnerved by all the people saying "terrific!" with their collars up. But they don't bite (despite their formidable buck teeth) so relax and enjoy a beer in The White Horse, known as the Sloaney Pony, or heavenly Sunday brunch at Duke on the Green.

Map 49

Coffee

Caffe Nero • 142 Wandsworth Bridge Rd
Starbucks • 95 Wandsworth Bridge Rd

Nightlife

Amuse Bouche • 51 Parsons Green Ln
The Establishment • Parsons Green Ln
The White Horse • 1 Parson's Green

Restaurants

De Cecco • 189 New King's Rd
Duke on the Green • 235 New Kings Rd
Ghillies • 271 New King's Rd
Kebab Kid • 90 New Kings Rd
Mao Tai • New King's Rd
Tendido Cuatro • 108 New King's Rd

Supermarkets

Tesco • 601 King's Rd

○ Landmarks

Lots Road Power Station • 27 Lots Rd

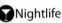 **Libraries**

Sands End Library • 59 Broughton Rd

♥ Nightlife

» **606 Club** • 90 Lots Rd

🍴 Restaurants

» **Deep** • The Boulevard, Imperial Wharf
» **Sands End** • 135 Stephendale Rd

MUSWELL HILL

Highgate Wood

Queen's Wood

HIGHGATE

CROUCH END

52

Hornsey

Hampstead Ln

51

Highgate Hill

Archway Rd

Waterlow Park

ARCH

Hampstead Heath

59

Junction Rd

Hampstead Heath

DARTMOUTH PARK

H

Parliament Hill

58

TU

56

HAMPSTEAD

Heath St

Rosslyn Hill

Agincourt Rd

Mansfield Rd

Highgate Rd

Fortess Rd

Kentish Town Rd

Bre

57

BELSIZE PARK

72

WEST HAMPSTEAD

Fitzjohn's Ave

67

Maitland Rd

KENT TO

66

SWISS COTTAGE

Haverstock Hill

71

St Pancras W

Adelaide Rd

65

Iverson Rd

West End Ln

Kilburn High Rd

SOUTH HAMPSTEAD

70

Finchley Rd

Quex Rd

Belsize Rd

Primrose Hill

PRIMROSE HILL

Camden High St

Roya

68

Avenue Rd

69

London Zoo

REGENT'S PARK

KILBURN

Maida Vale

Abbey Rd

Wellington Rd

Prince Albert Rd

Albany St

Hampstead Rd

77

ST. JOHN'S WOOD

Regent's Park

Park Rd

WEST KILBURN

LISSON GREEN ESTATE

EUSTO

KENSAL TOWN

MAIDA HILL

MAIDA VALE

St John's Wood Rd

Lisson Grove

Edgware Rd

76

MARYLEBONE

Marylebone Rd

FI

Map 51 · **Highgate**

1

2

Highgate
Golf Course

Highgate
Allotments

Storey Road

Yeatman Road

North Hill
Avenue

Archway Road A1

Highgate
Wood

Muswell Hill

A

Stormont Road

View Road

View Road

Church Road

Wood Lane

Highgate

Broadlands Road

Broadlands

HIGHGATE

The Park   The Park

Hillcrest

Jacksons Lane

52

Hampstead
Heath

PAGE
338

Hampstead Lane B519

Grimshaw Close

Castle
Yd

Southwood Lane B550

Southwood Avenue

Lawn   Road

58

Fitzroy Park

The Grove

West Hill

South Grove

Cholmeley

Crescent

Park lands

Park lands

B

West
Lane

Holly Lodge Gdns

Townsend Yd

Broadbent Close

Duke's Head Yd

Cholmeley Park

Winchester
Place

Winchester
Rd

Highgate
Cemetery

Highgate
Cemetery

○ **Highgate
Cemetery**

PAGE
340

Waterlow
Park

DARTMOUTH
PARK

Cromwell Avenue

59

Hornsey Lane

Makepeace
Avenue

○ **Karl Marx's Grave**

Highgate
Cemetery

Holbrook
Close

Waterlow   Road

Langbourne
Avenue

0.25 mile   0.25 km

Map 51

Compared to grimy Archway, Highgate's like a different planet. The streets are clean, the air doesn't taste funny, and people generally seem happy. Really. Grab a baguette and a bottle from The Corner Shop for picnic in Waterlow Park or head to the Flask for hearty pub food and real ales. Either way, it's just a different London--a less chaotic one.

£ Banks

- **Barclays** • 56 Highgate High St
- **Lloyds** • 51 Highgate High St

Coffee

- **Caffe Nero** • 62 Highgate High St
- **Costa** • 66 Highgate High St

Landmarks

- **Highgate Cemetery** • 1 Swain's Lane
- **Karl Marx's Grave** • Highgate Cemetry

Nightlife

- **The Angel Inn** • 37 Highgate High St
- **The Boogaloo** • 312 Archway Rd
- **The Flask** • 77 Highgate West Hill
- **Prince Of Wales** • 53 Highgate High St
- **The Victoria** • 28 N Hill
- **The Woodman** • 414 Archway Rd
- **The Wrestlers** • 98 North Rd

Post Offices

- **Highgate Near Station** • 361 Archway Rd

Restaurants

- **The Bull** • 13 North Hill Ave
- **Cafe Rouge** • 6 South Grove
- **Papa Del's** • 347 Archway Rd
- **Red Lion And Sun** • 25 North Rd

Shopping

- **The Corner Shop** • 88 Highgate High St
- **Dragonfly Wholefoods** • 24 Highgate High Street
- **Highgate Butchers** • 76 Highgate High St
- **Hops N Pops** • 389 Archway Rd
- **Le Chocolatier** • 78 Highgate High St
- **Mind** • 329 Archway Rd
- **Oxfam** • 80 Highgate High St
- **Second Layer Records** • 323 Archway Rd
- **Walter Castellazzo Design** • 84 Highgate High St
- **Wild Guitars** • 393 Archway Road

Map 52

omething unexpected is happening here. Designer boutiques keep popping up; shion labels we've never even heard of. Then there's Dean & Hudson, a café so shionably quirky it should really be in Shoreditch. But real change takes time and night this becomes even more obvious. The Winchester is still the only decent ub around and The Caipirinha still stays open very, very late.

Landmarks

Parkland Walk Nature Reserve • Parkland Walk
Suicide Bridge • Hornsey Ln & Archway Rd

Libraries

London Mennonite Centre Library •
14 Shepherds Hill Heights

Nightlife

Caipirinha Jazz Bar • 177 Archway Rd
The Winchester Pub Hotel • 206 Archway Rd

Restaurants

Bengal Berties • 172 Archway Rd
Dean & Hudson • 249 Archway Rd
Fahrenheit • 230 Archway Rd
The Lighthouse • 179 Archway Rd

Shopping

Archway Cycles • 183 Archway Rd
Archway Video • 220 Archway Rd
The Green Room • 192 Archway Rd
Pax Guns • 166 Archway Rd
Wine of Course • 216 Archway Rd

Crouch End gets a bit of a bad rep. It's boring, people say. Just prams and middle-class media types. But, you know--it could be a lot worse. It's safe, with plenty of decent pubs (The King's Head), eateries (Banners) and a great record shop (Flashback). It might be low on the hipster scale, but for plain ol' good livin' it ticks all the boxes.

Map 5

£ Banks

- **Abbey** • 5 The Broadway
- **Barclays** • 8 The Broadway
- **Lloyds** • 34 The Broadway

Coffee

Spiazzo • 26 The Broadway
Starbucks • 7 The Broadway

Landmarks

Abandoned Warehouse •
Parkland Walk & Crouch End Hill

Libraries

- **Highgate Library** • 1 Shepherds Hill
- **Hornsey Library** • Haringey Park

Nightlife

Harringay Arms • 153 Crouch Hill
The King's Head • 2 Tottenham Ln
The Queens Pub & Dining Rooms •
26 Broadway Parade
The Wishing Well • 22 Topsfield Parade, Tottenham Lane

Post Offices

- **Crouch End** • 28 Topsfield Parade

Restaurants

- **Arocaria** • 48 The Broadway
- **Banners** • 21 Park Rd
- **Hot Pepper Jelly** • 11 Broadway Parade
- **Milou's on the Hill** • 83 Hazellville Rd
- **Piya Cafe** • 59 The Broadway
- **Thaitanic** • 66 Crouch End Hill

Shopping

- **Flashback** • 144 Crouch Hill
- **Haelen Centre** • 41 The Broadway
- **Walter Purkis And Sons** • 17 The Broadway

Map 5

his is as residential as it gets and you'll struggle to find as much as an open corner hop. There's bit of action up at Tottenham Lane, but by then you're virtually in Crouch End. Ridge Café is worth a stop for a good cup of coffee and some cake while you're at it. The locals watch sport at the seriously unpretentious Hope and Anchor pub.

Libraries

Stroud Green Library • Quernmore Rd

Nightlife

The Hope & Anchor • 128 Tottenham Ln

Restaurants

Ridge Cafe • 97 Tottenham Ln

A walk up Green Lanes is a pretty grim experience. Roughly one gazillion kebab places, a bunch of jewellers, a horrid-looking wedding shop and, well, not much else. Eventually, the Garden Ladder provides a glimmer of hope with cheap guest ales and finally, at the very end of the ladder, there's a different culinary option at Muna's, London's premier Sudanese restaurant.

Map 5

Coffee

Cafe Delight · 351 Green Lanes
Mezzo Shisha Lounge · 64 Grand Parade

Nightlife

The Beaconsfield · 359 Green Lanes
The Garden Ladder · 501 Green Lanes
The Salisbury · 1 Grand Parade, Green Lanes

Post Offices

Harringay · 509 Green Lanes

Restaurants

Muna's · 599 Green Lanes
The Village · 421 Green Lanes

Supermarkets

Sainsbury's · 4 Williamson Rd

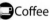

ure, leafy Hampstead Village is very posh and la-de-da, but there's still some fun
o be had. Head to Flask Walk for cute and eccentric local shops and, of course,
waffles at Slice of Ice. The Duke of Hamilton is as good a pub you're likely to find
nywhere and when they kick you out, Tinseltown does amazing milkshakes until
he early hours.

£ Banks

Barclays • 28 Hampstead High St
HSBC • 12 Hampstead High St
Lloyds • 40 Rosslyn Hill
NatWest • 25 Hampstead High St

Cinemas

Everyman Cinema Club • 5 Hollybush Vale

Coffee

Caffe Nero • 1 Hampstead High St
Ginger & White • 4 Perrin's Ct

Landmarks

Hampstead Observatory •
Lower Terrace & Hampstead Grove

Cinemas

Everyman Hampstead • 5 Hollybush Vale

Nightlife

• **The Duke of Hamilton** • 23 New End
• **The Flask** • 14 Flask Walk
• **The Freemasons Arms** • 32 Downshire Hill
• **Holly Bush** • 22 Holly Mount
• **The Rosslyn Arms** • 48 Rosslyn Hill

Restaurants

• **Bacchus Greek Taverna** • 37 Heath St
• **Carluccio's** • 34 Rosslyn Hill
• **La Creperie De Hampstead** • 77 Hampstead High St
• **The Louis Patisserie** • 32 Heath St
• **Tinseltown** • 104 Heath St

Map 56

Map 57

This area doesn't feel quite as posh as Hampstead Village, but that's mainly because the ugly Royal Free Hospital dominates the view. The bars and restaurants are all very upmarket, with prices to match. The beer garden at the Garden Gate is great for summer evenings (got heating as well, just in case) and any of the little restaurants on South End Road will fill you up nicely.

Coffee
Starbucks • 5 South End Rd

Emergency Rooms
Royal Free Hospital • Pond St & Fleet Rd

Landmarks
Keats' House • Keats Grove
Lawn Road Flats • Lawn Rd & Garnett Rd

Libraries
Heath Library • Keats Grove

Nightlife
The Garden Gate • 14 S End Rd
The Magdala • 2 South Hill Park
Roebuck • 15 Pond St

Restaurants
Hampstead Tea Rooms • 9 South End Rd
Osteria Emilia • 85 Fleet Rd
Paradise • 49 South End Rd
Polly's • 55 South End Rd

Shopping
Daunt Books • 51 South End Rd
Giocobazzi's Delicatessen • 150 Fleet Rd

Map 38 • **Parliament Hill / Dartmouth Park**

Holly Lodge Gdns

Highgate Cemetery

West Hill

Highgate West Hill

HIGHGATE

Oakeshott

Avenue

Makepeace

51

Langbourne

Avenue

Avenue

Bromwich Avenue

Chester

St. Anne's Close

Church Walk

Swains Lane

St. Albans Road

St. Albans Road

Kingswear Road

Brookfield Park

Croftdown Road

DARTMOUTH PARK

57

Woodsome Road

Laurier Road

Laurier Road

York Rise

Dartmouth Park Road

Glenhurst Avenue

Dartmouth Park Road

Bellgate Mews

Chetwynd

Mansfield Road B518

Gordon House Road B518

Twisden Road

Spencer Rise

GOSPEL OAK

Wesleyan Place

Churchill Road

Ingestre Road

59

Burghley Road

72

Sanderson Close

Lady Somerset Road

Oakford Road

Breaknock Road A5200

0.25 mile   0.25 km

Parliament Hill / Dartmouth Park

n area you stumble upon by accident, on your way somewhere else, probably ampstead Heath or Highgate Cemetery. Then you realize how nice it is. Maybe ou should try the little restaurants? Soon you find yourself having pizza at Al Parco ery week and trekking all across London just to find out what new ales they're rving at the Southampton Arms. You could live here. You really could.

Nightlife

ar Lorca • 156 Fortress Rd
he Bull and Last • 168 Highgate Rd
he Dartmouth Arms • 35 York Rise
uke of St. Albans • Highgate Road
he Southampton Arms • 139 Highgate Rd

Restaurants

l Parco • 2 Highgate West Hill
afe Mozart • 17 Swain's Ln
he Carob Tree • 15 Highgate Rd
alendar • 15 Swains Lane
tingray Cafe • 135 Fortress Rd

Shopping

orks • 9 Swain's Ln

Map 59

surrounded by the rougher Archway, Kentish Town, and Holloway—and immortalised by Simon Pegg in cult comedies Spaced and Shaun of the Dead-assuming Tufnell Park has been quietly fashionable for years. Unwind with a book and a coffee at Rustique, or hit The Star for a good selection of beers. The Dome hosts everything from the latest cutting-edge electronica to seasoned indie rock acts.

Emergency Rooms

Whittington Hospital •
Magdala Ave & Dartmouth Park Hill

Libraries

Highgate Library • Chester Rd

Nightlife

Boston Arms • 178 Junction Rd
The Dome • 178 Junction Rd
The Hideaway • 114 Junction Rd
The Lord Palmerston • 33 Dartmouth Park Hill
The Star • 47 Chester Rd

Restaurants

Charuwan • 110 Junction Rd
Rustique Cafe • 142 Fortess Rd
Spaghetti House • 169 Fortess Rd
The Spice • 161 Fortess Rd

Shopping

The Blue Carbuncle • 130 Junction Rd
The Hornsey Trust Charity Shop • 124 Fortess Rd
North London Adoption Centre • 135 Junction Rd

Map 60

grey and gritty as ever, Archway could really do with a fresh lick of paint. For
break from the grime try La Voute with their art exhibitions and awesome
eakfasts or RRC Thai for something spicier. At night, there are enough old man
oozers to keep you busy, but bear in mind, nicer places are only a short bus ride
ay.

 Banks

loyds • 19 Highgate Hill

 Coffee

afe Metro • 4 Junction Rd

Landmarks

anksy's Hitchhiking Charles Manson •
ally Ho Corner (off Highgate Hill)
ick Whittington's Cat • 89 Highgate Hill

Libraries

rchway Library • Highgate Hill

Nightlife

rchway Tavern • 1 Archway Close
he Mother Red Cap • 665 Holloway Rd

Restaurants

- **Archgate Café** • 5 Junction Rd
- **Iceland Fish Bar** • 11 Archway Rd
- **Junction Café** • 61 Junction Rd
- **La Voute** • 10 Archway Rd
- **Mosaic Café** • 24 Junction Rd
- **Nid Ting** • 533 Holloway Rd
- **RRC Thai Café** • 36 Highgate Hill
- **St Johns** • 91 Junction Rd
- **The Toll Gate** • 6 Archway Close

Shopping

- **Second Chance** • 7 St John's Way
- **Super Persia** • 621 Holloway Rd

Supermarkets

- **Co-Op** • 11 Junction Rd
- **Sainsbury's** • 643 Holloway Rd

The borough of Islington, in which North Holloway sits, is supposed to be either a byword for liberal middle class cosiness or else grim inner city deprivation, depending on who you talk to. This bit has neither, just lots of dull grey streets. The Shaftesbury brightens up Hornsey Road with good pub food and unusual beers, while El Molino (down on Holloway Road) is a great place for tapas.

Map 6

💲Banks
- Barclays • 403 Holloway Rd
- Halifax • 19 Seven Sisters Rd
- NatWest • 490 Holloway Rd

☕Coffee
- Caffe Nero • 400 Holloway Rd

🎬Cinemas
- Odeon Holloway • 419 Holloway Rd

📚Libraries
- North Library • Manor Gardens

🌃Nightlife
- Nambucca • 596 Holloway Rd
- The Quays • 471 Holloway Rd
- The Swimmer • 13 Eburne Rd

🍴Restaurants
- **El Molino** • 379 Holloway Rd
- **The Landseer** • 37 Landseer Rd
- **Orexi** • 236 Hornsey Rd
- **Tagine D' Or** • 92 Seven Sisters Rd

🛍Shopping
- **Michael's Fruiterers** • 56 Seven Sisters Rd

🛒Supermarkets
- **Iceland** • 442 Holloway Rd

Map 62

it's move to Finsbury Park,' newcomers say, 'why it's so near a park, a tube, AND a ...tion.' Then they get here. But there are twinkles—the park café, and the infamous ...sque now doing community outreach. Head to the Faltering Fullback for a pint, ...dleys for pancakes, the Happening Bagel Bakery for—well, you know—or run ...e gauntlet of Blackstock Road for bundles of mint and tasty lamachun.

Banks

atWest • 298 Seven Sisters Rd

Landmarks

...orth London Central Mosque (Finsbury Park) •
  St Thomas's Rd

Libraries

...4 Library • 26 Blackstock Road

Nightlife

...he Faultering Fullback • 19 Perth Rd

Post Offices

...troud Green Rd • 97 Stroud Green Rd

Restaurants

- **Dudley's Pancake House** • 119 Stroud Green Rd
- **Fassika** • 152 Seven Sisters Rd
- **Le Rif** • 172 Seven Sisters Rd
- **Petek** • 96 Stroud Green Rd

Shopping

- **The Happening Bagel Bakery** • 284 Seven Sisters Rd

Supermarkets

- **Tesco** • 105 Stroud Green Rd

Map 63

n't hang out near the 'scummy round the edges' station as it can get pretty
uesome at night, particularly round the horrific Manor Club. You might chance
on a warehouse party round here, but walk south, dodge the rats around the
servoir, admire the faux turrets of the Castle Climbing Centre and head to the New
ver Café for great fry-ups with views over the leafy oasis of Clissold Park.

Banks

Abbey • 304 7 Sisters Rd
Barclays • 254 7 Sisters Rd
HSBC • 312 7 Sisters Rd

Landmarks

The Castle Climbing Centre •
Green Lanes & Lordship Park

Libraries

Woodberry Down Library • 440 7 Sisters Rd

Nightlife

The Brownswood Park Tavern • 271 Green Lanes
The Manor Club • 277 Seven Sisters Rd

Post Offices

• **Woodberry Grove** • 107 Woodberry Grove

Restaurants

• **Il Bacio** • 178 Blackstock Rd
• **New River Café** • 271 Stoke Newington Church St

ned for its high square footage of creative types and three-wheeled buggies, s buzzing villagey 'hood has lost a lot of its Hackney edge but still has the d shooting to keep locals on their toes. Great beer and atmosphere (The akespeare), curry (Rasa N16), Sunday roast (Rose and Crown), and silver jewelry etal Crumble) to be found along mainly chain-free Stoke Newington Church reet.

Banks
- **Abbey** • 139 Stoke Newington Rd
- **Lloyds** • 133 Stoke Newington High St

Landmarks
- **Newington Green Church** • 39 Newington Green

Libraries
- **Stoke Newington Library** • Stoke Newington Church St

Nightlife
- **The Auld Shillelagh** • 105 Stoke Newington Church St
- **Londesborough** • 36 Barbauld Rd
- **Rose and Crown** • 199 Stoke Newington Church St
- **Ryan's Bar** • 181 Stoke Newington Church St
- **The Shakespeare** • 57 Allen Rd
- **White Hart** • 69 Stoke Newington High St

Post Offices
- **Church Street** • 170 Stoke Newington Church St
- **Stoke Newington** • Stoke Newington High St

Restaurants
- **Alistair's Brasserie** • 35 Stoke Newington Church St
- **Anglo Asian** • 60 Stoke Newington Church St
- **Blue Legume** • 101 Stoke Newington Church St
- **Fifty Six** • 56 Newington Green
- **Rasa N16** • 55 Stoke Newington Church St
- **Sariyer Balik** • 56 Green Lanes
- **Yum Yum** • 187 Stoke Newington High St

Shopping
- **Ark** • 161 Stoke Newington Rd
- **The Beaucatcher Salon** •
  44 Stoke Newington Church Street
- **Belle Epoque Boulangerie** • 37 Newington Green
- **Bridgewood & Neitzert** • 146 Stoke Newington Church St
- **Church Street Bookshop** •
  142 Stoke Newington Church St
- **Metal Crumble** • 13 Stoke Newington Church St
- **Mind** • 11 Stoke Newington Church St
- **Of Cabbages & Kings** • 34 Kersley Rd
- **Ribbons and Taylor** • 157 Stoke Newington Church St
- **Rosa Lingerie** • 3 Church Walk
- **Route 73 Kids** • 92 Stoke Newington Church St
- **S'graffiti** • 172 Stoke Newington Church St
- **Sacred Art** • 148 Albion Rd
- **The Spence Bakery** • 161 Stoke Newington Church St
- **Stoke Newington Farmers Market** • Stoke Newington Church St & Stoke Newington High St

Supermarkets
- **Whole Foods Market** • 32 Stoke Newington Church St
- **Iceland** • 17 Green Lanes

West Hampstead

...mpstead's ugly sister, West Hampstead is a leafy suburb that has absorbed some ...Kilburn's grittiness. Young urban nomads make up much of the population, as ...nt is moderate by London standards. Like the rest of London, West Hampstead ...s its fair share of Caffe Neros and Costa Coffees, but check out the Green Room ...r atmosphere and The Good Ship for music or comedy.

Map 65

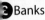 Banks

- **Barclays** • 83 Kilburn High Rd
- **Barclays** • 208 W End Ln
- **Halifax** • 149 Kilburn High Rd
- **Lloyds** • 106 Kilburn High Rd
- **NatWest** • 74 Kilburn High Rd

Coffee

- **Caffe Nero** • 101 Kilburn High Rd
- **Costa** • 203 W End Ln
- **Starbucks** • 201 W End Ln

Libraries

- **West Hampstead Library** • Dennington Park Rd

Nightlife

- **The Czech and Slovak Bar** • 74 West End Lane
- **The Good Ship** • 289 Kilburn High Rd
- **The Luminaire** • 311 High Rd

Post Offices

- **West Hampstead** • 128 W End Ln

Restaurants

- **The Green Room** • 182 Broadhurst Gardens
- **Small & Beautiful** • 351 Kilburn High Rd

Shopping

- **Party Party** • 206 Kilburn High Rd
- **Primark** • 54 Kilburn High Rd

Supermarkets

- **Sainsbury's** • 88 Kilburn High Rd
- **Sainsbury's** • 377 Kilburn High Rd

(141)

Map 66 • Finchley Road / Swiss Cottage

1

2

Mill Lane

West End Lane

Cannon Hill

West Cottages

West End Lane

Frognal

Lane

Greenaway Gardens

Oak Hill Park Ms

Frognal

Frognal

Mount Vernon

Holly Hill

Holly Wk

Church Row

Shepherds Wk

Hamps

Church Row

Ellerdale Road

Fitzjohn's Avenue

B511

Prince

Heath

Street

A

Cumberland
Lawn
Tennis Club

Hampstead
Cricket
Club

Frognal Close

WEST
HAMPSTEAD

Arkwright Road

Lithos Road

Rosemont Road

Frognal

Netherhall Gardens

Lyndhur

B511

B510

B520

West End Lane

Lymington Road

Dresden

West
Hampstead

West Hampstead

Frognal Way

SOUTH
HAMPSTEAD

65

Gardens

Broadhurst

Fairhazel Gardens

Canfield Gardens

Greencroft Gardens

Finchley Road A41

Frognal Court

Netherhall Way

Nutley Terrace

Fitzjohn's Avenue

B511

67

Burdett Ms

B

Aberdare Gardens

Goldhurst Terrace

Marston

Naseby

Belsize
Rd

College Crescent

Belsize Lane

Belsize Park

68

Belsize Road

B509

Fairfax Place

Fairfax Road

Belsize Road

Eton Avenue

Adamson Road

BELSIZE
PARK

Hilgrove Rd

Dobson Close

Finchley Road

Swiss Cottage

Fellows Road

South Hampstead
Rail Station

Adelaide Road

Winchester Road

A41

Hornby Close

69

Finchley Road / Swiss Cottage

Map 66

Although it is sandwiched between West Hampstead and Primrose Hill, this is simply not a great spot unless you're seeking bargains in the local pound shop. Finchley Road has a range of mediocre restaurants. Swiss Cottage has a good library and sports centre. The Camden Arts Centre and Freud Museum are jewels in this battered crown—it's worth braving the traffic to see them.

£ Banks

Abbey • 8 Finchley Rd
Barclays • 131 Finchley Rd
Halifax • 169 Finchley Rd
HSBC • 122 Finchley Rd
Lloyds • 145 Finchley Rd
NatWest • 106 Finchley Rd

Cinemas

Odeon Swiss Cottage • 96 Finchley Rd
Vue Finchley Road • Finchley Rd & Blackburn Rd

Coffee

Cafe Express • 25 Finchley Rd
Costa • 149 Finchley Rd
Starbucks • 255 Finchley Rd

Libraries

Swiss Cottage Library • 88 Avenue Rd

Nightlife

• **Ye Olde Swiss Cottage** • 98 Finchley Rd

Restaurants

• **Bradleys** • 25 Winchester Rd
• **Camden Arts Centre** • Arkwright Rd
• **Singapore Garden** • 83 Fairfax Rd

Supermarkets

• **Sainsbury's** • 255 Finchley Rd
• **Waitrose** • 199 Finchley Rd

Belsize Park

Map 67

Aggressively affluent rather than glamorous, Belsize Park is still not without its charm. Skip the upmarket chain restaurants by the tube and head to England's Lane. Nip in for coffee and cake at Violette's or something stronger at The Washington. When you're feeling peckish Belsize Lane has a great selection of eateries, but the grill at Retsina is hard to beat.

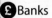 ## Banks

- **HSBC** • 147 Haverstock Hill
- **NatWest** • 185 Haverstock Hill

Cinemas

- **Everyman Belsize Park** • 203 Haverstock Hill

Coffee

- **Starbucks** • 57 England's Lane
- **Starbucks** • 202 Haverstock Hill

 ## Landmarks

- **Freud Statue** •
  Fitzjohn's Ave, opposite Maresfield Gardens Junction
- **St Stephen's** • Rosslyn Hill

Libraries

- **Belsize Library** • Antrim Rd

Nightlife

- **The Washington** • 50 England's Ln

Restaurants

- **Artigiano** • 12 Belsize Terrace
- **Brasserie Gerard** • 215 Haverstock Hill
- **Curry Manjil** • 34 England's Ln
- **Paradiso** • 36 England's Ln
- **Retsina** • 48 Belsize Ln
- **Violette Cafe** • 2 England's Ln

Shopping

- **Belsize Village Delicatessen** • 39 Belsize Ln
- **Lotus and Frog** • 32 England's Ln

Kilburn High Road / Abbey Road

Map 68

Opposites attract: to the east Abbey Road and dull suburbia beckon, while the west is dominated by grime and urban decay. For pockets of somethin' somethin' try The Clifton for drinkies or pig out at the delightful Little Bay. Better still, look up to the faded Art Deco grandeur of the State Building. Oh yeah, and remember it's just another bloody zebra crossing.

£ Banks

Barclays • 40 Wellington Rd
HSBC • 50 Kilburn High Rd
HSBC • 1 Finchley Rd
NatWest • 102 St John's Wood High St

Coffee

Starbucks • 79 St John's Wood High St

Landmarks

Abbey Road Zebra Crossing • 3 Abbey Rd

Libraries

Kilburn Library • 12 Kilburn High Rd
St John's Wood Library TEMPORARY LOCATION! • 20 Circus Rd

Y Nightlife

• **The Clifton** • 96 Clifton Hill

Post Offices

• **Kilburn** • 79 Kilburn High Rd
• **St Johns Wood** • 32 Circus Rd

Restaurants

• **Little Bay** • 228 Belsize Rd

Supermarkets

• **Tesco** • 115 Maida Vale

A leafy suburb for shy, retiring super-rich types. There's not much to do here (especially if you discount spotting hungover celebrities), but the leisure centre on Adelaide road is pretty swish with its climbing wall. To the west, Primrose Hill (and its hyper-bourgeois shops) is like Valhalla in North London and should be flocked to as soon as the sun shines.

 Nightlife

• **The Star** • 38 St. Johns Wood Terrace

 Restaurants

• **Tupelo Honey** • 27 Parkway, Camden

Map 70 · **Primrose Hill**

Primrose Hill

Map 70

The debauched Primrose Hill set, a gang of famous drug-taking, booze-swilling, partner-swapping models and actors, has upped sticks for St. John's Wood, but Primrose Hill retains a trendy appeal. Home of yummy mummies and their spouses and a few (older) artistic types, it has an excess of wonderful and expensive shops (Press, Shikasuki), restaurants (Lemonia) and coffee shops (Cafe 79, Primrose Bakery).

Landmarks
• **3 Chalcot Square** • 3 Chalcot Sq

Libraries
• **Chalk Farm Library** • 11 Sharples Hall St

Nightlife
• **The Albert** • 11 Princess Rd
• **Cecil Sharp House** • 2 Regents Park Rd
• **The Engineer** • 65 Gloucester Ave [Princess Road]
• **The Lansdowne** • 90 Gloucester Ave [Regent's Park Road]
• **Princess of Wales** • 22 Chalcot Rd
• **Queens No. 1** • 1 Edis St
• **Sir Richard Steele** • 97 Haverstock Hill

Post Offices
• **Regents Park Road** • 91 Regents Park Road

Restaurants
• **Cafe Seventy Nine** • 79 Regents Park Rd
• **The Hill Bar** • 94 Haverstock Hill
• **J Restaurant** • 148 Regents Park Rd
• **Legal Cafe** • 81 Haverstock Hill
• **Lemonia** • 89 Regents Park Rd
• **Manna** • 4 Erskine Rd [Regent's Park Road]
• **Melrose and Morgan** • 42 Gloucester Ave
• **Odette's** • 130 Regents Park Rd
• **Primrose Bakery** • 69 Gloucester Ave [Edis Street]
• **Trojka** • 101 Regents Park Rd
• **Two Brothers** • 297 Regents Park Rd

Shopping
• **Judith Michael & Daughter** • 73 Regents Park Rd
• **Miss Lala's Boudoir** • 148 Gloucester Ave
• **Nicolas (off licence)** • 67 Regents Park Rd
• **Press** • 3 Erskine Rd
• **Primrose Hill Books** • 134 Regent's Park Rd
• **Primrose Newsagent** • 91 Regents Park Rd
• **Richard Dare** • 93 Regents Park Rd
• **Shepherd Foods** • 59 Regents Park Rd
• **Shikasuki** • 67 Gloucester Ave
• **Sweet Pea** • 77 Gloucester Ave
• **Tann Rokka** • 123 Regent's Park Rd
• **Yeomans Grocers** • 152 Regent's Park Rd

We have a soft spot for Camden. Dull during the week and tourist hell-hole at the weekends, but somehow London just wouldn't be the same without it. Up The Video Junction is London's best DVD shop for obscure titles and Marine Ices do amazing ice cream and shakes. Camden at night is still all about live music, with enough venues to satisfy the weirdest of tastes.

£ Banks

- **Abbey** • 121 Camden High St
- **Barclays** • 193 Camden High St
- **HSBC** • 176 Camden High St
- **Lloyds** • 140 Camden High St
- **Royal Bank of Scotland** •
  189 Camden High St

Cinemas

- **Odeon Camden Town** • 14 Parkway

Coffee

- **Cafe La Cigale** • 47 Parkway
- **Cafe Metro** • 178 Camden High St
- **Caffe Nero** • 7 Jamestown Rd
- **Caffe Nero** • 11 Parkway
- **Costa** • 181 Camden High St
- **Eat.** • 185 Camden High St
- **Inhabition** • 15 Chalk Farm Rd
- **Pret A Manger** • 157 Camden High St
- **Pret A Manger** • 261 High St
- **Starbucks** •
  Parkway Camden & Arlington Rd

O Landmarks

- **Camden Market** • Camden Lock Pl
- **Grand Regents Canal** •
  Grand Regents Canal
- **The Roundhouse** •
  Chalk Farm Rd & Crogsland Rd

Libraries

- **Queen's Crescent Library** •
  165 Queen's Crescent

Nightlife

- **Bar Vinyl** • 6 Inverness St
- **Barfly** • 49 Chalk Farm Rd
- **Bartok** • 78 Chalk Farm Rd
- **The Constitution** • 42 St Pancras Way
- **Dingwalls** • Middle Yard
- **The Dublin Castle** • 94 Parkway
- **Electric Ballroom** • 184 Camden High St
- **The Enterprise** • 2 Haverstock Hill
- **Fiddlers Elbow** • 1 Malden Rd
- **Good Mixer** • 30 Inverness St
- **The Hawley Arms** • 2 Castlehaven Rd
- **Jazz Cafe** • 5 Parkway
- **Koko** • 1 Camden High St
- **The Lock Tavern** • 35 Chalk Farm Rd
- **Monkey Chews** • 2 Queen's Crescent
- **Oxford Arms** • 265 Camden High St
- **Proud Camden** • Chalk Farm Rd
- **Quinn's** • 65 Kentish Town Rd
- **The Underworld** • 174 Camden High St

Post Offices

- **Camden High Street** •
  112 Camden High St
- **Queen's Crescent** •
  139 Queen's Crescent

Restaurants

- **Andy's Taverna** • 81 Bayham St
- **Bar Gansa** • 2 Inverness St
- **Bar Solo** • 20 Inverness St
- **Bento Cafe** • 9 Parkway
- **Camden Bar And Kitchen** •
  102 Camden High St
- **Cotton's** • 55 Chalk Farm Rd
- **Gilgamesh** •
  The Stables Market, Chalk Farm Rd
- **The Green Note** • 106 Parkway
- **HachÉ** • 24 Inverness St
- **Kim's Vietnamese Food Hut** •
  Unit D, Camden Lock Palace
- **Limani** • 154 Regents Park Rd
- **Marathon Cafe** • 87 Chalk Farm Rd
- **Marine Ices** • 8 Haverstock Hill
- **Market** • 438 Parkway
- **Muang Thai** • 71 Chalk Farm Rd
- **My Village** • 37 Chalk Farm Rd
- **Thanh Binh** • 14 Chalk Farm Rd
- **Viet-anh Cafe** • 41 Parkway
- **Woody Grill** • 1 Camden Rd
- **Yumcha Tea Space** •
  91 Upper Walkway, West Yard,
  Camden Lock Market
- **Zorya Imperial Vodka Room** •
  48 Chalk Farm Rd

Shopping

- **Acumedic** • 101 Camden High St
- **Aldo Sale Shop** •
  231 Camden High St
- **Arckiv Vintage Eyewear** •
  Chalk Farm Rd & Castlehaven Rd
- **Black Rose** •
  The Stables Market, Chalk Farm Rd
- **Cyberdog** •
  Stables Market, Chalk Farm Rd
- **Episode** • 26 Chalk Farm Rd
- **Escapade** • 45 Chalk Farm Rd
- **Eye Contacts** • 10 Chalk Farm Rd
- **Fresh & Wild, Camden** • 49 Parkway
- **Graham and Green** •
  164 Regents Park Rd
- **Metal Militia** • 258 Camden High St
- **Music & Video Exchange** •
  208 Camden High St
- **Ray Man Music** • 54 Chalk Farm Rd
- **Rokit** • 225 Camden High St
- **Sounds That Swing** • 46 Inverness St
- **Traid** • 154 Camden High St
- **Up The Video Junction** •
  Middle Yard, Camden Lock Pl
- **Village Games** • 65 The West Yard
- **Whole Foods Market** • 49 Parkway

Supermarkets

- **Whole Foods Market** • 49 Parkway
- **Sainsbury's** • 77 Chalk Farm Rd
- **Sainsbury's** • 17 Camden St
- **Sainsbury's** • 10 Camden Rd

Kentish Town

Map 72

On first glance Kentish Town is just a grubby, horrible collection of pound shops and charity shops, but venture behind the high street and you'll find some of the most welcoming places North London has to offer. The Pineapple is a great little pub (if you can find it) and you might just bump into some hipster indie legend at Mario's Café.

Banks

- **Abbey** • 233 Kentish Town Rd
- **Barclays** • 230 Kentish Town Rd
- **HSBC** • 246 Kentish Town Rd

Coffee

- **Cafe Metro** • 180 Camden High St

Libraries

- **Kentish Town Library** • 262 Kentish Town Rd

Nightlife

- **The Abbey Tavern** • 124 Kentish Town Rd
- **The Assembly House** • 292 Kentish Town
- **The Bull & Gate** • 389 Kentish Town Rd
- **The Flowerpot** • 147 Kentish Town Rd
- **HMV Forum** • 9 Highgate Rd
- **The Lion and Unicorn** • 42 Gaisford St
- **The Pineapple** • 51 Leverton St
- **Rio's Health Spa** • 239 Kentish Town Rd

Restaurants

- **The Bengal Lancer** • 253 Kentish Town Rd
- **Bintang Cafe** • 93 Kentish Town Rd
- **Cafe Renoir** • 244 Kentish Town Rd
- **Eatzone** • 18 Fortess Rd
- **ITTA** • 225 Kentish Town Rd
- **Le Petit Prince** • 5 Holmes Rd
- **Mario's Cafe** • 6 Kelly St
- **The Oxford** • 256 Kentish Town Rd
- **Pane Vino** • 323 Kentish Town Rd
- **Phoenicia - Mediterranean Food Hall** • 186 Kentish Town Rd

Shopping

- **Blustons** • 213 Kentish Town Rd
- **Dots** • 132 St Pancras Way
- **Fish** • 161 Kentish Town Rd
- **Phoenicia** • 186 Kentish Town Rd
- **Pro Percussion** • 205 Kentish Town Rd

Supermarkets

- **Co-Op** • 250 Kentish Town Rd
- **EARTH natural foods** • 200 Kentish Town Rd
- **Iceland** • 301 Kentish Town Rd
- **Tesco/Esso** • 196 Camden Rd

Map 73 · **Holloway**

N

TUFNELL PARK

HOLLOWAY

LOWER HOLLOWAY

59

60

61

72

74

79

Tufnell Park Road

Tufnell Park Road

St Georges Avenue

Archibald Road

Anson Road

Carleton Road

Tabley Road

Brecknock Road

Parkhurst Road

Camden Road A503

Hilldrop Road

Hilmarton Road A503

Leighton Rd A5200

Camden Road A503

Torriano Avenue A5200

Brecknock Road A5200

Camden Park Road A5200

York Way A5200

Caledonian Road A503

Caledonian Road A5203

Camden Road A503

Caledonian Park

Caledonian Park

Market Road

Market Road Gardens

Brewery Road

Caledonian Road

Caledonian Road A5203

0.25 mile

0.25 km

Holloway is best known for its women's prison and not much else. To the west of Holloway Road it feels a bit like a sprawling backyard to gentrified Camden, Islington, and King's Cross. Nevertheless bars like The Lord Stanley and Shillibeers have gone all gastro, so it doesn't quite have the gritty vibe that it once had.

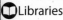
Libraries
• **John Barnes Library** • 275 Camden Rd

Nightlife
• **The Lord Stanley** • 51 Camden Park Rd
• **Shillibeers** • 1 Carpenter's Mews, North Rd

Post Offices
• **Brecknock Rd** • 20 Brecknock Rd

Shopping
• **Bumblebee Natural Foods** • 33 Brecknock Rd
• **DOC Records** • 5 Cardwell Terrace, Cardwell Rd

Supermarkets
• **Sainsbury's** • 4 Williamson St
• **Tesco/Esso** • 196 Camden Rd

Holloway Road / Arsenal

Map 74

ne of the universe's biggest football stadiums has been shoe-horned into this
ea of tidy terraces—red guttering anyone?—and on match days the streets make
sardine tin look roomy. This area also includes the first grotty stretch of Holloway
pad. For something different try House of Harlot for fetish fashion, El Comandante
r drinks, and Tbilisi for cheap eastern European eats.

Banks

- **Abbey** • 408 Holloway Rd
- **Lloyds** • 31 Holloway Rd

Coffee

- **Cafe Nero** • 348 Holloway Rd
- **Le Peche Mignon** • 6 Ronalds Rd

Landmarks

- **Gillespie Park** • 191 Drayton Park

Libraries

- **Central Library** • 2 Fieldway Crescent

Nightlife

- **The Coronet** • 338 Holloway Rd
- **El Comandante** • 10 Annette Rd
- **Hen and Chicken Theatre Bar** • 109 St Paul's Rd
- **The Relentless Garage** • 20 Highbury Corner

Post Offices

- **Highbury** • 5 Highbury Corner
- **Holloway Rd** • 118 Holloway Rd

Restaurants

- **Dastarkhan** • 203 Holloway Rd
- **Morgan M** • 489 Liverpool Rd
- **Tbilisi** • 91 Holloway Rd

Shopping

- **21st Century Retro** • 162 Holloway Rd
- **Fettered Pleasures** • 90 Holloway Rd
- **House of Harlot** • 90 Holloway Rd
- **Vivien of Holloway** • 294 Holloway Rd

Supermarkets

- **Waitrose** • 366 Holloway Rd

Map 75 · **Highbury**

N

1   2

Hurlock Street

Elwood Street

Conewood Street

Quadrant

Quadrant

Green Lanes A105

Brunswick Walk

Brunswick Walk

Collins Road

Sotheby   Road

63

Northolme

Archilaus Road

Aberdeen Road

Kelross Road

Burma

64

Highbury Hill

Aubert Road

Drakeley Court

Lucerne Road

Aubert Park

Aubert Park West

Hamilton Park West

Ronald

Highbury Park A1201

Rosa Mews

Kelross Road

Balfour Road

Highbury   Grange

Pega Lane

Petherton Road

Green Lanes

Jack Walker Court

Hamilton Park

Roseleigh Avenue

Picket Sq

Tavernung Sq

Stradbroke Road

Joiners Place

Coach House Lane

Highbury Hill

Kelvin

Balfour Road

Aberdeen Park

Aberdeen Park

Kingdom Way

Martineau Road

Framfield Road

Highbury Grove A1201

Melody Lane

Aberdeen

Park

Poets

Ferntower

Petherton Road

Whistler Street

HIGHBURY

Aberdeen

Aberdeen Lane

Searson Cres

Beresford Terrace

Pyrland

Beresford Road

74

Highbury Cres

Baalbec

Road

Highbury New Park

Van Park

Grosvenor Aven

Highbury Fields

Gallia Rd

Fergus Rd

Calabria Road

Calabria

Highbury Grove A1201

Grosvenor Avenue

Canonbury
Rail

Heaven Tree Close

Hope Close

Wallace Road

Harecourt

Blair Ct

Northampton Park

St. Paul's
Shrubbery

St. Paul's (North) Park

81

St. Paul's Road

80

Highbury &
Islington

Highbury
Corner

St. Paul's Road A1199

John Spencer

Alwyne Square

Alwyne Park North

Canonbury Park North

Prior Bolton Street

St. Mary's

Canonbury Park South

CANONBURY

Laycock Street Park

Laycock Street

| 0.25 mile | 0.25 km |

Map 7

quiet residential area in the main, blessed with the marvellous Highbury Fields or a hit of green and a thriving gay bar (Oak Bar). Bordered by busy St Paul's Road nd bustling Green Lanes—great for lamachun (Ustun) and the best auto parts op in the world (Cabbies Delight). All gets packed on match day, but try the nooty Fox for a quiet drink or San Daniele Del Friuli for classic Italian.

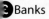

Banks

Abbey • 517 Green Lanes

Landmarks

St Paul's Shrubbery • St Paul's Rd & Northampton Park

Nightlife

Alwyne Castle • 83 St. Pauls Rd
Oak Bar • 79 Green Lanes
The Snooty Fox • 75 Grosvenor Avenue

Post Offices

Grosvenor Avenue • 91 Grosvenor Ave
Highbury Park • 12 Highbury Park

Restaurants

San Daniele Del Friuli • 72 Highbury Park
Ustun • 107 Green Lanes

Shopping

Cabbies Delight Auto Parts • 9 Green Lanes
La Fromagerie • 30 Highbury Park
Mother Earth • 282 St Paul's Rd

Map 76 • Edgeware Road / Marylebone (North)

Elm Tree Road

Wellington Place

Lord's Cricket Ground
PAGE 380

Lord's, Middlesex C.C.C. Practice Ground

St. John's Wood Church Gardens

Maida Vale A5

Clifton Road

27

Blomfield Road

Maida Avenue

St. John's Wood Road A5205

Wellington Road

Prince Albert Road

69

Lodge Road

North Bank

LISSON GROVE

Regent's Canal

Edgeware Road A5

Orchardson Street

Frampton Street

Crescent

Grove Gdns

Hanover Gate

Park Road A41

Church Street

Lisson Grove B507

Broadley Street

Portman Gate

Broadley Terrace

Harewood Avenue

Blandford Square

Marylebone Station
PAGE 413

31

Harrow Road A404

Edgware Road

Marylebone A501

Glentworth Street

Gloucester Place A41

Sherlock Holmes House

2

Baker Street

Old Marylebone Road A501

Seymour Place

Marylebone

1

2

0.25 mile   0.25 km

geware Road / Marylebone (North)

arylebone Road is noisy enough to have you running for the taps of the votwentytwo straight away. Things get calmer (meaning duller) further north, ut Mandalay's inexpensive Burmese treats save the north end of Edgware Road, while the Sea Shell of Lisson Grove does fine fish. And did we mention the great etective? Baker Street, dear Watson, Baker Street.

Map 76

£ Banks

Abbey • 388 Edgware Rd
HSBC • 186 Baker St
Lloyds • 185 Baker St
NatWest • 508 Edgware Rd
Royal Bank of Scotland • 119 Marylebone Rd

Coffee

Costa • 124 Baker St
Pret A Manger • 120 Baker St

Emergency Rooms

Western Eye Hospital • 173 Marylebone Rd

Landmarks

Sherlock Holmes' House • 221 Baker St

Libraries

Church Street Library • Church St
London Business School Library • 25 Taunton Pl
Marylebone Library • 109 Marylebone Rd

Nightlife

• twotwentytwo • 222 Marylebone Road
• The Perseverance • 11 Shroton Street
• Volunteer • 245 Baker St

Post Offices

• Edgware Rd • 354 Edgware Rd

Restaurants

• Mandalay • 444 Edgware Rd
• Sea Shell of Lisson Grove • 49 Lisson Grove

Shopping

• Alfie's Antiques Market • 25 Church St
• Archive Secondhand Books & Music • 83 Bell St
• Beatles London Store • 231 Baker St
• Elvisly Yours • 233 Baker St
• Lord's Cricket Shop •
  Lord's Cricket Ground, Lisson Grove

Supermarkets

• Tesco • 94 Church St

Map 77

med in by Regent's Park and Euston, this patch combines pretty streets with
r-block thoroughfares. Skip the din of Euston underpass for Drummond Street,
nden's 'little India'—decent dosas in Bhel Poori, Chutneys for veggies, the Crown
nchor for mugs of Black Sheep ale. Chow on tofu cheesecake with beatnik slam
ts in Green Note. Mingle al fresco with Edinboro Castle's yuppier folk.

Banks

tWest • 350 Euston Rd

Landmarks

ston Tower • 286 Euston Rd
eater London House • Hampstead Rd

Libraries

gents Park Library • Robert St [Compton Close]

Nightlife

wn & Anchor • 137 Drummond St
inboro Castle • 57 Mornington Terrace
een's Head and Artichoke • 30 Albany St

Restaurants

- **Chutneys** • 124 Drummond St
- **Diwana Bhel Poori** • 121 Drummond St
- **The Green Note** • 106 Parkway
- **Mestizo** • 103 Hampstead Rd

Shopping

- **Calumet Trading** • 93 Drummond St
- **Chess & Bridge** • 369 Euston Rd
- **Greens and Beans** • 131 Drummond St

Map 78 • Euston

N

Camden Town
Parkway A503
Camden Road A503
Kentish
Randolph Street
Agar Grove
Baynes Street
Wrotham Road
Agar Grove

72

Camden Street
Greenland Road
Greenland Street
Royal College Street
Lyme Street
St. Pancras Way A5202

71

Parkway
Arlington Road A503
Signmakers Yd
Pratt St
Bayham Street

Delancey Street
A503

Camden High Street

St. Martin's Gardens
St. Martins Close
Pratt Mews
Pratt Street
Georgiana Street

CAMDEN TOWN

Barker Drive

Mornington Street
Miller St
King's Terrace
Plender Street
Mandela Street
Camden Street A400
College Place
Royal College Street A5202
College Gro

KING'S CROSS

Arlington Road
Albert St
Carlow Street
Beatty St
Bayham Street
Bayham Place

Mornington Place
Mor Cres
Hampstead Road A400

27
21

Crowndale Road
Crowndale Road B512

St. Pancras Hospital

St. Pancras Way A5202
Granary

Mornington Crescent
Harrington Sq
Lid. Place A400
Oakley Square

77

Oakley Square
Chalton St
Goldington Cres
Goldington Street
Pancras Road A5202

St. Pancras Gardens

Camley Street

79

Cranleigh Street
Bridgeway St
Medburn Street
Penny Scrymss Street
Platt Street
Chenies PI

Werrington Street
Aldenham Street
Polygon Road
Cooper's Lane
Brill Place
Pancras Road A5202
Goods Way
Wharf Road

Bernby Street
Eversholt Street A200
Ossulston Street

Phoenix Road
Brill Place
Neville Close

SOMERS TOWN

Weller's Ct
Cheney Rd

Drummond Crescent
Doric Way
Chalton Street

St. Pancras Station

PAGE 414

Midland Road

Platform 9¾

Euston Station
PAGE 410

Lancing Street
Doric
Wellesley Place
Grafton PI
Chris. PI
Weirs Pas

The British Library

King's Cross Station
PAGE 411

York Way A5202
Caledonia

Euston Road
Reg. Blds
Euston Bldgs
Euston Square
Gower Place
Court Place

Grafton Place
Chalton Street
4

Euston Road A501
Bidborough Street
Argyle Street
Pancras Road A5202

2£

Pentonville
Crestfield
Birkenhead

5

Hastings Street
St. Chad's St
Gray's Inn

0.25 mile   0.25 km

Map 78

...ton's the first port of call for thousands of people each day, be it city workers ...m the Shires or pilgrims to the many erotic bookshops by the railway. Look ...ond the station—an ugly grey cube that dominates the area—and you find few ...ns. Students and bookish types head to the outstanding library (British that is), ...sters to the Wills-Moody Jumble Sale, and nobody to the in-station barber.

Banks

- ...rclays • 23 Euston Rd
- ...alifax • 96 Camden High St
- ...SBC • 31 Euston Rd

Coffee

- ...agel Factory • Euston Station
- ...e Espresso Bar • 96 Euston Rd
- ...et A Manger • 296 Pentonville Rd
- ...et A Manger • 117 Euston Rd
- ...arbucks • 296 Pentonville Rd

Landmarks

- ...e British Library • 96 Euston Rd
- ...amden High Street • Camden High St & Delancey St
- ...heney Road • Cheney Rd & Weller's Ct
- ...uston Station • Eversholt St & Doric Way
- ...atform 9¾ • King's Cross Station
- ... Pancras • Pancras Rd & Euston Rd
- ... Pancras Hospital • 4 St Pancras Way

Libraries

- ...e British Library • 96 Euston Rd
- ...amden Town Library • 218 Eversholt St
- ...ellcome Library • 183 Euston Rd

Nightlife

- The Camden Head • 100 Camden High St
- The Champagne Bar at St Pancras • Pancras Rd
- The Crown & Goose • 100 Arlington Rd
- Lincoln Lounge • 52 York Way
- Purple Turtle • 61 Crowndale Rd
- Scala • 275 Pentonville Rd

Post Offices

- Kings Cross • 21 Euston St

Restaurants

- Asakusa • 265 Eversholt St
- Banger Bros. • Euston Station
- Camino • 3 Varnisher's Yard
- Chop Chop Noodle Bar • 1 Euston Rd
- El Parador • 245 Eversholt St
- Great Nepalese • 48 Eversholt St
- Kitchin • 8 Caledonia St
- Rodon Live • 7 Pratt St
- The Somerstown Coffee House • 60 Chalton St
- Tony's Natural Foods • 10 Caledonian Rd

Shopping

- All Ages Records • 27 Pratt St
- Housmans Bookshop • 5 Caledonian Rd
- Peyton & Byrne • Pancras Rd
- Transformation • 52 Eversholt St
- Wills-Moody Jumble Sale • 21 Phoenix Road

Supermarkets

- Sainsbury's • 10 Camden High St

Map 79

m St Pancras Station, restored to its full former glory, to the futuristic new
mpus of Central St Martins, this wasteland-turned-construction site-turning-
er hub is changing so fast it's hard to keep track. Do some shopping and eating
Caledonian Road before heading to York Way and The Cross Kings for drinking
d dancing. The Lexington up Pentonville Road is fast becoming London's hippest
venue.

Libraries

wis Carroll Children's Library • 166 Copenhagen St
est Library • Bridgeman Road

Nightlife

he Big Chill House • 257 Pentonville Rd
anal 125 • 125 Caledonian Rd
entral Station • 37 Wharfdale Rd
ross Kings • 126 York Way
GG • 200 York Way
emingford Arms • 128 Hemingford Rd
he Lexington • 96 Pentonville Rd
ncoln Lounge • 52 York Way
armon • 270 Caledonian Rd

Post Offices

aledonian Road • 320 Caledonian Rd

Restaurants

ddis • 42 Caledonian Rd
allas Burger Bar • 257 Caledonian Rd
uro Café • 299 Caledonian Rd
arathon • 196 Caledonian Rd
enelik • 277 Caledonian Rd
he New Didar • 347 Caledonian Rd
z • 53 Caledonian Rd
um Yum • 48 Caledonian Rd

Shopping

• **Cosmo Cornelio** • 182 Caledonian Rd
• **King's Cross Continental Stores** • 26 Caledonian Rd

Supermarkets

• **Co-Op** • 303 Caledonian Rd
• **Iceland** • 259 Caledonian Rd

(169)

Map 80

area has everything. Welcoming bars full of lovely young things (Upper Street),
que shops full of lovely old things (Camden Passage), romance (Mem & Laz),
sion (Cuba Libre), chilled Sunday mornings (The Breakfast Club), and a great
of shops. And if that all sounds a little too peaceful, there's live music action
e Buffalo Bar every night.

Banks

bey • 15 Islington Park St
rclays • 38 Islington Green
rclays • 2 Highbury Corner
rclays • 14 Upper St
lifax • 1 Liverpool Rd
BC • 25 Islington High St
oyds • 19 Upper St
atWest • 218 Upper St
yal Bank of Scotland • 40 Islington High St

Cinemas

eryman Screen on the Green • 83 Islington Green
e Islington • 36 Parkfield St

Coffee

torick Gallery • 39 Canonbury Sq
phorium Bakery • 202 Upper St
et A Manger • 27 Islington High St
arbucks • 71 Upper St
arbucks • 30 Upper St
arbucks • 7 Islington High St
nderbox • 21 Upper St

Landmarks

agel Station Roof
e Bull • 100 Upper St

Nightlife

s Canonbury • 25 Canonbury Lane
bert & Pearl • 181 Upper St
e Angel • 3 Islington High St
e Angelic • 57 Liverpool Rd
uffalo Bar • 259 Upper St
amden Head • 2 Camden Walk
e Castle • 54 Pentonville Rd
ompton Arms • 4 Compton Ave
e Crown • 116 Cloudesley St
uba Libre • 72 Upper St
e Drapers Arms • 44 Barnsbury St
ectrowerkz • 7 Torrens St
e Florence • 50 Florence St
e Garage • 20 Highbury Corner
ope And Anchor • 207 Upper St
lington Academy • 16 Parkfield St
e Islington Tap • 80 Liverpool Rd
ury's Inn • 60 Pentonville Rd
eston Lodge • 131 Upper St
ng's Head Theatre & Pub • 115 Upper St
cky Voice • 173 Upper St
d Red Lion • 418 St John St
e Regent • 201 Liverpool Rd

• Round Midnight: Jazz and Blues Bar • 13 Liverpool Rd
• Slimelight • 7 Torrens St
• Union Chapel • Compton Terrace

Restaurants

• Afghan Kitchen • 35 Islington Green
• The Albion • 10 Thornhill Rd
• Alpino • 97 Chapel Market
• The Breakfast Club • 31 Camden Passage
• Candid Café • 3 Torrens St
• Desperados • 127 Upper St
• Elk in the Woods • 39 Camden Passage
• Fig and Olive • 151 Upper St
• Fine Burger Co • 330 Upper St
• Fredericks • Camden Passage
• Gem • 265 Upper St
• House • 63 Canonbury Rd
• Indian Veg Bhelpoori House • 93 Chapel Market
• Isarn • 119 Upper St
• Itsuka • 54 Islington Park St
• La Forchetta • 73 Upper St
• La Porchetta • 141 Upper St
• Le Mercury • 140 Upper St
• Masala Zone • 80 Upper St
• Mem & Laz • 8 Theberton St
• Metrogusto • 13 Theberton St
• Olive Grill • 61 Upper St
• Ottolenghi • 287 Upper St
• Pizzeria Oregano • 19 St Alban's Pl
• Pomegranate • 139 Upper St
• Rodizo Rico • 77 Upper St
• Tortilla • 13 Islington High St
• Vigata Ristorante • 70 Liverpool Rd
• Zaffrani • 47 Cross St

Shopping

• A Ferrari Deli • 48 Cross St
• After Noah • 121 Upper St
• Annie's Vintage Costume and Textiles •
  12 Camden Passage
• Camden Passage • Camden Passage
• Cass Art • 66 Colebrooke Row
• Gill Wing Kitchen Shop • 194 Upper St
• Monte's Deli • 23 Canonbury Lane
• Palette London • 21 Canonbury Ln
• Paul A Young Fine Chocolates • 33 Camden Passage
• Raymond Roe Fishmonger • 35 Chapel Market
• Twentytwentyone • 274 Upper St

Supermarkets

• Iceland • 62 Chapel Market

eady mix of leafy spacious streets with multi-million pound mansions, right
ext to some of London's poorest estates—London in a nutshell. Essex Road has
acking shops including the eccentric Get Stuffed for all your taxidermy needs.
odies are well catered for with real butchers (James Elliot), bakers (Raab's), and
reat ethnic eateries (Zigni House and Sabor).

Map 8

Landmarks

Gladiators Paving Slab • 10 Canonbury St

Libraries

South Library • 115 Essex Rd

Nightlife

Embassy Bar • 119 Essex Rd
Marquess Tavern • 32 Canonbury St
Myddleton Arms • 52 Canonbury Rd
The Green Man • 144 Essex Rd
The Lord Clyde • 342 Essex Rd

Restaurants

Angel Cafe • 100 Essex Rd
Raab's Bakery • 136 Essex Rd
Sabor • 108 Essex Rd
Zigni House • 330 Essex Rd

Shopping

Get Stuffed • 105 Essex Rd
Handmade and Found • 109 Essex Rd
HG Lockey & Sons • 8 Halton Cross St
James Elliot Master Butcher • 96 Essex Rd
Planet Organic • 64 Essex Rd
Raab's The Baker's • 136 Essex Rd
Sew Fantastic • 107 Essex Rd

Supermarkets

Co-Op • 132 Essex Rd

e Beauvoir is the buffer zone where swanky Islington merges into manic ackney. As such it's the best of both worlds. To the west, there's quiet squares nd gastropubs. But turn to the eastern edge for up-till-dawn boozing sessions. izarrely, it's also home to thousands of palm trees---so sit in de Beauvoir Square nd pretend you're on a tropical holiday.

Cinemas

Rio Cinema • 107 Kingsland High St

Coffee

2&4 Gallery • 4 Southgate Rd
Tina, We Salute You • 47 King Henry's Walk

Landmarks

Suleymaniye Mosque • 212 Kingsland Rd

Libraries

Mildmay Library • 21 Mildmay Park

Nightlife

Jazz Bar • 4 Bradbury St
The Northgate • 113 Southgate Rd
The Orwell • 382 Essex Rd
The Rosemary Branch • 2 Shepperton Rd
The Vortex • 11 Gillett Sq
The Duke of Wellington • 119 Balls Pond Rd

Restaurants

• Casaba • 162 Essex Rd
• Huong Viet • 12 Englefield Rd
• Puji Puji • 122 Balls Pond Rd

Shopping

• 2&4 Gallery • 4 Southgate Rd
• North One Garden Centre • 25 Englefield Rd

If you're bored of the bars on Upper Street or the ironic chic of Hoxton, the streets in between (along Essex Road or by the canal) are a better bet, with a more laid-back atmosphere. The Island Queen (NFT London's official birthplace!) is a cosy local pub and well worth a visit. One day they'll just have to give us one of those blue plaques.

Map 8

 Banks

Barclays • 146 City Rd

Coffee

Food Lab • 56 Essex Rd

Nightlife

Barrio North • 45 Essex Rd
The Charles Lamb • 16 Elia St
The Duke of Cambridge • 30 St Peter's St
Earl of Essex • 25 Danbury St
The Narrow Boat • 119 St.Peters St
Offside Bar and Gallery • 273 City Rd
The Island Queen • 87 Noel Rd
The Mucky Pup • 39 Queen's Head St
The Old Queenís Head • 44 Essex Rd
The Wenlock Arms • 26 Wenlock Rd

Restaurants

The Charles Lamb • 16 Elia St
Shepherdess Cafe • 221 City Rd
William IV • 7 Shepherdess

Shopping

Flashback • 50 Essex Rd
Haggle Vinyl • 114 Essex Rd
Past Caring • 54 Essex Rd

Map 8

Hoxton is still so happening anything we say here will be out of date within the next two minutes. Most of the good stuff radiates out from Hoxton Square (great for people watching in the summer) and Curtain Road—follow the trail of hipsters you can't miss them). Find modern art (White Cube), cheap Thai (Yelo), live music Cargo, Macbeth), and bars (The Foundry, Old Blue Last).

Coffee

Apostrophe • 42 Great Eastern St
Eat. • 59 Great Eastern St

Emergency Rooms

Moorfields Eye Hospital • 162 City Rd

Landmarks

Hoxton Square • Hoxton Sq
Village Underground • 54 Holywell Ln
White Cube • 48 Hoxton Square

Libraries

Shoredittch Library • 80 Hoxton St

Nightlife

333 • 333 Old St
Bedroom Bar • 62 Rivington St
The Bricklayer's Arms • 63 Charlotte Rd
Cantaloupe • 35 Charlotte Rd
Cargo • 83 Rivington St
Charlie Wright's International Bar • 45 Pitfield St
Club Aquarium • 256 Old St
Cocomo • 323 Old St
Comedy Cafe • 66 Rivington St
East Village • 89 Great Eastern St
The Elbow Room • 97 Curtain Rd
Electricity Showroom • 39 Hoxton Sq
Favela Chic • 91 Great Eastern St
The Foundry • 84 Great Eastern St
The Griffin • 93 Leonard St
Hoxton Square Bar and Kitchen • 2 Hoxton Sq
The Legion • 348 Old St
The Macbeth • 60 70 Hoxton St
The Old Blue Last • 38 Great Eastern St
Plastic People • 147 Curtain Rd
Red Lion • 41 Hoxton St
The Stag's Head • 55 Orsman Rd
Strongroom Bar • 120 Curtain Rd
Troy Bar • 10 Hoxton St

Restaurants

• **The Bean** • 126 Curtain Rd
• **The Diner** • 128 Curtain Rd
• **F. Cooke** • 150 Hoxton St
• **Fifteen** • 15 Westland Pl
• **Rivington Bar and Grill** • 28 Rivington St
• **Shish** • 313 Old St
• **Yelo** • 8 Hoxton Sq

Shopping

• **Favela Shop** • 12 Hoxton St
• **Good Hood** • 41 Coronet St
• **Sh!** • 57 Hoxton Sq

Supermarkets

• **Co-Op** • 136 New North Rd
• **Iceland** • 209 Hoxton St

Hovering over Dalston and Clapton like a ghost of the future, Stokey is where the trendos go when they've eaten too many pain au chocolat and are bursting out of their drainpipes. It's resplendent in dining options but try Testi first. For paying your respects or cruising, head to Abney Park Cemetery. For a bit of genteel warehouse-partying, check out Stoke Newington International Airport.

Banks

• **Halifax** • 173 Stoke Newington High St
• **HSBC** • 150 Stoke Newington High St
• **NatWest** • 196 Stoke Newington High St

Landmarks

• **Abney Park Cemetery** •
  Stoke Newington High St & Rectory Rd

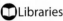Libraries

• **Clapton Library** • Northwold Road

Nightlife

• **The Birdcage** • 58 Stamford Hill
• **Blush** • 8 Cazenove Rd
• **The Royal Sovereign** • 64 Northwold Rd
• **Stoke Newington International Airport** •
  1-15 Leswin Place
• **White Hart** • 69 Stoke Newington High St

Post Offices

• **Stamford Hill** • 82 Stamford Hill
• **Stoke Newington** • 138 Stoke Newington High St

Restaurants

• **19 Numara Bos Cirrik** • 34 Stoke Newington Rd
• **Bagel House** • 2 Stoke Newington High St
• **Café Z Bar** • 58 Stoke Newington High St
• **Testi** • 38 Stoke Newington High St
• **Thai Cafe** • 3 Northwold Rd
• **Three Crowns** • 175 Stoke Newington Church St

Shopping

• **Bargain Bookshop** • 153 Stoke Newington High St
• **Hamdys** • 167 Stoke Newington High St
• **Stoke Newington Bookshop** •
  167 Stoke Newington High St
• **Rouge** • 158 Stoke Newington High St

Of course, now that the Guardian has named Dalston the coolest place in Britain, it's like sooo over. Well, not quite, but in 5 years this place'll be choking with bankers and mums. For the time being, Kingsland Road still feels like a Vice mag photoshoot. With hip bars like Dalston Superstore it's no wonder (but we still love the old skool Dalston Jazz Bar) and Cafe Oto is the experimental music cafe de jour.

Map 86

£ Banks

- **Abbey** • 86 Kingsland High St
- **Barclays** • 3 Kingsland High St
- **Halifax** • 81 Kingsland High St
- **NatWest** • 74 Kingsland High St

Cinemas

- **Lux** • 18 Shacklewell Ln

Coffee

- **Metolino Cafe** • 162 Stoke Newington Rd

O Landmarks

- **Centreprise** • 136 Kingsland High St
- **Holy Trinity, The Clowns Church** • Beechwood Rd & Kirkland Walk

Libraries

- **CLR James Library** • 30 Dalston Ln

Nightlife

- **Bar 23** • 23 Stoke Newington Rd
- **Bardens Boudoir** • 38 Stoke Newington Rd
- **Café Oto** • 18 Ashwin St
- **Dalston Superstore** • 117 Kingsland High St
- **The Haggerston** • 438 Kingsland Rd
- **Marquis of Lansdowne** • 48 Stoke Newington Rd
- **The Moustache Bar** • 58 Stoke Newington Rd
- **Passion** • 251 Amhurst Rd
- **The Prince George** • 40 Parkholme Rd

Post Offices

- **Kingsland High Street** • 118 Kingsland High St

Restaurants

- **The Best Turkish Kebab** • 125 Stoke Newington Rd
- **Dem Cafe** • 18 Stoke Newington Rd
- **Dalston Lane Café** • 170 Dalston Ln
- **Evin Bar and Café** • 115 Kingsland High St
- **LMNT** • 316 Queensbridge Rd
- **Mangal 1** • 10 Arcola St
- **Mangal 2** • 4 Stoke Newington Rd
- **El Panchos** • 176 Stoke Newington Rd
- **Peppers and Spice** • 20 Kingsland High St
- **Shanghai** • 41 Kingsland High St
- **Somine** • 131 Kingsland High St
- **Stone Cave** • 111 Kingsland High St
- **The Tea Rooms** • 155 Stoke Newington Rd

Shopping

- **Centre Supermarket** • 588 Kingsland Rd
- **Dalston Mill Fabrics** • 69 Ridley Rd
- **Oxfam** • 514 Kingsland Rd
- **Party Party** • 9 Ridley Rd
- **Ridley Road Food Market** • Ridley Rd
- **St Vincent's** • 484 Kingsland Rd
- **Turkish Food Centre** • 89 Ridley Rd

Map 87

A few years ago you couldn't move for house gigs and secret raves around the Downs but these days the area is devolving into the moody gangland it used to be. Lower Clapton on the other hand is ever on the up: Umit is a crazed film buff who sells rare films and sweets, Pogo is a right-on vegan punk place and the Parioli/Biddles Bros duet provides the perfect eat/drink double whammy.

£ Banks

- **Abbey** • 392 Mare St
- **Barclays** • 298 Mare St
- **Halifax** • 402 Mare St
- **HSBC** • 283 Mare St
- **NatWest** • 20 Amhurst Rd

Coffee

- **Gulluoglu** • 63 Lower Clapton Rd
- **Organic & Natural** • 191 Lower Clapton Rd

O Landmarks

- **London Orphan Asylum** •
  Lower Clapton Rd & Linscott Rd
- **The Strand Building** • 29 Urswick Rd
- **Sutton House** • 2 Homerton High St

Nightlife

- **Biddle Brothers** • 88 Lower Clapton Rd
- **Crooked Billet** • 84 Upper Clapton Rd
- **Hugo's Speaker Palace** • 14 Andre St
- **Pembury Tavern** • 90 Amhurst Rd

Post Offices

- **Dalston Lane** • 244 Dalston Ln
- **Hackney** • 382 Mare St

Restaurants

- **Dunya** • 199 Lower Clapton Rd
- **India Gate** • 75 Lower Clapton Rd
- **Mess Café** • 38 Amhurst Rd
- **Parioli** • 90 Lower Clapton Rd
- **Pogo Café** • 76 Clarence Rd

Shopping

- **Palm 2** • 152 Lower Clapton Rd
- **The Pet Shop** • 40 Amhurst Rd
- **Salvation Army Clapton** • 122 Lower Clapton Rd
- **Second Time Around** • 60 Lower Clapton Rd
- **Umit & Son** • 35 Lower Clapton Rd
- **Viktor Wynd's Shop of Horrors** • 11 Mare St

subsumed by the Hackney/Dalston/Stokey axis of cool, this area is a fashionable ash on a dirty backside. There are delicate highs in the Geffrye Museum but the lace belongs to seedy, trendy joints like the Russian Bar. You can really be 'artistic' ound Kingsland Road or at least get pissed with a bunch of people you're going despise come daylight.

Landmarks

Geffrye Museum • 136 Kingsland Rd

Nightlife

A10 (aka The Russian Bar) • 267 Kingsland Rd
The Fox • 372 Kingsland Rd
Passing Clouds • 440 Kingsland Rd
Plaza • 161 Kingsland Rd

Post Offices

Kingsland Road • 416 Kingsland Rd

Restaurants

Faulkner's • 424 Kingsland Rd
Hackney City Farm • 1 Goldsmiths Row
That Vietnamese Place • 134 Kingsland Rd
Uludag • 398 Kingsland Rd
Usha • 428 Kingsland Rd
Song Que • 134 Kingsland Rd
Viet Hoa Café • 70 Kingsland Rd

Shopping

KTS The Corner • 415 Kingsland Road

Hackney Central is a choked-up bus lane while London Fields is tarted-up Hackney. The lovely park hosts the Lido, where you can bump into a one-night stand doing breast stroke. The love it / hate it Broadway Market is dripping with boho 'charm' and admittedly great shops like Artvinyl and the traditional pie-and-mash F Cooke's. If only everyone wasn't so damn good looking.

Coffee

Caffe Nero • 22 London Lane
The Corner Deli • 121 Mare St
Wilton's • 63 Wilton Way

Landmarks

London Fields Lido • London Fields Westside

Libraries

Hackney Central Library • 1 Reading Lane

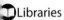Nightlife

Baxter's Court • 282 Mare St
The Dolphin • 165 Mare St
The Dove • 24 Broadway Market
The Old Ship • 2 Sylvester Path
Pub on the Park • 19 Martello St

Post Offices

London Fields • 39 Broadway Market
Wilton Way • 67 Wilton Way

Restaurants

- Buen Ayre • 50 Broadway Market
- Cafe Bohemia • 2 Bohemia Pl
- Cat and Mutton • 76 Broadway Market
- Corner Deli • 121 Mare St
- F. Cooke • 9 Broadway Market
- Hai Ha • 206 Mare St
- F. Cooke • 9 Broadway Market
- The Spurstowe Arms • 68 Greenwood Rd

Shopping

- Artvinyl • 13 Broadway Market
- Broadway Market • Broadway Market
- Burberry Factory Shop • 29 Chatham Pl
- Candle Factory • 184 Mare St
- L'eau a la Bouche • 49 Broadway Market London
- Lazy Days • 21 Mare St

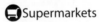Supermarkets

- Iceland • 150 Mare St
- Tesco • 55 Morning Ln

ackney heartlands with rows of terraces that get posher the nearer Vicky Park you
go. The gentrification fairy has sprinkled lots of magic dust on villagey Lauriston
oad – head to Sublime if you get a mega raise, Empress of India on payday and
oyal Inn on the Park or The Ginger Pig if you find a tenner on the floor. Homerton
like 'Badlands' but with nice houses and prams.

Emergency Rooms

Homerton University Hospital • Homerton Row

Libraries

Homerton Library • Homerton High St

Nightlife

Chats Palace Arts Centre • 42 Brooksby's Walk
The Lauriston • 162 Victoria Park Rd
Royal Inn on the Park • 111 Lauriston Rd

Post Offices

High Street • 226 Homerton High St
Victoria Park • 112 Lauriston Rd
Well Street • 188 Well St

Restaurants

• **The Empress of India** • 130 Lauriston Rd
• **The Fish House** • 126 Lauriston Rd

Shopping

• **Cheech Miller** • 227 Victoria Park Rd
• **The Ginger Pig** • 99 Lauriston Rd
• **Sublime** • 225 Victoria Park Rd
• **Work Shop** • 77 Lauriston Rd

Supermarkets

• **Tesco** • 180 Well St

oreditch / Brick Lane / Spitalfields

robbing with trend-lords on single-speed bikes, great curry houses and
ernative-lifestyle vomit, the trick is to sample Brick Lane and Shoreditch on
arket days for pure colour and bustle, but to avoid it on weekend eves. Shopping
abundant: Rough Trade, Beyond Retro and oodles of great little rag shacks. Head
wards Jaguar Shoes or Catch for booze. For a dash of authenticity, leave your
000 bike unlocked and see what happens.

Banks

atWest • 180 Shoreditch High St

Cinemas

ch Mix Centre •
4 Bethnal Green Rd
hort & Sweet • 91 Brick Ln

Coffee

offee @ • 154 Brick Ln
afe 1001 • 91 Brick Ln
offee@157 • 157 Brick Ln
ude Espresso • 26 Hanbury St
rufrock • 140 Shoreditch High St
me For Tea •
0 Shoreditch High St

Landmarks

ck Lane Mosque • 59 Brick Lane
hrist Church Spitalfields •
Fournier St
ennis Severs' House • 18 Folgate St
pitalfields Market •
05 Commercial St
weet Toof Graffiti Alley •
edley St & Brick Ln
n Bells • 84 Commercial St
uman's Brewery • Brick Lane

Libraries

orset Library • Ravenscroft St

Nightlife

Feet East • 150 Brick Ln
nda De Bridge • 42 Kingsland Rd
e Archers • 42 Osborn St
ar Kick • 127 Shoreditch High St
ar Music Hall • 134 Curtain Rd
droom Bar • 62 Rivington St
owns • 1 Hackney Rd
ay Walk off Brick Lane
afé 1001 • 91 Brick Lane
e Carpenters Arms • 73 Cheshire St

• Catch • 22 Kingsland Rd
• The Commercial Tavern •
142 Commercial St
• Comedy Cafe • 66 Rivington St
• Ditch Bar • 145 Shoreditch High St
• Exit • 174 Brick Lane
• The George & Dragon • Hackney Rd
• The Golden Heart • 110 Commercial St
• The Gramophone Bar •
60 Commercial St
• Green & Red • 51 Bethnal Green Rd
• Herbal • 10 Kingsland Rd
• Jaguar Shoes • 32 Kingsland Rd
• Joiners Arms • 116 Hackney Rd
• The Last Days of Decadence •
145 Shoreditch High St
• Loungelover • 1 Whiteby St
• The Old Shoreditch Station •
1 Kingsland Rd
• On the Rocks • 25 Kingsland Rd
• Owl & Pussycat • 34 Redchurch St
• Prague • 6 Kingsland Rd
• Pride of Spitalfields • 3 Heneage St
• Public Life • 82 Commercial St
• The Redchurch • 107 Redchurch St
• The Royal Oak • 73 Columbia Rd
• Shoreditch House • Ebor St
• T Bar • 18 Houndsditch
• Vibe Bar • 91 Brick Ln
• The Water Poet • 9 Folgate St
• Ye Olde Axe • 69 Hackney Rd

Post Offices

• Bethnal Green •
223 Bethnal Green Rd
• Hackney Road • 198 Hackney Rd

Restaurants

• Beigel Bakery • 155 Brick Lane
• Boundary • 2 Boundary St
• Brick Lane Clipper Restaurant •
104 Brick Ln
• Café Bangla • 128 Brick Lane
• Drunken Monkey •
222 Shoreditch High St
• Ethiopian Food Stall •
Sunday Upmarket, Truman's Brewery,
Brick Lane
• Gourmet San • 261 Bethnal Green Rd
• Green & Red • 51 Bethnal Green Rd
• Hanoi Cafe • 98 Kingsland Rd
• Hawksmoor • 157 Commercial St
• Jones Dairy Cafe • 23 Ezra St
• Le Taj • 96 Brick Ln
• Les Trois Garcons • 1 Club Row

• Noodle King • 185 Bethnal Green Rd
• Ping Pong • 3 Steward St
• The Premises • 209 Hackney Rd
• Que Viet • 102 Kingsland Rd
• Rootmaster • Elys Yard
• Rosa's • 12 Hanbury St
• St John Bread and Wine •
94 Commercial St
• Story Deli • 91 Brick Ln
• Tay Do • 60 Kingsland Rd
• Tay Do Cafe • 65 Kingsland Rd
• Viet Grill • 58 Kingsland Rd

Shopping

• A Butcher of Distinction • 91 Brick Ln
• Absolute Vintage • 15 Hanbury St
• Bangla City • 86 Brick Lane
• Bernstock Speirs • 234 Brick Lane
• Beyond Retro • 112 Cheshire St
• Blackmans • 44 Cheshire St
• Blackman's Shoes • 42 Cheshire St
• Brick Lane • Brick Lane
• Caravan • 3 Redchurch St
• A Child of The Jago •
10 Great Eastern St
• Columbia Road Flower Market •
Columbia Rd
• Columbia Road Market • Columbia Rd
• Comfort Station • 22 Cheshire St
• Duke of Uke • 22 Hanbury St
• FairyGothMother • 15 Lamb St
• The Grocery • 54 Kingsland Rd
• Hurwundeki • 98 Commerical St
• Junky Styling • 91 Brick Ln
• The Laden Showrooms •
103 Brick Lane
• Lapin & Me • 14 Ezra Street
• Labour & Wait • 18 Cheshire St
• Luna and Curious • 198 Brick Lane
• No One • 1 Kingsland Rd
• Nudge Records • 20 Hanbury St
• Prick Your Finger •
260 Bethnal Green Rd
• Rough Trade East • 91 Brick Ln
• Ryantown • 126 Columbia Road
• Scooter Emporium •
10 Dray Walk, Brick Lane,
• Second Thread • 261 Hackney Rd
• Shelf • 40 Cheshire Street
• Taj Stores • 112 Brick Lane
• Tatty Devine • 236 Brick Ln
• Taylor Taylor • 12 Cheshire St
• Taylor Taylor • 137 Commercial St
• Treacle • 110 Columbia Rd

h, you've got to love it. Blossoming from a caricature inner-city ghetto into lorious yummy-mummy media-worker land, you can sate pretty much any desire ere, dark or quaint. Columbia Flower Market and its tributary flea market lanes are lot of fun what with the buskers, mosaics and geezers selling flowers just like in ygmalion (but with men). The Star Of Bethnal Green is pretty cool for a pint-and-ander at young people. If that's your thing.

Map 9

£ Banks

- **Abbey** • 450 Bethnal Green Rd
- **Barclays** • 412 Bethnal Green Rd
- **Halifax** • 376 Bethnal Green Rd
- **HSBC** • 465 Bethnal Green Rd
- **Lloyds** • 404 Bethnal Green Rd
- **NatWest** • 403 Bethnal Green Rd

Coffee

- **Hurwendeki Cafe** • 299 Cambridge Heath Rd

Landmarks

- **Bethnal Green Tube Station** •
  Bethnal Green Tube Station
- **London Buddhist Centre** • 51 Roman Rd

Libraries

- **Bethnal Green Library** • Cambridge Heath Rd
- **Idea Store Bow** • Roman Rd

Nightlife

- **The Albion** • 94 Goldsmiths Row
- **The FymFyg Bar** • 231 Cambridge Heath Rd
- **Bethnal Green's Working Men's Club** • 44 Pollard Row
- **The Camel** • 277 Globe Rd
- **Florist** • 255 Globe Rd
- **Images** • 483 Hackney Rd
- **The Star Of Bethnal Green** • 359 Bethnal Green Rd

Post Offices

- **Bethnal Green Road** • 365 Bethnal Green Rd
- **Cambridge Heath** • 481 Cambridge Heath Rd

Restaurants

- **Bistrotheque** • 23 Wadeson St
- **E Pellicci** • 332 Bethnal Green Rd
- **Little Georgia** • 87 Goldsmiths Row
- **Wild Cherry** • 241 Globe Rd

Shopping

- **AP Fitzpatrick** • 142 Cambridge Heath Rd
- **Paul Mark Hatton** • 65 Roman Rd

Supermarkets

- **Tesco** • 361 Bethnal Green Rd

...ah Victoria Park is nice and all, but it's just a bunch of trees and grass innit? South
...? all that green sh** is an up-and-coming nabe with so many great little gems. So,
...he Palm Tree is the best pub in Britain. The Victoria is becoming a brilliant gig spot.
...inkles is East End seafood at its best. We'd move here if we had the balls in fact.

Banks

NatWest • 154 Roman Rd

Landmarks

Art Pavilion • 221 Grove Rd
Mile End Climbing Wall • Haverfield Rd & Grove Rd

Nightlife

The Approach Tavern • 47 Approach Rd
Fat Cat Cafe Bar • 221 Grove Rd
Jongleurs (Bow Wharf) • 221 Grove Rd
The Morgan Arms • 43 Morgan St
Palm Tree • 1 Haverfield Rd
The Victoria • 110 Grove Rd

Post Offices

Roman Road • 138 Roman Rd

Restaurants

Matsu • 558 Mile End Rd
The Morgan Arms • 43 Morgan St
Winkles • 238 Roman Rd

Map 94 • **Bow**

1

2

Victoria Park

PAGE
356

River Lee or Lea

Jodrell Road

Ollerton Grn

Candy Street

Hornbeam
Square

Gunmakers Lane

Barge Lane

Birdsfield

Tree Cl

Willow

Cedar
Clo

Parnell Road

Ruston Street

Waterloo
Close

Sycamore Avenue

Old Ford
Road
B118

Empire Wharf B118

Old Ford Road

Ruston
Street

Chisenhale Rd

Ripley
Street

Pulteney

Clo

Annie
Besant
Close

Chariot
Clo

Lea
Sq

Tamar
Clo

Garrison Road

Hadria
Clo

A

Ellesmere Road

Daling Way

Ford Street

Hewison Road

St. Stephen's Road

Beales
Road

Alice Lane

McCrown Rd

Armagh Road

Garrison Terrace

Forur
Clo

Vivian Road

Zealand Road

Driffield Road

Allen Road

Wrights Road

Beale Place

Libra Road

Forur
Clo

Tibe
Clo

Daling Way

Roman Sq
Market

McCullum Road

Usher
Road

£

Parnell Road B142

Hitchin Sq

Roman Road

Ewart
Place

Roman Road

Gladstone
Place

✉

✂

493

Lanfranc Road

Medway
Bldgs

Lyal Road

Norman Grove

St. Stephen's
Road

Cardigan Road

Hewison Street

Usher Road

B119

Rosse

Park Gdns

Medway Road

Stanfield Road

Selwyn Road

Saxon Road

Anglo Road

Vernon Road

Tredegar   Road

Four Seasons
Close

Arbery Road

Strahan Road

Athelstane Grove

Saxon Road

Stafford Road

Shetland Road

Mostyn Grove

Lacey Wk

Matilda Gdns

Morville Street

Redwood
Close

Mews

Primrose
Close

Antill Road

Cherrywood Close

Tredegar Road

Hereford Road

Ordell Road

Ceilia

Street

Springwood
Close

Lichfield Road

Malmesbury Road

B

Alloway Rd

Pembroke
Mews

Morgan Street

Tredegar Terrace

Tredegar
Mews

Benworth Street

Harley Grove

Alfred Street

Lawrence
Close

Caxton
Grove

Addington Road

Aberavon Road

Rhondda Grove

Tredegar Sq

Coborn Road

Coborn Street

Regal
Place

Denmark
Place

A1205

Lyn
Mews

98

99

Bow Road A11

Bow

£

Mile
End

Mile End Road A11

Wentworth
Mews

Burdett Road

Tiplin Street

0.25 mile

0.25 km

hat have the Romans ever done for us? Not much, you might think, walking
own Roman Road. But look closer and you'll find not only one of the oldest,
ost authentically East End jellied eels and mash eateries of the city, but also a
arket so cheap it'll knock even the most die-hard bargain hunters right out of
eir Centurion sandals. Pint? The haughty-sounding combo of The Young Prince
The Lord Mopeth.

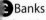 ## Banks

Barclays • 92 Bow Rd
Barclays • 611 Roman Rd

 ## Nightlife

The Coborn Arms • 8 Coborn Road
The Lord Morpeth • 402 Old Ford Road
The Young Prince • 448 Roman Road

Post Offices

Roman Road (603) • 603 Roman Rd

Restaurants

Chicchi • 516 Roman Rd
G.Kelly Pie & Mash shop • 526 Roman Rd
The Roman Tandoori • 432 Roman Road

Shopping

Pure • 430 Roman Rd
Roman Road Market • Roman Rd
Sew Amazing • 80 St Stephens Rd
South Molton Drugstore • 583 Roman Rd

Map 93 • Whitechapel (West) / St Katharine's Dock

0.25 mile

0.25 km

Whitechapel (West) / St Katharine's Dock

Map 95

Whitechapel Gallery has reclaimed its place as the jewel in the crown of this 'hood since its renovation. Much like a busty Page 3 girl (see if you can spot one totter out of The Sun's nearby offices) the gallery has burst out of its shackles to reveal something quite magnificent. The Rhythm Factory and The Castle are chaotic oozing dens – or head to Prohibition for drinkers dumb enough to believe it when you claim to captain one of the on-looking yachts.

£ Banks

Lloyds • 35 Whitechapel High St

Coffee

Oi Bagel • 45 Commercial Rd
Starbucks • 45 Whitechapel Rd

Landmarks

The Sun HQ • 1 Virginia Street

Nightlife

The Castle • 44 Commercial Rd
Dickens Inn • 1 St. Katharine Docks
Prohibition Bar and Grill • 1 St. Katherine's dock
Rhythm Factory • 16 Whitechapel Rd

Restaurants

Cafe Spice Namaste • 16 Prescot St
The Empress • 141 Leman St

Supermarkets

Waitrose • Thomas More St & Nesham St

...k-dockland Wapping now imports yuppies into its converted warehouses, ...ss gleaming Shadwell and Whitechapel keep more of the East End spirit alive. ...apping High Street is mainly residential, Whitechapel Road is more lively. Drink ...Indo if you're boho, stick with The Captain Kidd if not. Tayyab's is cracking—stick ...t the queues, or if curry's not your thing head to Il Bordello.

Banks

- **Abbey** • 40 Watney Warket
- **Barclays** • 240 Whitechapel Rd
- **HSBC** • 75 Whitechapel Rd
- **Lloyds** • 210 Commercial Rd
- **NatWest** • 130 Whitechapel High St
- **NatWest** • 45 Whitechapel Rd
- **NatWest** • 331 Whitechapel Rd

Emergency Rooms

- **Royal London Hospital** • Whitechapel Rd & Vallance Rd

Landmarks

- **Battle of Cable Street Mural, St George's Hall** • 236 Cable St
- **Blind Beggar Pub** • 337 Whitechapel Rd

Libraries

- **Idea Store Whitechapel** • 321 Whitechapel Rd
- **Watney Market Library** • 30 Watney Market

Nightlife

- **The Captain Kidd** • 108 Wapping High St
- **The Caxtons** • 50 The Highway
- **Indo** • 133 Whitechapel Rd
- **Town of Ramsgate** • 62 Wapping High St

Post Offices

- **Eastern** • 206 Whitechapel Rd
- **Philpot Street** • 12 Philpot St

Restaurants

- **Il Bordello** • 81 Wapping High Street
- **Tayyabs** • 83 Fieldgate St

Supermarkets

- **Iceland** • Watney St & Tarling St
- **Sainsbury's** • 1 Cambridge Heath Rd

Map 97 • **Stepney / Shadwell (East)**

Cockney geezers run into hipsters and smart new developments sit next to run-down estates. No one quite knows where this area is going. We know where we're going, though—to The George Tavern, mainly, for impromptu theatre, blue-collar poetry and other arty madness, or The Prospect of Whitby, if we're feeling nostalgic. Wapping Food, meanwhile, serves great fare inside a century-old power station.

 Cinemas

Genesis Mile End • 93 Mile End Rd

 Coffee

Popular Café • 536 Commercial Rd

 Nightlife

Cable Street Studios • 566 Cable St
The George Tavern • 373 Commercial Rd
The Prospect of Whitby • 57 Wapping Wall
Troxy • 490 Commerical Rd

Post Offices

Globe Road • 34 Globe Rd
Stepney • 502 Commercial Rd

 Restaurants

• **Wapping Food** • Wapping Wall

Shopping

• **John Lester Wigmakers** • 32 Globe Rd
• **East End Thrift Store** • 1 Assembly Passage

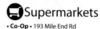 **Supermarkets**

• **Co-Op** • 193 Mile End Rd

Map 98 • Mile End (South) / Limehouse

1

2

Globe Road

Printing Way

Globe Road

Stepney Green

Alderney Road Cemetery (Jewish)

93

Mile End Road A11

Mile End

94

Wentworth Mews

Eric Street

Southern Grove

Louisa Street

Toby Lane

Union Drive

Hamlets Way

Maria Terrace

Eastbury Ter

Ernest Street

Solebay Street

Edmont Close

Treby Street

Ropery Street

English Street

Shandy Street

Commodore Street

Harford Street

Sandalwood Close

Stepney Green B121

Trafalgar

Shandy Park

Essian Street

Mile End Park

Bow Common Lane

Redman's Road

Rectory Sq

Bale Road

White Tower Way

PAGE 346

Portia Way

Wager Street

Joseph Street

A

Stepney Green Park

Masters Street

Bohn Road

Dongola Road

Candia St

Copperfield Road

Mile End Stadium

99

Stepping Stones Farm

Ben Jonson Road

B140

Haven Street

Revolution Karting

Belgrave Street

Walter Terrace

97

Our Our Bens Rd

Rhodes Oak Pl

Halley Street

Carr Street

St. Pauls Way

Turners Road

Rhodeswell Road

Clemence Street

B140

Booker Close

Wallwood Street

A1205

Cleveland Street

Redman's Road

White Horse Road B171

Gaselworthy Avenue

Repton Street

Dora Street

Agnes Street

Pixley Street

Burdett Road

Baythorne Street

Joseph Street

Butcher Row

Commercial Road A13

Limehouse

Norbiton Road

Southwater Ct

Copenhagen Place

100

Limehouse Cut

B

Branch Road A1017

The Highway A1203

Horseferry Road

Narrow Street

Bodhart Place

Salmon Lane

Island Row

Wharf Lane

St. Anne's Pass

Newell Street

Biccies Street

East India Dock Road

West India Dock Road

Jardine Road

River Thames

Limehouse Link

Ropemakers Field

Oak Lane

Ropemakers Fields

0.25 mile

0.25 km

Mile End (South) / Limehouse

Map 98

scary desolate landscapes and urban decay? Cool! Authenticity and Edge go hand-
and-hand 'round here until you get to the water, where it livens up and turns into a
'oxtons' wank fantasy. Still, The Grapes, The Narrow and La Figa are eats and drinks
'avens while the Ragged School Museum offers a glimpse of what it was like when
t was really grim round 'ere.

Landmarks

- **Ragged School Museum** • 46 Copperfield Rd

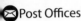Nightlife

- **The Grapes** • 76 Narrow Street

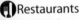Post Offices

- **Ben Jonson Road** • 52 Ben Jonson Rd
- **Mile End** • 1 Burdett Rd
- **Salmon Lane** • 127 Salmon Ln

Restaurants

- **La Figa** • 45 Narrow St
- **The Narrow** • 44 Narrow Street
- **Orange Room Café** • 63 Burdett Rd

Desolation Row pretty much. For hardy explorers kitted out with knives and/or chastity belts, the wonderfully overgrown and sh**-your-pants scary Tower Hamlets Cemetery Park is great. In fact, keep the afore-mentioned kit on if you intend creeping through the boarded-up council estates and general doom.

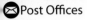 Post Offices

• **Poplar** • 22 Market Sq

Poplar (West) / Canary Wharf (West)

Now that we're officially out of the recession you can wander the wharf marveling at the 'scrapers without pesky ruined bankers landing on you. Ah yes, the smell of money has resurfaced around finance's engine room and the brilliantly futuristic landscape is once again replete with suits shopping at the bland mall under Cabot Square. They never left of course, they just got used to packed lunches like the rest of us.

£ Banks

Halifax • 350 Cabot Pl E
HSBC • Canary Wharf
HSBC • 45 Bank St
Lloyds • 230 Cabot Sq
NatWest • 54 Marsh Wall
NatWest • 20 Canada Sq

Cinemas

Cineworld West India Quay • 11 Hertsmere Rd

Coffee

• **Bagel Factory** • 7 Westferry Circus
• **Café Brera** • 45 Bank St
• **Café Brera** • 12 Cabot Sq
• **Café Brera** • 31 Westferry Circus
• **Coffee Republic** • 10 Cabot Square
• **Coffee Republic** • Hertsmere Rd
• **Fresco Café Bar** • 15 Cabot Sq
• **Fresco Café Bar** • 22 Canada Sq
• **Starbucks** • 1 Canada Sq
• **Starbucks** • 45 Bank St
• **Starbucks** • 8 Westferry Circus

O Landmarks

• **Canary Wharf Tower** • 1 Canada Sq
• **Canary Wharf Tube Station** • Canary Wharf

Nightlife

• **Bar 38** • West India Quay
• **Davy's at Canary Wharf** • 31 Canary Wharf
• **Dion Canary Wharf** •
   Port East Building, West India Quay
• **Via Fossa**• 18 Hertsmere Rd

Post Offices

• **Canary Wharf** • 5 Chancellor Passage

Restaurants

• **1802 Bar** • Hertsmere Rd
• **Browns** • Hertsmere Rd
• **Nicolas** • 480 One Canada Sq
• **Plateau** • Canada Pl
• **Tiffin Bites** • 22 Jubilee Place

Supermarkets

• **Tesco** • 15 Cabot Sq
• **Waitrose** • N Colonnade & Canada Sq

Map 100

Map 101

One day NFT lay down in the shadow of the Tower after a few in the Greenwich Pensioner and gazed up at the 'scraper, admiring its Philip K. Dickian splendour. A small plane buzzed by. Well-heeled bankers stuffed with pub grub from Gun strode by us. Then we got pulled up by the dreadlocks by a rozzer and got hoofed out for not reading the Financial Times. Serves us right.

 Banks

Barclays • 2 Churchill Pl
Barclays • 159 E India Dock Rd

 Libraries

• **Idea Store Canary Wharf** • Churchill Pl
• **Idea Store Chrisp Street** •
East India Dock Rd • 1 Vesey Path

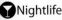 **Nightlife**

• **The Greenwich Pensioner** • 28 Bazely Street
• **The Resolute** • 210 Poplar High Street

 Post Offices

• **Churchill Place** • 2 Churchill Pl

 Restaurants

• **Gun** • 27 Coldharbour
• **Jamie's Italian** • 2 Churchill Pl

Map 102 · Millwall

N

ing Street

Marsh Wall

Strafford Street

100

Harbour Exchange Squa

'Hutchings'
Street

Havannah
Street

Mastmaker Road

Lightermans Road

Limeharbour

Malabar

Street

The Quarterdeck

Alpha Grove

Cassilis Road

Indescon Court

Lanterns
Court

Millharbour

Janet Street

Cheval
Street

Mellish
Street

Mellish Street

Muirfield
Cres
Pepper Street

Crossha
& Londo
Arena

A

Sir John
McDougall
Gardens

Westferry Road

Millwall Dock Road

Tiller Road

Muirfield
Cres

Claire Place

Starboard
Way

Green which View Place

Turnberry Quay

Glengall Causeway A1206

Arnhem Place

Wateridge
Close

Old Bellgate Place

The Docklands
Sailing &
Watersport
Centre

Millwall
Outer
Dock

Millwall
Inner
Dock

Saldson Way

East Ferry Road

Newton Pl

Crews Street

Claude Street

Cyclops
Mews

Charnwood Gdns

Severnake Close

Wheat Sheaf Close

Barnsdale Avenue

Epping Clo

Thames Cir

Sherwood
Gardens

Telegraph Place

Taeping
Street

Taeping
Street

Undine
Road

Undine
Road

Undine Road

Mudch

Homer Dr

Ironmongers
Pl

Spindrift Avenue

Taeping
Street

River
Thames

Mastmaker Terrace

Ferguson Close

Barnard Pl

Cahir Street

Amb
Sq

103

The mocogie La

Vulcan Square

Westferry Road

Harbinger Road

Hesperus
Cres

Vesta Cres

Chapel House St

Juliah
Place

Magellan
Pl

Lyndale Ct

Pointer's Clo

Brunel
Sq

Wharf
Sq

Wynan Road

Rainbow
Ave

Maritime Quay

Napier Avenue

Langbourne
Place

Westferry

Blaster Walk

St_Davids Sq

St_Davids

0.25 mile   0.25 km

Though Millwall has award winning Docklands Sailing Centre and decent community venue The Space (Hubbub Café and Bar), it doesn't really have much else. Bereft of tube, overground, or DLR, it doesn't even have Millwall FC anymore. Despite the potential of Canary Wharf on the doorstep and flush of luxury riverside apartments, it's still tainted with the whiff of BNP and football hooliganism. Buy now.

Map 10

O Landmarks

• **The Docklands Sailing & Watersport Centre** • 235 Westferry Rd

Nightlife

• **Hubbub** • 269 Westferry Rd

Post Offices

• **Westferry Rd** • 367 Westferry Rd

hough shaded by the skyscrapers of Canary Wharf and a rash of luxury evelopments, this corner of the Island is blessed by the marvellous Mudchute arm and Park (with the stand out Mudchute Kitchen and equestrian centre), not ne, not two, but three DLR stations, and a number of down-to-earth boozers (Lord elson, Waterman's Arms). Who let the Isle of Dogs out?

£ Banks

Lloyds • 24 Harbor Exchange

Libraries

Cubitt Town Library • Strattondale St

Nightlife

The Ferry House • 26 Ferry St
Lord Nelson • 1 Manchester Road
Waterman's Arms • 1 Glenaffric Avenue

Post Offices

Cubitt Town • 15 Castalia Sq
Isle Of Dogs • 159 Manchester Rd

Restaurants

Mudchute Kitchen • Pier Street

Supermarkets

ASDA • 151 E Ferry Rd

Hug the riverbank and you can culture 'till you puke. But you'll need stamina to survive; with such densely populated institutions your brain will give up long before your body. When it does, head for the cafe by day/bar by night, Concrete, tucked away behind the Southbank Centre, where the art installation du jour promises to have you wetting your pants in no time.

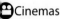

£ Banks

HSBC • 22 Stamford St
Lloyds • 2 York Rd
NatWest • 91 Westminster Bridge Rd

Cinemas

BFI London IMAX • 1 Charlie Chaplin Walk
BFI Southbank • Belverdere Rd & Waterloo Rd

Coffee

Bagel Factory • Waterloo Station
Benugo Bar & Kitchen • Belvedere Rd
Eat. • Belvedere Rd
Eat. • Barge House St
ScooterCaffe • 132 Lower Marsh
Starbucks • 3 Belvedere Rd

Landmarks

County Hall • Westminster Bridge Rd & Belvedere Rd
The Hayward Gallery • Southbank Centre
The London Eye • Westminster Bridge Rd
Low Tide at South Bank • Waterloo Rd & Upper Ground
National Theatre • South Bank
The Pier at OXO Tower •
Barge House St & Upper Ground
South Bank Book Market • Under Waterloo Bridge
Waterloo Bridge • Waterloo Bridge

Libraries

Imperial War Museum • Lambeth Road
Poetry Library • Royal Festival Hall
Waterloo Library • 114 Lower Marsh

Nightlife

The Anchor & Hope • 36 The Cut
Barrio • 14 W Square
Benugo Bar & Kitchen • Belvedere Rd
Concrete • Southbank Centre
Cubana • 48 Lower Marsh
The Cut Bar • 66 The Cut
Da Vinci's • 6 Baylis Rd
The Fire Station • 150 Waterloo Rd
The Pit Bar at the Old Vic • The Cut
Royal Festival Hall • Belvedere Rd
Skylon • Belvedere Rd

Restaurants

• **Anchor & Hope** • 32 The Cut
• **Canteen** • Royal Festival Hall, Belvedere Rd
• **Concrete** • Southbank Centre
• **The Cut Bar** • 66 The Cut
• **Enis's Cafe** • 79 Waterloo Rd
• **Giraffe** • Riverside Level 1
• **Livebait** • 45 The Cut
• **Marie's Cafe** • 90 Lower Marsh
• **Oxo Tower Wharf** • Barge House St
• **RSJ** • 33 Coin St
• **Skylon** • Belvedere Rd
• **Studio 6** • 56 Upper Ground
• **Tas Cut** • 33 The Cut

Shopping

• **Calder Bookshop** • 51 The Cut
• **Calder Bookshop - The Bookshop Theater** • 51 The Cut
• **I Knit London** • 106 Lower Marsh
• **Konditor & Cook** • 22 Cornwall Rd
• **Oasis** • 84 Lower Marsh
• **Radio Days** • 87 Lower Marsh
• **ScooterCaffe** • 132 Lower Marsh
• **Silverprint** • 12 Valentine Pl
• **Southbank Book Market** • Under Waterloo Bridge
• **Top Wind** • 2 Lower Marsh
• **Waterloo Camping** • 37 The Cut
• **What The Butler Wore** • 131 Lower Marsh

Supermarkets

• **Iceland** • 112 Lower Marsh
• **Marks & Spencer** • Waterloo Station
• **Sainsbury's** • 101 Waterloo Rd

...e Tate Modern, ladies and gents. It deserves all the praise it gets. And next door
...ere's the reconstruction of Shakespeare's famous playhouse, making this looked-
...er stretch of the Thames embankment a treasure for those hungry for culture.
...r those hungry for something else, you're spoilt with quirky options. Try Baltic
...r Polish Hunters' Stew, The Table for award-winning brunches, or Laughing Gravy
...a restaurant named after Laurel & Hardy's dog.

Coffee

- ...at. • Bankside
- ...ret A Manger • 2 Canvey St
- ...tarbucks • Emerson St (Units 1-3 Benbow House)

Landmarks

- ...uskers' Archway • Southbank
- ...ephant & Castle • Elephant & Castle
- ...ichael Faraday Memorial • Elephant & Castle
- ...he Ring • 72 Blackfriars Rd
- ...hakespeare's Globe • 21 New Globe Walk
- ...te Modern • Bankside

Nightlife

- ...bert Arms • 1 Gladstone St
- ...hibibe • 173 Blackfriars Rd
- ...inistry of Sound • 103 Gaunt St
- ...he Prince of Wales • 51 St George's Rd
- ...he Wine Theatre • 206 Union St

Post Offices

...ackfriars Road • 52 Blackfriars Rd

Restaurants

- **Baltic** • 74 Blackfriars Rd
- **Blackfriars Cafe** • 169 Blackfriars Rd
- **El Vergel** • 132 Webber St
- **Laughing Gravy** • 154 Blackfriars Rd
- **The Table** • 83 Southwark St
- **Tate Modern Restaurant** • Bankside

Shopping

- **Elephant & Castle Market** • Elephant & Castle

Supermarkets

- **Tesco** • Elephant & Castle Metro

Map 106 • Bankside (East) / Borough / Newington

◄105
107►
112
113

0.25 mile

0.25 km

Bankside (East) / Borough / Newington

Map 106

Shoreditch for grown-ups, these parts have become a bit suitified lately – and promises to be more so when the area is reborn as "London Bridge Quarter" under he Shard. Still, there's plenty of fun to be had.

£ Banks

- **Abbey** • 9 Southwark St
- **Barclays** • 29 Borough High St
- **HSBC** • 28 Borough High St
- **Lloyds** • 69 Borough High St
- **NatWest** • St Thomas St
- **NatWest** • 10 Southwark St

Coffee

- **Bagel Factory** • 12 Joiner St
- **Caffe Nero** • 3 Cathedral St
- **Costa** • 134 Borough High St
- **Patisserie Lila** • 1 Bedale St
- **Pret A Manger** • 8 London Bridge St
- **Pret A Manger** • 49 Tooley St
- **Starbucks** • Clink Wharf, Clink St

Landmarks

- **Cross Bones Graveyard** • Red Cross Way & Union St
- **Female Gladiator** • 159 Great Dover St
- **The Golden Hinde** • Clink St & Stoney St
- **The London Tombs** • 2 Tooley St
- **Mint Street Park** •
- Southwark Bridge Rd & Marshalsea Rd
- **Old Operating Theatre Museum** • 9 St Thomas St
- **Roman Cemetery** • 165 Great Dover St
- **Southwark Cathedral** • Cathedral St & Montague Close
- **St George the Martyr** • Borough High St & Tabard St
- **Winchester Palace** • Clink St & Storey St

Libraries

- **John Harvard Library** • 211 Borough High St

Nightlife

- **The Anchor** • 34 Park St
- **Belushi's** • 161 Borough High St
- **The Blue-Eyed Maid** • 173 Borough High St
- **Brew Wharf** • Brew Wharf Yard, Stoney St
- **The George Inn** • 77 Borough High St
- **The Globe** • 8 Bedale St
- **La Cave** • 6 Borough High St
- **The Market Porter** • 9 Stoney St
- **The Rake** • 14 Winchester Walk
- **The Roebuck** • 50 Great Dover St
- **The Rose** • 123 Snowfields
- **Roxy Bar and Screen** • 128 Borough High St

- **The Royal Oak** • 44 Tabard St
- **SeOne** • Weston St
- **Shunt Lounge** • 20 Stainer St
- **Southwark Tavern** • 22 Southwark St
- **Wine Wharf** • Stoney St

Post Offices

- **Great Dover Street** • 159 Great Dover St
- **London Bridge** • 19 Borough High St

Restaurants

- **Amano** • Clink St
- **Boot and Flogger** • 10 Redcross Way
- **Brew Wharf** • Brew Wharf Yard, Stoney St
- **Cantina Vinopolis** • 1 Bank End
- **Champor-Champor** • 62 Weston St
- **Feng Sushi** • 13 Stoney St
- **Fish!** • Cathedral St
- **Hing Loong** • 159 Borough High St
- **Nando's** • 215 Clink St
- **Roast** • The Floral Hall, Stoney St
- **Silka** • Southwark St
- **Tapas Brindisa** • 18 Southwark St
- **Tas Borough High Street** • 72 Borough High St
- **Wright Bros Oyster Bar** • 11 Stoney St

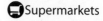 Shopping

- **Borough Market** • 8 Southwark St
- **Brindisa Retail** • Borough Market
- **German Deli** • 8 Southwark St
- **Paul Smith** • 13 Park St
- **Richer Sounds** • 2 London Bridge Walk
- **Vinopolis** • 1 Bank End

Supermarkets

- **Marks & Spencer** • London Bridge Station
- **Sainsbury's** • 116 Borough High St

Map 107 • **Shad Thames**

1

2

HMS Belfast

MORE
LONDON

City Hall

Potters
Fields Park

River
Thames

Duke Street Hill

London
Bridge
Station
PAGE
412

Tooley

Street A200

Queen Elizabeth St

Design
Museum

Shad
Thames

Floating
Gardens

St. Thomas Street A200

Crucifix

Lane

Tooley Street A200

Druid Street

Tanner Street A200

Druid Street A2207

Snowsfields

Fashion &
Textile
Museum

Tanner Street

106

108

Long Lane A2198

Newhams
Row

Market Yard
Ms

Stevens St

Abbey Street B202

Abbey Street A2198

Long Walk

Grange Road A2206

Bermondsey
Spa

Tower Bridge Road

Webb Street

Swan Mead

Old Kent Road A2

Stompie

113

114

New Kent Road A2

| 0.25 mile | | 0.25 km |

Map 105

...he elitist's Bermondsey, Shad Thames is home to ultra-hip boutiques, glass balconies, and ...onverted warehouses. No café dares exist without its own gallery. Bermondsey Street ...ossoms as an epicentre of creatives knocking out their latest bestseller over brunch, while ...e More London space by the Thames is an invigorating crowd-pleaser. Head to so-new-...s-still-burping-formula Shortwave for indie flicks, and The Scoop for top free events.

£ Banks

- **Barclays** • 104 Tower Bridge Rd
- **NatWest** • 201 Tooley St

Cinemas

- **Shortwave** • 10 Bermondsey Sq

Coffee

- **Caffe Nero** • 6 More Pl
- **Caphe House** • 114 Bermondsey St
- **Coffee @ Bermondsey** • 163 Bermondsey St
- **SoBo** • 83 Tower Bridge Rd

Landmarks

- **City Hall** • Queen's Walk, More London Development
- **Design Museum** • Shad Thames
- **Fashion and Textile Museum** • 83 Bermondsey St
- **Floating Gardens** • 31 Mill St
- **HMS Belfast** • Morgan's Lane & Tooley St
- **Stompie** • Mandela Way & Page's Walk
- **Tower Bridge** • Tower Bridge Road

Nightlife

- **Cable** • 33 Bermondsey St
- **The Hide** • 39 Bermondsey St
- **Hilton London Tower Bridge** • 5 Tooley St
- **Village East** • 171-173 Bermondsey St
- **The Wooipack** • 98 Bermondsey St

Restaurants

- **Butlers Wharf Chop House** • 36 Shad Thames
- **Delfina** • 50 Bermondsey St
- **Le Pont de la Tour** • 36 Shad Thames
- **M Manze Pie and Mash** • 87 Tower Bridge Rd
- **Magdalen** • 152 Tooley St
- **Village East** • 171-173 Bermondsey St

Shopping

- **Fine Foods** • 218 Long Lane
- **The Design Museum Shop** • 28 Shad Thames
- **Long Lane Deli** • 218 Long Ln
- **United Nude** • 124 Bermondsey St

Map 108 · **Bermondsey**

With its mixed bag of winding cobbled streets, council estates and posh new builds, you can imagine the awkwardness when the new-to-the-neighbourhood lean shirt steps into the the adamantly local Bermondsey boozer. The old-timers are sticking to their guns, and there is a definite dirty side to this on-the-cusp part of town. For quaint Japanese try PoppyHana on Jamaica Road.

Map 1

 # Banks

Barclays • 264 Southwark Park Rd
Lloyds • 255 Southwark Park Rd

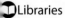 # Libraries

Blue Anchor Library • Southwark Park Rd

Post Offices

Jamaica Road • 158 Jamaica Rd
Southwark Park Road • 200 Southwark Park Rd

Restaurants

Poppy Hana • 169 Jamaica Rd

Supermarkets

Co-Op • 193 Southwark Park Rd
Iceland • 222 Southwark Park

Bordered by tower blocks and the unfortunate juxtaposition of a nursing home and undertaker's, you might toy with taking your picnic elsewhere. But step inside, because it's every bit the oasis that local hero Dr Salter hoped it would be. Well-spent investment has given it a boating lake, rose garden, wildlife area, and the inspired Café Gallery Projects. Nip to the Angel afterwards for cheap beers and river views.

Banks

Abbey • 210 Southwark

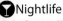Nightlife

Ancient Foresters • 282 Southwark Park Rd
The Angel • 101 Bermondsey Wall E

Map 110 • **Rotherhithe (West) / Canada Water**

Map 110

residential flats are your thing you'll love Rotherhithe West. Not if bars are our thing though. Or shops. Or life. But among the warren of apartments is the Mayflower, one of the greatest historical pubs in London, with the grave of the Mayflower ship's captain in the churchyard opposite. Entertain your dad at the Brunel Museum, and jog or snog your way along this serene stretch of Thames Path.

Coffee

Brunel Museum Café • Railway Ave

Landmarks

Brunel Museum • Railway Ave & Rotherhithe St

Libraries

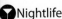

Rotherhithe Library • Albion St

Nightlife

The Albion • 20 Albion St
The Mayflower • 117 Rotherhithe St
Old Salt Quay • 163 Rotherhithe St
The Ship • 39 St Marychurch St

Post Offices

Lower Road Rotherhithe • 142 Lower Rd

Restaurants

Café Silka • 30 Albion St
Mayflower • 117 Rotherhithe St
The Rainbow • 33 Brunel Rd
Simplicity • 1 Tunnel Rd

Map 111 · **Rotherhithe (East) / Surrey Quays** Ⓝ

River Thames **1**   **2**

Sovereign Crescent

Rotherhithe Street
Rotherhithe Road

Edward Square

St. Paul's Ave

Byland's Close

St. Paul's Sports Ground

Lavender Road

Pitman Crescent

Rotherhithe Tunnel

Rotherhithe Street

Lavender Pond Nature Park

Bryater Place

Baxley Place

Heron Place

Acorn Walk

Salter Road B205

Lagado Mews

Katherine Close

Foundry Close

Globe Pond Road

Stave Yard Road

Staples Close

Buckters Rents

Farrins Rents

Silver Walk

Fisher Athletic (London) Football Club Ground (Surrey Docks Stadium)

Dean Road

Midship Close

Brunswood Walk

Fir Trees

Captian Way

Byfield Close

Surrey Water

Marlow Close

Hurley

Rupack

Crescent

Surrey Quays Road

Hull Close

Russia Dock Road

Redwood Close

Teak Close

Stephenson Way

Rotherhithe Street

A

Clarence Mews

Burnel Road

Clippa Road

Kinburn St

Wingrave

Clipper Cl

Schooner Cl

Bailey Court

Glengarrow

Gunwhale Close

Dock Hill Avenue

Timber Pond Road

Greenacre Square

Mellish Sports Ground

Stave Hill Ecological Park

Bryan Road

Holyoake Court

Christopher Close

Poolmans Street

Stalhouse Crescent

Fishermans Drive

Baltic Ct.

Stave Hill

Russia Dock Woodland

Downtown Road

Hamilton Close

Stears Way

Surrey Docks Farm

Vaughan Street

Spence Close

Wyatt Close

Needleman Street

Gatbr Way

Archangel Street

Victory Way

Way

Swan Road

Albatross Way

Roberts Close

Shipwright Road

Drain Road

Canada Street

Quebec Way

Lovell Place

Oslo Square

Redriff Est

◀110

Surrey Quays Road

Canada Water

ROTHERHITHE

Teredo Street

Edgar Street

Bergen Square

Guthrue Street

Elgar Street

Norway Gate

Plough Way Dock

Finland Street

109

Redriff Road A2202

Omega Gate

Helsinki Square

South Sea Street

B

A200

Brunswick Quay

Worgan Street

Trundleys Road

Greenland Dock

Rope Street

Calypso

118

Surrey Quays

Canute Gardens

Lower Road A200

Tawny Way

Mayflower

Greenland Quay

Sweden Gate

Plough Way

Hocker Gro

◀116

Cope Street

Plough Way B206

Trident St.

117 ▼

Boat Lifter Way

Lighter Close

Dunnage Crescent

Thevton Close

Plough Way

St. Georges Mews

St. Georges Square

0.25 mile   0.25 km

still has some dodgy estates, but Rotherhithe East is blossoming in a clean-cut city-worker kind of way. The docks are delightful and have resisted the chain bars, instead allowing great little independents like Wibbley Wobbley and Moby Dick to flourish. Trying to be healthy? Enjoy lunch among the goats at wholesome Café Nabo in Surrey Docks Farm, and visit Decathlon for sport equipment paradise.

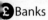

Banks

Halifax • 28 Redriff Rd
HSBC • Redriff Rd

Cinemas

Odeon Surrey Quays • Redriff Rd & Surrey Quays Rd

Landmarks

Surrey Docks Farm • Rotherhithe St

Nightlife

Blacksmith's Arms • 257 Rotherhithe St
Moby Dick • 6 Russell Place, off Greenland Dock
Ship & Whale • 2 Gulliver St
Whelan's • 11 Rotherhithe Old Rd
Wibbley Wobbley • South Dock Marina, Rope St

Restaurants

Café Nabo • Surrey Docks Farm, Rotherhithe St

Shopping

Decathlon • Surrey Quays Road

Supermarkets

Tesco • Redriff Rd

Change, at last, is promised for the infamous double roundabouts that make up Elephant and Castle. With a budget of £1.5 billion, this grisly area will soon be revamped into a global leader of "carbon positive" communities. Bill Clinton was so excited that he called Elephant and Castle "the future": a startling promise. While you wait for the future, learn about the past at the brilliant Imperial War museum.

Banks

• **Abbey** • 335 Elephant & Castle
• **Lloyds** • 245 Elephant and Castle

Libraries

• **Brandon Library** • Cooks Rd [Maddock Way]
• **Durning Library** • 167 Kennington Ln

Nightlife

• **Corsica Studios** • 5 Elephant Rd
• **Dog House** • 293 Kennington Rd
• **Prince of Wales** • Cleaver Sq

Post Offices

• **Kennington Park** • 410 Kennington Park Rd

Restaurants

• **Dragon Castle** • 114 Walworth Rd
• **Lobster Pot** • 3 Kennington Ln

Shopping

• **Pricebusters Hardware** •
  311 Elephant & Castle Shopping Centre
• **Recycling** • 110 Elephant Rd

Supermarkets

• **Iceland** • 300 Elephant & Castle

Map 1

Oh, Walworth. With all this about the Elephant and Castle redevelopment, why do we get the funny feeling you will never change? From the excessive amount of Gregg's bakeries along Walworth Road, to the 'who really buys these things?' tat at East Street Market, Walworth's lack of motivation is somehow endearing. La Luna or pizza is a find, as is the Beehive pub.

Banks

- **Abbey** • 347 Walworth Rd
- **Barclays** • 260 Walworth Rd
- **NatWest** • 290 Walworth Rd

Coffee

- **Ranya Café** • 314 Walworth Rd

O Landmarks

- **East Street Market** • Walworth Rd & East St
- **Heygate Estate** • Deacon Way & Heygate St

Libraries

- **Newington Library** • 157 Walworth Rd

Nightlife

- **Banana's Bar** • 374 Walworth Rd
- **The Beehive** • 60 Carter St
- **Red Lion** • 407 Walworth Rd
- **Temple Bar** • 286 Walworth Rd

Post Offices

- **Walworth Road** • 234 Walworth Rd

Restaurants

- **La Luna** • 380 Walworth Rd

Shopping

- **Mixed Blessings Caribbean Bakery** • 12 Camberwell Rd

Supermarkets

- **Iceland** • 332 Walworth Rd

With community action that captures the spirit of southeast London of yesteryear, locals successfully campaigned for £6 million funding to make Burgess Park fabulous. It's actually not bad as it is, with the lovely Chumleigh Gardens café, and even lovelier cheerleaders bouncing around the sports centre. But the real draw is the animatronic fireman above the fireplace shop across the way, clunkily waving his way into your nightmares.

 Coffee

• **Chumleigh Gardens Café** • Chumleigh Street

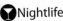 Landmarks

• **The Animatronic Fireman** • Old Kent Road
• **Peckham Library** • 122 Peckham Hill St

Nightlife

• **Auto-Italia South East** • 1 Glengall Rd
• **World Turned Upside Down** • 145 Old Kent Rd

Post Offices

• **Old Kent Road** • 240 Old Kent Rd

Restaurants

• **Pardis** • 280 Old Kent Rd
• **Parrilladas del Sur** • 186 Old Kent Rd

Shopping

• **Old Kent Road Food Centre** • 252 Old Kent Rd

Supermarkets

• **Tesco** • 107 Dunton Rd

There must be something to this portion of Old Kent Road, as the Pearly Kings and Queens won't shut up about the whole thing. As far as we can tell, it's not that much more than a giant Asda. Walk along Bird In Bush Road to laugh at its name and over to Peckham Park Road for a damn good fry-up at Roma Café.

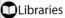

Libraries
• **East Street Library** • 168 Old Kent Rd

Restaurants
• **Roma Café** • 21 Peckham Park Rd

Supermarkets
• **ASDA** • Old Kent Rd & Ossory Rd

Map 116 · **South Bermondsey**

N

1

2

Southwark Park

Barnard Rd

Surrey Quays

Rotherhithe Old Rd A200

Lower Rd

Canute Rd

Hedrift

Bombay Street

Drummond Road

Fenner Close

Lenard Road

Frean Street

Beatson Walk

Hawkstone Road

Hornet Grove

Rol. New Road A200

Rol. Nev

Southwark Park Road

A2206

Raymouth Road

Almond Road

A2206

Frankland Close

Frankland Road

Neptune Road

Redfield Lane

Abbeyfield Rd

Rol. Nev

A2200 Rd Rotherhithe New Road A2208

Rotherhithe New Road A2208

Rol. Nev

Linsford

Oldfield Grove

A

Rosebery St

Roseberry St

Galleywall Road

Lynton Road

Amber St

Ainsley St

Corbetts Lane

Silwood Road

Millender Walk

Jarrow Road

Corbetts Passage

St. Helena Rd

Concorde Way

Island Road

Alpha Road

Resolver Road

Goldsworthy Gdns

Lambourne Grove

Sketchley Gdns

◀108

▲109

South Bermondsey Rail 🚉

Silwood Street

Sheppard Drive

Rossetti Road

Stevenson

Wealve Cl

B204

Rollin St

Rotherhithe New Road A2206

Verney Road

Stubbs Drive

Stubbs Drive

Hurst

Sharratt

Ryder Drive

Masters Dr

Masters Park

Birt Drive

Masters Cl

Crane St

Brass St

Daw St

Howland

Brim Gro

Del Rd

Delaford Road

Crasswell Rd

Ablett Street

Barkworth Road

Verney Road

Varcoe Road

Gomm Road

Eagle

Varcoe

Gerards Ct

Ilderton Road

Bolina Road

Zampa Road

Millwall FC (The Den) ○

117▶

Stockholm Road

Surrey Canal Rd

◀115

B

Record Street

Hatcham Road

Record Street

Rollins Street

Ormside Street

Rollins Street

Ilderton Road

Sharratt Street

Manor Grove

Sharratt Street

Hornshay Street

Lovelinch Close

Lovelinch Close

Lovelinch Close

Bridge Meadows

Bridge House Meadows

John William

Willow Grove

Sandgate Street

Ruby Triangle

Ruby Street

Hyndman Street

Murdock St

Old Kent Road A2

Elland Road

Pencraig Way

Camden Street

Alpine Rd

In Bush Road

Devon Street

Devonshire Grove

Sylvan Grove

Patterdale

124▼

Hunsdon Road

Water Lane

Water Lane

Farrow Lane

Old Ke

There may be more to this area than we've listed, but the fact is: we like you. We want to see you live to enjoy our favourite picks among these pages. If you make the wrong kind of eye contact as you tremble past the Millwall flags fluttering menacingly from the balconies, then we're worried we'll lose a much-loved reader. Swallow your valuables and back slowly away.

○ Landmarks

- **Millwall FC Stadium** • Zampa Road & Bolina Rd

Map 117 · **Deptford (West)**

N

1

2

Rotherhithe Old Road

Surrey Quays

Redriff Road A2208

Wogan Street

Greenland Quay

Greenland Quay Howland Quay

Trafalgar Close

Hawkstone Road

Canute Gardens

Hodnet Grove

Tawny Way

Trident Street

B206

Yeoman Street

Iceland Wharf

111

£

Plough Way

Cope Street

A

Rotherhithe New Road

Lower Road A200

Chilton Grove

Croft Street

Woodcroft Mews

Acasta Close

Wandon Street

St. Helena Road

Oldfield Grove

Haddonfield

Bush Road

Evelyn Street A200

Rainsbo

Concorde Way

Trundleys Terrace

Clayton Drive

ellender Walk

Eugenia Road

Island Road

John Silkin Lane

Crane Mead

Sybil Phoenix Close

Hicks Street

Alpine Road

Reculver Road

Oldfield Grove

Somerfield Street

Alloa Road

Crooke Road

Scawen Road

Silwood Street

Sketchley Gardens

Trundleys Road B207

116

Kezia Mews

118

Deptford Park

Millwall FC (The Den)

B

Greenland Mews

Scawen Road

Landmann Way

Grinstead Road

Canal Approach

holm Road

Bridge Meadows

Myers Lane

Mercury Way

Surrey Canal Road

Trundleys Road

Blackh

125

Juno

Folkestone Gardens

| 0.25 mile | 0.25 km |

Apparently, developers have their eye on Deptford West. You've really got to hope so. The Blitz did its best, but the area came back with hastily built and charmless 50s tower blocks. Still, like the rest of Deptford it's going through a gradual regeneration as young buyers move in to make their money stretch. The Yellow House offers salvation for eating out.

Map 1

Banks

Barclays • 1 Plough Way

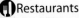Restaurants

Yellow House • 37 Plough Way

Map 118 · **Deptford (Central)**

When Christopher Marlowe was murdered in a Deptford tavern, Deptford hit its nightlife peak. That was 1593. Today, while the rest of London turns everything into a pub, Deptford turns its pubs into churches. Without beer, you may want to drown your sorrows in the Thames, but even that is thwarted: here the Thames path breaks to take you through neglected residential areas instead. Escape!

115 116 117 118
124 125 126 119 120
123 124

Map 1

Nightlife

▸ **The Lord Palmerston** • 81 Childers Street

Post Offices

▸ **Evelyn Street** • 301 Evelyn St

Map 119 • Deptfo

Map 119 • Deptfo

1   2

River Thames

A

Glaisher Street
Glaisher Street
Twinkle Park
Borthwick Street
Trevithick Mews
Caravel Mews
Watergate Street
Prince Street
Benbow Street
Hamilton Cresent
Bessey Way
Kessey Way
Glaisher Street
Greenwich Quay
Dacca Street
Henrietta Close
St. Nicholas House
Stowage
Creek Road A200
Prince Street
Car Street
New King Street
Frigate Mews
Deptford Green
Carrick Mews
Brig Mews

◀118

Evelyn Street A200
McMillan Street
Bruford Court
Berthon Street
Creek Road A200
Coppenas Street

Deptford Creek

Grinling Place
Lamerton Street
Deptford Church Street
Albury Street
Berthon Street
Bronze Street
Beech Close
Larch Close
Hyde Street
Mary Ann Gardens
St. Paul's Churchyard Gardens
Edward Street
Hamilton Street
Crossfield Street
Sue Godfrey Local Nature Reserve
Edward Place
Hinch Street
Payne Street
Hamilton Street
Deptford Rail
Resolution Way
A209
Creekside

◀12

B
Adolphus Street
Idonia Street
Octavius Street
Giffin Square Market
Vape Close
Amersham Vale
Turnpike Close
Rochdale Way
Giffin Street
Frankham Street
Douglas Way
Street Market
Margaret McMillan Park
Vaughan Williams Close
Margaret McMillan Park
Planet Close
Elgar Close
Wilson's Street
Glenville Grove
Baildon Street
Comet Street
Reginald Road
New Butt Lane
Fletcher Path
Reginald Square
Admiralty Close
Ravensbourne River
Mimford Mills
Greenwich High Road
Burgos Grove
Mornington Road
Stanley Street
Glenville Grove
Douglas Way

◀126

New Cross

New Cross Road A2
Deptford Broadway
Deptford Bridge A2
Blackheath R
Deptford High Street
Deptford Broadway
Deptford Bridge

0.25 mile   0.25 km

Deptford (East)

Map 119

As you arrive you may think twice about stepping out the comforting folds of the bendy bus. But toughen up: it's not all bad. Even if the clothes are nicked from your back, you can buy replacements from Deptford Market and still have change for pie & mushy peas from Manzes. The Dog & Bell is a rare local gem for a comforting pint while the Deptford Project is a flash of brilliance.

£ Banks

- **Barclays** • 80 Deptford High St
- **Halifax** • 93 Deptford High St
- **HSBC** • 90 Deptford High St

Coffee

- **The Deptford Project** • 121 Deptford High St

Nightlife

- **The Bird's Nest** • 32 Deptford Church St
- **Dog & Bell** • 116 Prince Street

Post Offices

- **New Cross** • 500 New Cross Rd

Restaurants

- **Kaya House** • 37 Deptford Broadway
- **Manzes** • 204 Deptford High St

Shopping

- **Deptford Market** • Deptford High St

Supermarkets

- **Iceland** • 112 Deptford High St

Map 120 · **Greenwich**

River
Thames

Cutty Sark
Gardens

Greenwich
Foot Tunnel

Naval
College
Gardens

Thames Street

Woodwharf

Thames Street

College
Approach

Greenwich Quay

Clavell Street

Durnford
Street

Romney Road A206

Creek Road A200

Cutty Sark

Nelson Road

National
Maritime
Museum Gar

Bardsley Lane

Basevi Way

Stowage

Thornham Street

Roan Street

Claremont Street

Greenwich
Park

Deptford
Creek

Roan Street

Randall Place

Straightsmouth

PAGE
336

Tarves Way

Burney Street

Crooms Hill

Greenwich High Road B209

Norman Road B209

Churchfields

Greenwich High Road A2211

Gloucester Circus

Crooms Hill Grove

Greenwich

119

Greenwich High Road A206

Maitland Close

Waller Way

Peyton
Place

Royal Hill B209

King George Street

Gloucester Circus

Circus Street

Prior Street

Ashburnham Place

St. Marks Close

Arlington
Place

Royal
Place

Georgette Place

Ashburnham Grove

Ashburnham
Retreat

Brand Street

Royal Hill

Hawks Mews

Hyde Vale B209

Devonshire Drive

Peabody
Close

Chesterfield

Egerton Drive B209

Guildford Grove

Admiral's Gate

Lindsell Street

Blissett Street

Winforton Street

Cade Place

Maidenstone Hill

Point Hill

Westgrove Lane

West Grove

Rangers Square

Burdon Grove

Catherine Grove

Greenwich South Street

Diamond Terrace

Clayton Mews

Friendly
Place

Plumbridge
Street

Dabin Cresent

Trafalgar Grove

Dutton Street

Hollymount Close

Point Close

Dartmouth Hill

Dartmouth Row

Shooters Hill

Blackheath Road A2

Blackheath Hill A2

Dartmouth Hill

Franklin Place

John Penn Street

Lewisham Road A21

Dartmouth Grove

Franklin Close

Morden Street

Sparta Street

Beck Close

0.25 mile   0.25 km

We're still sulking about the closure of one of London's best village markets here, and don't get us started on the delayed restoration of the Cutty Sark. But Greenwich is still one of the loveliest parts of London. Queue up to straddle the prime meridian, walk off your fish and chips through the foot tunnel, and round off with locally brewed chocolate beer at the Greenwich Union.

Map 1

£ Banks

- **HSBC** • 275 Greenwich High Rd
- **Lloyds** • 6 Crescent Arcade
- **NatWest** • 2 Greenwich Church St

Cinemas

- **Greenwich Picturehouse** • 180 Greenwich High Rd

Coffee

- **Rhodes Bakery** • 37 King William Walk
- **Starbucks** • 54 Greenwich Church St

O Landmarks

- **Cutty Sark Gardens** • King William Walk & Romney Rd
- **Greenwich Foot Tunnel** •
  Greenwich Church St & Thames St

Libraries

- **West Greenwich Library** • Greenwich High Rd

Nightlife

- **Bar du Musee** • 17 Nelson Rd
- **The Greenwich Union** • 56 Royal Hill
- **Up The Creek** • 302 Creek Rd

Post Offices

- **Greenwich** • 261 Greenwich High Rd

Restaurants

- **Goddard's Pie Shop Booth** •
  Fountain Court (off Greenwich Church Street)
- **Greenwich Park Bar & Grill** • 1 King William Walk
- **The Hill** • 89 Royal Hill
- **Inside** • 19 Greenwich South St
- **Piano Restaurant** • 131 Greenwich High Rd
- **Rivington Grill** • 178 Greenwich High Rd

Shopping

- **Belle** • 20 College Approach
- **Bullfrogs** • 22 Greenwich Church St
- **Cheeseboard** • 26 Royal Hill
- **Compendia** • 10 The Market
- **Emma Nissim** • 10 Greenwich Market
- **Johnny Rocket** • 10 College Approach
- **Meet Bernard** • 23 Nelson Rd
- **Mr Humbug** • Greenwich Market

his slowly reviving segment of Camberwell brings together a minority of polite arty types in the crumbling yet quaint town houses of Camberwell New Road with take-no-prisoners urbanites as seen in the chaos of Denmark Hill and its pointless Butterfly hopping Centre (why?). The neighbourhood good stuff includes music bargains (Rat ecords), killer Indian (New Dewaniam), and the new and unpronounceable Central sian eatery at the Pasha Hotel: Kazakh Kyrgyz Restaurant.

Map 1

Banks

HSBC • 23 Denmark Hill
NatWest • 70 Denmark Hill

Coffee

Kings Cafe • 120 Denmark Hill

Libraries

Minet Library • 52 Knatchbull Rd

Post Offices

Camberwell Green • 25 Denmark Hill

Restaurants

- **Kazakh Kyrgyz Restaurant** • 158 Camberwell Rd
- **New Dewaniam** • 225 Camberwell New Rd
- **Su-Thai** • 16 Coldharbour Ln

Shopping

- **Butterfly Walk Shopping Centre** • Denmark Hill
- **Rat Records** • 348 New Camberwell Rd

Supermarkets

- **Co-Op** • 177 Camberwell New Rd
- **Iceland** • 120 Camberwell Rd

Camberwell (East)

This lucky dip of a neighbourhood is home to a few gangs, art students, and the occasional Time Out editor. Anyone who wrinkles their nose at Camberwell has never experienced the bohemian opulence of Camberwell Grove (which does fade rather quickly into the familiar dodginess of Camberwell Church Street). For booze, up a pint at The Castle.

£ Banks

Barclays • 1 Butterfly Walk
Lloyds • 25 Camberwell Green

Libraries

Camberwell Library • 17 Camberwell Church St

Nightlife

The Castle • 65 Camberwell Church St

Post Offices

Southampton Way • 156 Southampton Way

Restaurants

Angels & Gypsies • 29 Camberwell Church St
Caravaggio's • 47 Camberwell Church St

Peckham: so many gang wars, so little time. But it's going up in the world: we've even had to hide a smirk as developers tentatively refer to it as Peckham Village. The library is over-enthusiastically garish but is first-class, and local boy Anthony Gormley has spruced the place up with some marvellously phallic Bollards. Which leads us neatly to recommending Bellenden Road for the local bit of bohemia.

Map 1

£ Banks

- **Abbey** • 97 Rye Ln
- **Barclays** • 28 Rye Ln
- **Barclays** • 223 Rye Ln
- **Halifax** • 24 Rye Ln
- **HSBC** • 47 Rye Ln
- **Lloyds** • 76 Rye Ln
- **NatWest** • 65 Peckham High St

Coffee

- **Petitou** • 63 Choumert Rd

Libraries

- **Peckham Library** • 122 Peckham Hill St

Movie Theaters

- **Peckham Multiplex** • 95 Rye Ln

Nightlife

- **Frank's Cafe and Campari Bar** • 95 Rye Ln

Post Offices

- **Peckham** • 121 Peckham High St
- **Rye Lane** • 199 Rye Ln

Restaurants

- **Bellenden Brasserie** • 168 Bellenden Rd

Shopping

- **Curious Science** • 5 Commercial Way
- **Persepolis** • 30 Peckham High St
- **Primark** • 51 Rye Lane

Supermarkets

- **Iceland** • 74 Rye Lane

(261)

Map 124

Never one to be cheery, the eastern side of Peckham surrounding the Queen's Road is a rather bleak landscape of monolithic tower blocks and sprawling council estates. But there is something refreshingly gritty and nonplussed about the area and its dedicated locals. For instance, the 805 Bar Restaurant has excellent African food and is a culinary oasis in an urban desert.

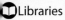
Libraries

Nunhead Library • Gordon Rd

Restaurants

• **805 Bar Restaurant** • 805 Old Kent Rd

Map 125 • **New Cr**

Rollins Street

1

Bridge
Meadows

2

Roll Street

Fo
G

Myers Lane

Juno Way

117

Lovelinch Close

Mercury Way

Bridge
House
Meadows

Samuel Close

Santord Walk

Sanford Street

Lovelinch Close

Cold Blow Lane

Knoyle
Street

Chubworthy Street

Whit

Hornshay Street

John Williams
Close

Coldblow Lane

Sterling Gardens

118

A

116

Hunsdon Road

Cottesbr
Street

Water Lane

Joseph Hardcastle Close

Nyn

Farrow Lane

Edric Road

Avonley Road

Monson Road

Camplin Street

Ba

Pump Lane

Wrigglesworth
Street

Tarragon Close

Sn

Heathfield Cl

Barlborough Street

Leyland Road

Robert Lowe Close

Goodwood

Wardalls Grove

Reaston Street

Eckington
Gardens

Ventnor Road

Auburn Close

New Cross Road A2

Hatfield Close

Casella Road

Egmont Street

Brocklehurst Street

124

Billington Road

Romney Close

Lubbock Street

Pankhurst
Close

Hatcham Park Road

Kender Street A202

Faulkner Street

Brians Street

Peters
Court

Nettleton Road

Harts Lane

126

Hatcham
B dens

Kenwood
Avenue

Besson Street A202

Hatcham Park Mews

New Cross G.

New Cross Road A2

Mylis Close

Lanchester Way

Troutbeck Road

Godley Close

Queens Road A202

Waller Road

Erlanger Road

Pepys Road

Jerningham Road

Drive

0.25 mile

0.25 km

Map 125

There used to be an urban myth that there are no cash machines in New Cross because of the muggings. Since then it's gone all art-student-cool but this bit is still quite rugged. Its biggest claim to fame is the fantastic Montague Arms, which looks like it was furnished by a drunken sailor-turned-taxidermist waking up and bellowing "bring me...stuff!"

£ Banks

• **Barclays** • 197 New Cross Rd

Y Nightlife

• **The Montague Arms** • 289 Queen's Rd

✉ Post Offices

• **New Cross Gate** • 199 New Cross Rd

🍴 Restaurants

• **Hong Kong City** • 43 New Cross Rd

Around here, the art student is king. In the shadow of the rather ugly Goldsmiths College Ben Pimlott Building, trendy young students enthralled to debauchery live out their art-school fantasies. Join them in the Hobgoblin for booze or try the decrepit New Cross Inn for your mate's band. Since its establishment in 2007 Amersham Arms is well on its way to becoming one of London's best music venues – leading the way to this neighbourhood's well-deserved revival.

O Landmarks

- **Ben Pimlott Building** · University of London, New Cross

Libraries

- **Goldsmiths Library** · Lewisham Wy

Nightlife

- **Amersham Arms** · 388 New Cross Rd
- **Hobgoblin** · 272 New Cross Rd
- **New Cross Inn** · 323 New Cross Rd

Post Offices

- **Lewisham Way** · 150 Lewisham Way
- **New Cross Road** · 500 New Cross Rd

Restaurants

- **Manzes** · 204 Deptford High St

Supermarkets

- **Iceland** · 277 New Cross Rd
- **Sainsbury's** · 263 New Cross Rd

here don't seem to be as many shootings on Coldharbour Lane as there used to e. Maybe the crack dealers are just quietly selling the stuff, as somebody on The Wire once sensibly advised. Or maybe they've all been converted by the pleasant onservatory at The Florence, invigorating swims at in the Brockwell Lido (p 328), nd handmade jams from the Blackbird Bakery. Yes, that's probably it.

Nightlife

The Commercial • 210 Railton Rd
Escape Bar and Art • 214 Railton Rd
The Florence • 133 Dulwich Rd
Prince Regent • 69 Dulwich Rd

Restaurants

Café Prov • 2 Half Moon Ln
Ichiban Sushi • 58 Atlantic Rd
New Fujiyama • 5 Vining St

Shopping

Blackbird Bakery • 208 Railton Rd

Coffee

Pullens • 293 Railton Rd

Denmark Hill / Herne Hill (East)

Map 128

There's something quaintly grounded about the leafy Victorian suburb of Herne Hill where funky neo-hippies settle into dreadlocked nuclear families. Denmark Hill sits at its top, with its imposing Salvation Army training grounds, following on to Ruskin Park for ornamental ponds and Edwardian ruins. Half Moon Lane plays main drag—get lost in a book at Tales on Moon Lane and lost in a bowl of noodles at Lombok.

Emergency Rooms

- **King's College Hospital** •
  Denmark Hill & Champion Park

Libraries

- **Carnegie Library** • 188 Herne Hill Rd

Post Offices

- **Crossthwaite Avenue** • 6 Crossthwaite Ave

Restaurants

- **Lombok** • 17 Half Moon Ln
- **Number 22** • 22 Half Moon Ln

Shopping

- **Tales on Moon Lane** • 25 Half Moon Ln

Supermarkets

- **Sainsbury's** • 132 Herne Hill

Map 1

East Dulwich is where your ex-flatmate finally settled down and now won't shut up about taramasalata, babies, and how he's only fifteen minutes from London Bridge by train over perfect cocktails at Black Cherry. Dodge baguettes, pushchairs, and delis along Lordship Lane, just don't get sucked in. Try the Sea Cow for fish & chips, a pint at the Palmerston, and a night out at Liquorish.

£ Banks

- **Barclays** • 68 Lordship Ln
- **HSBC** • 66 Lordship Ln

Coffee

- **Caffe Nero** • 8 Lordship Ln

Libraries

- **Grove Vale library** • 25 Grove Vale

Nightlife

- **Black Cherry** • 21 Lordship Ln
- **liquorish** • 123 Lordship Ln

Restaurants

- **The Palmerston** • 91 Lordship Ln
- **Sea Cow** • 37 Lordship Ln

Shopping

- **The Cheeseblock** • 69 Lordship Ln

Supermarkets

- **Iceland** • 84 Lordship Ln
- **Sainsbury's** • 80 Dog Kennel Hill

Map 130

A noticeboard on Peckham Rye Common alleges that ancient British Queen Boudicca was finally defeated by the Romans here. Anyone suggesting that the very middle class streets around North Cross Road—with its market, twee sweets at Hope and Greenwood, and lazy Sunday lunches at The Rye—have anything to do with Peckham as we know it might get the same treatment.

Coffee

Blue Mountain Café • 18 N Cross Rd

Nightlife

▸ **The Rye** • 31 Peckham Rye

Restaurants

Thai Corner Cafe • 44 Northcross Rd
▸ **The Rye** • 31 Peckham Rye

Shopping

Hope And Greenwood • 20 North Cross Rd

KENSINGTON

Holland Park

KN

SOUTH
KENSINGTON

BR

WEST
KENSINGTON

CHISWICK

HAMMERSMITH

EARLS
COURT

WEST
BROMPTON

CHELS

CASTELNAU

BARONS
COURT

Brompton
Cemetery

WALHAM
GREEN

SANDS
END

BARNES

FULHAM

PARSONS GREEN

MORTLAKE

Thames River

Putney Bridge Rd.

139

WANDSWORTH

136

137

138

PUTNEY

Wandsworth High St.

ROEHAMPTON

West Hill

WEST
HILL

146

Wandsworth
Cemetery

EARLSFIEL

Richmond
Park

SUMMEI

Deer Park

Wimbledon
Park

Wimbledon
Common

WIMBLEDON

Map 131 • Vauxhall / Albert Embankment

N

1 2

Westminster Bridge A302 Westminster Bridge Road

York Road

Leake Street

Lower Marsh

Grindal Street

Carlisle Lane

Launcelot Street

Murphy's Street

Frazier Street

Parman Street

Cooper Close

Greenham Close

Burden Street

Emery Street

Geridge Street

Webber Row

Morley Street

LAMBETH

104

Upper Marsh

Newnham Terrace

Baylis Road A302

Lambeth North

St. George's

Mead Row

King Edward Walk

King's College

PAGE 366

Royal Street

Centaur Street

Carlisle Lane

Hercules Road

McAuley Close

Kennington Road A23

Cosser Street

Morton Place

Geraldine Harmsworth

Tenn Cts

Victoria Tower Garden

River Thames

Lambeth Palace Gardens

Sports Grd

Archbishop's Park

Sieford Place

Lambeth Road A3203

Brook Drive

Walcot Square

Walcot Square

St. Mary's Gardens

Bishop's Terrace

St. Mary's Gardens

Abingdon Street

A3212

Lambeth Palace Road A3036

Lambeth Palace

Norfolk Row

Pratt Walk

Sail Street

Juxon Street

Badan Mews

Hornbeam Close

Walnut Tree Walk

Fitzalan Street

112

Lambeth Bridge A3203

Norfolk Row

Old Paradise Street

Lingham Close

Ravent Road

Lollard Street

Wincott Street

Lambeth Walk Open Space

Thorney Street

A3212

Millbank

River Thames

Lambeth High Street

Whitgift Street

Newport Street

Lambeth Walk

Gibson Road

Saunders

Lollard Street

Chester Way

Denny Street

Reedworth

Lambeth High Street

Lambeth Recreation Ground

Salamanca Place

Lilac Place

Loughton Close

Beaufoy Walk

Mayday Way

Distin Street

Lollard Street

Salamanca Street

Pedlars Park

Randall Row

Iyers Street

Black Prince Road

A23

Cleaver Street

Bowden Street

Wigton Place

Secret Intelligence Service HQ (MI6)

Randall Road

Cardigan Street

Tinworth Street

Jonathan Street

Wickham Street

Orsett Street

Sancroft Street

Newburn Street

Courtenay Street

Stables Way

Kennington Road

£

Glasshouse Walk

Laud Street

St Oswald's Place

Iyers Terrace

Worgan Street

Vauxhall Street

Wynyard Terrace

Aveline Street

Courtenay Square

Brangton Road

Windmill Row

New Spring Gardens Walk

Spring Gardens

Vauxhall City Farm

Vauxhall City Farm

Dolland Street

Kennington Lane A3204

135

Montford Place

Vauxhall City Farm

Godling Street

Auckland Street

Glyn Street

Durham Street

Braganza Street

Clayton Street

Kennington Oval

Bridgefoot A202

134

Vauxhall Rail

Vauxhall

A202

0.25 mile

0.25 km

Vauxhall / Albert Embankment

Map 131

he kiddies have their ponies at Vauxhall City Farm, spies have Vauxhall Cross (MI6 Q), dads have a pint at The Lavender, and mums the occasional up dog/down dog t The Lotus Exchange, but those who really rule the Vauxhall roost are the gays. experience "Gay Village" at its best, catch a cabaret at The Royal Vauxhall Tavern, heck out meat market Eagle London, or rave it out at Area.

£ Banks

HSBC • 20 Albert Embankment

✚ Emergency Rooms

St Thomas' Hospital •
Westminster Bridge Rd & Lambeth Palace Rd

Landmarks

Lambeth Palace • Lambeth Palace Rd & Lambeth Rd
Secret Intelligence Service HQ (MI6) •
85 Vauxhall Cross
Vauxhall City Farm • 165 Tyers St

Libraries

CILT Resources Library • 111 Vauxhall Bridge Rd
Lambeth Palace Library • Lambeth Palace Rd

Nightlife

Area • 67 Albert Embankment
Eagle London • 349 Kennington Ln
The Lavender • 112 Vauxhall Walk
The Royal Vauxhall Tavern • 372 Kennington Ln

Post Offices

Westminster Bridge Road • 125 Westminster Bridge Rd

Restaurants

Thai Pavillion East • 78 Kennington Rd

Supermarkets

Tesco • Kennington Ln

Map 132 · **Battersea (West)**

with no tubes or trains to attract the Hoi Polloi, Battersea West sits smugly hugging the River Thames, happily cut off from the hustle and bustle of the rest of London. However, despite being relatively central, the commute can be dire. Still, the masses flock--mostly for the spacious floor-to-ceiling glass apartments with killer river views. Soak in a Sunday afternoon at The Draft House Westbridge, the Woodman or Barrio.

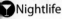 Nightlife

Barrio • 14 Battersea Sq
The Draft House Westbridge •
74 Battersea Bridge Road
The Greyhound • 136 Battersea High St
Le QuecumBar • 42 Battersea High St
The Woodman • 60 Battersea High St

✉ Post Offices

Battersea Bridge Road • 72 Battersea Bridge Rd
York Road • 583 Battersea Park Rd

🍴 Restaurants

The Greyhound • 136 Battersea High St
Ransom's Dock • 35 Parkgate Rd

🛒 Supermarkets

Sainsbury's • 326 Battersea Park Rd

n odd slice of post-industrial London dominated by the derelict Battersea Power
tation, there's naff all here until someone decides what to do with the old hulk
nd its surrounding domain. In the meantime, try registering for a new pooch at
e Dogs' Home or cycling around nearby Battersea Park from where you can rue
e slow death of the crumbling giant.

Banks

Barclays • 278 Queenstown Rd

Landmarks

Battersea Dogs' Home • 4 Battersea Park Rd
Battersea Park Gasometers •
Queenstown Rd & Prince of Wales Dr
Battersea Power Station • 188 Kirtling St

Libraries

Battersea Park Library • 309 Battersea Park Rd

Nightlife

The Chelsea Reach • 181 Battersea Park Rd

Post Offices

Battersea Park Road • 20 Battersea Park Rd

Shopping

London Recumbents • Battersea Park

Supermarkets

Sainsbury's • 326 Queenstown Rd

t ain't glamorous, but this neighbourhood still has a lot to offer. The gay scene at Vauxhall spills over into this southerly pocket of Lambeth, while 'Little Portugal' around South Lambeth Road boasts a number of great traditional tapas bars and restaurants. For great BYOB curries, head to Hot Stuff, and for hot stuff of another kind hit up Fire. Join the traders and head to New Covent Garden Market for fresh produce (get there early).

Map 1

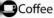 Coffee

Starbucks • 2 South Lambeth Rd

Libraries

South Lambeth Library • 180 S Lambeth Rd

Nightlife

Bar Estrella • 115 Old South Lambeth Rd
The Battersea Barge • Nine Elms Ln
Fire • 38 Parry St
Hoist • 47 S Lambeth Rd
The Vauxhall Griffin • 8 Wyvil Rd
Roller Disco @ Renaissance Rooms • 126 S Lambeth Rd

Post Offices

South Lambeth • 347 Wandsworth Rd

Restaurants

Bar Estrella • 115 Old South Lambeth Rd
Canton Arms • 177 S Lambeth Rd
Hot Stuff • 19 Wilcox Rd

Shopping

Lassco House & Garden • 30 Wandsworth Rd
New Covent Garden Market • Nine Elms Lane

Supermarkets

Sainsbury's • 62 Wandsworth Rd

osh town houses rub shoulders somewhat uneasily with housing estates here
and there's no denying the walk from Oval Station can be dodgy, but if you're a
an of cricket, the presence of the Oval cricket ground more than makes up for it.
/hen there's a match on, the area fills to the brim, but normally it's a modest and
nimposing neighbourhood. Organic foodies delight in the Oval Farmers' Market
nd vegan ex-squat The Bonnington Café.

Map 1

£ Banks

Barclays • 414 Kennington Rd

⬤ Coffee

Bonnington Cafe • 11 Vauxhall Grove

✉ Post Offices

Brixton Road • 82 Brixton Rd

🍴 Restaurants

Adulis • 44 Brixton Rd
The Bonnington Café • 11 Vauxhall Grove
Kebab and Hamburger Bar • 32 Clapham Rd

🍸 Nightlife

Fentiman Arms • 64 Fentiman Rd

Putney

Map 136

Putney has a bit of a bipolar personality disorder. On the one side, it's suburban middle England with its rugby and rowing types, on the other, it's increasingly vibrant and hip. The High Street's a bit genteel by day and young-up-for-it at night. Try Olé Restaurant and Bar or La Mancha for excellent Spanish, and Ma Goa for authentic Goan cuisine. For fab brunch head to celebrity chef's Wallace & Co or Moomba Bar & Kitchen.

£ Banks

- **Abbey** • 88 Putney High St
- **Barclays** • 159 Putney High St
- **Barclays** • 60 Putney High St
- **Halifax** • 171 Putney High St
- **HSBC** • 172 Upper Richmond Rd
- **Lloyds** • 110 Putney High St

Coffee

- **BB's Coffee and Muffins** • Putney High St & Chelverton Rd
- **Caffe Nero** • 95 Putney High St
- **Caffe Nero** • 112 Upper Richmond Rd
- **Costa** • 132 Putney High St
- **Pret A Manger** • 121 Putney High St
- **Starbucks** • 117 Putney High St

Libraries

- **Putney Library** • 5 Disraeli Rd

Movie Theaters

- **Odeon Putney** • 26 Putney High St

Nightlife

- **The Boathouse** • Brewhouse Lane
- **Duke's Head** • 8 Lower Richmond Rd
- **Jolly Gardeners** • 61 Lacy Rd
- **Star & Garter** • 4 Lower Richmond Rd

Post Offices

- **Putney** • 214 Upper Richmond Rd

Restaurants

- **Chakalaka** • 136 Upper Richmond Rd
- **La Mancha 32** • Putney High St
- **Ma Goa** • 242 Upper Richmond Rd
- **Moomba Bar & Kitchen** • 5 Lacy Rd
- **Olé Restaurant and Bar** • 240 Upper Richmond Rd
- **Talad Thai** • 320 Upper Richmond Rd
- **Wallace & Co** • 146 Upper Richmond Rd

Supermarkets

- **Sainsbury's** • 2 Werter Rd
- **Waitrose** • Putney High St & Lacy Rd

Map 137 · **Wandsworth (West)**

Disected by the busy Upper and Lower Richmond Roads, this bit of Wandsworth s a bit lifeless though pleasant enough. The pretty, riverside Wandsworth Park is a huge plus and heaves with locals with the first sniff of sunshine. Head to The Upper Lounge for a spot of liquid refreshment after a hard day's Frisbee chucking.

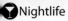Nightlife

• **The Upper Lounge** • 26 Upper Richmond Rd

Restaurants

• **Miraj** • 123 Putney Bridge Road
• **Yia Mas** • 40 Upper Richmond Rd

Map 138

This is East Wandsworth's poorer, uglier cousin--and you've got to feel sorry for it. It's got a drab shopping centre and a four-lane traffic system brings noise and air pollution. On the plus side, plenty of chain stores (Gap, Uniqlo etc.) and a Cineworld make life a little easier. To get away from it all, hibernate in the Old York Road. For the best Nepalese food in London, hit Kathmandu Valley.

Banks

- **Abbey** • 81 Wandsworth High St
- **Barclays** • 83 Wandsworth High St
- **Halifax** • 87 Wandsworth High St
- **HSBC** • 73 Wandsworth High St
- **Lloyds** • 159 Wandsworth High St

Cinemas

- **Cineworld Wandsworth** •
  Wandsworth High St & Ram St

Coffee

- **Caffe Nero** • Southside Shopping Centre
- **Coffee Republic** • Wandsworth High St

Nightlife

- **The Cat's Back** • 88 Point Pleasant
- **GJ's** • 89 Garratt Lane
- **The Queen Adelaide** • 35 Putney Bridge Rd

Post Offices

- **Wandsworth** • 1 Arndale Walk

Restaurants

- **Brady's** • 513 Old York Rd
- **Kathmandu Valley** • 5 West Hill

Supermarkets

- **Iceland** • Wandsworth High St & Buckhold Rd
- **Sainsbury's** • 45 Garratt Ln
- **Waitrose** • 66 Wandsworth High St

Wandsworth (East)

Map 139

Wandsworth East: a hodgepodge of extreme opulence and utter depravity. East Hill, locally known as "the Toast Rack", is home to a slew of celebrities. Check out St John's Hill for boutiques, bars and restaurants. Wanna learn how to bake? Cake Boy's your place. Gorge on great bistro food at Steam, if you can get past the naff bar, and hit up a well-to-do chippie at The Fish Club.

£ Banks

Halifax • 6 St John's Hill Grove

Libraries

York Gardens Library • 34 Lavender Rd

✉ Post Offices

St Johns Hill • 7 St John's Hill

Restaurants

The Fish Club • 189 St John's Hill
Steam • 55 E Hill

Shopping

Cake Boy • 2 Kingfisher House, Battersea Reach

2195

Map 140 · **Clapham Junction / Northcote Rd**

Map 140

Don't be fooled if your friend invites you to a house party in Clapham Junction she'll more than likely have mumbled the 'Junction' bit). The only reasons to plan a trip would be to nab a bargain at TK Maxx, plan a fancy dress outfit at Party Superstores, or take in some culture at the recently rescued Battersea Arts Centre. Otherwise…git along, little dogies.

£ Banks

- **Abbey** • 24 St John's Rd
- **Barclays** • 7 St John's Hill
- **HSBC** • 240 Lavender Hill
- **NatWest** • 66 St John's Rd

Coffee

- **Caffe Nero** • 20 St John's Rd
- **Caffe Nero** • 21 Battersea Rise
- **Starbucks** • 33 Northcote Rd

Landmarks

- **Northcote Road** • Northcote Rd

Libraries

- **Battersea Library** • 265 Lavender Hill
- **Northcote Library** • 155 Northcote Rd

Nightlife

- **adventure bar and lounge** • 91 Battersea Rise
- **B@1** • 85 Battersea Rise
- **Jongleurs (Battersea)** • 49 Lavender Gardens
- **The Peacock** • 148 Falcon Rd

Post Offices

- **Alfriston Road** • 99 Alfriston Rd
- **Battersea** • 202 Lavender Hill

Restaurants

- **Cafe Parisienne** • 225 Lavender Hill
- **I Sapori di Stefano Cavallini** • 146 Northcote Rd

Shopping

- **Anita's Vintage Fashion Fair** •
  Battersea Arts Centre, Lavender Hill
- **Dub Vendor** • 274 Lavender Hill
- **EF Russ** • 101 Battersea Rise
- **Huttons** • 29 Northcote Rd
- **Kiehls** • 20 Northcote Rd
- **Party Superstores** • 268 Lavender Hill
- **QT Toys and Games** • 90 Northcote Rd
- **Space NK Apothecary** • 46 Northcote Rd
- **Sweaty Betty** • 136 Northcote Rd
- **TK Maxx** • St John's Rd & Barnard Rd
- **Traid** • 28 St John's Rd
- **Vintage Market Place** • Battersea Arts Centre
- **Whole Foods Market** • 305 Lavender Hill

Supermarkets

- **ASDA** • 204 Lavender Hill
- **Whole Foods Market** • 305 Lavender Hill
- **Sainsbury's** • Clapham Junction Shopping Ctr

Map 141 • **Batters**

No one goes to Battersea South. You either live there, congratulating yourself on your nice Victorian conversion, or, you pass through on the way to Clapham or one of the lively bits of Battersea. Any of the 'action' happens around Lavender Hill. Lost Angel is an eccentrically fabulous boozer that would rather be a mile east or west.

Coffee

- **Captain Corelli** • 132 Battersea Park Rd

Nightlife

- **Halo** • 317 Battersea Park Rd
- **The Lost Angel** • 339 Battersea Park Rd

Restaurants

- **The Lavender** • 171 Lavender Hill

Shopping

- **Avalon Comics** • 143 Lavender Hill
- **Battersea Car Boot Sale** • 401 Battersea Park Rd
- **Comet Miniatures** • 44 Lavender Hill

The more genteel side of Clapham, Old Town hosts some fine restaurants (Trinity, Mooli), good watering-holes (The Prince of Wales, Frog and Forget-Me-Not) and one of London's best butchers (Moen's), all bordered by the green of Clapham Common. If you need more, and can resist Fish & Chips with free banter (Benny's), head to Queenstown Road for further fine dining establishments.

Coffee

- **The Roastery** • 789 Wandsworth Rd
- **Starbucks** • 40 Old Town

Libraries

- **Clapham Library** • 1 Clapham Common North Side

Nightlife

- **Frog and Forget-Me-Not** • 32 The Pavement
- **Lost Society** • 697 Wandsworth Rd
- **Prince of Wales** • 38 Clapham Old Town
- **Rose & Crown** • 2 The Polygon
- **The Sun** • 47 Old Town

Restaurants

- **Benny's** • 30 North St
- **Mooli** • 36 Old Town
- **Tom Ilic** • 123 Queenstown Rd
- **Trinity** • 4 The Polygon

Shopping

- **M. Moen & Sons** • 24 The Pavement
- **Puppet Planet** • 787 Wandsworth Rd

Supermarkets

- **Sainsbury's** • 646 Wandsworth Rd

Clapham is a microcosm of Cath Kidston mummies and their token gay best friends—watch them jog and brunch around the common in all weather. Stock up on al fresco goodies at Esca, down a pint at The Railway, and gorge on sushi at Tsunami or pizza at San Marco. Whatever you do, do not - we repeat, DO NOT - set foot in Infernos. We will find out and we will judge you.

Map 1

£ Banks

- **Abbey** • 164 Clapham High St
- **Barclays** • 188 Clapham High St
- **HSBC** • 154 Clapham High St
- **Lloyds** • 12 Clapham Common South Side
- **NatWest** • 145 Clapham High St

Cinemas

- **Clapham Picturehouse** • 76 Venn St

Coffee

- **Café Delight** • 19 Clapham High St
- **Caffe Nero** • 186 Clapham High St

O Landmarks

- **Clapham Common Air-Raid Shelter** • Clapham High St

Nightlife

- **The Alexandra** • 14 Clapham Common South Side
- **Bread & Roses** • 68 Clapham Manor St
- **The Clapham North** • 409 Clapham Rd
- **The Falcon** • 33 Bedford Rd
- **Green & Blue** • 20 Bedford Rd
- **Infernos** • 146 Clapham High St
- **Inn Clapham** • 15 The Pavement
- **The Loft** • 67 Clapham High St
- **The Railway** • 18 Clapham High St
- **Two Brewers** • 114 Clapham High St
- **The White House** • 65 Clapham Park Rd

Post Offices

- **Clapham Common** • 161 Clapham High St

Restaurants

- **Alba Pizzeria** • 3 Bedford Rd
- **Café Wanda** • 153 Clapham High St
- **The Fish Club** • 57 Clapham High St
- **Gastro** • 67 Venn St
- **The Pepper Tree** • 19 Clapham Common South Side
- **The Rapscallion** • 75 Venn St
- **San Marco Pizzeria** • 126 Clapham High St
- **Tsunami** • 5 Voltaire Rd

Shopping

- **Apex Cycles** • 40 Clapham High St
- **Esca** • 160 Clapham High St
- **M. Moen & Sons** • 24 The Pavement
- **Paws** • 62 Clapham High St
- **Today's Living Health Store** • 92 Clapham High St

Supermarkets

- **Iceland** • 4 The Pavement
- **Sainsbury's** • 133 Clapham High St
- **Sainsbury's** • 33 Clapham High St

While Stockwell continues to evolve from dodgy to night out de rigueur, the same can pretty much be said of Brixton, if you can ignore the crack dealers outside of KFC. Rock down to Electric Avenue and enjoy some great Caribbean market flavours, to-die-for pizza at Franco Manca, and organic deli food at the cutsie Rosie's Deli Cafe. On the subject of quaint, check out Lisa Stickley London for vintage-inspired tea towels.

Banks

Abbey • 498 Brixton Rd
Barclays • 463 Brixton Rd
Halifax • 393 Brixton Rd
HSBC • 512 Brixton Rd
NatWest • 358 S Lambeth Rd
NatWest • 395 Brixton Rd
NatWest • 504 Brixton Rd

Coffee

Rosie's Deli Cafe • 14 Market Row

Landmarks

Brixton Market • Electric Ave & Electric Ln
Electric Avenue • Electric Ave

Nightlife

Duke of Edinburgh • 204 Ferndale Rd
Plan B • 418 Brixton Rd
The Prince • 469 Brixton Rd
The Rest Is Noise • 442 Brixton Rd
The Swan • 215 Clapham Rd

Post Offices

Stockwell • 225 Clapham Rd

Restaurants

Franco Manca • 4 Electric Ln
Speedy Noodle • 506 Brixton Rd
SW9 Bar Cafe • 11 Dorrell Pl

Shopping

A&C Co Continental Grocers • 3 Atlantic Rd
Lisa Stickley London • 74 Landor Rd
The Old Post Office Bakery • 76 Landor Rd

Supermarkets

Iceland • 441 Brixton Rd
Iceland • 314 Clapham Rd
Sainsbury's • 425 Brixton Rd
Tesco • 330 Brixton Rd

Stockwell / Brixton (East)

Things have changed a bit since The Clash sang 'The Guns of Brixton' in '79 and race riots were a regular occurrence. While the middle classes have infiltrated most parts of Brixton, this neighbourhood still retains a defiant edge. Community spirit and close-knit neighbourhoods take precedence over trendy bars and pricey restaurants. Live music rules here; the legendary Brixton Academy still draws the hordes while Jamm offers an eclectic and worthy alternative.

Map 145

Landmarks

Stockwell Bowls • Stockwell Rd & Stockwell Park Walk

Libraries

Anti-Slavery International Library • Broomgrove Rd

Nightlife

Brixton Academy • 211 Stockwell Rd
The Grosvenor • 17 Sidney Rd
Jamm • 261 Brixton Rd

Sleepy little Earlsfield tends to mind its own business. It's a pretty sedate kind of place, slightly cut off by the lack of a tube stop. The well-heeled locals seem happy enough and make the most of what's on offer. Try Amaranth for great noodles before moving on to Bar 366 a few doors down for some chilled boozing.

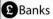 Banks

- **Barclays** • 376 Garratt Ln

Coffee

- **Caffe Nero** • 529 Garratt Ln
- **Refuel** • 515 Garratt Ln

Libraries

- **Alvering Library** • 2 Allfarthing Lane
- **Earlsfield Library** • 276 Magdalen Rd

Nightlife

- **Bar 366** • 366 Garratt Ln
- **Baraza** • 561 Garratt Ln
- **Halfway House** • 521 Garratt Ln
- **Le Gothique** • Windmill Rd & John Archer Wy

Restaurants

- **Amaranth Cafe & Noodle Bar** • 346 Garratt Ln
- **Carluccio's** • 537 Garratt Ln

Shopping

- **The Earlsfield Bookshop** • 513 Garratt Ln

Ensconced between the livelier Clapham and Tooting, this is a gentle slice of residential Southwest London. Bellevue Road offers a number of places to eat and drink overlooking Wandsworth Common, climaxing with the stupendous Chez Bruce. Nightingale Lane is terribly twee and hosts a few opportunities to shop organically and, you know, locally, or to stuff yourself silly at The Bombay Bicycle Club.

Map 14

Coffee

› **Caffe Nero** • 137 Balham High Rde

Nightlife

› **The Nightingale** • 97 Nightingale Lane

Restaurants

› **The Bombay Bicycle Club** • 95 Nightingale Lane
› **Chez Bruce** • 2 Bellevue Rd

Shopping

› **Bon Vivant** • 59 Nightingale Lane

The gentrification of Balham proceeds at pace but it hasn't yet killed off its character. Illegal all-nighters are a thing of the past but once the baby buggy crowds have finished their Waitrose run, Balham really comes alive. Diverse eating options (try Dish Dash for Persian treats), great pubs (Balham Bowls Club rules) and swanky bars (Harrison's darhling) all vie for your hard-earned nuggets.

£ Banks

- **Abbey** • 200 Balham High Rd
- **Barclays** • 169 Balham High Rd
- **Halifax** • 160 Balham High Rd
- **HSBC** • 117 Balham High Rd
- **Lloyds** • 125 Balham High Rd

Coffee

- **Starbucks** • 41 Bedford Hill

Libraries

- **Balham Library** • 16 Ramsden Rd

Nightlife

- **Balham Bowls Club** • 7 Ramsden Rd
- **The Bedford** • 77 Bedford Hill
- **The Exhibit** • 12 Balham Station Rd

Post Offices

- **Balham Hill** • 92 Balham Hill
- **Cavendish Road** • 273 Cavendish Rd

Restaurants

- **Dish Dash** • 11 Bedford Hill
- **The Exhibit** • 12 Balham Station Rd
- **Harrison's** • 15 Bedford Hill

Shopping

- **Moxon's** • Westbury Parade

Supermarkets

- **Sainsbury's** • 149 Balham High Rd
- **Sainsbury's** • 21 Balham Hill
- **Waitrose** • Balham High Rd & Ramsden Rd

Map 149 · **Clapham Park**

N

1   2

Clapham Common

PAGE
330

143

**CLAPHAM
PARK**

150

148

Worple Drive
Tabner Avenue
Almutt Way
Crescent Lane
Briarwood Road
West Road
Northmoore Drive
Maxford Road
Kings Mews
Park Hill
Allard Gardens
Holm Oak Mews

Shaftesbury Mews
Timothy Close
Waldo Close
St Gerards Close
Wakeford Close
Eagle Mews
Mandalay Road
Elms Road
Leppoc Road
Caldervale Road
Franconia Road
Elms Crescent
Common Close
Maple Close
Rosebery Road

Windmill Drive
Eagle Pond
Clapham Common South Side A3211
Cautley Avenue
Lessar Avenue
Lynette Avenue
Hambalt Road
Narbonne Avenue
Shandon Road
Bonneville Gardens
Trouville Road
Rodenhurst Road
Patto Close
Clarence
Morten Close
Clarence Avenue
Thornbury Road
Thorncliffe Road
Bourke Close

A

Cavendish Road
Englewood Road
Hazelbourne Road
Anchor Mews
Fernbank Mews
Joseph Powell Close
Gaskarth Road
Cathles Road
Dagnan Road
Yukon Road
Dinsmore Road
Krea Avenue
Gower Road
Westlands Terrace
Rudloe Road
Honeybrook Road
Poynders Gardens
Poynders Road A205
Rathmell Drive
Atkinson Avenue
Headlam Road
Maltby Close
Plummer Road
Atkins Road A205
King's Avenue B221

Lynn Road
Crows Road
Bells Street
Honey brook Rd
Atkins Road
Chelsham Close
Belthorn Crescent
Queensville Road
Scrutton Close
Langholm Close
Hannon Close
Kenilford Road
Langmead Road
Martindale Road
Ravenswood Road
Balham New Road
Old Devonshire Road
Weir Road
Pendle Road
Roseburn Close
Parkthorne Road
Copthorne Avenue
Adelina Mews

B

**GRANGE
MILLS**

Benjamin Mews
Mossbury Close
Hydethorpe Road
Ormeley Road
Tennor Road
Cambray Road
Midmoor Road
Thornton Gardens
Thornton Road B221
Thornton Avenue B221
Laitwood Road
Sistova Road
Rossiter Road
Rainmere Street
Scholars Road
Pentney Road
Haverhill Road
Burnbury Road
Teleford Avenue
Fieldhouse Road
Hydes Road

0.25 mile   0.25 km

This is where all the Claphamites settle down, have kids, move into their dream own house and one-up their friends with dinner parties and barbecues every other weekend. All this domesticity has left the locals' only restaurant options north on Clapham High Street or south in Balham. Still, you need fodder for your friends, so gourmet food shopping is where it's at at MacFarlenes and the Clapham armers' Market.

Map 14

Coffee

Starbucks • 39 Abbeville Rd

Post Offices

Clapham Park • 49 Poynders Rd

Shopping

MacFarlanes • 48 Abbeville Rd

...believe all the hysteria and Brixton is a nest of gun-toting crack heads. Problems ...exist but it's also one of London's most diverse and vibrant neighbourhoods. As ...Clapham rents rise, the yuppies are moving to the Acre Lane area, as evidenced by ...the proliferation of Havaianas flip-flopping around Grand Union. The Brixton Ritzy ...s one of the area's gems, offering much more than just film. Clubbers gravitate ...owards The Fridge (sweaty) and Mass (funky).

Map 15

£ Banks

Lloyds • 18 Acre Ln

Cinemas

Ritzy Picturehouse • Coldharbour Ln & Brixton Oval

Libraries

Brixton Library • Brixton Oval

Nightlife

The Dogstar • 389 Coldharbour Ln
The Effra • 38 Kellet Rd
Fridge Bar • 1 Town Hall Parade, Brixton Hill
Grand Union • 123 Acre Ln
Hootananny Brixton • 95 Effra Rd
Mango Landin' • 40 St Matthew's Rd
Mass • Brixton Hill
Prince Albert • 418 Coldharbour Ln
Upstairs at the Ritzy •
Ritzy Picturehouse • Brixton Oval, Coldharbour Lane
Satay • 447 Coldharbour Ln
St Matthews Church • Brixton Hill
The Windmill • 22 Blenheim Gardens

Post Offices

• **Brixton Hill** • 104 Brixton Hill

Restaurants

• **Asmara** • 386 Coldharbour Ln
• **Franco Manca** • 4 Market Row
• **Khan's** • 24 Brixton Water Lane
• **The Lounge** • 56 Atlantic Rd
• **Negril** • 132 Brixton Hill
• **Opus Café** • 89 Acre Ln
• **Upstairs Bar and Restaurant** • 89 Acre Ln

Shopping

• **Traid** • 2 Acre Ln

Supermarkets

• **Iceland** • 13 Winslade Rd

ot quite the Bec of beyond, this Tooting is the home of Europe's largest lido and
s a plethora of Asian grill bars for post-pub munchies. The best of the curry
ouses has to be Al Mirage, despite a popular following at Mirch Masala. For fairy
kes head to Bertie and Boo (we boo the name) and cocktails stop at Smoke. So
hat, you say? Sew buttons at the London Sewing Machine Museum no less.

$ Banks

Barclays • 29 Upper Tooting Rd

$ Coffee

Bertie and Boo • 162 Balham High Rd
Caffe Moka • 243 Balham High Rd

Nightlife

he Bec Bar • 26 Tooting Bec Rd
ing's Head • 84 Upper Tooting Rd
moke Bar • 14 Trinity Rd

Post Offices

pper Tooting • 63 Trinity Rd

Restaurants

l Mirage • 215 Upper Tooting Rd
Masaledar Kitchen • 121 Upper Tooting Rd
Mirch Masala • 213 Upper Tooting Rd
pice Village • 32 Upper Tooting Rd

Shopping

ussell's Hardware & DIY • 46 Upper Tooting Rd
Wandsworth Oasis HIV/AIDs Charity Shop •
0 Trinity Rd

Map 152

Decent rent, a Northern Line station and a grade one listed bingo hall: there's a lot here to like. Hit the High Street for curries and halal it all. Need anything else? Mitcham Road has the ticket. Local eat treats include Radha Krishna Bhavan, Sette Bello and Rick's Café, while Garden House and Tram & Social show that trendy pubs can indeed survive this far south.

Banks

- **Abbey** · 266 Upper Tooting Rd
- **Barclays** · 14 Mitcham Rd
- **Halifax** · 50 Tooting High St
- **HSBC** · 56 Tooting Broadway

Coffee

- **Cafee Manal** · 984 Garratt Ln
- **Urban Coffee** · 74 Tooting High St

O Landmarks

- **Gala Bingo Hall** · 50 Mitcham Road

Libraries

- **Tooting Library** · 75 Mitcham Rd

Nightlife

- **Garden House** · 196 Tooting High St
- **Ramble Inn** · 223 Mitcham Rd
- **Tooting Tram and Social** · 46 Mitcham Rd

Post Offices

- **London Road** · 47 London Rd
- **Tooting** · 2 Gatton Rd

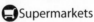 Restaurants

- **Jaffna House** · 90 Tooting High St
- **Radha Krishna Bhavan** · 86 Tooting High St
- **Rick's Cafe** · 122 Mitcham Rd
- **Sette Bello** · 8 Amen Corner
- **Urban Coffee** · 74 Tooting High St

Shopping

- **Tooting Market** · 21 Tooting High St

Supermarkets

- **Iceland** · 27 Tooting High St

General Information

Website: www.alexandrapalace.com
Phone: 020 8365 2121

Overview

If you fancy panoramic London views, exemplary Victorian architecture and an unrelenting stiff breeze to the face, the heights of Alexandra Park could be your cup of tea. With a fraction of the visitors of North London neighbours Hampstead Heath and Primrose Hill, Alexandra Park is nonetheless home to Ally Pally – Alexander Mackenzie's magnificent 1873 exhibition centre once renowned as the home of television after the BBC used it to broadcast the world's first high def transmissions in '36. It also boasts 196 acres of pristine, Green Flag-winning parkland, a two-hectare conservation area, and a fully functioning ice rink to boot.

Practicalities

Alexandra Park is well served by public transport: Alexandra Palace railway station is a short ride from King's Cross and Moorgate and sits directly next to the park's Wood Green entrance. You can also take the underground to Wood Green, catch the W3 direct to Ally Pally from just outside. You could also take advantage of the 2000 free parking spaces in the park itself if driving, though it's only a short walk from Muswell Hill town centre.

Nature

No doubt tempted by the reservoirs, 155 species of birds have been spotted in the park over the last 30 years. Nature fetishists should take in the two-hectare conservation area, which includes a wide array of animals including deer, donkeys, foxes and rabbits. In 1998, there was even a rare water vole sighting. There he was, large as life, like he owned the bloody place.

Architecture

For most Alexandra Park visitors it's all about the Palace, these days a thriving hub for exhibitions, concerts, farmer's markets and, uh, world darts tournaments. The Palace building itself was ravaged by fire in the 80s and has since been restored to its former glory, though nearby banqueting venue Blandford Hall succumbed to the same fate in 1971 and was completely destroyed. No matter: Ally Pally remains an impressive, domineering building well worth a nose-around. For the less active, admiring the view from the underrated Phoenix Bar (located in the south wing) is just as good.

Open Spaces

It's safe to say that Alexandra Park has more than enough grass to keep Cheech & Chong happy, being typified by the diverse range of landscaped grounds that can be found within. The Grove Garden actually pre-dates the park itself and there's also a good little café here if you fancy a quick bite. The Rose Garden is to the east side of the Palace and is even more aesthetically pleasing. Many newer small woodlands have been developing over the last few decades owing to the planting of large numbers of trees, producing an environment pleasing to both the rambler and runner.

Performance

The park often plays host to funfairs and circuses, but the Palace itself will usually be used at night for concerts. Its revival over recent years as a gig venue has led to the likes of the Arctic Monkeys and Paul Weller playing there, with its capacity being around 8,500, making it ideal for bands who've outgrown the Brixton Academy. Other parts of the Palace, such as the Great Hall, are used for classical music recitals.

The Palace also houses a theatre, which was dormant for over sixty-five years until a performance took place in 2004. It is still being restored and should be re-opened to the public for performances in the near future.

Check out Ally Pally's informative website (listed above) for a full calendar of upcoming events.

Sports

An indoor ice rink is housed within the Palace with a capacity of 1,250, with all manner of ice sports catered for (you can get further information by ringing 020 8365 4386). There is also a large boating lake with its own islands and fishing area (and even a smaller area for kids to boat on their own), with pedalos and rowing boats available for hire; being a seasonal facility, it's best to ring the operators Bluebird Boats Ltd. (020 7262 1330) beforehand. The boating pond is adjacent to a children's playground as well. For those who like golf with a view, the popular ten-hole pitch and putt course was recently revamped with an injection of Heritage Fund money: for prices and booking info see www.pitchnputt.co.uk or call 01245 257682. Alexandra Palace Park is also popular with cyclists, with the Parkland Walk a particular favourite, being a disued railway line that links up with Finsbury Park. In summertime the park is also a great place to get embroiled in countless spontaneous games of football and Frisbee, or to gawp/hurl insults at joggers.

General information

NFT Map: 7

Address: Barbican Centre, Silk St, London, EC2Y 8DS.

Phone: Box Office & Membership: 020 7638 8891 (9 am-8 pm daily); Switchboard: 020 7638 4141

Centre opening times:
Mon-Sat: 9 am-11 pm; Sun & Public Holidays: 12 pm-11 pm (although different parts of the centre may open at different times)

Website: www.barbican.org.uk

Overview

As terrifying as it is impressive, the Barbican Centre is a one-stop shop for all things cultural. At its best, the Barbican is utterly brilliant: a rambling collection of cinemas, galleries, bars, theatres, even a housing estate and a school. But stay after dark, when the culture vultures have left, and you can find yourself alone and lost in this city-within-a-city.

That the centre is brutally ugly makes what's inside even more splendid. The gallery space hosts world-class exhibitions and the cinemas show both mainstream and arthouse films. There's a world, classical and jazz music programme catering for everyone from scruffy backpackers to bearded professors. Most are sensible enough to leave before it gets too spooky. But plan your exit route in advance just in case.

Music

The heart of the Barbican monster is its music hall. A mecca for lovers of cerebral music, the centre's resident band is the London Symphony Orchestra: classical heavyweights who play year-round. The BBC Symphony Orchestra also has a base here, and the stage attracts biggies from around the world, including performances from Yo-Yo Ma, the Vienna Philharmonic and Cesaria Evora. But you don't need a high brow to find something to like: a flick through their listings—which last year included Silent Disco.

...uitar-playing finches and the Met Police—will ...on have you clicking Book Now.

...stivals are another key draw: not the ...ot-and-portacabin type, but impassioned ...lebrations. The Mostly Mozart festival reaches ...i-fi convention levels of fanaticism; the Great ...rformers Festival is an orgy of some of the ...orld's most spectacular musicians; and the ...zz Festival will have you feeling über hip (then ...erhaps a bit perplexed. And then, if you're 100% ...onest, rather wishing it was over). African, Latin, ...ontemporary and Opera festivals also sell out ...e near-2000 capacity venue.

...ilm

...ne programme has an arty bias but is so diverse ...at you're bound to find something inviting on ...ne of the three screens. Rule of thumb: silent ...ms, in. J-Lo, out. Subtitles, in. Mighty Duck ...logy, out. But they do offer the screens for ...rivate hire, so if you really want you can stick ...to 'em and have your own showing of Snakes ...n a Plane. The Barbican also hosts the annual ...ustralian Film and London Children's Film ...estivals, and runs constantly changing series. ...ecent favourites include the Bad Film Club ...r fans of the most reviled films, and Second ...hance Sunday so you can see on the big screen ...ms which you missed first time around.

...heatre and Dance

...on't be fooled by the Barbican's hulking ...xterior—the centre dabbles in the more ...elicate arts rather well. Its two theatres cater ...r both ends of the performance spectrum. The ...ain room, a shared home for acting and dance, ...eats over 1,000 punters and attracts some of ...e biggest names in high culture. Deep in the ...arbican's bowels the smaller Pit theatre is home ...o experimental and new acts. But be warned: ...ith just 200 seats the Pit is small enough for ...nyone dozing off to be highly visible.

...rt

...owhere else at the Barbican is the idea of ...aking culture accessible for all more apparent ...an their art spaces. The main gallery hosts ...mporary exhibitions, mixing all types of art into ...e cultural hot pot. In 2007, under the umbrella

of Art and Sex from Antiquity to Now, erotic Roman cutlery—that's right: erotic cutlery— shared a stage with impressionist paintings and an 11-minute film of someone's face as she was, ahem, attended to. Every first Thursday of the month the gallery opens for a nocturnal viewing, with talks, performances—burlesque dancers for the art and sex exhibition—and a themed bar. A second space, The Curve, winds its way round the ground floor where the exhibitions are generally free.

The Library

Libraries often get a bad press. They've got stuck with an image of frumpy, middle-aged women peering down their spectacles and telling youths to be quiet. But this couldn't be further removed from the reality of the Barbican Library. Alongside a decent array of books, there's a dazzling collection of live musical recordings. Some of these tracks are so rare that they can't be heard anywhere else in the world. Put some headphones on and rock out. Just don't get carried away and smash up the children's section.

How To Get There

By car: Parking is pricey with two hours costing £5 and each hour thereafter costing two or three quid more, though there's a flat weekend and evening (post-5.30 pm) fee of just a fiver.

By bus: The 153 (which runs from Liverpool Street to Finsbury Park) stops directly outside the Barbican at Silk Street; the following buses run nearby: 8, 11, 23, 26, 35, 42, 43, 47, 48, 55, 56, 76, 78, 100, 133, 141, 149, 172, 214, 242, 243, 271, 344 (seven days a week); 4, (Mon-Sat); 21, 25, 521 (Mon-Fri). If none of these buses can take you home then consider yourself extremely unlucky. By tube: Barbican stations runs on the Circle, District and Hammersmith & City lines. Other stations nearby are Moorgate, St Paul's, Bank, Liverpool Street and Mansion House.

By train: The nearest overland stations are Liverpool Street, Farringdon and Blackfriars. City Thameslink services run through Barbican, Moorgate and Cannon Street.

Practical Information

NFT Map: 132, 133, & 141
Official opening time is 8 am, although the gates are usually unlocked a little earlier than this. The park closes at dusk.
Friends of Battersea Park: www.batterseapark.org
Zoo: www.batterseaparkzoo.co.uk
Local council: www.wandsworth.gov.uk (see also for information on the Pump House Gallery)
Cycle hire: www.londonrecumbents.co.uk
BlueBird boat hire: www.bluebirdboats.co.uk

Overview

Opened in 1858 with the aim of giving the Victorian working classes something to do other than drinking gin, Battersea Park has developed to become one of London's prettiest, most popul and most usable parks. Squeezing a range gardens, cafes, animals, sports, cultural faciliti and even a peace pagoda into its diminutive 2 acres, the park is popular with everyone fro hordes of snotty little kids to wandering do walkers. It is also centrally located enough to easy to get to but still far enough from Centr London to retain a local feel.

The park is about two miles southwest fro Westminster and occupies the spot on the sou bank of the Thames between Albert and Chels bridges. Originally used for duelling, the Duke Wellington famously discharged upon the Ea of Winchelsea on the site in 1829. Rather tha the vast open and flat spaces that many Londo parks offer, Battersea is neatly divided into number of features and sections, making it fe much larger than it is.

Sporting Activities

Battersea has an incredibly good array of sporting facilities. The 'Millennium Arena' is a 400m 8-lane running track situated in the northeast corner of the park; it hosts athletic meets and training sessions and it benefited from an expensive overhaul in, you guessed it, 1999. Next to the arena are ten tennis courts and an all-weather football pitch whilst there are further all-weather astro-turf pitches in the southeast corner of the park marked for both hockey and football. The park also boasts cricket pitches and practice nets, a bowling green, smooth wide paths for skating and enough open spaces to invite impromptu sessions of pretty much any other sport. If you consider attacking fish a sport, and have a permit and rod licence, the park's lake offers fishing for nine months of the year. Rowing boats and pedaloes can also be taken out on to the lake during July and August (adults £4.50/hour, children £2). Bicycles can be hired from the London Recumbents shop, which is next to the Millennium Arena on the park's East Carriage Drive—but be warned: bikes can only be used in the park itself, and as it takes just 15 minutes for a leisurely pedal around the parameter, an hour's hire can become a little Groundhog Day.

Art

Battersea has fostered a creative relationship with the arts and has a number of sculptures dotted about, its own public gallery and a annual art fair. Taking pride of place next to the lake are two large Henry Moore and Barbara Hepworth sculptures, both of which are well worth rooting out. The Pumphouse Gallery is a Grade II-listed building, originally used to power the park's water works, which has been restored and converted into a gallery and information centre with six exhibitions throughout the year. The Gallery, located northeast of the lake, is also available for private hire and even has a licence to hold civil weddings. The park has hosted the Affordable Art Fair since 1999, which has become a leading showcase for art priced under £3,000.

Performance

In summer music aficionados should head down to La Gondola al Parco, the café by the lake, for free live concerts every Tuesday and Friday from 7pm. Entrance is free and there's also a BBQ and refreshments aplenty.

Nature and Children's Zoo

Battersea's varied landscapes ensure you stand a decent chance of seeing more than a rat or a pigeon while you saunter about. Squirrels, ducks and Canada geese are all too plentiful. More interesting potential sightings include woodpeckers, cormorants, Peregrine falcons, terrapins and, according to the RSPB, Pochards (whatever they are). If you don't come across any interesting wildlife, your only option is to cheat and visit the park's zoo. A five-minute stroll from the Chelsea Gate, the zoo is aimed at children and has a cool collection of small mammals, including lemurs, as well as small farm animals and some excitingly named birds, such as some 'Peach-faced Love birds'. In case you do fall in love with any of the zoo's inhabitants, most are available for adoption. Mice start at £10 for six months, pay-up and claim it's for your kid. The zoo is open throughout the year and entry costs £7.50 for adults, £6 for children.

How To Get There

By tube: Sloane Square (on the Circle and District lines) is the nearest Underground station at just under a mile away. From the station walk down Lower Sloane Street, which becomes Chelsea Bridge Road and leads to the Thames. Walk over Chelsea Bridge and you will see the park on your right. Alternatively take bus no 319.

By bus: From central London, buses run to the park from Liverpool Street (number 344), Notting Hill (452), Oxford Circus (137), Sloane Square (319, 137), Victoria Station (44) and Vauxhall (344).

By train: Battersea Park station is within sight of the park, trains run to both Clapham Junction and Victoria at high frequency. Queenstown Road is around 300m from the park. Trains from this station run to Waterloo and Clapham Junction and depart less often than from Battersea Park.

Chaos alert! As if it wasn't already hard enough to get there, the Albert Bridge closed from February 2010. Pedestrians and cyclists can still cross (cyclists must dismount), but bus routes have all gone squiffy. Check www.tfl.gov.uk to plan your best approach.

General Information

NFT Map: 127
Brockwell Park: www.brockwellpark.com
Brockwell Park Lido: www.brockwelllido.com
020 7274 3088

Overview

Brockwell Park may not be a household name when it comes to London Parks but for many South Londoners – not least residents of neighbouring Herne Hill – it's the pick of the bunch, all the lovelier for its unconventionality, tattiness and relative anonymity. It's eclectic, it's quirky, and it's impossible not to fall in love with.

History

By the end of the 19th century the local population was large, growing and in need of a serious park. Brockwell was secured for use by the public after MP Thomas Bristowe got wind of a private country estate that seemed just the ticket. Still, he might have over-exerted himself in the process: having taken a Bill through parliament to convert the land, led a committee to negotiate the price, and raised funds from across the community, Bristowe himself promptly collapsed and died on the steps of Brockwell Hall, moments after the opening ceremony in 1892.

Café

If that doesn't put you off your scones, nowadays, the ground floor of Brockwell Hall is a café where refreshments have been served ever since. Located at the top of the hill, it's a great place to stop for inexpensive cake, drinks etc. after some…

Activities!

There's heaps to do. A BMX track, tennis courts, bowling green, football and cricket pitches, basketball courts, outdoor theatre club, a children's play area and a paddling pool. Or you could chill by the ponds, in the walled garden, under the clock tower, at the picnic area, near the flower gardens, etc.

Brockwell Lido and Greenhouses

Built in 1937, Brockwell Lido is essentially an (unattractive) art deco building that replaced an old bathing pond. After experiencing financial difficulty it was restored and reopened in 2007. As well as a large outdoor pool, there is a gym and classes are held in yoga, pilates, tai-chi and meditation. For the under 5s, Whippersnappers have everything from acrobatics to puppets and African drumming. A Miniature Railway runs between Herne Hill Gate and the Lido. Run by a local enthusiast on a not-for-profit basis; it's only £1 for a round trip. May–Sept, Sat–Sun, 11am–5pm.

Brockwell also boasts a superb community greenhouse project open to volunteers. The greenhouses are open Sunday afternoons and give Londoners a rare chance to get green fingers and grow their own produce. Contact the greenhouse secretary at bpcgsecretary@gmail.com to get involved.

Annual Events

July: Lambeth Country Show is always good fun and involves medieval jousting, farm animals, live reggae/dub and rides, and there are homemade cake and jam contests, too. The Alternative Vegetable Animal Competition requires fruit and veg to be crafted into a famous person or building with a very entertaining adult category.
September: The annual Urban Green Fair helps teach London to become more sustainable.
November: The big fireworks show on Guy Fawkes Night is worth braving the cold for.

How to Get There

By rail/tube/foot: The park is a short walk from the following overland and underground stations:

Herne Hill Rail Station—5 mins
Tulse Hill Rail Station —15 mins
Brixton Tube —20 mins
Clapham North Tube —30 mins
By bus: The following all stop at Brockwell Park—2, 3, 37, 68, 196, 322, 468, P15

Overview

Lively and happening; youngish, professional, and trendy (in a safe way). Clapham Common reflects the area well.

Popular all year round, the Common truly comes alive in summer. On a warm weekend you'll find the park overflowing with picnickers sipping champagne and just plain lookin' good. It's a lovely scene made better by the relaxed, friendly atmosphere. And, when the sun finally sets, you're left with a seriously impressive choice of bars close by.

As well as drawing the usual funky sophisticates, the park is also family-friendly with lots of little ones enjoying the space.

Plenty of organised (or not) sport, kite flying, model boating, Ultimate Frisbee, and even fishing happens here too, but while the common is safe as houses during the day, at night-time its leafier enclaves are worth avoiding unless you're particularly keen on paying for a game of grown-up hide the sausage with other gentlemen.

History

Clapham began as a Saxon village. Back then it w called Clopp Ham, meaning the village (ham) by t short hill (clopp). The common was used by village to graze their livestock and as a source of firewood.

In the late 17th century the population began to gro as refugees arrived from the Great Plague of Londo (1665) and the fire of 1666. During this time, the ri gentry of London built a number of fine count houses around the common. When the railways we developed there was a sudden influx of commuter driving the upper class away to somewhere less, ur common.

Today, the surrounding area is one of the mo expensive in South London, partly because of i excellent transport links.

Clapham Sect

n the common is the Holy Trinity Church. This was a
eeting place of the Clapham Sect, a group of 19th-
ntury Evangelical Anglicans who fought for social
form. "Ugh" you say, but wait…

e Clapham Sect played a significant part in the
olition of slavery in England. They didn't stop there,
ing on to campaign for the eradication of slavery
orldwide. They also fought for reform in the penal
stem, focusing on unjust sentencing and the dire
ison conditions of the time.

Eateries

icero's on the Common (vegetarian)
Rookery Road, SW49QN, 020 7498 0770

afe Des Res (English/ Carribean)
The Pavement, SW4 0HY, 020 7622 6602

he Bowling Green Café (sandwiches, pasta etc)
lapham Common West Side, SW4 9AN, 020 7801
904

Three ponds

Mount Pond – is a fishing park pond about three
cres in size. It contains carp, roach, gudgeon and
els. Suggested baits include pellet, maggot, meat,
nd boilies, it says here.

agle Pond – is a smaller pond with a little island.
his one is also fishable. Stocks include carp, tench,
ream, roach, rudd, perch, chub and gudgeon. Best
aits are bread, pellet, maggot, hemp and castor, it
oes without saying.

ong Pond – has a century-old tradition of use for
nodel boating.

Activities

These days there are still some nice leafy pathways
ned by mature trees left for the strollers to enjoy.

Sporty types can go for the football, rugby, cricket,
softball, tennis, basketball, Aussie rules football,
croquet (!) or bowling.

Events

Some of the annual highlights include:

May: A Country Affair—is kinda interesting. There
are rides, bands, Morris dancing and lots of cleaner
than usual farm animals.

June/July: The Sprite Urban Games—Showcases
pro skateboarding, BMXing and breaking, with
(mostly hip hop) DJs providing the beats.

July: Ben 'n Jerry's Sundae On The Common—also
goes down well. If it sounds horribly corporate, it's
worth noting that a full restoration of the bandstand
in '05/'06 was partly funded by proceeds from this
festival. Or, just think of the free ice-cream…

**August: The Clapham Common Metro
Weekender**—Two successful, quality festivals have
joined forces. South West Four (progressive house,
trance, and breaks) and Get Loaded In the Park
(indie/dance) now happen side by side at the end
of August.

November: The Bonfire Night Fireworks—it's as
good as it gets here.

How to Get There

By train: Wandsworth Road Station (12 minutes),
Clapham High Street Station (12 minutes)

By tube: Clapham Common (4 minutes), Clapham
South (13 minutes)

By bus: 4, 35, 37, 88, 137, 155, 255, 345, 355,
417, G1

Overview

A lot is packed into this 54-acre park—mostly people. On a sunny day Clissold throngs with Stokenewingtonites; yummy mummies and three-wheeled buggies; gaggles of youths, with or without hoods; lads playing football; and assorted dog walkers. Visitors can see deer and goats in the animal enclosure, diamond doves and love birds in the aviary, and coots and moorhens in the nature ponds. Parents take little ones to the paddling pool (summer months only), toddlers group at the One O'clock Club or the well-equipped children's playground. The park hosts the usual hodgepodge of circuses and steam fairs as well as the famous arts festival, StokeFest, in the summer. On grey days, chilly days, or in the early hours, peace can be found - in the rose garden perhaps, or underneath one of the ancient trees.

Clissold Park Café

Phone:	0207 923 9797
Email:	info@clissoldparkcafe.com
Website:	www.clissoldparkcafe.com
Hours:	9 am–5.30 pm (winter)
	7.30 pm (summer)
Admission:	FREE

Clissold Mansion, the Grade II listed building ju‍ visible from Stoke Newington Church Street, home to a large, child-friendly cafe (that is, th cafe is large and child-friendly, not friendly on to the larger child). Herbal tea drinkers jostle wit‍ dripping ice-cream cone lickers on the sun tra‍ front veranda and circular lawn. The large insid‍ rooms are best avoided if you find children‍ chatter grating, but otherwise a lively spot to tu‍ into a plate of egg and chips. The building wa‍ constructed in the late 18th century on behalf family whose daughter was courted b‍ a local reverend—Augustus Clissold. He wooe‍ then married her, and swiftly changed the nam‍

of the estate to Clissold Place. Where is Catherine Cookson when you need her? A hundred years later when the land was up for redevelopment, two influential campaigners persuaded the Metropolitan Board of Works to create a public space, and Clissold Park was born on 24 July 1889. Now run by the London Borough of Hackney, Clissold is kept in check by the Clissold Park User Group, who recently secured a multi-million pound lottery bid to spruce the place up a bit and return it to its former 19th century splendour.

Sport in the Park

Year round you can hear the yells of football players churning up mud, the whine of iPods as joggers run in ever decreasing circles, the thwack of cricket ball against cricket bat, and the crunch of misthrown Frisbees hitting the litter bins. There is a basketball court and 10 tennis courts (two kiddies' sized) which are bookable by contacting the Park rangers (020 7254 4235) though they are impossible to get your hands on around Wimbledon—and they say TV doesn't affect our behaviour.

But one of the delights of this park is the more unusual sport that takes place. On misty mornings you can watch cotton-clad figures practice tai chi, and on warm weekends you can nearly always spot a group of hotties from the London School of Capoeira circling around each other. Then there is the occasional father/ daughter pair practising Taekwondo, or two dreadlocked crusties slinging up a line to get some tightrope practice in. Most recent addition to watchable sports in the park is run by 'Pushy Mothers'- groups of mums exercising with buggies. The buggy, with child on board, is pushed hither and thither by the panting parent. It's the ultimate in resistance training.

Nature and The Ponds

Hackney is one of the greenest inner-city boroughs and though relatively small, Clissold Park is still an important green, shady and watery spot for local wildlife, particularly waterfowl. The two nature ponds are named Beckmere and the Runtzmere in honour of the two principal founders (Beck and Runtz, in case you were wondering). The third pond in front of the cafe

is more of a 'canalette' and actually used to be part of the New River built in the early 1600s to supply drinking water to London.

The animal enclosure with its fuzzy-nosed deer, fluffy rabbits and bearded mini-goats are popular with visitors who stand stuffing chips and handfuls of poisonous leaves from nearby bushes through the fence directly under the signs saying: 'Please don't feed the animals—it will make them ill.'

Note: the paddling pool is not a nature pond and though you still can't let your dog in, hours spent gazing at its inhabitants are not looked on kindly.

How to Get There

By car: Don't. There isn't much in the way of parking. But if you really need to, from Newington Green head north along Green Lanes until you see a large green space with trees on your right. Or from the A10 turn left onto Stoke Newington Church St past all the cute shops and inviting pubs, until you get to the large church on your left. The park is on your right.

By tube: From Manor House, take exit 4 and walk south down Green Lanes for 10 minutes. The park is on your left.

By train: From Stoke Newington station, head south down the High St and turn right up Stoke Newington Church St, walk for 10 minutes until you see the park on your left just past Stoke Newington Town Hall.

By bus: The 341, 141, 73, 393, and 476 all stop at various entrances to the park.

Additional Information

London Borough of Hackney
www.hackney.gov.uk/cp-community-park.htm

Clissold Park User Group
www.clissoldpark.com

Stokefest
www.stokefest.co.uk

General Information

NFT Map: 55, 62, & 63
Website: www.haringey.gov.uk/
finsbury_park_leaflet.pdf

Overview

Sculpted from what was once a large woodland area on the fringes of London, Finsbury Park was baptized officially in the mid 19th century as a green escape for increasingly urbanized North Londoners. Today's Finsbury Park has been revamped to the tune of £5 million in an attempt to shake off the cloak of urban grime which descended during the 1970s. Though it certainly has cleaned up its act, the park is still a barren tundra-esque plain compared to Hyde or Regent's Park. More of a green scab on the city landscape that surrounds it, the sparse shrubbery and token trees are more suitable for football or running away from Staffordshire Terriers. Delve a little deeper, however, and there are quaint eccentricities and little gems dotted around.

Practicalities

You can enter this veritable urban Oz at Endymion Road, Seven Sisters Road, Green Lanes and Stroud Green Road. Two tube stops serve Finsbury Park: Manor House and the eponymous Finsbury Park. There are also overland trains at Harringey Green Lanes (grab an opulent Turkish meal on the way) and at Finsbury Park Stroud Green Road. Buses 4, 19, N19, 29, N29, 106, N106, 253, N253, 254, N279, W3 and W7 all touch the park at some point. Bear in mind that if you wish to travel in the area during an Arsenal match day you'd better take a stun gun and a red scarf to navigate the crowds!

Attractions

Quaint Englishness and sweaty sporting pursuits abound within the perimeters of Finsbury Park. There are many activities you can partake in from tennis (seven courts are available on a turn up and play basis) to running in the Heathside Athletics Club (020 8802 9139). There are even two American Football pitches. For a more twee time stroll up to the tiny boating pond and spend an hour in a beat-up boat circling the aviary island—home to exotic birds like ducks, some swans and, uh, ducks again. The kidz are catered for in the form of a skate park. Best of all is the amazing Parkland Walk, which snakes out from Finsbury Park to Alexandra Palace via Highgate.

Nature

The Arboretum and the Avenue of Mature Trees are the two main spots for tree watching. Granted, experienced botanists may find little to fire them up here, but on a mild Autumn day there are plenty of rich colours and textures that enrich any stroll through the park. There are no real 'wild' areas in the park, unlike Hampstead Heath, but there are some lovely quiet spots in the American Gardens which have been landscaped according to the original 19th century plans, with added kiddie play areas. There are some shrubs planted around the boating pond which Harringey Council calls the 'McKenzie Flower Garden' with capital letters which are barely merited.

Festivals

Recently the vast open spaces of the park have been used for music festivals and various other fairs. The Rise, Fleadh, and FinFest festivals are all fairly regular events. The park is also a popular venue for one off special music events—both the Sex Pistols and Morrissey have played controversial shows here. The steam and fun fairs are also worth going to for nostalgic or regressive fun.

Overview

Greenwich Park is the oldest enclosed Royal Park in Britain and has been an integral part of London life for centuries. Saxons built mounds here; Romans worshipped here; King Henry VIII and Anne Boleyn flirted here, and Charles II even built an observatory here. It's now a playground for ageing eccentrics escaping London, yuppie families with new puppies, and heaps of tourists trekking up the staggeringly steep hill towards the iconic Royal Observatory.

And it's worth the trek. The sweeping views from the highest point are spectacular and beat the London Eye hands down. London is revealed in all its glory, from the jutting skyline of Canary Wharf, to the sinuous turns of the Thames and the seemed-like-a-good-idea-at-the-time Millennium Dome. All in stark contrast with the neoclassical architecture of the Old Royal Observatory, Royal Naval College, National Maritime Museum and the Queen's House in the immediate foreground.

A well sought-after spot throughout history, the park has belonged to the Royal Family since 1427, and in the early 1600s, under James I, the park was given a makeover in the French style, which gave it its well-groomed tree-lined pathways. He then had Inigo Jones build the missus the stately Queen's House.

The Royal Observatory and Flamsteed House

Address: Greenwich Royal Park, Greenwich, London SE10
Phone: 020 8858 4422
Website: www.nmm.ac.uk
Hours: 10 am-5 pm daily
Admission: Free

Time begins, rather arbitrarily, here—on the Prime Meridian of the World, or Longitude 0°. Time all over the earth is based on a place's distance east or west from this imaginary line, outlined in metal so throngs of tourists can gawp at it. Thanks to Charles II's interest in science, Sir Christopher Wren was commissioned to build the Royal Observatory and Flamsteed House, the living quarters for the first Royal Astronomer. Time your visit to catch a workshop, talk, exhibition or planetarium show, which seek to give visitors a richer experience than simply straddling the Meridian with thumbs up.

Also notable is the Camera Obscura, which sits in a small building next to Flamsteed House. A predecessor to the modern camera, this small dark room displays a live image of the distant National Maritime Museum, projected using only a small hole in the roof.

National Maritime Museum

Address: Greenwich, London SE10 9NF
Phone: 020 8858 4422
Website: www.nmm.ac.uk
Hours: 10 am-5 pm daily
Admission: Free

Adjacent to the park's boundaries, this is a museum dedicated to all things nautical. It comprises the Royal Observatory, as well as the Queen's House, but its main components are the Maritime Galleries. Highlights include a collection of ships' figureheads, navigational charts, maps, medals, flags and models. They also host relics from Sir John Franklin's ill-fated Northwest Passage expedition (1845-1848) including a pair of his very old-school sunglasses.

Nature

Amongst the well-mowed green are trees of infinite varieties. The scented herb garden is best enjoyed in the summer time. The fallen remains of the 900 year-old Queen Elizabeth Oak can still be viewed and lie as proof of Henry VIII's passion for these grounds, he was said to have danced around the younger tree with Anne Boleyn (before he had her executed, obviously).

How to Get There

The nearest DLR station is Cutty Sark. It's fun too: push the excitable children out the way so you can sit in the front and pretend to be the driver – always a winner with the ladies. By bus, the 53, 177, 180, 188, 199 and 286 will all get you to points of suitable proximity.

You can also take the Greenwich foot tunnel from the Isle of Dogs, which runs beneath the Thames and is open 24 hours a day. Ignore the ominous drips: it's been sturdy for over 110 years, and even if it does at last succumb to the pressure of 50 ft of river above it, then you'll not have time to worry about it. So relax and enjoy!

Overview

Hampstead Heath is 791 acres of rambling woods and idyllic meadows worthy of much frolicking. It's the fact that its wilderness seems so, well, wild that makes this London park deceptive. You can be merrily re-enacting the Brothers Grimm, only to be spat out rather rudely onto Parliament Hill and confronted with gob-smacking views of St Paul's and the Gherkin. The Heath is truly nothing short of heaven—until you stumble over George Michael up to no good in the bushes. You can swim naked in its ponds, stroll amongst its tall grasses without seeing another living soul for twenty minutes or more and engage in a little sex scandal amongst the greenery. The park's common theme is one of a hidden countryside retreat right in the middle of it all.

Most likely because it *is* countryside. It's just the rest of London that's gone all urban around it. Long-established hedgerows and ancient trees attest to its lengthy history. The range of wildlife on show is impressive—kingfishers, parakeets, 400 species of fungi and several types of bat, to name a few. All sorts of famous people have enjoyed its leafy company through the years. Boudicca's Mound near the men's bathing pond (hmm... sounds dirty), is said to mark the ancient queen's burial chamber. Karl Marx and his family had a picnic here every Sunday while he lived in London and writer Wilkie Collins used the park as a backdrop for The Woman in White. All in all, the Heath has been a much-loved place of social gathering and strolling for centuries, a place of peace and perspective amongst the greater hustle and bustle of the Big Smoke.

Ponds, Ponds and... Oh Yeah, More Ponds...

It might be argued that losing your Heath virginity consists of swimming in one of its famous outdoor bathing ponds. These are open throughout the year and attract throngs of dedicated swimming fans. On the eastern side—closer to Highgate—are a series of eight 17th and 18th century reservoirs dotted between Parliament Hill Fields and Kenwood House. Amongst these is one swimming pond for guys, another for gals, a toy boat pond, a wildlife reserve pond, and a lake for fishing. On the western side of the Heath are three more, including the 'mixed pond', where you can have some underwater flirtations, should you wish.

Kenwood House

Address:	Hampstead - NW3 7JR
Phone:	0208 348 1286
Website:	www.english-heritage.org.uk/ server/show/conProperty.106
Hours:	April-October: 11 am-5 pm, Monday-Sunday, November-March: 11 am-4 pm, Monday-Sunday
Admission:	Free

Kenwood House, a 17th century manor in the middle of the park, adds very nicely to the Heath's countryside effect. Its striking classically white walls and landscaped grounds play backdrop to summer jazz festivals as well as a few scenes in the movie Notting Hill. Purchased by brewing magnate Edward Cecil Guinness in 1925, Kenwood House is more than just a pretty façade. Thanks to Guinness's fortune and interest in art, the manor house is also a very noteworthy art gallery featuring works by the likes of Rembrandt, Turner and Gainsborough.

Golders Hill Park

Golders Hill Park is the younger brother to the bigger Hampstead Heath, adjoining it on the western side. Where the latter is an icon of epic proportions, the former is more of a good ol' neighbourhood park. Its large expanse of grass was created rather suddenly when a house that stood on the grounds was bombed during the Blitz. It has a lot to offer for its size though, with a formal flower garden, a deer park and a small zoo (with alpacas no less). If you're feeling sporty, there are tennis courts, putting greens and plenty of jogging paths.

How to Get There

The closest tube stations are Hampstead, Golder's Green and Archway on the Northern Line. Nearby overland stations include Hampstead Heath and Gospel Oak. Bus numbers running to the park are the 168, 268 and 210, which cuts through on Spaniard's Road (where you may want to stop for a pint at the historic Spaniard's Inn).

Additional Information

City of London
www.cityoflondon.gov.uk
Information and booking tickets for swimming:
020 7485 5757
Heath and Hampstead Society:
www.heathandhampsteadsociety.org.uk

Highgate Cemetery
General Info

NFT Map: 51 & 59
Web: www.highgate-cemetery.org
Phone: 020 8340 1834

West Cemetery

The West Cemetery opened in 1839 and most of the original pathways and structures still exist. On weekdays, tours take place daily at 2 pm from March to November. There's a limit of 15 people so you'll need to book in advance on the number above. The weekends are a free-for-all with tours taking place hourly from 11 am until 4 pm April to November and until 3 pm December to March.

East Cemetery

The newer East Cemetery is located on the opposite side of the road to the West entrance. This side is open daily and for three pounds you get to roam unsupervised for as long as you please. It may not be as impressive as the West side, but it's still a place of breathtaking beauty. Although there are some well-trodden paths and proper walkways, large parts of the cemetery are almost completely overgrown, making it a wonderful place to go for a stroll.

Opening Hours

1st April to 31st October
Mon-Fri: 10 am-5 pm
Sat-Sun: 11 am-5 pm

1st November to 31st March
Mon-Fri: 10 am-4 pm
Sat-Sun: 11 am-4 pm

Famous Occupants

Quite a few notable people are buried here. The caretakers will be more than willing to inform you of the whereabouts of the following graves and plenty of others.

Douglas Adams, author. Most famous for the *Hitchhiker's Guide To The Galaxy* series of books.

George Eliot, English author and poet; also actually a woman.

Christina Rossetti, English poet.

Karl Marx. Philosopher; considered the father of communism.

Alexander Litvinenko, Russian ex-spy, famously murdered by radiation poisoning in a Soho sushi restaurant in 2006.

The Highgate Vampire

There have been numerous accounts of shapes, ghosts and supernatural figures seen on the cemetery grounds, and in the early 70s the media picked up on a theory involving a vampire and the legend of The Highgate Vampire was born. It caused quite a stir and soon mobs of 'vampire hunters' descended on the place (imagine something like the Thriller video, but with flares and tank tops). Finally, Sean Manchester, president and founder of the Vampire Research Society, claimed to have killed the fiend in 1973, when he tracked it to a nearby house. Manchester was also, in his spare time, patron of the Yorkshire Robin Hood society, and remains, in this publication's estimation, the single most compelling reason not to wander around Highgate Cemetery after dark.

Waterlow Park

Overview

Waterlow Park is a beautifully landscaped park located just next to the cemetery, making it a perfect spot for a pre- or post-gravespotting picnic. Often overlooked and overshadowed by nearby Hampstead Heath it is a charming and peaceful alternative. You can feed the ducks in one of the three ponds, hire tennis courts by the hour, admire the awesome view of London, wander in the rose garden, or just go look at the cool hollow tree at the bottom of the park.

Lauderdale House

Address: Highgate Hill, Waterlow Park
         London N6 5HG
Tel: 020 8348 8716
Web: www.lauderdalehouse.co.uk

Lauderdale House operates independently from the park, but is located on its grounds. The original house was built in 1582, but has gone through major alterations and restorations since then. In 1963 a major fire destroyed much of the old building and it was left untouched and unoccupied for 15 years. In 1978 it was finally repaired and reopened in its current incarnation. The house runs classes, concerts and exhibitions by local artists. There's also a small café. The House and the galleries are usually open Tue-Fri 11 am-4 pm, Sat 1.30 pm-5 pm & Sun 12 pm-5 pm, but you can always phone in advance to avoid disappointment.

How to Get There

Nearest tube station is Archway. Exit the station and turn left up Highgate Hill. Waterlow Park is about five minutes walk on your left hand side. To get to the cemetery, cross the park down to the Swain's Lane exit, which is adjacent to the East Cemetery gates.

(341)

General Information

Website: www.royalparks.org.uk/
             parks/hyde_park
Phone: 020 7298 2000

Overview

Hyde Park serves as the 'lungs of London'. For over 370 years it has been *the* place to go for oxygen-starved Londoners to take a breath of fresh air. As the city's grown, so has the desire to preserve this 350-acre mass of parkland and thankfully, Hyde Park has never been in better shape.

Eating

Perambulating through the park is bound to get that metabolism going, so stop off at one of the numerous food stalls to quench your thirst or down a plasticky hot-dog. Yum. For a more civilised affair check out one of the park's seated joints: the **Lido Café** (which also has a paddling pool) or **The Serpentine Bar & Kitchen**.

Nature, Architecture & Sculpture

The Serpentine Lake attracts the usual assortment of ducks and insects as well as some exotic additions, such as Egyptian Geese. **The Lookout Education Centre** holds informative talks about the park's wildlife. **The Grand Entrance** at Hyde Park Corner is an awe-inspiring arched construction of Greek influence, whilst the **Albert Memorial**, erected by Queen Victoria after her husband's death, is a true show of love. The **Diana, Princess of Wales Memorial Fountain**, remains one of the most visited areas in Hyde Park and is worth a look to satisfy curiosity, as is the **Peter Pan Memorial**. And pause to reflect at the heartbreaking 7 July Memorial, which pays tribute to each of the victims of the 2005 London Bombings.

Performance

The park attracts big musical events, and by big

we mean Live 8 big. It's only the musical deities that get their own special Hyde Park treatment— The Stones, Queen, Blur, but Summer means festival time and the annual 02 Wireless Festival and Capital FM Party In The Park. Brass band concerts are held throughout the summer at **The Bandstand**. **Speakers' Corner** is guaranteed to entertain. Since 1872 it's been the site of a verbal free-for-all stemming from the activities of the Reform League who marched for manhood suffrage in 1866. These days the topics aren't quite as revolutionary. Heather Mills sounded off here recently…ah, the injustice of having too much cash.

Sports

There are ample jogging paths, designated bike routes (see www.companioncycling.org.uk) and great paths for roller-blading and walking. Even more fun is boating on **The Serpentine Lake** from March to October. Informal games of rugby, football or cricket can be played on the **'Sports Field'** while **Hyde Park Tennis & Sports Centre** does exactly what it says on the tin. There's also a bowling green and horse riding at the **Manege.**

Kensington Gardens

The 111 hectares west of the Western Carriage Drive are known as Kensington Gardens. Annexed from the main park in 1689, the area retains a slightly more formal air, with regular tree-lined avenues to stroll down and less spaces for rambunctious sporting displays. This makes the Gardens an ideal spot for a picnic or a quiet ponder. Kensington Gardens also boasts the **Serpentine Gallery** (in between the Diana Fountain and the Albert Memorial), a toy-sized venue for renowned modern and contemporary art exhibitions, and the rather stunning **Kensington Palace**. Still a royal residence, the palace majestically overlooks some of the most well ordered green spaces London has to offer.

Parks & Places · **London Fields**

Overview

Best green space of the northeast? Victoria Park might still bag the accolade, but this relaxed, mid-sized park in the middle of Hackney is catching up. And quickly. It's lush and it's spacious and its latest addition, a smashing 50-metres Lido (see below), is hard to beat. Just off busy Mare Street and minutes from Regent's Canal, the park is easily reachable and easily manageable. There are two tennis courts, football, basketball and cricket pitches, and two well-equipped and well-maintained playgrounds, if you have kids in tow. London Fields does a nice job of attracting a pleasantly diverse mix of people, from Hoxton-refugee artists and rollie-smoking would-be philosophers, to pram-pushing mums and East End geezers with no teeth and big dogs. The architecture framing the tree-studded space is just as varied: bland high rises, pretty Victorians, depressing brick estates and fancy new developments, all modern Hackney is there.

The park's own drinking spot, imaginatively called Pub on the Park, is good for a relaxed outside pint, simple pub food or the footie. If you're after a slightly more refined meal, check the gastropub-ish Cat and Mutton at the park's bottom. This is also where Broadway Market begins, a traditional East End market street, now brimming with nice little shops, several pubs and original eateries. If the red wine you shared with your painter friends on their picnic blanket got you into serious party mood, head to the close-by (and late-night) Dolphin on Mare Street. Or just fall asleep in the shadows of those massive oak trees. Chances are, one of the dogs will lick you back to reality.

London Fields Lido

Address:	London Fields Westside, London E8 3EU
Phone:	020 7254 9038
Website:	http://www.hackney.gov.uk/c-londonfields-lido.htm
Hours:	Mon-Fri 6.45 am-6 pm; Sat-Sun 8 am-5 pm
Admission:	£4.10 for adults, £2.45 for kids

You might say that in a city where, essentially, you have the choice between stomach-turningly grotty leisure centre pools and hopelessly overpriced member gym versions, any new public swimming basin would be a winner. Fair enough. But WHAT a winner. Having mouldered closed for almost two decades, a £2.5m effort has restored this art deco gem to its former glory. In fact, it's probably better than ever: the 50-metre basin is nicely heated all year round (25C when we last checked), the changing rooms are modern and clean, admission's okay. Come during the week for a few pre-work lanes, when steam mysteriously hangs over the water, or jump in on the weekend, followed by a Sunday roast in one of the pubs close-by or a picnic in the park. Sounds nice? We know.

Sports

There's no shortage of things to do. The park's tennis courts can be booked for hourly slots (open 8.30 am-dusk; £5.50/h during peak times, £2.50/h off-peak; call 020 7254 4235 for more info). The Hackney Tennis Club (www.hackneycitytennisclub.co.uk) also offers classes and joint sessions. The football pitch (just come and play) is located in the middle, the basketball space (ditto) towards the south. Follow the sound of children for the playgrounds, one in the north, one in the south. If cricket is your cup of tea, get in touch with the London Fields Cricket Club (londonfieldscc@gmail.com), who keep the park's long-standing tradition as a cricket pitch alive (which, incidentally, is said to go back to 1800).

How to Get There

By bus: Most buses stop on Mare Street (get off at the London Fields stop), a few minutes walk from the actual park. From Liverpool Street Station, take 48 and 55, from Mile End or Bethnal Green grab the D6. The 106 takes you here from Finsbury Park, the 277 from Highbury & Islington. Two buses stop directly at the bottom of the park: the 236 (connecting to Dalston, Newington Green, Finsbury Park) and the 394 (Hackney Central, Homerton Hospital, Hoxton, Angel).

By train: The train is a great option, since London Fields station is located right next to the park. Train operator National Express East Anglia (formerly known as One Railway) serves the central Liverpool Street Station (via Cambridge Heath and Bethnal Green) and connects the Victoria Line tube stations Seven Sisters and Tottenham Hale further north. You can travel using your Oyster Card, for timetables check www.nationalexpresseastanglia.com.

Overview

Bordered at the north by the chain-ridden fake-a-rama, Bow Wharf, to the east and south by rat runs, and to the west by the dank waters of the Regent's Canal, this strange elongated park doesn't appear to have a lot going for it. However, this 32-hectare wiggle of green is more a string of mini parks—divided up by roads and railway lines—and each segment has hidden treasures worth digging for. There is an adventure playground, an arts pavilion with weird orange-and-white sculptural seats by Leona Matuszczak, an ecology park with moths and all sorts, a terraced garden and a sheltered children's playground. Clever landscaping and inventive use of space creates pockets of peace, and when the sun comes out, sparkling on the canal, bouncing off of the reflective jackets of the cyclists bombing past or laying its beams on giggling young couples, the park of many parks comes into its own.

It was created following the Second World War after the area was destroyed in the Blitz. The idea of Lord Abercombie, who envisioned a creepy-sounding 'finger of green' in amongst the rubble, Mile End really came into being in 1999 with Millennium Commission funding providing new areas, strange metal cross signage and an amazing green bridge—known by locals as the Banana. It actually has grass and shrubs taking walkers and cyclists over Mile End Road.

The remains of the Victorian terraces sit on the west side of the park, and one resilient pub, The Palm Tree, squats alone in the middle of a grey car park, a testament to the rows of two-up-two-downs which no longer flank the pub. This great local boozer is filled most nights with a mix of climbers and locals tucking into doorstep sandwiches and draft beer.

For those who want a bit more local history, The Ragged School Museum (www.raggedschoolmuseum.org.uk) on Copperfield St overlooks the southern tip of the park: a canal side slum that was transformed into a school for the local urchins by philanthropist Dr Barnado. It now has a mocked-up Victorian classroom and clunky little cafe. Only open Wednesday and Thursday and the occassional Sunday—check before you go.

Sports in the Park

The southern end of the park is a haven for sporty types with a refurbished stadium and ten all-weather pitches made from recycled car tyres, a go-kart track and the large Ikea-like Mile End Leisure Centre with all the usual sauna, gym, pool and verruca-infested changing rooms.

Mile End Climbing Wall is housed in an old pipe engineering works in the middle of the park, and is one of London's 'big three' (The Castle and the Westway are the others). It was opened in the 80s and some of its users seem unaware of time's passage, judging by their fetching leggings.

How to Get There

By tube: Turn left out of Mile End station, cross Grove Rd and you'll find yourself at one of the entrances to the middle section of the park.

By car: The park can be easily accessed from Bow Road, Grove Rd, or Mile End Rd, though according to London Borough of Tower Hamlets, 'The local streets operate a resident's parking permit system and are regularly patrolled by traffic wardens. Limited parking is available at Bow Wharf.'

By bus: The, D6, D7, 25, 205, 277, 323, 339 and all take you to various entrances around the park.

Additional Information

London Borough of Tower Hamlets
www.towerhamlets.gov.uk/data/discover/data/parks/mile-end/the-park-map.cfm

Mile End Climbing Wall
www.mileendwall.org.uk

General Information

Website: www.royalparks.org.uk/parks/
                   regents_park
Park Tel: 020 7486 7905
London Zoo: www.zsl.org
Open Air Theatre: www.openairtheatre.org

Overview

Whenever your quaint and backward country-dwelling friends are telling you the virtues of rural life, you can silence them with two words: Regent's Park. Let the yokels have their cleaner lungs, their maypoles and their children running barefoot and feral, because London may have its city drawbacks but it knows how to do a good park. When you stroll in Regent's Park, you're strolling on nothing less than Property of the Crown—you can see tigers and gorillas, play on the largest outdoor sports area in London, take in some Shakespeare, or, on a very good day, watch girls playing volleyball in bikinis. With 410 acres of parkland, you will always find a spot away from the (many thousands of) fellow visitors. It is the perfect space to take stock, step back and refresh, to sit in a deckchair with a good book, picnic with friends, breathe better air. Moreover, the same obnoxious people who wouldn't move down the tube to let you on or who pushed in the sandwich queue, are here relaxing with their families, lazing over a paper in a patch of sun, falling in love, throwing a Frisbee: it can be just what you need to re-bond with London when you're becoming jaded, and to get away from it all without leaving Zone One.

How to Get There

By tube:

Regent's Park – Bakerloo.
Great Portland St – Hammersmith & City, Circle, Metropolitan.
Baker St – Hammersmith & City, Jubilee, Metropolitan, Bakerloo.
St John's Wood – Jubilee.
Camden Town – Northern.

The Park is served by bus routes 2, 13, 18, 27, 30, 74, 82, 113, 139, 189, 274, 453 and C2.

Nature

The Park is a haven for the city's wildlife, thanks to a biodiversity which includes grassland, woodland, wetland, lakes and scrubs, as well as beautifully tended and fragrant gardens. Over 200 species of birds have been spotted in the Park, along with favourite garden mammals such as hedgehogs, squirrels and foxes. But if that's all just a bit too Beatrix Potter, you can get your fix of the more badass species at London Zoo in the Park's north-east end, where in addition to the normal enclosures, visitors can get closer to some of the animals with events like "Meet the Monkeys" or even help as a volunteer.

The Park's size and calm makes it a choice hangout for celebrities (not strictly nature, but dandelion richmandelion: spotting A-Listers doing tai chi in oversized sunglasses will impress more down the pub, and can there be a nobler calling?).

Performances and Events

The Park's permanent outdoor theatre is an absolute treat. The shows have a Shakespearian bias, but the venue also puts on non-bard performances, comedy nights and concerts. It is the experience more than the performance which will likely stay in your memory. Among the atmospheric trees of the park in the evening, with a bottle of wine and a blanket to snuggle up in (it is Britain after all—how many other theatres have an official "weather policy"?), it is a magical way to spend an evening. Outdoor does not mean free however: prices range from £10–£50 (Saturdays are the most expensive), and you pay theatre prices for food and drink. Cheaper to bring a picnic to enjoy in front of the theatre before the performance.

Regent's Park also hosts a number of big outdoor events. Notable regulars include Taste of London, the Innocent Smoothies Festival, and the Frieze art show. Check the website for one-off listings.

Primrose Hill

To the north of Regent's Park sits Primrose Hill, boasting corking views of much of Central and East London.

The former hunting ground for playboy king Henry VIII has a murky history, becoming the scene of a political feud in 1678, when magistrate Edmund Berry Godfrey was found dead there after being implicated in a plot to kill Charles II. In later generations Primrose Hill became the setting for duels: London lovers fought there over their ladies, while fops found it a good place to settle literary disagreements ("I say Dryden is naught but a one-trick satirist sir!" "Well then I say you are a cad and a scoundrel! Die you maggot!").

Celebrity voyeurs should keep 'em peeled for the likes of Kates Moss and, uh, writer Alan Bennett, while Primrose Hill in winter is the ideal spot to check out panoramic views of fireworks across the city on Guy Fawkes' night (5 November).

Overview

1625 Charles I brought his court to Richmond. He subsequently, with quite heroic selfishness, built wall 'round a large expanse of open grassland, nd created Richmond Park. These days the park thankfully accessible to the public, opening at 7 m (or 7.30 in the winter) and closing at dusk every ay. It's the biggest of the Royal Parks in London, nd is an obvious choice for long bike rides, picnics, formal sports and other wholesome pursuits for ur golden, happy days of youth.

Attractions

he park has a number of gardens and wooded eas, the most beautiful of which is probably the abella Plantation, an organic woodland garden at blooms with azaleas and rhododendrons. The en Ponds is another popular feature, as is Pembroke odge, the park's Georgian mansion, which can be nted out for weddings and conferences (www. embroke-lodge.co.uk or call 020 8940 8207). The djacent café also does a mean cream team.

Sports

here are three rugby pitches near the oehampton Gate that are available for rental on eekdays during winter (contact the Rosslyn Park ugby Club at 020 8948 3209), and two eighteen ole, pay and play golf courses (call 020 8876 1795 r info. and booking). Between 16 June and 14 larch you can purchase a fishing permit for the en Ponds (call 020 8948 3209 for information). Or r more extreme park-goers there is the option Power Kiting, whatever the hell that is (www. tevibe.com), and military-led Boot Camps to hape you up fast and mercilessly.

Kew

he Royal Botanic Gardens at Kew, begun in 1660, e not only easy on the eyes but an important entre for horticultural research and a UNESCO orld heritage site. The gardens are still going rong, with record amounts of visitors. The ardens are a hugely popular day trip destination r schoolchildren and adults alike and contain ch a surplus of sights and attractions that repeat sits are always surprising.

Attractions

Of course the main attractions here are the Gardens themselves. Between the formal gardens, smaller themed collections of plants and wildlife and conservation areas, there is enough walking and cooing to be done to justify any length of cake and sandwich sessions at one of the Gardens' eateries. There are also 39 Grade I and II listed buildings, all of which have some kind of historic significance. The 17th century Kew Palace (www.hrp.org.uk), is one of the most interesting of these, having previously been home to the notoriously 'mad' King George III. Other buildings in the gardens include the Chinese Pagoda of 1762, a traditional Japanese 'Minka' house and a number of museums. Decimus Burton's glasshouses (the Palm House and the Temperate) are iconic examples of this quintessentially Victorian architectural theme, and an essential part of any visit to Kew.

Events

Kew Gardens is run with great enthusiasm and has a packed programme of events throughout the year. These occur and change frequently so it's best to check the Kew website, which has comprehensive listings of everything that is going on in the Gardens, down to the blooming or blossoming of individual plant species: www. kew.org.

Several of the historic buildings, most spectacularly the Temperate Glasshouse, are available to rent for corporate and private parties.

How to Get There

Richmond station (overland trains, District Line) is a 20 minute walk from Richmond Park, or buses 371 and 65 both go from the station to the pedestrian gate at Petersham. Kew Gardens is (surprisingly) the closest station for Kew Gardens, London Overground trains stop here from across North and North West London. Trains from Waterloo stop at Kew Bridge station, a ten- minute walk from the gardens.

A large number of buses go from Hammersmith, Fulham, Clapham Junction, Wandsworth and Ealing to Richmond Park and to Kew Gardens.

River Thames

Victoria Embankment

Waterloo Bridge

Blackfriars Bridge

Oxo Tower Wharf

Gabriel's Wharf

Upper Ground

National Theatre

The London Studios

Stamford St

Blackfriars Rd

Hungerford Bridge

Queen Elizabeth Hall
Purcell Room

Upper Ground

Colin St

Derby St

Broadwall

Hatfields

Colombo

Colombo Sports Centre

Hayward Gallery

Royal Festival Hall

Doon St

Stamford St

Aquinas St

Meymott St

Belvedere Rd

BFI IMAX

Exton St

Roupell St

Southwark

Union S

Jubilee Gardens

Mepham St

Waterloo Rd

Cornwall Rd

Waterloo East Railway Station

British Airways
London Eye

York Rd

Chicheley St

Waterloo Station

The Young Vic

The Cut

London Aquarium

Addington St

The Old Vic

Lilford St

Pocock

Station Approach Rd

Lower Marsh

Webber St

Blackfriars Rd

Westminster Bridge

MAP 104

Florence Nightingale Museum

Westminster Bridge Rd

Baylis Rd

Pearman St

Morley St

Waterloo Rd

St George's

Bor

Lambeth North

Westminster Bridge Rd

Lambeth Palace Rd

Kennington Rd

Hercules Rd

Lambeth Rd

St George's Rd

Garden Row

Archbishop's Park

Lambeth Rd

Imperial War Museum

Lambeth Palace

Lambeth Wk

Brook Dr

Sayley St

Overview

A pedestrianised quarter formed of venues for theatre, music, cinema, art and various other artistically orientated entities, the South Bank is the realisation of a post-war dream of an arts-for-all hub in London. The area has its roots in 1951's Festival of Britain, a technicoloured marvel designed to showcase an optimistic future for Britons used to coal, Spitfires and fake mashed potato. The legacy of the Festival ensured that the surrounding area went on to grow into the playground that it has become today.

The South Bank Centre

The actual 'South Bank Centre' is officially formed of the Royal Festival Hall, the Queen Elizabeth Hall, the Purcell Room, the Hayward Gallery and the Saison Poetry Library, which are all concentrated in the centre of the South Bank. The Royal Festival Hall hosts a variety of musical and dance performances from its auditorium, whilst the Hall's foyer is an enormous and relaxed open-plan area with a bar, performance spaces and shop. The Queen Elizabeth Hall and Purcell Room offer further stages for musical recitals whilst the Saison Poetry Library houses a vast collection of poetry dating from 1912 onwards. The Hayward Gallery has an exterior of frightening ugliness, which shields a surprisingly spacious interior, devoted to exhibitions of the visual arts.

The National Theatre

The National Theatre is next-door to the South Bank Centre complex and is another gaping example of uncompromising architecture. Opened in 1963, it still looks slightly unhinged. The building consists of three theatres and puts on a range of productions from the established to the experimental. It also features an inviting foyer, and in the open spirit of the South Bank, offers back-stage tours, workshops, talks and costume and prop hire to Joe Schmo.

British Film Institute and IMAX

Nestling under Waterloo Bridge, the BFI promotes film and television through its archives, cinema screens, talks and festivals. It's a great alternative to the disgustingly over-priced and sticky-floored chain cinemas of central London and promotes an all-encompassing program from its three screens.

The Film Café and Benugo Bar & Kitchen do good pre- and post-flick munch. The BFI IMAX is the separate, rotund glass building situated around 200m south of the BFI. It shows films on Britain's biggest cinema screen accompanied by sound pumped from a gargantuan 11,600-watt sound system.

Everything Else

Beyond its theatres, music halls, galleries and cinemas, the South Bank has spawned a number of other attractions. The London Eye is an enormous Ferris wheel built in 2000 on the banks of the Thames adjacent to Westminster Bridge, it revolves at a leisurely 0.5 mph and offers brilliant views from its 135m-high peak. The London Aquarium is just opposite but with ticket prices roughly similar to the Eye, seeing big fish in small tanks starts to look a distinctly lame option. Less expensive attractions around South Bank include the open-air book market tucked under Waterloo Bridge and Gabriel's Wharf, a dinky enclave of small shops, bars and restaurants that offer succour to those cultured-out.

Getting There

By tube: Nearest stations are Waterloo (Northern, Bakerloo, Jubilee and Waterloo & City lines) and Embankment (Circle, District, Northern & Bakerloo lines). From Waterloo, head 50m towards the river. Embankment station is at the northern foot of Hungerford footbridge.

By train: Nearest stations are Waterloo & Charing Cross. For directions from Waterloo, see 'By Tube'. From Charing Cross, 100m down Villiers Street towards the river and then walk across the Hungerford footbridge.

By bus: The South Bank is on numerous bus routes. Buses stop on nearby Waterloo Bridge, York Road, Belvedere Road, Stamford Street and Waterloo Station. Most coming from the North get to South Bank via Holborn, The Strand or Victoria. From the South they come via Elephant and Castle or Lambeth North.

By boat: Festival Pier is adjacent to the London Eye. Pleasure boats dock here on cruises, as do riverboat services which sail west as far as Tate Britain and east as far as Woolwich Arsenal.

(353)

General Information

NFT Maps: 9 & 23
Website: www.royalparks.org.uk/
            parks/st_james_park
            www.royalparks.org.uk/
            parks/green_park
Free guided walks: 020 7930 1793
Inn the Park Café and Restaurant
(St. James's Park): 020 7451 9999

Overview

With Trafalgar Square at one end and Buck Palace at the other, both St. James's and Green Park are slap-bang in the heart of picture-postcard London. When the belching fumes of bendy buses and hordes of Oxford Street shoppers threaten both health and sanity, there's only one place to go. Zip past the crowds and pigeons in Trafalgar Square and head under the grand curve of Admiralty Arch into the stately calm of St. James's Park. Stand yourself on the bridge that crosses the lake, take a deep breath and marvel at the history surrounding you in the city's oldest

Royal Park, dating back to the days of Henry VIII.

The views: fairytale Buckingham Palace to the west, Downing Street, the seat of Parliament and Big Ben jutting out over Horse Guards' Parade to the east and the towers of Westminster Abbey to the south. There ain't nowhere else in London where you can view the icons of Church, State and Monarchy in one quick spin on your heels. Impressive. And when you're done marvelling, join the families, office workers, joggers and tourists in taking a stroll round the lake for pelican-spotting, duck-feeding, lunching and romancing.

A hop across the Mall and you'll find yourself in the rolling green of, yup, Green Park. Flowerbed free, this 53-acre patch of park with its aged plane trees is the more meditative of the two. A refuge from the noisy thoroughfare of Piccadilly and Hyde Park corner, its grounds soon fill with picnicking office-workers at the slightest suggestion of sun while the tree-lined Mall is the nearest you'll get to a Parisian boulevard.

Nature

The curving lake of St. James's park runs the length of the grounds and is perfect for indulging in some casual bird-spotting. Ever since the days of James I, the park has been home to an exotic menagerie, once including elephants, camels and even crocs.

While the crocs and ellies might be long gone, both Duck Island and the smaller West Island remain home to an impressive array of water birds. Beyond the humble duck and gulls, there are suitably stately black swans, rare golden eyes and the rather less-illustrious sounding shovelers, a close relative of the time-starved office-worker on lunch, we believe. But, with their gentlemanly swagger and mighty beaks, the five resident pelicans unquestionably steal the show. A gift from the Russian Ambassador in 1664, feeding time is worth a gander at 3pm daily. Known for their international antics—like flying to Regent's Park Zoo on fish-stealing sprees—one caused a media storm when, clearly lusting after a menu change, it swallowed a live pigeon whole, flapping feathers 'n' all.

Take some old bread and the park's tame, tubby squirrels will feast from your hand. Hang around 'til dusk and the bats come out to play.

Architecture & Sculpture

As if housing ol' Queenie's Buckingham Palace wasn't enough, the parks are surrounded by two more palaces—Westminster, now the Houses of Parliament, and St. James's. From the Regency elegance of the Mall's Carlton House, home to the Institute of Contemporary Arts (ICA), to the impressive frontage of Horse Guard's Parade, the parks are hemmed in by grandeur.

Once a swampy wasteland for grazing pigs, it's a tale with humble beginnings for London's most royal park. While each passing King and Queen slowly improved St. James's Park, it was Charles II that really put the work in, getting trees planted, lawns laid and then opening it up for the first time to us commoners.

Sobering war memorials in St. James's Park abound, including world war icons Mountbatten and Kitchener in Horse Guards' Parade, and an overblown marble statue of Queen Victoria complete with glitter and gates. Oh, and that grand old Duke of York, best-known for marching his men up and down some hill? He's here too, in bronze atop a mighty pillar by the ICA.

The Parks in Season

St. James's in spring is carpeted with crocuses and daffodils. Come summer, they're quickly replaced with a carpet of sun-starved Tom, Dick and Sallys, laid bare as they dare to catch some rays. For an instant upgrade from the rabble, head to Green Park by the tube and hire a stripy deck-chair at £1.50 a pop from April to September.

Between May and August, add a dash of high-brow culture to your day with free concerts at the bandstand every lunchtime and early evening.

Autumn days might be chilly but clear skies make for impressive sunsets while wintry strolls are all the more head-clearing, especially after a night on the Soho tiles.

Sports

With cycling and ball-games banned—*entirely* inappropriate in such stately surrounds!—jogging, morning tai chi, leisurely strolls and pigeon chasing are as energetic as it gets. Sundays are best for strolling when Constitution Hill is closed to traffic.

The Mall and Constitution Hill are cycle-friendly and make a pleasant cut through the West End. Join the Serpentine running club for regular jaunts through St. James's. (www.serpentine. org.uk).

Enjoy the sedate pace with free lunch-time guided walks twice a month, discussing anything from horticulture to royalty (booking line: 020 7930 1793).

General info

NFT Map: 90, 93, & 94
Website: http://www.towerhamlets.gov.uk/
               lgsl/451-500/461_parks_and_open_
               spaces/victoria_park.aspx
Information: 020 8985 1957

Overview

Look at all the joggers, skaters, cricketers and picnickers swarming in Victoria Park on any given weekend, and it seems hard to continue calling this 218-acres green space one of London's best-kept secrets. Yet, to many Londoners not living east, it still is. Lined by Regent's Canal in the south, London's third-largest cultivated green space is a nice blend of Regent's Park's beauty and the wilderness found in Hampstead Heath. It's also far enough off the Central London map to stay virtually tourist-free, while, at the same time, feeling reassuringly inner city urban, with the Gherkin and Canary Wharf's skyscrapers all in sight.

Divided into two handy bits by Grove Road, Victoria Park has much of what makes a park more than just grass and trees: excellent sporting facilities, ranging from athletics to rugby, several lakes, a deer enclosure, a secret garden—and plenty of decent drinking holes nearby. Designed in the 1840s to bring much needed greenery and breathing space to a soul-destroyingly grim East End, the "people's park" can also look back on an intriguing past of dissent, non-conformist rallying and all sorts of political mischief-making. And it's home to the oldest model boat racing club in the country. Come now, before the Olympics do. Once the squirrels start digging out amphetamines, the secret will be gone forever.

Nature

Ducks, swans, birds and god knows what else live around The Lake in the west, while deer and goats graze slightly further north. You're allowed to fish in the Old Lake, although we're not at all sure that there are really many fish in there. Pretty oak trees and hawthorns stud the whole place; colourful flowers and perfectly-groomed shrubs grow in the Old English Garden. It's a beautifully landscaped gem of a garden and one of this city's most peaceful spots—if you don't mind the odd greying philosopher, mumbling to himself.

Sports

...gging and skating are popular and, thanks to wide ...athways, possible throughout the park. There's a ...gby pitch, a large dedicated football area, four ...nnis courts (call 020 8986 5182) and three all-...eather cricket pitches, run by the esteemed Victoria ...ark Community Cricket League (www.vpccl.co.uk). ...e children's playgrounds are decent enough, and ...e athletic field is excellent. Get in touch with the ...ark's own athletics association (www.vphthac.org. ...k) for access to changing rooms, showers and its ...door training hall.

Architecture & sculpture

...sing in the middle of the park is a Grade-II listed ...inking fountain erected by Baroness Angela ...urdett-Coutts (England's wealthiest woman at ...me point, we're told), adorned by several half-...aked marble boys, smiling cheekily. The Hackney ...ick Great War Memorial, in the east part of the ...ark, is a reminder that this part of London was hit ...pecially hard by the bombings of the Second World ...ar. Close-by, you'll find two alcove-type fragments ...at survived the demolition of the old London ...idge Station. Fairly unremarkable, but good shelter ...en it's raining. Let's face it, no one comes here for ...chitecture.

Festivals

The hazy days when The Clash whipped up a beer-can-throwing frenzy in the park—heralding a new era called punk along the way—might be over, but Victoria Park has kept its musical tradition alive. Slightly more tamed and organised, the festivals taking place these days range from the trendy, village-feel Fields Day to the indie-and-electro-blending Lovebox Weekender, while big names (Radiohead for one) have also discovered a liking for the park's scenery and music-appreciating attitude.

Eat & drink

The park's café, next to The Lake, is tiny, but the organic cakes are a tasty lot. That aside, you have to venture to the park's fringes for food and drink, but fear not: a tap is never far. Leave behind the bog-standard, soulless pub that is The Victoria and opt for the East End earthiness of the Top of the Morning instead, near the Cadogan Gate. Good Ales, a real fireplace, and up-marketish pub food make The Royal Inn on the Park, near the Royal Gates, the usually busy favourite. The Fat Cat, a few minutes south of the park along Grove Road, is more restaurant than pub, a bit pricey but a good choice for high-quality pasta, burgers and steaks.

General Information

www.wpcc.org.uk

Overview

If London life starts to get you down, but trekking the countryside is too much hassle, then Wimbledon Common provides the best of both worlds. Incorporating Putney Heath to the north, Wimbledon Common offers over 1000 acres of old woodland, scrubland, heathland, ponds and well-tended, mown areas for sports and recreation. Bordered by the urban sprawls of Wimbledon, Putney and Richmond, the common has offered Londoners an escape from city life for centuries. Although thousands visit every weekend, the scale of the place is so vast that you can easily find a private haven for reading a book or a romantic picnic.

Unlike the micro-managed and perfectly structured central London parks, Wimbledon feels much more natural and random. Paths are unpaved and often little more than a muddy track leading off in unlikely directions. The untamed beauty of the common and the lack of traffic noise, or any noise for that matter, make it hard to believe you are still in London.

After a hard day of outdoor activity, or sunbathing, there are plenty of historic pubs to retire to in Wimbledon village. If you prefer your nature tamed and don't want to get your shoes dirty, head to the southeast corner of the common for Cannizaro House and gardens, a grand mansion converted into a boutique hotel and restaurant, with elegantly manicured gardens open to the public. In the summer, the friendly hotel bar opens onto a patio overlooking the grounds and makes a good spot for a sun-downer as you imagine being Lord or Lady of the Manor for the day.

Nature

The common is home to many animals including bats, badgers, and muntjac deer. It's also an important breeding ground for dragonflies and damselflies. For anyone wanting to find out more about the flora and fauna, the London Bat Group organises bat walks while the London Wildlife Trust organises guided walks. You can also take a self-guided wander along The Windmill Nature Trail. 800 metres long, the trail has been created with accessibility in mind and begins right next to the Windmill car park. The visitors' centre behind the Windmill has wildlife exhibits and also tells the history of the common. It also sells maps and booklets giving the low down on the nature on offer.

Recreation

There is loads of space on the common for pick-up games of rugby, football, Frisbee and cricket. If you fancy a 'real game', you can hire tennis courts by the hour, cricket pitches by the day (from as little as £100) or enjoy a round of golf on the two available courses. The common is very popular with runners and steeplechase events have been held here since 1867. Various running clubs such as the South London Harriers and Hercules Wimbledon use the Common. If you've ever fancied trying horse riding, there are a number of stables that make use of the 16 miles of trails—or bring your own nag with you.

Golf
www.wcgc.co.uk
www.londonscottishgolfclub.co.uk

Horse Riding
Wimbledon Village Stables: 020 8946 8579
Ridgway Stables: 020 8946 7400

Rugby, Football and Cricket Pitch Hire
020 8788 7655

How to Get There

By public transport:
The Northern Line goes to South Wimbledon where you can take a bus to central Wimbledon then change or walk to the village and common. Wimbledon station is much closer. Take the District Line from central London or over ground trains from Waterloo or London Bridge. If you are feeling fit, a ten-minute walk up Wimbledon Hill takes you to Wimbledon village and beyond that, the edge of the common. Regular buses serve the village. Alternatively, you can access Putney Heath which joins up with Wimbledon Common. To do this, take the District Line to Putney Bridge or East Putney overground to Putney mainline station and take a bus up Putney Hill.

It's likely that at some point during your London residence, you've been seized with the romantic notion of floating your way round a London market—savouring the smells, laughing with a vendor, flirting your way to some freebies. If you have, then your attempts to live that dream almost certainly resulted in you silently fuming as you crawled among a crowd of thousands, trekking for a cashpoint because you forgot that stalls don't accept cards, and getting crapped on by a pigeon. Don't be put off!

At the markets you can buy some of the most unique, quirky, fresh, stylish, grungy, exquisite, unusual items in London. Sometimes you'll get brilliant bargains, sometimes you'll pay high for something you fall in love with. And sometimes, yes, you'll be driven near to homicidal rampage. But they're one of London's great strengths: use them while you can, because the developers have their evil, dollar-signed eyes on them.

For groceries

The food in markets isn't necessarily locally grown, but you get a much more tempting choice than in most supermarkets. Expect fruit, veg, breads, cheeses, meats, spices and pastries, as well as stalls concocting irresistible snacks from around the world.

Borough (Map 106)

You don't come here for bargains: you come for ambiance, exquisite international foods, and to impress the person you woke up with. If you're rich and like the finer things in life, then here your weekly shop can consist of some of the freshest vegetables, plumpest fruit, sweetest patisseries and sockiest cheeses in London. If you're poor and just fancy a change from Saturday morning repeats of *Friends*, then head here for a hearty hog roast sandwich and to snaffle some free samples.

Broadway (Map 89)

As gorgeous as Borough, for a third of the price and a fifth of the crowds. It's a pain to get to stuck in one of the city's remaining quaintly retro spots not closely served by the tube (London Fields), but you'll want to move here by the en of your visit.

Ridley Road (Map 86)

If the gourmet markets are too poncey fo you, with their Bavarian organic rye bread an Malaysian honey from breast-fed bees, then ge down the Ridley Road. Here, in a market which bright, chaotic, grubby and bouncing to regga you can pick up an incredible array of Jamaican Turkish, African, Indian and Chinese foodstuf (and possibly e-coli).

For market-chic

You won't necessarily pay less than at the hig street, but you will have a choice of origina and irresistible items sold with passion an knowledge. Expect to leave these markets wit a lighter pocket (though try to make sure it's no because of the pickpockets…).

Spitalfields (Map 91)

Mecca for anyone looking for ethnic-hip an well-priced clothes, bags and jewellery. Her you can often chat to the maker of the clothe you're eyeing up and learn the story behind the designs. Which is all very inspiring, until you tr on their beloved creations, realise you're too fa for it, and reject it having slightly stretched i Because then it's just awkward.

Greenwich (Map 120)

Craft-tastic: a great place to go for beautifu handmade gifts which people love to receiv and then put in a cupboard for the rest of thei useful life. Here you'll find a gorgeous range o items for home and lifestyle: pictures, antiques candles, pottery, soft furnishings and clothes as well as some great food stalls, and an above average number of beautiful rich people than a most markets.

Portobello Road (Map 29)

Although famed for being the World's Largest Antiques Market, Portobello Road seems to sell *everything*. You'll need patience to work around its sprawling size and the crowds, but just about anything you're looking for is there somewhere or can be sourced by speaking to the right vendor. Stalls include clothes (from classy-vintage to student-cheap), jewellery, fabric, food, as well as 1500 antique stalls selling maps, medals, silverware, and things you never thought you needed (and which, after you've got them home, you realise you didn't).

Camden (Map 71)

Camden is actually home to six markets, though "chic" doesn't do any of them justice. Here you'll find a purse-emptying range of alternative fashions, vintage clothes, accessories, gifts, t-shirts, comedy hot water bottle covers, tie-dyed hippies, teeny-punks and chaps asking if you'd care for a nice bit of crack. Anything goes, and this open, free atmosphere makes it a major and exciting draw. Hit Camden Stables for brilliant international food stalls.

Fer findin a bit o Laaandon prop'a.

If you're a Londoner who "just adores the city", but oh dear *no*, wouldn't *dream* of bringing kids up here", then chances are you don't mingle much with the Prop'a Laandoner. This hardy breed whose family history is a Dickensian yarn of blitzes, TB and chimney sweeps are the core of this city, and the gradual nudging out of their jellied eels and pub sing-songs is tantamount to ethnic cleansing. Find them at London's Propa Markets before they vanish.

Smithfield (Map 15)

Smithfield Market is in full swing at 4 am, which makes it the perfect place to stumble into on your way home from clubbing. Unless you're vegetarian, because while frying bacon may have you yearning for looser morals, the smell of this 800 year old meat market will have you retching over your recycled sandals. It's the best place in London to pick up any meat you could hope for, including, in the 1500s, a barbecued Protestant or a topside of William Wallace, this being the site of hundreds of executions in its time. Some of the local pubs hold special early licenses, so on your way to the office you can swing in for breakfast over a pint with some of the meat porters: they'd just *love* it if you did.

Columbia Road (Map 91)

There's something deeply touching about an exquisite flower market being manned by some of the burliest Cockneys you'll see outside a Guy Ritchie film. Get there first thing on Sundays for the best choice, or in a low-cut top for the best bargains. And if the crowds and cries of the "daffs, dahlin'?" become too much, just slip into the enchanting boutiques lining Columbia Road.

Billingsgate (Map 101)

For the largest selection of fish in London, outside the London Aquarium (where they frown on you if you try to fry the fish. Bloody bureaucracy.), head to Billingsgate. People were buying their fish here long before London went all yuppie, and much the same stock is available—winkles, cockles, potted shrimp and things which smell ungodly. Today you'll find alongside them almost any fish you could hope for (though don't ask for goldfish), as well as poultry, oils and snacks.

General info

Address:	Southampton Row, London, WC1B 4AP
Phone:	020 7514 7022
Website:	www.csm.arts.ac.uk

Overview

Though hyped to infinity, and often lazily editorialised as the one vital source of all things up-and-coming in London, Central St Martins nevertheless has an undeniable history of producing graduates that tend to rocket to international fame upon leaving. The frequently cited list of alumni reads like a Who's Who of European art-and-design talent, and includes past superstars such as Alexander McQueen, Gilbert and George, and Anthony Gormley, as well as recent fashion darlings Christopher Kane, Gareth Pugh and Kim Jones, to name a few.

The school as it is today was formed in 1989 through the amalgamation of two prestigious 19th century institutions, the Central School of Arts and Crafts and St Martins School of Art. Since then it has annexed the Drama Center and the Byam Shaw School of Art in Archway, and as a result offers a huge range of courses covering most areas of the visual and performing arts. St Martins has a particularly formidable reputation for fashion design—it is the only university to show student collections as part of London Fashion Week— but it is well respected in all departments for its hyper-progressive ethos (expect to

hear words like 'challenging,' and 'risk-takin', liberally thrown around on open days). Th, college has recently revealed plans to move 1 a swish new building in King's Cross in 201 where student activity will be centralised ar, everyone will no doubt be even more fabulo, than before. Consequently, whether you fir, the whole thing pretentious and overrate, or are waiting in breathless anticipation fo the next St Martins wunderkind, it's goir to be very difficult to ignore the place in th coming years.

Campuses

Central St Martins

The majority of teaching for fine art, fashio, and design students takes place in the ve, centre of London, with one building o Southampton Row (nearest tube Holborn and one on Charing Cross Road (nea Tottenham Court Road). This means man, of sensitive creative souls find themselve struggling against tides of tourists, bu on the plus side they also get to inflic their frequently baffling artwork upon large section of the general public, whe on their way to Wetherspoons, are treate, to installations of varying quality in th front windows of the Charing Cross site. O course, being in the heart of Soho, most S Martins students are a moment away from cornucopia of incredibly trashy bars whe, they can lubricate their inner muses.

Drama Centre

The theatre types are based in Clerkenwell, some of Sadler's Wells and the Barbican, and mount public performances at the university-owned Cochrane Theatre in Holborn. The Drama Centre runs courses ranging from set design to classical acting, but also has a programme specifically designed for those wanting to act, direct or write in the film and television industries, and to this end is equipped with various studio and recording facilities. Pierce Brosnan went there but there's no need to let that put you off.

Byam Shaw

The Byam Shaw School of Art in Archway a fairly recent addition (2003) to Central St Martins, the 'Central' tag here being somewhat misleading as it's a good 20 minutes by tube from the other sites. Devoted solely to fine art, it runs a BA and more skills-based 2 year FdA as well as a variety of short and post-graduate courses.

College Culture

As is the case with most London institutions, the university community is massively subsumed by the bright lights of the city itself, but this is no bad thing. Though the college puts on frequent exhibitions, talks and events, there is no independent bar or central pub—students will instead inevitably find themselves taking advantage of the central location (which is, after all, a short walk from the National Gallery and ICA). The Student Union is not particular to Central St Martins but provides services for and represents all the art colleges in London (University of the Arts London) as a whole, and various services and societies (such as sports clubs) are run at this level. As far as the education part goes, it's not always easy being in the midst of the constant search for the next-big-thing, but at the same time the idiosyncratic slant of the teaching makes for a unique experience, and the generally high talent level of the students fosters a fantastic creative and social atmosphere.

Tuition

Fees for 2010/11 are £3,290 a year for UK/EU applicants taking an undergraduate or Foundation level degree. Some courses require payment of an additional course fee for materials. International students can expect to pay between £9,300 and £12,250 depending upon the type of course taken. Central St Martins offers a number of post-graduate level bursaries and scholarships.

Short Courses

Central St Martins also runs a large number of short courses for all aspirational (and rich) non-students wanting a piece of the action. Prices are high but the courses very popular, partly because of the college's reputation and partly because there are many interesting options to choose from. The courses run in evenings, weekends, or can be taken intensively as a Summer, Easter or Christmas school. Information: www.csm.arts.ac.uk or call 020 7514 7015.

Phone Numbers:

Charing Cross Road site: 020 7514 7190
Southampton Row site: 020 7514 7037
Drama Centre: 020 7514 8778
Byam Shaw School of Art: 020 7281 4111
Admissions—degree courses:
020 7514 7023
Admissions—short courses: 020 7514 7015
International Office: 020 7514 7027
Charing Cross Road Shop: 020 7514 7612
Southampton Row Shop: 020 7514 7017
Back Hill Shop: 020 7514 6851
University of the Arts Students' Union:
020 7514 6270

General info

Address: Northampton Square, London,
EC1V 0HB
Phone: 020 7040 5060
Website: www.city.ac.uk

Overview

In London, a place rich with academia, City University often gets overlooked. Unlike King's or LSE it has no grand halls, secret-handshakes or old-boys' networks. Its facilities are modest and its library short on fusty books. But it's carved out a reputation as a supplier of professionals, cementing its place in the top five for graduate employment in recent years.

Located on a pretty park on the edge of the City of London—the 'Square Mile' that's fast becoming the centre of the global economy—the university is overwhelmingly diverse. Ethnicities make up over half the student body, with young Chinese and wealthy Russians flocking to the business school. It's that section of the university that churns out workers for the finance industry—students who are so hell-bent on business success that they go to school in suits.

The university's first incarnation came in 1894 as an industrial college for the working classes. The on-site swimming pool was used when London hosted the 1908 Olympics, although it wasn't until 1966 that it gained full university status. It's maintained strong links with industry, with alumni including the founding father of budget Euro-travel, easyJet's Stelios (like Sting and Madonna he chooses to use only one name). Students at City may be lined up for good jobs when they graduate; but it comes at the cost of having to explain what their less well-known university is whenever they mention it.

Tuition

Undergraduate fees for 2010/11 are £3, 290 for home students (UK/EU). Maintenance and bursaries will remain at 2009/10 levels due to negative inflation in the economy. Those who receive full student loan allocation will be eligible for a bursary of £770 to help fund studies. Some students may receive partial bursary. Overseas student fees vary from course to course but are likely to be three times as much as 'home students'.

Postgraduate professional courses range form £4,305 (LLB) to £14,500 (Bar Professional Training Course) for UK students.

Culture

Culture in the traditional sense is a little thin on the ground. There are no museums or galleries to speak of, although one department did exhibit photos of prisoners at work last year. But as it included a con making sandwiches for 16p an hour this could've just been to get the wayward students to knuckle down.

Instead, the uni hosts some heavyweight lectures. The Students' Union offers limited clubs and societies with all the usual fare – tennis, chess, Christian Union. The Saddlers Wells Sport Centre is also home to the intramural team sports. 'Ten' (10 Northampton Square) is where the kids hang out, the social hub of City.

Departments

Admissions office (undergrad and postgrad):
020 7040 8716
Library   020 7040 8191
Saddler's Sports Centre   020 7040 5656
Student Union 020 7040 5600

1 Gloucester Building
2 Innovation Centre
3 School of Social Sciences
4 College Building
5 Centenary Building
6 Drysdale Building
7 Refectory Building
8 University Building
9 Tait Building
10 Goswell Place
11 Myddelton Building
12 Parkes Building
13 Health Centre
14 Walmsley Building
15 Paramount House
16 Saddlers Sports Centre
17 Finsbury Residence Hall
18 Heyworth Residence Hall
19 Peartree Court Residence Hall

General info

Address: Imperial College London
                  South Kensington Campus
                  London SW7 2AZ
Phone: 020 7589 5111
Website: www3.imperial.ac.uk

Overview

Imperial College really did have imperial beginnings with Prince Albert setting up the college as a research and learning centre of science, maths, medicine and engineering to enhance the image of the British Empire in 1887. In the Victorian age, and to this day, the college attracted the most enquiring of minds and was the central feature of what was once Prince Albert's successful push to create a centre of culture and learning, encompassing the nearby museums, Royal College of Music, Royal Geographical Society and the Royal Albert Hall. The university remains one of the best in the world, ranked 5th in 2009, and as such remains one of the most selective institutions in the UK with the application to admissions ratio being 7:1. Famous alumni include clever clogs Brian May (Queen), HG Wells and Alexander Fleming. In 2007 Imperial College became independent from the University of London and now awards its own degrees.

Departments

The pride and soul of the college are three faculties, each headed by a principal: engineering, medicine and natural sciences. The Tanaka Business School doesn't offer undergraduate degrees, but does allow undergraduate students to study management modules towards their degrees. The main purpose of the Humanities department is to provide elective subjects and language courses for the science students. For medical students Imperial is also associated with various London hospitals including St Mary's Hospital and Charing Cross Hospital.

Campus Culture

Imperial may have a 'heads down' atmosphere but there is still that unwritten rule that if you work hard you play hard. Imperial College Union (ICU) offers numerous clubs and societies from Bellydancing to Wakeboarding to Backgammon. The Union bar is also well used, and is particularly lively on an afternoon when a football or rugby match is screened. The free student paper, Felix (http://felixonline.co.uk/), is a popular and useful resource for keeping up to date with campus life and aims to be independent from the College itself. Imperial also has its own student TV station, Stoic, and radio station ICRadio (1134 AM or www.icradio.com). There are also regular public lectures on a variety of subjects.

Facilities

Imperial's main campus in South Kensington is surrounded by many of London's best museums including the Natural History Museum, Science Museum and Victoria & Albert Museum. Being in the thick of it also means a close proximity to the shops and cafes of South Ken and High Street Kensington and being a stone's throw from Hyde Park.

The main campus boats some of the best facilities of the London universities. As well as the usual on-campus shops (including bookshop, cafes, travel agents and bank) there are some impressive sports facilities on offer. The brand, spanking new ETHOS centre contains not only a fully equipped gym but also an inside climbing wall, swimming pool, squash courts, sports hall and a treatment room offering massages and physiotherapy. On top of that there's a boathouse and a 60-acre athletic ground. Naturally, there's a well-stocked central library and various smaller departmental libraries.

Tuition

Home students' (UK/EU) annual fees for 2010/11 are £3,290 for undergraduate programmes. International students can expect to pay the whopping amount of between £19, 800 and £39, 150 depending upon the subject studied. Students from England may be eligible for a means tested maintenance grant of £2, 906.

General Information

Address:	King's College London
	Strand
	London
	WC2R 2LS
Phone:	020 7836 5454
Website:	www. kcl.ac.uk

Overview

Kings College is one of the 19 colleges that make up the colossus that is the University of London. King's (or KCL, as otherwise known) has nearly 20,000 students and five campuses—the Strand, Guy's, Waterloo, St. Thomas' and Denmark Hill. In 2011 the school of law will move into the East Wing of the magnificent Somerset House. It has an excellent academic reputation and ranks in the top ten UK universities. Unlike some of the other University of London colleges, King's is equally well known for its arts and science courses.

Its religious affiliation is now less central, but back in 1829 King's was founded as a Church of England institution to counter University College London, or "the godless college in Gower Street." The beautifully designed chapel at the Strand campus testifies to its pious beginnings, though few students would consider it a motivation for attending the college. The student body is diverse, as the societies list reflects—it includes a Catholic society, a Christian Union, a Krishna Consciousness group, and a Nomads society, amongst a myriad others.

King's boasts a number of famous alumni. Keats studied apothecary there (he didn't like it much), and Florence Nightingale set up the world's first school of nursing at St. Thomas' Hospital, now the Florence Nightingale School of Nursing and Midwifery. In the 1960s, Archbishop Desmond Tutu spent time in its halls. The KCL student union nightclub, Tutu's—a pretty grungy place but one of the few open past 2 am in the Strand on a Saturday—is named after him.

London prices may take their toll on the student purse, but King's students at least benefit from a prime location. As well as the nightclub, the college has two bars, one at Guy's Campus and one at the Strand. The Waterfront bar at the Strand looks directly onto the Thames, giving a view of everything from Westminster to the Oxo Tower. It's also a great gig venue—Alanis Morissette, Richard Ashcroft, and Beth Orton have all played there.

Sports

The college's sports facilities are impressive. It caters to almost anything—it has a swimming pool, gym, and even rifle range. Although King's cannot rival the Oxbridge rowing tradition, its sports do have a history—two of the men's rugby clubs, Guy's and St. Thomas', are the oldest in the world. To access the sports grounds students must leave Zone 1; the grounds are in Dulwich, Surrey, and South London.

Culture

Kings has numerous dramatic societies where amateur thespians can hone their skills, especially with the recent acquisition of the Grade I listed Anatomy Theatre and Museum. More unusually, its classics department stages a play in ancient Greek every year, and is the only classics department in the UK to do so. The college's religious origins are evident in its wonderful choral music. 25 choral scholars uphold this tradition.

Tuition

Undergraduate tuition fees are £3,290 per year for home students (UK/EU) for 2010/11. Postgraduate fees range between £3,450 and £5,550 depending upon the subject.

Contact details

General Enquiries 020 7836 5454
Social Science and Public Policy .020 7848 1495
Physical Sciences and Engineering ....
...........................020 7848 2267/2268
Nursing and Midwifery 020 7848 4698
Medicine 020 7848 6501
Law.............................020 7836 5454
Institute of Psychiatry 020 7836 5454
Humanities 020 7848 2350
Dental Institute ....020 7848 6512 (undergrad),
....................020 7848 6703 (postgrad)
Biomedical and Health Sciences.............
.... 020 7848 6400 (Guy's)
..................020 7848 4172 (Waterloo)

Libraries:
Maughan Chancery Lane....020 7848 2430
Waterloo...................020 7848 3000
St. Thomas.................020 7188 3740
Guy's 020 7848 6900
Denmark Hill 020 7848 5740
Student Union 020 7848 1588

MAP 104

Waterloo Campus

Doon St

Cornwall Rd

Franklin-Wilkins Building

Waterloo Bridge Wing

Stamford St

K4 Fitness Centre

Stamford Street Apartments

James Clark Maxwell Building

Secker St

Waterloo Rd

Waterloo Station

Exton St

General Information

Address: Houghton Street,
             London WC2A 2AE
Phone: 020 7405 7686
Website: www.lse.ac.uk

Overview

The London School of Economics and Political Science, or LSE as it is commonly known, is a single faculty college focused on the social sciences; world-renowned for its highly prestigious programmes and distinguished alumni. Located amidst a hub of academic activity with UCL, Kings College, SOAS and Birkbeck nearby, the college is affiliated with the University of London and stands apart due to its high proportion of postgraduate students. LSE was founded in 1895 by the intellectual socialist movement, the Fabian Society, with the aim of bettering society through the education of Britain's business and political elite. Today it remains a strongly political institution, with considerable influence in government through both its research programmes and campaigns. Its alumni are also highly represented in business and law spheres. While best known for its economics and politics degrees, the broad range of social science programmes offered complements the international ethos of the school and it remains at the cutting edge in terms of research.

The college enrolls around 8,000 students who represent over 140 different countries; over half of these are postgraduates who arely leave the library unless attending high-brow seminars on globalization and inequality. Its starry alumni includes Nobel laureates, international Heads of State, outstanding academics, and a notable proportion of British MP's. And of course Mick Jagger.

Culture On Campus

Despite its reputation for academic excellence, LSE's social activities are mainly fuelled by a lively undergraduate population who also know how to enjoy themselves. With over 170 eclectic student societies, ranging from 'Catalan' to 'Taiwanese'; from 'United Nations' to 'Anti-Authoritarian' and from 'Maths&Stats' to good old fashioned 'Lager&Real Ale', the broad international and diverse facets of the student population is encompassed. An atmosphere of work hard/play hard prevails and nightly events lure the undergraduates from the libraries and keep the campus buzzing. The large postgraduate population tends to shuffle by however, books in hand; the days of cheesy music, luminous drinks in shot glasses and ill-conceived experimental fashions behind them while they actually do some work. LSE also hosts numerous public lectures with acclaimed speakers at the forefront of the subject discussed. Past speakers have included Noam Chomsky, Kofi Annan, David Cameron and architect Richard Rogers.

Sports

Not to be let down by its central, and somewhat geographically limited campus, LSE manages to maintain a thriving sports culture through the Athletics Union. Football and rugby seem to top the bill, with provision for some of the less mainstream athletic pursuits such as capoeira and Ultimate Frisbee. The college makes use of its affiliation with the University of London Union, which broadens the scope for sports participation alongside students of other universities.

Tuition

Undergraduate tuition fees are £3,290 for home students (UK/EU) and £13,680 for overseas students. Home postgraduate students can expect to pay between £6,432 for home and £23,928 for MA and year long professional courses (Finance courses are the most expensive). International students should expect to pay between £13,092 and £23,928 per year for postgraduate study.

Departments

Undergraduate Admissions Office . . . .
. . . . 020 7955 7125
. . . . 020 7955 7757
Graduate Admissions Office . . . .
. . . . 020 7955 7160
Library. 020 7955 6733
Students' Union 020 7955 7158

General Information

Address: Gower Street
           London WC1E 6BT
Phone: 020 7679 2000
Website: www.ucl.ac.uk

Overview

UCL, a constituent college of the University of London, has been a place of diversity from the word go—living very much up to its status as London's Global University. University College London was founded in 1826 by Jeremy Bentham as a progressive alternative to Oxford and Cambridge's social exclusivity and religious restrictions. Thus, it was the first university in England to admit students of any race, class or religion and welcome women on equal standing with men. International students have been a part of the college's

fabric since day one and it was the first English university to offer the systematic teaching of law, architecture and medicine. Bentham even requested in his will that his body be preserved in the name of science and stored in a wooden cabinet, which is on display to this day in the main building of the College. Creepy.

UCL consistently ranks among the top five universities in Britain and is currently in the top ten universities globally. To this day, the science, law and medical departments are still some of its strongest. 20 Nobel prizes have been awarded to UCL academics and students, ten of which were in Physiology & Medicine alone. However, UCL degrees in anthropology, history and the arts are also very highly regarded in their fields.

UCL's many networks of libraries are impressive and an easy place to get lost. The Main Library, designed by William Wilkins, who also designed the similar National Gallery building, focuses on arts and humanities, history, economics, public policy and law. The Special Collections include medieval manuscripts and first editions of works by George Orwell, James Joyce's *Ulysses*, Newton's *Principia* and Darwin's *Origin of the Species*.

There's no such thing as a typical UCL student, as it's such a diverse place. The only thing students have in common is their intelligence and London. Because it's a university with great academics right in the heart of Bloomsbury, it makes for some pretty interesting alums. Where else can you have such diverse graduates as Alexander Graham Bell, Mahatma Gandhi, Ricky Gervais, and all four members of Coldplay?

Tuition

Undergraduate home students (UK/EU) can expect to pay £3,290 per year while overseas students will pay £12,770 per year. The UK government recently decided to not fund university places where the student is studying for an equivalent or lower qualification than they have already achieved. UCL is one of the few London universities who charge only one rate of tuition fee regardless of this. Postgraduate study, therefore, will set you back between £1,705 to £4,865 depending upon subject and level studied. UCL offer numerous bursaries and scholarships for all types of students.

Sports

UCL's sports are as diverse as its students—everything from hockey, rowing and women's rugby to Kung Fu, skateboarding and water polo. The UCLU (University College London Union) is your one-stop shop for campus sports teams and clubs. If you're looking for football, The 90-acre UCL sports ground at Shenley, Hertfordshire, has very high quality pitches. Watford football club even train there. The Union gym (Bloomsbury Fitness) offers facilities for activities such as basketball and personal fitness programmes.

Culture

Being right in the centre of London means that you're never short of something cultural to do. However, UCL stands up quite well. It even has its own museum—the Petrie Museum of Egyptian Archaeology—accessible from the Science Library. Here you're even given your own torch to explore the collection of over 80,000 rare objects DIY (or Indiana Jones) style. UCL also has its own West End theatre, the UCL Bloomsbury, wedged into the maze of main buildings. It's a must-stop for top comedian tours. Jimmy Carr and Ricky Gervais have been known to shoot their stand-up DVDs there. The UCL Union has access to the theatre for at least ten weeks a year, where it is dedicated to student drama and music society performances. Although neither drama, music nor dance are formally taught at UCL, this does not stop the Union's drama club from making it to the Edinburgh Fringe Festival. At UCL, despite the fact that students can really go out just about anywhere in London, many stay loyal to the bars within the Union, and it's usually a great place to meet before a bigger night out.

Departments

Undergraduate & Postgraduate Admissions
.... 020 7679 7742
Student Information Centre . 020 7679 3000
UCL Union 020 7387 3611
UCL Bloomsbury Theatre 020 7388 8822
Petrie Museum.............. 020 7679 2884

General Information

Address: Thornhaugh Street, Russell Square, London WC1H 0XG

Phone: 020 7637 2388

Website: www.soas.ac.uk

Overview

The School of African and Oriental Studies is a specialist college which focuses on the languages, cultures, law and social studies of Africa, Asia, and the Near and Middle East. SOAS, as it is commonly known, is part of the University of London and is the only institution of its kind in the United Kingdom. It has an excellent reputation as one of the leading authorities on African and Asian studies in the world and ranks highly in university charts on the strength of its programmes Originally founded in 1916 to educate and inform British citizens bound for overseas postings, the school began with an Oriental studies' focus and later incorporated African studies. SOAS is nestled in the corner of Russell Square, with another campus up close to King's Cross; its diversity complements the hotbed of academic activity that makes up this part of London.

The college enrolls over 4,000 students and nearly half of the postgraduates are from countries outside of the UK or the EU. They are often seen sitting in Russell Square eating their organic lunch, and chatting (in Swahili or Taiwanese) about their UNICEF internships. SOAS's alumni include members of parliament and royalty of a range of countries from Ghana to Burma. The Crown Princess of Norway went here. Well of course she did. The Norwegians are so PC. Except for whale hunting.

Culture On Campus

One thing to be said about SOAS students is they are serious. The Students Union has a reputation of leaning heavily to the left and is very politically active. SOAS students have been a notable presence at anti-war protests and they are also now rather concerned with environmental causes—campaigning for the reduction of carbon footprints, among other issues. Societies at the college, unsurprisingly, have a very international, 'right-on' flavour, and include the obvious 'Amnesty International Society', 'Campaign for Human Rights in the Philippines Society', 'Model United Nations' and of course the 'Natural Remedies Society' for when these guys need to let their hair down and knock back an entire bottle of Echinacea.

Tuition

Undergraduates home students (UK/EU) can expect to pay around £3,150 per year for a bachelors degree while international students will pay around £11,460. Postgraduate fees for home students are between £2,550 and £12,200 depending upon the subject studied. International students can expect to pay around £12,600 per year.

Departments

Undergraduate Admissions Office
020 7898 4301/ 4306

Graduate Admissions office
020 7898 4300/ 4311/ 4322/ 4361

Library
020 7898 4197

Students Welfare Office
020 7074 5014

General Information

University of London Students Union (ULU),
Malet Street, WC1E 7HY
www.ulu.co.uk
www.thebarflyclub.com/ulu (The Venue)

Overview

Students are the same the world over and in London they ain't no different. In amongst the banter over Bronte and misunderstandings about Marx stands beer, boogying and burgers. Luckily, for over 100,000 of the University of London's students there's a central place to go to make your university years active and sociable—ULU.

You will need to be a member of ULU to get into some of the events, although grabbing a cheeky cheap sarnie in the café shouldn't pose too much of a problem for clued-up Londoners. There are 20 University of London colleges that are eligible for ULU membership including Kings College and UCL. If you are a student at one of the lucky 20 then you've got it made. If not, use your powers of persuasion to get the gold dust of cheap beer and food.

Practicalities

You cannot really get more central. There are a plethora of tube stations and lines within a 5-10 minutes walk, not to mention Oxford Street. The nearest tube, however, is Russell Square (Piccadilly Line) or Goodge Street (Northern Line).

Clubs & Societies (non-sport)

The range of clubs and societies on offer at ULU change more often than Europe's borders. Reason being the turnover of students and the lure from students' own colleges – all the more reason to get down there and sign up now! You've got the usual suspects such as Drama club but it would not be Londontown without a few obscure offerings – Revelation Rock Gospel Choir anyone? Hell, yeah.

Sports

ULU has to cater for thousands of students, but also attract students away from sports clubs in their particular college. Sports, and the bar afterward, is the place to mix with students from the other colleges. Sportswise there's the usual fare – tennis, football, swimming and martial arts – may come in handy for students living in Severn Sisters. There's also Energybase which contains a gym and pool. Amongst other things take your pick from salsa, breakdancing, fencing or rifle club. Now there's one for the CV…

Food & Bars

Lunch Box is ULU's coffee shop, perfectly located on the ground floor for those who want to grab a quick (Fair Trade) coffee or a bargain meal deal—you even get fruit—how healthy. The aptly named **Duck 'n Dive** bar is, erm, a bit of a dive in that usual charming student way, but does have a lively atmosphere and loads of events. There's also **The Gallery Bar** which, despite the rather odd sheets hanging from the ceiling, serves up some wallet and taste bud satisfying treats until 11pm.

Facilities

The **Student Print Centre** will resolve all your reprographics and binding troubles. Wander into the **Student Union Shop** with a clear conscience to grab a Fair Trade snack or a recycled notepad. Open until 7pm on weekdays.

Events

You'll never be without events at ULU. You've got the **Duck 'n Dive** for regular events but there's also live music at **The Venue** hosting up and coming unsigned bands as well as the odd better-known act. For gigs enter ULU on Byng Place.

Learning in the capital has a long and venerable history. University College London (UCL) was the third university founded in England after Cambridge and Oxford and the first to admit students of any race or religion. It even let women in, showing scant regard for their swooning nature and feeble minds. Now there are hundreds of universities, colleges and adult education centres offering a mind-boggling array of courses.

The first port of call for those with a lust for learning or even an empty Tuesday night to fill is Floodlight (www.floodlight. co.uk), which lists 40,000 courses. Fancy brushing up your motorbike maintenance skills at Hackney Community College, getting an NVQ in sugar modelling at the National Bakery School, learning how to create the ultimate kitchen garden at the English Gardening School or studying the nonsense verse of Lear and Carroll at City Lit? The sky is your oyster.

Continuing Education and Professional Development

University College London
Gower Street, WC1E 6BT
020 7679 2000
www.ucl.ac.uk

City University
Northampton Square, EC1V 0HB
020 7040 5060
www.city.ac.uk

London South Bank University
103 Borough Road, SE22 0HU
020 7815 7815
www.lsbu.ac.uk

London Metropolitan University
31 Jewry Street, EC3N 2EY
020 7423 0000
www.londonmet.ac.uk

University of East London
4 University Way, E16 2RD
020 8223 2420
www.uel.ac.uk

University of Greenwich
Park Row, SE10 9LS
020 8331 8000
www.gre.ac.uk

A Little Bit of Everything…

Birkbeck
26 Russell Square, WC1B 5DQ
0845 601 0174
www.bbk.ac.uk/ce/aboutus

Open University
Your home
0845 300 60 90
www.open.ac.uk

Bishopsgate Institute
230 Bishopsgate, EC2M 4QH
020 7392 9200
www.bishopsgate.org.uk

Arts and Lifestyle

University of the Arts London
65 Davies Street, W1K 5DA
020 7514 6000
www.arts.ac.uk

Leiths School of Food and Wine
16-20 Wendell Road, W12 9RT
020 8749 6400
www.leiths.com

The London School of Journalism
126 Shirland Road, W9 2BT
020 7289 7777
www.lsj.org

Glass Blowing Courses
15 Forest Trading Estate, E17 6AL
020 8418 5900
www.glassblowingcourses.co.uk

English Gardening School
66 Royal Hospital Road, SW3 4HS
020 7352 4347
www.englishgardeningschool.co.uk/

London School Of Beauty & Make-Up
47-50 Margaret Street, W1W 8SB
020 7636 1893
www.lond-est.com

Institute Francais
17 Queensbury Place SW7 2DT
020 7073 1350
www.institut-francais.org.uk

London Buddhist Centre
51 Roman Road, E2 0HU
084 5458 4716
www.lbc.org.uk

Athletics and Dance

Circus Space
Coronet Street, London, N1 6HD
020 7613 4141
www.thecircusspace.co.uk

Tokei Martial Arts
28 Magdalen Street, SE1 2EN
020 7403 5979
www.tokeicentre.org

Jump and Dance
400 York Way, N7 9LR
020 7700 7722
www.jumpanddance.com

Regents Canoe Club
Regents Canal, Graham Street, N1
www.regentscanoeclub.co.uk

Docklands Sailing & Watersport Centre
235a Westferry Road, E14 3QS
020 7537 2626
www.dswc.org

London School of Capoeira
1 & 2 Leeds Place, N4 3RF
020 7281 2020
www.londonschoolofcapoeira.co.uk

General Information

NFT Map: 74
Website: www.arsenal.com
Phone: 020 7704 4000
Box office: 020 7704 4040
Location: Highbury House, 75 Drayton Park,
London N5 1BU

Overview

On the British sporting landscape, few other institutions continue to dominate proceedings more than Arsenal Football Club. Arsene Wenger continues to avoid splashing the cash on top names; building a young, thriving team out of foreign, enthusiastic players and homegrown talent. As the club's longest serving manager part of the sport of being an Arsenal fan is counting all Wenger's new grey hairs as he fumes in moody Francais style. The club holds numerous national records and has a trophy room packed with more silver than any other, save Manchester United. T'was not always thus of course. From humble beginnings south of the river, Arsenal built themselves up from roots level, with glory years seeming to come in waves. The mid 80s saw the instatement of George Graham, a hugely popular former player, who began a powerful, muscular side captained by local hero Tony Adams. Wenger has brought in a continental flavour to the team and an invigorating playing style—once a byword for boring defensive football. Following Arsenal is not always an easy ride. It's surprising that so many people still flock to the new Emirates stadium in Holloway given the stupendous ticket prices (anywhere between £30 and £75), and that's if you can even get one, given the six year Membership waiting list. If you're lucky enough to have the £1000s needed for a decent season ticket then you get to sit in a huge, soulless stadium named after an airline company to watch what are ostensibly a bunch of bloody foreigners. On the plus side, those bloody foreigners play some of the most dazzling football in Europe.

How to Get There

By Car: The Arsenal website states: 'Supporters are strongly advised not to drive to Emirates Stadium. The ground is situated in a mainly residential area with an extensive Event Day Parking Scheme in operation. Only car owners with resident's permits will be allowed to park on-street in the designated areas and any cars parked illegally will be towed away'. In other words, don't bother bringing a car.

By Public Transport: Arsenal (Piccadilly Line) is the nearest tube station, around three minutes walk from the ground. Finsbury Park (Victoria, Piccadilly Lines and Great Northern rail) and Highbury & Islington (Victoria Line, North London Line and Great Northern rail) stations are around a 10-minute walk - these should be slightly less crowded.

How to Get Tickets

As Arsenal play some damn sexy football, tickets are not easy to come by. However, in the new, swanky Emirates stadium there is always going to be one or two no-shows or corporate tickets that have slipped into the wrong hands. Members have first dibs on tickets and snap them up but the less scrupulous ones sell them on to make a fast buck. Try Gumtree or matchday touts if you really must. To be honest, it's probably one of the rare instances where it really is worth the hassle.

General Information

Phone: 0871 226 1905
Website: www.cafc.co.uk
Location: The Valley, Floyd Road,
          Charlton, London SE7 8BL

Overview

Thinking of a day out at Charlton? You're a few years late. Back in 2007, The Addicks were mixing it with the big boys. But after several seasons in freefall, Charlton now find themselves in football's third tier. A day out at The Valley isn't even fun for the fans any more.

Where did it all go wrong? It's all gone downhill since Iain Dowie, officially football's ugliest man, took the reigns. He played a brand of football to go with his grotesque looks and got the boot (no, not to his face, that's just how he looks). Inexplicably, Les Reed got the job next – a man with no managerial experience. He lasted a month.

That year they went down to the Championship. And guess what? Last year, they were relegated again.

Charlton used to have a reputation as being a family club. Sadly, these days they're more like that creepy uncle who lives on his own.

How to Get There

By Car: You can leave the M25 at Junction 2 in order to access the A2, heading towards London. When the A2 becomes the A102 (M), take the right hand exit at the roundabout into the A206 Woolwich Road. After passing the major set of traffic lights at the junction of Anchor and Hope Lane and Charlton Church Lane, turn right at the second roundabout into Charlton Lane. Go over the railway crossing then take the first right into Harvey Gardens, with the road leading to the ground. From central London, travel along the A13 until it becomes the East India Dock Road, then take the A102 through the Blackwall Tunnel. Come off at the second junction and take the first exit at the roundabout, then go along the A206 Woolwich Road into Charlton Lane as detailed above. Thanks to the local residents' parking scheme, you'll be hard pushed to find a parking space; try Westmoor Street, Eastmoor Street, Warspite Road and Ruston Road.

By Public Transport: The ground is within walking distance of Charlton railway station, with the Southeastern line running services from mainline stations Charing Cross and London Bridge and services from Cannon Street on Saturdays. You can also take the Jubilee Line to North Greenwich, and then take a short ride on buses 161, 472 or 486 to get to the Valley. Moderate masochists can walk from the tube station.

How to Get Tickets

Unless the unlikely event arises of a successful cup run, getting to see a match shouldn't be an issue. Tickets can be ordered by phone from the Box Office, via the internet at the club's website or in person at The Valley.

General Information

NFT Map: 43
Phone: 0871 984 1905
Website: www.chelseafc.com
Location: Stamford Bridge,
Fulham Road,
London, SW6 1HS

Overview

Stamford Bridge, home to one of the Premiership's 'big four' clubs, is now one of Europe's most glamorous stadiums. However, 'The Bridge' was once an unappealing and daunting shit-hole more used to hosting pitch invasions and fighting hooligans than the well-heeled city types and Russian oligarchs of today. In the '70s and '80s, it was the violent 'headhunters' that made the club unpopular, but as 'The Blues' never won anything, no one took much notice. In recent years, Chelsea have succeeded in wrestling the mantle of most-hated team in England away from Manchester United, largely due to winning things with the never-ending supply of money from Roman Abramovich. The hooligans have all but gone, either priced out or grown up, but the antics of Prima Donna players and their sitcom private lives have been placing cement shoes on the club's image of late. While Chelsea's coffers have meant they've been able to import expensive foreign players, leading to back-to-back title wins in 2004-2006, their homegrown players have spent more time on tabloid front covers than on football pitches. John Terry and Ashley Cole's bed-hopping adventures will make a great airport novel one day but they've left a lot of fans disappointed in the meantime. These are trouble times indeed for the blues; after the departure of celebrated manager Mourinho the top position has seen its own share of turbulence. With superstar coach Scolari sacked and the silverware drying up it seems money can't buy you everything. However, the club continue to qualify for European and domestic titles so at least fans get a chance to see the players excorise their personal demons on the pitch.

How to Get There

By Car: It is possible to drive to Stamford Bridge on match days but it's pretty pointless to do so. Traffic snarls up badly and the effects are felt throughout Southwest London. If you do brave the traffic, remember that Fulham Road is closed off on match days. Parking is a nightmare with most zones given over to residents. Gangs of eager traffic wardens are on hand to make your Saturday afternoon miserable.

By Public Transport: Stamford Bridge is a two-minute stroll from Fulham Broadway tube station. Regular district line underground trains deliver the hordes from central London in a matter of minutes. If the idea of a packed train full of sweaty football fans isn't your idea of heaven, many fans descend at Ealing Broadway and take the ten-minute walk to the stadium instead.

How to Get Tickets

With so many competitions and cups, getting tickets is easier than you might think. The 'big' fixtures—London derby's, Man U, Liverpool and the later cup stages are either impossible to get or crazily priced, but tickets for the less glamorous ties can be picked up from the Chelsea website or box office. Otherwise, cheeky geezers will be on hand to fleece you on match day. You will probably end up in the new West Stand alongside Japanese and American tourists, but that might be preferable to a fat skinhead in the 'Shed.'

General Information

NFT Map: 47
Tickets: 0870 442 1222
Website: www.fulhamfc.com
Location: Craven Cottage, Stevenage Road,
London SW6 6HH

Overview

Fulham like to think of themselves as a family club. The have a quaint little stadium by the Thames; their manager has a speech impediment; they play in Fulham for God's sake. Overlook their sexually charged nickname—The Cottagers—and all seems hunky dory.

That, in part, is why their recent recovery has been so lovely. When Roy Hodgson took the reigns in 2008 they were doomed. But he rescued The Cottagers—seriously. That is easily the most X-rated nickname in football —from relegation and, in 2009, guided them into Europe. The perfect family feel-good story.

That is, it would be—except the club's sugadaddy is barmy passport-chaser Mohamed Al-Fayed. That's the same Mo who owns Harrods, and whose son died with Princess Diana. The same Mo who tried suing, er, Prince Phillip for killing his boy.

That aside, though, Roy has done a sterling job. Craven Cottage is still one of the nicest grounds in London and tickets are relatively easy to come by. Just be wary of that hole in the gents.

How to Get There

By Car: Craven Cottage sits in a leafy, riverside suburb of Fulham. Parking is relatively easy around the ground with plenty of parking meters, although reaching the ground could be difficult as weekend traffic in London is never fun to negotiate.

By Public Transport: Putney Bridge on the District Line is your best bet. Putney also has a mainline station with connections from Clapham Junction and direct trains from Waterloo. Cross the road opposite Putney station and hop on any passing bus. Alternatively, a ten-minute walk down the high street and over the river will get you to the ground.

How to Get Tickets

One of the 'joys' of watching Fulham is that tickets are easy to get your hands on. Many games are available on general sale through the club website. For the biggest matches, priority is given to members but persevere and you should be rewarded. If you can't get a ticket legitimately, you can always take your chance with a tout on match day. Try haggling; due to Fulham's fortunes, you could get lucky.

General Information

NFT Map: 76
Main switchboard: 020 7616 8500
Ticketline: 020 7616 8700
Lord's website: www.lords.org
England Cricket Board website:
www.ecb.co.uk
Middlesex CCC website:
www.middlesexccc.com
Location: St John's Wood,
London, NW8 8QN.

Overview

Even if you know nothing about cricket, don't be put off coming to Lord's. Yes, some games last for five days, and yes, it can still be a draw at the end of it. But as much as anything else Lord's is a fabulous place to come and have a drink. On a hot day the ground is paradise. The sunburnt crowd get slowly boozed up and by the time the players break for tea—yes, tea—few people are concerned at what's going on in the middle. With the polite hum of chatter building up to full-blown drunken singing, it's worth going to Lord's for the atmosphere alone. But when the rabble have calmed down, Lord's is a very genteel place. It's widely seen as the Home of Cricket, and used to house the international governing body. It hosts a heap of England games every year and it's the home ground of county side Middlesex. There's also a year-round gym—you don't even have to be posh to use it—and an indoor training centre. There's even a museum to amuse you when rain stops play. And, rest assured, at some point rain WILL stop play. At the moment Lords holds two Test matches (the marathon international five-dayers) and a handful of England one-day games. These are the ground's showpiece events, where the crowd are at their most boisterous. Middlesex games rarely attract many spectators, and unless you're an old man or a dog you may be in a minority.

How to Get There

By Car: There's little parking around Lord's so, as you'll be parked up all day, public transport will always be cheaper. If you must drive, the ground is off the A4, which turns into the M4.

By Public Transport: The nearest station is St John's Wood (Jubilee Line). Marylebone (Bakerloo) and Baker Street (Bakerloo, Jubilee, Hammersmith and City, Metropolitan and Circle) are both nearby. Marylebone mainline station serves the north and west of the country. London Paddington is a short bus ride away. Dozens of buses run to Baker Street, many of which stop right outside the ground: 13, 82, 113, 139, 189, 755, 757, 758, 768, 771, 772, 773, 797

How to Get Tickets

Getting your hands on England tickets can be tricky. The first few days of a Test match tend to sell out months in advance, though tickets for the last day never go on pre-sale (as the game could be over by then). Similarly, One Day Internationals are normally sell-outs, so it does take a little planning to get in. Check the website over the preceding winter and you might get lucky. If there are less than ten overs in a day due to rain, or if the game's already over, you can claim the full ticket price back. If the weather limits play to between 10.1-24.5 overs (in English, that's up to 149 balls played) you get a 50 per cent refund. Any more than that and you're deemed to have got your money's worth. Middlesex games rarely sell out, however, so you can just rock up on the day, beers in hand, and enjoy the Lord's village.

General Information

NFT Map: 135
Telephone: 020 7582 6660
Website: www.surreycricket.com
the-brit-oval
Location: The Brit Oval, Kennington,
London, SE11 5SS

Overview

What better way to while away a sunny summer's day than at The Oval cricket ground, typically alongside hundreds of other shirkers who also called in sick? The Oval is one of London's twin icons of the game, alongside Lord's in North London, and boasts a rich history stretching all the way back to 1846, when it was converted from cabbage patch to cricket pitch. It now plays host to Surrey County and international test matches, including the biennial England-Australia slugfest 'The Ashes.' Live international cricket remains a boozy, good natured affair with English fanbase 'The Barmy Army' typically belting out salty chants and cheering occasional streakers. County cricket is a mellower, no less enjoyable event, with readily available tickets and a good portion of the crowd more interested in today's paper than the action in front of them. Taxing it ain't.

How to Get There

By Car: Driving to the Oval is not ideal, because parking is near impossible. Should you be willing to risk it, it's situated on the A202, near the junction with the A3 and A24, south of Vauxhall Bridge. As ever with London driving, you'll need your A to Z and nerves of steel.

By Public Transport: The Oval boasts its own, eponymous tube stop on the Northern Line, from which the stadium is a few hundred yards walk. Determinedly overground travellers should alight at Vauxhall, from which Oval is a ten minute jaunt, tops. Buses 36, 185 and 436 stop right outside the ground too.

How to Get Tickets

Tickets for Surrey county matches are relatively easy to get hold of, though seats for some fixtures can only be bought on site on the day of the match. Check www.surreycricket.com/tickets/domestic for a list of fixtures and availability. International matches tend to sell out very quickly indeed—touts or online sales sites like eBay and Gumtree are usually the best option, at a price. Check out www.surreycricket.com/tickets/international for more info. Ticketmaster also offers tickets to all Oval fixtures at www.ticketmaster.co.uk/venue/147862.

General Information

NFT Map: 32
Telephone: 020 8743 0262
Ticket hotline: 08444 777 007
Website: www.qpr.
premiumtv.co.uk
Location: Loftus Road Stadium,
South Africa Road,
Shepherds Bush,
W12 7PA

Overview

Once-itinerant football club Queen's Park Rangers have called Loftus Road—based, confusingly, in Shepherd's Bush—home since 1917, give or take a few seasons. Their footballing fortunes have yo-yoed through the decades: once a whisker away from winning Division One in the years before it became the Premiership; they now scuffle about in the Championship (or second division, in layman's terms), with one eye fixed anxiously on the precipitous drop to Football League One (or third division, it says here). New ownership, including pint-sized F1 oligarch Bernie Eccleston, injected some much needed glamour into the club (prior to the takeover, Pete Doherty was the Hoop's most famous fan). But, amid wacky boasts of Euro domination, Bernie was cut down to size. The years following the sacking of their Italian boss De Canio has seen the hoops' top spot resemble a revolving door in a busy brothel. eight different managers and caretakers have come and gone in two years resulting in tumult on the pitch, too. They're still in the Championship for a start, better stick to cars Bernie.

How to Get There

By Car: Whether you're approaching Loftus Road from the North (from the M1 through the A406 and A40), East (via the A40(M)), South (from the A3 and A219) or West (up the M4 via the A315 and A402 on a wing and a prayer), all routes lead through White City. Once there, turn right off Wood Lane into South Africa Road. Don't even set off withou your NFT Map, or emergency rations For the brave, full details of all journeys are available at QPR's official website listed above.

By Public Transport: The majority of QPR fans are local and rely either on nearby tube stops (White City on the Central Line, Shepherd's Bush on the Hammersmith and City Line), any of buses 72, 95, or 220 to White City Station, or overground train to Acton Central, followed by a quick bus ride.

How to Get Tickets

As long as QPR are knee deep in the Championship, tickets are relatively easy to get hold of, either via the Rangers' ticket website (eticketing.co.uk/qpr) or phone numbers listed above, or by visiting the Loftus Road box office on game days. They're around £25 per person.

General Information

Ticketline: 0844 499 5000
Website: www.spurs.co.uk
Location: Bill Nicholson Way,
748 High Road,
London, N17 0AP

Overview

Even the Spurs die-hard would admit that White Hart Lane is a little scruffy. The team moved into the stadium over a century ago, and it's been growing slowly more dog-eared ever since. Few grounds in the capital are located farther from a tube stop, and it's in a corner of London where even the police dogs walk in pairs. But that's part of the old ground's charm. More than most fans, the Spurs faithful have a tight grasp of history (which could be because there's been no league title there since 1961). And it shows at the stadium—supporters even chant about what a grand old team Spurs are. But that song only gets sporadic outings. Most of the chants that ring around White Hart Lane are about how much the fans hate Arsenal. It's a rivalry that's as intense as any in football—and as Arsenal started out in the south of the city, only moving across the river in 1913, Spurs claim of being Kings of North London isn't such a wild one. And the division has grown deeper since Arsenal moved into their corporate-branded Emirates Stadium. While Spurs have remained in touch with their Jewish roots—old ladies still sell bagels inside the ground—Arsenal have become the bourgeoisie of football. Their fans may sneer down their lattes at the Spurs supporters who piss in the sinks, but be honest—the queue's huge, the game's kicking off: wouldn't you?

How to Get There

By Car: The area's congested at the best of times; on match days, traffic can grind to a standstill. But if you don't mind a bit of gridlock, White Hart Lane is on the Tottenham High Road (A1010) a mile south of the North Circular (A406). This is

easily accessible from junction 25 of the M25, in itself a temple to traffic.

By Public Transport: The nearest tube is Seven Sisters (Victoria Line), which is a 25 minute walk away. But at least if you work up a hunger from all that walking there's hundreds of kebab shops en route. White Hart Lane overland station, which runs from Liverpool Street through Seven Sisters, is a five-minute walk from the ground. Bus routes 279, 349, 149, 259 run closest to the stadium, but many more pass nearby.

How to Get Tickets

Although home games normally sell out, tickets are fairly easy to get hold of. Club members get first refusal at tickets (it costs £32 to join), ten days before going on sale to the public. But few games sell out before this stage, and if you're savvy about the on-sale dates, snapping up tickets is reasonably simple. To get on the season ticket waiting list, you have to become a One Hotspur Bronze Member. This costs £47; but as the club's fortunes are on the rise, the wait could be some time.

General Information

Website: www.rfu.com
Phone: 0870 405 2000
Location: Twickenham Stadium,
Rugby Road, Twickenham, TW1 1DZ

Overview

The home of English rugby, Twickenham is a behemoth of a stadium. An ugly chunk of concrete seemingly dumped from a great height onto a quiet London suburb, Twickenham lacks the charm and character of Ireland's Landsdowne Road and Scotland's Murrayfield, and has been all but pushed to the sidelines by the magnificent Millennium Stadium in Wales. However, the stadium has largely remained a fortress when it comes to England Internationals. Cheered on by 82,000 well-spoken, white-shirted fans booming out 'Swing Low Sweet Chariot' probably helps. Maybe the England players absorb the unfussy and uncompromising nature of their surroundings into their psyche on match days. Critics would argue that their style of rugby is as ugly and bland as the stadium they play in. This would be harsh if England hadn't consistently under-performed after carrying off the Rugby World Cup in 2003. Twickenham also hosts a series of Rugby tournaments and exhibition matches, including the famous 'Sevens', in addition to the occasional Premiership fixture. Outside the Rugby season, the stadium is given over to rock concerts for international bands like Bon Jovi and R.E.M.

How to Get There

By Car: Twickenham is very accessible by road - if you live in the South. The M3 motorway turns into the A316 that passes the stadium, carrying on into central London. Certain roads get closed down on match days so drivers should allow plenty of time. Parking at the stadium is extremely limited and should be booked in advance. Resident permits are helpfully required for all roads bordering the stadium so the best thing to do is park in the general vicinity and walk the rest of the way.

By Public Transport: Mainline trains run to Twickenham station from Waterloo and Reading. London Underground runs to Richmond on the District Line where shuttle buses will take

fans to the stadium (50p outbound. Free return). Hounslow is an alternative Underground station but shuttle buses only run from Twickenham to Hounslow station so you will have to make it to the stadium under your own steam. Bus numbers 281, 267 and H22 all have regular services passing close to the stadium.

How to Get Tickets

England rugby tickets are hot property, commanding higher prices than top football games. As competition games are relatively infrequent, tickets sell out well in advance so keep checking the website for updates on ticket releases. Premiership tickets and friendly matches are easier to come by but will generally sell out. If you don't get lucky in advance, rugby touts (slightly less aggressive than their football cousins) will happily make your wallet lighter for you. Ticketmaster is the best option for concerts or Gumtree and Craigslist for re-sales and swaps.

General Information

Website: www.whufc.com
Phone: 020 8548 2794
Location: Boleyn Ground,
Green Street,
London E13 9AZ

Overview

When bald biscuit king Eggert Magnusson bought the Hammers everything looked rosy. But then the world went tits up. The recession meant Icelander Eggert's companies were suddenly worth nothing. He went bankrupt—and West Ham became Scandinavian IOU. While boss Gianfranco Zola was leading a revolution on the pitch—shepherding a young team to the brinks of Europe—there were real dangers the club would fold.

Currently, West Ham is owned by a consortium that seized the club off Magnusson—made up of, er, Icelandic banks. Not really where you want your money right now. But if they survive, the Irons are on the way up. If you can find the ground in deepest East London they're well worth a look.

Over the years, West Ham has been unfairly tainted by association with the ICF hooligan firm. Largely active in the '70s and '80s, 2005 film, 'Green Street' did its best to rekindle unwanted memories. The drama was undermined slightly by giving the lead role to a hobbit. Such unfortunate associations continue to dog the club, as recent clashes with famed hooligan rivals Millwall brought riots to the streets and pitch invasions inside the stadium. That being said, the appointment of Italian ex-striker extraordinaire Zola as the manager has meant their game results have been more positive of late.

How to Get There

By Car: Driving in London is a waste of time even on the best of days, but try it on match

days and you are asking for trouble. East London is a warren of one way streets, dead ends and no through roads. You are likely to either miss kick-off or get a parking ticket or both.

By Public Transport: The district line will 'whisk' you from central London to Upton Park in half an hour or so. The Boleyn Ground is 5 minutes walk from the underground station.

How to Get Tickets

Unless you want to pay through the nose for tickets against the big clubs, you should be able to find spares for the smaller fixtures. West Ham is a relatively small ground with a dedicated, hardcore following. Being less glamorous than Chelsea et al means that casual fans have a better chance of watching a game for a decent price.

General Information

Phone: 0844 980 8001
Website: www.wembleystadium.com
Location: Wembley Stadium,
Wembley HA9 0WS

Overview

Wembley Stadium enjoys a strang position in the British psyche. For footba fans it's most significant as the scene c England's only World Cup win back in 1966, as well as numerous pitch invasion by angry / jubilant Scottish fans wheneve their national team came down to play Plus, a generation of British bands have grown up dreaming of the day they'd bellow: "hello Wem-ber-ley, are you ready to rock?!!" to tens of thousands of people who've just paid a fiver for a chewy patty of minced spleen 'n' testicles in a dry bun. For these sentimental reasons, then, very few people complained that the National Stadium was a bit of a crap-hole stuck in an inaccessible suburb of West London. By the late '90s the place was looking a bit battered, so they knocked it down and then very, very slowly, and at tremendous, tabloid-scandalising expense, built a replacement on the same site. The result is, just about, worth it. There are none of the blind spots for spectators that the old stadium used to have, plus it has far greater leg-room for 90-thousand-plus people and much more comfortable seating. It also looks fantastically imposing as you walk out of Wembley Park tube with its massive arch curving into the sky. A trip here might not make your knees go "all trembly" as fans used to sing but for football lovers it's one of the world's great venues. They also have a special removable running track for athletics and, to the disgust of "soccer" tourists, they've even let American football" teams play here, too.

How to Get There

By Car: Short of hiring snipers to pick drivers off as they approach the mighty arch, the Stadium could hardly do more to discourage visitors from driving. "Wembley Stadium is a public transport destination. Please leave your car behind," the website primly advises. However, if you are some kind of die-hard, planet-raping petrol-head you'll see signs pointing to the stadium from Great Central Way

onwards. There are very few parking spaces at the Stadium itself and these need to be booked in advance for £25 or £12 for disabled users and, despite the prices, they often sell out. On match days, or when there's anything else happening, the local area becomes residents' parking only, too. Yes, they really don't want you to bring your car.

By Public Transport: The nearest Tube is Wembley Park on the Metropolitan and Jubilee line. Wembley Central (on the Bakerloo line) is about 10–15 minutes walk and there's also Wembley Stadium mainline train station with links all over the country. If you're travelling from outside London there are National Express coaches from 43 different towns and cities.

How to Get Tickets

Easier said than done. 'Club Wembley' have kindly created a 'ten year seat licence'—no doubt to re-coup the massive overspend that accompanied completion of the stadium. These licences give owners access to all major events hosted at Wembley and its worth going on the website to laugh at the ridiculous prices. A 'one-off licence fee' costs from £1,650 to £19,226. Annual season tickets are on top of that. Cloud Cuckoo Land. 'Normal' people can buy tickets to England games through the FA (you need to be a member), for football and rugby cup games through the respective clubs and tickets for one off events and shows through Ticketmaster. It's always worth checking Gumtree.com as you never know who might be flogging off a golden ticket to the highest bidder.

Practice Courts

Aorangi Pavilion

Buses

Aorangi Terrace ("Henman Hill")

No. 1 Court (see right)

Court 18

Court 19

Church Rd

Wimbledon Park

Newstead Wy

Museum

The Wimbledon Shop

Long & Lawn Buffet

Court 14

Court 15

Court 16

Court 17

Centre Court (see right)

Millennium Building

Car Park 3

Somerset Rd

Covered Courts/ Car Park 2

Car Park 1

Maryat Rd

Court 3

Court 4

Court 5

Court 6

Café Pergola

Car Park 5 →

Wimbledon Park →

Court 7

Court 8

Court 9

Court 10

Court 11

Court 12

No. 2 Court

Buses

No. 1 Court

43 1
39 41 36 2 3 5
37 34 4
32 6
35 30 8
33 28 26 10 11
31 24 12
29 A 14 15
27 22 20 18 16 17
25
23 21

Centre Court

512
509 510 511 513
508 308 309 310 311 514
507 307 205 206 207 208 312 515
506 306 204 107 108 109 110 315 516
505 105 209 314 517
504 104 111 519
503 305 203 103 112 520
502 304 102 113 210 315 521
501 303 202 101 114 211 316 522
302 201 Royal Box 212 523
301 318 317

General Information

Telephone: 020 8944 1066
Website: www.wimbledon.org
Location: The All England Lawn
Tennis and Croquet Club,
Church Road, Wimbledon,
SW19 5AE

Overview

New balls please! If it's not pissing it down—which is a big if—Wimbledon's All England Tennis and Croquet Club is the place to witness the world's finest tennis players do battle on rye grass courts, home as it is to the oldest major Championship in the game each June/July. But this is also a place to be seen and to be merry—sure, it's about the tennis, but it's also about strawberries and cream (of which 62,000 pounds and 1,540 gallons worth are sold each year respectively), the free flowing champagne, the celebrity crowd, and the Ralph Lauren-designed ballboy and ballgirl outfits. And if you can't actually get a ticket for the tournament—and the All England Club makes approximately 1,500 of them available each day, if you're prepared to camp out overnight in the queue—you can always sit yourself on Henman Hill at the northern end of the complex, where a vast television screen allows you to watch British players systematically eliminated in typically heartbreaking fashion. Really, we should stick to darts.

How to Get There

By Car: During the tournament, traffic and parking are nightmarish propositions, and you're better off using public transport. Nonetheless, the determined will need to take the A219 from the A3, and turn off left onto Church Road once in Wimbledon itself.

By Public Transport: Wimbledon railway station is a short journey from both Waterloo and Clapham Junction, and is otherwise serviced (Vicar!) by trains from towns right across the South of England. From here, board the London General shuttle bus straight to the grounds; they depart every five minutes or so during the tournament. Tube users should head for Southfields on the District Line, from where a London General shuttle also operates. Those who prefer to saunter can mosey on down Wimbledon Park Road heading south for ten minutes or so, and you can also walk it from Wimbledon Park tube station, heading north-west.

How to Get Tickets

You can (legally) come by tickets to Wimbledon in two ways—one, apply in advance to the public 'ballot', via the website above, in the hope you are selected at random to purchase tickets (closing date end of December). Two, join the serpentine, overnight queues for on-the-day tickets, of which five hundred are usually made available for each of Centre, Number One and Number Two Courts. Then, of course, there are all the other methods of which you're already no doubt aware.

Sports · **Bowling**

Overview

Any bowling buff will tell you that there are two types of bowling in this country. Ten Pin Bowling, the ghastly Americanized import, is by far the most popular among Londoners and the generally disrespectful 'Youth Of Today.' Crown Green Bowling is a far more serene, (elderly) gentlemanly pursuit complete with its own rules and rituals. Of course, bowlers of both persuasions are served in London, ensuring that violent confrontations between the two groups are kept to a minimum.

London's ten pin bowlers are spoiled rotten. As it's now a trendy pastime shot through with irony, there are plenty of old, large basements converted into pristine bowling alleys designed to look retro. There's no chavs in tracksuits on speed around here: the All Star Lanes franchises are heaving with immaculately dressed trendos and hen/stag nights drunkenly bowling and singing in the karaoke booths. However, at a peak rate of £8.50 per person per game (your average game is a mere 10 minutes) you'll have to asses whether it's worth blowing the rent money on one night of fun. Bloomsbury Bowling Lanes does the American chic thing a bit better and its lanes are £36 an hour, which

works out cheaper in a group. They also host cool gigs and DJs occasionally.

For families and the penniless, London has plenty of more 'traditional' British bowling lanes. By this, of course, we mean cavernous warehouses with pumping chart music, scary underage drinkers and sticky air hockey tables. Try the classic Rowans (Finsbury Park) which at its priciest is a mere £3.70 per person per game or Queens (Bayswater) which has also has an ice rink to cool off those skittle blues.

And what of Green Bowling? Well, being an outdoor pursuit in Britain, it's safe to say it is primarily a Summer affair. When the sun is out you'll find bowling greens in all the major parks; Hyde Park offers a set of woods for £5 (with no time limit) May till October.

After suffering at the hands of boho and cheapo Ten Pin bowling facilities you may find that there can be no better way to waste an afternoon than to sit around a bowling green in Finsbury Park with a beer in hand, laughing at your idiot friends' attempts to hit the 'jack.' Maybe those elderly gentlemen are on to something...

Bowling	Address	Phone	Map
All Star Lanes	95 Brick Ln	020 7426 9200	91
All Star Lanes	Victoria House, Bloomsbury Pl	020 7025 2676	4
All Star Lanes	6 Porchester Gardens	020 7313 8363	30
Bloomsbury Bowling Lanes	Bedford Way	020 7183 1979	4
Hyde Park	Hyde Park	020 7262 3474	n/a
Queens	17 Queensway	020 7229 0172	30
Rowans	10 Stroud Green Rd	020 8800 1950	62

Overview

Nothing combines relaxation and hypertension quite like golf, nor indeed knee-length socks, spats and flat caps. For golfing Londoners, opportunities to play must be sought towards the outskirts of the capital, where the city shore is lapped once more by greenery and open space. You can, of course, take your one wood out onto London's pavements and practise your fade drive there, but you're odds on to be arrested if you do.

You'll be better received moving clockwise around London from the North, at establishments such as the Highgate Golf Club and Muswell Hill Golf Club. Both are highbrow member institutions with epic fairways, open nonetheless to the public, as long as that public is wearing a decent shirt. Eighteen holes at each are in the £30-40 range, which is also the case at the Hampstead Golf Club, home of one of England's toughest front nines. Nearby Finchley Golf Club is similarly priced for visitors but also offers some neat specials such as winter green fees in the £25 range and knockdown prices for twelve holes of 'twilight golf'. A little further north, Mill Hill Golf Club is a shade cheaper though no less satisfying.

In the south-east, the Royal Blackheath Golf Club positions itself as the oldest in the world, which might be why playing eighteen holes as a visitor requires a small trust fund, at £50 during summer weekdays. Moving further west, the Central London Golf Centre is a no-nonsense 'pay-and-play' establishment offering nine full-length holes to golfers of all standards for little more than a tenner. The Wimbledon Park Golf Club is another quality members club open to visitors, while nearby Royal Wimbledon Golf Club terms itself a 'very private' club—visitors are welcome but will be required to apply in writing, prove handicap and, in all likelihood, undergo some kind of permanently scarring initiation ritual. Access to each of these Wimbledon clubs kicks off at a chokingly high £70 for eighteen holes. You could buy a second hand Playstation for that. The London Scottish Golf Club on Wimbledon Common is much more like it, at £20 a round, though a pillar-box red top is compulsory for all. Out west, Dukes Meadows Golf Club in Chiswick offers nine three-par holes, a driving range and function rooms, all at a reasonable price.

For golfers who really are determined not to leave Zone One, there is one option after all. Urban Golf, with venues in Soho (W1) and Smithfield (EC1), is the last word in golf simulation, with the chance to play, virtual-style, some of the world's top courses. It also boasts well-stocked bars and chic lounge areas. You just know the purists will loathe it.

Golf Clubs	Address	Phone	Map
Central London Golf Centre	Burntwood Ln	020 8871 2468	n/a
Dukes Meadows Golf Club	Dukes Meadow	020 8995 0537	n/a
Finchley	Frith Ln	020 8346 1133	n/a
Hampstead Golf Club	82 Winnington Rd	020 8455 0203	n/a
Highgate Golf Club	Denewood Rd	020 8340 3745	n/a
Holland Park	Ilchester Pl	020 7602 2226	34
London Scottish Golf Club	Windmill Rd	020 8788 0135	n/a
Mill Hill Golf Club	100 Barnet Way	020 8959 2339	n/a
Muswell Hill Golf Club	Rhodes Ave	020 8888 1764	n/a
Royal Blackheath Golf Club	Court Rd	020 8550 1795	n/a
Urban Golf	33 Great Pulteney St	020 7434 4300	10
Urban Golf	12 Smithfield St	020 7248 8600	15
Wilbledon Park Golf Club	Home Park Rd	020 8946 1250	n/a

Overview

Remember the Levi's ad in the pool hall? The one which had The Clash's *Should I Stay Or Should I Go?* as the soundtrack? Yeah, that one. It conjured up a pretty cool image, right? Unfortunately London's pool halls have not had the retro revamp (is that an oxymoron?) that bowling is currently enjoying (All Star Lanes, Bloomsbury Bowling) so it's rare to actually find a place where you can stand around looking like James Dean, kissing your teeth, chewing on a tooth pick, and generally inviting any hustler to take you on without like, really being taken on by someone from the Russian/Turkish mafia. Of course, if you just want to chill, have a few beers and play some 8-ball with your buddies there is the ever reliable Elbow Rooms (Shoreditch/ Islington/Westbourne Grove) and the slightly less groovy but no less functional Riley's (Victoria/Clapham/Lewisham). The Islington Elbow Room has experienced a couple of shootings of the gun variety in recent years, so try not to spill your pint on anyone as you go from bar to pool table. The Shoreditch Elbow Room has a ping pong table in the summer. Why it is a seasonal attraction is uncertain but us Brits tend to associate sports according to weather it seems. We also inextricably link shooting some pool with having a drink or two, but it is often the lesser red and yellow-balled "pub" pool table (funnily enough) rather than the greater spotted (and striped) genuine American pool table which is found within the confines of the few remaining non-chain traditional pubs in London.The Westbury Bar in Kilburn however, has three American pool tables in a rather swank environment of leather Chesterfields, parquet flooring and red lampshades. Food is pan-Asian and roasts are served on Sundays, adding to a pub vibe. 19:20 in Clerkenwell has more of a pool hall feel with media types taking their game a little more seriously at the end of the working day. If you do fancy something a little more louche, there are many a pool and snooker hall to be found on the edges of central London which can offer a grittier atmosphere. Bomonti on the Kingsland Road is a Russian Bar where various art "happenings", poetry readings and live music nights occur as well as being a near-open all hours venue to play pool. The fact that Pete Doherty has been known to frequent the premises will either pique your interest or put you right off.

Pool & Snooker	Address	Phone	Map
19:20	20 Great Sutton St	020 7253 1920	6
Bomonti	340 Kingsland Rd	020 7923 1548	88
The Elbow Room	97 Curtain Rd	020 7613 1316	84
The Elbow Room	89 Chapel Market	020 7278 3244	80
The Elbow Room	103 Westbourne Grove	020 7221 5211	30
Riley's	638 Wandsworth Rd	020 7498 0432	142
Riley's	16 Semley Pl	020 7824 8261	19
Rowans	10 Stroud Green Rd	020 8800 1950	62
The Westbury	34 Kilburn High Rd	020 7625 7500	68

Tennis

Ah…the other beautiful game, beloved of park fence jumpers and upper class grunters alike. Like many popular sports, tennis may have originated in Britain, but we're pretty consistent in our ineptitude at it. This is not for the lack of trying: the country's capital is packed full of tennis clubs, outdoor park courts and large sports complexes.

Tennis is certainly not as exclusive as it once was, with an hour's playing a lot cheaper than ten-pin bowling, for example. You can mince about amidst leafy surroundings in Hyde Park (Hyde Park Sports Centre, 020 7262 3474), flail in the dark depths of Finsbury Park on a turn-up-and-play basis, or in the luxury of the historic Queens Club (www.queensclub.co.uk, 020 7386 3429 for membership information). Also commendable are the Paddington Sports Club (020 7286 8448) in Maida Vale and the courts in Regent's Park: go to www.tennisintheparks.co.uk for information on, uh, playing tennis in parks. Indicative of the new equalitarian nature of the game are Tennis London International (www.tennislondon.com) who take pride in being 'the largest gay and lesbian tennis group in the UK.' But it's not all democratic: there's always Wimbledon (www.wimbledon.org, which due to the jaw dropping ticket prices, still is as exclusive as it's always been. If you still want to get caught up in the annual tennis frenzy, head to Henman Hill, or Murray Mound, or whatever it's called these days. Essentially a hill outside Centre Court, here you can sit on the grass and watch the action on video screens with all the other poor proles who don't have any kidneys left to trade for a ticket.

Squash

Like some weird secret society, squash players spend their time locked indoors, organised into little private clubs and engaged in an activity which will eventually mess them up. Squash is hard—just ask your poor knees. The squash court is a high-octane containment tank swimming in adrenalin, which explains why Londoners have taken to it with such gusto. A court at Sobell Center (020 7609 2166) in Finsbury Park for example, is near impossible to book at peak times. In Shepherd's Bush, there's the exclusive squash club New Grampians (020 7603 4255) which is lush, but there are sizeable membership fees to match. Be warned—a lot of sports centres don't have squash facilities, but somewhere like the Oasis Sports Centre (0207 831 1804) in Tottenham Court Road is a church to all things sweaty and squashy…and you can go for an outdoor swim afterwards too. For a quirkier court try Maiden Lane (020-7267 9586)—a community centre in a housing estate, which has one beat-up court for £6 an hour. If there isn't a yoga class in progress, that is.

Badminton/Table Tennis

They may be worlds apart in many ways, but badminton and table tennis are usually offered in the same place, and both are 'genteel' sports in which it is almost acceptable to be beaten by the opposite sex (whichever sex you are). Badminton is especially popular across the board, with almost all sizeable sports centres offering courts and equipment. However, if you've any experience in attempting to book a court at most public sports complexes you'll know of the often depressing amount of phone wrangling and frustration that arises from these exchanges. Chief perpetrator is Kings Hall Sports Centre (020 8985 2158) in Lower Clapton, who will test your patience to inhumane limits. The Brixton Recreation Centre (020 7926 9779) caters for badminton and squash players but always sound like they can't wait to get you off the phone; their rates are around £7 for badminton, which is pretty competitive. The Sobell Centre, as mentioned above, also caters for table tennis (doesn't ping pong sound nicer?) and badminton. The best strategy is to phone your local centre to ascertain which racquet sports they cater for and then prepare yourself to be either double-booked, misinformed or given a free session depending on the ability of the desk assistant!

Overview

As the nascent city of 'Londinium' was being named by the Romans in AD 43, in Asia the practice of yoga was entering its third or fourth millennium. Nineteen hundred years on, at last it found its way out west, and London's yoga establishments have flourished ever since. Essentially, the capital's schools can be divided into those concerned primarily with physical fitness—often the larger institutions offering a range of styles—and those with a more spiritual bent. Of the former, Go Yoga in Shepherd's Bush is a fine example, offering yoga and pilates for adults and kids alike, while the popular Triyoga centres in Primrose Hill and Covent Garden are one-stop holistic shops for the upwardly mobile set. More specialised centres include Bikram Yoga College of India in Kentish Town, and its partner Bikram Yoga City—

bring water and a towel for hard wearing specially heated sessions—and the Iyengar Yoga Institute in Maida Vale, which offers a free introductory class. Special mention also goes to Fulham Yogashala, a newish venture offering all sorts including, unnervingly, 'power yoga'. Still, entering the peaceful surroundings of Yogashala is, according to one client, like getting a hug. Those more spiritual schools include the wonderful Sivanada Yoga Centre, an oasis of serenity in the midst of Putney boasting resident yogi teachers, and the Satyananda Yoga Centre in Clapham with its deep focus on yoga-meditation techniques. Shanti Sadam, out west, is also more concerned with inner stillness than downward dogs. And hidden away in Archway, the Kriya Centre runs a series of kundalini yoga classes in humble but hospitable surroundings—Ohm tastic!

Yoga Centers	Address	Phone	Website	Map
Alchemy	Stables Market	020 7267 6188	www.alchemythecentre.co.uk	71
Battersea Yoga	152 Northcote Rd	020 7978 7995	www.batterseayoga.com	140
Bikram Yoga City	6 Vestry St	020 7336 6330	www.bikramyoga.co.uk/studio_city.html	84
Bikram's Yoga College of India	173 Queen's Crescent	020 7692 6900	www.bikramyoga.co.uk/studio_north.html	71
Fulham Yogashala	11 Lettice St	079 5609 1696	www.fulhamyogashala.co.uk	48
Go Yoga	140 Percy Rd	020 8740 1989	www.go-yoga.co.uk	n/a
The Hidden Space	93 Falkland Rd	020 8347 3400	www.thehiddenspace.co.uk	55
Islington Yoga	357 City Rd	020 7704 6796	www.islingtonyoga.com	83
Iyengar Yoga Institute	223 Randolph Ave	020 7624 3080	www.iyi.org.uk	27
Jamyang Buddhist Centre	43 Renfrew Rd	020 7820 8787	www.jamyang.co.uk	112
The Kriya Centre	25 Bickerton Rd	020 7272 5811	www.karamkriya.co.uk	59
The Lotus Exchange	Black Prince Rd	020 7463 2234	www.lotusexchange.com	131
North London Buddhist Centre	72 Holloway Rd	020 7700 1177	www.northlondonbuddhistcentre.com	74
Satyananda Yoga Centre	70 Thurleigh Rd	020 8673 4869	www.syclondon.com	147
The Shala	26 Voltaire Rd	020 8670 0925	www.theshala.co.uk	143
Shanti Sadan Yoga Centre	29 Chepstow Villas	020 7727 7846	www.shantisadan.org	29
Shoreditch Studio	49 Curtain Rd	020 7012 1238	www.shoreditchstudio.co.uk	8
Siddha Yoga Sangham Of Europe	63 Collier St	020 7278 0567		79
Sivananda Yoga	51 Felsham Rd	020 8426 9795	www.sivananda.co.uk	136
Surya Yoga Studio	9 Park Hill	020 7622 4257	www.suryayoga.com	149
Synchronicity	157 Hubert Grove	07956 945 417	www.synchronicitylondon.com	144
Templeton House Yoga Studio,	34 Chiswell St	020 7074 6000	www.templetonhouse.co.uk	7
Triyoga	6 Erskine Road	020 7483 3344	www.triyoga.co.uk	70
Urban Bikram	24 Shacklewell Ln	020 7254 3060		86
Yoga Place	449 Bethnal Green Rd	020 7739 5195	www.yogaplace.co.uk	93
Yoga Therapy Center	92 Pentonville Rd	020 7689 3040	www.yogatherapy.org	80

There's nothing quite like an obesity epidemic to make a city sporty. We're constantly being told that we're swelling to huge new levels. The message is worrying: buck up fatties, or you won't even fit into your own coffin. But with a London Olympics on the horizon, grassroots sport has been thrust into the spotlight. Part of the package that won the Games was to build a sporting legacy. And in the hope that we won't all be housebound when the Olympics rolls into town, lower-level sport is seeing increased investment. London's sizeable ethnic communities have also brought weird and wonderful games with them (American Football? In London? Not in our lifetimes). Dozens of leagues, in dozens of sports, gather every evening to try and beat the bulge.

General tips

A good starting point is the Gumtree website (www. gumtree.com). Their sports and community section is full of ads trying to fills gaps in sports teams. And as it was started by born-to-sweat Aussies, it never lets up in sheer quantity of athletic opportunities. The local press is also a decent bet. All London boroughs have their own newspapers, who cover amateur sports with as much enthusiasm as the professionals. You may never make it in the big leagues, but at least you can be a hero in Camden. But one area where London struggles is with the concept of pick-up games. Perhaps it's part of our reserved nature, but it's unusual to just rock up at a park and challenge whoever's there. By all means try, but you may get rebuked by a stiff upper lip.

Football

Sunday league football in London used to have a reputation of being rough. For many years it was the preserve of hungover builders, who wanted ninety minutes letting off steam by kicking people around. But it's moved on slightly from those days, with a more general acceptance of skill and less emphasis placed on pain. The spiritual home of recreational football is Hackney Marshes. The east London site has a whopping 87 pitches—so many leagues and teams play there that it's worth just turning up and asking around. If you draw a blank there, then the FA website (www.thefa.com) has a club locator search. Regardless of where you live, you'll get a mammoth list of clubs. The hardest part of finding a team in London is narrowing down who it is you want to play for. Five-a-side football is also booming in London. In the city centre, where space is at a premium, it's often the only way of getting in a game. Powerleague (www.powerleague.co.uk) organise leagues around the capital, though these can be pricey. A cheaper option is to head to a leisure centre with a five-a-side pitch. They often run leagues and are less profit-driven than the private companies. Lists of leisure centres can be found on specific borough's website (such as Islington's www. islington.gov.uk).

Rugby

Don't mind drinking pints of your team-mates' urine? Enjoy a good eye-gouging? Then you must be a rugby fan! The Rugby in London website (www.rugbyinlondon. co.uk) is a Bible for lovers of casual violence, as it lists hundreds of clubs, contact details and even training venues and times. Female fans of egg chasing are also well represented. Most teams play around Southwest London, though there's a few more dotted around the city. A full list is on the RFU Women's website (www.rfuwlonse.co.uk). If you don't fancy the full-on ear-biting code of the sport there's a flourishing touch rugby scene in London. In this form of the game tackling is represented by tagging your opponent. It's an altogether less bloody type of rugby, although you're still allowed to indulge in the booze-fuelled rituals that the contact players enjoy. In2Touch (www.in2touch.com) lists a few of these leagues.

Cricket

As a sport that takes up plenty of space, you have to head slightly out of town to play cricket. Most London clubs play in either the Essex, Middlesex or Surrey leagues, in the outskirts of the capital. The Play-Cricket website (www. play-cricket.co.uk) has a full rundown on London clubs.

Athletics and the London Marathon

Every spring, London's runners dust down their gorilla costumes and tackle the London Marathon. If you feel up to it then you have to plan ahead; places are limited and dished out via a ballot. If you need a helping hand in the run up to the race, there's a list of jogging and road-running clubs at www.onesite.co.uk/find/running. As well as getting you in shape, so you don't die after 20 miles, they can help you get a spot in the starting line-up. And if you catch the bug of competitive athletics, there are six clubs who compete in the London Inter Club Challenge (www.licc.co.uk).

Miscellaneous

For fans of all things Irish, there's the London Gaelic Sports Association (www.londongaa.org); American footballers can get their fix with the British American Football League (www.bafl.org.uk); and if tight shorts and sleeveless shirts are your thing there's the British Aussie Rules Association (www.barfl.co.uk; or you could just join the navy).

Airline	Terminal	Phone Number
Adria Airways	North	020 8099 7254
Aer Lingus	South	0871 521 2772
Afriqiyah	South	0870 040 5040
Air Algerie	South	0870 111 1111
Air Baltic	North	0870 190 0737
Air Comet	North	0870 111 1111
Air Europa	South	0844 493 0787
Air Malta	South	0844 493 0787
Air Namibia	South	0870 066 1472
Air Southwest	North	0870 111 1111
Air Transat	South	0870 190 0737
Air Zimbabwe	South	0870 040 5040
Atlas Blue	North	0870 111 1111
Aurigny	South	0870 190 0737
Azerbaijan Airlines	South	0870 190 0737
Belavia Belarusian Airlines	South	020 7752 0445
BH Air (Balkan Holidays)	South	0845 600 0950
bmi	South	0870 066 1472
British Airways	North	0870 574 7747
British Jet	South	0800 091 4444
Brussels Airlines	North	0870 190 0737
Bulgaria Air	South	0870 111 1111
Cimber Sterling	South	0870 111 1111
Clickair	North	0870 190 0737
Croatia Airlines	South	0870 066 1472
Cubana	South	0844 493 0787
Daallo Airlines	North	0870 243 2222
Delta Air Lines	North	0870 876 5000
easyJet	North & South	0870 111 1111
Emirates	North	0870 040 5040
Estonian Air	North	0870 111 1111
Eurocypria	South	0870 190 0737
Flybe	South	0870 111 1111
flyglobespan	South	0870 111 1111
flyLAL Lithuanian Airlines	North	01293 579 900

Airline	Terminal	Phone Number
Flystar Astraeus	North	01293 819 800
Ghana International Airlines	South	0870 60 70 555
Iceland Express	South	0870 066 1472
Karthago	South	0870 111 1111
Kibris Turkish Airlines	North	0870 190 0737
Malev	North	0871 737 8155
Meridiana Airlines	South	01293 596 609
Mexicana	South	0870 574 7747
Monarch Airlines	South	0870 876 5000
Montenegro Airlines	South	0870 040 5040
norwegian.no	South	0870 190 0737
Olympic Airlines	South	0870 111 1111
Onur Air	South	0870 190 0737
Pakistan International Airlines	South	0800 587 1023
Qatar Airways	North	0870 190 0737
Rossiya Airlines	South	0844 493 0787
Ryanair	South	0870 876 5000
SAS	South	020 7393 1201
SATA International	South	0870 066 1472
TAP Air Portugal	South	0845 601 0932
Tarom	North	0870 111 1111
Thomas Cook	South	0870 190 0737
Thomson Airways	North	0844 493 0787
Ukraine International Airlines	South	0870 190 0737
US Airways	South	0844 493 0787
Viking Airlines	South	0844 493 0787
Virgin Atlantic Airways	South	0870 876 5000
Virgin Nigeria	North	0844 412 1788
Wizz Air	South	+48 22 351 9499
XL Airways	South	0870 169 0169
Zoom Airlines	South	0870 240 0055

General Information

West Sussex
RH6 0NP
General enquiries: 0870 000 2468
Lost property: 01293 503 162
www.gatwickairport.com

Overview

"Gatwick is the busiest single-runway airport in the world." No shit. And they say that like it's a good thing. Basically if you've ever had to go to Spain in high summer, you know the reasons why you shouldn't go to Gatwick: it's not on the Tube and, more importantly, the check-in zone is a sweat-filled free-for-all. Realistically, if being in an airport really was some kind of holiday, you wouldn't need to fly out of the place. Gatwick, though clunkier than some of the bigger, flashier airports, is not so bad to deal with if you have patience. There's light at the end of the world's largest air passenger bridge however as BAA sold the airport to Global Infrastructure Partners (of London City Airport fame). GIP have promised a billion-pound overhaul of the airport and its services (don't they all) and speculation in the financial world is that the owners' connections and experience will lead to more flights and airlines using the airport once it's been done up. In even-more-layman's terms, things can only get better innit?

As far as amenities go, the usual suspects are all present, with convivial times available at Britain's premier diluting station, J.D. Wetherspoons, and the glamour of Knightsbridge miraculously squeezed into one of those little airport branches of Harrods—just in case you feel the need to inflict one of their god-awful teddy bears on another country. As far as eating's concerned, you could try something apart from McDonald's but then again why pretend to yourself that you're having a nice time when it's clearly not on the cards for the next few hours?

Which Terminal?

Trains arrive at the South Terminal, and there are more shops here – but if your flight is from the North Terminal, a free automated train will take you on the five minute transfer.

Getting There

A refreshingly good train service—the creatively-titled Gatwick Express (www.gatwickexpress.com) —runs from Victoria every 15 minutes 5.20 am–12:50 am; and hourly during the night. It takes 30 minutes and if you're near the rail hubs it is by far the most pleasant way to get there—though a single journey is going to set you back around £16. First Capital Connect run trains to Gatwick from St Pancras International and London Bridge which costs closer to £8 and take only about 45 minutes. Easybus

coaches from Victoria Coach Station get to Gatwick in 40 minutes, and cost around £2–6 for a single.
To drive to Gatwick from the M25 you need to leave at Junction 7 and carry on southwards along the M23, following the signs. Leave the M23 at junction 9 and again, follow those handy signs to get to the appropriate terminal.

Parking

The short stay car park is recommended for up to five hours at a time, and is incremented every 15 minutes then every hour, with a maximum charge of £22.20 per 24 hours. For long stays there are several parks located 5-15 minutes away (via bus transfers) from the airport. These are best booked in advance. For the official Gatwick car park, charges are £9 per day for drive-up, but much cheaper if you book online.

Car Hire

All the big names are represented, or you can try generic websites such as www.travelsupermarket. com/carhire.

Shops

There is the usual wide range of shops ranging from chemists to food/drink to fashion. Retail stores include Harrods, Monsoon, Nike, Quiksilver, Ray Ban, and Yo! Sushi.

Hotels

Alexander House
Arora International
Cambridge Hotel
Clarion Hotel
Copthorne Hotel
Corner House Hotel
Effingham Park Hotel
Europa Hotel
Express
Felbridge Hotel
George Hotel
Hilton
Holiday Inn
Ibis Hotel
Langshott Manor
Moathouse Hotel
Premier Travel Inn
Ramada Plaza
Renaissance Hotel
Russ Hill
Skylane Hotel
Sofitel Hotel
Thistle
Travelodge
Whitehouse
Worth Hotel

Airline	Terminal	Phone Number
Aer Lingus	1	0870 876 5000
Aeroflot	2	020 7355 2233
Air Algerie	2	020 8750 3300
Air Astana	2	01293 596 622
Air Canada	3	0871 220 1111
Air China	3	020 8745 4624
Air France	2	0870 142 4343
Air India	3	020 8560 9996
Air Malta	4	0906 103 0012
Air Mauritius	3	020 7434 4375
Air New Zealand	1	0800 028 4149
Air Seychelles	2	01293 596 656
Air Transat	2	020 7616 9187
Alitalia	2	0870 544 8259
All Nippon Airways	3	+44 (0)870 837 8811
American Airlines	3	+44 (0)20 7365 0777
Arik Air	2	08444 822324
Asiana Airlines	1	020 7304 9900
Atlas Blue	2	020 7307 5803
Austrian Airlines	2	020 7766 0300
Azerbaijan Airlines	2	0870 760 5757
Bellview Airlines	2	020 7372 3770
Biman Bangladesh Airlines	3	020 7629 0252
Blue1 (SAS Group)	3	0906 294 2016
bmi	1	0870 60 70 555
bmi	3	0870 60 70 555
British Airways	3 & 4 but mainly 5	0844 493 0787
Bulgaria Air	2	020 7637 7637
Cathay Pacific Airways	3	020 8834 8888
China Eastern	2	020 7935 2676
Clickair	3	00 800 25425247
Continental Airlines	4	0845 607 6760
Croatia Airlines	2	020 8563 0022
CSA Czech Airlines	2	0870 444 3747
Cyprus Airways	1	020 8359 1333
Delta Air Lines	4	0845 600 0950
Egypt Air	3	020 8759 3635
El Al Israel Airlines	1	020 7957 4100
Emirates	3	0870 243 2222
Ethiopian Airlines	3	020 8745 4235

Airline	Terminal	Phone Number
Etihad Airways	3	0870 241 7121
Eva Air	3	020 7380 8300
Finnair	3	0870 241 4411
Gulf Air	3	0870 777 1717
Iberia	3	0870 609 0500
Icelandair	1	0870 787 4020
Iran Air	3	020 8759 0921
Japan Airlines	3	0845 774 7700
JAT Airways	2	020 8745 0899
Jet Airways	3	0808 101 1199
Kenya Airways	4	020 8283 1818
Kibris Turkish Airlines	3	020 7930 4851
Kingfisher Airlines	4	0800 047 0810
KLM Royal Dutch Airlines	4	0870 507 4074
Korean Air	3	0800 413 000
Kuwait Airways	3	020 8745 7772
Libyan Arab Airlines	2	020 8750 4066
LOT Polish Airlines	1	0845 601 0949
Lufthansa	1	0871 945 9747
Malaysia Airlines System	3	0870 607 9090
MEA Middle East Airlines	3	020 7467 8000
Northwest Airlines	4	0870 507 4074
Pakistan International Airlines	3	0800 587 1023
Qantas	4	0845 774 7767
Qatar Airways	3	020 7896 3636
Singapore Airlines	3	0844 800 2380
South African Airways	1	0870 747 1111
Sri Lankan Airlines	4	020 8538 2000
Swiss International Airlines	2	0845 601 0956
Syrianair	2	020 7493 2851
Transaero Airlines	1	0870 850 7767
Tunisair	2	020 7734 7644
Turkish Airlines	3	0844 800 6666
Turkmenistan Airlines	3	020 8577 2211
United Airlines	1	0845 844 4777
US Airways	1	0845 600 3300
Uzbekistan Airways	2	020 7935 4775
Virgin Atlantic Airways	3	0870 574 7747
Yemenia Yemen Airways	2	0870 732 3213

General Information

234 Bath Road, Hayes, Middlesex, UB3 5AP
General enquiries: 0870 000 0123
Lost property: 020 8745 7727
www.heathrowairport.com

Overview

We all *love* airports, especially Heathrow. You can play all those xenophobic guessing games with the nationalities of the passengers and mix in a bit of class snobbery concerning which airline they're taking. Then there's all the anticipation and fervour in the air, the relaxed vibes in arrivals department. Yes, we're being sarcastic. Heathrow is resplendent in all the main offenders: infinite queues, bad food, draconian security and the acrid scent of 'the British on holiday,' which should fill every Briton with fear and dismay It's way overcrowded and has tiresome security checks; delays; queues; overpriced shops; terrible food and a tendency to lose baggage. Even our ex-mayor Ken Livingstone has accused Heathrow of keeping people "prisoner" in its "ghastly shopping mall." There does seem to be slow, gradual improvement but it's still a long way from what it should be, and gives a poor first impression of the UK.

For years Heathrow has been stretched beyond its capacity but is currently in mid-transformation. Terminals 1 and 2 are being turned into something called Heathrow East while Terminal 5 has picked up the baton following a chaotic opening a few years and tears ago. The new terminal has taken the annual passenger count to 90 million, placing the airport in contention for busiest in the world. Talking of new terminals there's yet another on the cards along with a controversial third runway. The local residents might not like it but at least they don't have to suffer an hour on the tube to catch a flight. On a positive note the transport services have been vastly improved: new motorway access, a terminal 5 stop on the tube and, uh, well that's it for now.

Which Terminal?

Heathrow is in a seemingly constant state of flux, so confirm before you travel.

Terminal 1 is due to be demolished in a few years but currently deals with domestic flights, UK airline flights to Europe, EL AL, South African and United. **Terminal 2** has retired in the corner, waiting to be demolished. **Terminal 3** is the long haul terminal for Asian and Asia Pacific airlines, US and South American, plus most African and Middle Eastern carriers. **Terminal 4** deals with North African, European airlines and miscellaneous other rogue airlines. **Terminal 5** is pretty much the throne of British Airways.

Terminals 1-3 are within walking distance of each other (up to 15 minutes) so just follow the signs. You can transfer (for free) to T4 on the Heathrow Connect train and T5 on the Heathrow Express. There is also a free bus which connects T4 and T5, every 6 minutes.

Getting There

The London Underground's Piccadilly Line can get you to central London in less than an hour for only about £4. The wait time for a train is generally no more than 10 minutes. Heathrow has three underground stations; one servicing terminal 1, 2 & 3, and one each for terminals 4&5.

Heathrow Express is a non-stop train between the airport and Paddington every 15 minutes, "In 15 minutes— every 15 minutes". It stops at Heathrow Central Station (T1-3) and the new T5. £16.50 one way

Heathrow Connect follows the same route into west London, but serves intermediate stations making its journey time 25 minutes. Trains depart Paddington every 30 minutes from Platform 12, stopping at Heathrow Central (Terminal 1,2,3) and Terminal 4. £7.90 one way. Passengers arriving at T5 may catch the Heathrow Express free of charge to Central station if they wish to use Heathrow Connect into town.

Both these trains run between approx 5 am–12 am. There are also three tube stations—a cheaper and slower option. Roughly £4 for an hour's journey to central London. During rush hour it gets packed with commuters.

National Express run a bargain bus from London Victoria station which only costs £5 one way. It takes anywhere from 45-75 minutes and drops you off at Heathrow Central bus terminal (T1,2,3)

Driving from Central London takes about 45-60 minutes—well anything really—depending on traffic. When leaving Terminals 1–3, follow exit signs to the access/exit tunnel. Then follow signs to the M4 motorway, which will eventually bring you into London. A taxi to central London takes 45-60 minutes and costs £35+.

Car Parking

There are short-term and long-term car parks, both are expensive. An hour at the short stay is £4.30, 48 hours is £93.80. The long stay car park is about 10 minutes away by courtesy bus and the drive-up price is £15.60 per day.

General Information:

Royal Docks,
London, E16 2PX
General Enquiries: 020 7646 0000/88
www.londoncityairport.com

Overview

With its one wee runway squeezed over the water between the old George V and Royal Albert Docks, City is London's smallest and most central airport (6 miles from the City of London). Where once stevedores ate pie and mash, stockbrokers are now whisked off to lunchtime meetings on dinky short take-off jets. Primarily used by business types, its small size and short runway means City only serves European destinations (20 in total, although British Airways do have a flight to New York in the pipeline) from its single terminal and 22 check-in desks. Still, this means much faster check-in times and fewer delays than at the comparative behemoths of Heathrow and Gatwick.

Getting There

In 2005 someone, somewhere, saw the light and extended the DLR (Docklands Light Railway) to City. The airport now couldn't be simpler to get to by public transport: get on the DLR at Bank; make sure you take a train destined for the King George V branch (these are marked "via City Airport"); and you'll arrive at the airport's station in 25 minutes. A slightly quicker route is to take the Jubilee Underground line to Canning Town and take the DLR a mere three stops westbound from there. There is a taxi rank directly outside the terminal exit, expect to pay at least £35 for a black cab to go

to or from the West End. Don't expect the journey to be much faster than on the DLR/Underground. Pre-booked cabs should be a little cheaper, try Airport Executive (020 8838 3333) or the trusty Addison Lee (020 7387 8888).

If you're driving—given its central location—there's no obvious route to City. A useful general rule is to point your wheels at the eastern end of Central London and then keep going that way from Tower Hill on the A1203 (East Smithfield/The Highway). The airport is signposted from this road. If you're getting there from the South East, head through the Blackwall tunnel and follow signs once you emerge into the daylight. If you're near the M25 and like traffic jams, crawl your way to junction 30 and take the Thames Gateway to the airport from there.

Parking

Short stay is directly next to the terminal and rates start at £8 for one hour going up to £82 for 48 hours.

You can also have your car valet-parked for no extra cost (apart from having to tip the man entrusted with not scratching your pride and joy).

The long stay carpark is a short walk from the terminal and will relieve you of £14 for up to four hours, £24 for 4-12 hours, £36 from 12-24 hours, or £72 per day if you stay two or more days.

So parking is expensive. If you still feel the need to park and can book in advance, get in touch with BCP airport parking for a (slightly) cheaper option at www.parkbcp.co.uk.

Car Hire

Avis 020 7646 0832
Europcar................ 020 7646 0844
Hertz 020 7476 9646

Hotels

Etap Hotel London City Airport,
North Woolwich Road, Silvertown,
London, E16 2EE
020 7474 9106

Custom House Hotel Excel Docklands,
272-283 Victoria Dock Road, London,
E16 3BY
020 7474 0011

Premier Travel Inn
Excel East, Royal Victoria Docks, Canning
Town, E16 1SL
0870 238 3322

Novotel London Excel
7 Western Gateway Royal Victoria Dock,
London, E16 1AA
020 7540 9700

Ibis London Excel
9 Western Gateway, London, E16 1AB
020 7055 2300

Sunborn Yacht Hotel
1 Royal Victoria Dock, London, E16 1SL
020 70599100

Holiday Inn Express
1 Silvertown Way, Docklands, London,
E16 1EA
020 75404040

Travelodge London City Airport Hotel
Hartmann Road, Silvertown, London
E16 2BZ
0871 9846290

Airlines:

Aer Arann

British Airways

CityJet

KLM

Lufthansa

Luxair

SAS

SunAir

Swiss International Air Lines

VLM Airlines

General Information

London Luton Airport
Navigation House
Airport Way
Luton, Bedfordshire LU2 9LY
General enquiries including lost property:
01582 405100
www.london-luton.co.uk

Overview

To call Luton Airport a 'London' airport is surely one HUGE marketing scam. In fact, calling Luton Airport an 'Airport' is pushing it: the reality is it's one huge shit pit that airplanes depart and arrive from occasionally. The same tragedy happens everyday: the unsuspecting traveller smugly enters their credit card details as they book their £2.99 easyJet flight to some godforsaken club 18-30 resort on the Spanish coast, thinking they got the best deal *ever*. One big problem. The flight's from Luton Airport—which should stop any celebrating London traveller dead. Unless you live in North London, getting to and from Luton by public transport is awful. It consists of taking an unreliable half-hour train service from St Pancras or London Bridge to Luton Parkway. After your train journey, if you're lucky, you'll be met at Luton Parkway by a shuttle bus. Be sure to purchase your rail tickets with London Luton Airport as your final destination. If your plane is delayed past midnight, which most budget airlines

tend to be, God help you. Where's the Luton Express you might wonder? Ha ha. Good question...

Once you get to the one-terminal airport, your travelling companions will be the kind of people who hunt down the absolute cheapest airfares for their raucous stag or hen nights. Inside security, the few shops and cafés of the Pret a Manger and Dixons variety, will be teeming with these unsavoury characters. So next time you select 'all London airports' when booking your weekend getaway—think carefully!

Getting There

This can be extremely tricky and there's really no easy way. What with a Tube journey to St Pancras or London Bridge station, a train journey, and finally a shuttle bus, you better pack light. Also, you really don't want to get stuck sleeping in the airport when the shuttle bus stops at midnight.

Coach services, such as the 757 Greenline (collaborating with Terravision), easyBus and National Express are good alternatives that will at least get you home if your flight comes in late. Greenline & Terravision are probably your best bet (0990 747 777) with pick-up and drop-off points on Buckingham Palace Road, Marble Arch and Baker Street. Prices are from £13 and it takes about an hour, but it runs pretty regularly through the night. The National Express (08705 80 80 80) service 421 also operates between Luton, Heathrow Airport and London Victoria.

London Luton Airport is somewhat accessible from both the M1 and M25. If you have a choice, go for the M1, as the airport is only about five minutes from junction 10. Without traffic, it can take c. 45 minutes from central London. This can sometimes be longer when there are extensive road works, which tends to be always. When using Sat Nav systems, use the postcode LU2 9QT.

How To Get There – Really

Seriously. You've paid next to nothing for your airfare, splash out on a private cab. If you book a licensed mini-cab ahead of time, the service is often cheaper than the equivalent black cab fare and definitely easier, as they'll meet you at the arrivals hall. A consistently cheap company is Simply Airports (020 7701 4321) which is usually under £55, but you may want to get a quote from your own local company. If you leave it to the last minute, and must take a black cab, get ready to shell out at least £85 (with their meters, can increase with traffic) plus a meeting fee if you want them to wait for you. Cab rides from central London usually take about an hour.

Parking

Short Term Parking is pricier but situated closest to the terminal, with prices ranging from £3 for 15 minutes, to £480 for 16 days. Mid-term is ideal for stays of around five days and is about a five-minute transfer by bus. Prices can vary from £11.25 to £17.00 per day dependent on length of stay. Long-term parking is about 10 minutes from the terminal by bus, and can be booked ahead of time online (www.ncp.co.uk) to save money. Prices range from £12.50 per day for up to four days to £90 for eight days. NCP can be reached on 01582 395484 (9 am–4 pm) and 07734 595560 in an emergency.

Rental Cars

Hertz Rent A Car 01582 450333
Avis Rent A Car Ltd 01582 454040
Thrifty Car Rental 01582 416222
National Car Rental. 01582 454554

Shops

Luton has a small selection of shops and is slowly getting better, but don't expect too much. There is a Boots (chemist/drugstore), a newsagent, and somewhere to eat/drink.

Hotels

Chiltern Hotel Luton
73 Beechwood Road; 01582 575911

Days Hotel Luton
Regent Street; 01582 878 090

Express by Holiday Inn Hotel
2 Percival Way; 01582 589 100

Holiday Inn Luton South
London Road; 0870 443171

Menzies Strathmore Hotel Luton
The Luton Arndale Centre; 01582 734199

Airlines

Aer Arann

Blue Air

easyJet

El Al

Flybe

Monarch

Ryanair

SkyEurope

Thomson

transavia.com

Wizz Air

General Information

Address: Stansted Airport,
Essex CM24 1QW
General enquiries: 0 870 000 0303
Lost property: 0 1279 663 293
Left luggage: 0 1279 663 213
Police: 0 1245 452 450
Website: www.stanstedairport.com

Overview

It might be tucked away in the middle of the dull Essex countryside, but Stansted Airport has one thing going for it—it's amazingly simple. One terminal (and quite a nice one too, Norman Foster saluted), one check-in area, one security gate. Take that, Heathrow. Around 20 airlines, most of them budget, fly more than 20 million passengers from here to a growing list of mainly domestic and short-haul destinations. If you're budget-crazy enough to fly in the middle of the night, there are several breakfast opportunities. Eating options are generally better before security—unless you like tiny, overpriced ciabatta baguettes or the sugar-drenched fare offered by the big coffee chains. But once through, you can settle for a few surprisingly average-priced pints at Est Bar Est and grab a sandwich on the run once you hear your name being called for the third time. On the downside, the ridiculously long walk to your gate is often obstructed by screaming children or singing hen-night crowds. And the queue at border control is, at most times, long enough to make you reconsider the whole affair and just run back to your plane.

Getting There

Public Transport

Stansted might seem a long way from London, but getting there by public transport is surprisingly easy. All you have to do is choose between the train (fast) and the bus (cheap). Several train operators serve the airport from Liverpool Street Station. But before you start struggling with too many timetables for trains that stop at too many stops, opt for the dedicated Stansted Express (www.stanstedexpress.com; 08456 007 245). The service runs every 15 minutes and takes you to the airport in 45 minutes straight. Tickets start at £18 and can be bought online, from the ticket office or a ticket machine. Buses will take an hour to take you to the airport, and longer if there's a lot of traffic, but single tickets start at £2. A number of operators fight for your custom, the main ones are: Terravision (01279 680 028; www.terravision.eu) leaves from Liverpool Street Station and Victoria Station. The slightly more expensive National Express (08705 747 777; www.nationalexpress.com) connects to the same stations but some buses also stop in Stratford and Golders Green. Easybus (www.easybus.co.uk) gives you the intimacy of a small mini-van, stopping in Baker Street and Victoria

Station. If you're traveling during the rush hour, take a book. Whitechapel Road is one of London's most bustling streets, but it will get boring at some point.

Driving

If you're fortunate enough to have a car, or managed to convince your dad-in-law to lend you his, find your way out of the city via Stratford and hit the M11. It's a straight drive from here and amid Essex' greenery, the airport is hard to miss. Cab drivers will know how to get you to the airport, but will probably charge you a small fortune for it.

Parking

Daily parking rates start at £2.50 for the first half-hour and rise in steps to £26.40 for 24 hours. Long-term parking, in the intriguingly christened Pink Elephant car park, will cost you £9 a day. If you're in for a weekend trip, opt for the mid-stay car park, which is closer to the terminal than the Elephant and charges £12.50/day. The airport recently introduced valet parking, which can be pre-booked on 08708 502 825. Once there, drop your car at the end of Set Down Lane; the pick-up point is next to the Fast Track car park. For discounts on all Stansted parking options, call BAA Advance on 0121 410 5228 and book your parking lot before you head off.

Car Rental

Hertz, Check-In Concourse............ 0 8708 460 005
Budget, Check-In Concourse.......... 0 1279 681 396
Avis, Check-In Concourse 0 8706 086 364
Europcar, Check-In Concourse 0 1279 680 240
National, International Arrivals Concourse ....
.... 0 1279 506 534

Shops

Stansted has the usual selection of 'small airport shops', more aimed at passing the time than serious purchases.

Hotels

Hilton National Hotel, Enterprise House, Bassingbourne Road, Essex CM24 1QW , 0 08700 000 303

Radisson SAS Hotel, Waltham Close, London Stansted Airport, Essex CM24 1PP, 0 1279 661 012

Express by Holiday Inn, Thremhall Avenue, Stansted, Essex CM24 1PY, 0 1279 680 015

Airlines

Aegean Airlines	norwegian.no
Air Arabia Maroc	Pakistan International
Air Berlin	Pegasus Airlines
Air Malta	Ryanair
Air Moldova	Snowjet
Air Asia X	Turkish Airlines
Atlantic Airways	(There's only one
Aurigny	terminal)
Blue Air	
Cyprus Airways	
easyJet	
El Al Israel Airlines	
Esprit Ski	
Germanwings	
Kibris Turkish Airlines	

Overview

If the Underground had a motto it wouldn't be "Mind the gap" but "Sorry for any inconvenience caused." But as we grumble and ponder if anyone is ever actually sorry for squeezing you 30m below the surface, in a sweat-box held together by dust, rust and expensive fares, the magnificence of the 'Tube' network should really be appreciated. Across its 250-odd miles of track the Underground will take you to 275 stations spread the length and breadth of London (although with disproportionately few lines reaching into south London). The system is well integrated with the bus and overground train networks and—with the advent of the Oyster card—most of these share a common ticketing system.

When fully functioning, the Underground will get you across town quicker than the bus and without the complicated timetables and schedules of overground trains. When it is struck by signal failures and breakdowns, which is very often, it can be excruciatingly slow and get very overcrowded, very quickly. In conclusion: the Underground won't necessarily get you anywhere on time, in style or in comfort, but it will (eventually) get you pretty much anywhere.

Fares

The vast majority of the network is divided into concentric fare rings or zones (1-6). Zone 1 covers central London, zone 6 covers the outskirts of London. Fares are dependent on how many zones your journey includes and there's a premium for travelling in zone 1. Peak fares (Monday to Friday from 4.30-9.30 am and 4-7 pm) are from 50p to a few pounds more than off-peak, although journeys limited to zone 1 do not benefit from the off-peak discount. Your best bet is to get an Oyster Card—lowest single fare is £1.60 off-peak (£2 peak) instead of £4 if you pay by cash. Oyster Cards are available for just £3 from vending machines. It's a total no-brainer. The total amount that can be deducted from your Oyster card is also capped over a 24-hour period to match the equivalent cost of a one day travel card.

So the fare system is complicated, but if you take £1.60 (which will get you a single journey within zone 1 with an Oyster card) as a base rate, and add to this the further out of zone 1 you travel, things become clearer. If you feel the need to marvel at the full intricacy of the fares and ticketing system, give yourself eye-strain at Transport for London's website www.tfl.gov.uk.

Frequency and Quality of Service

The vast majority of centrally-located stations will have a train at least every three minutes most of the day. At the very beginning and end of the day service frequency tails-off and can get as low as eight minutes between trains. Trains are also much less frequent at the further reaches of some lines—the Metropolitan line has trains only every 20 minutes from its most north-western stations, even during peak times. Almost all lines have a reduced frequency on Sundays. First trains are 05:00-05:30, last trains are between midnight and 12.30. Last trains are generally safe; expect a slightly raucous mix of pickled after-workers and overly obsequious rough-sleepers rather than any real troublemakers. Mayor Boris Johnson's initially controversial booze ban seems to have been accepted now. The whole network is currently having £5bn thrown at it to try to get things ship-shape for the 2012 Olympics. As a result, line closures are common at weekends, so check before you travel.

Lines

Bakerloo: (Brown coloured on maps) Runs from Harrow & Wealdstone in the north west to Elephant & Castle in the south east.

Central: (Red) Runs from West Ruislip in the east to Epping in the far north east. The central section is buried under Oxford Street and has four stops on the street, the quietest usually being Bond Street.

Circle: (Yellow) Notoriously slow and unreliable. Circles the circumference of the city centre. Shares almost all of its track and stations with other lines so don't necessarily bother waiting specifically for a dedicated Circle Line train. Look out for the 'Platform for Art' as you pass Gloucester Road station.

District: (Green) One of the few lines to serve deepest south London, branches run into Richmond and Wimbledon in the southwest and also to Ealing. The line continues up to Upminster in the northeast. Almost all of the branches of this fragmented line come together at Earls Court station into an infuriating mess, so plan ahead if changing there.

East London: (Orange) Currently chewing up North East London with its expansion into Dalston.

Hammersmith & City: (Pink) Starts at Hammersmith in the west of the city before heading north to Paddington and continuing east to Barking. Take it to Ladbroke Grove if heading to the Portobello market.

Jubilee: (Silver) Silver coloured as it opened in the year of the Queen's Silver Jubilee in 1977, the line serves northwest, central and east London, including the Canary Wharf business district. The section east of Green Park is the most recent addition to the network (it opened in 1999) and has a number of architecturally exemplary stations.

Metropolitan: (Dark Purple) The oldest of all the lines, this granddaddy of metropolitan underground railways strikes far out in the suburbs and countryside northwest of the city from its central root at Aldgate.

Northern: (Black) Presumably given black as its colour to reflect the dark mood of anyone unlucky enough to have to commute on it, the Northern line is the overcrowded spine of London, covering vast swathes of the city centre, the north and the south.

Piccadilly: (Dark Blue) From Cockfosters in the far northeast this line trundles all the way to Heathrow airport, with some of the most popular tourist spots in between. It's a very cheap way to the airport but is also the slowest. Southgate and Arnos Grove stations are both 1930s modernist brilliance.

Victoria: (Light Blue) Runs from Walthamstow in the north to Brixton in the south. This musty line is currently undergoing refurbishment and will feature new trains and track by 2011. In the meantime, check for early closing and shutdowns, particularly during weekends.

Waterloo & City: (Turquoise) No-one has ever met anyone who has been on this line. Erm, it has two stations, Waterloo and Bank, and is designed for suited and booted commuters coming in by train from Waterloo. No trains on Sundays.

London Overground: (Orange) TfL took over part of the overground rail network, notably the somewhat shabby and North London Line which runs from Richmond to Stratford. Just think of it as an extension to the tube network.

Bicycles

Bicycles are generally only allowed on the tube outside peak hours and only from stations outside central London. They are not permitted on the Victoria or Waterloo and City lines at all. Folding bicycles can be taken on all sections of the Tube free of charge.

General Info

Website: www.tfl.gov.uk/dlr
Phone: 020 7363 9700
Lost property: 020 7363 9550

Overview

Not quite a tram, tube or train, it's simply the Docklands Light Railway, a nifty little thing that makes getting to places like Greenwich Village and City Airport easy and cheap. Launched in 1987 with a modest 11 trains and only 15 stations, the regeneration of the Docklands area has seen it grow to 94 trains covering 38 stations and counting. Serving the east and Southeast of the city, it is pretty much as pleasant as London public transport gets. It's reliable, less noisy than the tube, generally less crowded and it's pretty well air-conditioned. The DLR is also fully-automated and most of the time there is no driver, meaning that you can take the front seat and pretend that you're actually driving the thing.

The DLR provides a key service for London's suits, with the Bank to Canary Wharf journey taking just over ten minutes. For normal people, Canary Wharf also makes an interesting/unusual weekend destination. Almost completely deserted, a stroll amongst the abandoned skyscrapers is a strangely satisfying way to spend a Sunday afternoon.

With the Olympic games invading East London in 2012, there's quite a bit of engineering work going on. Stations are being adapted to cope with longer trains and they're also building an extension to the new Stratford International Station and the nearby Olympic Park. Expect some disruptions to service over the next few years and check the website before you travel.

Fares

As on the rest of London's public transport you're best off with an Oyster card. One thing to remember is that there are no barriers at DLR stations and instead Oyster readers are located at station exits and entrances. To avoid getting slapped with a fine and to ensure you're charged the right amount, remember to touch in and out correctly. The prices are similar to the tube, so cash works out more expensive, though not as expensive as the tube with its £4 cash single.

Hours

The DLR runs 5.30 am–12.30 am, with train frequencies depending on the time of day. During peak hours, there's usually a train every three minutes or so, but even on Sundays you shouldn't have to wait more than 10 minutes.

General Information

National Rail Enquiries 08457 48 49 50
Tickets. www.thetrainline.com;
. . . . .also websites of individual franchisees
Eurostar . . . . .08705 186 186 or
. . . . .0 1233 617 575
. . . . www.eurostar.com

Overview

The railways are one of the great British inventions but, unfortunately, the Victorians who built the network in this country did slightly too good a job. Every generation since has taken one look at the massively expensive task of modernising them and scuttled back into their Ford Fiestas. So, while France, Germany and Japan got on with building super-speed bullet trains Britain was stuck with an uneasy compromise between the technologies of 1950 and 1850. This doesn't mean that you shouldn't use trains. It just means that it's probably best to avoid them at peak times. That's when London plays a cruel trick on people who choose to live in places with names like 'Gravesend' and 'Slough' by making them lurch slowly with less personal space than the legal minimum for cattle. During off-

peak times train travel can, in contrast, be positively pleasant. It's a great way to see the countryside, every city and major town in the country is connected, and, if you book far enough in advance and shop around on sites like www.megatrain.com it can be less expensive than you'd think. In London itself, the Thameslink improvement programme will help a little; Crossrail will (eventually) arrive; and pay as you go Oyster will be grudgingly accepted by all train operators.

Stations

Broadly speaking, Euston and King's Cross stations serve the north of the country, Liverpool Street the east, Victoria the south, Paddington and Marylebone the west.

Eurostar

The King's Cross area is also home to the splendid St Pancras—the terminal for the Eurostar train service which connects Britain with the rest of Europe. Since November 2007 it's been possible to get from here to Paris or Brussels in around two hours—with connecting trains to Siberia and beyond.

Charing Cross Station

NFT Map:	24
Address:	12-30 The Strand, London WC2N 6RQ
General enquiries:	020 7839 2576
South Eastern Trains:	08706 030405
Southern Trains:	0845 123 7770

Overview

Perched at the top of the Strand amidst popular tourist attractions such as Trafalgar Square and with the majestic 1865 Charing Cross Hotel being part of the station, you may presume that a cornucopia of ornate delights lies within. Well, it's a dump; the chances of "Brief Encounter" being remade here are pretty slim. But your chances of being barged by a curmudgeonly office worker are very good, what with it being the fifth busiest rail terminal in London. Still, can you blame them for wanting to get out of the place so quickly?

With services to south London and Kent, even the pigeons give the concourse here a wide berth. It's also home to possibly the worst station pub in the country; "The Boadicea" excels in the areas of soullessness and morbidity, likely to satisfy only the hardened alcoholic on their third liver with a preference for pubs that reek of urine. If only Dante had been able to sample this place…

Tickets

There is a small ticket office open some 20 hours per day, and three banks of ticket machines in or around the concourse.

Services

If you're in need of a quick bite, there's a decent variety of food outlets to cater for all tastes, whether burger-lover (Burger King) or health food freak (Cranberry). Indulge your Schadenfreude by watching the beleaguered information guy having to dispense a plethora of poor excuses as to why the 17.34 to Margate was cancelled. And those kinky souls with a tie fetish will love Tie Rack.

Natwest and Bank of Scotland cash machines can be found on the concourse, as well as a Barclays in the front entrance.

Public Transport

The station is easily accessible by Charing Cross station (Northern & Bakerloo lines) and also the adjoining Embankment station (Circle & District lines). The nearby Trafalgar Square is a major hub for buses—especially night buses for post-West End madness—which inch their way out to places as far apart as Harrow and Crystal Palace.

Euston Station

NFT Map:	78
Address:	Euston Road NW1 2RT
General enquiries:	020 7922 6482
Lost property:	020 7247 4297
First Scotrail:	0845 601 5929
London Midland:	0844 811 0133
London Overground:	020 7222 5600
Virgin Trains :	08457 222 333

Overview

Easily the ugliest station in London, Euston creeps up as you nervously edge along Euston Road. The first inter-city terminal built in London, it was originally constructed in 1837, but the lovely original was demolished to make way for the monstrous concrete-and-glass coffin which now squats next to the mail depot. Since privatisation the interior has become an identi-kit British rail station with more chain businesses per head than is morally decent. Thanks Network Rail.

It's not all doom and gloom, however. Within this architectural eyesore you'll find a scarily concise summation of human nature. Like most busy stations, there's plenty of eccentricity and electricity here: abandoned Tube tunnels; stressed-out coffee guzzling power-commuters; fresh-faced backpackers sprawled out on the floor ; and the infamous beggar who — to the delight of football lovers everywhere except in Manchester — was arrested for punching Manchester Utd manager Sir Alex Ferguson.

The station is London's gateway to the north west of England and Scotland, and also North Wales. As such it is the point of entry for Scousers, Mancunians, Glaswegians and more. Virgin trains (www.virgintrains.co.uk) to Glasgow can take as little as 4 hrs 10 mins.

Tickets

The ticket cashiers may have the glazed look of Kafka-esque zombies but the cleaning staff are often more helpful. Just use the Fasttrack machines!

Services

There's plenty of eating and drinking options, all of the 'chain' variety. Of this motley crew Paul and Upper Crust are as good as it gets. If you're determined to hang around, check out the Doric Arch (1 Eversholt St; 020 7388 2221) which is a shoddy little boozer with a cool 'end of the world' vibe. The left luggage office is at the top of the ramp to platforms 16–18 and is open between 7 am–11 pm.

Public Transport

As an actual railway station it is adequate. Served by two Tube lines and nine bus routes, it's nothing if not convenient.

King's Cross Station

NFT Map:	78
Address:	Euston Rd & Pancras Rd N1 9AP
General enquiries:	0207 922 4931
Lost property:	0207 2783310
National Express East Coast:	08457 225 225
First Capital Connect:	0845 676 9904

Overview

Previously a dingy playground for prostitutes, drug dealers, and all sorts of similarly bad kids, King's Cross Station has scrubbed up a bit in recent years, thanks to lots of chin scratching and typically panicked spending on the government's part. Built in 1852 on the site of a former smallpox hospital, it is one of the busiest and most well-connected stations in the country: running trains to Edinburgh; Newcastle; the East coast; as well as six Tube lines. Zany trivia about the station includes the fact that it is supposedly built on top of legendary Fembot-Queen Boudicea's grave (most probably a total lie) and that it has a tacky little shrine to Harry Potter at what has been designated 'Platform 9 3/4' (oh God).

Nearly all long distance train services leave from the overground platforms under the arches straight ahead of you as you enter from Euston Road. The Tube is also accessible from steps at this entrance and at what used to be the Thameslink station next to the Scala on Pentonville Road. From the main Tube entrance there is a pedestrian subway that comes up on the other side of Euston road just outside Macdonald's. This is handy for crossing the road at busy times, and of course for getting chips. There is a Spartan waiting lounge just outside the entrance.

Tickets

Tube tickets, including Oyster top ups and season tickets, can be purchased from the machines in front of the Tube entry gates, located just at the bottom of both sets of stairs at the station. For railcard discounts and more specific enquiries you'll have to queue at the manned ticket desks next to the machines. For all other tickets go to the upstairs ticket hall which is to the left of the main Euston Road entrance.

Services

Food options are pretty poor, consisting of a small array of chain stores with prices hiked just enough so that people in a rush will not notice they're being ripped off. If you're not one of those people, it's probably best to just pop across the road and get some noodles from Chop Chop, which is fast, cheap and dirty, like the best rail travel.

Public Transport

King's Cross crosses more Tube lines (six) than any other station, and is serviced by at least twice as many buses, many of which run all night. For full details of bus routes look at the bus maps for Camden on the Transport for London website: http://www.tfl.gov.uk/tfl/gettingaround/maps/buses/.

Liverpool Street Station

NFT Map:	8
Address:	EC2M 7QH
General enquiries:	020 7295 2789
Lost property:	020 7247 4297
One Railway:	0845 6007245
Natl Express East Anglia Railway	0845 6007245

Overview

Scene of drunken anarchy at the infamous Facebook party that preceded Boris's booze ban, it's not that Liverpool Street is particularly ugly, but if it's architectural beauty you're after, you're much better off heading to Paddington or the newly re-opened St. Pancras International. In comparison to these two icons of British train design, Liverpool Street is extremely modest, boring even. Clean, modern and easy to navigate around, it is simply a good train station. With the markets, bars and restaurants of Spitalfields and Brick Lane just around the corner, the station is the perfect starting point to explore east London. First opened to the public in 1874, it is now the second-busiest station in London (after Waterloo) with an estimated 123m visitors each year. With 18 platforms, the station mainly serves destinations in the east of England, including daytrip favourites such as Cambridge and Southend on Sea.

It is also the home of the Stansted Express, providing easy airport access with departures every 15 minutes. If you're travelling with a group of people a taxi might work out slightly cheaper, but the train is much quicker and more reliable. The Tube station, with its main entrance centrally located on the main concourse, makes all of London easily accessible with the Central, Hammersmith & City, Circle and Metropolitan lines all passing through. Being the fifth busiest station on the underground network, rush hour can get nasty and is best avoided.

Tickets

The ticket office is located on the main concourse, on your left hand side if entering from Bishopsgate. Ticket windows are open for immediate travel 24/7 with advance ticket purchases available between 7.30 am–7.30 pm. There are also several express ticket machines scattered throughout the station. Tickets for the Stansted Express can be purchased from designated ticket machines opposite platforms 5-6. A cluster of cash machines can be found by the stairs leading up to the Old Broad Street exit. There are payphones on both levels and most are located on the Bishopsgate side of the station.

Services

With Brick Lane just around the corner, eating, drinking and shopping here should really be a last resort. The regular big-chain fast food joints are scattered (some of them repeatedly) throughout the station with the usual selection of coffee, burgers, sandwiches and sweets. The main shopping area is on the lower level around the Broadgate and Exchange Square exits, offering everything from toiletries and birthday cards to Italian silk ties and double-glazed windows.

Passengers are invited to wait for their trains in the so-called "food court," which really isn't much more than a few cramped tables between Burger King and The Wren, one of the station's two shitty pubs. There's a small but nicer waiting lounge located adjacent to platform 10. Here you also find the left luggage, a bureau de change, a less busy cash machine and access to the main taxi rank. Smoking is prohibited at all times throughout the station.

Public Transport

The main bus station is located on the upper level of the station (Broadgate end), and provides a large number of services to destinations throughout London. Plenty of buses also stop on the street just outside the Bishopsgate exit.

London Bridge Station

NFT Map:	106
Address:	Station Approach SE1 9SP
General enquiries:	020 7234 1209
Lost property:	020 7234 1247
Southern Trains:	0845 123 7770
South East Trains:	0845 000 2211
First Capital Connect:	0845 026 4700
South Eastern disabled contact:	0800 783 4524

Overview

Around in one form or other since 1836, when steam trains filled the air with smoke, London Bridge is the city's oldest station. Sounds romantic? It's anything but. Hopelessly overcrowded, with 42 million people elbowing their way through the tunnel-like walkways every year, and crumbling on its grey concrete edges, London Bridge has long been SCREAMING for a makeover. Someone finally heard the call, and £3.5m is earmarked to get this vital commuter hub (connecting south London, Sussex and Kent) up to scratch. The ambitious revamp will also see the construction of one of Europe's highest skyscrapers—a massive arrowhead of a building, hosting 7,000 people once completed.

It's a good starting point for weekend trips to Kent's countryside or days on Brighton's beach. Operators Southeastern and Southern cover the south east, while First Capital Connect operates (little-known) connections to the airports Gatwick and Luton. The station couldn't be better connected to public transport, with two Tube lines and a plethora of buses at the doorstep. The catacombs underneath the station—said to be haunted—have been turned into the museum-cum-gore-fest London Bridge Experience, adding to the spooky entertainment already provided by the London Dungeon next door—just in case a cancelled or delayed train leaves you with too much time on your hands. Does happen, we're told.

Tickets

The main office is located next to the main entrance (London Bridge Street) or there are machines situated throughout the station. Jump the queues by booking online at www.nationalrail.co.uk.

Services

The main concourse is lined with eating and shopping options. Grab Cornish pasties, sandwiches, donuts; and the usual burgers from the usual chains. Bodyshop, M&S and WH Smith lead the list of practical, but terribly unexciting shop names. There are toilets on platforms 1-2 and 5-6. The caverns connecting the Underground station with the national trains is teeming with better food options however - some even non-chain.

Public Transport

Connections are excellent. London Bridge Station is served by the Jubilee Line and the Bank branch of the Northern Line. Escalators take you down from the main concourse. Step outside the main entrance for the massive bus station, where buses leave in all directions of the city, except its far western reaches.

Marylebone Train Station

NFT Map:	76
Address:	Great Central House
	Melcombe Place
	NW1 6JJ
Central number:	08456 005165

Overview

Despite Monopoly-board notoriety, Marylebone railway station fell into neglect in the mid to late-twentieth century, spurned as a rundown piggy-in-the-middle wedged haplessly between neighbours Paddington and Euston. But it's an aimless drifter no more. A refurb' in the 90s and again in 2006 saw Marylebone reinvigorated, with a thorough sprucing up and two new platforms. Servicing the Midlands, it now threads as far as Birmingham, Shakespeare's Stratford-Upon-Avon, Leamington Spa, Aylesbury, and High Wycombe, amongst others. It remains the runt of the London train station litter, but is a popular location for television filming (Doctor Who; Magnum PI; Green Wing; Peep Show) at a mere £500 per hour—half the price of King's Cross. In its bowels, Bakerloo Line trains rumble through an underground station of the same name.

Tickets

Rail ticket windows are to the north of Marylebone's relatively petite concourse and open Monday-Saturday 06.30–22:10 or Sunday 07.30–21.30. As with all mainline train stations, self-service ticket machines are in abundance should ticket offices be closed or queues too long. Sturdy padded-barriers ensure buying tickets on board the train, or getting away without them, is not an option. Underground tickets can be purchased from windows or machines alike within the Tube station itself.

Services

The usual plethora of railway station chains are on hand: newsagent WH Smith, baguette bakers Upper Crust, supermarket Marks & Spencer, and pasty purveyors the West Cornwall Company among them. More individually, Marylebone also hosts AMT Coffee, a café with a seating area at the centre of the concourse, the nifty Chiltern Flowers on the south wall, and The V&A free house in the west passageway—an old man's boozer in the classic, wood panelled style. Cash points and payphones are in this same walkway, and toilets are situated on the south wall.

Public Transport

Marylebone underground station lies directly beneath Marylebone overground, and is serviced (Matron!) by the Bakerloo Line, while buses 2, 205 and 453 stop directly outside the main entrance. A taxi stand is also situated out front. Baker Street and Edgware tube stations are a short walk away.

Paddington Station

NFT Map:	31
Address:	Paddington, London, W2 1HQ
General enquiries:	020 7922 6793
Lost property:	020 7247 4297
First Great Western:	084 5700 0125
Heathrow Express:	084 5600 1515
Chiltern Railways:	084 5600 5165

Overview

If you're in that small minority of people who love stations, then Paddington's paradise. Designed by engineering legend Isambard Kingdom Brunel—his middle name is Kingdom for God's sake, of course his work's going to be magnificent—this barn-like structure harks back to an era when train travel retained a little glamour. If it wasn't for the on-site Burger King you could easily imagine tearful ladies waving silk handkerchiefs at dapper gents.

The station also occupies a unique place in literary heritage. Every British child in the last half-century knows the tales of Paddington Bear. From "deepest darkest Peru", he was left unattended at the station; but a kind family picked him up, took him in, and named him after it. No other station name can inspire such genuine warmth. It certainly wouldn't have worked if he'd been found at Clapham Junction.

Heathrow Express

The super-fast link to Heathrow runs from Paddington. Be warned, though; it's far from cheap. At £32 return it could end up being more than your flight (and works out at £24 more than taking the tube). Ouch.

Tickets

A ticket office and machines are located near platforms 9-10, and there are other machines and an information point near the Eastbourne Terrace entrance and also underneath the mezzanine.

Services

If you have any money left from your ticket—unlikely at today's prices—there are plenty of sharks who can take it off you. Burger King and Upper Crust will overcharge you for burgers or baguettes and there's an 'offie' (off-license) for expensive booze. There's also a pub that resembles a building site (Portakabin). If you find yourself drinking in there you've got some serious questions to ask yourself.

There are other ways of staying amused; as it's the main portal for commuters entering London from the west and Wales) there's WiFi, a supermarket, a bookshop and curiously, a lingerie shop. Just what sort of a job do you have if you get to the station and realise: "Bollocks! No suspenders!"? Certainly not one compatible with Paddington's place in children's lit, that's for sure.

Public Transport

The Bakerloo, Circle, District, and Hammersmith & City Tube lines all stop at Paddington. Buses serve west and north west London.

St Pancras International

NFT Map:	78
Address:	Pancras Road, London, NW1 2QP
Central number:	020 7843 4250
Eurostar:	08705 186 186
Midland Mainline:	08457 125678

Overview

The newly souped-up St Pancras station has been generating waves of breathless excitement ever since its opening ceremony in 2007, which was by all accounts a pretty histrionic affair. This "Cathedral of Transport" situated next door to King's Cross station, is now home to the Eurostar international train service and has domestic connections (via First Capital Connect's Thameslink trains) to Luton Airport, Bedford and Brighton; as well as Midland Mainline connections to places like Leicester and Sheffield. As the first major project of a huge scheme to redevelop the area, St Pancras has been marketed as so-much-more-than-a-station. Alongside its rail platforms it features Europe's longest Champagne bar, a farmers market, and an arcade of pointedly-classy shops. All this is housed within beautiful listed buildings dating from 1868, with an extension for the long Eurostar trains designed by British starchitect Norman Foster—presumably on time out from his usual business of making pleasure domes for the world's nastiest totalitarian governments.

Tickets

The Eurostar ticket office and travel centre is located at the Euston Road end of the long arcade, while self-service machines (for collecting pre-booked tickets) can be found outside the Eurostar departure lounge further along the arcade and to the right. Opening times for the Eurostar ticket office are 4.30 am–9 pm (Mon-Fri), 5.30 am–9 pm (Sat) and 6.30 am–9 pm (Sun). For National Rail services, you will need to buy tickets from machines, or a manned ticket desk at the designated area at the far end of the Arcade, next to that horrific kissing statue.

Services

At St Pancras International there are more than 40 places to eat, drink and shop, with a fair number of chain stores as well as some exclusives, such as the Champagne Bar and Gastro Pub. The station has its own dedicated shopping arcade with branches of classic London stores Hamleys and Foyles, as well as a market area and another brace of shops at the north end of the station ('The Circle'). Everything is shiny, new and upmarket, so expect your money to vanish pretty damn quickly. The Betjeman Arms pub – named after the famous poet whose petition saved the listed buildings from the same fate as Euston's arch – hosts beer festivals and music/literature events.

Public Transport

St Pancras can be reached by Tube (via adjacent King's Cross Station) on the Victoria, Hammersmith & City, Circle, Piccadilly, Northern and Metropolitan Lines. A large number of buses also stop along Euston Road day and night. For route details check the bus maps for Camden borough at www.tfl.gov.uk/tfl/gettingaround/maps/buses/.

Victoria Station

NFT Map:	20
Address:	Buckingham Palace Road SW1V 1JU
General enquiries:	020 7922 6214
Lost property:	020 7963 0957
Gatwick Express:	0845 850 1530
Southern:	08451 27 29 20
Southeastern:	0845 000 2222

Overview

80 million people use London Victoria per year, making it one of the UK's busiest stations. Hit it at rush hour and it will feel like those 80 million are all there with you. Built a century ago for a less populous, less rushed and less demanding city, it struggles with crowds of commuters who jostle for platform space. Now it enforces crowd-control measures at peak times: prepare to be patient. Nevertheless, it is well laid-out with services clearly sign-posted, and a major upgrade is planned to improve its capacity.

Victoria's main train operators are Southeastern, Southern and Gatwick Express, who between them will whisk you to Brighton, Portsmouth, Hastings and Gatwick, among other Southeastern towns. Or if you're looking for a romantic break and the Victoria route to Bognor Regis is just a little too obvious for you, you can earn yourself brownie points and a hefty overdraft by taking the Orient Express from this station.

The building itself is impressive: look above the modern shop fascias to enjoy century-old architecture. But if that is all a little too high-brow, look up anyway, as the entrance to the South East building sports four caryatids: columns shaped like women, whose tunics saucily hang open so a gratuitous nipple can pop out to cheer the commuters. Rule Britannia!

Tickets

If you haven't booked in advance (why? Why?!), then head for the 24 hour ticket office in the central concourse, where you will queue for anything up to a year to buy your journey for much more money than you'd have paid online a week earlier. If you don't require assistance from a ticket officer, use the automated machines dotted round the concourse: their queues always move faster (unless the person in front of you is a newbie who can't figure out the buttons, which is guaranteed if you have less than five minutes to catch your train). Keep your ticket handy as all platforms are guarded by ticket barriers, and add a few extra minutes to reach platforms 15–19.

Services

All the predictable station fare is available in the main concourse for your journey's usual sandwich, loofah and tie needs. Food options have mercifully diversified so in addition to the obligatory artery-cloggers you can now grab sushi from the Wasabi stand or maintain your body's temple-status at the Camden Food Co. If it's a meal you're after and you must remain at the station, head up to the food court via Victoria Place for a choice of what could charitably be described as restaurants. Victoria Place itself boasts the ubiquitous high street shops to help you kill time or for any last minute gifts (as long as you don't really like the person you're buying for). Station loos are 20p—even up in the food court you can't pee for free—and showers are available if you're getting a bit ripe. Victoria also has a left luggage service, WiFi (charged) and photo booths.

Public Transport

Victoria is on the Victoria, Circle and District lines; entrance to the underground is opposite platform 7. The bus terminus is just outside the main entrance. It is also next door to London's national bus depot for cheapo travel to/from other parts of the UK. The main taxi rank is outside the main entrance, but if it has a heart-sinking queue then head up to the Plaza exit for an alternative rank.

Waterloo Station

NFT Map:	104
Address:	Waterloo, London, SE1 8H
Train company:	South West Trains
General enquiries:	020 7922 2545
Lost property:	0845 330 9882
	0845 6000 650
Website:	www.southwesttrains.co.uk

Overview

Until 2007, Waterloo was the first port of call for 'Europeans' arriving by train. Thousands of chic foreigners, clutching manbags and sporting huge sunglasses, would arrive at the station every week. But not any more. Nearly 200 years after the British triumphed in the first battle of Waterloo—a town in Belgium—the French got their revenge. Last November Eurostar gave the two fingers to the British Waterloo and promiscuously buggered off to St Pancras. Rumour has it that ex-PM Margaret Thatcher had specifically ordered that Eurostar terminate at a station named after a famous French defeat; but things have moved on a little since the "Iron Lady" left office. We're all Europeans now…

In truth, perhaps it's not that bad a thing. Even though no other British station covers as much space, Waterloo feels like it's at bursting point. Even without the Eurostar it has a whopping 19 platforms—in almost constant use—and four Tube lines. It's calmed down slightly since the international terminal was put out to stud, but it's still pretty manic.

The station services London's south western suburbs (as can be seen by the swathes of well dressed commuters) and, further afield, the towns south west of the capital.

Waterloo East

NFT Map:	104
Address:	Sandell St, SE8 8H
Central number:	0871 200 49650

Overview

If the south west isn't your bag, you can disappear to England's south east—Kent, Sussex and SE London—from Waterloo East. There's an escalator next to Burger King, opposite platform 12, that makes a trip to the south east look far more alluring than it really is.

Tickets

The main office is opposite platforms 16–17. And it's open 24 hours—so why not charm them into giving you a free ticket after a few drinks? They can't have heard it before, right?

Services

A delay is just unplanned "me time", so make the most of it by buying a newspaper, eating your own weight in overpriced pasties and cookies; then wash it down with a few pints of generic football-sponsor lager in Bonaparte's pub before buying your loved-one a novelty tie/'cute' socks to make up for being late. And drunk. And flatulent. And tasteless. There's a left luggage office between platforms 11-12.

Public Transportation

Waterloo is served by four underground lines: Bakerloo, Jubilee, Northern, Waterloo & City; and approximately 20 bus routes. See tfl.gov.uk for details.

Overview

there's one thing that screams London, it's g red buses -loads of 'em- preferably passing neath Big Ben for maximum iconic impact. e was an almighty roar from Londoners when e Routemaster was scrapped: panoramas ewed from the Oxo tower were dotted with ts clutching rolled-up Time Outs shaking at mayoral offices. The accordion buses which placed them were met with similar anger but ey've now to be scrapped: one can only guess the amount of revenue lost by fare dodgers.

hatever you think of the death of the bendy s and Boris' reinvention of the Routemaster hich is apparently to feature a glass roof) one ing is certain: you're going to spend a lot of ne on buses, around them, dodging them or oaning about them. Let's have a quick run- own of things to drop in a London bus convo: rivers take pleasure in driving off just as you t to the stop, 'Why do they always drive so fast/ ow?' 'They're earning up to £500 a week? Why e they so grumpy all the time?' ad infinitum. a Londoner, your list of hobbies and interests w includes transport: deal with it.

rmer mayor Ken Livingstone always had a ing for buses and we make 6m journeys every y. There are a variety of different operating mpanies, but to us they're all the same, all the ay out to the frontiers of Zone 6. Get on at the ont, get off at the middle.

big red bus featured in the Beijing Olympics osing ceremony, as the world looked to London 12. And new(ish) boy Boris has taken up the s baton with a new design set to enter service 2011. At procurement stage, a key design quirement was an open platform – so the spirit the Routemaster looks set to live on after all. A duction in those nasty diesel particulates has so been specified, as excuses for capital car ivers become ever weaker.

Fares

In an effort to make the city more efficient and to cut down on theft-based attacks on drivers, Transport for London (TfL) introduced the Oyster card. Now people only beat up drivers for fun. The Oyster ("The world's your..."—geddit?) is an electronic swipe card that can be bought at all 275 Tube stations and some 4,000 other outlets such as newsagents.

The card can carry a mixture of travel passes (often referred to as travelcards in a nod to the pre-electronic age of cardboard); and pay-as-you-go cash value. Note that if you choose pay-as-you-go, and you end up making more journeys than you anticipated; once it reaches the equivalent cost of a one-day travelcard, it will cap itself so you don't spend more.

Unless you are making a small number of journeys it usually works out cheaper to get a travelcard. In a further move towards the cashless society, coins are still accepted—but you will pay more for a journey. A single ticket costs £1.20 with Oyster or £2 with cash. On some bus routes you will not be allowed to purchase a ticket on the bus, but instead there will be a roadside ticket machine. Believe us, Oyster's just easier...

When you get on, don't forget to push your card against the scanner by the drivers' window. Sure, you're on camera 300 times per day, and every journey you make is recorded. But if you're paranoid, try another city, because they *are* watching you here.

You can buy a bus and tram pass (£16.60 p/w), or you can buy a bus/tube travelcard (prices vary by zones). If you don't work or socialise in the centre, and you only buy, let's say a Zone 2-3 bus travelcard, you can still use this on all buses in Zones 1-6. Which is nice. An Oyster card costs £3 to get, but you'll soon recoup that. Concessions are also available for the unemployed and for full-time students.

417

24-Hour Services

You'll not hear London referred to as "the other city which never sleeps". Partly because it's unwieldy, but mostly because it's not true. After a hard night's binge-drinking and fighting in taxi ranks, we like our kip.

But for those of you that are hardcore no-sleep-till-Brockley types, there is a network of 24-hour services. There are also a large number of night buses. They're just like day buses, except the route number is prefixed by a large 'N' and the view is less interesting.

Information

TfL's website (tfl.gov.uk) is an essential reference. Fare information and travel updates are available, plus PDFs of routes and timetables. As you get closer to central London, many routes operate on a frequency-basis rather than at fixed times.

The main reason to visit TfL's site is the Journey Planner. Enter your start and end points and it will (usually) calculate the best options. A word of warning though, computers are fallible and some route maps are schematics—so do check your own map and use common sense. Like those idiots that follow their GPS even when it tells them to drive into a river, it's frustrating to take three buses in a big circuit then realise you could have walked it in five minutes…

If you do want to live out your 1940s film fantasies, you can still catch the quaint old Routemasters doddering along 'Heritage Routes' 9 and 15. If you're wondering who this guy is that keeps bugging you at the door-less rear step, it's the conductor and he only wants your money. It's the silent guy in the corner who wants your soul that you have to watch out for…

Safety

Like all big cities, London has its fair sha of oddballs and criminals. And then a fe institution-loads more in case things eve get boring. But CCTV in every bus and th creation of Safer Transport teams is havir an effect—and not just on the share price video camera manufacturers. TfL claimed a 11% reduction in reported crime at the er of 2007 and a ratio of 15 crimes per millic journeys. Also, bus crime is concentrated particular areas on particular routes. An you'll soon get to know the 'usual suspects' don't worry. Night buses can get a bit lairy, s follow a few tips below to make sure the on stress you suffer is traffic-related. Gangste may wish to laugh at the following; Moth Theresas may wish to tattoo it on the insic of their eyelids:

Avoid the top deck when possible. Sit on th left so the driver can see you (he has a rad link to base). Don't fall asleep. Use the sam stop at night and know your surroundings s you can be confident. Keep your belonging close to you and be switched on. Get to kno the 'hot spots' so you can be aware.

For more info, see our fabulous fold out bu map.

Overview

Coaches are traditionally associated with the grimier side of travel. But London's biggest coach company, National Express, are desperately trying to shake their image as a purveyor of seedy transport. They're rebranding themselves as quick, comfortable and green. Their fleet of coaches are shiny and the drivers slightly less grumpy than they used to be.

National Express' nemesis is the Megabus. There's a few misconceptions about these guys and they are: that all their fares are £1 and that they're shoddy scum buckets on wheels. Their advertising screams the £1 thing but they release only a handful of these tickets for each journey and then the fare rises the closer you get to your preferred date. However, they're not as bad as they used to be: the coaches are now pretty much as good as National Express. In addition, National Express have started a super cheap ticket campaign: pretty soon both companies will merge in holy matrimony and we won't need to choose between them anymore. What you have to bear in mind is that if you use coaches in general you will be showered with sick by old turkey junkies at the back and you will have to take a gas mask if you're sat within a coach lengths of the portal of hell that is the toilet. Just sit back, for an additional 4 hours, and think of the £10 you've spent on not taking the train.

The main coach hub is near Victoria train station. You can buy tickets for both Megabus and National Express—the two main operators who run from Victoria Coach Station—from the same booths just inside the station. But, like plane tickets, (only without that last shred of glamour that air travel still has) if you buy in advance, you can get some super-cheap prices. National Express has an office on the road between the train and bus stations.

London's other main hub is Golder's Green. This is the last stop for services heading north (or the first stop for buses coming down into London). If you live in north London, it's worth jumping off here, as it's on the Northern Line and can shave an hour off the trip.

There's also a healthy trade in coaches to Oxford. The Oxford Tube competes with National Express on the route from Victoria; travelling via Marble Arch, Notting Hill and Shepherd's Bush. Tickets normally cost about £13 and you can buy on board. They also run through the night—so if you get drunk and have the urge to go on an impromptu holiday—well, Oxford it is.

Beyond Tooting, Croydon's trams will take you from places like Wimbledon to shop – lemming-like with the locals – at the Ampere Way IKEA. The trams accept Oyster and use a similar charging scale to buses. Once you get back on the map, your flatpacked sideboard will win admiring glances but few friends as you trail home on busy tubes.

National Express

Unit 6/7 Collonades Walk
123 Buckingham Palace Road, SW1W 1SH
08717 818181
www.nationalexpress.com

Megabus
0900 160 0900
www.megabus.co.uk

Oxford Tube
01865 772250
www.oxfordtube.com

There's a war going on out there, one with real casualties and collateral damage. When Tory leader David Cameron was spotted going through a red light on his bicycle, it threw into sharp relief a low level conflict which has been going on for decades. Bikes v. Cars: with hapless pedestrians caught in the middle.

Cycling around London is not for the faint-hearted, but recent improvements—like Boris' cycling revolution campaigning and the hard work of the London Cycling Campaign (www.lcc.org.uk) are encouraging people to drop their Oyster cards and jump on their bikes. Indeed, the Tory mayor has begun work on 2 of the 12 proposed 'Cycle Superhighways' and has already introduced the city cycle-hire program: a brilliant system based on European models in which users pick up a bike and then drop it off when finished at a suitable point in the city. Some of the routes highlighted in the brilliant (and free) maps produced by LCC and Transport for London have become so popular, cycling along them is like taking part in the Tour de France (albeit slower and with slightly fewer drugs). There's even a Velib'-style communal bike scheme planned to start in May 2010 and tangle-haired tearaway Boris upset skivers everywhere by leading a mass ride-to-work to beat the tube strike.

But cycling does hold some risks. As well as the nightmare of walking around all day with 'helmet hair' you've got accidents and theft. LCC's website has details of road-confidence training and lists local cycling groups who run social events and cycle maintenance classes. They will sometimes cycle your new route to work with you to help you negotiate the difficult bits. Aren't they nice?

For those new to cycling on London roads, basic rules include: stay door length (or stride) away from the pavement or parked cars; watch out for distracted office drones leaping into the road and into black cabs; don't undertake bendy-buses or HGVs; don't use your phone while moving; and if in doubt on a tricky junction, transform yourself into a pedestrian—get off and push your bike wherever you need to go. For debate around riding on pavements, wearing helmets and jumping red lights check on www.cyclechat.co.uk/forums.

Bolt-cutting 'tea-leaves' steal thousands of bikes every year. You have three options to reduce this particular risk. One, buy a rubbish bike that no-one would want to steal and lock it with one lock. Two, get a decent bike, carry around a D-lock and two other locks and spend 20 mins each time you stop. Three, get a shit-hot bike and never take it out.

Where to Ride Bikes

There are plenty of great rides around town and a happy cyclist is one who has been able to incorporate one into the commute. The cycling maps mentioned above give colour-coded help, look for the brown routes (separate from the traffic) or even better the green routes (separate from the traffic and passing through parks, beside canals or rivers.)

Good options are the short but scenic Parkland Walk Nature Reserve, which links Finsbury Park to Highgate via an abandoned railway line; a Saturday morning cycle takes you to one of Highgate's wonderful pubs for lunch and a lazy pint. The City, normally snarled with cabs, buses and kamikaze pedestrians, a dream on a Sunday morning.

Though not continuous, the path along the Regent's Canal linking Paddington with Canary Wharf takes cyclists away from traffic and along some surprisingly gorgeous stretches of canal (which also sport some top notch graffiti)—as well as some godawful, festering dumps. A useful section of the canal links the west side of Regent's Park with Paddington via Lisson Grove and Warwick Avenue. Watch out for super-fast cyclists determined to slice a second off their PB, especially where the path narrows under bridges or around ramps. Also recent yellow crime signs around London Fields spoke of a gang of youths pushing cyclists into the canal for fun. Watch out for them too.

A jaunt through any of the capital's great parks seems an obvious choice, but beware, some parks (notably Hampstead Heath) ban bikes on almost all paths,

thanks to selfish cyclists of the past who went too fast and frightened the jumpy pedestrians.

The new anarchic FreeWheel Event is a real highlight, where great swathes of normally packed roads along the Embankment and up to St James's Park are closed to all but cyclists every September (we fervently hope this will remain forever). And the London Critical Mass meet at 6 pm on the last Friday of the month by the National Film Theatre, if you can't wait that long.

www.londonfreewheel.com
www.criticalmasslondon.org.uk

Bike Shops	Address	Phone
Apex Cycles	40-42 Clapham High St, SW4 7UR	020 7622 1334
Archway Cycles	183 Archway Rd	020 8340 9696
Bicycle Magic	6 Greatorex St, E1 5NF	020 7375 2993
Bikefix	48 Lamb's Conduit St, WC1N 3LJ	020 7405 1218
Brick Lane Bikes	118 Bethnal Green Rd, E2 6DG	020 7033 9053
Bobbin Bicycles	397 St John St	020 7837 3370
Brixton Cycles	145 Stockwell Rd, SW9 9TN	020 7733 6055
Cheech Miller	227 Victoria Park Rd	020 8985 9900
Condor Cycles	51 Gray's Inn Rd, WC1X 8PP	020 7269 6820
Decathlon	Surrey Quays Rd	020 7394 2000
Evans (Spitalfields)	The Cavern, 1 Market St, E1 6AA	020 7426 0391
Holloway Cycles	290 Holloway Rd, N7 6NJ	020 7700 6611
London Fields Cycles	281 Mare St, E8 1PJ	020 8525 0077
London Recumbents	Battersea Park	020 7498 6543
Mosquito	123 Essex Rd, N1 2SN	020 7226 8765
ReCycling	110 Elephant Rd, SE17 1LB	020 7703 7001

To consider taking a taxi in London you either need (a) a trust fund, or (b) to be drunk. If you are both, congratulations: prepare to be taken for a ride in more ways than one.

Dating back to the mid-17th Century (kind of), London's 'black cabs' (www.londonblackcabs.co.uk), or 'Hackneys', are the world's oldest taxi service and are as representative of London as Routemasters, Big Ben and robbery. They are the most visible, the most iconic and probably the most expensive taxi service in London. While this flag-down option is great (they are the only company licensed to pick up on the street) budgeting for a black cab is tricky. Their prices are designed to confuse passengers into parting with huge wads for what often feels like a round-the-block trip. A whole range of metaphysical problems contribute to that huge sum waiting to be paid at jouney's end; all fares start at £2.20 and then go up according to the time of day, speed, and the time spent in the cab. There's also an airport surcharge and the 'puke charge' of £40. Keep it in!

Black cabs are operated by many different companies who are all regulated and licensed by the Public Carriage Office (PCO). Generally speaking, the service you receive doesn't vary much from company to company, though some boast little add-ons to capture your fare. Big, well organized companies like Dial-A-Cab (www.dialacab.co.uk; 020 7253 5000) and Radio Taxis (www.radiotaxis.co.uk; 020 7272 0272) offer online booking, carbon neutral trips, and friendly service. All black cab drivers must pass 'The Knowledge' test to get their license, so every driver will have a labyrinthine understanding of London and most will not be shy in sharing this with you.

Though a cheaper option, going private can be a minefield. Since 2001 all tax services in London are required by law to be licensed by the PCO: this includes the city's thousands of private-hire minicabs. Private hire companies are everywhere you look and often take the form of nicotine-stained shoddily-built little offices with lots of bored men milling about. Every neighbourhood has plenty of local services and it's really trial and error to find one that doesn't rip you off or drive barely roadworthy chariots of rust. The drivers of these little companies can be pretty eccentric—you can be regaled by tales of times past, given essential life advice or simply receive the disdainful silent treatment. The website www.taxinumber.com offers a list of local minicabs for every postcode in the UK.

The 'private taxi sector' does do upmarket however. By far the most efficient and elegant service is that offered by Addison Lee, (www.addisonlee.com; 020 7387 8888) who text you twice, have huge gleaming six-seaters and perfectly-manicured drivers. Fares are pretty cheap over longer distances but the minimum is around £10. E-london Cars are almost as good (www.elondoncars.co.uk; 020 7494 4004). Of course, you can also sup from the cup of bad taste by ordering a stretch hummer or pink limo at Book A Limo (www.booklimo.co.uk; 020 8965 1724).

A word of warning: London is awash with rogue taxi-drivers who are not licensed and who will attempt to pick you up from outside a club or theatre. These guys will either charge you more than you agreed upon, not know where they are going, or they will be driving beat-up death-traps. There are also many stories of attacks on women, so if in doubt, don't get in!

Helicopter Services

Westland Heliport
020 7228 0181 www.helipad.co.uk

SW11's very own heliport! Aerial tours of London can be made online with Helipad running from Westland Heliport in Battersea, Elstree and London City Airport. The nearest tube is Clapham Junction.

EBG Helicopters
01737 823 282 www.ebghelipcopters.co.uk

Running helicopter tours of London and charter flights from Redhill Airport in Surrey, 10 minutes by car from Gatwick Airport. £140 will get you 35 minutes over London, the only downside is getting to Surrey. Flights are between 10-4pm. Also offers charters for weddings and corporate events. Flying from Heathrow? Take a 20 minute sky ride for a cool £1,200.

Helicopter Days
08704 430 555 www.helicopterdays.co.uk

Operating out of Biggin Hill, 30-minute flights over Canary Wharf and Westminster start at £125 per person and you can cram up to 5 friends in with you. Lessons are available for less than £200. For drivers the helipad's close to M25 or you can be picked up by a helicopter from another location!

Elstree Aerodrome
020 8953 7480 www.egtr.net

A variety of charters operate out of Elstree offering sky tours, as well as flight academies for those who want to take the wheel. On site is The Elstree Bar & Café, plus it's close to M1.

Ferries/Boat Tours, Rentals & Charters

London River Services (LRS)
020 7222 1234
www.tfl.gov.uk/gettingaround

Provides commuter river transportation on the Thames. This runs in the East from Masthouse Terrace Pier to Savoy Pier at Embankment. In peak hours services run to Woolwich Arsenal with a further service from Blackfriars Millenium Pier in the City to Putney Pier in the west costing £15 return. WiFi is available on boats serving Woolwich. Services run every 20 minutes. All are wheelchair friendly.

Thames Clippers
0870 7815049
www.thamesclippers.com

London's answer to the NYC water taxis, primarily serving the O2 stadium from Waterloo, Embankment and Tower Bridge. Conveniently runs later than the Tube meaning you can actually stay right to the end of a show

without the worry of being stranded on the south side of the river. Single tickets cost between £3-5 with Oyster Card holders getting 1/3 off. Boats leave every 15 minutes.

Bateux London
020 7925 2215
www.bateuxlondon.com.

Dinner, lunch and charter cruises from Embankment Pier. Yes, there's even a jazz cruise.

Westminster Passenger Services Association
020 7930 2062
www.wpsa.co.uk

One of the only popular charters to offer services upriver to Kew, Richmond and Hampton Court.

City Cruises
020 7740 0400
www.citycruises.com.

Hop on hop off services primarily aimed at tourists and with tourist prices. Tickets start from £11

return for adults from Greenwich to Westminster/Waterloo Pier.

Heritage Boat Charters
01932 224 800
www.heritageboatcharters.com

For something different, try messing about on the river in one of these historic wooden numbers. On offer are skippered cruises down the Thames starting at £825. Formal dinner on board is available.

Silver Fleet Woods River Cruises
020 7481 2711
www.silverfleet.co.uk

Luxury chartered boats. Particularly good at putting on top-notch corporate events.

Thames Cruises
020 7928 9009
www.thamescruises.com

Two words—disco cruise. Hot pants are not required for dinner cruises.

Marinas/Passenger Ship Terminal

Chelsea Marina
07770 542 783
www.chelseaharbourmarina.
com

Despite being in upmarket Chelsea, the prices for mooring your boat here are incredibly generous—£2 per metre a night or £300 a year with space for 60 boats. Secure subterranean parking also available.

Chiswick Quay Marina
020 8994 8743
www.chiswickquay.com/marina

Great, secluded spot for West Londoners near Chiswick Bridge. A little far from a tube station, yet Chiswick overland station is within walking distance with services to Waterloo. Prices are on an annual basis at £162 per metre including a resident harbourmaster, shower block, mains water and electricity.

Gallions Point Marina
020 7476 7054
www.gallionspointmarina.co.uk

In London's Docklands and therefore perfect for those working in the city.

St Katharine Haven
020 7481 8350
www.stkaths.co.uk

One of London's best marinas. Great location by Tower Bridge, close to the quayside bars and restaurants and reasonable London prices—£3.60 per metre, per day.

Welcome Floating Terminal in Greenwich
01474 562 200
www.portoflondon.co.uk

Built in 2004 and believed to be the world's first floating terminal. Welcome has on-site immigration and custom services for cruise ship passengers entering or leaving London.

London Cruise Terminal at Tilbury
01375 852 360
www.londoncruiseterminal.
com

The most popular regional departure point for passenger liners is 25 miles from Central London in Essex. Its close proximity to the M25 makes it easy for Londoners to get to. Current destinations from here include Scandinavia and continental Europe.

With London's Congestion Charge, Low Emission Zone, pricey parking, kamikaze bus drivers, dreaded speed bumps, speed cameras and a road layout that would give Spock the night terrors—"it's so illogical Captain"—driving around town is something to be avoided. Combine this with over 7.5 million people who just want to get from A to B without anyone getting in their frickin' way, and you can see where problems arise.

But, there are times when a four-wheeler is the only option, and for those times here are some things to watch out for:

Pedestrians love to stride purposefully into the road with nary a thought for their safety. Keep a weather eye out, one foot over the brake and one hand over the horn.

Cyclists are ever-increasing in number—give them plenty of space and remember for the one speedhound jumping the lights there are hundreds of law abiders that you just don't notice. Try to focus on them.

Motorbikes and Scooters are not all ridden by leather clad Hells Angels or Jamie Oliver clones; most just want get about and avoid the Congestion Charge. As with cyclists, give plenty of space and check your blind spots.

Black Cabs, these roving London landmarks have been known, on occasion, to pull up to the curb, do a 'U-ie' and even advertise the FT without sufficient warning.

Traffic Wardens A.K.A. 'council revenue generating units'. Make sure you avoid illegal parking—unless you are an ambassador.

Driving Statistics

Speed Limit: **30 mph**

Average speed in rush hour: **6 mph** (estimates vary)

Amount stolen from Westminster parking meters: **Over £50,000 a week**

Increase in congestion predicted by 2015: **25%**

Amount of UK Carbon emissions coming from road traffic: **21%**

Worst day of the week for accidents: **Friday**

Ways to make it bearable

Most of the stress caused by driving in London, apart from the sheer volume of traffic, is caused by lack of consideration for others—usually as drivers are running late. So make sure you leave PLENTY of time for your journey, try not to block junctions, and let people out if you have a chance.

Get a tiny car that you can park sideways. Ha! That'll show 'em.

Join a car club like Street Car or WhizzGo– then you can drive whenever you want at a fraction of the cost of owning a car.

Try and avoid rush hour. Morning rush lasts from 7 am to 10.30 am, lunch rush from 11 am to 2.30 pm, school run rush from 2.45 pm to 4.15 pm and afternoon rush from 4.30 pm to 8.45 pm. Bonne chance…

Driving in the Congestion Charge Zone and the Low Emission Zone

The Congestion Zone, introduced in 2003, meant the centre of town was remarkably less congested—for about twenty minutes if the Daily Mail is to be believed. The charge is currently £8 if you enter the zone between 07:00 and 18:00, Monday to Friday. Bank Holidays don't count. If you pay a day late the charge goes up to £10. After that, hefty fines apply. Huge red Cs in circles alert drivers to the start of the zone, if you miss them you should consider a swift visit to your optician. Check the website for exemptions. There is ongoing debate over the actual impact of the charge, and whether the zone will expand, or be removed altogether.

The Low Emission Zone (LEZ) was introduced in February 2008 to deter large lorries, buses, coaches and vans from dragging their belching exhausts through town. It covers a much larger area than the Congestion Charge: almost all of London within the M25 and applies 24/7. The charge varies between £100 and £200. A DAY.

Key Roads

A1

Running straight north from St Paul's Cathedral in the City through Islington, Archway, Highgate and beyond, this old Roman Road has some freer stretches allowing the frustrated drive to accelerate to 43 mph for 3 seconds, get a speeding ticket and then slam on the brakes. Ends (eventually) in Princes Street, Edinburgh, Scotland.

North Circular/South Circular (A406)

This is the M25's angrier and twisted little brother. Circling Outer London it has some of the busiest stretches of road in London and even includes a ferry across the river at Woolwich. The way dwindles to one exhausted lane in certain sections, causing great clots of traffic every day in rush hour. See left for rush hour times.

Euston Rd/Marylebone Road (A501)

Running east-west past King's Cross and Euston, this wide road skirts the northern edge of the congestion zone. It gets very crowded, because it's a feeder road to the relatively breezy start of the A40 heading out of London.

Embankment

The view as you drive along the Embankment along the north bank of the Thames is breathtaking. It needs to be to keep you occupied as you inch forward for hours. Runs from Chelsea (A4) to Tower Bridge.

Vauxhall Bridge Rd/Grovesnor Place/Park Lane/Edgware Rd (A5)

Running roughly north-west from Vauxhall Bridge Rd, around Victoria, past Hyde Park Corner and Marble Arch and out to join the A40, this route is a free corridor through the Congestion zone – free from charge rather than free from traffic. Be prepared—it's rammed.

Old Kent Rd / New Cross Rd / Lewisham Way / etc. (A2/A20)

Running south-west from The Bricklayers Arms roundabout and eventually down to Dover, where you catch the ferry to France; the Old Kent Rd, despite being the cheapest Monopoly property, is totally free from traffic at all times. No wait—that can't be right.

A3

Starting at London Bridge, this road eventually ends up in Portsmouth, but you have to struggle past Elephant and Castle, Clapham Common and Wimbledon Common along with everyone else trying to get to Guildford.

Traffic Hot Spots

Angel, Elephant and Castle, Hanger Lane Gyratory, Vauxhall Gyratory, Trafalgar Square, Parliament Square, Hammersmith Gyratory, everywhere else.

Useful links

TfL Interactive Traffic Map:
trafficalerts.tfl.gov.uk/microsite

Capital FM for traffic news from the Flying Eye 95.8 FM

Parking for Cars
www.park-up.com

Parking for Motorbikes and Scooters:
www.parkingforbikes.com

Route Planner:
www.theaa.com/travelwatch/planner_main.jsp

Congestion Charge:
www.tfl.gov.uk/roadusers/congestioncharging

Parking Ticket Appeals:
www.ticketbusters.co.uk

The great thing about being a Londoner is there's really no need to have a car. Except on those few occasions where you're cursing yourself for hauling a flat-packed Ikea coffee table on the shitty Croydon tram service. This is where joining a membership-based carsharing company, such as Streetcar (www.streetcar.co.uk; 0845 644 8475), Zipcar (www.zipcar.co.uk; 0800 011 2555), City Car Club (www.citycarclub.co.uk; 0845 330 1234) or fledgling Connect by Hertz (www.connectbyhertz.com; 08708 45 45 45) comes in handy.

Streetcar and Zipcar are your best bet, as they offer self-service cars and vans to members, billable by the hour, day, week or month. The beauty of this service is there's probably either a Zipcar or Streetcar parked around the corner from wherever you are in central London, which means you don't have to hike to a car rental centre, stand in a queue or deal with annoying upselling at a counter. Plus,

if you get thrown out of your girlfriend's flat at 2 am and need a ride, you're in luck. Both offer a 24/7, 365 day a year self-service. For a membership fee of £50-60 a year, you have access to a fleet of cars, where all you have to do is enter the PIN, grab the keys from the glovebox and away you go.

On top of the membership fee, prices vary from £3.95 to £7.50 p/h depending on the company. The difference between Streetcar and Zipcar is the car. Streetcar offers only Volkswagens but their prices are pretty standardised. With Zipcar, you can have fun varying the car, with Minis, environmentally-friendly hybrids and BMWs on offer—but this means prices can vary too.

If you must go the conventional route, there are, of course, Hertz, National, and Avis centres aplenty, but for a smart Londoner who only wants a car sometimes—go for a carshare.

Company	Address	Phone	Map
Avis	8 Balderton St	0870 153 9104	2
Avis	88 Eversholt St	0840 010 7967	78
Avis	20 Seagrave Rd	0870 010 7968	43
Avis	86 St Katharines Wy	0207 423 8875	95
Avis	33 York Rd	0870 608 6369	104
Easy Car	Elms Mews	0871 0500 444	30
Easy Car	20 Seagrave Rd	0871 0500 444	43
Easy Car	88 Eversholt St	0871 0500 444	78
Easy Car	77 Britannia Rd	0871 0500 444	43
Easy Car	37 Munster Rd	0871 0500 444	48
Easy Car	68 Clapham Rd	0871 0500 444	135
Easy Car	136 Pentonville Rd	0871 0500 444	79
Easy Car	1 Brewery Rd	0871 0500 444	73
Easy Car	7 Bryanston St	0871 0500 444	1
Easy Car	171 Battersea Park Rd	0871 0500 444	133
Easy Car	43 York Rd	0871 0500 444	104
Easy Car	131 Belsize Rd	0871 0500 444	68
Easy Car	8 Balderton St	0871 0500 444	2
Easy Car	12 Semley Pl	0871 0500 444	19
Easy Car	33 York Rd	0871 0500 444	104
Easy Car	245 Warwick Rd	0871 0500 444	34
Enterprise	145 Bow Rd	02089805600	94
Enterprise	131 Belsize Rd	02073280200	68
Enterprise	200 King St	02085637400	40
Enterprise	59 Royal Mint St	02076809944	95
Enterprise	202 Ilderton Rd	02077323838	116
Enterprise	49 Woburn Pl	02076314700	94
Hertz	156 Southampton Row	087 0850 2664	4
Hertz	200 Buckingham Palace Rd	0870 8460002	20
Hertz	35 Edgware Rd	0870 8460011	1
Hertz	79 Clapham Rd	0207 582 5775	135
Hertz	713 Old Kent Rd	020 76392121	116
National	68 Clapham Rd	44 207 8200202	135
National	150 Pentonville Rd	44 20 72782273	79
National	7 Bryanston St	44 207 4081255	1
National	12 Semley Pl	44 207 2 59 16 00	19
National	43 York Rd	44 207 9282725	104
Thrifty	131 Belsize Rd	44 20 76253556	68
Thrifty	Sloane Ave	44 02072622223	46
Thrifty	178 Tower Bridge Rd	44 02074033458	107

Petrol Stations	Address	Map
Total	170 Marylebone Rd	2
et	30 Clipstone St	3
P	Russell Ct & Woburn Pl	4
hell	198 Old St	7
P	Park Ln & Mount St	9
P	Vauxhall Bridge Rd & Udall St	21
sso	115 Sutherland Ave	27
hell	104 Bayswater Rd	30
exaco	383 Edgware Rd	31
P	383 Edgware Rd	31
P	1 Westwick Gardens	33
P	Shepherds Bush Green & Rockley Rd	33
otal	137 Chiswick High Rd	38
otal	372 Goldhawk Rd	39
P	Great West Rd & Oil Mill Ln	39
P	372 Goldhawk Rd	39
et	182 Goldhawk Rd	40
P	Talgarth Rd & Gliddon Rd	41
esco	459 Fulham Rd	43
hell	49 Tadema Rd	44
hell	106 Old Brompton Rd	45
esco	601 King's Rd	49
otal	31 N Rd	51
hell	89 Hornsey Rise	53
ainsbury's	4 Williamson Rd	55
sso	640 Holloway Rd	60
exaco	73 Stapleton Hall Rd	62
et	314 7 Sisters Rd	63
otal	409 Kilburn High Rd	65
P	Finchley Rd & College Crescent	66
P	Haverstock Hill & Oman Rd	67
P	Wellington Rd & Wellington Pl	68
esco	115 Maida Vale	68
sso	33 Chalk Farm Rd	71
P	142 Camden Rd	72
esco	196 Camden Rd	72
ainsbury's	4 Williamson St	73
otal	109 York Wy	73
hell	104 Holloway Rd	74
	Hampstead Rd & Cardington St	77
P	Goodsway & Camley St	78
hell	276 Upper St	80
et	43 Stamford Hill	83
P	144 Stoke Newington Rd	86
exaco	168 Shoreditch High St	91

Petrol Stations	Address	Map
Total	112 Vallance Rd	91
BP	Cambridge Heath Rd & Paradise Row	92
Sainsbury's	1 Cambridge Heath Rd	92
Texaco	51 Grove Rd	93
Texaco	127 Bow Rd	94
Texaco	77 The Highway	95
Texaco	102 The Hwy	96
Shell	139 Whitechapel Rd	96
ASDA	151 E Ferry Rd	103
Shell	101 Southwark Bridge Rd	106
Shell	137 Walworth Rd	113
BP	New Kent Rd & Balfour St	113
Total	234 Old Kent Rd	114
Tesco	107 Dunton Rd	114
Total	272 St James Rd	115
Jet	747 Old Kent Rd	116
Shell	101 Evelyn St	118
Jet	179 Creek Rd	119
Jet	25 Greenwich High Rd	120
BP	Camberwell Rd & Albany Rd	121
BP	Peckham Rd & Southampton Wy	122
Total	38 Peckham Rd	122
BP	New Cross Rd & Pomeroy St	125
Sainsbury's	263 New Cross Rd	125
Jet	42 Hinton Rd	127
Jet	13 E Dulwich Rd	130
Texaco	213 Kennington Rd	131
BP	238 Kennington Ln	131
Shell	326 Queenstown Rd	133
Esso	2 Battersea Park Rd	133
Esso	54 Wandsworth Rd	134
Sainsbury's	62 Wandsworth Rd	134
Esso	77 Clapham Rd	135
Total	257 Upper Richmond Rd	136
BP	Swandon Wy & Smugglers Wy	138
Texaco	474 Wandsworth Rd	142
Tesco	330 Brixton Rd	144
Esso	243 Brixton Rd	145
Total	39 Nightingale Ln	147
Total	40 Balham Hill	148
BP	124 Brixton Hill	150
BP	Marius Rd & Rowfant Rd	151

January

- **New Year's Day Parade** · Big Ben to Piccadilly Circus · Marching band and thousands of kids. How better to cure a hangover?
- **London Boat Show** · ExCel Exhibition Centre · Like we always say: you can never have too many yachts.
- **Russian Winter Festival** · Trafalgar Square · Magical Russian Winterland replaces the normal Pigeon-Crap Land.
- **London Art Fair** · Business Design Centre · Pick up something to hide that patch of mould.
- **London International Mime Festival** · Southbank Centre · Even weirder when you see it for real.
- **Charles I Commemoration Ceremony** · Trafalgar Sq - St James' Palace · Thousands of uniformed Cavaliers confuse the tourists.

February

- **Chinese New Year** · West End · Party like it's 4707.
- **Destinations: Holiday and Travel Show** · Earls Court Exhibition Centre · Chase away the Winter Blues.
- **London Fashion Week** · Natural History Museum · Far Too Thin.
- **National Wedding Show** · Olympia · Perfect day out for a first date.
- **Lifted** · Harrods · A bizarre annual exhibition inside Harrod's lifts.
- **The Great Spitalfields Pancake Race** · Old Truman Brewery · Now even The Great Unwashed can buy art!
- **Blessing the Throats** · St Etheldreda's Church, Ely Place · Lemsip not working? Sore throats cured by holy candle.
- **Clowns' Service** · Holy Trinity, Dalston · Because God likes clowns too.
- **Kinetica Art Fair** · P3 · Carnivorous lampshades and pole-dancing robots? We're there.
- **BAFTAs** · London Palladium · Ten points per autograph.

March

- **Affordable Art Fair** · The Marquee, Battersea Park · Now even The Great Unwashed can buy art!
- **Ideal Home Show** · Earls Court Exhibition Centre · Make your home ideal (or a bit less grotty).
- **St Patrick's Day Parade** · Park Lane · Shamrocks, river-dancing, big fluffy Guinness hats: true Irish tradition.

- **East Festival** · East London · Because East London isn't just for muggers.
- **London Drinker Beer & Cider Festival** · The Camden Centre · Get rat-arsed on Pressed Rat & Warthog.
- **La Dolce Vita** · Business Design Centre · Get your sampling face on
- **Move It** · Olympia · Put on your dancing shoes.
- **The International Food & Drink Event** · Olympia · This gorge-fest happens biannually, so start starving yourself now.
- **The Country Living Spring Fair** · Business Design Centre · For those with time for wooden chicken eggs
- **JobServe Live!** · Olympia · Career ideas and thousands of vacancies.

April

- **Oxford & Cambridge Boat Race** · River Thames · Hole up in a pub by the river and cheer over a beer.
- **Virgin London Marathon** · Greenwich – The Mall · 35,000 pairs of bleeding nipples.
- **London Book Fair** · Earl's Court · The publishing industry's main event. Occasionally stuff for free.
- **Alternative Fashion Week** · Old Spitalfields Market · Huge range of cutting edge fashion. And fetishwear.
- **Queen's Birthday Gun Salute** · Hyde Park · Who said the monarchy is archaic?
- **St George's Day** · Covent Garden / Cenotaph / Shakespeare's Globe · Brush up your Morris dancing skills.
- **The Real Food Festival** · Earl's Court Exhibition Centre · Real Food: much nicer than fake food.
- **Hot Cross Bun Service** · St Bartholomew-the-Great, Smithfield · Widows get a free hot cross bun. Worth losing the husband.
- **London Independent Film Festival** · Various West and Central Cinemas · Cool celebration of cinematographic indieness without The Man. Or something.
- **Sci-Fi Festival** · London Apollo · The UK's only Sci-Fi Festival. Thank god.

May

- **Freedom of the City** · Central London · Frequently awesome improv and experimental festival attracting top names.
- **Baishakhi Mela** · Brick Lane · Celebrate the Bengali New Year in the British tradition: vindaloo.

- **Mind, Body, Spirit Festival** · Royal Horticultural Halls · Make up for all the time in the pub.
- **Camden Crawl** · Throughout Camden · If you're not crawling by the end, you haven't done it right.
- **Chelsea Flower Show** · Royal Hospital Chelsea · You'll go for the flowers. You'll stay for the Pimms.
- **The Drag Olympics** · The Way Out Club · Drag Queens are put throug their pedicured, high-heeled paces

June

- **City of London Festival** · The City · Bringing High Culture to a bunch o bankers.
- **Start of Open Air Theatre season** · Regent's Park · Ignore the climate and take in an outdoor play.
- **Taste of London** · Regent's Park · The best picnic in the world.
- **Wimbledon** · All England Lawn Tennis and Croquet Club · Short skirts and grunting. Marvellous.
- **Trooping the Colour** · Horse Guard's Parade · Hundreds of chaps in uniforms. Ohhhhh yes.
- **Meltdown Festival** · Southbank Centre · Eclectic music festival curated by major musicians.
- **Royal Academy Summer Exhibition** · Royal Academy · Lots and lots and LOTS of art.
- **Arts Festival Chelsea** · Chelsea · The artists formerly known as 'The Chelsea Festival'.
- **Big Sexy Festy Party** · Finsbury Park · So good-natured you'll want to hug a tree. And it's FREE!
- **Naked Bike Ride** · Hyde Park · Don think about the bums on seats.

July

- **The Big Dance (biennial: even years)** · Various around London · London learns to dance.
- **Dogget's Coat & Badge Race** · Thames: London Bridge to Chelsea · Intense boat race to win a badge. Hardly seems worth it.
- **Pimms Urban Regatta** · Finsbury Square · People full of Pimms race on land in bottomless boats. Bloody Ozzies.
- **Pride London** · Trafalgar Square · One of Britain's biggest, funnest street parties.
- **The British 10k London Run** · Hyde Park - Whitehall · Work off the pies.
- **Hampton Court Palace Show** · Hampton Court · Stock up your garden / flowerpot / imagination.

The Chap Olympics · Bedford Square Gardens · Olympics for gentleman—no sportswear please.

Rise Festival · Finsbury Park · Celebrating the best of multicultural London, for free.

Swan Upping · River Thames · Census of swans. For goodness sake.

Opening of Buckingham Palace · Buckingham Palace · The Plebeians allowed in to see how their taxes (and steep entrance fees) are spent.

Wireless Festival · Hyde Park · Big names vibrate the Serpentine.

Greenwich Beer & Jazz Festival · Old Royal Naval College · An odd paring that somehow works.

Shoreditch Festival · Shoreditch. Because you can never have too many local festivals. Apparently.

August

Innocent Smoothies Festival · Regent's Park · You wouldn't think fun could be this wholesome.

Great British Beer Festival · Earls Court Exhibition Centre · A festival that puts the Great in Britain.

Trafalgar Square Festival · Trafalgar Square · 3 weeks of music, theatre, dance and art.

Carnaval del Pueblo · Burgess Park · Thousands of Latino lovelies. That's all you need to know, right?

London Triathlon · Docklands · Marathons are for pussies.

London Mela · Gunnersbury Park · Partaaaay, Asia-style.

Metro Weekender · Clapham Common · Dance music Saturday, bands on Sunday, chilled all weekend.

Notting Hill Carnival · Ladbroke Grove · Party till your wallet gets nicked.

Kids Week · West End · West End shows free for kids. Soooo unfaaaaiiiir.

Bathing the Buddha · Leicester Square · Buddha gets a birthday bath.

Tiger Beer Singapore Chilli Crab Festival · Truman Brewery · Cold beer, hot food and cool sounds.

September

The Great British Duck Race · The Thames · Like the Oxbridge boat race. But with 165,000 rubber ducks.

Horseman's Sunday · Hyde Park Crescent · London's horses say their Hail Maries. Yes, really.

Oyster & Seafood Fair · Hays Galleria · The romance of oysters with the unholy stink of kippers.

· Thames Festival · Tower Bridge - Westminster · Fireworks, costumes, river races, carnivals. Kids like it.

· Last Night of the Proms · Royal Albert Hall · Camp overnight if you want tickets.

· Spitalfields Show & Green Fair · Buxton Street · Who has the biggest marrow?

· Open House Weekend · Various around London · Over 600 architectural landmarks open for a nosey.

· Fashion Week · Natural History Museum · the September instalment of the famous frockfest.

· Great Gorilla Run · Start at London Underwriting Centre · Raise £400 for the Gorilla Organisation and the costume's yours.

October

· The Big Draw · Museum of Childhood · Pencils, not guns. Unfortunately.

· 'Original Pearly Kings & Queens Association Harvest Festival · Church of St Martin-in-the-Fields · Affordable Art Fair.

· London Tattoo Convention · Old Truman Brewery · Who cares if it looks crap when you're 80?

· International Halloween Festival · Queen Mary College · Witches, druids and shamans unite for Europe's biggest Pagan festival.

· Halloween · London Dungeon · Trick Or Treating is for pussies.

· Frieze Art Fair · Regent's Park · Air kisses all round.

· London Film Festival · BFI Southbank · Two weeks of the best new films and lectures from A-Listers.

· Metro Ski & Snowboard Show · Olympia · London hosts the world's biggest winter sport show. Naturally.

· Shell Wildlife Photographer of the Year (exhibition opens, for 6mths) · Natural History Museum Puts your arty market photos to shame.

· The Yoga Show · Olympia · Bendy people upon bendy people. Literally.

· Turner Prize Exhibition · Tate Britain · Get to know the next Hirst or Emin.

November

· London's Christmas Ice Rinks · Venues across London · Much more romantic in your head than in reality.

· Brighton Veteran Car Run · Starts Hyde Park · Century-old bangers potter their way to Brighton.

· Erotica Show · Olympia · 31,000 horny adults pretend they're just browsing.

· Bonfire Night · Venues across London · Hundreds of thousands of pounds go pop.

· Royal British Legion Festival of Remembrance · Royal Albert Hall · Take tissues.

· Lord Mayor's Show · Central London · Running for over 800 years and yet still a bit crap.

· London Jazz Festival · South Bank Centre · Start practising your jazz hands.

· Winter Wonderland · Hyde Park · Grottos and Glühweins galore.

December

· Satan's Grotto · London Dungeon · Tortured elves and spit-roasting robins.

· Trafalgar Square Christmas Tree · Trafalgar Square · The only thing everyone knows about Oslo.

· Blackrock Masters Tennis · Royal Albert Hall · Former World No.1s wheeze their way through a tournament.

· Peter Pan Cup · Serpentine Lido, Hyde Park · Freeze your nipples off on Christmas morning.

· Great Christmas Pudding Race · Covent Garden · We're mad, us! What are we like? Crazy!

· Christmas Carol Sing-along · Royal Albert Hall · Belt out your favourites and get in the mood.

· International Horse Show · Olympia · Not just for posh people. But mostly.

· Midnight Mass at St Paul's · St Paul's · Eats the other Midnight Masses for breakfast.

· New Year's Eve Fireworks · Jubilee Gardens · Oooooh. And, of course, aaaaaaah.

Tactics

Finding somewhere to live in London is a ruthless and cutthroat business. Make sure you have plenty of red bull, cigarettes and patience. Also take a week off. And hire a driver, maybe.

Ok, so these precautions aren't completely necessary, but you will have to work in mysterious and multifarious ways if you don't want to spend the next six months paying through your gullible nose for mice and verrucas. A good place to start is by harassing your friends, your friends' friends, and your friends' friends' friends. Send out a group email and hope it gets passed around, and make sure you Tweet like mad about it. Twitter is a great place to get your request passed around. Who knows? Stephen Fry might have a room to let. Estate agents (see below for a list) will invariably try and rip you off but, then again, so will everyone else, so it's worth registering with all the big ones, as well as any whose office you see in the street, or you spot in newspapers, on TV or the internet. After uncovering a fair few completely brazen lies in the property listings on www.gumtree.com you will find that many of the smaller businesses place adverts for (sometimes fake) properties here. Don't be put off by the lies though, because this can be a good way of finding an agent (or getting in direct contact with a landlord) who is keen to make a deal with you, or who will try and match the prices advertised, even if they have nothing that fits the bill at the exact moment of lying. Of course, some of these listings are also genuine, and a good way to find rooms/apartments at lower than usual rates. Just bare in mind that a LOT of people use this site.

General sites

www.gumtree.com
www.findaproperty.co.uk
www.craigslist.org
www.rightmove.co.uk
www.propertyfinder.com

Estate Agents

There are hundreds of Estate Agents an Letting Agents across the city, some of th larger players (good and bad) include:

www.foxtons.co.uk - Offices all over London
www.keatons.co.uk - Bow, Hackney, Harringey, Kentish Town, Stratford.
www.black-katz.com - Lettings only agency numerous offices.
www.fjlord.co.uk - Numerous offices, specialise in uncooperative staff.
www.nelsonslettings.com - South and central London.
www.atkinsonmcleod.com - City and Docklands.

If you do end up using an agent, they wi of course want to charge you an additiona fee beyond any deposits or advance ren required by the landlord. But, as many of th agents in central London are close togethe it's possible that they may be competing wit each other to sell/rent the same properties This will enable you to get a better deal. S shop around, be devious, and backstab a much as possible.

Council Tax

Council Tax is an annoying hidden cos that always comes as a bit of a surprise. I is worked out by your local council and i based on the value of your house/flat, whic the council will already have placed in to on of 8 tax bands (bands are A–G, G covering the most valuable properties).There ar several ways to determine the value of property, but the easiest is probably to go t the website of the valuation office at www voa.gov.uk. Having done that, it's possibl to weigh up the benefits of different area by comparing the council tax in equivalen bands charged by different local councils. It fairly laborious, but worth it in the long rur if you can be bothered.

Because council tax is based on the property, not the people inside it, the rate is constant no matter how many people live in the house. This means that it's much cheaper to live in a big house with lots of people to split the tax with, than on your own, when you are liable for the full amount. Students do not have to pay council tax at all, but if they are sharing with one or more non-students then there will still be council tax to pay. A single non-student in a house full of students receives a 25% discount on his/her council tax bill, but if there is more than one non-student then all non-students are liable to pay full whack.

Alternative Options

In a city where house prices have been soaring through the roof some time now (although it's calmed down somewhat recently), of course people do things like squat, have dreadlocks and go vegan. If you're not willing to go the whole way but fancy an adventure, or simply don't have much money, then it might be worth taking a look at being a guardian for Camelot. This company aims to fill vacant properties with responsible people who will prevent them from being abused. You must have good references, a job, and be over eighteen, as well as be ok with sharing with an indeterminate number of strangers, but the benefits are the unusual properties (e.g. schools, disused churches), the often large spaces and the ridiculously cheap rent (£25–60 pw inclusive of all bills). Of course loads of people want to do this, and properties in London are not always available, but it's nevertheless a good idea to keep an eye on their site if the idea excites you: www.camelotproperty.co.uk.

WAREHOUSES

As with Starbucks and obesity, us Brits have finally caught on to the American craze for warehouse 'live/work' spaces. Okay we may have had the likes of Tracey Emin and other artists living in old carpet factories

since the YBA days, but recently a whole crop of established estate agents have been refurbishing lofts and factories for letting at a premium. Any established warehouser will tell you the way to go is independent, through enthusiastic urban explorers who renovate and convert these old buildings for love and enjoyment. Often the only way into this secret brotherhood of the leaky roof is by simply ending up at a huge party at 4am in one of these spaces and asking the residents politely. The freedom of living in these places can be exhilarating if you've spent years toeing the line with grumpy neighbours and grumpier landlords.

CANAL-BOATS

If all this land lubbing is bringing you down, there's always the option of dropping anchor at Little Venice or the Lea Valley Harbour and sampling London's canal networks. More and more skint artsy fartsy folk are squeezing their possessions into canal boats and living a romantic life on the water. A casual stroll down Regent's Canal may convince you this is the way to live, but bare in mind the hidden cons of London nautical life: mooring fees, fuel, unlit walks down leafy paths frequented by degenerates… Don't say we didn't warn you!

The best of the best

London is full of interactive children's pursuits, and nothing beats discovering all the joys that the city has to offer to the little ones, so we thought we'd give you some inside tips on what there is!

- **Best Rainy Day Activity:** The Science Museum (Exhibition Road, SW7 2DD, 0870 870 4868) is great fun and one of London's most interactive museums. Don't miss the Launchpad gallery, which is full of hands-on exhibits to tinker with, simulators and a face morphing machine. The museum's occasional Science Nights are activity filled, with overnight camping in the building included. Entry is free. Open 7 days a week from 10am to 6pm.

- **Coolest Cinema:** The BFI London IMAX Cinema (1 Charlie Chaplin Walk, SE1 8XR, 020 7902 1234) has the largest screen (20 metres) in the country, as well as an 11,600-watt digital surround sound system with which to deafen your children. With most of the cinema's 3D programming dedicated to children's films, they'll be spoilt rotten by the whole experience; even the entrance to the place is cool, with futuristic blue lighting paving your way through the tunnels.

- **Goriest Tourist Haunt:** The London Dungeon (28-34 Tooley Street, SE1 2SZ, 020 7403 7221) specialises in the darker side of English history and has a preponderance of gruesome waxworks, theme rides and costumed staff to scare the bejesus out of your children, which they'll love (unless you've brought them up to be softly). Open all week from 11am to 5pm.

- **Best Tour For Budding Media Moguls:** The BBC Television Centre Tour (Wood Lane, W12 7RJ, 0870 603 0304) provides a chance for children 9 and over to take a behind the scenes look at the world of TV, as well as a chance to play in an interactive studio. A separate tour (ages 7 and over) entitled "The CBBC Experience" is based on the BBC's kids' channel and offers visitors the chance to roam around the Blue Peter garden, amongst other things. Regular tours are conducted every day except Sunday.

- **Best Ice Cream:** It's no secret that kids love ice cream, but the plethora of dodgy "Mr Whippy" vans selling their frozen wares in London can be improved upon. For outstanding homemade gourmet sorbets and exotic ice cream cones, there is no better place than the kiosk to the side

of Golders Hill Park Refreshment House (North End Road, NW3 7HD, 020 8455 8010); prices are very reasonable and the park is a gorgeous setting within which to consume such tasty delights.

- **Best One To Keep The Boys Happy:** The Arsenal Emirates Stadium Tour (Ashburton Grove, N7 7AF, 020 7704 4504). Surely even Spurs fans would appreciate a look behind the scenes at London's newest and most aesthetic football venue. Poke around the first team dressing room, walk down the player's tunnel and sample a unique pitchside view of the stadium; under 5s get in free.

- **Best For Halloween Costumes:** Escapade (150 Camden High Street, NW1 0NE, 020 7485 7384) has been kitting kids out in all manner of costumes since 1982, and offers wigs (maybe one for Dad?), hats, masks, make-up, jokes and magic tricks. Perfect for trick or treat, or for those already bored of their child's ugly face.

- **Best Eatery For Families:** Maxwell's (8-9 James Street, WC2E 8BH) lies deep in the heart of Covent Garden and specialises in burgers (does any child not like burgers?) which won't break parents' banks. A kids' menu is provided, as well as activities and games.

Rainy day activities

Especially for when the infamous London weather puts a dampener on outdoor activities…

- **Cartoon Museum** (35 Little Russell Street, WC1A 2HH, 020 7580 8155) This fascinating place archives the development of cartoon art in Britain, from the 18th century through to the present day; best of all, the Young Artists' Gallery lets children try their hands at animation and claymation.

- **London Aquarium** (County Hall, Westminster Bridge Road, SE1 7PB, 020 7967 8000) One of the largest aquariums in the world, over 400 species of aquatic life (including the only zebra sharks in the U.K.) can be found within this building. With three floors, piranhas, and pools where you can prod things, there's more than enough to keep even the most jaded parent happy.

- **London Eye** (Jubilee Gardens, South Bank, SE1 7PB, 0870 500 0600) This 135-metre high riverside Ferris wheel offers breathtaking views of London in up to 25 miles in each direction, all from the vantage point of an air-conditioned glass pod. Book online to beat the queues.

- **Natural History Museum** (Cromwell Road, SW7 5BD, 020 7942 5000) Ever wanted to see a replica skeleton of a 26-metre long Diplodocus dinosaur? It's one of the 70 million items housed within this excellent museum, which also includes the Darwin Centre, a must for any budding paleontologists; non-nerds should love it too.

- **Madame Tussaud's** (Marylebone Road, NW1 5LR, 0870 999 0046) Infamous exhibition of waxworks, with recently introduced interactive exhibits giving you the chance to score a goal for England or sing with Britney Spears (she'll be the one lip-syncing). Worth booking online to avoid the often long queues.

- **Museum Of London** (150 London Wall, EC2Y 5HN, 0870 444 3852, some galleries undergoing renovation and due to re-open late 2009) Explains the history of London in vivid detail; the innovative layout consists of a chain of chronological galleries (no skipping to 1945, OK?) Also has fragments of the old London Wall in the grounds.

- **Peter Harrison Planetarium** (Royal Observatory Greenwich, Greenwich Park, SE10 9NF, 020 8312 8565) Open since 2007 and the only planetarium in London seats 120 and uses the latest technology to take you on an armchair tour of the universe. Children aged 4 and under will not be admitted.

- **Queens Ice And Bowl** (17 Queensway, W2 4QP, 020 7229 0172) An ice rink, ten pin bowling alleys and a pizza restaurant, it's the perfect opportunity for kids to stuff their faces whilst watching their Dad break a bone on the rink. Children's skating classes available.

- **Topsy Turvy World** (Brent Cross Shopping Centre, Prince Charles Drive, NW4 3FP, 020 8359 9920) A huge indoor playground in the middle of one of London's busiest shopping centres. There's more to this place than just bouncy things and over-excitement, it also offers baking activities (might as well get your children cooking for you early) and various classes.

- **Tower Of London** (Tower Hill, EC3N 4AB, 0870 756 7070) A cornucopia of royal history and English culture lies within the Tower's ancient walls, with royal jewels aplenty. Good for the whole family, and under 5s get in free. Avoid the queues by booking ahead.

- **The V&A Museum Of Childhood** (Cambridge Heath Road, E2 9PA, 020 8983 5200) This lesser known gem of the Victoria & Albert Museum houses the national childhood collection, which basically means it's full of toys, games, dolls, dollhouses, nursery antiques and children's costumes. There's no shortage of activities and events going on here to keep your kids occupied, and it's free.

Classes

A recent resurgence in the amount of out of school programmes being implemented in the capital means that there's more for your kids to do than ever before.

- **Art Club** (Orleans House Gallery, Riverside, TW1 3DJ, 020 8831 6000) A rare opportunity for 5-10 year olds to work with practicing artists and explore new techniques and materials. Every Wednesday and Thursday from 3.45-5pm.

- **Barnsbury One O'Clock Club** (Barnard Park, Hemingford Road, N1 0JU, 020 7278 9494) Fun and games for the under 5s.

- **Brixton Recreation Centre** (27 Brixton Station Road, SW9 8QQ, 020 7926 9779) Recently refurbished, this centre includes The Energy Zone (ages 5-15) for ball games and The Fitness Zone (ages 8-15) with SHOKK fitness equipment specifically designed for the younger body builder/steroid abuser.

- **Camden Square Play Centre** (Camden Square, NW1 9RE, 020 7485 6827) After school (and school holiday) centre with fun activities for children aged 4-12.

- **Camden Swiss Cottage Swimming Club** (Swiss Cottage Leisure Centre, Winchester Road, NW3 3NR, 020 7974 5440) Swimming lessons for children aged 4 and upward.

- **Chang's Hapkido Academy** (Topnotch Health Club, 3 Tudor Street, EC4Y 0AH, 07951 535876) Martial arts school with classes for ages 12 and upward.

- **The Circus Space** (Coronet Street, N1 6HD, 020 7613 4141) Prepare your children for a life in the circus with The Circus Space's variety of classes and workshops for all ages.

- **Crazee Kids** (Jackson Lane Community Centre, Archway Road, N6 5AA, Tuesdays), (Union Church & Community Centre, Weston Park, N8 9TA, Saturdays) 020 8444 5333, Weekly term-time dance, drama and music classes. Summer workshops.
- **Harringay Club** (Hornsey YMCA, 50 Tottenham Lane, N8 7EE, 020 8348 2124) A range of things to do for those aged up to 15, including a pre-school programme, gymnastics, ballet, street dance and kickboxing.
- **The Kids' Cookery School** (107 Gunnersbury Len W3 8HQ, 020 8992 8882) Get your kids cooking at this fine venue which offers classes and workshops for those aged 3 and upwards.
- **Kite Art Studios** (Priory Mews, 2B Bassein Park Road, W12 9RY, 020 8576 6278) Courses and workshops on painting, pottery and jewellery making amongst other fun activities for kids of all ages. Mother and toddler sessions too.
- **London Irish Centre** (50-52 Camden Square, NW1 9XB, 020 7916 7222) Irish dancing classes for beginners upwards, every Monday at 6pm, courtesy of the Barrett Semple-Morris School.
- **The Little Angel Theatre (**14 Dagmar Passage, Cross Street, N1 2DN, 020 7226 1787) Children's theatre offering after-school courses in puppet making, the art of puppetry performance and a Saturday Puppet Club.
- **The Little Gym** (Compass House, Riverside West, Smugglers Way, SW18 1DB, 020 8874 6567) Gymnastics and skills development within a relaxed environment for children aged up to 12.
- **Music House For Children** (Bush Hall, 310 Uxbridge Road, W12 7LJ, 020 8932 2652) Whether it's instrumental or singing lessons, this wonderful place can provide individual and group tuition and even caters for 1 year olds!
- **Painted Earth** (Arch 65, The Catacombs, Stables Market, NW1 8AH, 020 7424 8983) Ceramic arts classes supervised by staff. Children can make their own mugs and plates.
- **Richmond Junior Chess Club** (ETNA Community Centre, 13 Rosslyn Road, TW1 2AR, 07720 716336) Chess classes with a mixture of instruction and play for those up to the age of 18.
- **Sobell Leisure Centre** (Hornsey Road, N7 7NY, 020 7609 2166) No need to book, just turn up for coached sessions in basketball, badminton, football and ice hockey amongst other sports.

Children aged 7 and under must be accompanied by an adult.

- **Tricycle Theatre** (269 Kilburn High Road, NW6 7JR, 020 7328 1000) Not just a theatre/cinema/gallery, the Tricycle also runs term-time workshops in drama, storytelling and music.
- **Triyoga** (6 Erskine Road, NW3 3AJ, 020 7483 3344) Let the kids get their Zen on at after school yoga classes for ages 5 and over.
- **Westway Stables** (20 Stable Way, Latimer Road, W11 6QX, 020 8964 2140) Horse riding lessons for the over 5s in the heart of Notting Hill.

Babysitting/nanny/services

- **Nannies Unlimited** 11 Chelveton Road, SW15 1RN, 020 8788 9640
- **Nanny Search** 1st Floor, 1 Shepherds Hill, N6 5QJ, 020 8348 4111
- **Sleeptight Nannies** 20 Nursery Road, N14 5QB, 020 8292 2618
- **Top Notch Nannies** 49 Harrington Gardens, SW7 4JU, 020 7259 2626

Where to go for more info

www.kidslovelondon.com

Shopping essentials

- **Baby Dior** 6 Harriet Street, SW1X 9JW, 020 7823 2039 – Encourage label envy as soon as possible.
- **Baby Munchkins** 186 Hoxton Street, N1 5LH, 020 7684 5994 – Baby wear.
- **Balloonland** 12 Hale Lane, NW7 3NX, 020 8906 3302 – Balloons and party supplies.
- **Benjamin Pollock's Toyshop** 44 The Piazza, Covent Garden WC2E 8RF, 020 7379 7866 – Toys.
- **Biff** 43 Dulwich Village, SE21 7BN, 020 8299 0911 – Designer and street brands.
- **Boomerang** 69 Blythe Road, W14 0HP, 020 7610 5232 – Clothes and necessities for tots.
- **Bonpoint** Chic clothes.
  17 Victoria Grove, W8 5RW – 020 7584 5131
  197 Westbourne Grove, W11 2SE – 020 7792 2515
  256 Brompton Road, SW3 2AS – 020 3263 5057
  35B Sloane Street, SW1X 9LP – 020 7235 1441
  38 Old Bond Street, W1S 4QW – 020 7495 1680

Burberry 21-23 New Bond Street, W1S 2RE, 020 7839 5222 – Clothes.

Caramel 291 Brompton Road, SW3 2DY, 020 7589 7001 – Cool clothes.

Catamini – Babies and children's clothes. 33C King's Road, SW3 4LX – 020 7824 8897, 52 South Molton Street, W1Y 1HF – 020 7629 8099

Cheeky Monkeys – Mainly wooden toys. 202 Kensington Park Road, W11 1NR – 020 7792 9022, 94 Kings Road, SW6 4UL – 020 7731 3037

Children's Book Centre 237 Kensington High Street, W8 6SA, 020 7937 7497 – Books.

Coco Children's Boutique 27A Devonshire Street, W1G 6PN, 020 7935 3554 – Children's boutique (fancy that!).

D2 Leisure 201-203 Roman Road, E2 0QY, 020 8980 4966 – Bicycle shop.

Daisy & Tom 181 King's Road, SW3 5EB, 020 7352 5000 – Clothes, toys and a carousel.

Davenports Magic Shop 7 Adelaide Street, WC2N 4HZ, 020 7836 0408 – Magic shop.

Early Learning Centre 36 King's Road, SW3 4UD, 020 7581 5764 – Educational toyshop.

Disney Store – Disney merchandise.

Unit 10, The Piazza, WC2E 8HD – 020 7836 5037

22A & 26 The Broadway Shopping Centre, W6 9YD – 020 8748 8886

360-366 Oxford Street, W1N 9HA – 020 7491 9136

Eric Snook's Toyshop 32 Covent Garden Market, WC1 8RE, 020 7379 7681 – Toys and teddies.

Escapade 150 Camden High Street, NW1 0NE, 020 7485 7384 – Costumes and masks.

The Farmyard 63 Barnes High Street, SW13 9LF, 020 8878 7338 – Toys for younger children and babies.

GapKids/Baby Gap

35 Hampstead High Street, NW3 1QE – 020 7794 9182

146-148 Regent Street, W1B 5SH – 020 7287 5095

Brent Cross Shopping Centre, NW4 3FB – 020 8203 9696

122 King's Road, SW3 4TR – 020 7823 7272

4 Queens Road, SW19 8YE- 020 8947 9074

101-111 Kensington High Street, W8 5SA – 020 7368 2900

260-262 Chiswick High Road, W4 1PD – 020 8995 3255

47-49 St John's Wood High Street, NW8 7NJ – 020 7586 6123

151 Queensway, W2 4YL – 020 7221 8039

330-340 Cabot Place East, E14 4QT – 020 7513 0241

121-123 Long Acre, WC2E 9PA – 020 7836 0646

Green Rabbit 20 Briston Grove, N8 9EX, 020 8348 3770 – Contemporary kids' wear.

Hamley's 188-196 Regent Street, W1B 5BT, 020 7153 9000 – Toys galore, tourists galore.

Happy Returns 36 Rosslyn Hill, NW3 1NH, 020 7435 2431 – Toys again!

Honeyjam 267 Portobello Road, W11 1LR, 020 7243 0449 – Retro and vintage toys and rocking horses.

Igloo Kids Wide range of kids' clothes. 300 Upper Street, N1 2TU – 020 7354 7300, 80 St John's Wood, NW8 7SH – 020 7483 2332

Infantasia Unit 103 Wood Green Shopping City, N22 6YA, 020 8889 1494 – Furniture and bedding.

International Magic 89 Clerkenwell Road, EC1R 5BX, 020 7405 7324 – Magic shop.

Joujou & Lucy 32 Clifton Road, W9 1ST, 020 7289 0866 – Children's boutique.

Kent & Carey 154 Wandsworth Bridge Road, SW6 2UH, 020 7736 5554 – Classic children's clothes.

Little Stinkies 15 Victoria Grove, W8 5RW, 020 7052 0077 – Dolls' houses, toys and puppet theatres.

Marie Chantal 148 Walton Street, SW3 2JJ, 020 7838 1111 – Children's fashion.

MIMMO 602 Fulham Road, SW6 5PA, 020 7731 4706 – Designer duds.

Mothercare – The leading chain for baby stuff in the UK; will sell you everything but the baby.

Brent Cross Shopping Centre, NW4 3FD – 020 8202 5377

416 Brixton Road, SW9 7AY – 020 7733 1494

Unit 7, The Waterglade Centre, 1-8 The Broadway, W5 2ND – 0208 579 6181

Ravenside Retail Park, Angel Road, N18 3HA – 020 8807 5518

146 High Street, SE9 1BJ – 020 8859 7957

4 Palace Gardens, EN2 6SN – 020 8367 1188

316 North End Road, SW6 1NG – 020 7381 6387

Kings Mall Shopping Centre, W6 0PZ – 020 8600 2860

448 Holloway Road, N7 6QA – 020 7607 0915

112 High Street, TW3 1NA – 020 8577 1767

Unit 1A, Richmond Retail Park, Mortlake Road, Kew – 020 8878 3758

41 Riverdale High Street, SE13 7EP – 020 8852 2167

526-528 Oxford Street, W1C 1LW – 0845 365 0515

Unit 2, Aylesham Centre, Rye Lane, SE15 5EW – 020 7358 0093

33-34 The Mall, E15 1XD – 020 8534 5714

BHS Surrey Quays Shopping Centre, Redriff Road, SE16 7LL – 020 7237 2025

Unit 59, Southside Shopping Centre, SW18 4TF – 020 8877 4180

Unit Lsu4, Centre Court, SW19 8YA – 020 8944 5296

38-40 High Road, N22 6BX – 020 8888 6920

62 Powis Street, SE18 1LQ – 020 8854 3540

- **Never Never Land** 3 Mildhurst Parade, Fortis Green, N10 3EJ, 020 883 3997 – Toys and dolls.

- **Olive Loves Alfie** 84 Stoke Newington Church Street, N16 0AP, 020 7241 4212 – Children's lifestyle shop.

- **Patrick's Toys & Models** 107 Lillie Road, SW6 7SX, 020 7385 9864 – Outdoor games and equipment.

- **Patrizia Wigan** 19 Walton Street, SW3 2HX, 020 7823 7080 – Clothing boutique.

- **Petit Bateau** 62 South Molton Street, W1K 5SR, 020 7491 4498 – Luxurious baby wear.

- **Petite Ange** 6 Harriet Street, SW1X 9JW, 020 7235 7737 – Exclusive clothing.

- **Please Mum** 85 Knightsbridge, SW1X 7RB, 020 7486 1380 – Expensive clothing.

- **Pom D'Api** 3 Blenheim Crescent, W11 2EE, 020 7243 0535 – Classy shoes.

- **QT Toys** 90 Northcote Road, SW11 6QN, 020 7223 8637 – Toys, games and gifts.

- **Rachel Riley** 14 Pont Street, SW1X 9EN, 020 7935 7007 – Clothes.

- **Rainbow** 253 Archway Road, N6 5BS, 020 8340 9700 – Toys, games and clothes.

- **Showroom** 64 Titchfield Street, W1W 7QH, 020 7636 2501 – Funky children's clothes.

- **Soup Dragon** 27 Topsfield Parade, Tottenham Lane, N8 8PT, 020 8348 0224 – Toys and clothes.

- **The Shoe Station** 3 Station Approach, Kew Gardens, TW9 3QB, 020 8940 9905 – Shoes and footwear.

- **Their Nibs** 214 Kensington Park Road, W11 1NR, 020 7221 4263 – Designer clothes and bedding.

- **Tots** 39 Turnham Green Terrace, W4 1RG, 020 8995 0520 – Clothes boutique.

- **Toys R Us** - Toys, toys, toys.
  Tilling Road (opposite Brent Cross Shopping Centre), NW2 1LW – 020 8209 0019
  Great Cambridge Road, EN1 3RN – 020 8364 6600
  Hayes Road, UB2 5LN – 020 8561 4681
  760 Old Kent Road, SE15 1NJ – 020 7732 7322

- **Traditional Toys** Chelsea Green, 53 Godfrey Street, SW3 3SX, 020 7352 1718 – Timeless toys.

- **The Little White Company** 261 Pavillion Road, SW1X 0BP, 020 7881 0783 – Clothing, bed linen and furniture.

General Information · **Internet & WiFi**

For many, the Internet is *the* key to the city. Before the dawning of the Internet, we Dickensian scamps had to scurry around in the filth foraging for information in 'books' and by talking to actual people'. Now that the future is here, Londoners can navigate their city's streets, explore its dark history, organise a debauched weekend in Chiswick or, as is more likely, peer over the shoulder of men in raincoats in Internet Cafes.

Internet Cafes are *everywhere*. In fact you probably live in one. They can range from the dimly lit 'Money Transfer' shacks that have an air of illegality, to the over-orange **Easyeverything** chain that dominated the market before home internet use skyrocketed in the late 90s. You can escape the grim D.I.Y. flea pits in chic coffee outlets like **Coffee @** (155 Brick Lane 020 7247 6735) but sharpen your elbows as space is tight. **Cyberia Cafe** near Goodge Street (39 Whitfield Street Tel No – 020 7209 0984) claims to have been the first Internet Cafe in the world and is still very plush. To be fair, internet use in these places is usually criminally cheap : as low as 50p per hour in the non-tourist areas. For a large list of London internet cafes check out http://www.allinlondon.co.uk/directory/1166.php.

London was recently crowned WiFi capital of the world, owing to its astronomical rate of increase in WiFi networks. It is becoming more and more difficult to relax in your local cafe without catching the sharp edge of a laptop. The **Apostrophe Cafe** chain is efficient, expensive and has WiFi as standard. Like many WiFi-compatible eateries, wireless access is limited to an hour and they give out passwords to paying customers only. If you wish to cook your internal organs with your PowerBook you can do so in hundreds of cafes in London; for a decent online map of WiFi locations check out http://londonist.com/2007/05/free_wifi_in_lo.php. Of course there is always the pirate option—dodging the Community Officers and fiendishly stealing a neighbours connection. Beware however, in 2007 a man was arrested in what was the first case of WiFi theft—he was balancing his laptop on his garden wall!

Useful And/Or Fun London Links:

www.notfortourists.com/London.aspx
www.fedbybirds.com
www.royalparks.org.uk
www.tfl.gov.uk
www.londonist.com
www.londonfreelist.com
www.davehill.typepad.com
www.shadyoldlady.com
www.derelictlondon.com
www.walk-london.blogspot.com
www.hiddenlondon.com
www.londonbloggers.iamcal.com
www.london-underground.blogspot.com
www.fancyapint.com
www.dailycandy.com/london
www.gumtree.com
www.timeout.com
www.brickads.blogspot.com
www. wildinlondon.blogspot.com
www. westlondonblogger.blogspot.com
www. dalstonoxfamshop.blogspot.com
www.viewlondon.co.uk
www.lecool.com/cities/london
www.deadcafesociety.org.uk
www.londonreviewofbreakfasts.blogspot.com
www.beerintheevening.com
www.london-se1.co.uk
www.talkonthetube.com
www.london.thewayweseeit.org
londoncabby.blogspot.com

The doom-sayers have less cause to complain about the decline of Gayhood in London recently, what with **Heaven** (London's self-proclaimed most famous gay club) hanging on and new nights popping up everywhere. Yes, popular indie discos **Popstarz** and **Rebel Rebel** have relocated but **Girl's Action** at Ghetto promises great things and we are so in love with 'polysexual' club **Dalston Supermarket** at the moment. Of course every time one door (read: gay club) closes another one opens, and let's face it, the latter will probably open later and sell you even cheaper Red Bull and vodka.

One of the most exciting developments in the past few years has been the advent of what has been dubbed London's new 'Gay Village'—the cluster of clubs, saunas and after-hours hangover incubators that have sprung up in Vauxhall. Now it's possible, though still just as unadvisable, to party from Thursday through to Tuesday without stopping to reapply deodorant, or think about the consequences of what you're doing—hooray. The small outcrop of gay and 'polysexual' nights in the East End, (which until recently included the notoriously wonderful, but necessarily short-lived 'Boombox') is still thriving, and offers another refreshing alternative to Soho for those in search of an aggressive fashion consciousness and a less cruisy atmosphere. This said, if you can handle bright lights, pop music, tight t-shirts and a lot of hair gel, you'll still have massive amounts of fun around Soho and Old Compton Street, the traditional central London gay epicentre. This area is always buzzing, day and night, and is a great place to sit back and do some people watching as well as to go out and, y'know, go crazy.

For girls there is still room for improvement, with options fewer and less centralised but **The Minories'** new Girls' night is a blast and the continuing women-only nights at **Village** and **Element** are cause for celebration. Many mixed and polysexual nights (such as Motherfucker at **Barden's Boudoir**) also draw large female crowds, and though dedicated lesbian bars and clubs are few and far between, there is enough going on in the city to make any day of the week a possible night out.

Websites

www.dirtydirtydancing.com - Super-airbrushed photos from many of the trendier Soho and east London nights.

http://scene-out.com - Comprehensive mainstream scene guide.

www.gaylondon.co.uk - Online gay and lesbian community for London.

www.gingerbeer.co.uk - Lesbian guide to London.

www.girlguidelondon.co.uk - Does what it says on the tin.

www.gmfa.org.uk - Gay men's health charity.

www.pinkdate.com - Speed dating events for gay men and women in central London.

Publications

The following are all free listings/scene magazine that can be found in most gay shops and venue (anywhere on Old Compton Street should have some copies lying around):

Boyz Magazine - Weekly scene news and listings, out Thursdays. www.boyz.co.uk

G3 Magazine - Lesbian scene, monthly. www.g3mag.co.uk

Out in the City Mag - Monthly London lifestyle magazine for gay men. www.outmag.co.uk

Qx Magazine - Gay men's mag. www.qxmagazine.com

Shops

Gay's the Word, 66 Marchmont Street, WC1N 1AB 020 7278 7654, http://freespace.virgin.net/gays.theword/, The only dedicated Gay and Lesbian Bookshop in London, recently threatened by rising rent. Visit whilst it's still there!

Foyles, 113–119 Charing Cross Road, WC2H 0EB, 020 7437 5660, www.foyles.co.uk, Huge bookshop with large gay and lesbian section.

Prowler, 5–7 Brewer Street, W1F 0RF, 020 7734 4031 The ultimate gay men's shop, stocking everything from (skimpy) clothes to sex toys plus mountains of lube, pornography, and the other usual suspects.

Sexual Health

A comprehensive list of London clinics that offer same day HIV testing and PEP treatments for gay/ bisexual men is available at www.gmfa.org.uk/ londonservices/clinics. CLASH, below, is particularly recommended.

LASH (Central London Action on Street Health), 1 Warwick Street, W1B 5NA, 020 7734 1794, Friday night clinic for gay men, with incredibly friendly staff who will offer comfort and advice. Same day (often instant) HIV testing, PEP treatment. Fridays, - 8.30pm, call for an appointment.

Support Organizations

gain, a more comprehensive list can be found at the GMFA website: www.gmfa.org.uk/londonservices/support-groups/index

Stonewall, Tower Building, York Road, SE1 7NX, www.stonewall.org.uk, Gay rights charity and lobbying group.

PACE Youthwork Service, 34 Hartham Road, N7 9LJ, 020 7700 1323, www.outzone.org, Support organization for gay and lesbian youths under 25. Organizes regular social events and offers one to one consultations with advisors: phone or visit the website to get involved.

London Friend, 86 Caledonian Road, N1 9DN, 020 833 1674, www.londonfriend.org.uk, Voluntary organization which runs several helplines, group workshops and social events, as well as offering advice on reporting hate crime.

London Lesbian and Gay Switchboard, 020 837 7324 (helpline), 020 7689 8501 (Volunteers), Counselling and information service.

Kairos in Soho, Unit 10, 10-11 Archer Street, W1D AZ, 020 7437 6063, www.kairosinsoho.org.uk, Gay and lesbian charity which organises a variety of recreational events to promote the health, well being and development of the LGBT community.

Naz Project London, Palingswick House, 241 King Street, W6 9LP, 020 8741 1879 www.naz.org.uk, Charity that organizes support and sexual health services for black and ethnic minority communities in London. Various services, including free one-on-one counselling and support groups are available, phone or check website for details.

GALOP, PO Box 32810, N1 3ZD, 020 7704 6767, www.galop.org.uk, Charity specialising in advice about reporting hate crime.

Annual Events

Pride London, www.pridelondon.org, Large pride festival, takes place every July.

London Lesbian and Gay Film Festival, www.bfi.org.uk/llgff, Film festival at the BFI on South Bank, March–April.

Bistrotheque Annual Drag Ball, www.myspace.com/trannylipsync or www.bistrotheque.com, Annual team-based drag contest. Open entry but fierce competition!

London LGBT History Month, www.lgbthistorymonth.co.uk, Nationwide awareness month, with various talks and events staged in London, every February.

Gay/mixed venues

Soho:

79CXR, 79 Charing Cross Road, WC2H 0NE, 020 7734 0769, Dingy bar with middle aged crowd.

The Admiral Duncan, 54 Old Compton Street, W1D 4UB, 020 7437 5300

Barcode Soho, 3-4 Archer Street W1D 7AT, 020 7734 3342

Box, 32–34 Monmouth Street, WC2H 9HA, 020 7240 5828, Civilised bar and eatery.

Comptons, 53–57 Old Compton Street, W1D 6HN, 020 7479 7961, Crammed gay pub.

Duke of Wellington, 77 Wardour Street, W1D 6QA

The Edge, 11 Soho Square, W1D 3QF, 020 7439 1313

G-A-Y Bar, 30 Old Compton Street, W1D 5JX, 020 7494 2756, Poptastic bunker. Video walls and cheap drinks.

G-A-Y Late, 5 Goslett Yard, WC2H 0ER, 020 7734 9858, Cheap drinks and pop videos wipe out brain functions 'til 3am.

Ghetto, Falconberg Court, W1D 3AB, 020 7287 3726, Loud electro at this busy gay club. Thursday is ladies night.

Halfway to Heaven, 7 Duncannon Street, WC2N 4JF, 020 7321 2791.

Heaven, Under the Arches, Villiers Street, WC2N 6NG, 020 7930 2020, Legendary gay club. An institution.

Ku Bar, 30 Lisle Street, WC2H 7BA, 020 7437 4303, Newly relocated bar for the young and clueless.

Kudos, 10 Adelaide Street, WC2N 4HZ, 020 7379 4573

Profile, 56–57 Frith Street, W1D 3JG, 020 7734 8300

Shadow Lounge, 5 Brewer Street, W1F, 020 7439 4089, Supposed to be a shi-shi cocktail lounge. Hmmmm.

Soho Revue Bar, 11 Walkers Court, Brewer Street, W1F 0ED, Cabaret acts followed by dancing 'til late.

The Village, 81 Wardour Street, W1D 6QD, 020 7434 2124, Tacky, flirtatious bar spread across two floors.

Trash Palace, 11 Wardour Street, W1D 6PG, 020 7734 0522, Bratty queer indie bar.

North:

Cosmo Lounge, 43 Essex Road, N1 2SF, 020 7688 0051, Subdued bar, normally full of regulars.

Central Station, 37 Wharfdale Road, N1 9SD, 020 7278 3294. Pub/club with ominously blacked out windows.

The Green, 74 Upper Street N1 0NY, 0871 971 4097, Innocuous gay bar/restaurant frequented by many unsuspecting straight couples.

King Edward VI Pub, 25 Bromfield Street, N1 0PZ

The Black Cap, 171 Camden High Street, NW1 7JY, 020 7428 2721, Slightly crummy gay pub.

East:

Bistrotheque, 23–27 Wadeson Street, E2 9DR, Jonny Woo's restaurant, great food and drag acts.

The Black Horse, 168 Mile End Road, E1 4LJ, 020 7790 1684

George and Dragon, 2 Hackney Road, E2 7NS, Small, atmospheric pub full of trendy boys and girls.

Joiners Arms, 116–118, Hackney Road, E2 7Q, Late opening free-for-all with a wonderfully mixed crowd. ('til 2/3am most nights)

South:

Area, 67–68 Albert Embankment, SE1 7TP

Barcode Vauxhall, 69 Albert Embankment, 020 7582 4180

The Two Brewers, 114 Clapham High Street, SW4 7UJ, 020 7498 4971

Depot, 66 Albert Embankment, SE11 7TP, Sister club of Area, with a more cruisy vibe.

Fire, South Lambeth Road, SW8 1RT, 020 7434 1113, The quintessential Vauxhall club. Open pretty much forever, bulging muscles everywhere.

The Fort, 131 Grange Road, Bermondsey, SE1 3AL - Themed cruising/fetish/sex bar.

Kazbar Clapham, 50 Clapham High Street, SW4 7UL, 020 7622 0070

Little Apple Bar, 98 Kennington Lane, SE11 4XD Mixed/lesbian bar.

Man Bar, 82 Great Suffolk Street, SE1 0BE, 020 7928 3223, Cruise bar.

The Powder Monkey, 22 King William Walk, SE10 PHU, 020 8293 5928, thepowdermonkey.net

Royal Vauxhall Tavern, 372 Kennington Lane, SE11 5HY, 020 7820 1222

South Central, 349 Kennington Lane, SE11 5QY, 020 7793 0903

Substation South, 9 Brighton Terrace, SW9 8DJ, 020 7737 2095

XXL, 51–53 Southwark Street, SE1 1TE, www. fatsandsmalls.com, Busy bear club.

West:

Bromptons, 294 Old Brompton Road, SW5 9JF, 020 77370 1344

The Coleherne, 261 Old Brompton Road, SW5 9JA020 7244 5951

Recommended Nights

Club Motherfucker, second Saturdays @ Barden's Boudoir, 38 Stoke Newington Road, Dalston, N16 7XJ, Polysexual band night. Sweaty, noisy, very much about the music.

Circus, Fridays @ Soho Revue Bar, 11 Walkers Court, Brewer Street, W1F 0ED, Drag Queen Jodie Harsh's long running night attracts its fair share of celebrities from both on and off the scene. Get there early or be prepared to queue.

DTPM, www.myspace.com/dtpm, Legendary event, no longer with a fixed location. See site for details of upcoming parties.

For3ign, Saturdays @ Bar Music Hall, 134 Curtain Road, EC2A 3AR, 020 7613 5951, Outlandish costumes and, of course, thumping electro.

Horsemeat Disco, Sundays @ South Central, Italo and 70s Disco bring all sorts to this fantastic night, originally a bear love club.

Icon, Sundays @ Essence, 562a Mile End Road, E3 4PH, 0208 980 6427, mob 07843 440 443 (weekly), New night in the East End. Yet to prove itself.

Issue, monthly (check site for details) @ Electricity Showrooms, 39a Hoxton Square, N1 6NN, issueclub.blogspot.com. Polysexual parties to coincide with the launch of this scene/fashion magazine.

Matinee, monthly (check site) @ Fabric, 77a Charterhouse Street, EC1M 3HN, 020 7335 8898, www.matineelondon.com, Irregular gay night at this enormous club in Farringdon.

Popstarz, Fridays @ Sin, 144 Charing Cross Road, WC2H 0LB, 020 7240 1900, Gay indie institution, recently relocated.

Trailer Trash, Fridays @ On the Rocks, 25 Kingsland Road, E2 8AA, 020 7688 0339, The dirtiest electro and the drunkest you've ever been. Crammed with sweating fashionistas.

Wet Yourself, Sundays @ Aquarium, 256–264 Old Street, EC1V 9DD, 020 7251 6136, This used to be the place to be after Boombox. It's lost only a little of its charm since (mixed polysexual crowd).

Lesbian Venues

Blush Bar, 8 Cazenove Road, Stoke Newington N16, 020 7923 9202, www.blushbar.co.uk

Candy Bar, 23-24 Bateman Street, W1V 5HR, 020 7437 1977, The reluctant epicentre of the Lesbian scene in Soho.

First Out Café Bar, Soho - 52 St Giles High St, WC2H 8LH, 020 7240 8042, Cafe with nightly events. All girls on Friday.

Oak Bar, 79 Green Lanes, N16, www.oakbar.co.uk, 020 7354 2791,

The Star At Night, 22 Great Chapel Street, Soho, W1 8FR, 020 7434 3749, Mixed cocktail bar with a predominantly female crowd.

Recommended Nights

100% Babe, Bank Holiday Sundays @ The Roxy, 3 Rathbone Place, W1P 1DA, 020 7636 1598, Irregular party for fans of funky house, R&B, old skool and electropop.

Blue Light, last Saturdays @ Bar Med, Triton Court, 14 Finsbury Square, EC2, 020 7588 3056

Club Wotever, first Saturday of the month @ The Masters Club, 12 Denman Street, Piccadilly, W1D 7HH, 020 7734 4243, Draggy night with a large 'King' quota.

Code, irregular night @ the Enclave, 25–27 Brewer Street, W1F 0RR, www.club-code.net - check website for details.

Girls on Girls, Wednesdays @ Village, 81 Wardour Street, W1D 6QD, 020 7434 2124

Lounge, second Thursdays @ Vertigo, 1 Leicester Square, WC2H 7NA, 020 7734 0900, Relaxed cocktail night at this swish Leicester Square club.

Miss Shapes, Thursdays @ Ghetto, Falconberg Court, W1D 3AB, 020 7287 3726, Popular girls-only indie night.

Pink, Wednesdays @ Element, 4-5 Greek Street, W1D 4DD, 020 7434 3323.

Play, irregular night @ Bar Rumba, 35 Shaftesbury Ave, W1D 7EP, 020 7287 2715, www.myspace. com/_clubplay

Rumours, last Saturday of the month @ 64–73 Minories, EC3, 07949 477 804

Smack, irregular night @ various venues, check website, www.myspace.com/smackclub

Wish, first Saturdays @ Gramophone, 60–62 Commercial Street, E1 6LT, Style conscious night for young techno-heads and indie girls.

Women's Anarchist Nuisance Cafe, Penultimate wednesdays @ the RampART Creative Centre and Social Space, Rampart St, Aldgate, E1 2LA, Social group and cooperative vegan women's cafe.

Stickier Options

Club Fukk, second Fridays @ Central Station, 37 Wharfdale Road, N1 9SD, 020 7278 3294, www. centralstation.co.uk or www.woteverworld.com/ id17.html, Predominantly Lesbian fetish/play club. One of many sex/cruising nights at the venue – check site for details.

Chariots, www.gaysauna.co.uk, Popular chain of gay saunas, with branches at the following locations: *Shoreditch*: 1 Fairchild Street, EC2A 3NS, *Waterloo*: 101 Lower Marsh, SE1 7AB, 020 7401 8484, *Limehouse*: 574 Commercial Road, E14 7JD, 020 7791 2808, *Streatham*: 292 [rear of] Streatham High Road, SW16 6HG, 020 8696 0929, *Farringdon*: 57 Cowcross Street, EC1M 6BX, 020 7251 5553, *Vauxhall*: 63-64 Albert Embankment, SE1, 020 7247 5333

The Fort,131 Grange Road, Bermondsey, SE1 3AL , Themed cruising/fetish/sex bar.

Hard On, monthly @ Hidden, 100 Tinworth Street, SE11 5EQ, www.hardonclub.co.uk, Rubber and fetish sex club for gay and bisexual men and women.

The Hoist, Arch 47b & 47c, South Lambeth Road, SW8 1RH, 020 7735 9972, www.thehoist.co.uk, Fetish sex club with strict dress codes, check website for details.

Man Bar, 82 Great Suffolk Street, SE1 0BE, 020 7928 3223, www.manbar.info, Cruise bar.

Nudity, first Fridays @ Hidden, 100 Tinworth Street, SE11 5EQ, Nude men's dance/play club.

Purrrr, 87 Fortess Road, Kentish Town NW5, www. purrrr.co.uk, Monthly S&M play club for Lesbians.

London Timeline

A timeline of significant events in London's history.

50: The Romans found Londinium, building the first London Bridge.

61: Queen Boudicca burns Londinium down.

100: Londinium becomes the capital of Roman Britain.

200: The Romans build the London Wall.

410: Roman occupation ends and Londinium is largely abandoned for many years.

604: King Aethelbert of Kent completes the first St Paul's Cathedral.

700: The Saxons build Lundenwic a mile to the west of old Londinium.

851: The Vikings burn Lundenwic down (starting to see a pattern, here?)

878: Alfred The Great defeats the Vikings and establishes a new settlement within the Roman Walls.

1013: The Viking King Canute besieges London.

1066: William The Conqueror becomes the first king to be crowned at Westminster Abbey.

1088: William The Conqueror builds the Tower Of London.

1097: William Rufus builds Westminster Hall—later part of the Houses Of Parliament.

1176: The wooden London Bridge is replaced by a stone structure.

1343: 'The Canterbury Tales' author Geoffrey Chaucer is born in London.

1348: The Black Death wipes out between a third and half of London's population in 18 months.

1381: Peasants revolt, storming the Tower Of London.

1599: William Shakespeare's theatre company The Chamberlain's Men build the Globe Theatre.

1605: Guy Fawkes' Gunpowder Plot fails to blow up the Palace Of Westminster.

1635: Hyde Park opens to the public.

1649: King Charles I is beheaded at Whitehall.

1665: The Great Plague kills a fifth of London's population (starting to see another pattern, here?)

1666: The Fire of London destroys 60% of the city, including St Paul's Cathedral, but wipes out the plague. This really must have been a great year.

1708: The new St Paul's Cathedral is completed by Sir Christopher Wren.

1732: Downing Street becomes the home of the Prime Minister.

1750: Westminster Bridge is built.

1814: Lord's Cricket Ground is opened.

1829: Robert Peel establishes the Metropolitan Police force, policemen known as 'Bobbies' or 'Peelers'.

1831: London becomes the world's biggest city.

1834: The Houses Of Parliament are built.

1843: Nelson's Column is completed in Trafalgar Square.

1851: Six million people gawp at newfangled technology and design at The Great Exhibition.

1858: The Great Stink inspires the 19th century's biggest civil engineering project—London's sewerage system.

London Timeline

1863: The first London Underground line is built.

1876: The Albert Memorial to Queen Victoria's husband Prince Albert is completed.

1884: An imaginary line through Greenwich Royal Observatory is internationally accepted as the Prime Meridian. Except by the French.

1887: Arthur Conan Doyle publishes the first Sherlock Holmes story 'A Study In Scarlet.'

1888: Jack The Ripper's first victim, Mary Ann Nichols, is murdered.

1908: London hosts the Olympics for the first time.

1915: German Zeppelin airships launch first air raids on London, ultimately killing over 700 people.

1923: Wembley Stadium is built in 300 days, costing £750,000.

1940: The Blitz begins—German bombs kill over 30,000 Londoners by the end of WW2 and destroy large areas of the city.

1946: Heathrow Airport opens for commercial flights.

1948: The second London Olympics is held.

1951: The Royal Festival Hall is built as part of the Festival Of Britain.

1952: The Great Smog, caused by a combination of fog and coal smoke, kills 4000 people in five days.

1956: The Clean Air Act puts an end to London's smog problems.

1965: The Notting Hill Carnival is established by West London's Caribbean community.

1969: The Beatles play their last ever gig on the roof of the Apple building.

1976: The Sex Pistols play at the first 'International Punk Festival' at the 100 Club on Oxford Street.

1981: The first London Marathon.

1983: Six people are killed when the IRA bombs Harrods.

1991: London's tallest building, One Canada Square (better known as Canary Wharf), is completed.

2000: Ken Livingstone becomes London's first directly-elected Mayor.

2005: 52 people are killed by four suicide bombers on Underground trains and a bus.

2007: The rebuilt Wembley Stadium is completed after four years, costing £778 million.

2008: Boris Johnson defeats Red Ken in the London Mayoral Election with a promise to re-instate the Routemaster.

2012: London's third Olympics to be held, expectations of a bumper haul of medals remains low.

London is an egotist—it just *loves* to talk about itself. As you might expect, there's a vast array of print and online publications, not to mention radio stations, designed to let the city do exactly that. Single-handedly forcing the environmental movement back twenty years are freebie dailies **The Metro** and the more fiscally orientated **City A.M.** Free weeklies to look out for include **Stylist** on Wednesday for girls and **Shortlist** on Thursdays for boys. The Aussies are pushing **TNT** at tube stations on Monday, but it lacks the wider appeal. The new addition to the freesheet line-up is now the substantial **Evening Standard**, which went free in January of last year and is the preferred news-roundup du jour of suburbanites and city types alike, if only for the sudoku and quick crossword puzzles. Online, **www.thisislocallondon.co.uk** condenses forty local newspapers into 'one online voice'. On the wireless, **Capital Radio** broadcasts an irksome parade of popular hits and frenetic DJs, whilst **Heart** and **Magic** corner the market on lip-trembling power ballads, mid-paced chart rock and wacky quizzes. All of the British Broadcasting Corporation's national radio stations—including the snazzy, young(ish) **Radio 1** and ovaltine-drinkers' choice **Radio 2**—are based in London, as is (surprisingly) **BBC London**, a decent option for weekend sports coverage. Cooler, urban types are more likely to be tuning into **Kiss FM** (dance, hip hop), **Smooth FM** (jazz, soul) or **Choice** (dancehall, roots), while alternative rockers tune their dials anguishedly over at **XFM**, and the talkative indulge in unreserved subjectivity over at **LBC**. Of course, the undisputed king of alternative London broadcasting is **Resonance FM**, a 'community run' station which has just been granted a permanent licence: expect everything from 'Calling All Pensioners' to live psycho-geographic wanders around city's warped dark streets. Un-licensed and illegal pirate radio stations offer a slightly un-hinged ear into the fringes of London's musical society. Twiddle your dials around the extreme ends of the FM spectrum for pirate stalwarts **Rude FM** and **Kool FM**. On the goggle-box, the latest news is spoon-fed to you in ITV's **London Tonight** show and delivered in short slots at the end of the BBC and ITV national news programs. For those actually risking going outside, **Time Out** remains the socialite's sacred text.

Print

The Evening Standard Northcliffe House, 2 Derry Street, W8 5TT, 020 7938 6000, Newly reinstated as a freesheet, it continues to be London's favourite journey home read.

Metro Northcliffe House, 2 Derry Street, W8 5TT, 020 7651 5200, Free underground daily from same stable.

City AM New London Bridge House, 25 London Bridge St, SE1 9SG, 020 7015 1200, Free morning business bulletin for city-goers.

Sport Third Floor, Courtyard Building, 11 Curtain Road, EC2A 3LT, 0207 375 3175 Free sports overview every Friday.

TimeOut London 251-255 Tottenham Court Road, Universal House, W1T 7AB, 0207 813 3000, Listings & reviews across the city. Pretty damned comprehensive.

London Gazette PO Box 7923, SE1 5ZH, 020 7394 4517, Capital's oldest paper—official journals record of the government.

London Literary Review 44 Lexington Street, W1 0LW, 020 7437 9392, Fortnightly publication for the bookish.

The London Magazine 32 Addison Grove, W4 1ER, 020 8400 5882, Bi-monthly Arts reviews.

TNT London 14-15 Childs Place, Earls Court, SW5 9RX, 020 7373 3377, Info and opinion for the antipodean set.

Loot 31 John Street, WC1N 2AT, 0871 222 5000, Classifieds: flats, bought/sold and lonely hearts.

The Voice GV Media Group Ltd, Northern & Shell Tower, 6th Floor, 4 Selsdon Way, E14 9GL, 020 7510 0340, African-British national.

London Bichitra Bangalink Media, 272 Holton Road, Barry, CF63 4HU, Bengali monthly.

Polish Express 603 Cumberland House, 80 Scrubs Lane, NW10 6RF, 020 8964 4488 , News and info for the Polish community.

Reflect Magazine 130 Stroud Green Road, N4 3RZ, 020 7272 8502, For 'thinking, young Muslims'.

Live Listings Magazine Keith Villa (House), 102 Mallinson Rd, SW11 1BN, 020 7207 2734 Guide to what's on in multicultural London.

ShortList 6 Emerald Street, London, WC1N 3QA, 020 7242 5873, A Thursday freebie for metrosexuals.

Stylist 6 Emerald Street, London, WC1N 3QA, 020 7242 5873, London's first free women's glossy. Handed out on Wednesdays.

Public Radio

FM

89.1 BBC Radio Two: Middle-aged music and chat.
91.3 BBC Radio Three: Classical.
93.5 BBC Radio Four: Current affairs, comfort listening.
94.9 BBC London: Chat, sport.
95.8 Capital FM: Chart, capers.
96.9 Choice FM: Hip Hop, R&B.
97.3 LBC: Phone in, chat.
98.8 BBC Radio 1: Pop, rock, more pop.
100.0 Kiss FM: Dance, urban.
100.9 Classic FM: Classical.
102.2 Smooth FM: Jazz, soul.
102.6 Essex FM: Audible in East London.
103.3 London Greek Radio: Um, Greek.
103.5 BBC Essex: Audible out East.
104.4 Resonance FM: Always bizzare, always brilliant.
104.9 Xfm: Alternative, rock.
105.4 Magic: Pop, slush.
105.8 Virgin Radio: Pop, rock.
106.2 Heart: Chart, pop.
106.6 Time: West London only.
107.3 Time: South East London only.

AM

252 Atlantic: Rock.
558 Spectrum International: Multi-ethnic.
648 BBC World Service: Global.
720 BBC Radio Four: Spoken word.
909 BBC Radio Five Live: Sport, phone in.
963 Liberty Radio: 70s, 80s pop.
1035 Ritz: Country.
1089 talkSPORT: Sports phone in.
1152 LBC News: News, weather.
1215 Virgin Radio: Pop, rock.
1305 Premier Radio: Christian.
1458 Sunrise: Asian.
1548 Capital Gold: Rock 'gold', sport.
1584 London Turkish Radio: Turkish community.

Essential London Books

The Diary of Samuel Pepys (1825): Samuel Pepys: eyewitness accounts of the Restoration, Great Plague and Fire of London from noted sixteenth century scribbler.

Oliver Twist; Hard Times; Great Expectations (1837, 1854, 1860): Charles Dickens: any Dickens novel paints Victorian London at its most exacting.

The Strange Case of Dr. Jekyll and Mr. Hyde (1886): Robert Louis Stevenson: the book that enthralled a city unnerved by Jack the Ripper.

The Adventures of Sherlock Holmes; The Hound of the

Baskervilles (1892): Arthur Conan Doyle: classic whodunits featuring Holmes and Watson.

The Inimitable Jeeves (1923): P.G. Wodehouse: prewar upper-class tomfoolery in London Town.

Mrs Dalloway (1925): Virginia Woolf If you know London, you can follow Clarissa Dalloway every step of the way – in real time.

V For Vendetta (1982-1989): Alan Moore, The world's greatest comic writer blows up London in a fit of Anarchist fantasies.

London Fields (1989): Martin Amis: post-modern jaunt through London at the end of the millennium.

London – The Biography, and *Illustrated London* (2000): Peter Ackroyd: definitive, eight hundred page mother lode of remarkable city history, and lavish pictorial version.

London's Disused Underground Stations (2001): JE Connor: documenting forgotten, ghostly tube stations beneath the pavements.

London Orbital and Hackney That Rose Red Empire (2002): Iain Sinclair: London's premier scribe continues to fill our brains with joy despite being ripped off by devotee Peter Ackroyd.

The Clerkenwell Tales (2003): Peter Ackroyd: corking murder mystery set in the time of Chaucer.

Brick Lane (2003): Monica Ali: award winning coming-of-age tale centred on Brick Lane's Muslim community.

Art Deco London (2003): Colin Michael Hines: Wistful but enjoyable stroll around London's Art Deco heritage.

Intimate Adventures of a London Call Girl (2005): Belle de Jour: steamy, real-life shenanigans ahoy.

From Here to Here (2005): Simmons, Taylor, Lynham, Rich: 31 top notch short stories about Circle Line destinations, includes Simon Armitage.

Secret London: Exploring the Hidden City, with Original Walks and Unusual Places to Visit (2006): Andrew Duncan: an explorer's dream.

The London Bombings: An Independent Inquiry (2006): Nafeez Mosaddeq Ahmed: balanced, subtle overview of 2005 Underground bombings.

Around London with Kids – 68 Great Things to See and Do (3rd edition; 2006): Eugene Fodor: should keep the little rascals from breaking into cars.

I Never Knew That About London (2007): Christopher Winn: Well, did you?

The London Encyclopaedia (2008): Ben Weinreb and Christopher Hibbert: London's history and culture documented in minutest detail

Derelict London (2008): Paul Talling: The urban explorers' bible!

Essential London Songs

Lambeth Walk, Noel Gay/Douglas Furber (1937): All together! *Doing the Lambeth Walk! Oi!*

A Nightingale Sang in Berkeley Square, Judy Campbell (1940): Wartime cheer made famous by Vera Lynn.

London Pride, Sir Noel Coward (1941): Written during the Blitz, this sensational ballad gave comfort to Londoners being bombed nightly.

Maybe It's Because I'm a Londoner, Hubert Gregg (1944): Pearly Queen favourite crammed with WWII spirit.

A Foggy Day (In London Town), Ella Fitzgerald (1956): Definitive recording of Gershwin classic.

Waterloo Sunset, The Kinks (1967): Timeless paean to the nation's capital.

Consider Yourself, Lionel Bart (1968): Oliver Twist hoodwinked into a life of crime by the Artful Dodger, the rascal.

Primrose Hill, John and Beverly Martyn (1970). Folk rock's second couple never had to deal with Katie Frost and Kate Moss when they were watching the sun set, did they?

Streets Of London, Ralph McTell (1974). Cool folk dude destroys credibility forever with international monster hit.

Baker Street, Gerry Rafferty (1978): Feel that sax line, air that guitar.

London Calling, The Clash (1979): Joe Strummer paints an apocalyptic vision of a city in post-punk transition.

Electric Avenue, Eddy Grant (1983): Roots-rock champion name checks 80s Brixton scene.

London, The Smiths (1983): Morrissey lugubriously debates a trip south. Miserable shite.

West End Girls, Pet Shop Boys (1986): East London working class meets West London affluence in electro-pop classic.

Pump Up London, Mr. Lee (1988). Squelchy Chicago House dude makes London sound amazing whilst name checking every British town he can think of: Leeds! Manchester! Scatland!

Parklife, Blur (1994): Home counties-boys get cockney makeover while eyeing London's jogging scene.

Sunny Goodge Street, Donovan (2002): Folk crooner sings of a hippy London goneby.

Essential London Films

The 39 Steps (1935): Hitchcock adaptation of John Buchan novel.

Pygmalion (1938): Leslie Howard as Henry Higgins and Wendy Hiller as Eliza Doolittle prove Shaw's classic comedy does very well without music.

Great Expectations (1946): Rare Richard Attenborough acting in classic Dickens adaptation.

The Ladykillers (1955): Superb black comedy from the Ealing canon, with pre-Obi Wan Alec Guinness.

One Hundred and One Dalmations (1961): Innocent pelt-seeker tortured by 101 belligerent pups. For shame.

Mary Poppins (1964): Notable for Dick Van Dyke's confounding, lanky turn as cockney chimney sweep.

A Hard Day's Night (1964): Classic, swinging 60s' comedy from the Fab Four.

Alfie (1966): Caine in much-lauded role as audience-addressing lothario.

Carry On Doctor (1967): Critically-panned, guilty-pleasure raunchfest from Pinewood Studios.

The London Nobody Knows (1967): The greatest film about London ever. Period.

Oliver! (1968): Sprightly musical adaptation of Dickens classic.

The Elephant Man (1980): John Merrick 'accepted' by London's polite Victorian-era society in David Lynch masterpiece.

An American Werewolf in London (1981): US student attacked on moors; gets haunted; romps with Jenny Agutter; becomes werewolf; slaughters innocents; is shot in alley; credits roll.

My Beautiful Launderette (1985): Hanif Kureishi's controversial depiction of cross-culture, same-gender love in the Thatcher-era.

Muppet Christmas Carol (1992): That Michael Caine, he sure can act. But he sure can't sing.

London (1994): Patrick Kellier's abstract ramble through 'the most unsociable and reactionary of cities.'

Lock, Stock and Two Smoking Barrels (1998): East End crime capers from Madonna's (not from the East End) husband.

Notting Hill (1999): Hugh Grant as mumbling, bumbling, lovesick fop.

Bridget Jones's Diary (2001): Rene Zellweger goes Sloane in adaptation of Helen Fielding novel.

28 Days Later (2002): Us Londoners finally erupt in pandemic rage at how slow tourists are on the tube.

Love Actually (2003): Expansive Richard Curtis romcom with Grant in slightly-less mumbly, slightly-more bumbly form.

Shaun of the Dead (2003): Fighting off zombies at the local pub. Hilarious.

There can't be anything worse than the inconvenience of trying to find a convenience when nature takes an unexpected hold of your nether regions; you may choose to follow the lead of many a Saturday evening reveller and use a public doorway, but is it really worth the £80 fine that will be levied if caught in the act (and let's face it, it's hard to conceal the evidence)?

Unfortunately, London has seen a recent decline in the provision of public toilet facilities, as local councils seem to have decided that they are under no obligation to provide such a service; you'll also be hard pushed to find a toilet attendant manning a lavatory these days, and the dubious goings-on in some loos may not be quite what you had in mind, unless your name has a "Michael" in it. Most surviving public toilets seem also to emit their own particular aroma of…well, you don't really have to use your imagination. But don't get down in the dumps!

The most obvious place to go to when in need is McDonald's. Despite what some may say about their food, their outlets are the place to go when caught short and not wishing to pay to pee. Usually maintained and cleaned throughout opening hours, they can also be used inconspicuously and without purchasing anything; and let's face it, you can't move for McDonalds in London. It's also a safe bet to use Starbucks, Caffe Nero and Costa Coffee bars, although they often have a policy of access to toilets by key only, which can be a bit of a bummer (groan).

It may seem like a good idea to visit pubs or bars solely for their toilets, but you might find yourself being hauled out by an irked landlord mid-act. Furthermore, don't expect luxury; pub toilets are usually fairly scummy and often not furnished with toilet paper. It's also unlikely to find a men's cubicle that will have a working lock in it; do you really wish to have an unwanted visitor whilst on the throne? Exceptions are the Wetherspoon's chain, which prides itself on having toilets cleaned on the hour, and the nicest of gastro pubs, which can offer commodious and clean facilities (at least during the day). Otherwise, if desperate, at least go for a pub or bar that's busy.

Also bear in mind that if you find yourself in need in the City of Westminster, you can use a toilet text service from your mobile phone! Known as SatLav, texting the word 'Toilet' to 80097 will result in a message being sent to your phone informing you of the nearest public convenience. It may prove to be the most relieving 25p you'll ever spend in London…

A good and extensive list of London public toilets can be found at www.lastrounds.co.uk/public_toilets.html.

If none of the afore-mentioned places are available, there are other options:

Other street public toilets—yes, those bizarre futuristic looking structures on some of London's central streets are toilets. Known as sanisettes or "superloos", there is a charge to use them and once in, you've got 15 minutes before the door automatically opens (don't get extended stage-fright). They're self-cleaning, which usually means that they're in a right state, and are also quite popular with junkies and prostitutes, so best saved for when extremely desperate.

There are also a few pop-up toilets which, intended for night use, disappear underground during the day. These are only suitable for (drunk) men and rise to the challenge of channelling away an evening's excesses from 7pm to 6am. Located at notorious 'wet spots' in the West End, they are linked to the main sewerage system; taking the piss, indeed…

Stations—including almost all large railway stations and a few central London tube stations. There will usually be a cost for these facilities though (around 20p).

Department Stores—All the large ones, including John Lewis, Selfridges, Debenhams and Harrods. Smaller shops rarely have toilets for public use.

Supermarkets—many larger branches of Sainsbury's and Marks & Spencer.

Museums—the majority of London's large museums and galleries are free to enter (erm, and have toilets).

Libraries—most libraries will have an area of salvation for the needy.

Universities and Colleges—and you get to pass yourself off as a student or lecturer (in need of the loo).

Hospitals—you can also drop in on that relative that you always meant to visit, or maybe leave a stool sample; just try not to leave with a superbug.

Parks—not on the grass, please.

Hotels—larger hotels shouldn't pose a problem.

London has some of the finest hospitals in the world, attracting top-notch specialists who carry-out state-of-the-art procedures—the trick is, getting in to see one of them. An appointment at a specific hospital, or with a specialist, requires a referral from your GP and plenty of patience. In an emergency go to your nearest A&E—bring a book and some earplugs. On the weekends after eleven, waiting times for non-urgent problems can be measured in aeons, but rest assured, if something is seriously wrong you'll be seen very quickly—lucky ol' you. For non serious injuries or illnesses, find your nearest Minor Injuries Unit or Walk-in Centre on www.nhs.uk. You'll spend less time hanging around and free up A&E for critical cases and over-cidered teens needing stomach pumps. The ever-friendly 24 hr NHS Direct 0845 4647 is also always available for advice.

If you have the money, numerous private sector hospitals and clinics are available to cure what ails you, or to pander to your hypochondriacal needs. You won't necessarily get better treatment, but there'll be less waiting, more pampering and more grapes by your bedside. For information, start at www.privatehealth.co.uk.

A & E	Address	Phone	Map
Charing Cross Hospital	Fulham Palace Rd & St Dunstan's Rd	020 3311 1234	41
Chelsea and Westminster Hospital	369 Fulham Rd	020 8746 8000	43
Homerton University Hospital	Homerton Row	020 8510 5555	90
King's College Hospital	Denmark Hill & Champion Park	020 3299 9000	128
Moorfields Eye Hospital	162 City Rd	020 7253 3411	84
Royal Free Hospital	Pond St & Fleet Rd	020 7794 0500	57
Royal London Hospital	Whitechapel Rd & Vallance Rd	020 7377 7000	96
St Mary's Hospital	Praed St & Winsland St	020 3312 6666	31
St Thomas' Hospital	Westminster Bridge Rd & Lambeth Palace Rd	020 7188 7188	131
University College Hospital	235 Euston Rd	0845 155 5000	4
Western Eye Hospital	173 Marylebone Rd	020 7886 6666	2
Whittington Hospital	Magdala Ave	020 7272 3070	59

Other Hospitals	Address	Phone	Map
Bupa Cromwell Hospital	162 Cromwell Rd	020 7460 2000	35
Capio Chelsea	1 Radnor Walk	020 7351 7098	45
Capio Eye	114 Harley St	020 7034 1030	2
Capio Nightingale Hospital	11 Lisson Grove	020 7535 7700	76
Charing Cross Hospital	Fulham Palace Rd & St Dunstan's Rd	020 3311 1234	41
Chelsea and Westminster Hospital	369 Fulham Rd	020 8746 8000	43
Eastman Dental Hospital	256 Gray's Inn Rd	020 7915 1000	5
Elizabeth Garrett Anderson Hospital	Huntley St	0845 155 5000	4
Gordon Hospital	Bloomburg St & Vauxhall Bridge Rd	020 8746 8733	21
Great Ormond St Children's Hospital	34 Great Ormond St	020 7405 9200	5
Guy's Hospital	Great Maze Pond & St Thomas St	020 7188 7188	106
Heart Hospital	16 Westmoreland St	020 7573 8888	2
Highgate Private Hospital	17 View Rd	020 8341 4182	51
Homerton University Hospital	Homerton Row	020 8510 5555	90

Other Hospitals	Address	Phone	Map
Hospital For Tropical Diseases	Martimer Market & Capper St	0845 155 5000	4
Hospital of St John and St Elizabeth	60 Grove End Rd	020 7806 4000	68
King Edward VII Hospital For Officers	5 Beaumont St	020 7486 4411	2
King's College Hospital	Denmark Hill & Champion Park	020 3299 9000	128
Lambeth Hospital	108 Landor Rd	020 3228 6000	144
Lister Hospital	Chelsea Bridge Rd	020 7730 7733	20
London Bridge Hospital	27 Tooley St	020 7407 3100	106
London Chest Hospital	Bonner Rd & Approach Rd	020 7377 7000	93
London Independent Hospital	1 Beaumont Sq	020 7780 2400	97
London Welbeck Hospital	25 Welbeck St	020 7224 2242	2
Mildmay Mission Hospital	Hackney Rd & Columbia Rd	020 7613 6309	91
Mile End Hospital	Bancroft Rd & Alderney Rd	020 7377 7000	93
Moorfields Eye Hospital	162 City Rd	020 7253 3411	84
National Hospital for Neorology and Neurosciences	Queen Sq & Great Ormond St	0845 155 5000	5
Portland Hospital For women and Children	209 Great Portland St	020 7580 4400	3
Princess Grace Hospital	42 Nottingham Pl	020 7486 1234	2
The Rosenheim Building	25 Grafton Way	0845 155 5000	4
Royal Brompton Hospital	Sydney St & Cale St	020 7352 8121	45
Royal Free Hospital	Pond St & Fleet Rd	020 7794 0500	57
Royal London Homeopathic Hospital	60 Great Ormond St	020 7391 8888	5
Royal London Hospital	Whitechapel Rd & Vallance Rd	020 7377 7000	96
Royal Marsden Hospital	Fulham Rd & Sydney Close	020 7352 8171	45
Royal National Orthopaedic Hospital	51 Bolsover St	020 8954 2300	3
Royal National Throat, Nose and Ear Hospital	330 Gray's Inn Rd	020 7915 1300	5
St Bartholomew's	West Smithfield & Hosier Ln	020 7377 7000	15
Fitzroy Square Hospital	14 Fitzroy Sq	020 7388 4954	3
St Mary's Hospital	Praed St & Winsland St	020 3312 6666	31
St Pancras Hospital	4 St Pancras Way	020 7530 3500	78
St Thomas' Hospital	Westminster Bridge Rd & Lambeth Palace Rd	020 7188 7188	131
University College Hospital	235 Euston Rd	0845 155 5000	4
Wellington Hospital	8 Wellington Pl	020 7586 5959	76
Western Eye Hospital	173 Marylebone Rd	020 3312 6666	2
Whittington Hospital	Magdala Ave & Dartmouth Park Hill	020 7272 3070	59

General Information · **Libraries**

Overview

Librarians love nothing more than a warm cardigan and a complex cataloguing system, nevertheless, they've done themselves proud with London's libraries. London boasts an enormous, if somewhat eccentric and confusing, network of over 360 libraries. NFT have tried to make things a little clearer with a starter guide below, but check www.londonlibraries.org for a great searchable database to match your needs with the right library.

London's libraries vary enormously in subject, range and facilities, with some accessible for free, some for a fee, some with an appointment and some only if you are very very nice and give the curator a chocolate digestive. But the treat of such a large network, apart from the world-class breadth, depth and quality of collections, is that many of the libraries have a unique personality to make them a treasured part of London. For example, £10 will get you a day's membership of the **London Library (Map 23)**, an atmospheric labyrinth where you can browse alongside ghosts of past members including Dickens, Tennyson and Darwin, and feel several IQ points higher than before you went in. In Tower Hamlets, libraries are now **"Ideas Stores" (Map 92, 101, 96)**, because Tower Hamlets is, like, cool. In addition to the books, magazines, music and internet facilities which are available at most public libraries, these superb spaces also offer activities such as free PopLaw legal advice clinics, homework clubs and jazz classes. The borough has built four of these wonders; find them in Bow, Whitechapel, Canary Wharf and on East India Dock Road. London linguists are spoiled with the excellent **French Institute**

(Map 36), **Instituto Cervantes (Map 19)** and the **Goethe Institut (Map 37)**, while more cunning linguists may prefer the eye-opening gynaecological collection among the 2.5 million medical-related works in the **Wellcome Library (Map 4)**. Poets should meander their way to the **Saison Poetry Library (Map 104)**, ensconced within the South Bank Centre, for a little inspiration. Artists will enjoy the **National Art Library (Map 36)**, which nestles within the V&A Museum. You can use many of London's academic and specialist libraries through the Inspire London scheme, which grants one-day reference access to collections throughout London; ask your local library to refer you.

However, the Daddy of them all is the **British Library (Map 78)**. This behemoth receives a copy of every publication printed in the UK and Ireland, and requires 625km of shelving space to accommodate its 150million items. But it's just such a tease. You cannot borrow books, and to even access the collections you need to obtain a Reader Pass, via an introductory discussion to establish why you need it and whether you're likely to doodle on the books. This requires two forms of ID, no compromise: refer to www.bl.uk for the latest guidelines. Once you have your pass you can access the Reading Rooms, albeit with your personal belongings in a clear plastic bag (or stored in a locker). But if you just fancy seeing the Magna Carta, Shakespeare in Quarto or some Beatles manuscripts, you can access the book-free visitor areas without appointment and still gain an impressive look at one of the world's greatest information resources.

General Information

Important phone numbers:
All emergencies: 999
Non-emergencies: 101
Anti-terrorism hotline: 0800 789 321
Crime Stoppers: 0800 555 111
Neighbourhood Watch: 020 79934709
Missing Persons: 0500 700 700
Complaints: 08453 002 002
Websites:
www.met.police.uk
www.cityoflondon.police.uk (Separate police force specifically covering the Square Mile).
www.btp.police.uk (Separate police force specifically covering public transport).

Statistics* (Greater London)

	2007/08	2007/06	2006/05	2005/04
Murder	123	142	142	155
Rapes	1,558	1,977	2,001	2,035
GBH	3,785	4,380	4,702	4,496
Burglary (res)	49,946	50,193	53,939	52,693
Vehicle Crime	100,678	109,436	114,501	114,698

* taken from a report from the Metropolitan Police Performance Directorate

Police Stations

	Address	Phone	Map
Albany Street Police Station	60 Albany St	030 0123 1212	77
Battersea Police Station	112 Battersea Bridge	030 0123 1212	132
Belgravia Police Station	202 Buckingham Palace Rd	030 0123 1212	20
Brixton Police Station	367 Brixton Rd	030 0123 1212	144
Camberwell Police Station	22 Camberwell Church St	030 0123 1212	122
Cavendish Road Police Station	47 Cavendish Parade	030 0123 1212	149
Charing Cross Police Station	Agar St & Strand	030 0123 1212	24
Chelsea Police Station	2 Lucan Pl	030 0123 1212	46
Chiswick Police Station	209 Chiswick High Rd	030 0123 1212	38
Deptford Police Station	114 Amersham Vale	020 8297 1212	126
East Dulwich Police Station	173 Lordship Ln	030 0123 1212	129
Greenwich Police Station	31 Royal Hill	030 0123 1212	120
Hampstead Police Station	26 Rosslyn Hill	030 0123 1212	56
Harrow Road Police Station	325 Harrow Rd	030 0123 1212	26
Holborn Police Station	10 Lamb's Conduit St	030 0123 1212	5
Holloway Police Station	284 Hornsey Rd	030 0123 1212	61
Hornsey Police Station	98 Tottenham Ln	030 0123 1212	54
Islington Police Station	2 Tolpuddle St	030 0123 1212	80
Kennington Police Station	49 Kennington Rd	030 0123 1212	104
Kensington Police Station	72 Earl's Court Rd	030 0123 1212	35
Kentish Town Police	12 Holmes Rd	030 0123 1212	72
Lavender Hill Police Station	176 Lavender Hill	030 0123 1212	140
Marylebone Police Station	1 Seymour St	030 0123 1212	1
Notting Hill Police Station	100 Ladbroke Grove	030 0123 1212	28
Paddington Green Police Station	2 Harrow Rd	030 0123 1212	31
Peckham Police Station	177 Peckham High St	030 0123 1212	123
Rotherhithe Police Station	99 Lower Rd	020 7378 1212	110
Southwark Police Station	323 Borough High St	030 0123 1212	106
St John's Wood Police Station	20 Newcourt St	030 0123 1212	69
Tooting Police Station	251 Mitcham Rd	030 0123 1212	152
Walworth Police Station	12 Manor Pl	030 0123 1212	113
Wandsworth Police Station	146 Wandsworth High St	030 0123 1212	138
West End Central Police Station	27 Savile Row	030 0123 1212	10

Overview

London hotels can be sources of hopelessly romantic creativity. In 1899 Claude Monet painted the Houses of Parliament from his balcony at the Savoy hotel. About 100 years later, Fay Weldon moved in with her typewriter as writer in residence. If you've got visitors in town, fancy giving Claude a run for his money, or just can't face going back to your dump of a flat, you'll need the services of a hotel. When choosing your hotel, think carefully about what kind of London you're looking to experience and whom the room is for. We've identified a few of the usual suspects for whom you may find yourself booking a hotel room, and heartily offer you our best suggestions for each. Just don't expect to emerge from any of them clutching a masterpiece penned overnight.

Only the best, Daah-ling

So you need to find a hotel for a VIP client who will accept nothing but the best. Where to start? Since you don't have to cover the bill yourself, here is where you can really dig into London hospitality at its most deluxe. Start by trying to book **The Ritz (Map 9)**, with its amazing views of Green Park, Rococo detailing and killer high tea. **Brown's (Map 9)** is a stunning five-star and was the first hotel in London to have a lift. There is also the **Dorchester (Map 9)**, and its neighbour the **Hilton Park Lane (Map 9)**, where you may see a celebrity stumbling back to their quarters at four in the morning, if you're very, very lucky. **The Landmark (Map 76)** is a wonderfully Victorian retreat in the centre of ritzy Marylebone and has a rather fine atrium. But the granddaddy of luxury London must be the **Savoy (Map 24)**. This elegant old-timer stunk of old money until its temporary closure in 2007 for a £100 million spruce-up. It was built on the location of the Savoy Palace, which burned down during the Peasants' Revolt in 1381. We say let them eat cake (and tea).

A Dirty Weekend

This can be any weekend where a Londoner decides booze-goggled sex and/or quick-to-bed access after a night of clubbing is worthy of dishing out the dosh on an über-chic central hotel. It's one (giant) step up from splurging on a taxi and is the realm of the London boutique hotel where location is everything. **Hazlitt's (Map 12)** is right in the middle of Soho yet still wonderfully intimate. **Andaz Hotel (Map 8) (formerly Great Eastern Hotel)** is in the heart of the City, with funky Shoreditch on its doorstep, whilst the 'modern English' style of the **Charlotte Street Hotel (Map 3)** is painfully hip and sophisticated.

The Tea-and-Crumpet Tourist

Then there's the hotel for your sweetly naïve cousin that sees London through rose-tinted Ray Bans: full of scones, Mary Poppins and the chimes of Big Ben. You wouldn't want to burst her cute little bubble, would you? Not to worry, there are plenty of hotels to satisfy the Harrods tourist. **San Domenico House London (Map 46)** is a Chelsea boutique hotel that is about as warm and cuddly as a cup of sugary tea. **The Rookery (Map 15)**, built amongst a row of once derelict Georgian townhouses in Clerkenwell, is cluttered with museum-worthy furniture, open fires and ye oldey worldey frippery. Or, if she can't bear to be too far away from Buckingham Palace, there's the nearby **Windermere (Map 20)**.

Parents in Town?

If your parents have spent their nest egg on bailing you out of your London-induced debt, they will probably want to get the most out of London for the least money possible. But if the hotel you pick for their stay is anything short of perfect, you'll never hear the end of it. If they have loyalty cards with any of the bigger hotel chains, now is a good time to use them. **The London Bridge Hotel (Map 22)** is an independent four-star that usually has good deals and is conveniently close to Borough Market and London Bridge station. Gower

Street has a wealth of small family-run hotels at reasonable prices, including the **Cavendish (Map 23)**, within stumbling distance of the British Museum. There's also the nearby **Crescent Hotel (Map 4)**, next to Russell Square. If you miss home cooking, get your 'rents a serviced apartment with a kitchenette. Marlin Apartments and Think London have a few different properties, often ripe for the celeb sighting as pop stars are known to hitch up their wagons there during drawn-out tours.

In Lieu of a Couch to Crash On

Then you get your university friend still in strong denial of the real world, who refuses to get a real job. The amount of times this sponger has crashed on your sofa has been enough to send your might-be-the-one girl/boyfriend packing. Instead of blaming him/her for your future life of loneliness, banish them from the flat and call in the services of one of London's cheapies. They do exist, you just have to look hard. The **Hoxton Hotel (Map 84)**, an urban cheap boutique founded by the owner of Pret a Manger, is famous for its £1 hotel room sales. Cheap but cheerful chain Premier Inn (multiple locations) boasts rooms from £29 a night. Sometimes short-term rental companies, like **Best London Rent**, offer shared-facility flats at very cheap prices. This is perfect if it's going to be for a week or more, and although the locations aren't too central, this can be a good alternative to endless weeks of friends imposing on your hospitality.

Where to Stick Your Best Friend From School
(And Her Husband, Two Perfect Kids and a Dog)

Unfortunately, for some people visiting London a dodgy guesthouse isn't going to cut it. You want to show them how your city can be just as perfect as their countryside home and how not jealous you are of them! Of course, they don't see the point in paying tons either. This is where the few and far between bed and breakfasts come out of the woodwork. Most of these are small, so book in advance. London's best is the warm and welcoming **Bay Tree House and Annex B&B (Out of coverage)**. Great for families or singletons alike, it's in New Southgate (about 25 minutes by tube from central London but can be a relaxing retreat. **Barclay House (Map 43)** is a hidden gem in Fulham Broadway (make sure you write down the address as it's not signposted and can blend in). **Aster House (Map 45)** is a bit pricier but close enough to posh High Street Kensington to give a glimpse of how the other half live.

With all these hotels, compare prices online ask for their best rate and/or call for last minute deals, you may be surprised at the reductions available. Good offers mean you can pay less than you'd think for the best, and London does really have the best.

Map 1 · Marylebone (West)

	Address	Phone	Price in £
22 York St	22 York St	020 7224 2990	89
Boston Court Hotel	26 Upper Berkeley St	020 7723 1445	89
The Cumberland	Great Cumberland Pl	087 1376 9014	110
Edward Lear	28 Seymour St	020 7402 5401	50
Hadleigh Hotel	24 Upper Berkeley St	020 7262 4084	81
Hotel 82	82 Gloucester Pl	020 7486 3679	110
The Leonard	15 Seymour St	020 7935 2010	100
Sherlock Holmes Hotel	108 Baker St	020 7486 6161	117
Thistle Marble Arch	Bryanston St Marble Arch	0871 376 9027	149

Map 2 · Marylebone (East)

	Address	Phone	Price in £
Claridges	Brook St	020 7629 8860	167
Hotel La Place	17 Nottingham Pl	020 7486 2323	99
Marylebone	47 Welbeck St	020 7486 6600	120
The Langham	1 Portland Pl	020 7636 1000	198
No. 5 Maddox	5 Maddox St	020 7647 0200	270

General Information · **Hotels**

Map 3 · Fitzrovia	Address	Phone	Price in £
Charlotte Street Hotel	15 Charlotte Street	020 7806 2000	270
Grange Fitzrovia Hotel	20 Bolsover St	020 7467 7000	101
Sanderson Hotel	50 Berners St	020 7300 1400	214

Map 4 · Bloomsbury (West)	Address	Phone	Price in £
Academy	21 Gower St	020 7631 4115	200
Ambassadors Hotel	12 Upper Woburn Pl	020 7693 5400	112
Arosfa	83 Gower St	020 7636 2115	55
Bloomsbury Park Hotel	126 Southampton Row	084 5305 8307	99
Crescent Hotel	49 Cartwright Gardens	020 7387 1515	100
Hotel Cavendish	75 Gower St	020 7636 9079	95
Hotel Russell	1 Russell Square	020 7837 6470	119
The Montague	15 Montague St	020 7637 1001	135
Myhotel Bloomsbury	11 Bayley St	020 7667 6000	186
Radisson	97 Great Russell St	020 7637 3477	142
St Giles	Bedford Ave	020 7300 3000	88

Map 5 · Bloomsbury (East)	Address	Phone	Price in £
Comfort Inn	2 St Chad's St	020 7837 1940	98
Generator Hostel	37 Tavistock Pl	020 7388 7666	17

Map 7 · Barbican / City Road (South)	Address	Phone	Price in £
Barbican Hotel	120 Central St	084 5305 8304	71
Citadines Hotel	7 Goswell Rd	020 7566 8000	99

Map 8 · Liverpool Street / Broadgate	Address	Phone	Price in £
Andaz Hotel	40 Liverpool St	020 7961 1234	160

Map 9 · Mayfair / Green Park	Address	Phone	Price in £
Athenaeum Hotel	116 Piccadilly	020 7499 3464	153
Brown's Hotel	1 Albemarle St	020 7493 6020	239
Chesterfield	35 Charles St	020 7491 2622	116
The Connaught	Carlos Pl	020 7499 7070	188
Curzon Plaza Hotel	56 Curzon St	020 7499 4121	122
The Dorchester	53 Park Ln	020 7629 8888	245
Flemings Mayfair Hotel	7 Half Moon St	020 7499 2964	134
Grosvenor House	86 Park Ln	020 7499 6363	175
Hilton Park Lane	22 Park Ln	020 7493 8000	226
The Intercontinental	1 Hamilton Pl	020 7409 3131	198
May Fair Hotel	Stratton St	020 7769 4041	173
Metropolitan	Old Park Lane	020 7447 1047	191
Millennium Hotel	44 Grosvenor Square	020 7629 9400	145
The Ritz	150 Piccadilly	020 7493 8181	265

Map 11 · Soho (Central)	Address	Phone	Price in £
The Shaftesbury	65 Shaftesbury Ave	020 7871 6000	164
The Soho Hotel	4 Richmond Mews	020 7559 3000	240

Map 12 · Soho (East)	Address	Phone	Price in £
Hazlitt's Hotel	6 Frith St	020 7434 1771	159

Map 13 · Covent Garden	Address	Phone	Price in £
Covent Garden Hotel	10 Monmouth St	020 7806 1000	235
Fielding	4 Broad Ct	020 7836 8305	85
The Radisson	20 Monmouth St	020 7836 4300	150

Map 14 · Holborn / Temple

	Address	Phone	Price in
Citadines Hotel	94 High Holborn	020 7395 8800	99
One Aldwych	1 Aldwych	020 7300 1000	240
Renaissance Chancery Court	252 High Holborn	020 7829 9888	340

Map 15 · Blackfriars / Farringdon

		Phone	Price in £
Club Quarters	24 Ludgate Hill	020 7651 2200	84
Malmaison	18 Charterhouse Sq	020 7012 3700	225
The Rookery	12 Peter's Ln	020 7336 0931	128

Map 17 · Square Mile (East)

	Address	Phone	Price in £
Club Quarters	7 Gracechurch St	020 7666 1620	79
Threadneedles Hotel	5 Threadneedle St	020 7657 8080	153

Map 18 · Tower Hill / Aldgate

	Address	Phone	Price in £
Apex Hotel	1 Seething Ln	013 1441 0440	86
Chamberlain	130 Minories	020 7680 1500	94
Novotel Tower Bridge	10 Pepys St	020 7265 6000	145

Map 19 · Belgravia

	Address	Phone	Price in £
B&B Belgravia	64 Ebury St	020 7259 8570	99
The Berkeley	Wilton Pl	020 7235 6000	255
The Halkin	Halkin St	020 7333 1000	390
Morgan Guest House	120 Ebury St	020 7730 2384	52
Sheraton Belgravia	20 Chesham Pl	020 7235 6040	178

Map 20 · Victoria / Pimlico (West)

		Phone	Price in £
41	41 Buckingham Palace Rd	020 7300 0041	255
Caswell Hotel	25 Gloucester St	020 7834 6345	63
Central House	39 Belgrave Rd	020 7834 8036	122
Days Hotel	80 Belgrave Rd	020 7828 8661	102
Dover Hotel	42 Belgrave Rd	020 7821 9085	63
Durrants Hotel	26 George St	020 7935 8131	153
Elizabeth Hotel and Apartments	37 Eccleston Square	020 7828 6812	85
Enrico Hotel	77 Warwick Way	020 7834 9538	56
Goring	15 Beeston Pl	020 7396 9000	279
Hart House Hotel	51 Gloucester St	020 7935 2288	85
Hesperia London Victoria Hotel	2 Bridge Pl	087 0225 4134	114
Windermere	144 Warwick Way	020 7834 5163	90

Map 21 · Pimlico (East)

	Address	Phone	Price in £
Best Western	85 Belgrave Rd	020 7828 9279	76
City Inn Westminster	30 John Islip Street	020 7630 1000	140
Corbigoe Hotel	101 Belgrave Rd	020 7834 9790	46
Dolphin House Hotel	Chichester St	020 7798 8000	52
Wellington	71 Vincent Square	020 7834 4740	62

Map 22 · Westminster

	Address	Phone	Price in £
51 Buckingham Gate	51 Buckingham Gate	020 7769 7766	326
London Bridge Hotel	8 Bridge St	020 7855 2200	172
Vandon House Hotel	1 Vandon St	020 7799 6780	45

Map 23 • St. James's	Address	Phone	Price in
The Cavendish Hotel	81 Jermyn St	020 7930 2111	142
Dukes Hotel	35 St James's St	020 7491 4840	185
Radisson	3 St Martin's St	020 7930 8641	167
Radisson Edwardian Hampshire	31 Leicester Square	020 7839 9399	160
The Stafford	16 St James's Pl	020 7493 0111	290
Thistle Trafalgar Hotel	Whitcomb St	087 1376 9037	114

Map 24 • Trafalgar Square / The Strand		Phone	Price in £
Guoman Charing Cross	The Strand	020 7839 7282	111
The Savoy	Strand	020 7836 4343	TBD
The Strand Palace	372 Strand	020 7836 8080	115

Map 27 • Maida Vale	Address	Phone	Price in £
Colonnade	2 Warrington Crescent	020 7286 1052	270
The Royal Park	3 Westbourne Terrace Rd	020 7479 6600	140

Map 29 • Notting Hill Gate	Address	Phone	Price in £
Guesthouse West	165 Westbourne Grove	020 7792 9800	155
The Lennox	34 Pembridge Gardens	020 7229 9977	190
The Main House	6 Colville Rd	020 7221 9691	50
Miller's Residence	111 Westbourne Grove	020 7243 1024	150
The Portobello Hotel	22 Stanley Gardens	020 7727 2777	145

Map 30 • Bayswater	Address	Phone	Price in £
Bayswater Inn	8 Princes Square	020 7727 8621	91
Best Western	27 Devonshire Terrace	020 7745 1200	102
Best Western Mornington	12 Lancaster Gate	020 7262 7361	130
Best Western Phoenix Hotel	1 Kensington Gardens Sq	020 7229 2494	91
Blakemore Hotel	30 Leinster Gardens	020 7262 4591	102
Caesar Hotel	26 Queen's Gardens	020 7262 0022	91
Central Park Hotel	49 Queensborough Terrace	020 7229 2424	61
Comfort Inn	19 Craven Hill Gardens	020 7262 6644	72
Commodore Hotel	50 Lancaster Gate	020 7402 5291	102
Craven Gardens Hotel	16 Leinster Terrace	020 7402 4101	56
Duke of Leinster Hotel	20 Leinster Gardens	020 7298 3850	89
Dylan House	14 Devonshire Terrace	020 7723 3280	117
Garden Court	30 Kensington Gardens Square	020 7229 2553	48
Hempel Hotel	31 Craven Hill Gardens	020 7298 9000	173
Henry VIII Hotel	19 Leinster Gardens	020 7262 0117	101
Hyde Park Premier	14 Craven Hill	020 7262 0111	132
Paddington Court Hotel	27 Devonshire Terrace	020 7262 1212	113
Pembridge Palace Hotel	55 Princes Square	020 7229 6262	87
Princes Square Hotel	23 Prince's Sq	020 7229 9876	115
Royal Lancaster Hotel	1 Lancaster Terrace	020 7262 6737	145
Thistle Hyde Park	90 Lancaster Gate	0871 376 9022	86
Vancouver Studios	30 Prince's Square	020 7243 1270	85

Map 31 • Paddington	Address	Phone	Price in £
Castleton	164 Sussex Gardens	020 7706 4666	76
Chrysos Hotel	25 Norfolk Square	020 7262 2417	102
The Delmere	130 Sussex Gardens	020 7706 3344	99
Edward Hotel	1 Spring St	020 7262 2671	95
Hilton	225 Edgware Rd	020 7402 4141	117
Hilton	146 Praed St	020 7850 0500	153
Pavilion Hotel	36 Sussex Gardens	020 7262 0905	60
Queensway Hotel	147 Sussex Gardens	020 7723 7749	61

Map 35 · Kensington

	Address	Phone	Price in £
Best Western	33 Hogarth Rd	020 7370 6831	119
Comfort Inn	22 West Cromwell Rd	020 7373 3300	68
Copthorne Tara Hotel	Scarsdale Place	020 7937 7211	117
Derby Hotel	155 Cromwell Rd	020 7262 0022	103
Garden View Hotel	29 Nevern Square	020 7835 1900	135
Majestic	160 Cromwell Rd	020 7373 3083	57
The Milestone Hotel	1 Kensington Ct Pl	020 7917 1010	265
Radisson	68 W Cromwell Rd	020 7761 9000	98
The Rockwell	181 W Cromwell Rd	020 7244 2000	120
Warwick House Hotel	109 Warwick Rd	020 7373 9584	67

Map 36 · South Kensington / Gloucester Rd

		Phone	Price in £
Baglioni Hotel	60 Hyde Park Gate	020 7368 5700	357
Best Western	4 Queens Gate	020 7808 8400	122
Citadines Hotel	35 Gloucester Rd	0207 543 7878	107
Fraser Place Hotel	39 Queen's Gate Gardens	020 7969 3555	115
Gainsborough Hotel	7 Queensberry Pl	020 7957 0000	91
Gallery Hotel	8 Queensberry Pl	020 7915 0000	112
The Gore	190 Queen's Gate	020 7584 6601	178
Grange Hotel	41 Queen's Gate Gardens	020 7584 0512	90
Grosvenor Kensington Hotel	2 Harrington Rd	020 8859 3333	119
Holiday Inn	97 Cromwell Rd	0877 228 7143	99
Millennium Hotel	140 Gloucester Rd	020 7373 6000	110
Park International Hotel	117 Cromwell Rd	020 7370 5711	101

Map 37 · Knightsbridge

	Address	Phone	Price in £
Cadogan Hotel	75 Sloane St	020 7235 7141	178
The Capital Hotel and Apartments	22 Basil St	020 7589 5171	230
Durley House Hotel	115 Sloane St	020 7235 5537	459
The Franklin Hotel	22 Egerton Gardens	020 7584 5533	200
The Knightsbridge	10 Beaufort Gardens	020 7584 6300	170
Knightsbridge Green Hotel	159 Knightsbridge	020 7584 6274	150
The Rembrandt Hotel	11 Thurloe Pl	020 7589 8100	142

Map 42 · Barons Court

	Address	Phone	Price in £
Holiday Inn Express	295 North End Rd	020 7384 5151	109

Map 43 · West Brompton / Fulham Broadway / Earl's Court

			Price in £
Barclay House	21 Barclay Rd	020 7384 3390	66
Best Western	18 Barkston Gardens	020 7373 3151	74
City Continental London	11 Penywern Rd	020 7373 6514	106
Enterprise Hotel	15 Hogarth Rd	020 7373 4502	68
Garden View Hotel	29 Nevern Square	020 7244 6466	68
Mayflower Hotel	26 Trebovir Rd	020 7370 0991	170
Rushmore	11 Trebovir Rd	020 7370 3839	164
Twenty Nevern Square	20 Nevern Square	020 7565 9555	79

Map 44 · Chelsea

	Address	Phone	Price in £
Astons Apartments Hotel	31 Rosary Gardens	020 7590 6000	97
Blakes Hotel	33 Roland Gardens	020 7370 6701	175

Map 45 · Chelsea (East)

	Address	Phone	Price in £
Aster House	3 Sumner Pl	020 7581 5888	99
Myhotel Chelsea	35 Ixworth Pl	020 7225 7500	222
Regency	100 Queens Gate	020 7373 7878	114
Sydney House	9 Sydney St	020 7376 7711	160

General Information · **Hotels**

Map 46 · Sloane Square	Address	Phone	Price in £
Draycott Hotel	26 Cadogan Gardens	020 773 06466	306
San Domenico House	29 Draycott Pl	020 7581 5757	210

Map 56 · Hampstead Village	Address	Phone	Price in £
Hampstead Village Guesthouse	2 Kemplay Rd	020 7586 9573	65

Map 69 · St. John's Wood	Address	Phone	Price in £
Marriot	128 King Henry's Rd	020 7722 7711	127

Map 70 · Primrose Hill	Address	Phone	Price in £
Hampstead Britannia Hotel	Primrose Hill Rd	087 1222 0043	76

Map 76 · Edgeware Road / Marylebone (North)	Address	Phone	Price in £
Danubius Hotel	18 Lodge Rd	0207 722 7722	84
Dorset Square Hotel	39 Dorset Sq	020 7723 7874	160
Four Seasons Hotel	173 Gloucester Pl	020 7724 3461	96
Landmark	222 Marylebone Rd	020 7631 8000	210

Map 77 · Mornington Crescent / Regent's Park	Address	Phone	Price in £
Melia White House Hotel	Albany St	020 7391 3000	109

Map 84 · Hoxton		Phone	Price in £
Hoxton Hotel	81 Great Eastern St	020 7550 1000	89

Map 91 · Shoreditch / Brick Lane / Spitalfields	Address	Phone	Price in £
City Hotel	12-20 Osborn St	020 7247 3313	102
Hotel St Gregory	100 Shoreditch High St	020 7613 9800	137

Map 98 · Mile End (South) / Limehouse	Address	Phone	Price in £
Holiday Inn Express	469 The Highway	020 7791 3850	133

Map 100 · Poplar (West) / Canary Wharf (West)	Address	Phone	Price in £
The Hilton	Marsh Wall	020 3002 2350	104
International Hotel	163 Marsh Wall	0871 222 0042	81
Marriot	22 Hertsmere Rd	020 7093 1000	119

Map 104 · South Bank / Waterloo / Lambeth North	Address	Phone	Price in £
Marriott County Hall	Westminster Bridge Rd	020 7928 5200	189
Travel Inn London County Hall	Belverdere Rd	0870 238 3300	104

105 · Southwark / Bankside (West)		Phone	Price in £
The Mad Hatter Hotel	3 Stamford St	020 7401 9222	115

Map 106 · Bankside (East) / Borough / Newington		Phone	Price in £
Novotel London City South	61 Southwark Bridge Rd	020 7089 0400	98
Southwark Rose Hotel	47 Southwark Bridge Rd	020 7015 1480	105

Map 113 · Walworth	Address	Phone	Price in £
Express by Eurotraveller Hotel	18 Amelia St	020 7358 4898	79

Map 120 · Greenwich	Address	Phone	Price in £
Novotel Greenwich	173 Greenwich High Rd	020 8312 6800	145

Map 121 · Camberwell (West)	Address	Phone	Price in £
Park Plaza Hotel	1 Addington Square	020 7021 1800	127

Map 131 · Vauxhall / Albert Embankment		Phone	Price in £
Days Hotel	54 Kennington Rd	020 7922 1331	97
Park Plaza Hotel	18 Albert Embankment	020 7958 8000	119
Plaza on the River	18 Albert Embankment	020 7769 2525	224

Map 134 · South Lambeth	Address	Phone	Price in £
Comfort Inn	87 S Lambeth Rd	020 7735 9494	74

Map 137 · Wandsworth (West)	Address	Phone	Price in £
Best Western	52 Upper Richmond Rd	020 8874 1598	97

As you might expect from a site constantly inhabited since the Roman invasion of Britain, and probably before, London has managed to assemble a vast array of good, bad and ugly landmarks. The city is, in fact, stuffed with them, and the following is a slightly subjective rumination on a small proportion of some of the most noteworthy.

Historical

London gracefully bears a massive weight of history, and many of its landmarks reflect this. One of the oldest is the remains of the **Temple of Mithras (Map 16)** on Walbrook, built by the Romans when London was Londinium. Parts of the **London Wall (Map 18)**, also originally built by the Romans, still exist, the best fragments are around Tower Hill station. In Medieval times London became a bustling place; celebrate one of its most beautiful churches by visiting the oddly named **St Giles' Cripplegate (Map 7)**, which is ensconced within the brutal **Barbican Centre (Map 7)**, a landmark itself. By the 1600s, London was bustling so hard it got the plague and then some idiot burnt the entire city down in 1666. Celebrate three days of the Great Fire by climbing to the top of the 202 feet high **Monument (Map 18)**, before visiting post-fire architect Christopher Wren's masterpiece, **St Paul's Cathedral (Map 16)**. Into the 18th century, things became a little more sophisticated and some of London's prettiest domestic architecture bloomed. Stroll down Bloomsbury's **Doughty Street (Map 5)**, stopping at Charles Dickens' House, for perfectly proportioned Georgian elegance. The Victorians had a huge impact on London, with whole tracts of the city bearing the stamp of the starched times of chimney sweeps and empire bashing. For the lighter side of Victorian London, poke about the museums quarter from the **Victoria & Albert Museum (Map 37)** up to the **Albert Memorial (Map 36)**. For the darker, dodge the elderly at the **St Pancras Hospital (Map 78)**, an ex-workhouse.

Tourist Bait

London has a host of over-exposed landmarks that are honey to the swarms of tourist worker-bees but over-rated in the eyes of many Londoners. We don't necessarily share this view, but if you want to venture beyond the crowds at **Big Ben (Map 22)**, try some of the following. The aforementioned **St Paul's Cathedral (Map 16)** is an absolute wonder, although try the smaller **Southwark Cathedral (Map 106)** for a more intimate option. **The British Museum (Map 4)** is a beauty made fairer by its recent courtyard renovation; peruse the library to see where Marx pondered upon 'Das Kapital'. **The Burlington Arcade (Map 10)** is how shopping should be. The crypt under **St Mary-le-Bow Church (Map 16)** is 11th century weirdness complete with its own vegetarian restaurant. The Thames is long enough to provide you with your own spot of riverside tranquillity. If you're scared of bridges, burrow under the river at the **Greenwich Foot Tunnel (Map 120)**, or chug across it on the free Woolwich Ferry. For a weekend mooch, try the **Grand Regent's Canal (Map 71)**.

Modern Landmarks

The 20th century blessed the city with some opinion splitting contributions. **The Hayward Gallery (Map 104)** and **National Theatre (Map 104)** are both concrete frighteners which we are learning to love. Despite originally housing a power station, **Tate Modern (Map 105)** has been more graciously received. Meanwhile, further down the river, disused **Battersea Power Station (Map 133)** continues to crumble. The **BT Tower (Map 3)** is like a 1960s lighthouse for central London drunks. **The Lloyds Building (Map 18)** and **Tower 42 (Map 18)** are both absorbing odes to the banker and glare menacingly at new rival **One Canada Square (or Canary Wharf Tower) (Map 100)**. A more recent contribution to the city is the **Canary Wharf Underground Station (Map 100)**.

Lowbrow

In these clean times of starchitects, steel and glass, a few minutes spent gawping at **Elephant and Castle (Map 105)** shopping centre is enough to remind anyone how awry a landmark can go. Even a quick squizz at the nearby **Faraday Memorial (Map 105)** may not lift your gloom, largely as it now forms the body of a clogged roundabout. However, London can do lowbrow with the best of them, starting with the **Westway Flyover (Map 31)**: a noisy, dusty shard of concrete to remind you that the car is still king. The disused **Kingsway Tram Tunnel (Map 4)** is a forgotten piece of prime underground real estate and **Centre Point (Map 4)** and **Millbank**

Tower (Map 21) are good examples of dodgy skyscrapers that no-one needed. **Battersea Park Gasometers (Map 133)** are imposing monsters, whereas **Lots Road Power Station (Map 50)** is fast becoming London's trendiest disused power station. If you must jump upon band wagons, keep your eyes peeled around east London for art left on walls by Banksy. Mobile lowbrow starts with a trip on a Routemaster, despite the buses being withdrawn in 2005, two heritage routes are still running. Lowbrow (along with logic, aesthetic quality and planning) finishes with **Euston Station (Map 78)**, which is, simply, disgusting.

Map 1 · Marylebone (West)

Marble Arch	Oxford St & Park Ln	Randomly plonked gateway to nowhere.
Speakers' Corner	Cumberland Gate & Park Ln	It's easy—stand on the corner and listen to the 'speeches.'

Map 2 · Marylebone (East)

Hertford House	Manchester Sq & Hinde St	Terribly twee home of the Wallace Collection.
Jimi Hendrix Memorial Blue Plaque	23 Brook St	Jimi lived here. Some bloke called Handel lived next door.

Map 3 · Fitzrovia

BT Tower	60 Cleveland St	A 574 foot tall official government secret until 1993.
Charlotte Street	Charlotte St	Restaurant strip for the advertising in-crowd.
Middlesex Hospital	Mortimer St & Cleveland St	Closed-down and spooky-looking.
Pollock's Toy Museum	1 Scala St	Brimming with delightful, traditional toys and Dickensian atmosphere.
Sinner Winner Man	216 Oxford St	Are you a sinner? Or a winner? London's top preacher's patch.
Tottenham Court Road	Tottenham Ct Rd	Buy your electronics 'ere, innit?

Map 4 · Bloomsbury (West)

The British Museum	Great Russell St & Museum St	Newly-covered Great Court is architectural manna.
Centre Point	101 New Oxford St	Ugly skyscraper looking kinda out of place.
Kingsway Tram Tunnel	Theobalds Rd & Southampton Row	Spooky remnant of London's defunct Tram network.
Senate House	Malet St & Torrington Sq	Ominous art deco building; Orwell's Ministry of Truth.
Tavistock Square	Tavistock Sq	Has a statue of Gandhi looking as cool as ever.

Map 5 · Bloomsbury (East)

The Dickens House Museum	48 Doughty St	Unassuming from the outside, mecca for Dickens' fans on the inside.
Doughty Street	Doughty St & Guilford St	Exquisite Georgian street in heart of literary land.
Gray's Inn Field	Theobald's Rd	Holborn Hideaway.

Map 7 · Barbican / City Road (South)

Barbican Centre	Silk St & Whitecross St	An architectural eyesore. Bloody good events though.
Bunhill Fields	38 City Rd	120 thousand dead people, including William Blake. All buried, luckily.
Church of Saint Bartholomew	6 Kinghorn St	Stroll in for your daily dose of frankincense and choir song.
LSO St Luke's	161 Old St	Home to the London Symphony Orchestra. Peaceful gardens for relaxation.
St. Giles-without-Cripplegate	Fore St & Wood St	Medieval church which defied the Blitz. Catch an organ recital.

General Information · **Landmarks**

Map 8 · Liverpool Street / Broadgate

Fulcrum at Broadgate	Broadgate	Richard Serra's overwhelming steel megalith.

Map 9 · Mayfair / Green Park

50 Berkeley Square	50 Berkeley Sq	The most haunted house in all of London town!
Apsley House	149 Piccadilly	"Number One, London"—former hip address of Duke of Wellington.
Buckingham Palace	The Mall	Unofficial HQ for Fathers For Justice.
Down Street Station	Down St & Piccadilly	Bricked-up Underground station. The Turtles didn't live here.

Map 10 · Piccadilly / Soho (West)

Burlington Arcade	Burlington Arcade & Piccadilly	Welcoming shoppers since 1819.
Carnaby Street	Carnaby St	Will anything innovative ever come from here again?
Kingly Court	Kingly St & Foubert's Pl	Flash the cash to cut a dash.
Statue of Eros	Piccadilly Circus	God of Love, smothered in pigeon crap: a cautionary tale.

Map 11 · Soho (Central)

Huge Tree In Pub (Waxy O'Connor's)	14 Rupert St	No, you're not drunk, it really is a tree.
John Snow Water Pump	Broadwick Street	Source of 1854 Cholera outbreak identified by Snow.
Berwick Street Market	Berwick St & Rupert St	Arrive early for traditional Cockney trader songs / off-duty hookers.

Map 12 · Soho (East)

Denmark Street	Denmark St & Charing Cross Rd	Guitar land. 'Enter Sandman' forbidden in most stores.
FA Headquarters	25 Soho Sq	Home of English football's top brass.
Old Compton Street	Old Compton St	Dubious gay hub.
The Phoenix Garden	21 Stacey St	A beautiful green mini-oasis in the middle of the city.
Soho Square	Soho Sq	Great atmosphere on hot summer days.

Map 13 · Covent Garden

Oasis Lido	32 Endell St	A lido in central London! In a 50s housing estate!
Seven Dials	Upper St Martin's Ln & Earlham St	Slum area in the past. Now great for shopping!

Map 14 · Holborn / Temple

Aldwych tube station	Strand & Surrey St	Creepy abandoned tube station. With a photo booth... of doom?
BBC Bush House	Aldwych & Kingsway	London calling the world, since 1940.
Hatton Garden	Hatton Garden	Historic jewelry and diamond district
Inner Temple Garden	Inner Temple	So peaceful even the lawyers look relaxed.
Lincoln's Inn Fields	High Holborn & Chancery Ln	Largest public square in London.
The Old Curiosity Shop	13 Portsmouth St	The oldest shop in London is truly Dickensesque.
Royal Courts of Justice	Strand & Bell Yard	Witness justice meted out to all, even the McCartneys.
Sir John Soane's Museum	13 Lincoln's Inn Fields	Spooky museum dedicated to the great 18th century architect.
Site of Sweeny Todd's Barber Shop	186 Fleet St	Swing by for a demon haircut and lovely pie.
Somerset House	Strand	18th century palace, beautiful fountains; has various modern functions.

Map 15 · Blackfriars / Farringdon

Daily Express Building	121 Fleet St	Art Deco sleeper.
Millennium Bridge	Millennium Bridge	Footbridge famous for wobbling alarmingly when it was opened.
Postman's Park	King Edward St & Little Britain	Tile memorial for 'average' people who did really cool things.

Map 16 · Square Mile (West)

The Guildhall	Gresham St & Basinghall St	Big, posh, old... Like Prince Phillip but less entertaining.
St Mary le Bow Church	Cheapside & Bow Ln	A historic place for City tycoons to save their souls.
St. Paul's Cathedral	St. Paul's Church Yard & Cannon St	Magnificence since 604AD.
Temple of Mithras	Queen Victoria St & Queen St	3rd century Roman temple foundations. Discovered 1954 and moved here.

465

General Information • **Landmarks**

Map 17 • Square Mile (East)

Bank of England	Threadneedle St	The 'Old Lady' still churns out the pounds.
London Stone	111 Cannon St	Possibly used by Romans to measure all distances in Britannia.
Threadneedle Street	Threadneedle St & Prince's St	London's original Grope Cunt Lane. Seriously, it's a true story.

Map 18 • Tower Hill / Aldgate

The Gherkin	30 St Mary Axe	Phwoar.
Leadenhall Market	Leadenhall Market	Designed by Horace Jones (Billingsgate and Smithfield Markets)
The Lloyds Building	1 Lime St	Dystopia's nicer side.
London Wall	Cooper's Row & Trinity Sq	Ruins, should be re-built to keep Northerners out.
The Monument	Monument St & Fish St Hill	Climb 311 coronary-inducing steps for unique, unsung London views.
Pudding Lane	Pudding Ln	Starting point for Great Fire of 1666. No smoking.
Royal Raven Lodgings	Wakefield Tower	Want to upgrade your pokey flat? Become a raven.
Soup Kitchen for the Jewish Poor	Brune St & Tenter Ground	The kitchen's gone; the stunning ornate façade is still there.
Thames Clipper	Tower Pier	
Tower 42 (Natwest Tower)	25 Old Broad St	One of London's skyscrapers. Great view (and restaurant) at top.
Tower of London	The Tower of London	Kings and Queens. Surprisingly insightful, annoyingly expensive.

Map 20 • Victoria / Pimlico (West)

Little Ben	Victoria St & Vauxhall Bridge Rd	Big Ben's runty kid brother.
Westminster Cathedral	42 Francis St	Yep, impressive.

Map 21 • Pimlico (East)

Millbank Tower	21 Millbank	Ugly sore thumb. And Labour Party HQ!
The Shard Building Site	32 Vauxhall Bridge Rd	Site of the super tall skyscraper to be.

Map 22 • Westminster

Big Ben	House of Commons	The world's most famous clock and pretty damn cool.
Bolan Rock Shrine	Queen's Ride, Putney	Memorial shrine where 70s rock star Marc Bolan died.
Field of Remembrance	Victoria St & Dean's Yard	Sea of crosses and poppies to honour veterans.
New Scotland Yard Sign	8 Broadway	It spins!! Just like on the telly!!
Smith Square	Smith Sq	Square with great concert venue--watch out for MPs.
UK Parliament	Victoria St & Abingdon St	Parliament buildings where you can watch government debates.
Westminster Tube Station	Bridge St & Victoria Embankment	A daunting, soulless, engineering playground. Good and bad both extinct here...

Map 23 • St. James's

Economist Plaza	25 St James's St	Rotating sculpture installations from bratty young artists.
Giro the Nazi Dog	9 Carlton House Terrace	London's sole Nazi memorial. You'd think there'd be more…
Leicester Square	Leicester Sq	Tragic, tacky, always inexplicably heaving. Avoid.
TKTS	Leicester Square & St Martin's St	Cheapo tickets to sometimes worth-seeing shows.

Map 24 • Trafalgar Square / The Strand

10 Downing Street	10 Downing St	The Prime Minister's house.
The Actors' Church	29 Bedford St	Somewhat hidden and unique church long-associated with thesps.
The Banqueting House	Whitehall & Horse Guards Ave	Unsullied Renaissance cum-shot. Still does private parties.
Cleopatra's Needle	Embankment	Ancient-Egyptian Empire esoterica, with additional Luftwaffe 'distressed' styling.
Eleanor Cross	Charing Cross Station, The Strand	A mourning King's tribute to his expired Queen.
Jane Austen Residence	10 Henrietta St	The first Bridget Jones' bachelorette crashed here for a time.
Right-hand Drive Street	Savoy Ct	Britain's only right-hand-drive street. Like being on holiday! (ish)
Sewer Lamp	Carting Lane & Strand	Lit by the power of your bowels.
St Martin-in-the-Fields	St Martin's Pl & Duncannon St	Was indeed surrounded by fields once. Just TRY to imagine!

General Information · **Landmarks**

Top Secret Tunnels	6 Craig's Ct	Government's WWII tunnels, 100ft below London. But shhh: top secret.
Trafalgar Square	Trafalgar Sq	Hardly an oasis but space to sit, look and think.

Map 25 · Kensal Town

Trellick Tower	5 Golborne Rd	Grade II listed 1960s council estate inspiring love/hate reactions.

Map 29 · Notting Hill Gate

Portobello Road Market	223 Portobello Rd	Antiques, clothes, food and more. A London institution.

Map 31 · Paddington

Paddington Bear Statue	Paddington Station	The statue's pleasant. But they're milking it with the crap shop.
Tony Blair's house	Connaught Square & Seymour St	Promise not to do anything naughty now.
Westway Flyover		Coolest car route into London

Map 33 · Shepherd's Bush

BBC Television Centre	Wood Ln & Ring Rd	Treasure it before the BBC moves out in 2013.

Map 34 · West Kensington / Olympia

Kyoto Garden (Holland Park)	100 Holland Park Ave	Traditional Japanese Garden in Holland Park offering peace and tranquility.

Map 35 · Kensington

Kensington Palace Gardens	Kensington Palace Gardens	Billionaire's Row. Stunning street to amble down and gawp at the mansions.

Map 36 · South Kensington / Gloucester Rd

Albert Memorial	Kensington Gardens	The shiniest balding head in town.
Royal Albert Hall	Kensington Gore	One stunner of a music hall, inside and out.

Map 37 · Knightsbridge

Holy Trinity Brompton	Brompton Rd & Knightsbridge	Historic HTB is home to the Alpha course. Even Guy Ritchie's been!
Victoria & Albert Museum	Cromwell Rd & Thurloe Pl	Victorian treasure trove, building a beauty itself.

Map 42 · Baron's Court

Empress State Buidling	Lillie Rd & North End Rd	Awesome Art Deco building now a scary cult center.

Map 43 · West Brompton / Fulham Broadway / Earl's Court

Stamford Bridge	Fulham Road & Moore Park Rd	That's not sweat you smell but money at Chelsea FC's HQ.

Map 46 · Sloane Square

Saatchi Gallery	Duke of York HQ, King's Rd	See rich dude's great art collection, for free.

Map 48 · Fulham

Putney Bridge Tube Pill Box	Putney Bridge Station	"We will fight them on the platforms!"

Map 50 · Sand's End

Lots Road Power Station	27 Lots Rd	Pint-sized power station, now disued.

Map 51 · Highgate

Highgate Cemetery	1 Swain's Ln	Eerily gothic home to Karl Marx and The Highgate Vampire.
Karl Marx's grave	Highgate Cemetry	Exactly what it says on the tin.

Map 52 · Archway (North)

Parkland Walk Nature Reserve	Parkland Walk	Hedgehogs and graffiti to be spotted along this abandoned railway.
Suicide Bridge	Hornsey Ln & Archway Rd	Former London entry point, now very much an exit point.

Map 53 · Crouch End

| Abandoned Warehouse | Parkland Walk & Crouch End Hill | Dereliction galore along one of the best walks in London. |

Map 56 · Hampstead Village

| Hampstead Observatory | Lower Terrace & Hampstead Grove | The highest point in London, and open to the public! |

Map 57 · Hampstead Heath

| Keats' House | Keats Grove | Beautiful buildin' where some bloke wrote some poem. Innit. |
| Lawn Road Flats | Lawn Rd & Garnett Rd | c.1934 modern living. Learn to love concrete. |

Map 60 · Archway

| Banksy's Hitchhiking Charles Manson | Tally Ho Corner (off Highgate Hill) | Early stencil by internationally renowned graff artist. |
| Dick Whittington's Cat | 89 Highgate Hill | Small stone statue of obscure Mayor's cat. |

Map 62 · Finsbury Park

| North London Central Mosque (Finsbury Park) | 7 St Thomas's Rd | New name, ethos for once controversial, now myth-dispelling, mosque. |

Map 63 · Manor House

| The Castle Climbing Centre | Green Lanes & Lordship Park | Fake castle, real climbers. |

Map 64 · Stoke Newington

| Newington Green Church | 39 Newington Green | 'ERECTED 1708, ENLARGED 1860'...well, it made us laugh. |

Map 67 · Belsize Park

| Freud Statue | Fitzjohn's Ave, opposite Maresfield Gardens Junction | Statue by Oscar Nemon near the psychoanalyst's Hampstead home. |
| St Stephen's | Rosslyn Hill | Gothic awesomeness. Currently being restored to its former glory. |

Map 68 · Kilburn High Road / Abbey Road

| Abbey Road Zebra Crossing | 3 Abbey Rd | Go on. Take THAT photo. You know you want to. |

Map 70 · Primrose Hill

| 3 Chalcot Square | 3 Chalcot Sq | Home of poet Sylvia Plath, 1960-61. |

Map 71 · Camden Town / Chalk Farm / Kentish Town (West)

Camden Market	Camden Lock Pl	Shop, hang, drink, listen, pose, watch, chill, rock, laugh.
Grand Regents Canal	Grand Regents Canal	London's best bike lane. Or canoe to Birmingham.
The Roundhouse	Chalk Farm Rd & Crogsland Rd	Prominent round building and historic performance venue.

Map 74 · Holloway Road / Arsenal

| Gillespie Park | 191 Drayton Park | Weird and wonderful nature park along the train tracks. |

Map 75 · Highbury

| St Paul's Shrubbery | St Paul's Rd & Northampton Park | All Monty Python jokes welcome, in fact, positively encouraged. |

Map 76 · Edgeware Road / Marylebone (North)

| Sherlock Holmes' House | 221 Baker St | It's elementary my dear Watson! |

Map 77 · Mornington Crescent / Regent's Park

| Euston Tower | 286 Euston Rd | Quite an impressive erection. |
| Greater London House | 180 Hampstead Rd | Crazy Art Deco building. |

Map 78 · Euston

The British Library	96 Euston Rd	Prestigious research library with unmatched collection.
Camden High Street	Camden High St & Delancey St	'Alternative' tourist mecca.
Cheney Road	Cheney Rd & Weller's Ct	"Chaplin, 'Alfie' and many more were filmed on these cobbles.

General Information · Landmarks

Euston Station	Eversholt St & Doric Way	So ugly it's oogly.
Platform 9¾	King's Cross Station	This Harry Potter thing has gone way too f'ing far.
St Pancras Station	St Pancras Way	Listed Gothic frontage, massive modern Eurostar hangar behind.
St Pancras	Pancras Rd & Euston Rd	Ex-Victorian workhouse turned superbug den.

Map 80 · Angel / Upper St

Angel Station Roof	Angel	You can get on the roof here, you epic teens.
The Bull	100 Upper St	Hands up: who loves beer?

Map 81 · Canonbury

Gladiators Paving Slab	10 Canonbury St	Logo of fighty telly show built into pavement. Me neither.

Map 82 · De Beauvoir Town / Kingsland

Suleymaniye Mosque	212 Kingsland Rd	Striking minaret silhouetted against Shoreditch Church spire and Broadgate Tower.

Map 84 · Hoxton

Hoxton Square	Hoxton Sq	Great in summer. Buy some cans and join the hipsters.
Village Underground	54 Holywell Ln	How did they get the trains up there?
White Cube	48 Hoxton Sq	Jay Jopling's homage to modern art

Map 85 · Stoke Newington (East)

Abney Park Cemetery	Stoke Newington High St & Rectory Rd	Egyptian revival-style, spooky nature reserve.

Map 86 · Dalston / Kingsland

Centreprise	136 Kingsland High St	Multi-cultural art centre, cafe, bookshop and venue.
Holy Trinity, The Clowns Church	Beechwood Rd & Kirkland Walk	Every Feb, clowns mourn Grimaldi. In full costume.

Map 87 · Hackney Downs / Lower Clapton

London Orphan Asylum	Lower Clapton Rd & Linscott Rd	Grandiose remains of historic site now beloved of enviornmental artists.
The Strand Building	29 Urswick Rd	Beautiful Art Deco building, NOT the subject of Roxy Music song.
Sutton House	2 Homerton High St	Music and arts in the oldest house in East London.

Map 88 · Haggerston / Queensbridge Rd

Geffrye Museum	136 Kingsland Rd	English interior design from 1600 to today.

Map 89 · London Fields / Hackney Central

London Fields Lido	London Fields Westside	Open-air swimming for hardy Hackney folk.

Map 91 · Shoreditch / Brick Lane / Spitalfields

Brick Lane Mosque	59 Brick Ln	The area's changes reflect on the building - once a synagogue, now a mosque.
Christ Church Spitalfields	2 Fournier St	Star architect Nicholas Hawksmoor's pretty masterpiece.
Dennis Severs' House	18 Folgate St	Candle-lit cellar, parlour, smoking room - step 300 years back in time.
Spitalfields Market	105 Commercial St	No bargains but certainly one-of-a-kind fashions.
Sweet Toof Graffiti Alley	Pedley St & Brick Ln	Signature sweeties and skulls – just off Brick Lane.
Ten Bells	84 Commercial St	Where Jack the Ripper got his victims.
Truman's Brewery	91 Brick Lane	Beautiful old building now a hip weekend market. That's progress...

Map 92 · Bethnal Green

Bethnal Green Tube Station	Bethnal Green Tube Station	Scene of the worst civilian loss of the Second World War.
London Buddhist Centre	51 Roman Rd	Get your freak om.

Map 93 · Globe Town / Mile End (North)

Art Pavillion	221 Grove Rd	Arts center seemingly designed by the Teletubbies.
Mile End Climbing Wall	Haverfield Rd & Grove Rd	Classic climbing centre - one of London's big three.

Map 95 · De Beauvoir Town / Kingsland

The Sun HQ	1 Virginia Street	It's probably not legal to stake out Page 3 girls.

Map 96 · Whitechapel (East) / Shadwell (West) / Wapping

Battle of Cable Street Mural, St George's Hall	236 Cable St	Celebrating an almighty multi-faith bashing of a 1930s fascist march.
Blind Beggar Pub	337 Whitechapel Rd	A killing here finally led to Ronnie Kray doing porridge.

Map 98 · Mile End (South) / Limehouse

Ragged School Museum	46 Copperfield Rd	Barnado's school 'for the deserving poor' turned East End museum.

Map 100 · Poplar (West) / Canary Wharf (West)

Canary Wharf Tower	1 Canada Sq	You can smell the money yards away. Look, don't touch.
Canary Wharf Tube Station	Canary Wharf	Norman Foster's Jewel in the Jubilee Line Extension.

Map 102 · Millwall

The Docklands Sailing & Watersport Centre	235 Westferry Rd	Award-winning sailing centre.

Map 104 · South Bank / Waterloo / Lambeth North

County Hall	Westminster Bridge Rd & Belvedere Rd	One of London's most historical and vast buildings.
The Hayward Gallery	Southbank Centre	Revered and reviled bruiser.
The London Eye	Westminster Bridge Rd	Two words: Tourist. Trap. Nice view though.
Low Tide at South Bank	South Bank	Go for a walk on the exposed riverbed.
National Theatre	Waterloo Rd & Upper Ground	South Bank centre-piece, looked like it was from 2050 in 1960.
The Pier at OXO Tower	Barge House St & Upper Ground	Screw OXO! Have a picnic on the pier instead.
South Bank Book Market	Under Waterloo Bridge	Little-known outdoor market; heaps of vintage and second-hand reads.
Waterloo Bridge	Waterloo Bridge	When tired with London, come here and watch the sunset.

Map 105 · Southwark / Bankside (West)

Buskers' Archway	Southbank	Excellent acoustics make the decorated tunnel a coveted buskers' spot.
Elephant & Castle	Elephant & Castle	Everything that was wrong with 60s town planning. Concrete hell.
Michael Faraday Memorial	Elephant & Castle	He gave us electromagnetism, we gave him a roundabout.
The Ring	72 Blackfriars Rd	London's first boxing ring was here; now a characterful pub.
Shakespeare's Globe	21 New Globe Walk	The Bard's famous playhouse reconstructed.
Tate Modern	Bankside	Herzog and de Meuron dazzler.

Map 106 · Bankside (East) / Borough / Newington

Borough Market	8 Southwark St	London's best food market. Enjoy the free samples.
Cross Bones Graveyard	Redcross Way & Union St	Medieval resting place for London's ladies of the night.
Female Gladiator	159 Great Dover St	1st centruy AD grave of London's very own Xena.
The Golden Hinde	Clink St & Stoney St	Amazing replica of Francis Drake's Tudor war ship.
The London Tombs	2 Tooley St	Lesser known Tower experience—beware the plague pits.
Mint Street Park	Southwark Bridge Rd & Marshalsea Rd	Open space on the site of the old Evelina Children's Hospital.
Old Operating Theatre Museum	9 St Thomas St	Macabre ancient operating theatre, with gallery for eager spectators.
Southwark Cathedral	Cathedral St & Montague Close	Worth the diversion to see Chaucer and Shakespeare's stomping grounds.
St George the Martyr	Borough High St & Tabard St	
Winchester Palace	Clink St & Storey St	Random 13th century ruins with remarkable rose window.

Map 107 · Shad Thames

City Hall	Queen's Walk, More London	Dubbed 'The Testicle' by Mayor Ken Livingstone. Nice.
Design Museum	Shad Thames	Fairly unsatisfying shows - drool-worthy bookshop.
Fashion and Textile Museum	83 Bermondsey St	DAH-ling, it's just fabulous!
Floating Gardens	31 Mill St	Gardens. Mad tramps. On Boats. What else do you want?
HMS Belfast	Morgan's Lane & Tooley St	Floating WW2 killing machine, much beloved of children.

Stompie	Mandela Way & Page's Walk	Sounds like a baby elephant. But it's a Soviet tank.
Tower Bridge	Tower Bridge Road	Messing about on the water.

Map 110 • Rotherhithe (West) / Canada Water

Brunel Museum	Railway Ave & Rotherhithe St	Where engineering geeks can seek refuge from being picked on.

Map 111 • Rotherhithe (East) Surrey Quays

Surrey Docks Farm	Rotherhithe St & Salter Rd	Show the kids what their bacon used to look like.

Map 113 • Walworth

East Street Market	Walworth Rd & East St	Gloriously useless stuff.
Heygate Estate	Deacon Way & Heygate St	A testament to urban planning gone horribly wrong.

Map 114 • Old Kent Road (West) / Burgess Park

The Animatronic Fireman	Old Kent Rd	Be afraid. Be very afraid.
Peckham Library	122 Peckham Hill St	Groundbreaking modern architecture or huge, carelessly dropped Tetris block?

Map 116 • South Bermondsey

Millwall FC Stadium	Zampa Road & Bolina Rd	A football mecca for somebody?

Map 120 • Greenwich

Cutty Sark Gardens	King William Walk & Romney Rd	Where the Archbishop of Canterbury was murdered in 1012.
Greenwich Foot Tunnel	Greenwich Church St & Thames St	Walk/crawl/skip/limp under the Thames.

Map 126 • New Cross

Ben Pimlott Building	University of London, New Cross	A building of cheerful, dreary, warped, modern fascist fun.

Map 131 • Vauxhall / Albert Embankment

Lambeth Palace	Lambeth Palace Rd & Lambeth Rd	Where the Archbishop of Canterbury lives; no, not in Canterbury, stupid.
Secret Intelligence Service HQ (MI6)	85 Vauxhall Cross	Real life James Bonds in a not-so-secret location.
Vauxhall City Farm	165 Tyers St	So that's where an egg comes from.

Map 133 • Battersea (East)

Battersea Dogs' Home	4 Battersea Park Rd	Re-house a pooch. Now does cats too.
Battersea Park Gasometers	Queenstown Rd & Prince of Wales Dr	Rusting monsters.
Battersea Power Station	188 Kirtling St	The world's most beautiful power station, surely.

Map 140 • Clapham Junction / Northcote Rd

Northcote Road	Northcote Rd	Middle-class marketing-types mecca.

Map 143 • Clapham High Street

Clapham Common Air-Raid Shelter	Clapham High St	The depths of government paranoia.

Map 144 • Stockwell / Brixton (West)

Brixton Market	Electric Ave & Electric Ln	Caribbean flavours, smells and sounds.
Electric Avenue	Electric Ave & Brixton Rd	First shopping area in Britain lit by electricity, in 1880.

Map 145 • Stockwell / Brixton (East)

Stockwell Bowls	Stockwell Rd & Stockwell Park Walk	70's concrete skatepark, take quads and get beaten-up.

Map 152 • Tooting Broadway

Gala Bingo Hall	50 Mitcham Rd	Bingo hall with Grade One listed interior.

MAP
37

Level 6

137 138 139 140 141 142 143 144 145

118 118a
119
120
122b 122a 122c
121 122 123 125c 125
125

level 4

128a
127 128 129 131

Europe
Asia
Modern
Materials & Techniques
Special Exhibitions

81 87 94 95
82 88 96
70a 65 66 67 68 69 88a 97
89 90 98
70 90a 102 99
71 83 100
level 3 101
72 84 109 107 108
73
74 National Art Library 85
111
40a
113 114a 114b 114c 114d 114e
116 117 112

52 52b
52a
53 53a
54
54a 54a 58b
55 56 57 58

level 2

151 156

51
21 21a 22 23 24 25
40
41 42 44 45 46a 46 46b
47a 47b 47c 47d 47e 47f 47g
48a 49 50a 50b

11 16a
17 27 Special
18 26 Exhibitions
19 Level 1 32 38a
20 Shop 33

1
2
3 Level 0
4 5 6 7 8 9

General Information

NFT Map:	37
Address:	Cromwell Road
	London SW7 2RL
Phone:	020 7942 2000
Website:	www.vam.ac.uk
Hours:	10 am–6 pm daily,
	Wednesdays until 9 pm.

Admission: Free to the permanent collection. There is a charge for temporary exhibitions. Tickets have an allotted time slot and although they can be purchased on the day, it is recommended you book ahead of time by phone or online, especially with the more popular exhibitions.

Overview

The Victoria and Albert Museum, or the V&A, calls itself the world's greatest museum of art and design and nowhere has there ever been such an eclectic collection of objects inducing so many 'ooooohs', 'aaaaahs' and 'holy shits!'. With a permanent collection of over 4.5 million objects, pretty much all on display in the 145 galleries, you can go everyday for a lifetime and be blown over by something you hadn't noticed before. For the tourist and non-tourist alike, the V&A is a wonderful maze of cultural ramblings. You'll get lost, overwhelmed and flustered, but we promise you won't get bored.

The V&A is a cabinet of curiosities of gargantuan proportions, boasting 5000 years of art and design, in every medium imaginable (from wax dioramas to a little black dress made of bras), spread over seven levels and organised by five themes—Asia, Europe, Materials & Techniques, Modern and Exhibitions. The trouble is where to start. You'll no doubt spend the first 10 minutes mesmerised by the glass Chihuly chandelier over the information booth, but what you do afterwards depends on how much time you've got. Got hours? Avoid structure and just wander. Got an hour? Take a look at the map, see what strikes your fancy and head straight there. Just don't forget to hit up the gift shop afterwards—it's killer.

The Greatest Hits

There's no real method to the V&A's madness. Despite their best efforts to categorise everything, Vivienne Westwood gowns are just a stumble away from 1000 year-old Buddhas. But this is a great thing. The best advice is really to ditch the guidebook and go with your instincts. To make sure you take in the best stuff, start in the basement (having arrived through the Tunnel Entrance from the tube station), where you'll find the 17th century **Cabinet of Curiosities**—predecessors to the modern museum—which will get you in the right mind set. Weaving past bits and pieces of **Versailles**, you emerge onto the ground floor (Level 1) which covers fashion, Asia and both Medieval and Renaissance Europe. Highlights of which include the **cast courts**, which boast a life-size replica of **Trajan's Column** in plaster, then onto ancient **samurai swords** and spectacular **kimonos** in Asia, the **Ardabil Carpet**—the largest and most amazing Islamic carpets in existence dating from 1539 (lit up on the hour and half-hour), an extensive costume room covering everything from **18th century crinolines** to **Juicy Couture** worthy of Paris Hilton, and lastly, **Raphael's cartoons**—massive sketches for a 1515 commission of tapestries that now hang in the Vatican. Before heading on, stop for a tea in the **Morris, Gamble & Poynter Rooms** café for teacakes in 1860s arts and crafts surroundings. Level 2 consists of the tucked away **British Galleries**, including the **Great Bed of Ware** as well as the endearing **Lord and Lady Clapham** dolls bedecked in miniature turn-of-the-18th century outfits. Up again on Level 3, you'll find the Materials & Techniques rooms, with its vast collections of **silver, ironwork and musical instruments**, as well as some dynamite paintings. Don't miss **Rossetti's The Daydream** and then **Ron Arad's Chair** in the modern rooms. This floor also houses the **National Art Library** (an art history student's research dream (you have to get a reading pass to study here though). Level 4 has a wonderfully tactile display of **glasswork**, as well as **architecture** and more **British Galleries from 1760-1900**. If you've made it this far, you deserve a knighthood.

MAP 4

Upper Floors

Restaurant

Main Floor

Montague Place Entrance

Lower Floor

Restaurant

Reading Room

Great Court

Clore Education Centre

Ford Centre for Young Visitors

Main Entrance Great Russell Street

Paul Hamlyn Library

Ancient Greece & Rome
Middle East
Asia
Egypt
Enlightenment
North & Central America
Africa
Exhibitions and changing displays
Europe
⊠ Lift
||| Stairs

General Information

NFT Map: 4

Address: Great Russell Street, WC1B 3DG

Phone: 020 7323 8299 (information) or
020 7323 8181 (exhibition tickets)

Website: www.britishmuseum.org

Hours: The galleries open daily 10 am–
5.30 pm, with selected galleries open
until 8.30 pm Thu & Fri (see website
for details). The Great Court is open
9 am–6 pm. Jan 1, Good Friday,
Dec 24-26: closed.

Admission: Free, with a charge for some
special exhibitions.

Overview

Unless you're Indiana Jones, combining archaeological expertise with the swashbuckling energy to defeat obnoxious school groups, then do not attempt to cover the British Museum in a day. With 13 million items covering two million years of human history in almost 100 permanent and temporary galleries, you are better off treating yourself to different sections when the mood takes you—a perk of having one of the world's largest museums on your doorstep and open for free.

At 250 years, it is also the oldest museum in the world, but forget preconceptions of dusty urns and endless Roman coins—they're there if that's your bag, but this is a very modern organisation. The permanent displays include some of the world's most fascinating treasures, while the temporary exhibitions bring London a chance to break and lose artefacts which have seen some of the greatest moments of history, such as the recent display of drawings by Michelangelo, Raphael, Leonardo, and some other Renaissance scribblers who didn't make Ninja Turtle status.

However, while preserving artefacts to inspire its visitors, the Museum can also be seen as a testament to the great British pastime of looting. Some of the shining lights of its collection were acquired under the shadiest of circumstances, and the countries which were plundered so that snotty kids could chortle at the genitalia of their sculptures are increasingly vocal about getting the items back. For example the Elgin Marbles,

rechristened with their pleasantly playful English name after the earl who helped himself to them, are huge slabs hacked from the 2500 year old Athenian Parthenon (albeit Elgin's entire nose later rotted off due to syphilis: a gratifying example of one-upmanship by nature). The legality of this move is hotly debated, but apart from the damage to the Parthenon, the Marbles undeniably suffered when they were cut into smaller pieces for transport to Britain, and when rowdy schoolboys bopped the leg off a centaur in 1961. The Museum holds firm that returning debated items would empty the museums of the world, but it has extended the occasional olive branch to ease the controversy; compensation was paid for the display of drawings stolen by Nazis, and they returned the Tasmanian Ashes (aboriginal human remains) to Australia after a 20-year battle.

The Greatest Hits

The **Great Court** is not just a Greatest Hit of the Museum, but of London as a whole. Being "the world's largest covered public square" may sound too niche an accolade to be impressive, but it really is stunning. The 150 year old **Reading Room** at its centre is a delight, both for the excellent library and for the wall-mounted list of major historical figures who have sought inspiration within its round walls. Whatever your ethics on plunder, some of the most morally-dubious exhibits are among the absolute must-sees: the **Elgin Marbles** in Room 18 are remarkable, while the **Rosetta Stone** in Room 4 gives you the irresistible buzz of seeing something so legendary up close, or as close as the backpacked hordes will allow, in your own town. A whole **Moai Statue** from Easter Island is in Room 24, the **Lewis Chessmen** set is in Room 42, and the **Mausoleum of Halikarnassos** exhibition displays some of the last remaining fragments of one of the Seven Wonders of the World. However, it is the stories of heartache, adventure, mystery and passion behind the items which bring them to life. Asking the steward of Rooms 62-3 how the **mummies** came to be in the museum, or seeing the pages from **The Book of the Dead** which recorded lives of the deceased, is a fascinating way to gain insight to people around the world and throughout time. And if that's a bit too deep, just head to one of the four **shops** for a mummy-shaped pencil case or replica Rosetta Stone.

General Information

NFT Map: 36
Address: Cromwell Road, SW7 5BD
Phone: 020 7942 5000
Website: www.nhm.ac.uk
Hours: Daily 10 am–5.50 pm
               (Last admission 17.30)
               "After Hours" events run on the
               last Friday of each month
               during Nov–Apr.
               24–26 Dec: closed.
Admission: Free access to most of the
               Museum. Fee charged for
               some special exhibitions
               (free to Members).

Overview

Visiting the Natural History Museum is like reading National Geographic, if it was edited by JK Rowling. As imagination-tingling to adults as it is to kids, you can mull over serious questions about genetic modification and the environmental cost of modern life, while walking inside a termite mound or knocking on a petrified tree.

With more than 70 million specimens in their collection, you simply won't see it all at once, or for most of us—ever. But with free entry, regularly refreshed exhibits and unforgettable special exhibitions, it's worth dropping in when you have the opportunity. Grab a free map at the entrance to work out your route, which is colour-coded for a slightly) easier life: Red Zone for the planet and forces of nature; Green for ecology and the environment; Blue for dinosaurs, mammals and biology; and Orange for the Wildlife Garden and behind-the-scenes peeks.

Weekends are inevitably heaving with hyperactive button-pressing families, spellbound tourists and Londoners trying to rebuild the brain cells they killed off with the night before's drinking; weekdays are amok with school groups. But don't let this put you off. If there's a queue outside the main entrance on Cromwell Road, and you don't fancy killing time by spotting all the different creatures carved around the entrance arch, nip 'round the side to Exhibition Road entrance and you'll fast-track yourself in. You can go early or late for fewer crowds, or stick with the permanent exhibitions, which are superb but not as sexy as the world-class special exhibitions which draw in the masses. Or, if all else fails, just shove the kids out the way: they're smaller than you and the buttons are *so much fun* to press.

The Greatest Hits

Anyone who didn't see the **Dinosaur Exhibition** as a child really missed out: run here and rectify the situation immediately if you haven't been, or revisit and enjoy the modernised exhibits if you have. The **Mammals Exhibition** will get you wondering exactly *how* someone stuffs a giraffe, and gives you a chance to get close to the gaping jaws of a hippo. For a different perspective on this room, go up to the balcony around it: watching people stare agog at the brilliantly-displayed **blue whale** is as entertaining as the exhibits themselves. For proof that even history geeks can make the earth move for you, visit the **Power Within** exhibition which recreates an earthquake (though don't expect a Universal Studios experience. The will is there, bless, but the budget just isn't...). Watch blushing parents introduce their kids to the birds and the bees in the **Human Biology** section, where an 8-times-life sized model of a **foetus** will put you off pregnancy forever. The **Wildlife Garden** is an oasis of

serenity open from April–October, or you can impress a date (or not, depending on your coordination) by **ice-skating** next to the stunning Victorian building from November–January.

The Museum's Special Exhibitions are superb—check the website for current information. The annual **Veolia Wildlife Photographer of the Year**, October–April, is utterly inspirational, while a varying daily programme of events includes **lectures, behind the scenes tours** of the botany department, and **fossil workshops** for kids.

"Like the creatures it displays (except for the Dodo—you'll find one in the Green Zone), the museum keeps evolving. Aptly, the latest major development is the Darwin Centre, where you can stoke your nightmares by checking out the giant tarantulas, experience life in a cocoon (like life in a London flat, but more spacious), and watch scientists at work. You might not think that watching scientists analysing and cataloguing bits of plant would be much of a spectator sport, but an hour in the centre will whiz by and leave you bursting with new knowledge to irritate your mates with.

5
Medicine
Veterinary

MAP
36

4
Glimpses
of Medical
History

3
Launchpad
Motionride
Stimulators
Flight
In
Future
Wellcome
Wing
Science in
the 18th
Century
Health matters

2
Computing
Maths
Shipping
Docks &
Diving
Wellcome
Wing
Energy -
Fuelling
the future

1
Challenge of
Materials
Agriculture
Measuring time
Wellcome
Wing

G
Energy Hall
Exploring
Space
Making the
Modern World
Talking Points
Pattern Pod
Force Field
Wellcome
Wing
Main
Entrance

B
Garden
Secret life
of the home
Café

General Information

NFT Map: 36

Address: Exhibition Road, South
               Kensington, London
               SW7 2DD.

Phone: 0870 870 4868

Website: www.sciencemuseum.org.uk

Hours: Open 10 am–6 pm every day
               except 24 to 26 December.

Admission: Free, but charges apply to
               IMAX 3D Cinema, simulators &
               a few special exhibitions.

Overview

Museum and Science. Two words known to strike fear into the heart of many a child. And many a grown-up, come to that. But the Science Museum is one of the most visited museums in London. How so? Perhaps it's the heady mix of mildly erotic pistons and shafts; 60s room-sized computers and Bakelite ashtrays; special affects simulators and the mighty IMAX theatre? Or maybe it is the multitude of buttons; red and blue and green actual buttons, as well as Minority Report-style touch screens? We know they're aimed at kids, but we like. Oh and levers, did we mention levers?

The museum has its origins in the popular Great Exhibition of 1851. Prince Albert (no laughing in the back please) suggested the extra cash made by the Exhibition be used to found a number of educational establishments. Following a number of building moves and expansions the Science Museum as we know and love it opened in 1885.

The Greatest Hits

The museum's 300,000 gidgets, gadgets and gizmos attract 2.5 million visitors a minute or something, but venture above the third floor, to the **medical floors**, and you will have the place almost to yourself. The most popular area is the main drag along the ground floor which includes **Exploring Space** hung with real life space probes and other relics that look like they've come from the Doctor Who costume and props department, and **Making of the Modern World** featuring **Stephenson's Rocket**, to titillate your dormant trainspotter.

The third floor's **Launchpad** area has as many interactive displays as an 8-year-old could ever want. Parents hope their little darlings are actually learning something as they race from exhibit to exhibit whirling wheels, spinning liquids in plastic tubes and grimacing through head-sized lenses till tiredness or RSI sets in. For younger kids the tactile **Pattern Pod** on the ground floor makes up for its lack of buttons by its immensely pleasing shape.

The museum has its own Imax to impress the grown-ups and to make whimpering children cower as 3D Rexes loom into their faces. Don't even think about going in with a hangover. A huge silver hoop joins the **Energy exhibition** on the second to the ground floor. Answer a question on a nearby monitor, (don't worry they are easy) and watch your initials and age whiz around the inside of the ring. But what's that BUZZ? Like a huge electric fly killer? It's the inspired **'don't touch' display**— irresistible for the naughtiest in the class, one small electric shock later, the rest of the lemmings race over for a turn. Hilarious.

Arts & Entertainment • **The Tates**

Tate Modern

7
Bar | East Room

6
Members Room

5
8 | 9 | 10 | 12 | 11 | 10 | 9 | 8
7 | 2 | 3 | 7
6 | 5 | 3 | 1 | 1 | 2 | 4 | 5 | 6

4
Espresso Bar

3
6 | 7 | 2 | 9 | 10 | Scale | 9 | 8 | 7
5 | 4 | 3 | 2 | 1 | 3 | 6
1 | 2 | 4 | 5

River Entrance

2
Café | Seminar Room | Gallery
Starr Auditorium

1
Shop
Gallery
Main Entrance

MAP 105

Level 5
States of Flux
Energy and Process
Conceptual Models

Level 4
Exhibitions

Level 3
Poetry and Dream
Material Gestures

‖‖‖ Stairs
▭▭▭ Escalators

Tate Britain

5 | 4
6 | 3
2 | Duveen Galleries
7 | 8
9 | Octagon | 28 | 27
10 | 11 | 12 | Art Now | 26
14 | 13 | 23 | 24 | 25
15 | 18 | 22 | 21 | T4 | T5 | T10
16 | 17 | 19 | 20 | T1 | T3 | T7
T2 | T6

Millbank Entrance

MAP 21

Manton Entrance (Atterbury St)

Restaurant | Cafe

Auditorium

Sculpture Court

Clore Entrance

Level 3
Level 2
Level 1

General Information

Tate Britain:

NFT Map:	21
Address:	London SW1P 4RG
Phone:	020 7887 8888
Website:	www.tate.org.uk/britain
Hours:	Daily 10 am–5.50 pm; until 10 pm on the first Friday of each month for Late at Tate Britain.

Tate Modern:

NFT Map:	105
Address:	London SE1 9TG
Phone:	020 7887 8888
Website:	www.tate.org.uk/modern
Hours:	Sunday–Thursday 10 am–6 pm, Friday and Saturday 10 am–10 pm. Last admission into exhibitions is 5.15 pm (Friday and Saturday 8.15 pm).

Overview

In a city renowned for its galleries and museums, London's Tate galleries shine from the banks of the Thames. The first Tate was founded in 1897 as the National Gallery of British Art, but was renamed soon afterwards after its main patron Henry Tate—he of Tate and Lyle and the sugar cube. Originally on the site of the former Milbank Prison (where Tate Britain remains), the gallery gradually expanded and divided its collection over the four sites, two in London, one in Liverpool and the last in St Ives. In London, Tate Britain houses British art dating from 1500 to the present day, while Tate Modern was created to house—yes you've guessed it—more modern work from 1900 to the present day.

The two Tates carry the same trendy Tate logo and the shops contain much of the same avant-garde merchandise with a great range of children's stuff available in both. But while the more traditional Tate Britain more closely resembles the National Gallery in architectural and artistic flavour, Tate Modern has a very hip feel and draws a slightly broader audience, in part due to its location on the increasingly buzzy South Bank.

Both museums have popular restaurants and cafes, but to encourage those without a membership to sign up, each offers an exclusive members' room. These provide the best views, nicest toilets, designated staff and ever so slightly self-important customers, and are always a safe bet to impress a date.

Tate Modern

Based in the former Bankside Power Station, Tate Modern has proved to be an extremely popular attraction for tourists and Londoners alike since its opening in 2000. It houses the national collection of modern art, so expect plenty of inspirational and challenging works alongside exhibits that look like your cat sicked them up. The temporary art installations of the five-storey tall Turbine Hall provide much of the draw to the gallery. This huge space displays specially commissioned works from October to April of each year—a programme which was intended to run for only five years, but was extended due to its popularity. Quirky exhibitions fill the vast Turbine Hall, like Olafur Eliasson's 'Weather Project' which encouraged visitors to lie back on the floor in their thousands, gazing at the shadows cast by the synthetic sun. At the time of going to press we await confirmation of the next commission, but for now we're having a great time scaring our mates in Miroslaw Balka's How It Is. Acclaimed for an earlier sculpture made of live maggots, Balka's contribution to the Turbine is an intense dark space which delights shrieking kids, deep thinkers and sex pests alike. But if it all seems like you could have created better art yourself, then try one of the gallery's excellent workshops or courses and give it a go.

Tate Britain

The Tate Britain boasts the most comprehensive collection of British art in the world, and is home to the annual and unmissable Turner Prize show. Stone steps lead up to the portico and once inside, the Duveen Galleries' ethereal sculptures lie straight ahead, giving the first taste of a breathtaking collection of artwork. Tate Britain's collection is divided chronologically and dedicates space exclusively to notable artists, such as Turner, Blake and Constable. The gallery also includes significant works by William Hogarth, Stanley Spencer and Francis Bacon. While lacking the hip ambience of its sister gallery down the river, Tate Britain has been attempting to trend-ify itself with 'Late at Tate Britain' between 6pm and 10pm on the first Friday of every month, which aims to lure young'uns from the pub for some after-hours art-appreciation with exhibitions, performances, music, talks and films.

Look out for the themed guides to suit your mood, such as "The I've Just Split Up", "The I'm In A Hurry" and "The I Haven't Been Here For Ages" collections: a highly endearing way ease you through the 500 years of exhibits.

General Information

NFT Map: 24
Address: Trafalgar Square
           London WC2N 5DN
Phone: 020 7747 2885
Website: www.nationalgallery.org.uk
Hours: 10 am–6 pm daily,
           Fridays until 9 pm.

Admission: Free to the permanent collection and temporary exhibitions in the Sunley Room, Room 1 and The Space on Level 2. There is a charge for temporary exhibitions held on Level 2 in the Sainsbury Wing. Tickets have an allotted time slot and although they can be purchased on the day, it is recommended you book them ahead of time online, especially with the more popular exhibitions.

Overview

The National Gallery is home to one of the best and largest collections of Western European painting in the world, coming in at around 2100 paintings on display at any one time. An emphasis on *Western* and *painting* is needed. If you're looking for Roman antiquities or Persian miniatures, head for the British Museum or the V&A—this is not where you're going to get it. Furthermore, if you're into anything post-Impressionist, make an about face for the Tate Britain. This is a celebration of the arts of Europe in all their old-school occidental glory. Taking the surprisingly manageable tour around the galleries (most of which are on one floor) will leave you wowed by how many works of art you will recognise. This is a collection that has been branded deep into your subconscious—with its oh-yeah-that-one Turners, Hogarths, Rembrandts and Leonardos. Bring a date and even the most culturally challenged will be able to impress.

The collection came into being in 1824 when the House of Commons paid £57,000 for 38 paintings belonging to a banker, using his Pall Mall home as the exhibition space. Compared to the Louvre, calling a few paintings in some guy's house the National Gallery was a little too embarrassing for the British public. So the great and the good demanded the Government pull their finger out and get to work on a purpose-built gallery worthy of a national art collection. In 1832, architect William Wilkins was given the job, constructing the recognisable porticoed façade in an up-and-coming area known as Trafalgar Square, called by one trustee 'the very gangway of London'. The most recent addition to the gallery is the Sainsbury Wing, designed in 1991 by leading contemporary architects Robert Venturi and Scott Brown after much controversy. Prince Charles, notoriously fussy when it comes to architecture, dismissed one suggested design as "a monstrous carbuncle on the face of a much-loved and elegant friend".

The National Gallery can be tackled in one exhausting afternoon, if you put your mind to it. Take advantage of the fancy benches, as many of the more epic paintings are best viewed from a distance. Be sure to get lost in the many smaller galleries, which house some dynamite, lesser-known, works. If you're feeling hungry, the National Dining Rooms is a critically acclaimed (read: expensive) restaurant, serving up the best in British fare. If you're feeling like a little culinary nationalism, the more casual National Café serves a very good cream tea.

The Greatest Hits

Starting with the Sainsbury Wing, the collection snakes around, covering European painting in chronological order from 1250 to 1900. There are a lot of paintings and it can get slightly overwhelming, so if you're pressed for time and want to make sure you've 'done' the National Gallery, try one of their 60 minute taster tours or pick up their guide to the 30 must-see paintings. Don't miss the **Arnolfini Portrait** (signed with 'Van Eyck was here' above the mirror—hilarious), **Botticelli's Venus and Mars, The Wilton Diptych**, and **Uccello's The Battle of San Romano**. Moving onto the 1500-1600 range, you'll recognise **Leonardo's cartoon of The Virgin and Child with St Anne and St John the Baptist**, **'The Ambassadors'** by Hans Holbein the younger (the one where you have to crouch to see the skull), the still-hilarious portrait of **A Grotesque Old Woman** by Quinten Massys (a 1664 example of the classic conundrum—a 64 year-old trying desperately to look 16) and **Titian's Bacchus and Ariadne**. Moving on, the collection houses a rather large collection of Dutch masters, including **Rembrandt, Rubens and van Dyck**. If you're sick of 2-D, a rather cool contraption is **Samuel von Hoogstraten's peepshow**. Peer through the peep hole in this painted box for an eye-popping view of the interior of a Dutch house. Very cool. A trip to the museum is never complete without viewing a **Gainsborough, Turner and Hogarth**, all of which are housed in the 1700-1900 galleries. Do not miss Hogarth's **Marriage a la Mode** a comical rendition of an 18th century arranged marriage—in a series of six paintings. Last but not least, onto the juxtaposition of three epic 19th century history paintings depicting corporal punishment with chilling realism—**Manet's Execution of Maximillian, Delaroche's Lady Jane Gray and Puvis de Chavanne's Beheading of St John the Baptist**. What a way to end it all, quite literally.

General Information

Address:	Peninsula Square, London, SE10 0DX
Website:	www.theO2.co.uk
General Information:	020 8463 2000
Tickets:	0871 984 0002

Overview

Exactly how the Millennium Dome transformed itself from national embarrassment and vortex for millions of taxpayers' money to the slick new home of groovy events is a bit of a mystery. Or maybe it's blindingly obvious—suits are better than politicians at this kind of thing. Anyway, on the outside it looks the same—the oversized lovechild of a jellyfish and hedgehog. Inside, gone are the attractions and concepts of 1999, aimed at celebrating all things British, so visionary that visitors stayed away in droves. Instead, the contents of an above-average high street have been stuffed inside—generic bistro food and wine bars, a multi-screen cinema. Whoope-doo you might think. But hold on—people come for the music. No really, they do.

Enter the O2 Arena or its little sis, the IndigO2 (see what they did there?) and be very impressed. The Arena has been engineered to provide sight lines that older venues can only dream of. The air conditioning—usually a rarity at London gigs, actually works. The acoustics have to be heard to be believed. It might not be a destination venue for mosh-loving purists and those who like the sweat and beer to fly, but if you like your music with a bit of comfort and luxury, you know, like toilets that work and don't stink of piss (548 of them!) then the O2 is well worth a look. Wheelchair users are catered for with fully accessible facilities. London seems to have its first venue that feels like some real thought has gone into its creation. If the organisers get their act together and diversify the bands appearing, including more that veer away from mainstream bands then it could become unstoppable.

How to Get There—Driving

Driving to the O2 isn't as daft as it might sound considering its location—previously un-chartered industrial wastelands of south east London. 2,000 parking spaces can be reserved in advance. With decent road links, traveling after rush hour should be bearable. The A102 linking north and south London runs through the Blackwall Tunnel, right next to the venue.

How to Get There—Mass Transit

In theory, the O2 has excellent transport links no matter how you travel. In practice, there's a good chance that your gig coincides with engineers digging up the precise bit of track you need to travel on. Check www.tfl.gov.uk before you travel. But when everything is working, then the Jubilee line at nearby North Greenwich connects directly with Waterloo and London Bridge. The Docklands Light Railway is one stop away and several bus routes drop off right outside. But the best way to arrive has to be by boat—the high speed Thames Clipper runs every 15 minutes from several piers including Greenwich, Embankment and Waterloo. It's not only relaxing, but you get to see London at its best on the trip.

How to Get Tickets

Ticketmaster. Naturally. Try Gumtree and Craigslist for swaps, unwanted tickets and scum-of-the-earth touts.

Life in London can sometimes seem like one continuous, eventful film, but if you like your plots to take place on screen then the city has a lot to offer. Going to catch a flick in London can often unravel like some kind of Indiana Jones-esque adventure—the Holy Grail being a reasonably-priced ticket in a clean, comfortable theatre, that can only be sought after battling hundreds of tourists and fellow Londoners all with the same thought. Every year 164 million people visit London's cinemas; now that's a fair few ticket stubs. Thankfully, by leaving The Twilight Zone (a.k.a. the tourist trap of the West End) there are plenty of cinematic treasures to be plundered. Whatever genre of film takes your fancy, whatever time of night and whether you want a velour seat and popcorn or a leather chair and glass of champagne, you are sure to find it in the nation's capital.

For those who are desperate to catch Spielberg's latest offering, and are crazy enough to stick it out in the West End, chain cinemas abound. You'll find **Odeon (Maps 1, 4, 23, 30, 35, 61, 66, 71, 111 & 136)**, **Vue (Maps 12, 33, 43, 66 & 80)** and **Cineworld (Maps 11, 23, 40, 43, 45, 100 & 138)** theatres all over London. If you're brave, or just fancy seeing a star or two at one of the regular premiers, **Odeon Leicester Square (Map 23)** (made up of two separate theatres) could be for you. Another monster on the square is the historic **Empire (Map 11)**, seating an impressive 1,300 patrons is a landmark in itself, although she is a slightly faded leading lady these days. Beware though. While the price of a cinema ticket in the big smoke is normally enough to make you choke on your Butterkist, wandering into any of the theatres in Leicester Square may force you to re-mortgage with prices as high as £22.50 a ticket at peak times. **Apollo West End Multiplex (Map 23)** on Lower Regent Street was formerly the home of Paramount Pictures in the UK but now houses five small, luxurious theatres showing the latest flicks on general release.

It's not hard to find cinemas offering art house and independent films in London. Finding a good one, however, can be more of a challenge. The **Barbican (Map 7)** is always a good bet, and you can take in an exhibition before your film to really beef up your grey matter. We highly recommend the **Curzon Soho (Map 11)** offering not only a wide range of cinematic gems but also a plush bar to loosen you up for that three hour Kurasawa number. Remember if the queue is snaking along the pavement, tickets can be bought at the bar

downstairs too. Check out the cinema's cousin in **Mayfair (Map 9)** as well as the slightly shabby **Renoir (Map 5)** in Brunswick Square. **Cineworld Chelsea (Map 45)** on the lustrous King's Road is one of London's premier art houses with two-seaters available for the perfect smooching experience. **The Gate (Map 29)** in Notting Hill was created from a restaurant in 1911 and now offers independent releases in a luxurious setting. **BFI Southbank (Map 104)** specializes in film through the ages as well as hosting frequent events. Who would have thought old Charlie would help us save our pennies? **The Prince Charles Cinema (Map 11)** off Leicester Square sits in a perfect location and offers revivals, cult and foreign language films for as low as £1.50. Now that's a bloody bargain. For those with a penchant for 'le cine' courtesy of our French neighbours visit **Cine Lumiere (Map 36)** in South Kensington. Uber-cool Clapham has an equally trendy art house cinema, the **Clapham Picturehouse (Map 143)**, Dalston's Art Deco gem the **Rio Cinema (Map 86)** is worth a look, while Bloomsbury offers up **The Horse Hospital (Map 4)**—the name's almost as avant-garde as the films they show. Just leave Dobbin behind.

There are some wonderful cinematic experiences to be had too. **BFI IMAX (Map 104)** is housed in a curious circular building, south of Waterloo Bridge, with the biggest screen in the UK—the size of five double-decker buses. Then there are those three magic words—**The Electric Cinema (Map 29)** on Portobello Road. Grab a Pinot Grigio, rest your derriere on a soft leather seat and munch away at home-made ice cream all the way from sunny Hampshire while watching the latest Polish release. We now have the first British cinema to be opened in the 21st century: **Shortwave (Map 107)**, popped up in 2009 in the stylish Bermondsey Square, and among its 50 seats are some which were shrewdly rehoused from the Electric Cinema. For those who are lured by bling, bling, bling and the power of exclusivity, get down to Soho's private member's joint, **Rex Cinema and Bar (Map 11)**, where miniature hamburgers and reclining leather seats await you for a mere £250 a year. And treat your mates to another round and a packet of crisps, because there are increasing numbers of mini-cinemas in pubs, such as **The Garrison (Map 107)**.".

Remember Londoners! Those on the Orange phone network get 2 for 1 on Wednesday nights—an ideal opportunity to save some precious pounds.

Cinemas	Address	Phone	Map
Aldwych Film	1 Aldwych	020 7300 1000	14
Apollo Cinema Piccadilly Circus	19 Lower Regent St	0871 2233 444	23
Barbican Centre Cinema	Silk St & Whitecross St	020 7638 4141	7
BFI London IMAX	1 Charlie Chaplin Walk	0870 787 2525	104
BFI Southbank	Belverdere Rd & Waterloo Rd	020 7928 3232	104
Cine Lumiere	17 Queensberry Pl	020 7073 1350	36
Cineworld Chelsea	279 King's Rd	0871 200 2000	45
Cineworld Fulham Road	142 Fulham Rd	0871 200 2000	43
Cineworld Hammersmith	207 King St	0871 200 2000	40
Cineworld Haymarket	63 Haymarket	0871 200 2000	23
Cineworld Shaftesbury Avenue	13 Coventry St	0871 200 2000	11
Cineworld Wandsworth	Wandsworth High St & Ram St	0871 220 8000	138
Cineworld West India Quay	11 Hertsmere Rd	0871 200 2000	100
Clapham Picturehouse	76 Venn St	020 7498 2242	143
Curzon Chelsea	206 King's Rd	020 7351 3742	45
Curzon Mayfair	38 Curzon St	020 7495 0501	9
Curzon Soho	99 Shaftesbury Ave	020 7292 1686	11
The Electric Cinema	191 Portobello Rd	020 7908 9696	29
Empire Leicester Square	5 Leicester Square	020 7437 9011	11
Everyman Baker Street	96 Baker St	020 3145 0565	1
Everyman Belsize Park	203 Haverstock Hill	020 3145 0520	67
Everyman Hampstead	5 Hollybush Vale	0870 066 4777	56
Everyman Screen on the Green	83 Islington Green	020 3145 0525	80
Frontline Club	13 Norfolk Pl	020 7479 8950	31
Gate Picturehouse	87 Notting Hill Gate	020 7727 4043	29
Genesis Mile End	93 Mile End Rd	020 7780 2000	97
Greenwich Picturehouse	180 Greenwich High Rd	087 0755 0065	120
Horse Hospital	30 Colonnade	020 7833 3644	4
ICA Cinema	The Mall & Horse Guards Rd	020 7930 3647	23
Lux	18 Shacklewell Ln	020 7503 3980	86
Notting Hill Coronet	103 Notting Hill Gate	020 7727 6705	29
Odeon Camden Town	14 Parkway	020 7482 4576	71
Odeon Holloway	419 Holloway Rd	0871 22 44 007	61
Odeon Kensington	Kensington High St & Edwards Sq	0871 22 44 007	35
Odeon Leicester Square	24 Leicester Sq	0871 22 44 007	23
Odeon Marble Arch	10 Edgware Rd	0871 22 44 007	1
Odeon Panton Street	11 Panton St	0871 22 44 007	23
Odeon Putney	26 Putney High St	0871 22 44 007	136
Odeon Surrey Quays	Redriff Rd & Surrey Quays Rd	0871 22 44 007	111
Odeon Swiss Cottage	96 Finchley Rd	0871 22 44 007	66
Odeon Tottenham Court	30 Tottenham Ct Rd	0871 22 44 007	4
Odeon West End Cinema	40 Leicester Sq	0871 22 44 007	23
Odeon Whiteleys	Queensway & Porchester Gardens	0871 22 44 007	30
Peckham Multiplex	95 Rye Ln	0870 0420 299	123
Phoenix Cinema	52 High Rd	020 8444 6789	na
Prince Charles Cinema	7 Leicester Pl	020 7494 3654	11
Renoir Cinema	1 Brunswick Sq	0870 0420 299	5
Rich Mix Centre	34 Bethnal Green Rd	020 7613 7490	91
Rio Cinema	107 Kingsland High St	020 7241 9410	82
Ritzy Picturehouse	Coldharbour Ln & Brixton Oval	020 7733 2229	150
Riverside Studios	Crisp Rd & Queen Caroline St	020 8237 1111	41
Short & Sweet	91 Brick Ln	020 7247 6166	91
Shortwave	10 Bermondsey Square	0207 357 6845	107
Vue Finchley Road	Finchley Rd & Blackburn Rd	08712 240 240	66
Vue Fulham	Fulham Rd & Cedarne Rd	08712 240240	43
Vue Islington	36 Parkfield St	08712 240240	80
Vue Shepherds Bush	Shepherds Bush Green & Rockley Rd	08712 240 240	33
Vue West End Cinema	3 Cranbourn St	08712 240 240	12

It seems that every pub, bench and bridge in London has a tale to tell of past literary greats mulling over their troubles, weeping over lovers lost or launching themselves into the Thames. Ours is a city saturated in literary history and literature-lovers, with an abundance of bookshops and diversity of readers. While so many other retailers are homogenising, our independent bookshops—with their knowledgeable staffs and their often narrow focus—remain as eclectic and enthusiastic as ever. As well as a great selection of specialist independent stores, London is also home to dozens of second-hand bookshops, book markets, a literature festival, a major international book trade fair, and Europe's largest bookshop.

General

The **Foyles** flagship store on Charing Cross Road **(Map 12)** is a London institution, with a history as eccentric as its stock. Along with mainstream books and best-sellers, it offers a great range of second hand and out-of-print books, as well as a specialist Antiquarian department and a chilled jazz café. Venerable **Hatchard's (Map 10)** has been hawking books for over 200 years, making it London's oldest bookshop. The **London Review Bookshop (Map 4)** offers a huge range of constantly updated books with an intellectual bent and intellectual staff. **Metropolitan Books (Map 6)** is small but perfectly stocked, and Phil the owner makes time for any customer seeking advice or a friendly chat. Kids can find a bookshop wonderland in **Tales on Moon Lane (Map 128)** while parents can find the books they grew up with at **Ripping Yarns (Map 51)**. The excellence of the independent stores has meant the chains have had to up their game—and loath though we are to say it, some, such as **Borders (Maps 10, 12, 43 & 80)** and academic specialists **Blackwells (Maps 4, 12 & 74)** have got it very right indeed. In particular, **Waterstone's** in Piccadilly **(Map 23)** attracts all sorts of excitable superlatives, being the largest bookshop in Europe, running a range of literary activities to complement their stock, and even hosting a bar with some of the finest views of London.

Second Hand

Sadly, the world-renowned status Charing Cross Road used to command as the Mecca of second-hand bookstores is fading, and those who go looking for the genteel expertise immortalised in Helene Hanff's bestseller *84 Charing Cross Road* will find a "Med Kitchen" (shudder) at number 84. Many shops still cling to their ideals however, such as **Any Amount of Books (Map 12)** selling titles from as little £1 and offering a leather-binding service so your books can furnish your room as well as your mind. Good places to start if you are scouting for quality second-hand bookshops are: the tardis-like **The Bookshop (Map 129)** staffed by bookworms who have read *everything* (or so it seems) and can always help you find a gem; **John Sandoe (Map 46)** for true bookshop charm (rickety staircases, passionate staff, enchanting atmosphere); and the **Trinity Hospice (Map 136)** and **Oxfam Bookshops (Maps 38, 51, 86)**—not only an astonishingly cheap and broad collection of works, but all for charidee.

Specialist

Finding a bookshop devoted to your passion is like finding a club of old friends, and London caters for all tastes. Bored of cheese toasties? **Books for Cooks (Map 29)** smells as good as the recipes look, as they're tested in their kitchen first, while in-store cooking workshops teach new skills to avid customers. Sci-Fi nerds will be in their element at **Forbidden Planet (Map 179)**. **Gekoski (Map 4)** stocks a good range of modern first editions, or for older and rarer first editions try **Henry Sotheran (Map 10)**: a unique, but pricey, treat for any enthusiast. Head to **Atlantis (Map 4)** for all your occult needs (though no doubt the Spirits had already tipped you off on that one). Arty types are extensively catered for: **The Photographers' Gallery (Map 3)**, a treat in itself, has a substantial shop stocking photography titles, artists' monographs and unusual cameras; the **ICA Bookshop (Map 23)** is a great destination for art and film fans, and you can take in an exhibition while you're there; **Travis & Emery (Map 24)** stocks a vast range of music books and scores; comic geeks can get their fix at **Gosh! (Map 4)**. And for those with a passion for passion, pop along to the book section of **Coco de Mer (Map 13)**. Head to **Artwords (Map 84)** for books on—nope, I'll see if you can guess. Or to **Chappell (Map 11)** to supplement your Abba Hits keyboard book with some of their 50,000 music titles. **Motor Books (Map 24)**, surprisingly London's only shop dedicated to motoring, rail, aviation and military books, is the ideal repository for your menfolk when you need some peace.

Travel

Feeling lethargic? Head to one of the city's superb travel bookshops to have your energy restored. **Stanford's (Map 13)** has been inspiring London for 150 years, with its enormous collection of travel books and maps. A bookshop for travellers who like to read, **Daunt Books (Maps 2, 28, 57 & 67)** arranges all its books by geographical location, so even its fiction, cookbooks and history are shelved by country. Or to learn any of over 150 languages, head to **Grant & Cutler (Map 10)**, the UK's largest foreign-language specialist.

Politics

Bookmarks (Map 4) stocks left-leaning works on a huge range of issues and takes a lively role in political activism, giving it a real and infectious

sense of purpose. Also hugely right-on, both representing and driving several lefty social movements, is **Housmans (Map 78)**. Or for a more balanced approach with political works across the parties and even the odd Minister browsing for ideas, try **Westminster Bookshop (Map 22)**.

Talks and events

Publishing is a cut-throat business, and many writers have to sell their soul to get noticed. For them, it means an endless round of book signings and talks; for us, it means a fabulous chance to hobnob with our favourite authors. Most bookshops host occasional signings, but for regular events from the most celebrated authors, the big boys predictably have all the clout. **Foyles (Maps 12, 33, 78, 104)** and **Waterstone's (see p.489)** attract huge names: recent guests have included JK Rowling, Louis de Bernières, Salman Rushdie and AS Byatt. **Stanford's (Map 13)** offers opportunities to hear well-known travel editors, writers and photographers for an inspirational and sometimes career-changing evening. For intellectually stimulating debates and literary discussions, check out the **London Review Bookshop (Map 4)** and **Bookmarks (Map 4)**. Some events are free, some as much as a theatre ticket, but all should be booked in advance to ensure a place.

Bookshops	Address	Phone	Map
Any Amount of Books	56 Charing Cross Rd	020 7836 3697	12
Artwords	65 Rivington St	020 7729 2000	84
Atlantis	49 Museum St	020 7405 2120	4
Bargain Bookshop	153 Stoke Newington High Street	020 7249 8983	85
Bertram Rota	31 Long Acre	020 7836 0723	13
Blackwell	119 London Road	020 7928 5378	105
Blackwell Business + Law Bookshop	243 High Holborn	020 7831 9501	14
Blackwell Medical Bookshop	St Thomas Street	020 7403 5259	106
Blackwells	183 Euston Road	020 7611 2160	4
Blackwells	100 Charing Cross Rd	020 7292 5100	12
Blackwells	158 Holloway Road	020 7700 4786	74
Bookmarks	1 Bloomsbury St	020 7637 1848	4
Bolingbroke Bookshop	147 Northcote Rd	020 7223 9344	140
Books etc.	30 Broadgate Circle	020 7628 8944	8
Books etc.	115 Buckingham Plalace Road	020 7630 6244	20
Books etc.	66 Victoria St	020 7931 0677	22
Books etc.	Queensway	020 7229 3865	30
Books etc.	28 Broadway shopping centre	020 8764 3912	41
Books etc.	Cabot Place East	020 7513 0060	100
Books etc.	Southside Shopping Centre	020 8874 4587	138
Books for Cooks	4 Blenheim Crescent	020 7221 1992	29
The Bookshop	1 Calton Ave	020 8693 2808	129
Chappell of Bond St	152 Wardour St	020 7432 4400	11
Coco de Mer	23 Monmouth St	020 7836 8882	13

Bookshops	Address	Phone	Map
Daunt Books	83 Marylebone High St	020 7224 2295	2
Daunt Books	193 Haverstock Hill	020 7794 4006	67
Daunt Books	51 S End Rd	020 7794 8206	57
Daunt Books	112 Holland Park Ave	020 7727 7022	28
The Dover Bookshop	18 Earlham St	020 7836 2111	12
Forbidden Planet	179 Shaftesbury Ave	020 7420 3666	12
Foyles	113 Charing Cross Rd	020 7437 5660	12
Foyles	Upper Ground	020 7440 3212	104
Foyles	Pancras Road	020 3206 2650	78
Foyles	Westfield	020 3206 2656	33
Gosh! Comics	39 Great Russell St	020 7636 1011	4
Grant & Cutler	57 Great Marlborough Street	020 7734 2012	10
Hatchard's	187 Piccadilly	020 7439 9921	10
Henry Sotheran	2 Sackville St	020 7439 6151	10
Highgate Bookshop	9 Highgate Highstreet	020 8348 8202	n/a
Housmans Bookshop	5 Caledonian Rd	020 7837 4473	78
ICA Bookshop	The Mall	020 7766 1452	23
John Sandoe	10 Blacklands Terrace	020 7589 9473	46
The Lion and Unicorn Bookshop	19 King Street	020 8940 0483	n/a
London Review Bookshop	14 Bury Pl	020 7269 9030	4
Magma	8 Earlham St	020 7240 8498	12
Metropolitan Books	64 Exmouth Market	020 7278 6900	6
Motor Books	13 Cecil Court	020 7836 5376	24
Oxfam	80 Highgate High St	020 8340 3888	51
Owl Books	209 Kentish Town Rd	020 7485 7793	72
Pages of Hackney	70 Lower Clapton Rd	020 8525 1452	87
The Photographers' Gallery	16 Ramillies St	020 7831 1772	10
Quinto	72 Charing Cross Rd	020 7379 7669	12
R. A. Gekoski	15 Bloomsbury Square	020 7706 2735	4
Ripping Yarns	355 Archway Rd	020 8341 6111	51
Southbank Book Market	Under Waterloo Bridge	0871 663 2501	104
Stanford's	Long Acre	020 7836 1321	13
Stoke Newington Bookshop	159 Stoke Newington High Street	020 7249 2808	85
Tales on Moon Lane	25 Half Moon Ln	020 7274 5759	128
Travis & Emery	17 Cecil Ct	020 7240 2129	24
Trinity Hospice Bookshop	208 Upper Richmond Rd	020 8780 0737	136
Village Books	1 Calton Ave	020 8693 2808	129
Waterstone's	421 Oxford St	020 7495 8507	2
Waterstone's	82 Gower St	020 7636 1577	4
Waterstone's	Spencer Street	020 7608 0706	6
Waterstone's	9 Garrick St	020 7836 6757	13
Waterstone's	176 Fleet St	020 7353 5939	14
Waterstone's	Ludgate Circus	020 7236 5858	15
Waterstone's	54 London Wall	020 7628 9708	17
Waterstone's	1 Whittington Ave	020 7220 7882	18
Waterstone's	206 Piccadilly	020 7851 2400	23
Waterstone's	Trafalgar Square	020 7839 4411	24
Waterstone's	Exhibition Rd	020 7942 4481	36
Waterstone's	87 Brompton Rd	020 7730 1234	37
Waterstone's	151 King's Rd	020 7351 2023	45
Waterstone's	255 Finchley Road	020 7433 3299	66
Waterstone's	128 Camden High Street	020 7284 4948	78
Waterstone's	45 Bank Street	020 7719 0688	100
Waterstone's Economists' Bookshop	Clare Market	020 7405 5531	14
Westminster Bookshop	8 Artillery Row	020 7802 0018	22
WHSmith	124 High Holborn	020 7242 0535	14
WHSmith	Cannon Street Station	020 7626 5643	16
WHSmith	Fenchurch Street Station	020 7480 7295	18
WHSmith	Surrey Quays Shopping Centre	020 7237 5235	111
WHSmith	Elephant and Castle Shopping Centre	020 7703 8525	112

Yep you've heard the news. Theatre in the capital is all commercial. Predictable. Repetitive. Uncontroversial. If you believe the whingers, it's all fucking boring stuff. Don't, because it's not. Yes, the West End, that heartland of commercial theatre around Shaftesbury Avenue, is filled with tourist-grabbing, crowd-pleasing musicals. Yes, there are more star-dominated, tried-and-tested plays than ever. Yes, the Mousetrap is still taking up the space at St Martin's after 58 years of we-bloody-well-know-whodunit.

But all that's only half the story. To find the other half, look beyond the glittering billboard signs to find the daring, small West End theatres, such as the **Donmar Warehouse (Map 13)**, bringing the innovative and unusual to Theatreland. There are the Off-West End theatres that proudly fly the flag for new writers, unafraid of being political, controversial and in-yer-face: **The Royal Court (Map 19)**, **The Soho (Map 11)**, **The Bush (Map 33)**. There are the unconventional, anarchic ensemble companies, such as PunchDrunk, shaking up things all the way from the fringe to the West End, while innovative short-play evenings are popping up at pubs across the city (see below).

But let's not forget the cracking double-whammy of the **National Theatre (Map 104)** and **The Old Vic (Map 104)**, two artistic powerhouses currently going from strength to strength. At the National, the unstoppable Nicholas Hytner brings original works to this Southbank concrete colossus (coupled with a £10-tickets offer), while down the road, Hollywood-star-turned-theatre-connoisseur Kevin Spacey is returning the Old Vic into its former glory. The refurbished **Young Vic (Map 104)**, meanwhile, is one of the best places to see fresh, new theatre (and get drunk afterwards). And, whatever you do, you're never far from a good Shakespeare production.

Keeping It Real In The West End

The Donmar Warehouse (Map 13), the West End's smallest theatre, has gained a reputation for being one of Theatreland's most innovative, yet still crowd-pleasing houses. It's quite common for good new plays that have successfully kicked off at a fringe or Off-West End venue to transfer to the West End, such as Tom Stoppard's guitars-meet-politics cracker Rock'n'Roll. **Dean Street's**

Soho Theatre (Map 11) hunts out some of the most original, fearless or hilarious theatre around, while the **Comedy Theatre (Map 23)** may play it a little more safe but packs its shows with jaw-dropping casts. The West End is also a great place to catch up on those classics you always wanted to see but never got round to: from Beckett to Shakespeare.

Off-West End & The Fringe – The Best

The underground-led, breakneck guerrilla heyday might be over, but theatre outside the West End is in rude health. Head to rough-around-the-edges Dalston, where the **Arcola Theatre (Map 86)** continues to thrive in its scruffy ex-factory home, thanks to eclectic programming, an early-fringe-days feel and heaps of creative energy. The tiny **Bush Theatre (Map 33)** has long been a fierce champion of new work, and after being rescued by a star-studded tantrum in the face of funding cuts in 2008 it will doubtless continue to discover exciting new talent. So will **The Royal Court (Map 19)** on Sloane Square, which is one of London's finest. For new, innovative work, also keep your eyes on the **Battersea Arts Centre (Map 140)**, to watch what others will pay £50 to see next year (such as its premiere of Jerry Springer The Opera while other theatres nervously wrung their hands).

Theatre can't change society? Try telling that to the conviction-led crew of Kilburn's **The Tricycle (Map 65)**—easily London's most radical and most dedicated, political theatre. Islington's **Almeida (Map 80)** is far more conventional, but pretty—and that's got to count for something. If you're up for a laugh, check **The Hackney Empire (Map 87)**, a turn-of-the-century music hall, hosting some of London's best variety shows. **The Old Red Lion (Map 80)**, home inside an Islington pub, stubbornly clings to its unconventional, ale-fuelled fringe attitude, while **Battersea's Theatre 503 (Map 132)** is as provocative as ever. Be surprised.

If the thought of being in a theatre at all is too bourgeois for you, then you're still well catered for. London thesps it up wherever it can so you're never too far from a performance and its sometimes unwitting audience. Recent outings have included an opera about domesticity and flatpack furniture in the Wembley Ikea, and a thriller performed in an office while the audience watch with binoculars and audiophones from the terrace above. Or if it's sunny, squeeze among the crowds and their bottles of rosé for the occasional performances at **The Scoop**.

Tickets

If you know what you're after, check the theatre's website—they will either have their own system, a link to a ticket selling site, or provide a phone number. If not, check www.officiallondontheatre.co.uk, which lists shows by name, theatre and genre. The site also displays shows that are just opening, or just closing, and links straight to the appropriate ticketing website, once you have made your mind up. There's a handy map of all West End venues, too.

Fancy a bargain? The iconic TKTS ticket booth on Leicester Square sells on-the-day tickets for most big shows, half-price. The queue can be mind-boggling, so go early. There's a £2.50 booking fee, but it's included in the price shown. Many theatres also have their own discount schemes. If you don't mind standing, you can get Royal Court tickets for as little as 50p. Yes, that's 50p. Just show up between 6 pm and 6.30 pm on the day of the performance. The National has £5 standing tickets for all shows, but the view ain't always great.

Exciting & New

Enter the ensemble. They are multi-skilled, imaginative and are shaking the cosy, venue-obsessed Theatreland with a vengeance. Ensemble companies like PunchDrunk and Kneehigh are touring their way through London's venues in vigorously anarchic fashion. The result is increasingly physical, increasingly unconventional—and increasingly exciting theatre, which you'd be mad to miss.

PunchDrunk (www.punchdrunk.org.uk) have gained a reputation for site-specific productions, inviting the audience to walk around and follow actors and themes as they please. Their 2006 treatment of Goethe's Faust at the National Theatre was widely hailed as one of the best things to have happened to British theatre in years. Kneehigh (www.kneehigh.co.uk) enjoy

setting their nightmarish productions in outside mystical locations, but aren't afraid of West End constraints either. The award-winning Cheek by Jowl (www.cheekbyjowl.com), which have been producing Shakespeare and European classics since 1982, keep discovering hot talent—and ways to innovate.

If that's not grassroots enough, visit one of the themed short-play evenings that are popping up across town. Bringing together writers, actors and directors for twenty-minutes-or-so mini-shows, they have become a popular theatre alternative. Take your pick: Established organisers Nabokov (www.nabokov-online.com) have found a West End home at the **Trafalgar Studios (Map 24)**, SourFeast (www.sourfeast.co.uk) are based at Brixton's **Dogstar Pub (Map 150)**, and relative newcomers DryWrite have made Whitechapel's **The George Tavern (Map 97)** their own. The message is spreading. What you thought was a boozer, really is a stage. The possibilities are endless.

Contemporary Dance

From small company shows to big stage spectacles, contemporary dance is having one hell of a ride. **Sadlers Wells (Map 6)** (www.sadlerswells.com), the grand old lady of dance venues, is still doing a fine job bringing some of the world's best dance to London. Check their Sadler's Wells Sampled programme, showcasing dazzling future talent for as little as £10. **The Barbican (Map 7)** (www.barbican.org.uk) has established itself as a reliable source of powerful dance performances, while the **Royal Festival Hall (Map 104)** attracts increasingly bold and interesting works to its refurbished riverside location. For London's most innovative dance performances, check **The Place (Map 4)**, a stylish venue that combines performance, training and dance education (www.theplace.org.uk).

Theatres	Address	Phone	Type	Map
Adelphi Theatre	The Strand	087 0403 0303	West End	24
Aldwych Theatre	49 Aldwych	0870 4000 805	West End	14
Almeida Theatre	Almeida St	020 7359 4404	Fringe	80
Ambassadors Theatre	West St	084 4811 2334	West End	12
Apollo Theatre	Shaftesbury Ave	084 4579 1971	West End	11
Apollo Victoria Theatre	17 Wilton Rd	020 7834 6318	West End	20
Arcola Theatre	27 Arcola St	020 7503 1646	Fringe	86
Arts Theatre	6 Great Newport St	084 5017 5584	West End	12
Barbican Centre	Silk St & Whitecross St	020 7638 4141	Performing Arts	7
Barons Court Theatre	28 Comeragh Rd	020 8932 4747	Fringe	42
Battersea Arts Centre	Lavender Hill & Theatre St	020 7223 2223	Fringe	140
Bloomsbury Theatre	15 Gordon St	020 7388 8822	Fringe	4
Brixton Academy	211 Stockwell Rd	020 7771 3000	Performing Arts	145
Bush Theatre	2 Shepherd's Bush Rd	020 8743 3584	Fringe	33
Cadogan Hall	5 Sloane Terrace	020 7730 4500	Performing Arts	19
Cambridge Theatre	Earlham St	084 4412 4652	West End	13
Chats Palace Arts Centre	42 Brooksby's Walk	020 8533 0227	Performing Arts	90
Comedy Theatre	Panton St	087 1297 5454	West End	23
Criterion Theatre	218 Piccadilly	087 0060 2313	West End	10
The Dogstar	389 Coldharbour Ln	020 7733 7515	Fringe	150
Dominion Theatre	268 Tottenham Court Rd	020 7413 3546	West End	4
Donmar Warehouse Theatre	41 Earlham St	020 7438 9200	West End	13
The Drill Hall	16 Chenies St	020 7307 5060	Fringe	4
Duchess Theatre	Catherine St	084 5434 9290	West End	14
Duke of York's Theatre	St Martin's Ln	087 0060 6623	West End	24
Etcetera	265 Camden High St	020 7482 4857	Fringe	71
Fortune Theatre	Russell St	020 7369 1737	West End	13
Garrick Theatre	Charing Cross Rd	020 7520 5690	West End	24
Gate Theatre	11 Pembridge Rd	020 7229 0706	Fringe	29
The George Tavern	373 Commercial Rd	020 7790 7335	Fringe	97
Gielgud Theatre	Shaftesbury Ave	084 4482 5130	West End	11
Greenwich Theatre	Crooms Hill & Nevada St	020 8858 7755	Fringe	120
Hackney Empire	291 Mare St	020 8985 2424	Fringe	89
Hampstead Theatre	Eton Ave	020 7722 9301	Fringe	66
Her Majesty's Theatre	Haymarket	0844 412 2707	West End	23
Indigo2	Millenium Way	020 8463 2000	Performing Arts	na
Jermyn Street Theatre	16 Jermyn St	020 7287 2875	Fringe	23
King's Head Theatre & Pub	115 Upper St	020 7226 1916	Fringe	80
Koko	1 Camden High St	087 0432 5527	Performing Arts	71
Leicester Square Theatre	5 Leicester Pl	020 7534 1740	West End	11
Hammersmith Apollo Theatre	Queen Caroline St	020 8563 3800	West End	41
Her Majesty's Theatre	Haymarket	084 4412 4653	West End	23
HMV Forum	9 Highgate Rd	020 7428 4099	Performing Arts	72
Little Angel Theatre	14 Dagmar Passage	020 7226 1787	Performing Arts	80
London Palladium	Argyll St	020 7494 5020	West End	10
Lyceum Theatre	21 Wellington St	020 7432 4220	West End	14
Lyric Theatre	29 Shaftesbury Ave	020 7494 5045	West End	11
National Theatre	South Bank	020 7452 3400	West End	104
New London Theatre	Drury Ln	0870 890 0141	West End	13
Noël Coward Theatre	St Martin's Ln	084 4482 5140	West End	24
Novello Theatre	Aldwych	084 4482 5170	West End	14

Theatres	Address	Phone	Type	Map
Old Red Lion	418 St John St	020 7837 7816	Fringe	6
The Old Vic Theatre	103 The Cut	084 4871 7628	West End	104
Palace Theatre	Shaftesbury Ave	087 0890 0142	West End	12
Phoenix Theatre	Charing Cross Rd	087 0060 6629	West End	12
Piccadilly Theatre	16 Denman St	020 7478 8800	West End	10
The Place	17 Duke's Rd	020 7121 1000	Performing Arts	4
Playhouse Theatre	Northumberland Ave	084 4871 7631	West End	24
Prince Edward Theatre	28 Old Compton St	084 4482 5151	West End	12
Prince of Wales Theatre	Coventry St	084 4482 5115	West End	11
Queen Elizabeth Hall	South Bank Centre	020 7960 4200	Performing Arts	104
Queen's Theatre	Shaftesbury Ave	084 4482 5160	West End	11
Riverside Studios	Crisp Rd & Queen Caroline St	020 8237 1111	Fringe	41
Ronnie Scott's	47 Frith St	020 7439 0747	Performing Arts	12
The Roundhouse	Chalk Farm Rd & Crogsland Rd	020 7424 9991	Performing Arts	71
Royal Albert Hall	Kensington Gore	020 7589 8212	Performing Arts	36
Royal Court Theatre	Sloane Sq	020 7565 5000	West End	19
Royal Festival Hall	Belvedere Rd	084 4875 0073	Performing Arts	104
Royal Opera House	Bow St	020 7304 4000	Performing Arts	13
Sadler's Wells	Rosebery Ave	084 4412 4300	Performing Arts	6
Savoy Theatre	The Strand	0870 164 8787	West End	24
Scala	275 Pentonville Rd	020 7833 2022	Performing Arts	78
The Scoop	The Queen's Walk	020 7403 4866	Performing Arts	107
Shaftesbury Theatre	210 Shaftesbury Ave	020 7379 5399	West End	13
Shakespeare's Globe	21 New Globe Walk	020 7902 1400	West End	105
Shepherd's Bush Empire	56 Shepherd's Bush Green	084 4477 2000	Performing Arts	33
Soho Theatre	21 Dean St	020 7478 0100	Fringe	11
The Space	269 Westferry Rd	020 7515 7799	Fringe, Performing Arts	na
St John's	Smith Square	020 7222 1061	Performing Arts	22
St Martin's Theatre	West St	020 7836 1443	West End	12
Sutton House	2 Homerton High St	020 8986 2264	Performing Arts	87
Theatre 503	503 Battersea Park Rd	020 7978 7040	Fringe	132
Theatre Royal Drury Lane	Catherine St	087 0890 6002	West End	13
Theatre Royal Haymarket	Haymarket	020 7930 8890	West End	23
Toynbee Studios	28 Commercial St	020 7650 2350	Fringe	91
Trafalgar Studios	14 Whitehall	087 0060 6632	West End	24
The Tricycle Theatre	259 Kilburn High Rd	020 7372 6611	Fringe	65
Vaudeville Theatre	404 Strand	087 0890 0511	West End	24
Victoria Palace Theatre	Victoria St	084 4248 5000	West End	20
Wembley Stadium	Wembley Hill Rd	084 4980 8001	Performing Arts	na
Wigmore Hall	36 Wigmore St	020 7935 2141	Performing Arts	2
Wilton's Music Hall	Graces Alley & Ensign St	020 7702 2789	Fringe	95
Wyndham's Theatre	32 Charing Cross Rd	084 4482 5120	West End	12
The Young Vic Theatre	66 The Cut	020 7922 2922	West End	104

There are many great things about London's vibrant art world. The best? It's free. Granted, if you want to see some of the big show-stopping exhibitions that pass through the **Tates** (Maps 21 & 105), **British Museum** (Map 4), **National Gallery** (Map 23) and **Royal Academy** (Map 2) you'll have to pay quite a hefty sum, but overall, you can experience virtual arts throughout the capital without coughing up much dough. This might be a contributing factor to London's sprawling art scene, as it is so easy to duck in and out of the capital's 300+ museums and galleries on a lunch break.

Of course, there are concentrations of art in locations around Piccadilly and Bond Street (check out Cork Street for its galleries, such as **Messum** (Map 10) and the **Adam Gallery** (Map 10), running parallel with Savile Row), the East End (funkier affair and an artistic hipster breeding ground—check out Vyner Street in Bethnal Green), South Kensington/Chelsea (a major culture scene as a result of the Great Exhibition of 1851) and various institutions dotted along the Thames (as seen from the Tate to Tate boat service). But great art is all over the this city, so get out your Oyster Card, and get ready to cover a lot of ground.

Starting with London's modern art, the **Tate Modern** (Map 105), with its massive smoke stack, has become a major London landmark. This is despite it only existing as a separate entity from the **Tate Britain** (Map 21) since 2000. Check out its spacious turbine hall, with often spectacular installations.

It's not surprising that the Tate Modern is often the London tourist's first stop these days, as the city has become well-known for contemporary art. Due in part to the too-cool-for-school London art scene of the 1990s, which saw the establishment of Turner Prizers Tracy Emin, Rachel Whiteread and Damien Hirst, and made a major mark under Saatchi's guiding light. This light has faded somewhat, as the movement's personalities have slowly sold out a little (Emin designing for Longchamp is a case in point). But certain London galleries remain as monuments to this explosion of counter-culture, and, in addition to the **Saatchi Gallery** (Map 46), these include the **Serpentine Gallery** (Map 30), **Haunch of Venison** (Map 10), and **Victoria Miro** (Map 31). Other inspiring alternatives include the **Riflemaker** (Map 10), **South London Gallery** (Map 122), **Camden Arts Centre** (Map 66), the **White Cube** at Mason's Yard (Map 23) and **Hoxton Square** (Map 84).

London is a city with a lot on offer, and if you're looking for something a bit more traditional, start with the **National Gallery** (Map 24) in Trafalgar Square, moving onto the **National Portrait Gallery** (Map 24) next door, which presents you with a who's who of British culture past and present. Stroll up Charing Cross Road to the awesome **British Museum** (Map 4) with its jaw-dropping two acre roof over the Great Court (yet another example of Norman Foster's obsession with glass and geometry). Be sure to take in the Parthenon Marbles, aka Elgin Marbles, before the Greek government makes any attempt to get them back. Then over to the not-nearly-praised-enough **Wallace Collection** (Map 2) behind Selfridge's for some tea and Watteau action. A traditional art-lover's tour of London is not over without a trip to the **Royal Academy** (Map 2) with its epic exhibitions and finally to the **Tate Britain** (Map 21), where the Pre-Raphaelites reign supreme.

Feeling a little non-conformist? London has a brilliant array of cultural institutions that offer more than just marble and canvas. From ceramics to dolls houses, kimonos to plaster casts of just about every great sculpture in the world—the VA has it all (not to mention an awesome gift shop). Other alternatives to the mainstream include **The Photographers' Gallery** (Map 13) by Leicester Square, which not only squeezes in the best photographic exhibitions in town, but also boasts the best bookshop on the subject. Odd in its own way is the **Museum of London** (Map 7), which walks you through the history of the city from prehistoric times to the present day. Recent London museum gems also include the newly renovated **London Transport Museum** (Map 24), **Fashion and Textile Museum** (Map 107), **Museum of Brands, Packaging and Advertising** (Map 29) and the **Design Museum** (Map 107), with cars and video games in case you're stuck entertaining your nephew. The Horniman (*snigger*) Museum is a legacy of Victorian curiosity, starring an overstuffed walrus whose taxidermist didn't realise that walruses are supposed to have wrinkles.

A lot of the capital's best museum and gallery treasures are off the beaten path and may even require a trip in a bendy bus (gasp!). The **Geffreye Museum** (Map 88) is a good one to check out when you're in Shoreditch and tired of being hip. Just up Kingsland Road from **Flowers** (Map 91) (a good British contemporary art gallery), this museum of domestic interiors runs through the history of Britain one living room at a time. Somewhat forgotten are the weird and wonderful **Sir John Soane's Museum** (Map 14), **Leighton House** (Map 35) and **Dennis Severs' House** (Map 91)—but we'll let you discover these gems for yourself.

So forget Pret a Manger—feed your soul in one of London's many museums and galleries. They certainly have more to offer than one of those crappy no bread sandwiches, anyway.

Museums & Galleries	Address	Phone	Map
2 Willow Road	2 Willow Road	020 7435 6166	56
19 Princelet Street - Museum of Immigration and Diversity	19 Princelet St	020 7247 5352	91
7 Hammersmith Terrace	7 Hammersmith Terrace	0208 741 4104	39
Adam Gallery	24 Cork St	020 7439 6633	10
Apsley House	149 Piccadilly	020 7499 5676	9
Arsenal Museum and Stadium Tour	Drayton Park	020 7704 4504	74
Bank of England Museum	Threadneedle Street	020 7601 5545	17
The Banqueting House	Whitehall & Horse Guards Ave	020 3166 6000	24
Benjamin Franklin House	36 Craven St	020 7839 2006	24
The Bramah Museum of Tea and Coffee	40 Southwark Street	020 7403 5650	106
Britain At War Experience	66 Tooley Street	020 7403 3171	107
The British Library	96 Euston Rd	084 3208 1144	78
The British Museum	Great Russell St & Museum St	020 7323 8299	4
Brunel Museum	Railway Ave & Rotherhithe St	020 7231 3840	110
Brunswick House	30 Wandsworth Rd	020 7394 2100	134
Camden Arts Centre	Arkwright Rd	020 7472 5500	66
Cartoon Museum	35 Little Russell St	020 7580 8155	4
Chelsea FC Museum and Stadium Tour	Stamford Bridge	087 1984 1955	43
Chelsea Physic Garden	66 Royal Hospital Rd	020 7352 5646	45
Churchill Museum and Cabinet War Rooms	King Charles Street	020 7930 6961	24
Clink Prison Museum	1 Clink St	020 7403 0900	106
Clockmakers' Museum	Aldermanbury	020 7332 1868	16
Cuming Museum	151 Walworth Rd	020 7525 2332	113
Dennis Severs' House	18 Folgate St	020 7247 4013	91
Design Museum	Shad Thames	020 7403 6933	107
The Dickens House Museum	48 Doughty St	020 7405 2127	5
Dr Johnson's House	17 Gough Square	020 7353 3745	15
Fan Museum	12 Croom's Hill	020 8305 1441	120
Fashion and Textile Museum	83 Bermondsey St	020 7407 8664	107
Florence Nightingale Museum	2 Lambeth Palace Rd	020 7620 0374	131
Flowers	82 Kingsland Rd	020 7920 7777	91
Foundling Museum	40 Brunswick Square	020 7841 3600	5
Freud Museum	20 Maresfield Gardens	020 7435 2002	66
Geffrye Museum	136 Kingsland Rd	020 7739 9893	88
Grant Museum of Zoology	Malet Place	020 7679 2647	4
Guards Museum	Birdcage Walk	020 7414 3428	22
Hampstead Museum	New End Square	020 7431 0144	56
Handel House Museum	25 Brook St	020 7495 1685	2
Haunch of Venison	6 Burlington Gardens	020 7495 5050	10
Hayward Gallery	Belvedere Rd	0871 663 2501	104
Horniman Museum & Gardens	100 London Rd	020 8699 1872	n/a
Hunterian Museum	35 Lincoln's Inn Fields	020 7869 6560	14
Imperial War Museum	Lambeth Road	020 7416 5000	104
Jewish Museum	129 Albert St	020 7284 7384	71
King's Place Gallery	90 York Way	020 7520 1485	79
Kirkaldy Testing Museum	99 Southwark St	013 2233 2195	105
Leighton House Museum	12 Holland Park Rd	020 7602 3316	34
The Library and Museum of Freemasonry	60 Great Queen St	020 7395 9251	13
Linley Sambourne House	18 Stafford Terrace	020 7602 3316	35
London Canal Museum	12 New Wharf Rd	020 7713 0836	79
London Dungeon	29 Tooley St	020 7403 7221	106
London Fire Brigade Museum	94 Southwark Bridge Rd	020 8555 1200	106

Museums & Galleries	Address	Phone	Map
London Sewing Machine Museum	293 Balham High Rd	020 8767 4724	151
London Transport Museum	Covent Garden Piazza	020 7379 6344	24
Marylebone Cricket Club Museum	St John's Wood Rd	020 7616 8656	76
Messum	8 Cork St	020 7437 5545	10
Museum in Docklands	Hertsmere Road	020 7001 9844	100
Museum of Brands, Packaging and Advertising	2 Colville Mews	020 7908 0880	29
Museum Of Childhood	Cambridge Heath Road	020 8983 5200	92
Museum of Fulham Palace	Bishops Avenue	020 7736 3233	48
Museum of Garden History	Lambeth Palace Road	020 7401 8865	131
Museum of London	150 London Wall	020 7001 9844	7
Museum of Methodism & Wesley's Chapel	49 City Rd	020 7253 2262	7
Museum of the Order of St John	26 St John's Ln	020 7324 4005	15
Museum of the Royal Pharmaceutical Society	1 Lambeth High St	020 7572 2210	131
National Army Museum	Royal Hospital Road	020 7881 2455	46
National Gallery	Trafalgar Square	020 7747 2885	24
National Maritime Museum	Park Row	020 8312 6565	n/a
National Portrait Gallery	St Martin's Place	020 7306 0055	24
Natural History Museum	Cromwell Rd	020 7942 5460	36
The Old Operating Theatre, Museum & Herb Garret Venue	9 St Thomas St	020 7188 2679	106
Petrie Museum of Egyptian Archaeology	Gower St	020 7679 2884	4
Pollock's Toy Museum	1 Scala St	020 7636 3452	3
Ragged School Museum	46 Copperfield Rd	020 8980 6405	98
Riflemaker Gallery	74 Beak St	020 7439 0000	10
Rootstein Hopkins Parade Ground	16 John Islip St	020 7514 8514	21
Rotherhithe Picture Research Library	82 Marychurch St	020 7237 2010	109
Royal Academy of Music Museum	Marylebone Rd	020 7873 7373	2
Saatchi Gallery	King's Road	020 7823 2332	46
Science Museum	Exhibition Rd	087 0870 4868	36
Serpentine Gallery	Kensington Gardens	020 7402 6075	30
Sherlock Holmes Museum	221 Baker St	020 7224 3688	76
Sikorski Museum	20 Princes Gate	020 7589 9249	37
Sir John Soane's Museum	13 Lincoln's Inn Fields	020 7440 4263	14
Smythson Stationery Museum	40 New Bond St	020 7629 8558	10
South London Gallery	65 Peckham Rd	020 7703 6120	122
Spencer House	27 St James's Pl	020 7499 8620	23
St Bartholomew's Hospital Museum	West Smithfield	020 7601 8152	15
Tate Britain	Millbank	020 7887 8888	21
Tate Modern	Bankside	020 7887 8888	105
Tower Bridge Exhibition	Tower Bridge	020 7403 3761	107
Victoria & Albert Museum	Cromwell Rd & Thurloe Pl	020 7942 2000	37
Victoria Miro Gallery	16 S Wharf Rd	020 7336 8109	31
Wallace Collection	Manchester Square	020 7563 9500	2
Wellcome Collection	183 Euston Rd	020 7611 2222	4
Westminster Abbey	Parliament Square	020 7222 5152	22
White Cube	26 Mason's Yard	020 7930 5373	23
White Cube	48 Hoxton Square	020 7930 5373	84

Overview

Stumbling out bleary-eyed into the light, pallid skin wrecked by long hours in darkness and surrounded by strangers, it's hard to believe that this time last year we were counting out our coppers and begging our friends to buy us another drink. Okay, so we're not completely in the red and London's cash registers may not be overflowing with moolah as they once were but we've managed to open new bars, forget about old ones, sing ourselves raw in amateur karaoke sessions, break a few bones dancing in scary clubs we shouldn't be in—you know, the usual. What is scary though is how fast the night-time landscape is changing around us. These days walking around Soho is like picking your way through a warzone; with the Astoria and its surrounding area now bulldozed, it sometimes feels the heart of London's soul has been ripped out by greedy developers. Maybe it has, but we're not dwelling on all those bad vibes: we're too busy digging amateur folk in Stokey, or quaffing luxurious cocktails in the depths of Old Street, or down the front at some dingy gig hellhole in the depths of Brixton having the time of our sorry little lives. As you may have gathered by now, London's options are as endlessly varied as our tastes. And being children of the post-modern age (or is that post-post-modern age?) we've given up caring about tribalism and consistency and have dived head-first into everything at once. Economy, what economy?

Local Pubs For Local People

'The local' in London doesn't have any meaning until you get to Zone 3, let's be honest. Inner city London's inhabitants are quite zealous in their marauding into alien territory and raiding their pubs, but many pubs do have a strong whiff of what your local would be like if you lived on Fleet Street. **Ye Olde Cheshire Cheese (Map 15)**, a dark Victorian Dickens was fond of, is still too dark for major tourism issues while Borough's **George Inn (Map 106)**, with a dazzling selection of ales, is as ancient as they get. **The Lamb (Map 14)** is where to go after your office job if you want to pretend you're a writer, while the Grade II-listed **Princess Louise (Map 4)** is sparkling with old man-ness but in the heart of London. In Hampstead, it's got to be the pretty, and pretty hidden, **Holly Bush (Map 56)**. And while it's

been gentrified since it was run by the Kray's mum, **The Carpenter's Arms (Map 91)**, is still a great, tiny little foreign beer-heaven. Modern rot has yet to set in at Highgate's old-school **The Winchester (Map 52)** and you can eyeball woodworm in the brilliant **The Compton Arms (Map 80)**. The old-timers in Rotherhithe's dream-of-your-dad **The Mayflower (Map 109)**, and Brixton's **The Effra (Map 150)** will have never heard of the Interwebs, never mind Facebook, flashmobs or Twitter.

Keep it Real Ale

Terribly authentic Northerners often berate us Southerners' fancy ways and cocktail quaffing. But we have Pride (sic) in our real ale credentials! **The Wenlock Arms (Map 83)** proves we can do down-to-earth ale-enthusiast and **The Jerusalem Tavern (Map 3)** shows we can do fake ye olde times with amazing beer selection as well as any Lancashire local. Borough's **Market Porter (Map 106)** has a great selection, and is full of market traders counting their cash. Lovers of the Belgian stuff (and trendy Hackney-ites) will feel at home in **The Dove (Map 89)** and those after an even greater selection of European ales without the pretentiousness should head to **Quinns (Map 71)** in Camden. Too fancy? For great ale selections, there's **The Royal Oak (Map 106)** also in Borough, where the taps come courtesy of the Harveys brewery. Pitfield, Freedom and St Peter's, meanwhile, supply Islington's **Duke of Cambridge (Map 83)** with organic beer, if you like that kind of stuff. In Parson's Green **The White Horse (Map 49)** is a Victorian gem and the **John Snow (Map 10)** serves the full Sam Smiths range (delicious and cheap) in the heart of Soho.

Good Mixers

Actually maybe those Northerners have a point. We do love cocktails. But what's not to love? Extreme amounts of alcohol in small glasses, mixed with exotic things we've never heard of and won't remember, all costing the same amount as a house in Bolton. For aesthetic hedonism we love **Lounge Bohemia (Map 8)** but for tequilas head to **Green & Red (Map 91)**. Martinis? You'll find us at the **Charlotte Street Hotel (Map 3)**. At **5th View (Map 10)** there's vistas of Big Ben with your Kir Royal and the NYC-esque **Milk & Honey (Map 10)** comes with eight handy house rules, including "no star fucking". We like Soho's **22 Below (Map 10)** for its down-to-earth attitude, and the plush Art Deco heaven that is **Claridge's Bar (Map 2)** for the opposite. **Montgomery Place (Map 29)** does extremely well serving Notting Hill. If you find yourself on Clapham High Street then you could do a lot worse than heading to **The Loft (Map 143)**—a modern, lush escape. We would also love to praise **The Cinnamon Club (Map 22)**, inside the Old Westminster Library. If only we could find it.

Weirdos

Let's face it, sometimes the booze just isn't enough to keep you entertained. Destroying your internal organs with the stuff is just sometimes a little boring, right? Well just walk past the New Cross Inn and head to the **Montague Arms (Map 125)** for some pirate-themed taxidermy action. **The Foundry (Map 84)** is pretty weird with an outsider art chic, and **Public Life (Map 91)**, a refurbished toilet, is literally a shithole. **Stoke Newington Airport (Map 85)** and Jamboree at **Cable Street Studios (Map 97)** are artist-run warehouse spaces that do mannered bohemian and hipster rave-offs respectively. **The Windmill (Map 150)** of Brixton is a handmade weirdo magnet and **The Battersea Barge (Map 134)** is a friendly old pub. On a very thin barge. **The Coronet (Map 74)** in Holloway has a desolate, nostalgic charm as does perhaps the weirdest pub of them all, the **Palm Tree (Map 93)**, a celebration of British antiquity with crooners of a certain age most nights.

Smoker-Friendly

If the merciless prohibition regime of 2007 hasn't resulted in reluctant surrender, don't despair: from provisionally erected patios to all-year beer gardens to secret backdoors, London's ban-bashing creativity knows no boundaries. Great fag spots include the terrace at **Proud (Map 71)**, overlooking Camden's roofs, the barbeque-and-beer-can courtyard of **93 Feet East (Map 91)** and the tree-shaded garden of the **Edinboro Castle (Map 77)**. Hang out in front of Highgate favourite **The Flask (Map 51)** or combine a late-

night pint with a rollie in the backyard of the **The Dolphin (Map 89)**. For clubbing, consider **EGG (Map 79)**, where you're allowed to smoke in the massive garden. **The Owl & Pussycat (Map 91)** is not just a surprisingly pleasant pub in Shoreditch, it's also got a surprisingly nice garden, where smoking is not just allowed, dear friends, but encouraged.

We're Raving We're Raving

Just as we're getting over The End closing, now **Plastic People (Map 84)** is looking unsure on its feet. Over at **Fabric (Map 15)**, the grandaddy of London clubbing, things are still going strong with inventive and provocative programming. For the groovier (can you still say groovy?), smaller joint try **Guanabara (Map 13)** or the swanky **Images (Map 92)**. The ever-so-eclectic **Notting Hill Arts Club (Map 29)** continues to come up with good nights, as does Brick Lane's **93 Feet East (Map 91)** and **333 (Map 84)**. **Madame Jojo's (Map 11)** provides exactly the kind of decadence we demand from Soho clubbing, while Piccadilly's **Pigalle Club (Map 10)** swoops us back to the '40s. As long as lip fuzz is stilll trendy there's always the **Moustache Bar (Map 86)** and for quirky, extra fartsery head to **Passing Clouds (Map 88)**, both in Dalston, natch. For serious rockabilly, find **Ye Olde Axe (Map 91)** gentlemen's club on Hackney Road, where the rock 'n' roll starts as soon as the last naked girl has disappeared behind the big-mirrored wall.

Great Bars

George Orwell's ideal pub was all about "draught stout, open fires, cheap meals, motherly barmaids and no radio." These days we'd maybe add music straight from a blog, handmade decor and a dangerous vibe. For some if not all of these try up-beat **Jaguar Shoes (Map 13)** or **Freud (Map 13)** or the **French House (Map 11)** in the West End are also solid contenders for boho shlock. But there's so much more: crawl from **Barrio North (Map 83)** caravan to the country-house of **Lost Society (Map 142)**, from the **Island Queen (Map 83)** to the Moijto-fuelled **Mau Mau (Map 29)**. We like standing next to (would-be) artists at the **ICA Bar (Map 23)** and actor types on the terrace of **The Cut Bar (Map 104)**. Or in front of a movie screen, at **Roxy Bar and Screen (Map 106)**. Later on, you'll find us nibbling cheese in Dalston's **Jazz Bar (Map 82)**, or dancing to trashy music at **Da Vinci's (Map 104)**.

Best Of The Rest

Want to feel exclusive? Members-only clubs are not only becoming ever more popula, but also ever more accessible. So there. Escape Shoreditch's terrifying hordes to the rooftop swimming pool of **Shoreditch House (Map 91)** or the boredom of Shepherd's Bush to the underground ex-toilets that have become **Ginglik (Map 33)**. Of course, most of those in the know will drag you to the various warehouse raves that fire up every weekend. People like **Real Gold** (http://wearerealgold.com) are a good place to start if you fancy some of this awfulness. Remember it's not who you know but, oh wait, it is who you know.

To create your own entertainment and/or embarrass yourself **Lucky Voice (Maps 10, 80)** is one of many joints offering private karaoke booths for you and some people who will most probably cease to be your friends after they hear you massacre 'Time After Time.' If relying on that notoriously joke-cracking ex-friend of a friend for your evening's amusement sounds a bit risky, consider these alternatives: The standard-setting **Comedy Store (Map 11)** (book in advance), Bethnal Green's **FymFyg Bar (Map 92)** and Covent Garden **Comedy Club (Map 24)**, or, at the pub end of things, **The Bedford (Map 148)** and the **Camden Head (Map 80)**. If you think that YOU should in fact provide the evening's amusement, well, the **Poetry Café (Map 13)** gives you the stage. Or stay at home and talk to yourself; it's cheaper.

Music, Sweet Music

More than anything else, London's veins are pumped by its jack-hammer rhythms, its mellifluous melodies, the sneers of angry young men or the coos of sweet maidens. Whether you're popping class As in the dark or jamming along at folk night there'll be something to hear at any given night of the week.

Strummin' Mental

As always our Rock, Pop, Indie and 'Alternative' scenes are in a constant state of flux with bands, venues and styles falling in and out of cool lists quicker than a Ramones song. What never changes is that everywhere you look (ok maybe not everywhere) there's some schmuck with a guitar and half a voice pining over some schmuckette to a bunch of schmucks. The good news is that there are so many great places to do this in. Yes we've got our share of corporate cesspits (hello 02) but for every church of Carling there are two or three brilliant dives like the punky **Grosvenor (Map 145)** or the ever-mobbed **Stag's Head (Map 84)**.

For the sweatily inclined there are infinite choices. Bethnal Green's **Star of Bethnal Green (Map 92)** (formerly the Pleasure Unit), Highgate's **Buffalo Bar (Map 80)** and Angel's **Lexington (Map 79)** are as pant-wettingly indie as they come, but if you like harder or weirder stuff, the **Camden Underworld (Map 71)** and **Slimelight (Map 80)** does all the metals, while **Cafe Oto (Map 86)** handles experimental and improv. **The MacBeth (Map 84)** is very popular yet somehow suffers from a fun bypass but **Monto Water Rats (Map 5)** is an unshakeable legend. The refurbished **Old Blue Last (Map 84)** or Vice Magazine party HQ has surfed to the crest of the trend wave fueled by young kids attempting to be sexually harassed by older men like in their favourite adverts for American Apparel. Mid-sized venues for mid-fame bands? **The Scala (Map 78)** is a brilliant converted cinema, The **Luminaire (Map 65)** is a great venue, but **The Dome (Map 59)** is fast becoming our favourite school hall-like venue. The now legal **Barden's Boudoir (Map 86)** has come a long way since it was a dingy dive run by gangsters and of course the **ICA (Map 23)** is the 'art-space' par excellence for all artistes who insist on that 'e' at the end of 'artist.' The **Amersham Arms (Map 126)** and **The Rest Is Noise (Map 144)** are owned by the same hipster morons but they're good places to watch some twonks you've been told to like by Dazed. The city's electronic music scene generally piggy-backs the guitars except for new places like **Cable (Map 107)** and **The Lightbox (Map 134)**.

As for the classics, the **Shepherd's Bush Empire (Map 33)** and the breathtakingly beautiful **Bush Hall (Map 32)** remain West London's finest, while Camden stalwart **Koko (Map 71)** keeps rocking in the free world. **Brixton Academy (Map 145)** might be slightly overrated, but its sky-like ceiling remains awesome. If you have to do stadium-size, do stadium-size in style and get your seat in the **Royal Albert Hall (Map 36)**, which is increasingly luring good non-classical acts. The refurbishment of the **Royal Festival Hall (Map 104)**, meanwhile, has kick-started more pop-oriented programming on the South Bank.

A World of Jazz And Blues

Camden's intimate **Jazz Café (Map 71)** seems to have no intention of stopping its relentless stream of first-rate jazz performances, getting in more soul, funk and pop at the same time, while **Ronnie Scott's Jazz Club (Map 12)**, London's undisputed jazz original, is equally determined to keep up the good programming. For some of the freshest jazz, alongside great contemporary folk and world music, head to Dalston, where the plush **Vortex (Map 82)** is a-buzz with free-spirited legends. On the other side of town, Chelsea's **606 Club (Map 50)** is a fine, small jazz venue with crammed, small tables within slobbering distance from the saxes. Catch excellent blues and singer/songwriter stuff every night of the week at **Ain't Nothing But The Blues Bar (Map 10)**, or Denmark Street's **12 Bar Club (Map 12)**. Latin jazz lurks at Archway's **Caipirinha Jazz Bar (Map 52)**. For world music, the **Barbican Centre (Map 7)** leads the pack, but is easily beaten in atmosphere stakes by the **Union Chapel (Map 80)**, an Islington church doubling as one of London's most beautiful venues and in scummy stakes by **Dingwalls (Map 71)** who continue to expand their programming. The home of folk is the brilliant **Cecil Sharp House (Map 70)**. If classical music is your cup of tea, look beyond the obvious venues and settle amid the great acoustics of Chelsea's **Cadogan Hall (Map 19)**, the historical brilliance of Hackney's **Sutton House (Map 87)** or the magnificent **Wigmore Hall (Map 2)**, in Mayfair.

Map 1 · Marylebone (West)

Ruby Lo	23 Orchard St	020 7486 3671	Dimly-lit, sexy bar with kick ass Mojitos.

Map 2 · Marylebone (East)

Claridge's Bar	55 Brook St	020 7629 8860	Posh and plush and Art Deco. More champagne!
Inn 1888 East	21 Devonshire St	020 7486 7420	Quiet pint perfection.
Moors Bar	57 Paddington St	020 8348 4161	Hub for well-off media types with films, music and booze.
The Phoenix	37 Cavendish Sq	020 7493 8003	A quirky gem amidst an ocean of crappy chain bars.

Map 3 · Fitzrovia   *Address*

100 Club	100 Oxford St	020 7636 0933	Ancient club that's seen off Nazi bombs and Sex Pistols.
The Albany	240 Great Portland St	020 7387 0221	Swanky, but nice. And the music's good.
Bourne & Hollingsworth	28 Rathbone Pl	020 7636 8228	Fine Fitzrovian basement boutique.
Bradleys Spanish Bar	42 Hanway St	020 7636 0359	60's rock joint with awesome jukebox and disgusting toilets.
Bricklayers Arms	31 Gresse St	020 7636 5593	Advertising types fake no-nonsense boozing.
Charlotte Street Hotel	15 Charlotte St	020 7806 2000	Dirty gossip over dirty martinis.
The Fitzroy Tavern	16 Charlotte St	020 7580 3714	Sam Smith's, anyone?
Hakkasan	8 Hanway Pl	020 7927 7000	Sleek, blue-lit boutique. For saketinis and rose petal martinis.
The Jerusalem Tavern	55 Britton St	020 7490 4281	A tiny old wooden gem of a pub. And organic ale.
Market Place	11 Market Pl	020 7079 2020	Warm buzz. Hot crowd. Cool prices.
Northumberland Arms	43 Goodge St	020 7637 3806	Cosy, old-style bar with a local feel.
Punk	14 Soho St0	084 5094 5195	Starf***er central. But kinda fun.
The Rising Sun	46 Tottenham Ct Rd	020 7636 6530	Bordering studentland and Fitzrovia; pretty name, less pretty pub.
The Roxy	3 Rathbone Pl	020 7255 1098	Hip subterranean hangout. More chicks than dicks.
The Social	5 Little Portland St	020 7636 4992	Fab music, nonchalant surroundings and plenty of trendsters.
The Yorkshire Grey	46 Langham St	020 7636 4788	Upstairs is perfect when Oxford Street's pissing you off.

Map 4 · Bloomsbury (West)

All Star Lanes	Victoria House, Bloomsbury Pl	020 7025 2676	You'll be bowled over. Oh yes you will.
Bloomsbury Bowling Lanes	Bedford Way	020 7183 1979	As cool as bowling gets.

The Fly	36 New Oxford	020 7688 8994	For your quick indie fix on New Oxford.
Marquis of Cornwallis	31 Marchmont St	020 7278 8355	Chilled couches.
Old Crown	33 New Oxford St	020 7836 9121	After-work bar that takes itself very seriously.
The Plough	27 Museum St	020 7636 7964	Fancy a bite? Vampyre Society meetings held here monthly.
Point 101	101 New Oxford St	020 7379 3112	Even mass murderers on day-release get in here.
The Princess Louise	208 High Holborn	020 7405 8816	Victorian gin palace now serving cheap but good lager.
ULU	1 Malet St	020 7664 2000	Student union, student prices, student bands.

Map 5 · Bloomsbury (East)

06 St Chad's Place	6 St Chad's Pl	020 7278 3355	Stylish wine bar with plastic chairs! SOOO avant-garde, dahhhling!
The Blue Lion	13 Gray's Inn Rd	020 7405 4422	Pool table!
Calthorpe Arms	25 Gray's Inn Rd	020 7278 4732	Impressive old man pub.
Duke of York	156 Clerkenwell Rd	020 7837 8548	You and a hundred cycle couriers.
King's Cross Social Club	2 Brittania Street	020 7278 4252	Where to go and be social in King's Cross apparently
Monto Water Rats	328 Gray's Inn Rd	020 7837 4412	No rats here, only the best up-and-coming bands.
The Perseverance	63 Lamb's Conduit St	020 7405 8278	Bustling, young and semi-trendy.
Smithy's	15 Leeke St	020 7278 5949	Our lunchtime to late-night-wind-down friend.

Map 6 · Clerkenwell

Bandstand Busking	Northampton Sq		Free acoustic gigs in summer. Dreamy.
The Betsey Trotwood	56 Farringdon Rd	020 7253 4285	Thoroughly likable Shepherd Neame pub renowned for live music.
The Boadicea	292 St John St	020 7354 9993	Full of students paying their lecturers off with pints.
Café Kick	43 Exmouth Market	020 7837 8077	Creaky, Latin American table football café.
Cicada	132 St John St	020 7608 1550	Gorgeous Art Deco interior, original and classic cocktails.
Dollar Grills and Martinis	2 Exmouth Market	020 7278 0077	Forget the grills, go with the martinis.
The Dovetail	9 Jerusalem Passage	020 7490 7321	Small, but perfectly formed Clerkenwell sister to Broadway Market's The Dove.
Filthy McNasty's	68 Amwell St	020 7837 6067	Disappointingly un-filthy or nasty. Sigh.
The Harlequin	27 Arlington Way	079 7565 2669	Livingroom boozer.
Old Red Lion	418 St John St	020 7837 7816	Theatre pub legend.
The Slaughtered Lamb	34 Great Sutton St	020 7253 1516	Dimly-lit pub that's still packing in the Clerkenwell crowd.
The Three Kings	7 Clerkenwell Close	020 7253 0483	Quirky pub that dies on weekends.
The Wilmington Arms	69 Rosebery Ave	020 7837 1384	Staff have 'arsehole' tattooed on their foreheads. .

Map 8 · Liverpool Street / Broadgate

The Light	233 Shoreditch High St	020 7247 8989	Light at the end of the tunnel for city revellers.
Lounge Bohemia	1 Great Eastern St	077 2070 7000	Vintage martinis whizz up for neo-avant-garde pretenses.
The Red Lion	1 Eldon St	020 7247 5381	Drinkers near Moorgate can't be choosers. So there.
Sosho	2 Tabernacle St	020 7920 0701	It's so Sosho darhling.

Map 9 · Mayfair / Green Park

1707 Wine Bar	181 Piccadilly	020 7734 8040	Empty Fortnum & Mason's wine cellar.
bbar	43 Buckingham Palace Rd	020 7958 7000	Get drunk liberally with Elizabeth's back.
Funky Buddah	15 Berkeley St	020 7495 2596	Overpriced, overrated, tacky Z-list haunt. Apart from that, it's great!
Mahiki	1 Dover St	020 7493 9529	Crushingly tropical cocktail bar. Pineapples a-go-go.
Shepherd's Tavern	50 Hertford St	020 7499 3017	For drinking within Shepherd's Market.

Map 10 · Piccadilly / Soho (West)

22 Below	22 Great Marlborough St	020 7437 4106	Table-service cocktail lounge - without being snooty. We love it.
5th View	203 Piccadilly	020 7851 2433	Spill Bloody Marys over books in full view of Big Ben.
Ain't Nothing But The Blues Bar	20 Kingly St	020 7287 0514	Bracingly raw music in a tiny frontroom.
Cheers Bar	72 Regent St	020 7494 3322	Sitcom-themed Americana; wags shouting 'Norm!' at regular intervals.
Courthouse Bar	19 Great Marlborough St	020 7297 5555	Drink where Oscar Wilde was in the clink.
Green and Red	51 Bethnal Green Rd	020 7749 9670	Tequila bar worth its post-shot salt - you're spoilt for choice.
John Snow	39 Broadwick St	020 7437 1344	Soho drinkers! Sam Smith's full range and a relaxed upstairs!
Lucky Voice	52 Poland St	020 7439 3660	Why is this London's best karaoke bar? The dress up box.
Milk & Honey	61 Poland St	020 7065 6840	The promised land of after-hours cocktails. Members club, so join.
The Pigalle Club	215 Piccadilly	020 7644 1420	Ladies and gentleman, welcome to the 40s.
Red	5 Kingly St	020 7434 3417	Soho cocktail madness. Plush, sexy and red.
Strawberry Moons	15 Heddon St	020 7437 7300	Dig the cheese, with your new squeeze.

Map 11 · Soho (Central)

Blue Posts	22 Berwick St	020 7437 5008	Unreformed, scuzzy boozer.
The Blue Posts	28 Rupert St	020 7437 1415	Hey, a decent pub in Soho.
Cafe Boheme	13 Old Compton St	020 7734 0623	Beautiful bar to prop up and people watch.
Candy Bar	4 Carlisle St	020 7287 5041	Soho's premier all-girl venue.

Arts & Entertainment • **Nightlife**

The Comedy Store	1 Oxendon St	084 4847 1728	It ain't world famous for no reason, chuckles.
De Hems	11 Macclesfield St	020 7437 2494	Dutch bar with brain-cell-annihilatingly strong beer. Hic!
The Endurance	90 Berwick St	020 7437 2944	Hang-out for loud media twats.
Freedom	66 Wardour St	020 7734 0071	Neon green cocktail kitsch.
The French House	49 Dean St	020 7437 2799	Boho Soho hang-out for eccentrics.
LVPO	50 Dean St	020 7317 9260	A labyrinth of candlelit corners and sophisticated conversation.
Madame Jojo's	8 Brewer St	020 7734 3040	Unpretentious club where you won't remain single for too long.
Shadow Lounge	5 Brewer St	020 7317 9270	Gay chi chi lounge.
Village	81 Wardour St	020 7478 0530	Tacky, flirtatious Soho gay bar.

Map 12 • Soho (East)

12 Bar Club	22 Denmark St	020 7240 2622	Ludicrously tiny live club with singer/songwriter focus.
The Borderline	16 Manette St	020 7734 5547	Cool basement club, bizarrely got up in Tex-Mex decor.
Comptons	53 Old Compton St	020 7479 7961	Crammed gay pub.
Crobar	17 Manette St	020 7439 0831	Heavy metal and cheap bourbon. Be a man for once.
G-A-Y Bar	30 Old Compton St	020 7494 2756	Poptastic gay boozer.
G-A-Y Late	5 Goslett Yard	020 7734 9858	Cheap drinks and pop videos wipe out brain functions 'til 3 am.
Garlic & Shots	14 Frith St	020 7734 9505	Drunken vampires beware.
Green Carnation	5 Greek St	020 7434 3323	Sexy, Oscar Wilde-inspired lounge that Oscar would have approved of.
Jazz After Dark	9 Greek St	020 7734 0545	Tunes and cheap drinks, until LATE.
Karaoke Box	18 Frith St	020 7494 3878	A bit gritty but one of London's cheaper karaoke bars.
Ku Bar	30 Lisle St	020 7437 4303	Newly relocated gay bar for the young and clueless.
Lab	12 Old Compton St	020 7437 7820	London Academy of Bartending - they know how to make martinis.
Montagu Pyke	105 Charing Cross Rd	020 7287 6039	Cheap beer - in the West End.
Ronnie Scott's Jazz Club	47 Frith St	020 7439 0747	Original, and still the best.
The Royal George	133 Charing Cross Rd, Goslett Yard	020 7734 8837	Busy, but the crowd's nice. Board games and food.
The Toucan	19 Carlisle St	020 7437 4123	Small and snug central bolthole for Guinness.

Map 13 • Covent Garden

AKA	18 W Central St	020 7836 0110	Proper drinks and proper DJs. And pizza for in-between.
Bunker	41 Earlham St	020 7240 0606	Beer brewed in front of your eyes.
The Cross Keys	31 Endell St	020 7836 5185	Tiny old-school boozer.
The End	18 W Central St	020 7419 9199	The beginning is the beginning. This pioneering club's still rockin' it.
Freud	198 Shaftesbury Ave	020 7240 9933	Intimate basement bar that used to be Alex of Blur's living room. Literally.
Guanabara	Parker St	020 7242 8600	Brasil. But in Holborn.
The Lamb and Flag	33 Rose St	020 7497 9504	Cobbled lane leads to a crowded but gloriously timeless inn.
Poetry Cafe	22 Betterton St	020 7420 9887	Eat, drink, write, listen or yes, PERFORM!

Map 14 • Holborn / Temple

Cittie of Yorke	22 High Holborn	020 7242 7670	Soe olde it's name has extra e's. A marvellouse pube.
The Enterprise	38 Red Lion St	020 7269 5901	More Captain Cook than Captain Kirk.
The Lamb	92 Lamb's Conduit St	020 7405 0713	Legendary little place with Victorian touches.
Na Zdrowie The Polish Bar	11 Little Turnstile	020 7831 9679	With 50 types of vodka, even beetroot soup tastes good.
The Seven Stars	53 Carey St	020 7242 8521	Tiny, slightly dusty bar frequented by barristers.
Temple Bar Bar	Temple Pl	020 7836 3555	A touch of Bertie Wooster open to all.
Tutu's	Surrey St	020 7848 1588	King's College students' very own nightclub.
Volupte	9 Norwich St	020 7831 1622	They call it burlesque, we call it strippers with tassles.

Map 15 • Blackfriars / Farringdon

Corney & Barrow	10 Paternoster Sq	020 7618 9520	Champagne breakfast, anyone?
The Deux Beers	3 Hatton Wall	020 7405 9777	Home of the original politically incorrect 100 shooter list.
Fabric	77 Charterhouse St	020 7336 8898	Debauched club mecca for gurners of all persuasions.
Fox and Anchor	115 Charterhouse St	020 7012 3702	Amazing interior and the tankards make up for the wankers.
The Hat and Tun	3 Hatton Wall	020 7242 4747	Home of the original politically incorrect 100 shooter list.
Smithfield Bar & Grill	2 W Smithfield	020 7246 0900	Suits, suits, suits. And chandeliers, jazz and cocktails. And suits.
Ye Olde Cheshire Cheese	154 Fleet St	020 7353 6170	Get tanked up where Dickens used to. Historic.
Ye Olde London	42 Ludgate Hill	020 7248 1852	It ain't Olde, really, but it sells beer.
Ye Olde Mitre	1 Ely Ct	020 7405 4751	Elizabeth I used to dance here, don't you know?!

Map 16 · Square Mile (West)

Hatchet	28 Garlick Hill	020 7236 0720	Lost in the City? Escape here.
The Mansion House	44 Cannon St	020 7248 1700	Out of the tube, into the House.
The Samuel Pepys	48 Upper Thames St	020 7489 1871	Find it and be rewarded with Thames views.
Ye Olde Watling	29 Watling St	020 7653 9971	Squeeze in.

Map 17 · Square Mile (East)

The Counting House	50 Cornhill	020 7283 7123	A truly magnificent (former) bank. That sells beer now.
Grand Cafe & Bar	The Ctyard, Royal Exchange	020 7618 2480	The courtyard of the Royal Exchange. Fancy, eh?

Map 18 · Tower Hill / Aldgate

Dion City	52 Leadenhall St	020 7702 9111	Veuve Clicquot La Grande Dame Rose, anyone?
Kenza	10 Devonshire Sq	020 7929 5533	Belly-dancers, cocktails & couscous.
Mary Janes	64 Minories	020 7481 8195	Inconspicuous perspex floor catches out the knickerless.
The Minories	64-73 Minories	020 7702 1658	Cavernous boozer by day, thumping disco by night.
Pepys Bar at the Novotel Hotel	10 Pepys St	020 7265 6000	Get on the Kir Royales and kiss tomorrow goodbye.
Prism	147 Leadenhall St	020 7256 3875	Cocktails underneath the former Bank of New York.
Revolution	140 Leadenhall St	020 7929 4233	Vodka-drenched, vault-like DJ bar that couldn't care less about the revolution.
1f Bar	18 Houndsditch	020 7729 2973	Does cool well.

Map 19 · Belgravia

The Blue Bar	The Berkeley Hotel, Wilton Pl	020 7235 6000	It's blue. Mindbogglingly so.
Nag's Head	53 Kinnerton St	020 7235 1135	No mobiles allowed. Says it all.
The Plumber's Arms	14 Lower Belgrave St	020 7730 4067	Tradesman's pub from days of yore. Ask about Lord Lucan.
Wilton Arms	71 Kinnerton St	020 7235 4854	A Shepherd Neame pub? In Belgravia?

Map 20 · Victoria / Pimlico (West)

The Cardinal	23 Francis St	020 7834 7260	Easier to like than to find.
Cask & Glass	39 Palace St	020 7834 7630	Teeny tiny, English country garden-esque drinking hole. Flower-festooned frontage, real ale.

Map 21 · Pimlico (East)

Morpeth Arms	58 Millbank	020 7834 6442	Where Millbank prisoners used to escape to.

Map 22 · Westminster

The Albert	52 Victoria St	020 7222 5577	Distinguished, well-preserved period pub. Tourist haunt but rightly so.
The Cinnamon Club	30 Great Smith St	020 7222 2555	Cocktail classiness inside the Old Westminster Library. Try finding it.
The Speaker	46 Great Peter St	020 7222 1749	Good after-worker with guest ales.
St. Stephen's Tavern	10 Bridge St	020 7925 2286	Tiny pub with character, despite being on tourist trail.
Two Chairmen	39 Dartmouth St	020 7222 8694	Public servants galore! Decent pub for this area though.

Map 23 · St. James's

Aura	48 St James's St	020 7499 9999	If you ain't on the list, you ain't coming in. Seriously.
ICA	The Mall	020 7930 3647	Cutting edge arts complex/bar, weirdly stuck on the upper-crust Mall.
The Sports Cafe	80 Haymarket	020 7766 4687	Umpteen screens of international sport distract from appalling service/grub.

Map 24 · Trafalgar Square / The Strand

Asia de Cuba	45 St Martin's Lane	020 7300 5588	For rum-drinking with the jet set.
The Chandos	29 St Martins Lane	020 7836 1401	All Trafalgar Square pubs are tourist traps? Think again.
The Coal Hole	91 Strand	020 7379 9883	Genuine old style.
Covent Garden Comedy Club	The Arches, Off Villiers St	079 6007 1340	Good acts play to a friendly crowd drinking awful beer.
Gordon's Wine Bar	47 Villiers St	020 7930 1408	Candle-lit vaults. Romantic perfection.
Heaven	Under the Arches, off Villiers St	020 7930 2020	Epicentre of London's late night gay scene.
Maple Leaf	41 Maiden Ln	020 7240 2843	Just don't ask which State they're from.
Punch & Judy	The Covent Garden Piazza	020 7379 0923	Naff, naff, naff. 'Nuff said?
Retro Bar	2 George Ct	020 7321 2811	Chilled gay bar down from Charing Cross in a small alley.
Roadhouse	35 The Piazza	020 7240 6001	"You're the one that I want, ooh-ooh-ooh"
The Sherlock Holmes	10 Northumberland St	020 7930 2644	Unintentionally sinister, must-see Holmes waxwork upstairs. Expect bad dreams.
The Ship and Shovell	1 Craven Passage	020 7839 1311	A pub made of two pubs, both obsessed with Sherlock Holmes.
Zoo Bar & Club	13 Bear St	020 7839 4188	Wake up with someone new.

Map 26 · Maida Hill

The Skiddaw	46 Chippenham Rd	020 7286 7815	West London trendy hang out. Great Sunday roast.

Map 27 · Maida Vale

The Bridge House	13 Westbourne Terrace Rd	020 7266 4326	Canal views and comedy. Lovely.
E Bar	2 Warrington Crescent	020 7432 8455	Basement lounge for a quiet drink.
Robert Browning	15 Clifton Rd	020 7286 2732	Cheapo boozer in posh surroundings.
The Warwick Castle	6 Warwick Pl	020 7266 0921	Down-to-earth drinking in Maida Vale. Indeed.
The Waterway	54 Formosa St	020 7266 3557	Try not to fall into the canal.

Map 28 · Ladbroke Grove / Notting Hill (West)

Julie's Bar	135 Portland Rd	020 7229 8331	Pleasantly posh wine bar full of pleasantly posh ladies.

Map 29 · Notting Hill Gate

Black Cherry	21 Lordship Ln	020 8299 8877	Oh ya, only the boutique-iest of cocktails here.
Mau Mau	265 Portobello Rd	020 7229 8528	Ace mojitos and Thursdays open-mic. Wear your dancing shoes.
Montgomery Place	31 Kensington Park Rd	020 7792 3921	The mixers rock. And they know it.
Notting Hill Arts Club	21 Notting Hill Gate	020 7460 4459	Indie cave with bands, lurid projections and teenagers.
Sun in Splendour	7 Portobello Rd	020 7792 0914	Notting Hill denizens' choice.
Uxbridge Arms	13 Uxbridge St	020 7727 7326	Warm little place full of eccentric old toffs.
Windsor Castle	114 Campden Hill Rd	020 7243 8797	A wood-panelled piece of pub history.

Map 30 · Bayswater

The Cow	89 Westbourne Park Rd	020 7221 0021	Lovely pub. Let down by braying trustafarians.

Map 31 · Paddington

The Royal Exchange	26 Sale Pl	020 7723 3781	Irish boozer; amazing homemade pies

Map 32 · Shepherd's Bush (West)

Bush Hall	310 Uxbridge Rd	020 8222 6955	The red carpet, the ornate walls…the sheer beauty!
The Goldhawk	122 Goldhawk Rd	020 8576 6921	A pub, ladies and gentleman.
The Queen Adelaide	412 Uxbridge Rd	020 8746 2573	Chic gastropub serving the West Bush.
White Horse	31 Uxbridge Rd	020 8723 4531	Did you call my pint a slag? Outside, now!

Map 33 · Shepherd's Bush

Albertine	1 Wood Ln	020 8743 9593	Drink wine with the Beep set.
Ginglik	1 Shepherd's Bush Green	020 7348 8968	Members-only underground ex-toilets. Join free on the door.
Shepherd's Bush Empire	Shepherd's Bush Green	020 8354 3300	Still among London venueland's finest.

Map 34 · West Kensington / Olympia

The Cumberland Arms	29 N End Rd	020 7371 6806	Where long hard days become good again.
Famous 3 Kings	171 North End Rd	020 7603 6071	Brilliant atmosphere for big matches, especially rugby. Pool tables too.
Plum Bar	380 Kensington High St	020 7603 3333	Dying for a drink in Kensington? Well there.

Map 35 · Kensington

Builders Arms	1 Kensington Ct Pl	020 7937 6213	Boozy haven from High Street Kensington's shopping madness.

Map 36 · South Kensington / Gloucester Rd

Boujis	43 Thurloe St	020 7584 2000	If you want to see the two princes drunk. And only then.

Map 38 · Chiswick

Carvosso's	210 Chiswick High Rd	020 8995 9121	For a glass of wine before dinner.
George IV	185 Chiswick High Rd	020 8994 4624	Fullers pies, real ale and a comedy club on the High Road? Sweet.
The Packhorse & Talbot	145 Chiswick High Rd	020 8994 0360	A Chiswick institution. Proper British pub…with live jazz?! Truly.

Map 39 · Stamford Brook

The Raven	375 Goldhawk Rd	020 8748 6977	A bit grubby on the outside but £4 handmade pies are part of the appeal.

Map 40 · Goldhawk Rd / Ravenscourt Park

The Dove	19 Upper Mall	020 8748 9474	So perfect for dates that Charles II brought Nell Gwynne here.
Ruby Grand	227 King St	020 8748 3391	Self-proclaimed purveyor of elegance.

Map 41 · Hammersmith

Brook Green Hotel	170 Shepherd's Bush Rd	020 7603 2516	Lost between Hammersmith and Shepherd's Bush? Fear not.
The Distillers	64 Fulham Palace Rd	020 8748 2834	Chandelier clad pub-bar with ace live music and comedy in The Regal Room.
Hammersmith Apollo	45 Queen Caroline St	084 4844 4748	Still West London's best music venue
Lyric Hammersmith	King St	087 1221 1729	Hammersmith's hottest home of hentertainment..

Map 42 · Baron's Court

Colton Arms	187 Greyhound Road	020 7385 6956	If you're not already a regular, you'll wish you were.
The Curtains Up	28 Comeragh Rd	020 7386 7543	Pub which keeps actors in the basement.
The Fulham Mitre	81 Dawes Rd	020 7386 8877	Young, trendy Fulhamites like it. We don't.
Queen's Arms	171 Greyhound Rd	020 7386 5078	Relaxed and comfy local boozer with tip top Sunday roasts.

Map 44 · Chelsea

Brinkley's	47 Hollywood Rd	020 7351 1683	Enter the cougar's lair.
The Duke of Clarence	148 Old Brompton Rd	020 7373 1285	All leather seats and wooden floors. Cool spot for a drink after work.
Rumi	531 Kings Rd	020 7823 3362	Fulham's secret, chic and cosy jewel.

Map 45 · Chelsea (East)

The Anglesea Arms	15 Selwood Terrace	020 7373 7960	4th Best Pub in the UK, says The Morning Advertiser Industry.
Apartment 195	195 Kings Rd	020 7349 4468	Hire your personal Kings Road party apartment.
Chelsea Potter	119 Kings Rd	020 7352 9479	Chelsea old school.
The Drayton Arms	153 Old Brompton Rd	020 7835 2301	Low-lit Victorian pub with mismatched chairs and a great beer selection.
The Pig's Ear	35 Old Church St	020 7352 2908	Quirky, restored boozer. Deep fried pigs ear anyone? Seriously.

Map 47 · Fulham (West)

The Crabtree Tavern	Rainville Rd	020 7385 3929	Great riverside location. So-so pub.

Map 48 · Fulham

Wheatsheaf	582 Fulham Rd	020 7384 1444	Slouch sofas and soft lighting with great food. Quiz on Thursday evenings.

Map 49 · Parson's Green

Amuse Bouche	51 Parsons Green Lane	020 7371 8517	Fizzy fun.
Duke on the Green	235 New Kings Road	020 7736 2777	If only all pub food was this good (but half the price).
The Establishment	45-47 Parsons Green Ln	020 7384 2418	British favourites meet retro cool. Pie and...Pimms anyone?
The White Horse	1 Parson's Green	020 7736 2115	Victorian pub and a beer drinker's heaven. Book a table.

Map 50 · Sand's End

606 Club	90 Lots Rd	020 7352 5953	Great jazz venue. If you like ten minute sax solos.

Map 51 · Sand's End

The Angel Inn	37 Highgate High St	020 8341 5913	Lively local with board games and unusual beers.
The Boogaloo	312 Archway Rd	020 8340 2928	Not as cool as it thinks it is.
The Flask	77 Highgate West Hill	020 8348 7346	Great beers, great food, great place. Really, it is.
Prince Of Wales	53 Highgate High St	020 8340 0445	Friendly local for posh Highgaters and their even posher dogs.
The Victoria	28 N Hill	020 8340 6091	Try to catch the Sunday sing-along sessions.
The Woodman	414 Archway Rd	020 8340 3016	Reformed fight club with gastropub intentions.
The Wrestlers	98 North Rd	020 8340 4297	Branded "best pub in Highgate" by residents.

Map 52 · Archway (North)

Caipirinha Jazz Bar	177 Archway Rd	020 8342 8146	Cosiness! Cocktails! Latin jazz! Sherpa required to find it!
The Winchester Pub Hotel	206 Archway Rd	020 8374 1690	Wonky-floored palace of boozy delight.

Map 53 · Crouch End

Harringay Arms	153 Crouch Hill	020 8340 4243	No music, plenty of beer.
The Hope & Anchor	128 Tottenham Ln	020 8340 3051	Proper local.
The King's Head	2 Tottenham Ln	020 8340 102	Plenty of funny business.
The Queens Pub & Dining Rooms	26 Broadway Parade	020 8340 2031	God save the Queens.
The Wishing Well	22 Topsfield Parade, Tottenham Lane	020 8340 1096	Goodbye Crouch End gastropub, hello Hornsey cheap boozer.

Map 55 · Harringay

The Beaconsfield	359 Green Lanes	020 8800 2153	Friendly local. The footy's always on!
The Garden Ladder	501 Green Lanes	020 8348 8553	Relaxed place with interesting guest ales.
The Salisbury	1 Grand Parade, Green Lanes	020 8800 9617	A local's secret...no longer! Exceptional.

Map 56 · Hampstead Village

The Flask	14 Flask Walk	020 7435 4580	Hampstead alleyway classic that's been refitted. But nicely so.
The Freemasons Arms	32 Downshire Hill	020 7433 6811	Lovely beer garden.
Holly Bush	22 Holly Mount	020 7435 2892	It's hidden. It's a gem. Really.

Map 57 · Hampstead Heath

The Garden Gate	14S End Rd	020 7435 4938	Nice pub with garden for those sunny days. (yeah right)
The Magdala	2 South Hill Park	020 7435 2503	Gastropub and site of Ruth Ellis's infamous shooting of husband outside the joint.
Roebuck	15 Pond St	020 7433 6871	Somewhere between cosy pub and stylish bar. And good at it.
The White Horse	154 Fleet Rd	020 7485 2112	Yet another pub on the Thai food bandwagon.

Map 58 · Parliament Hill / Dartmouth Park

Bar Lorca	156 Fortress Rd	020 7485 1314	Spanish beer. Spanish tapas.
The Bull and Last	168 Highgate Rd	020 7267 3641	Good place for a post-Heath pint.
The Dartmouth Arms	35 York Rise	020 7485 3267	A fire. Dogs. Old gits. The perfect local.
Duke of St. Albans	Highgate Road	020 7209 0385	Pretty dodgy at times, but also the only pub around.

Map 59 · Tufnell Park

Boston Arms	178 Junction Rd	020 7272 8153	Ferociously scruffy but friendly Irish pub, with rock pit attached.
The Dome	178 Junction Rd	020 7272 8153	Fast becoming our favourite venue!
The Hideaway	114 Junction Rd	020 7561 0779	Beer, pizza, dancing. What else do you need?
The Lord Palmerston	33 Dartmouth Park Hill	020 7485 1578	Gone a bit plastic, but still worth it.
The Star	47 Chester Rd	020 7263 9067	It's a star.

Map 60 · Archway

Archway Tavern	1 Archway Close	020 7272 2840	Cheap beer, plentiful fisticuffs.
The Mother Red Cap	665 Holloway Rd	020 7263 7082	Begorra! Bejesus! Be better off going to another boozer!

Map 61 · Holloway (North)

Nambucca	596 Holloway Rd	020 7272 7366	Self-proclaimed cult venue.
The Quays	471 Holloway Rd	020 7272 3634	Into bad U2 cover bands? Then you'll love it here.
The Swimmer	13 Eburne Rd	020 7281 4632	No running, diving in the shallow end, or heavy petting.

Map 62 · Finsbury Park

The Faltering Fullback	19 Perth Rd	020 7272 5834	Tardis-like local. Avoid match nights unless you're a Gooner

Map 63 · Manor House

The Brownswood Park Tavern	271 Green Lanes	020 8809 2846	Enter, before Manor House drives you mad.
The Manor Club	277 Seven Sisters Rd	078 2823 2869	Once a historic pub, now a strip club. No brainer.

Map 64 · Stoke Newington

The Auld Shillelagh	105 Stoke Newington Church St	020 7249 5951	The best Guinness in London; you won't leave standing up.
Londesborough	36 Barbauld Rd	020 7254 5865	Stokey trendies on leather sofas.
Rose and Crown	199 Stoke Newington Church St	020 7254 7497	Sunday roasts to die for and step-back-in-time décor.
Ryan's Bar	Stoke Newington Church S	020 7275 7807	Boho cafe and venue with a noise limiter! Pussies.

| The Shakespeare | 57 Allen Rd | 020 7254 4190 | The Bard would be proud. |
| White Hart | 69 Stoke Newington High St | 020 7254 6626 | Huge pub, huge beer garden—really it's huge. |

Map 65 • West Hampstead

The Czech and Slovak Bar	74 West End Lane	020 7372 0131	Go Czech.
The Good Ship	289 Kilburn High Rd	079 4900 8253	Where Kilburn takes music seriously.
The Luminaire	311 High Rd	020 7372 7123	Regular winner of "best live venue" awards, despite the weird decor.

Map 66 • Finchley Road / Swiss Cottage

| Ye Olde Swiss Cottage | 98 Finchley Rd | 020 7722 3487 | What can we say. |

Map 67 • Belsize Park

| The Washington | 50 England's Ln | 020 7722 8842 | Monday night is pub quiz night. |

Map 68 • Kilburn High Road / Abbey Road

| The Clifton | 96 Clifton Hill | 020 7372 3427 | Not as secret as they want you to believe. But very nice. |

Map 69 • St. John's Wood

| The Star | 38 St. Johns Wood Terrace | 020 7722 1051 | Drink face-to-face with a huge Highland Terrier. |

Map 70 • Primrose Hill

The Albert	11 Princess Rd	020 7722 1886	A local. Cosy and relaxed.
Cecil Sharp House	2 Regents Park Rd	020 7485 2206	Sword dancing and Olde Stuffe.
The Engineer	65 Gloucester Ave	020 7722 0950	The classy chandeliers say it all.
The Lansdowne	90 Gloucester Ave	020 7483 0409	Home of the beautiful people.
Princess of Wales	22 Chalcot Rd	020 7722 0354	Traditional pub with occasional jazz performances.
Queens No. 1	1 Edis St	020 7586 3049	Comfy, quiet local.
Sir Richard Steele	97 Haverstock Hill	020 7483 1261	Friendly local with quirky decor.

Map 71 • Camden Town / Chalk Farm / Kentish Town (West)

Bar Vinyl	6 Inverness St	020 7482 5545	DJ Bar. And good coffee.
Bartok	78 Chalk Farm Rd	020 7916 0595	Hip, late-night bar with chilled-out sofa feel.
The Constitution	42 St Pancras Way	020 7387 4805	Proper boozer away from the madness of Camden Taaahn.
Dingwalls	Middle Yard	019 2082 3098	Camden Lock's guitar-smashing heartland.
The Dublin Castle	94 Parkway	020 7485 1773	Famous, small, LOUD.
Electric Ballroom	184 Camden High St	020 7485 9006	Scruffy but essential rock haunt, perennially threatened by developers.
The Enterprise	2 Haverstock Hill	020 7485 2659	Literary Irish pub with tiny indie venue upstairs.
Fiddlers Elbow	1 Malden Rd	020 7485 3269	Live music venue pub sans pretention.
Good Mixer	30 Inverness St	020 7916 7929	Ah, remember those halcyon days of Britpop?
The Hawley Arms	2 Castlehaven Rd	020 7428 5979	The Hawley will rise from the ashes. Camden needs it.
Jazz Cafe	5 Parkway	020 7485 6834	A relentless stream of excellent gigs.
Koko	1 Camden High St	087 0432 5527	From Charlie Chaplin to Lenny Kravitz, playing Koko still kicks ass.
The Lock Tavern	35 Chalk Farm Rd	020 7482 7163	Great gigs, Sunday roasts and (unpainfully) hip clientele.
Monkey Chews	2 Queen's Crescent	020 7267 6406	Dark and intimate bar and music venue.
Oxford Arms	265 Camden High St	020 7267 4945	Theatre pub where you may stumble upon Amy Winehouse, maybe.
Proud Camden	Chalk Farm Rd	020 7482 3867	Oh-so-casual, trendy little bar. Fairy lights and arty types.
Quinn's	65 Kentish Town Rd	020 7267 8240	More German beer than you can pronounce.
The Underworld	174 Camden High St	020 7482 1932	Throbbing pit of angry rock and even angrier metal.

Map 72 • Kentish Town

The Abbey Tavern	124 Kentish Town Rd	020 7267 9449	Fairy-lit, casual beer garden with talented DJs on Saturdays.
The Assembly House	292 Kentish Town Rd	020 7485 2031	Massive pub with friendly atmosphere.
The Bull & Gate	389 Kentish Town Rd	020 8826 5000	A gigging institution.
HMV Forum	9 Highgate Rd	020 7428 4099	Good venue for medium-sized bands.
The Pineapple	51 Leverton St	020 7284 4631	Backstreet Victorian with good beers and Thai grub.
Rio's Health Spa	239 Kentish Town Rd	020 7485 0607	Bored of your wife? Swap her here.

Map 73 • Holloway

| The Lord Stanley | 51 Camden Park Rd | 020 7428 9488 | Dark wood, Edwardian interior, fireplace and secret walled garden. |
| Shillibeers | 1 Carpenter's Mews, North Rd | 020 7700 1858 | For relaxed drinking on comfy couches. |

Map 74 • Holloway Road / Arsenal

The Coronet	338 Holloway Rd	020 7609 5014	The smell of old men's piss is abound, but it's cheap!
El Comandante	10 Annette Rd	020 7607 3961	South American vibe in a Victorian pub.
The Garage	20 Highbury Corner	020 7619 6720	Bad sound and a guaranteed black hole in your evening.
Hen and Chickens Theatre Bar	109 St. Paul's Rd	020 7704 2001	All the best pubs have theatres. Fact.

Map 75 • Highbury

Alwyne Castle	83 St Pauls Rd	020 7359 7351	Alright for a pint.
Oak Bar	79 Green Lanes	020 7354 2791	Eclectic programme of events at this mixed/lesbian venue.
The Snooty Fox	75 Grosvenor Avenue	020 7354 9532	Strangely empty - shame for such a great pub.

Map 76 • Edgeware Road / Marylebone (North)

The Perseverance	11 Shroton St	020 7723 7469	Perseverance in finding it will be rewarded.
twotwentytwo	222 Marylebone Rd	020 7631 8000	Grand is the word.
The Volunteer	245 Baker St	020 7486 4091	Grand old Victorian taphouse great for a lively post-work pint.

Map 77 • Mornington Crescent / Regent's Park

The Crown & Anchor	137 Drummond St	020 7383 2681	A pub makeover masterpiece.
Edinboro Castle	57 Mornington Terrace	020 7255 9651	Huge outdoors bit, great BBQ on summer weekends.
Queen's Head & Artichoke	30 Albany St	020 7916 6206	The pinchos are addictive. We have warned, friends.

Map 78 • Euston

The Champagne Bar at St Pancras	Pancras Rd	020 7870 9900	Miss your train!
The Crown & Goose	100 Arlington Rd	020 7485 8008	Delightfully old-fashioned pub with good grub and an open fire.
Lincoln Lounge	52 York Way	020 7837 9339	Arty, quirky and cool. Does King's Cross proud.
Purple Turtle	61 Crowndale Rd	020 7383 4976	Rock club that looks like a wacky goth spaceship.
Scala	275 Pentonville Rd	020 7833 2022	Historic venue with plush edges. If these walls could talk...

Map 79 • King's Cross

The Big Chill House	257 Pentonville Rd	020 7427 2540	Allow staff 28 working days to process your drinks order.
Canal 125	125 Caledonian Rd	020 7837 1924	Upmarket bar that draws a swanky crowd.
Central Station	37 Wharfdale Rd	020 7278 3294	Ominous looking cabaret bar-cum-cruise emporium. Check site first.
Cross Kings	126 York Way	020 7278 8318	Nice little place that tries but usually fails to be 'edgy'.
EGG	200 York Way	020 7609 8364	Big club, big garden, big night out.
Hemingford Arms	128 Hemingford Rd	020 7607 3303	Full of local aleheads.
The Lexington	96 Pentonville Rd	020 7837 5371	Come and support your boyfriend's shit band.
Tarmon	270 Caledonian Rd	020 7607 3242	Character. Lots of character.

Map 80 • Angel / Upper St

25 Canonbury	25 Canonbury Ln	020 7226 0955	You'll never love it as much as it loves itself.
Albert and Pearl	181 Upper St	020 7354 9993	Classy when dark. Garish when lit.
The Angel	3 Islington High St	020 7837 2218	Students. The elderly. The unemployed.
The Angelic	57 Liverpool Rd	020 7278 8433	A sophisticated boozer.
Buffalo Bar	259 Upper St	020 7359 6191	Sweaty, small venue. You'll see them here first.
Camden Head	2 Camden Walk	020 7359 0851	Comedians debut new gags upstairs. Cheap—and mostly cheerful.
The Castle	54 Pentonville Rd	020 7713 1858	Needs breaking in.
Compton Arms	4 Compton Ave	020 7359 6883	Islington's only real pub—or so they say.
The Crown	116 Cloudesley Rd	020 7837 7107	Jovial spot for a quiet pint and Sunday roasts.
Cuba Libre	72 Upper St	020 7354 9998	Tank up with mojitos. Salsa with the barman.
The Drapers Arms	44 Bransbury St	020 7619 0348	Celeb backlash against new CCTV. Big Brother is really watching.
Electrowerkz	7 Torrens St	020 7837 6419	Crumbling rave labyrinth.
Embassy Bar	119 Essex St	020 7226 7901	Wannabe DJs' last real hope.
The Florence	50 Florence St	020 7354 5633	Refurbed, warm Georgian boozer.
The Green Man	144 Essex Rd	020 7226 2692	Eerie inside, scary punters.
Hope And Anchor	207 Upper St	020 7704 2689	Scuzzy pub with even scuzzier bands in the basement.
Islington Academy	16 Parkfield St	020 7288 4400	Grubby live music. Slap on some skinny jeans first.
Islington Tap	80 Liverpool St	020 7354 5111	Vast, ornate ceilings and over-priced beer.
Jury's Inn	60 Pentonville Rd	020 7282 5500	Really? Why did you even buy this book?
Keston Lodge	131 Upper St	020 7354 9535	Just the right side of poncy.
King's Head Theatre & Pub	115 Upper St	020 7226 8561	Proper, good-time boozer.
The Lord Clyde	342 Essex Rd	020 7288 9850	Like boozing in Land of Leather.
Lucky Voice	173 Upper St	020 7354 6280	Singing in private? Like a bathroom with beer.
Marquess Tavern	32 Canonbury St	020 7354 2975	Scruffy locals live on despite gastro revolution.
Myddleton Arms	52 Canonbury Rd	020 7226 4595	Don't those people have, y'know, jobs?

Old Red Lion	418 St John St	020 7837 7816	Theatre pub legend.
The Regent	201 Liverpool Rd	020 7700 2725	Good news: it's finally starting to fray.
Round Midnight: Jazz and Blues Bar	13 Liverpool Rd		Great music and a good atmosphere.
Union Chapel	Compton Terrace	020 7226 3750	God's favourite music venue. Hell, everyone's.

Map 81 · Marquess Tavern

Marquess Tavern	32 Canonbury St	020 7354 2975	Scruffy locals live on, despite gastro revolution.

Map 82 · De Beauvoir Town / Kingsland

Jazz Bar	4 Bradbury St	020 7254 9728	Funk and free cheese. Until 5. Need we say more?
The Northgate	113 Southgate Rd	020 7359 7392	Reliable local despite being—gasp!—a gastro.
The Orwell	382 Essex Rd	020 7288 1914	Drinking in the day. George would be proud.
The Rosemary Branch	2 Shepperton Rd	020 7704 2730	Theatre pub with great selection of ales and hearty fare.
The Vortex	11 Gillett Sq	020 7254 4097	Dalston's only real jazz bar.
The Duke of Wellington	119 Balls Pond Rd	020 7275 7640	Nice little boozer, as they say.

Map 83 · Angel (East) / City Rd (North)

Barrio North	45 Essex Rd	020 7688 2882	Groovy little bar with friendly international vibe. And a caravan!
The Charles Lamb	16 Elia St	020 7837 5040	It's not big, but it's clever.
The Duke of Cambridge	30 St Peter's St	020 7359 3066	Feel self-righteous in the world's first organic pub.
Earl of Essex	25 Danbury St	020 7226 3608	For drinking in the day. In the dark.
The Island Queen	87 Noel Rd	020 7354 8741	Where NFT planned the London guide. Sweet.
The Mucky Pup	39 Queen's Head St	020 7226 2572	The dog's bollocks.
The Narrow Boat	119 St Peters St	020 7288 0572	Cheerful canal-side pub for lazy pints and people-watching.
Offside Bar and Gallery	273 City Rd	020 7253 3306	Like a football stadium, but without anyone pissing in the sinks.
The Old Queen's Head	44 Essex Rd	020 7354 9993	Trendier than the name suggests.
The Wenlock Arms	26 Wenlock Rd	020 7608 3406	Threadbare, battered old boozer with a magnificent range of real ales.

Map 84 · Hoxton

333	333 Old St	020 7739 5949	The Shoreditch grandfather.
The Bricklayer's Arms	63 Charlotte Rd	087 2148 3675	Double bypass heart of 90s Britart scene. Barely still beating.
Cantaloupe	35 Charlotte Rd	020 7729 5566	Of course YOU'RE not a corporate whore.
Cargo	83 Rivington St	020 7739 3440	Cavernous, sterile hole with bad sound but good gigs. Natch.
Charlie Wright's International Bar	45 Pitfield St	020 7490 8345	Does anyone turn up here sober?
Club Aquarium	256 Old St	020 7253 3558	After-hours swimming pool scuzzfest.
Cocomo	323 Old St	020 7613 0315	Cocktail bar with cakes, comfy sofas and scrumptious staff.
East Village	89 Great Eastern St	020 7739 5173	Shoreditch clubbing novice where the DJ is king.
The Elbow Room	97 Curtain Rd	020 7613 1316	Pricey, mildly funky pool joint.
Electricity Showroom	39 Hoxton Sq	020 7739 3939	Shark-infested waters.
Favela Chic	91 Great Eastern St	020 7613 4228	Caipirinha-iovin', shabby-chic bar full of clothes-swapping kwaziness.
The Foundry	84 Great Eastern St	020 7739 6900	Like a pretentious art student's dream bar. In a good way.
The Griffin	93 Leonard St	020 7739 6719	NOT the strip bar of the same name...
Hoxton Square Bar & Kitchen	2 Hoxton Sq	020 7613 0709	Snotty bands and doormen. Wear something uber.
The Legion	348 Old St	020 7729 4441	Free jukebox, quality DJs, cheap beer. Happy times.
The Macbeth	60 70 Hoxton St	020 7749 0600	Hot new bands love it. And so do we.
The Old Blue Last	38 Great Eastern St	020 7739 7033	Until the bass drum WILL bring down that pub ceiling.
Plastic People	147 Curtain Rd	020 7739 6471	Tiny, pitch black musical adventure.
Red Lion	41 Hoxton St	020 7729 7920	Stay forever if you bag the chaise lounge...
The Stag's Head	55 Orsman Rd	020 7739 6741	Run down boozer currently being used for hip gigs.
Strongroom Bar	120 Curtain Rd	020 7426 5103	Shoreditch's last stronghold of unpretentiousness?
Troy Bar	10 Hoxton St	020 7739 6695	A semi-hidden gem with soul and funk music most nights.

Map 85 · Stoke Newington (East)

The Birdcage	58 Stamford Hill	020 8806 6740	High-ceilinged pub with squishy sofas and lived-in feel.
Blush	8 Cazenove Rd	020 7923 9202	Pink pint-parlour with poker and personable patrons (oh please!)
The Royal Sovereign	64 Northwold Rd	020 8806 2449	Drink with the locals.
Stoke Newington Int'l Airport	1-15Leswin Place	079 7128 4912	Eclectic live entertainment is always on the menu.

Map 86 · Dalston / Kingsland

Bar 23	23 Stoke Newington Rd	020 7241 2060	A slice of weirdness with wacked out DJing and drinking.
Bardens Boudoir	38 Stoke Newington Rd	020 7249 9557	Anything can happen in this basement. The beating heart of Dalston's music shenanigans.
Cafe Oto	18 Ashwin St	020 7923 1231	Mysterious new venue importing music from the hinterlands of psychedelia.
Dalston Superstore	117 Kingsland High St	020 7254 2273	Uber hip polysexual squelch-a-thon.
The Haggerston	438 Kingsland Rd	020 7923 3206	Artist-run flea pit. Chaotic crowd surfing most nights.
Marquis of Lansdowne	48 Stoke Newington Rd	020 7254 1104	Pleases long-standing locals and hip Hackneyites alike.
The Moustache Bar	58 Stoke Newington Rd		Follow the moustache (sticker) trail to this trendy/grimy subterranean bar.
Passion	251 Amhurst Rd	020 7254 3667	Tiny basement venue that hosts massive all-nighters.
The Prince George	40 Parkholme Rd	087 1934 1384	Buzzing local favourite. Renowned Monday quiz night, great jukebox.

Map 87 · Hackney Downs / Lower Clapton

Biddle Brothers	88 Lower Clapton Rd	020 8985 7052	Almost trendy oasis for the trendy in an eccentric neighbourhood.
Crooked Billet	84 Upper Clapton Rd	020 8806 2747	Proof that Clapton can still be f***ing terrifying.
Hugo's Speaker Palace	14 Andre St	020 8968 5704	Clandestine speaker cemetery. Very hush-hush and very cool.
Pembury Tavern	90 Amhurst Rd	020 8986 8597	Large selection of microbrews.

Map 88 · Haggerston / Queensbridge Rd

A10 (aka The Russian Bar)	267 Kingsland Rd	n/a	It's hell and it's heaven and we can't make our f'ing minds up.
The Fox	372 Kingsland Rd	020 3215 2093	Half-way stop for Shoreditch-to-Dalston pub crawls.
Passing Clouds	440 Kingsland Rd	020 7168 7146	Back alley arts collective and live venue.
Plaza	161 Kingsland Rd	020 7613 1319	Sometime gig venue, all-the-time scary East End boozer.

Map 89 · London Fields / Hackney Central

Baxter's Court	282 Mare St	020 8525 9010	A chain pub, okay, okay. But check the ladies' toilets!
The Dolphin	165 Mare St	020 8985 3727	Pathos-sodden karaoke occasionally ruined by post-opening art people.
The Dove	24 Broadway Market	020 7275 7617	Belgian beer paradise.
Pub on the Park	19 Martello St	020 7275 9586	Tap for London Fields.
The Old Ship	2 Sylvester Path	020 8986 1641	Nicely refurbed ex-dive.

Map 90 · Homerton / Victoria Park North

Chats Palace Arts Centre	42 Brooksby's Walk	020 8533 0227	Fantastic community arts venue—Hackney classic.
The Lauriston	162 Victoria Park Rd	020 8985 5404	As vamped up as its would-be-village surroundings.
Royal Inn on the Park	111 Lauriston Rd	020 8985 3321	Victoria Park's prime boozer.

Map 91 · Shoreditch / Brick Lane / Spitalfields

93 Feet East	150 Brick Ln	020 7247 3293	Enthusiastic, trendy club (to impress out-of-towners).
Anda De Bridge	42 Kingsland Rd	020 7503 9651	Cocktail party, Caribbean-style.
The Archers	42 Osborn St	020 7247 3826	Nice ole pub that's resisted Shoreditchification. Perfect for pre-curry pints.
Bar Kick	127 Shoreditch High St	020 7739 8700	Lemon-yellow table football gaff.
Bar Music Hall	134 Curtain St	020 7613 5951	Nice wallpaper, free music. Who's complaining?
Bedroom Bar	62 Rivington St	020 7613 5637	Saturday's DJ'n'sax players mean dancing til dawn.
Bethnal Green Working Men's Club	44 Pollard Row	020 7739 7170	Saucy amateur burlesque that still confuses the resident Working Men.
The Big Chill Bar	Dray Walk off Brick Lane	020 7392 9180	Still among Brick Lane's better drinking spots.
Browns	1 Hackney Rd	020 7739 4653	Now really. What would your mother say?
Café 1001	91 Brick Ln`	020 7247 6166	Like a house party. But one where cans cost £3.
The Carpenter's Arms	73 Cheshire St	020 7739 6342	No longer run by the Kray twins' mother, still felonious fun.
Catch	22 Kingsland Rd	020 7729 6097	Reliable active dancefloor, reliable silly hats, reliable good fun.
Comedy Cafe	66 Rivington St	020 7739 5706	Fun venue, but invariably a dud in the line-up.
The Commercial Tavern	142 Commercial St	020 7247 1888	Trusty Shoreditch traditional.
Ditch Bar	145 Shoreditch High St	020 7739 4018	Noisy electro bar/scrum.
Exit	174 Brick Lane	020 7377 2088	Sit in a row with fellow Brick Lane trendies.
The George & Dragon	2 Blackheath Hill	020 8691 3764	Witness the E2 gay clique rev up for imminent carnage.
The Golden Heart	110 Commercial St	020 7247 2158	Has it all: fires, pints and a lazy resident dog.
The Gramophone Bar	60 Commercial St	020 7377 5332	Dark basement venue.
Green & Red	51 Bethnal Green Rd	020 7749 9670	Tequila bar worth its post-shot salt—you're spoilt for choice.
Herbal	10 Kingsland Rd	020 7613 4462	It's small enough to shout at the DJ. And groovy.
Jaguar Shoes	32 Kingsland Rd	020 7729 5830	Happy hipsters behind wide windows.
Joiners Arms	116 Hackney Rd	020 7739 9397	Popular gay pub that knows how to have fun.
Loungelover	1 Whiteby St	020 7012 1234	Kitsch-colonial glitter-ball of a cocktail bar.

The Old Shoreditch Station	1 Kingsland Rd	020 7729 5188	Used to be cool. When it was a train station.
On the Rocks	25 Kingsland Rd	020 7688 0339	Come face to face with oblivion every Friday.
Owl & Pussycat	34 Redchurch St	020 7613 3628	Crooked little place, tucked in the folds of Shoreditch's blubber.
Prague	6 Kingsland Rd	020 7739 9110	The closest you'll ever get to a romantic bar in Shoreditch.
Pride of Spitalfields	3 Heneage St	020 7247 8933	The only East End boozer left on Brick Lane.
Public Life	82 Commercial St	020 7375 1631	Used to be a toilet. Kinda still is. Moronic fun.
The Redchurch	107 Redchurch St	020 7729 8333	Late, loud DJ box.
The Royal Oak	73 Columbia Rd	020 7729 2220	Gentrifying, gentrifying... gentrified.
Shoreditch House	Ebor St	020 7739 5040	Last one in the rooftop pool buys the drinks!
Vibe Bar	91 Brick Ln	020 7247 3479	Bar in a brewery. Feel the vibe?
The Water Poet	9 Folgate St	020 7426 0495	Mismatched chairs, over-stuffed sofas, philosophy and beer.
Ye Olde Axe	69 Hackney Rd	020 7729 5137	Rockabilly-only weekends. That's right: rockabilly-only. Occasional gentleman's club.

Map 92 • Bethnal Green

The Albion	94 Goldsmiths Row	020 7739 0185	Friendly, footy-mad local. All welcome.
Bethnal Green Working Men's Club	44 Pollard Row	020 7739 7170	Saucy amateur burlesque that still confuses the resident Working Men.
The Camel	277 Globe Rd	020 8983 9888	Bethnal Green's best kept secret... D'oh!
Florist	255 Globe Rd	020 8981 1100	The Camel's naughty little sister.
The FymFyg Bar	231 Cambridge Heath Rd	020 7613 1057	The comedian's comedy house: this one knows what it's doing.
Images	483 Hackney Rd	020 7739 5213	When the lapdancing's over, the clubbing madness begins.
The Star of Bethnal Green	359 Bethnal Green Rd	020 7729 0167	Formerly the Pleasure Unit. Still Bethnal Green's live music best.

Map 93 • Globe Town / Mile End (North)

The Approach Tavern	47 Approach Rd	0208 983 3878	Great if you can tolerate the ironic haircuts crew.
The Fat Cat Cafe Bar	221 Grove Rd	020 8983 4353	No fat cats, but a good mix of locals and trendies.
Jongleurs (Bow Wharf)	221 Grove Rd	0844 499 4062	Blandard comedy chain.
The Morgan Arms	43 Morgan St	020 8980 6389	Grab a pint with some gourmet food.
Palm Tree	1 Haverfield Rd	020 8980 2918	Brass walls and retired crooners! Amazingly old-fashioned boozer.
The Victoria	110 Grove Rd	020 8980 6609	Coolified old man's boozer turned hipster joint.

Map 94 • Bow

The Coborn Arms	8 Coborn Rd	020 8980 3793	Nice ales, nice beer garden.
The Young Prince	448 Roman Rd	020 8980 1292	If on Roman Road...

Map 95 • Whitechapel (West) / St Katharine's Dock

The Castle	44 Commercial Rd	020 7481 2361	East End fortress holding it against the City.
Dickens Inn	St Katharine's Way	020 7488 2208	Proof that an awesome location can conquer all.
Prohibition Bar & Grill	1 St. Katherine's Docks	020 7702 4210	Gormless bar.
Rhythm Factory	16 Whitechapel Rd	020 7375 3774	The Libertines' old haunt, with all the grimy 'chic' that implies.

Map 96 • Whitechapel (East) / Shadwell (West) / Wapping

The Captain Kidd	108 Wapping High St	020 7480 5759	Pub with nice Thames-side beer garden.
The Caxton	50 The Highway	020 7481 2961	Opens weekdays at 4am. Depressing, but come here to kick-on.
Indo	133 Whitechapel Rd	020 7247 4926	Very narrow and everything but narrow-minded.
Town of Ramsgate	62 Wapping High St	020 7481 8000	Get nautical.

Map 97 • Stepney / Shadwell (East)

Cable Street Studios	56 Cable St	020 7790 1309	'Artists.' 'Warehouse studios.' 'Parties.' It'll never work.
The George Tavern	373 Commercial Rd	020 7790 7335	Old men, hipsters and blue-collar poets in imperfect harmony.
The Prospect of Whitby	57 Wapping Wall	020 7481 1095	Ye olde pub(e) on ye Thames(e).
Troxy	490 Commercial Rd	020 7790 9000	Glorious art deco palace.

Map 98 • Mile End (South) / Limehouse

The Grapes	76 Narrow St	020 7987 4396	True to its roots East End boozer—natural survivor.

Map 100 • Poplar (West) / Canary Wharf (West)

Bar 38	West India Quay	020 7515 8361	Great inside and out.
Davy's at Canary Wharf	31 Canary Wharf	020 7363 6633	Traditional-style with fine ales, wine and food.
Dion Canary Wharf	Port East Building, West India Quay	020 7987 0001	Docklands warehouse-turned-champagne heaven.
Via Fossa	18 Hertsmere Rd	020 7515 8549	Three floors of bankers...

Map 101 · Poplar (East) / Canary Wharf (East)

The Greenwich Pensioner	28 Bazely St	020 7987 4414	No pensioners and not in Greenwich.
The Resolute	210 Poplar High St	020 7987 1429	In Poplar? Desperate for a drink?

Map 102 · Millwall

Hubbub	269 Westferry Rd	020 7515 5577	Oasis in Docklands desert.

Map 103 · Cubitt Town / Mudchute

The Ferry House	26 Ferry St	020 7537 9587	Beer-drenched docks time capsule.
Lord Nelson	1 Manchester Rd	020 7987 1970	Can I have a half, Nelson?
Waterman's Arms	1 Glenaffric Ave	020 7093 2885	Proper boozer on the Island.

Map 104 · South Bank / Waterloo / Lambeth North

The Anchor & Hope	36 The Cut	020 7928 9898	For that intellectual pre-theatre/dinner chat.
Benugo Bar & Kitchen	Belvedere Rd	020 7401 9000	Cheerily mismatched armchairs welcome students and film buffs alike.
Barrio	14 W Square	020 7801 9548	What balmy Sunday evenings were made for.
Concrete	Southbank Centre	020 7928 4123	Restaurant/bar features Russian beer, food, absinthe.
Cubana	48 Lower Marsh	020 7928 8778	Still riding the mojito trend. But good at them.
The Cut Bar	66 The Cut	020 7928 4400	Enjoy the outdoor terrace with trendy media types and thesps.
Da Vinci's	6 Baylis Rd	020 7928 8099	Cheesy and bizarre late-night fun.
The Fire Station	150 Waterloo Rd	020 7620 2226	Only fun when you're desperate.
The Pit Bar at The Old Vic	The Cut	020 7928 2975	Guzzle champagne with Kevin Spacey and friends.
Royal Festival Hall	Belvedere Rd	084 4875 0073	Increasingly exciting programming amid nicely refurbished surroundings.
Skylon	Belvedere Rd	020 7654 7800	Impress someone with the view, then split the bill.

Map 105 · Southwark / Bankside (West)

Albert Arms	1 Gladstone St	020 7928 6517	Where yuppies meet students meet blow-ins meet locals.
Imbibe	173 Blackfriars Rd	020 7928 3693	Studenty feel, mid-week. Shouty after-workers, otherwise.
Ministry of Sound	103 Gaunt St	087 0060 0010	The sound really IS amazing.
The Prince of Wales	51 St George's Rd	020 7582 9696	Cheap local with downright scary karaoke.
The White Theatre	206 Union St	020 7261 0209	Free aperitivo food excuses their 'TWT' abbreviation.

Map 106 · Bankside (East) / Borough / Newington

The Anchor	34 Park St	020 7407 1577	Did Samuel Johnson have to battle this many tourists?
Belushi's	161 Borough High St	020 7939 9700	Drunk Antipodeans. Karaoke. General carnage.
The Blue-Eyed Maid	173 Borough High St	020 7378 8259	It's never too late for a last drink in Borough.
Brew Wharf	Brew Wharf Yard, Stoney St	020 7378 6601	Beer lovers' heaven.
The George Inn	77 Borough High St	020 7407 2056	Grab a home brew in the dazzlingly ancient George Inn.
The Globe	8 Bedale St	020 7407 0043	Bridget Jones' home? Do we care?
La Cave	6 Borough High St	020 7378 0788	So delightful you'll even start liking the French. Briefly.
The Market Porter	9 Stoney St	020 7407 2495	Market traders and suits neck real ale. Smell the testosterone.
The Rake	14 Winchester Walk	020 7407 0557	Tiny place with a hundred different beers. Honestly, a hundred.
The Roebuck	50 Great Dover St	020 7357 7324	Cool but calm drinkerie for a pre-night-out drink.
The Rose	123 Snowfields	020 7378 6660	Superb backstreet boozer full of human oddities.
Roxy Bar and Screen	128 Borough High St	020 7407 4057	Mingle with baby yuppies at the Roxy Bar & Screen.
The Royal Oak	44 Tabard St	020 7357 7173	Possibly the friendliest landlords in London.
SeOne	Weston St	020 7407 1617	Loud music & louder people.
Shunt Lounge	20 Stainer St	020 7378 7776	Dusty dancing under the railway arches. Membership required.
Southwark Tavern	22 Southwark St	020 7403 0257	Traditional ambience and ordinary fare in ye olde Southwark Tavern.
Wine Wharf	Stoney St	087 0899 8856	If you're as crazy about wine as they are.

Map 107 · Shad Thames

Cable	33 Bermondsey St	020 7403 7730	Get messed up in a dark tunnel. Again.
The Hide	39 Bermondsey St	020 7403 6655	Slightly odd vibe, but cracking drinks.
Hilton London Tower Bridge	5 Tooley St	020 3002 4300	Super-chilled, low-lit relaxation zone for the wealthy.
The Woolpack	98 Bermondsey St	020 7357 9269	Filling lunches, comfy sofas, great garden. Job done.

Map 109 · Southwark Park

Ancient Foresters	282 Southwark Park Rd	020 7394 1633	Surprise charmer in an otherwise grimy area.
The Angel	101 Bermondsey Wall E	020 7394 3214	Sam Smith pub with great views across the river
The Mayflower	117 Rotherhithe St	020 7237 4088	Used to be The Shippe from whenst the Mayflower departed
The Ship	39 St Marychurch St	020 7237 4103	Sunny day? Settle in with a beer and a sarnie.

Map 110 • Rotherhithe (West) / Canada Water

The Albion	20 Albion St	020 72370182	Only if three generations of your family drank here first.
Old Salt Quay	163 Rotherhithe St	020 7394 7108	Pub-by-numbers, but the riverside patio of dreams.

Map 111 • Rotherhithe (East) Surrey Quays

Blacksmith's Arms	257 Rotherhithe St	020 7237 1349	Good enough for the Queen Mum: good enough for us.
Moby Dick	6 Russell Pl, off Greenland Dock	020 7231 6719	Once here, it's hard to leave. Because it's really far from the tube.
Ship & Whale	2 Gulliver St	020 7237 7072	So good we even come for breakfast.
Whelan's	11 Rotherhithe Old Rd	020 7237 9425	Looks rough around the edges, but you could do worse.
Wibbley Wobbley	South Dock Marina, Rope St	020 7232 2320	Great dinky boat-bar, for short people.

Map 112 • Kennington / Elephant and Castle

Corsica Studios	5 Elephant Rd	020 7703 4760	Sweaty music venue with 'home-made' vibe.
Dog House	293 Kennington Rd	020 7820 9310	Like your scruffy, unpretentious younger brother. Made for chill-axing.
Prince of Wales	43 Cleaver Sq	020 7735 9916	Stuart's favourite pub in Kennington.

Map 113 • Walworth

Temple Bar	286 Walworth Rd	020 7703 4117	Only when you really, REALLY need a drink.
The Beehive	60 Carter St	020 7703 4992	The local bit of nice.

Map 114 • Old Kent Road (West) / Burgess Park

Auto-Italia South East	1 Glengall Rd		Frankly amazing artist-run space in an old car showroom!
World Turned Upside Down	145 Old Kent Rd	020 7237 4181	Original headquarters of the Pearly Kings & Queens.

Map 118 • Deptford (Central)

The Lord Palmerston	81 Childers St	020 8692 1575	Fewer brawls than your average Deptford pub.

Map 119 • Deptford (East)

The Bird's Nest	32 Deptford Church St	020 8694 1852	Hilarious 'locals vs. trendies' vibe. Go for monthly Flesh Dunce!
Dog & Bell	116 Prince St	020 8692 5664	Now why can't ALL pubs in Deptford be like this?

Map 120 • Greenwich

Bar du Musee	17 Nelson Rd	020 8858 4710	"You have beautiful eyes, you know that?"
The Greenwich Union	56 Royal Hill	020 8692 6258	Beers galore.
Up The Creek	30 Creek Rd	0208 858 4581	Comedy club (plus comedy dancing at the disco)

Map 122 • Camberwell (East)

The Castle	65 Camberwell Church St	020 7277 2601	Locals, board games and disco.

Map 123 • Peckham

Frank's Cafe and Campari Bar	95 Rye Ln	07943 379 726	Cheap Campari cocktails in a multi-story car park. Pure class.

Map 125 • New Cross Gate

The Montague Arms	289 Queen's Rd	020 7639 4923	Semi-legendary, bizarrely decorated local, staffed by the world's oldest barmen and women.

Map 126 • New Cross *Address*

Amersham Arms	388 New Cross Rd	020 8469 1499	Art school hipdom in grimy New Cross's coolest venue.
Hobgoblin	272 New Cross Rd	020 8692 3193	Get drunk with the Goldsmiths crowd.
New Cross Inn	323 New Cross Rd	020 8691 7222	Someone's gotta keep "the scene" going.

Map 127 • Coldharbour Lane / Herne Hill (West)

The Commercial	210 Railton Rd	020 7733 8783	Roaring fire and mulled wine in winter. Fits like a glove.
Escape Bar and Art	214 Railton Rd	020 7737 0333	The bar's alright, the art's excellent.
The Florence	133 Dulwich Rd	020 7326 4987	Microbrewery on premises.
Prince Regent	69 Dulwich Rd	020 7274 1567	Life drawing on Wednesdays to titillate posh diners.

Map 129 · East Dulwich

liquorish	123 Lordship Ln	020 8693 7744	Good things happen here.

Map 130 · Peckham Rye

The Rye	31 Peckham Rye	020 7639 5397	For lazy lunches on summer Sundays. A pocket of delicious East Dulwich swank Peckham-side.

Map 131 · Vauxhall / Albert Embankment

Area	67 Albert Embankment	020 3242 0040	Another massive Vauxhall rave hole. Serious gay clientele.
Eagle London	349 Kennington Ln	020 7793 0903	Fur on tap throughout the week. Sundays recommended.
The Lavender	112 Vauxhall Walk	020 7735 4440	Just popping to the Lav.
The Royal Vauxhall Tavern	372 Kennington Ln	020 7820 1222	Fun gay pub with trashy cabaret.

Map 132 · Battersea (West)

Barrio	14 Battersea Sq	020 7801 9548	What balmy Sunday evenings were made for.
The Draft House Westbridge	74 Battersea Bridge Road	020 7228 6482	A great pub well worth the trek.
The Greyhound	136 Battersea High St	020 7978 7021	1000-bottle wine list? Not your normal pub.
Le QuecumBar	42 Battersea High St	020 7787 2227	Gypsy jazz, honkytonk and frogs legs in bygone Parisian chic.
The Woodman	60 Battersea High St	020 7228 2968	A nice fire. Pint of Badger. Luverleee.

Map 134 · South Lambeth

Bar Estrela	115 Old South Lambeth Rd	020 7793 1051	Like mama used to make. Probably.
The Battersea Barge	Nine Elms Ln	020 7498 0004	Bouncy, buoyant, thrilled to see you—the Labrador puppy of venues.
Fire	38 Parry St	020 7820 0550	Legendary gay terrordrome with LED ceiling.
Hoist	47 S Lambeth Rd	020 7735 9972	Slap on some leather and get hoisted up.
The Lightbox	6S Lambeth Pl	075 0066 7874	15,000 LED lights. Enough to give us all seizures.
Roller Disco @ Renaissance Rooms	126 S Lambeth Rd	084 4736 5375	Roller skates, alcohol, and a very nervous Health & Safety officer.
The Vauxhall Griffin	8 Wyvil Rd	020 7622 0222	Theme nights to knock your socks off

Map 135 · Oval

Fentiman Arms	64 Fentiman Rd	020 7793 9796	The staff believe that smiles kill kittens.

Map 136 · Putney

The Boathouse	Brewhouse Ln	020 8789 0476	Riverside pub with loadsa outdoor space.
Duke's Head	8 Lower Richmond Rd	020 8788 2552	Typical gastro pub upstairs. Dark DJ bar downstairs.
Jolly Gardeners	61 Lacy Rd	020 8789 2539	Like all good pubs. And sock monkey classes on Wednesdays.
Star & Garter	4 Lower Richmond Rd	020 8788 0345	Upscale Saturday night hotspot on the Thames.

Map 137 · Wandsworth (West)

The Upper Lounge	26 Upper Richmond Rd	020 8875 0269	Utterly likeable. Except Thursdays when it heaves with excitable Saffas.

Map 138 · Wandsworth (Central)

The Cat's Back	88 Point Pleasant	020 8877 0818	Atmospheric and busy with loadsa obscure decoration.
GJ's	89 Garratt Ln	020 8874 2271	Party with snow bunnies.
The Upper Lounge	35 Putney Bridge Rd	020 8874 1695	Good beer selection. Mixed crowd. Decent Sunday Roast.

Map 139 · Wandsworth (East)

Adventure Bar and Lounge	91 Battersea Rise	020 7223 1700	Laid back lounging. Friendly crowd. Poncey cocktails.

Map 140 · Clapham Junction / Northcote Rd

B@1	85 Battersea Rise	020 7978 6595	Be at one with a cocktail menu the size of a book.
Jongleurs (Battersea)	49 Lavender Gardens	0844 499 4062	Lots and lots of laughs. Turns into a scary club.
The Peacock	148 Falcon Rd	020 7223 9633	Burlesque off the beaten track

Map 141 · Battersea (South)

Halo	317 Battersea Park Rd	020 7801 8683	A halo isn't enough. Give this bar a sainthood.
The Lost Angel	339 Battersea Park Rd	020 7622 2112	Put this in your pipe and smoke it, Shoreditch.

Map 142 · Clapham Old Town

Frog and Forget-Me-Not	32 The Pavement	020 7622 5230	A first floor terrace that's just made for summer.
Lost Society	697 Wandsworth Rd	020 7652 6526	Country-house drinking, in Clapham.
Prince of Wales	38 Old Town	020 7622 3530	Eccentric, friendly. Run by a magpie.

Arts & Entertainment · **Nightlife**

ose & Crown	2 The Polygon	020 7720 8265	For the CAMRA purists.
he Sun	47 Clapham Old Town	020 7622 4980	Nice pub. Ruined by surfeit of twats.

Map 143 · Clapham High Street

he Alexandra	14 Clapham Common South Side	020 7627 5102	Join an up-for-it crowd as multinational as the sport here.
read and Roses	68 Clapham Manor St	020 7498 1779	Surprisingly pleasant socialist boozer. Without Clapham tossers.
he Clapham North	409 Clapham Rd	020 7274 2472	A bit 'Clapham', but pretty likable really.
he Falcon	33 Bedford Rd	020 7274 2428	"I told Daddy, I've nowhere to even PARK a GTi!"
reen & Blue	20 Bedford Rd	020 7498 9648	For the finest wine. Because you're worth it.
nfernos	146 Clapham High St	020 7720 7633	Oh God no.
nn Clapham	15 The Pavement	020 7652 2948	Charmingly tatty and full of French people.
he Loft	67 Clapham High St	020 7627 0792	A welcome oasis from Clapham High Street.
he Railway	18 Clapham High St	020 7622 4077	Half-trendy, half-local, three-quarters cool.
wo Brewers	114 Clapham High St	020 7819 9539	Club nights, gay cabaret, lots of fu-un!
he White House	65 Clapham Park Rd	020 7498 3388	Manhattan in Clapham? Erm, O.K.

Map 144 · Stockwell / Brixton (West)

uke of Edinburgh	204 Ferndale Rd	020 7924 0509	Warm, traditional pub with massive beer garden.
lan B	418 Brixton Rd	087 0116 5421	Has made a name for itself, but pretty lame really.
he Prince	469 Brixton Rd	020 7326 4455	Behind dealers chanting skunk lies a nothin' special pub.
he Rest Is Noise	44 Brixton Rd	020 7346 8521	New hip wank-ahol frequented by your worst nightmare.
he Swan	215 Clapham Rd	020 7978 9778	Don't worry about spitting on the floor.

Map 145 · Stockwell / Brixton (East)

rixton Academy	211 Stockwell Rd	020 7771 3000	Overrated, but still a tad awesome.
he Grosvenor	17 Sidney Rd	020 7733 1799	Rough n' ready local with amazing crust/noise/punk gigs.
amm	261 Brixton Rd	020 7274 5537	The real deal a little way out.

Map 146 · Earlsfield

ar 366	366 Garratt Ln	020 8944 9591	Chilled, lounge-type bar.
araza	561 Garratt Ln	020 8944 9009	Teeny, funky bar with cocktails-a-go-go.
alfway House	521 Garratt Ln	020 8946 2788	Slinky, chardonnay-swilling pub with terrific terrace.
e Gothique	Windmill Rd & John Archer Wy	020 8870 6567	The answer to: "Open a bar! What could go wrong?"

Map 147 · Balham (West)

he Nightingale	97 Nightingale Ln	020 8673 1637	Untrendified local. Long may it stay so.

Map 148 · Balham (East)

alham Bowls Club	7 Ramsden Rd	020 8673 4700	A pub. In a bowling club circa 1950. Genius.
he Bedford	77 Bedford Hill	020 8682 8940	Music and comedy pub with great bands but crappy beer.
he Exhibit	12 Balham Station Rd	020 8772 6556	Cool, up-market venue. Friendly, laid back vibe.

Map 150 · Brixton

he Dogstar	389 Coldharbour Ln	020 7733 7515	The burritos are great, but leave before the tunes get cheesy.
he Effra	38 Kellet Rd	020 7274 4180	A slice of the real Brixton.
ridge Bar	1 Town Hall Parade	020 7326 5100	Techno, trance, hardcore venue avec occasional stabbing.
rand Union	123 Acre Ln	020 7274 8794	Come for the tiki shacks and burgers.
ootananny Brixton	95 Effra Rd	020 7737 7273	Great gigs - many for free
ango Landin'	40 St Matthew's Rd	020 7737 3044	Reggae-tinged alternative bar.
ass	Brixton Hill	020 7738 7875	Drum and Bass + Hard House + Fetish Nights = Hedonist Heaven
rince Albert	418 Coldharbour Ln	020 7274 3771	It's charming, trust us. In a not too obvious kindaway.
atay	447 Coldharbour Ln	020 7326 5001	Cocktails to suit the snobbiest of drinks connoisseurs
he Windmill	22 Blenheim Gardens	020 8671 0700	Rough-edged weirdo magnet. Unique and brilliant.
pstairs at the Ritzy	Brixton Oval, Coldharbour Lane (above Ritzy cinema)	020 7733 2229	Where Brixton sparkles. Cinema, bar, café and free live music.

Map 151 · Tooting Bec

he Bec Bar	26 Tooting Bec Rd	020 8672 7722	Pleasant enough. Go for sport.
ing's Head	84 Upper Tooting Rd	020 8767 6708	Former gin palace brings yesteryear flair to the wasteland.
moke Bar	14 Trinity Rd	020 8767 3902	Standard, compact DJ bar.

Map 152 · Tooting Broadway

arden House	196 Tooting High St	020 8767 6582	Revived Victorian local. Live music and log fire.
amble Inn	223 Mitcham Rd	020 8767 4040	Irish/locals bullcrap-free boozer.
ooting Tram and Social	46 Mitcham Rd	020 8767 0278	Cavernous, funky and cool without trying.

It's hard to judge Londoners by their favourite restaurants. We all have a fully stocked larder of eateries we frequent—adapting to every culinary occasion like cosmopolitan chameleons. We'll rough it over a hangover-challenging fry-up by day (**E Pellicci (Map 92)**), camp it up deluxe style by night (**Ruby & Sequoia (Map 29)**) and blow most of our wage on a bottle of champagne over Sunday lunch, just to celebrate pay day in the first place. The truth is—there's so much choice, we can't really help it. We don't pay out extortionate rents just to cook spag bol ourselves, like the rest of the country. No. We choose to live in London, where the disproportionate amount of restaurants per capita leaves us no choice but to accept our fate and embrace the restaurant as foreplay to a damn good night out. After all, we have restaurants to suit every imaginable situation. Everyone has their local Italian; die-hard curry house; girly bistro where rosé becomes acceptable; guaranteed-a-shag-later candlelit brasserie; close-that-deal power lunch spot; greasy caff; and of course, that Sunday lunch gastropub where you can think about all of this over a massive Yorkshire pudding. Probably you don't need us, but we know how fickle London can be. We swear by our local one day, but the minute Gordon opens another reasonably over-priced gastropub, there goes that old favourite.

Eating For Britain

From pie shops to posh Sunday lunches, great British food has become our little pièce de résistance in the global restaurant scene. And like everything else, we do it with a bit of a nudge nudge wink wink. We rule the gastropub roost—especially when the likes of **The Eagle (Map 6)**, **Anchor & Hope (Map 104)** and **Great Queen Street (Map 13)** opened their doors, taking a new look at British cuisine and putting it on our tables in ways we'd never seen it before, while other old standards refuse to budge from doing what they do best—partly because there's no one else on earth that can do it like them. The pie and mash at **Clarks Pie and Mash (Map 6)**, for instance, is so good they'd have made Queen Victoria demanding: "Please sir, may I have some more?"

With the aftermath of the recession leaving u crying for mummy under piles of rejected bank loans, London's appetite for the most comforting of comfort foods on every corner is still running rampant. From the Raclette man oozing cheese over hot potatoes at **Borough Market (Map 106)** to **Banger Bros. (Map 78)** pitching up their stall outside of Euston Station—comfort food is everywhere. If you're in need of a gastronomical tribute to ol' Blighty try **Roast (Map 106)** for its native breed Mondays (promising only to use British meat); **Boot and Flogger (Map 106)**, fo some whiffy, yet delicious, Stilton and Port; and **The Carpenter's Arms (Map 39)** for gastropub fare that's as good as it gets.

For a Sunday lunch to savour try **The Charles Lamb (Map 83)** for a long drawn out afternoon. Last but not least, London has some of the most sophisticated fish & chips around with über-fresh ingredients like at **Brady's (Map 138)**, **Fisher's Chips (Map 48)**, **Tom's (Map 45)**, **Sea Cow (Map 129)**, and **Rock & Sole Plaice (Map 13)**. London is still a great place to eat British.

Caffs And Breakfast Joints

Few of us have time to actually eat it during the week, but nothing beats a breakfast when a hangover has descended. From a posh crumpet brunch at the **Wolseley (Map 9)** to the most traditional of caffs like **Shepherdess Cafe (Map 83)** or those that think outside of sausage n' egg box like the Monte Cristo sandwich with maple syrup at **Fish! (Map 106)** of all places, breakfast really has become the most important meal of any Londoner's Saturday morning, anyway. All these are well and good, but if you can discover one of those rarities like the absolutely knock-you-on the floor-delicious Latin breakfast at **El Vergel (Map 105)**, you know you must have rock-hard London karma. If you like people watching, there's **Bar Italia (Map 12)** or **Smiths of Smithfield (Map 15)**. For healthier fare try **The Larder (Map 15)** For a Turkish take on a fry-up try **Archgate Cafe (Map 60)** or if you like your morning meal more Yank than rank try anything at **The Breakfast Club (Map 80)**. The best greasy spoons include **Jeff's Café (Map 18)**, **Mario's Café (Map 72)**, and **Marie's Café (Map 104)**.

Credit Crunch Lunches

The recession has had its way with us, leaving a path of destruction in its wake and although the so-called 'credit crunch' is passée, we're still suffering in the ways of the wallet. Furthermore, there's this nasty rumour—spread mostly by those out-of-towners who resent their commute yet insist on living two hours away—that London is no place for the impoverished restaurant lover, particularly in these economically unstable times. Such slanderers should be stopped at the M25 and made to pay double congestion charge. The truth is, if you know London, you know how to eat out for under £20 (and even under a tenner when particularly skint). We have plenty of true gems where you can boldly shout "I'll get this one!" all smugly moving ahead in the old restaurant rounds game, with your accompanying party none the wiser. We have to sing the praises of **Cha Cha Moon (Map 10)**, once boasting a price of £3.50 for everything on the menu when it first opened, punters still don't have to reach too deeply in their wallets for spot-on char kway teow. Craving cheap as chips ciabattas? Try **Bada Bing! (Map 6)**. Grab a bento for a fiver at **Little Japan (Map 36)**. If you have no qualms re: pretense and just want to eat cheap try **Sandwichman (Map 6)** with its .65p gourmet, you guessed it, sandwiches, **Tortilla (Map 80)** for a quick burrito, **Icco Pizza (Map 3)** for £3.50 a pie and low-wonga wurst at **Kurz + Lang (Map 15)**. Stuck in Chelsea without a trust fund? Try **Le Columbier (Map 45)**. Now, go cash in on that overdraft and keep reading...

Eating On Trend

London du jour is one of tightening purse strings. Gone are the glory days of "putting it on expenses" ever since the media descended upon the MPs' love of fudging budgets. So while the yummy mummies and Sloane Rangers still roam, fashionable eating has become about being in-the-know over chic, "my little discovery" eateries where how much dosh you dish falls second fiddle to dishing the right nosh.

While Michelin-starred institutions like **Gordon Ramsay at Claridge's (Map 2)**, **Alain Ducasse at the Dorchester (Map 9)** and **Rhodes 24 (Map 17)** still matter in this town, celebrities are now seen frequenting holes in the wall, as we hear Marc Jacobs likes slurping noodles at Hackney's **Que Viet (Map 91)**. The real Big Smoke cognoscenti

make their way to **Beas of Bloomsbury (Map 5)** for artisan cupcakes, **Negozio Classica (Map 29)** for latenight luxuriating over vino and sharing platters at **Bocca di Lupo (Map 11)**—with its sophisticated yet somehow affordable Italian fare. We've always been a city that loves a "bargain" alternative—like Jimmy Choo at H&M's—and we're still proud to say that for every celebrity chef hot spot, there's a high street version. If you can't afford the £95 per person price at **Gordon Ramsay (Map 46)** (and that's without splashing out on the £10,000 bottles of wine), you'll love **York & Albany (Map 77)**. And if you lust over Tom Aikens, try **Tom's Kitchen (Map 45)**, an ever-popular brasserie that still has a lot to write home about. Our current favourite, however, has to be **Jamie's Italian (Map 101)** for its awesome antipasti. So in this sprawling city, you can still eat like a king while the rest of the world moans about its financial woes.

For classically chic and delicious, try **The Bleeding Heart (Map 15)**—the bistro's better than the restaurant—or **Galvin Bistrot de Luxe (Map 2)**. For a view, **Galvin at Windows (Map 9)**, **Skylon (Map 104)**, and **Oxo Tower Wharf (Map 104)** still reign supreme over London's skyline. If you're a visiting footballer's wife lurching around in 10-inch heels, try **Balans (Map 11)**, **Deep (Map 50)**, or **Eight Over Eight (Map 44)**. Hipster deluxe joints include **Village East (Map 107)**, **The Market (Map 71)** and **Bistrotheque (Map 92)**. For absolutely delicious hype, try **Moro (Map 6)**. Take mummy dearest to **Aubergine (Map 44)** or **Morgan M (Map 74)** when she's in town and if you like anything with a label, try **J Sheekey (Map 24)**. But, if you want something worth every penny try **Le Cercle (Map 46)** or **Wild Honey (Map 10)**. Pretty soon you'll be able to enter your fave fashionable joint and exchange noisy bisoux with the maitre d' (that's when you know you're in).

Going For A.. (Fill In The Blank / Ethnic Food)

In such an ethnically diverse capital as this one, we savour our wide-range of foreign grub. For Londoners 'going for a curry' is an adventure which can encompass such a wide range of cuisines from Nepalese at **Kathmandu Valley (Map 138)** to Eritrean at **Adulis (Map 135)** and a kebab at **Tayyabs (Map 96)** or Beirut

Express (Map 1) is more than just an ill-advised stop on the way to the night bus. We choose our indulgences carefully. We know how to avoid the incessant menu hawkers along Brick Lane on our way to the **Beigel Shop (Map 91)**. After all, the best curry houses are rarely on this over-hyped thoroughfare—if you have to, try **The Clipper (Map 91)**—but tucked away on neighbouring streets are places like **The Empress (Map 95)** and **Cafe Spice Namaste (Map 95)** (get yourself dhal-ed up) or those a good tube ride away at **Masaledar Kitchen (Map 151)**, **Mirch Masala (Map 151)**, and **The Punjab (Map 13)**.

The best Chinese food can be found around Chinatown, but you have to hunt. Your first stop should be **Leong's Legends (Map 11)** for to die for Taiwanese. Also try **Friendly Inn (Map 12)**, **Royal China (Map 30)**, **Haozhan (Map 12)**,or delicious **New World (Map 12)** for killer custard dumplings. But why settle for Chinese when there are so many other Asian foods to try? Thai at **Yum Yum (Maps 79, 64)**, **Esarn Kheaw (Map 32)**, **Thai Pavillion East (Map 131)** and **Su-Thai (Map 121)**; cheap and cheerful Malaysian at **Malaysia Kopi Tiam (Map 12)**; greasy spoon Korean at **Assa (Map 12)** and over karaoke at **Corean Chilli (Map 12)**; Singaporean at **Singapore Garden (Map 66)**; Vietnamese at **Hai Ha (Map 89)** and **Que Viet (Map 91)**; Japanese skewers at **Bincho Soho (Map 12)**. And of course, because we're London, for every down-and-out corner spot, there's its posh cousin. Try glamorous Indian at **Amaya (Map 19)**, stylish Thai at **Crazy Bear (Map 3)**, and gourmet Malaysian at **Champor-Champor (Map 106)**.

If you're looking for a neighbourhood Italian, try **Metrogusto (Map 80)** for its home-made pasta (ignore the art on the walls), **Il Bordello (Map 96)** and **Tentazioni (Map 10)**. Mexican continues to thrive with **Green & Red (Map 91)**, **Taqueria (Map 29)** and **Crazy Homies (Map 29)**. In terms of French, if you haven't noticed, this is the cuisine of choice for any Michelin-starred restaurant in this town worth its salt. But for those of us on a smaller budget there's **Le Petit Prince (Map 72)**, **Le Beaujolais (Map 12)** and **Savoir Faire (Map 4)**. For extraordinary tapas combinations right every time try **The Providores (Map 2)**. One cuisine boom, which reflects that of the population, is of the Eastern European variety. For Polish, try (we're not kidding) **Lowiczanka Polish Cultural Centre (Map 40)** or Russian

try **Trojka (Map 70)**. If you can't decide, opt for one of London's craziest fusions that somehow works—Brazilian and Japanese at **Sushinho (Map 45)**. Mango sushi anyone?

Eating Meat

Here's where we implore you, begging you on both knees, not to let yourself EVER stumble into one of those steakhouse chains, mainly around Leicester Square, that shall not be named. If we succeed in anything with this guide, it should be at least to give carnivores a decent alternative. If you're stuck on the Aberdeen Angus variety of beef, try the **Popeseye Steakhouse (Map 33)**. But if you're open to other options, Argentinian steakhouses are really where it's at right now, with **Gaucho (Map 8)** at the forefront and **Buen Ayre (Map 89)** not far behind. If you want steak with a heart of gold (read: ethically sourced) try **Hawksmoor (Map 91)**.

If you like your meat on a bun, go for **The Diner's (Map 84)** blue cheese burgers, **Byron (Map 35)** for the best local, and **Haché (Map 71)**. If you'd rather someone else fired up your barbie, go for **Bodean's (Map 43)** or **Rodizio Rico (Map 80)**. If you're into eating things the rest of us see at the zoo, try **Archipelago (Map 3)** and **Chakalaka (Map 136)**.

Eating Veggie

In a town full of yoga bunnies, eco warriors and Madonna, veggie restaurants are pretty prevalent. And lucky for us, they're not just serving up nut roast. There are places that even sworn meat-eaters love. Get your carnivorous best mate to try the sweet potato curry at **Mildred's (Map 10)** or the veggie food by the pound at **Tibits (Map 10)**. If you're looking for a place to impress your new vegan girlfriend (you swear she's the one!), try **Rootmaster (Map 91)**. But there are plenty of other goodies like **Beetroot (Map 11)** and **Alara (Map 4)**. Also, remember Indian is always a good bet, like **Rasa N16 (Map 64)**, **Diwana Bhelpoori (Map 77)** or **Indian Veg Bhelpoori House (Map 80)**.

Our Guiltiest Pleasures

OK, so we avoid the golden arches at all costs, steer clear of corporate coffee houses, and duck out of lame pubs, but every Londoner has their guilty chain restaurant secret. Let's get this straight: few of us are comfortable giving into these rare pleasures, and they most certainly aren't your average High Street hiccup (please kindly leave this book at the door if you're going to partake in a Wetherspoon Curry Club). These are a carefully vetted bunch that, after endlessly refuting their existence, we gave into without even realising it ("What? They have free Wi-Fi!"). **Nando's (Map 106)** for example. No one realises their friends also like this Portuguese chicken joint until they spot their best mate dribbling over his Perinaise sauce at their local. Or there, **Gourmet Burger Kitchen (Map 24)**, featuring meat mountains in buns to rival Kylie. On the other end of the spectrum is **Le Pain Quotidien (Map 10)**. Try a tartine with a bowl of hot chocolate and graduate to a glass of wine—no one will judge, and we're pretty sure you'll never want to leave.

Our Favourite Restaurant (Because we're still skint!)

While every Londoner loves a good clean white table cloth, extensive tasting menus and a waiter at your every beck and call—let's face it:

we're broke. It seems almost with the pain of the recession in mind (although the cheery and energetic staff act all but oblivious to the outside world) that **Franco Manca (Map 144)** opened its doors in Brixton Market to very hungry punters. The pizza here is perfect, and worth every moment on the endless queue that moves along in famished anticipation of the sour dough crusts and organic, ethically sourced chorizo toppings. While awaiting our table underneath the diffused light of the marketplace's arches, a passerby challenges the growing crowd of would-be diners with: "All this, for pizza?" Only to be berated, almost in unison, by the dedicated many: "Yes, but this is pizza from the gods." If it were not enough that the pizzas here come as cheaply as £4 and the flowing red wine for £1.40 a glass, everything here—from the flour to the toppings, beer and cloudy lemonade—is made from only the best ingredients, all somehow good for the earth and our pockets at the same time. Now with a second branch opening in Chiswick **(Map 38)** and the potential for even more cropping up around the capital, we worry that the rough-around-the-edges authenticity to this London gem may not last forever but we hope we're proven very wrong.

Key: £: Under £10 / ££: £10–£20 / £££: £20–£30 / ££££: £30–£40 / £££££: £40+
* : Does not accept credit cards./ †: Accepts only American Express / ††: Accepts only Visa and Mastercard
Time listed refers to kitchen closing time on weekend nights

Map 1 • Marylebone (West)

Abu Ali Cafe	136 George St	020 7724 6338	£		Good cheap 'n cheerful Lebanese joint among many similar in the area!
Beirut Express	112 Edgware Rd	020 7724 2700	££	2 am	Chaotic, rude and the best Lebanese in town.
Maroush IV	68 Edgware Rd	020 7224 9339	££	12 am	Wax philosophical while smoking a hookah out front.
Locanda Locatelli	8 Seymour St	020 7935 9088	££££	11.30 pm	Outstanding Italian food.
Nippon Tuk	225 Edgware Rd	020 7616 6496	££££	11.15 pm	One to avoid for vertigo sufferers—astounding, 23rd floor views.

Map 2 • Marylebone (East)

Comptoir Libanais	65 Wigmore St	020 7935 1110	£	8 pm	Uncompromisingly cheap and cheerful mezes.
Diwan	31 Thayer St	020 7935 2445	££	11 pm	Lebanese gorge spot.
Galvin Bistrot de Luxe	66 Baker Street	020 7935 4007	£££	11 pm	Veloutés, ballantines, tartares and escargots. Delicieux? Mais oui.
The Golden Hind	73 Marylebone Ln	020 7486 3644	££	10 pm	Fish and chips from the top-drawer. Can do BYOB.
Gordon Ramsay at Claridge's	Brook St	020 7499 0099	£££££	11 pm	A rich perfectionist's culinary art deco dream.
Hush Brasserie	8 Lancashire Ct	020 7659 1500	££££	11 pm	European food al fresco. Go on a lunch hour holiday.
No. 5 Cavendish Square	5 Cavendish Square	087 1223 5000	££££	11 pm	A No. 5 desperately trying to be as opulent as Chanel's.
Patisserie Valerie	105 Marylebone High St	020 7935 6240	£	9 pm	Boho coffee and pastry.
The Providores	109 Marylebone High St	020 7935 6175	££	11 pm	Sip Rioja and gorge on tapas for the cognoscenti.
Sakura	9 Hanover St	020 7629 2961	££	10 pm	Authentic Japanese queue. Worth it for the food.

Arts & Entertainment · **Restaurants**

Key: £ : Under £10 / ££ : £10–£20 / £££ : £20–£30 / ££££ : £30–£40 / £££££ : £40+
* : Does not accept credit cards./ † : Accepts only American Express / †† : Accepts only Visa and Mastercard
Time listed refers to kitchen closing time on weekend nights

Map 3 · Fitzrovia

Archipelago	110 Whitfield St	020 7383 3346	£££££	10.30 pm London's best, alright only, chocolate-covered scorpions and crocodile steaks.
Ask	48 Grafton Way	020 7388 8108	£	11.30 pm ...for pizza.
Carluccio's	8 Market Pl	020 7636 2228	£££	11 pm Pretty good for a chain. Have the espresso and ice cream.
Chutney & Lager	43 Great Titchfield St	0207 636 5737	££	11 pm Indian tapas restaurant and lounge bar.
Crazy Bear	26 Whitfield St	020 7631 0088	£££££	10.30 pm Thai deluxe. Where the media world feeds its clients.
Eagle Bar Diner	3 Rathbone Pl	020 7637 1418	££	11 pm Trendy modern American diner; two words: Crocodile Burger.
Elena's L'Etoile	30 Charlotte St	020 7636 7189	£££££	11 pm Old school French sophistication, politicians and journos.
Govinda's	9 Soho St	020 7437 4928	£*	8 pm Cheap Krishna food. You know the deal.
Hakkasan	8 Hanway Pl	020 7927 7000	££££	12 am Soho's sexiest subterranean Chinese. China-chic dining for the beautiful people.
Icco Pizza	46 Goodge St	020 7580 9250	£	11 pm Zen it is not—but who cares at £3.50 a pizza?
Latium	21 Berners St	020 7323 9123	£££	10.30 pm Romantic (and pricey) first date place.
Market Place	11 Market Pl	020 7079 2020	£	1 am Warm buzz all day/night. Hot clientele/tepid prices.
Navarro's	67 Charlotte St	020 7637 7713	££	10 pm Delicioso! Smells like Seville, tastes like Seville.
Ragam	57 Cleveland St	020 7636 9098	££	10.45 pm Can't dis these dosas (potato crepes) at very decent prices.
Rasa Express	5 Rathbone St	020 7637 0222	£	11 pm Take-away-priced Indian lunch boxes, seating included.
Roka	37 Charlotte St	020 7580 6464	£££	11 pm Dazzling Izakaya concept Japanese.
Salt Yard	54 Goodge St	020 7637 0657	£££	11 pm Intimate and sexy. Take a date. Get laid. Possibly.
Sardo	45 Grafton Way	020 7387 2521	££	10 pm Hit after hit. Try the crab pasta.
Squat & Gobble	69 Charlotte St	020 7580 5338	£	4.30 pm Scrumptious, cheap, tiny. Just squat and, um, gobble.
Stef's	3 Berners St	020 3073 1041	££	11 pm You can't knock the gnocchi.
Thai Metro	36 Charlotte St	020 7436 4201	££	11 pm Thai food, cooked well, served well, job done.

Map 4 · Bloomsbury (West)

Alara	58 Marchmont St	020 7837 1172	£££	7 pm Hardcore veggie/vegan mecca, surprisingly good.
Bi Won	24 Coptic St	020 7580 2660	£	10 pm Manhandling staff but great food.
Savoir Faire	42 New Oxford St	020 7436 0707	££	10.30 pm Sweet little rustic restaurant, a stroll from Soho.

Map 5 · Bloomsbury (East)

Acorn House	69 Swinton St	020 7812 1842	£££	10.30 pm Eco-chic: the Gwyneth Paltrow of restaurants.
Aki Bistro	182 Gray's Inn Rd	020 7837 9281	££	11 pm Almost too Japanese Japanese.
Beas of Bloomsbury	44 Theobald's Rd	020 7242 8330	£	6 pm You can watch the chefs create artisan cupcake masterpieces here.
Bread and Butter Sandwich Bar	100 Judd St	020 7713 7767	£*	9 pm Notable for its very cheap al fresco fry-ups.
Ciao Bella	86 Lamb's Conduit St	020 7242 4119	££	11 pm Authentic, rustic feel Italian complete with piano.
Cigala	54 Lamb's Conduit St	020 7405 1717	££	10.45pm Great service and gorgeous salty Spanish bread.
The Food Bazaar	59 Gray's Inn Rd	020 7242 6578	£*	9 pm Casual and friendly with great hot food selection.
Fryer's Delight	19 Theobald's Rd	020 7405 4114	£*	10 pm No frills chippie; big portions of chunky, salty, greasy tastiness.
Konstam	2 Acton St	020 7833 5040	££	10 pm All food sourced within London. Should be grim—actually delicious.
La Provence	63 Gray's Inn Rd	020 7404 4920	£	10 pm Super-friendly staff and a generous hot food deal.
Malletti	174 Clerkenwell Rd	020 7713 8665	£	4.30 pm Pizza served al taglio like in Italia.
Mary Ward Centre	42 Queen Sq	020 7269 6000	£*	5 pm Hippy educational centre with a great organic cafe.
Paolina Thai Snack Bar	181 King's Cross Rd	020 7278 8176	£*	11 pm Grotty exterior disguises this diamond of cheerful authentic Thai.
The Perseverance	63 Lamb's Conduit St	020 7405 8278	££	10.30pm Good quality gastropub food.

| Swintons | 61 Swinton St | 020 7837 3995 | ££ | 9.30 pm | If Heaven made fishfinger sandwiches, they'd use Swintons' recipe. |
| Thai Candle | 38 Lamb's Conduit St | 020 7430 2472 | £££ | 10 pm | Cosy, cheerful with a nice lunchtime meal deal. |

Map 6 · Clerkenwell

Bada Bing!	120 St John St	020 7253 3723	£	4 pm	Excellent lunch joint. The toasted ciabattas are divine.
Clarks Pie and Mash	46 Exmouth Market	020 7837 1974	£*	5.30 pm	A last bastion of a lost London.
Dans Le Noir	30 Clerkenwell Green	020 7253 1100	££££	9 pm	Blind waiters serve in pitch darkness: don't wear white.
The Eagle	159 Farringdon Rd		££	10.30 pm	London's first gastro pub—just look what they started.
Little Bay	171 Farringdon Rd	020 7278 1234	££	12 am	Posh-people food at pikey-people prices.
Moro	34 Exmouth Market	020 7833 8336	££££	11 pm	DO believe the hype.
The Quality Chop House	94 Farringdon Rd	020 7837 5093	££	10.45pm	OMG it's so BRITISH. Meat and potatoes like nowhere else.
Sandwichman	23 Easton St	020 7833 9001	£*	2.30 pm	Office delivery returns. Gourmet—and just 65p. Best lunch in London.

Map 7 · Barbican / City Road (South)

Bavarian Beerhouse	190 City Rd	0844 330 2005	££	11 pm	Unlace your lederhausen for some serious schnitzel madness.
Carnevale	135 Whitecross St	020 7250 3452	££	11.00 pm	Veggie on the cheap.
De Santis	11 Old St	020 7689 5626	££	9.30 pm	Like being in Milan; owner Enzo takes care of you
NUSA Kitchen	9 Old St	020 7253 3135	£*	5 pm	People queuing? For ages? For soup? Now I've seen everything.

Map 8 · Liverpool Street / Broadgate

Damascu Bite Kebab	21 Shoreditch High St	020 7247 0207	£*	1 am	It's the way they grill them from the outside.
Eyre Brothers	70 Leonard St	020 7613 5346	££	10.45 pm	Great place run by the Eyre brothers—Jane no relation.
Gaucho Broadgate	5 Finsbury Ave	020 7256 6877	££££	11 pm	Divine, ohmigod, melt-in-your-mouth steak. Oops, drooling!
Ponti's Caffe	176 Bishopsgate	020 7283 4889	£	24 hrs	24 hour cafe for the inebriated insomniac.
Rivington Bar and Grill	28 Rivington St	020 7729 7053	££	11 pm	Emin on the walls, meat in the buns.

Map 9 · Mayfair / Green Park

Alain Ducasse at The Dorchester	Park Ln	020 7629 8866	££££	10 pm	Better known for its extortionate prices than Michelin-starred food.
El Pirata of Mayfair	5 Down St	020 7491 3810	£££	11.30 pm	Don't be put off by stuffy location—these are f'ing good tapas.
The English Tea Room at Browns	Albemarle Street	020 7518 4155	££££	11 pm	Ah, so that's what a £48 cup of tea tastes like.
Galvin at Windows	28th Floor, Hilton Park Lane	020 7208 4021	£££££	11 pm	Art Deco French overlooking Buckingham Palace. We're not worthy!
Kiplings	2 Hill St	020 8340 1719	££	11.30 pm	Swanky curry joint boasts Raffles Hotel stylings including resident pianist.
L'Autre	5 Shepherd St	020 7499 4680	£££	11 pm	Polish meets Mexican. Surprisingly well.
Nobu	19 Old Park Ln	020 7447 4747	£££££	12 am	Rob a bank on the way as it's bloody expensive!
The Ritz	150 Piccadilly	020 7300 8765	£££££	11 pm	High tea amidst ornaments and swank - resist temptation to swipe towels.
Theo Randall at the InterContinental	1 Hamilton Pl	020 7318 8747	£££££	11 pm	Sincere and stylish cuisine unfortunately hidden behind a hotel façade.
The Wolseley	160 Piccadilly	020 7499 6996	££££	12 am	Over-hyped. There. We said it.

Map 10 · Piccadilly / Soho (West)

Bob Bob Ricard	1 Upper James St	020 3145 1000	£££	11.30 pm	Proper posh British diner serving Cornish crab cake and...Ribena.
Cecconi's	5 Burlington Gardens	020 7434 1500	££££	11.15 pm	All-day menu for the spoilt. Delicious breakfasts.
Cha Cha Moon	15 Ganton St	020 7297 9800	££	11 pm	Like Wagamamas but for Chinese.
Chowki	2 Denman St	020 7439 1330	£££	11.30 pm	Rotating regional cuisines of India; brilliant.
Dehesa	25 Ganton St	020 7494 4170	£££	11 pm	Faux-rustic protein-rich tapas, sweetie.
Fernandez and Wells Coffee Bar	73 Beak St	020 7287 8124	£*	6 pm	Perfect pasteis de nata and locally made ice-cream. Delightfully friendly!
Kulu Kulu	76 Brewer St	020 7734 7316	£	10 pm	Great, fresh, fast sushi for people on the go. Sit down is 45 minutes only.

Key: £ : Under £10 : ££ : £10–£20 : £££ : £20–£30 : ££££ : £30–£40 / £££££: £40+
* : Does not accept credit cards / † : Accepts only American Express / †† : Accepts only Visa and Mastercard
Time listed refers to kitchen closing time on weekend nights

Le Pain Quotidien	18 Great Marlborough St	020 7486 6154	£	10 pm	Feel like a right old tartine.
Mildred's	45 Lexington St	020 7494 1634	££	10.30 pm	Great house, sometimes crap service. Get the sweet potato curry to takeaway!
Mosaico	13 Albermale St	020 7409 1011	£££	11 pm	Stylish Italian. Prices more for the Mayfair Mamas.
Nordic Bakery	14 Golden Sq	020 3230 1077	£	7 pm	Authentic sticky cinnamon buns, Karelian pies and smoked Moomin.
The Photographers' Gallery	16 Ramillies St	020 7831 1772	£*	6 pm	Artsy coffee spot with photos on view.
Ping Pong	45 Great Marlborough St	020 7851 6969	££	11 pm	Don't leave without trying a char sui bun!
Pure California	39 Beak St	020 7287 3708	£	6 pm	As pure a salad/juice as you'd find in the Sunshine State all made to order.
Sartoria	20 Saville Row	020 7534 7000	£££££	11 pm	The pick of the Conran restaurants.
Sketch	9 Conduit St	020 7659 4500	£££	1 am	Colossally trendy kitsch palace.
Taro	61 Brewer St	020 7734 5826	££	10.30 pm	Where London's Japanese locals eat sushi.
Ten Ten Tei	56 Brewer St	020 7287 1738	£££££	10 pm	The Japanese restaurant Japanese people love.
Tentazioni Restaurant	2 Mill St	0207 237 1100	££	10.45 pm	Stunningly sophisticated for a neighbourhood eaterie.
Thanks for Franks	26 Fouberts Pl	020 7494 2434	£*	6 pm	Good sandwiches.
Tibits	12 Heddon St	020 7758 4110	££	10 pm	Buffet: sans meat, sold by weight. Genius!
Toku @ The Japan Centre	212 Piccadilly	020 7255 8255	££	10 pm	The best gyoza outside of Tokyo.
Wagamama	10 Lexington St	020 7292 0990	£	11 pm	Reliable, speedy noodle chain.
Wild Honey	12 St George St	020 7758 9160	£££	10.30 pm	Miss Michelin star's got skillz (and a damn good tête-de-veau).
Yauatcha	15 Broadwick St	020 7494 8888	£££££	11.45 pm	Traditional Chinese tea-house meets star-spangled media haunt.
Yoshino	3 Piccadilly place	020 7287 6622	££	10 pm	Back alley bentos so good you'll pretend they were your discovery.

Map 11 · Soho (Central)

Balans	60 Old Compton St	020 7439 2183	££	3 am	Share a 4am breakfast with the likes of Amy Winehouse.
Bar Bruno	101 Wardour St	020 7734 3750	£*	10 pm	Hidden Italian cafe gem. Authentically loud and friendly.
Beetroot	92 Berwick St	020 7437 8591	£	10 pm	Awesome veggie/vegan place.
Bocca di Lupo	12 Archer St	020 7734 2223	£££	12 am	Italian for 'break a leg'; authentic fare gets your bocca watering.
Busaba Eathai	110 Wardour St	020 7255 8686	£££	11 pm	Never mind the shared benches, the food's too yummy.
Cafe Espana	63 Old Compton St	020 7494 1271	££	11 pm	Highly recommended. 10% off for eating with castanets (possibly).
Grace	42 Great Windmill St	020 7851 0800	££££	10.30 pm	Wannabe a WAG? Get in 'ere!
Hummus Bros	88 Wardour St	020 7734 1311	£	11 pm	Where hummus is the main dish.
Imli	167 Wardour St	020 7287 4243	£	11 pm	Tapas + curry. Fusion gone insane but somehow works.
Italian Graffiti	163 Wardour St	020 7439 4668	£££	11 am	Less 'street' than the name suggest. Nice though.
Jerk City	189 Wardour St	020 7287 2878	£	10 pm	Jamaican fast food. In doubt? Go for ackee and saltfish.
Leong's Legends	4 Macclesfield St	020 7287 0288	££	11 pm	A Taiwanese Chinatown legend.
Malletti	26 Noel St	020 7439 4096	£*	3 pm	Amazing! Use your mobile and you won't get served.
Maoz	43 Old Compton St	020 7851 1586	£*	1 am	Falafeltastic!
Melati	30 Peter St	020 7437 2011	££	11.30 pm	Enthusiastic staff and greased up curry/noodle hybrids.
Paul	49 Old Compton St	020 7287 6261	£	10 pm	French cafe/bakery chain. Amazing baguettes!
Pizza Express Jazz Club	10 Dean St	020 7439 8722	£	11 pm	Surprisingly, jazz takes the mediocre chain up a notch.
Randall & Aubin	16 Brewer St	020 7287 4447	£££	11 pm	Over-indulgently carnal seafood delights which only call for champagne.
Red Veg	95 Dean St	020 7437 3109	£*	10 pm	Veggie fast food joint.
Snog	9 Brewer St	020 7494 3301	£*	12 am	If they had yoghurt and not milk in Clockwork Orange.
Soho Thai	27 St. Annes Ct	020 7287 2000	££	11 pm	Thai with a good range. In set meals: go for starter NOT dessert.
St Moritz	161 Wardour St	020 7734 3324	££££	11.30 pm	Swiss cheese heaven.

Won Kei	41 Wardour St	020 7437 8408	££	10 pm	AKA Wonky's: institutionally rude service, cheap fast Chinese.
Yoshino Delicatessen	59 Shaftesbury Ave	020 7434 3610	£	10 pm	Cheap as chips but with sushi.

Map 12 · Soho (East)

Abeno Too	17 Great Newport St	020 7379 1160	££	11 pm	Addictive Okonomiyaki (pancakes) flipped and fried on the table.
Arbutus	63 Frith St	020 7734 4545	£££	11 pm	Chocolate soup! Worth it for that alone.
Assa	53 St Giles High St	020 7240 8256	££	12 am	Cheerful eager-to-please Korean cafe
Bar Italia	22 Frith St	020 7437 4520	££	4.30 am	Soho institution; perfect for people watching at any hour.
Barrafina	54 Frith St	020 7813 8016	££	11 pm	Seriously, the best (and hippest) place for tapas.
Bincho Soho	16 Old Compton St	020 7287 9111	££	11.30 pm	Save on skewers every Tuesday
Boheme Kitchen and Bar	19 Old Compton St	020 7734 5656	£££	11.45 pm	You want frites with that? Deliciously snobby comfort food.
Café Emm	17 Frith St	020 7437 0723	£££	10.30 pm	Double-take cheap prices and wholesome fare. Wins popular vote.
Chinese Experience	118 Shaftesbury Ave	020 7437 0377	£££	11 pm	Popular for a reason. Overwhelmed? Go for the always-great set menu.
Corean Chilli	51 Charing Cross Rd	020 7734 6737	££	12 am	Karaoke and stir-fries with the Korean cool kids.
Ed's Easy Diner	12 Moor St	020 7434 4439	££	11 pm	It's like, you know? Soooo, like, American? You know?
Friendly Inn	47 Gerrard St	020 7437 4170	£	1 am	Where Londoners go for Chinese in Soho.
Gaby's	30 Charing Cross Rd	020 7836 4233	££	10 pm	High on tradition, low on frills. Authentically spartan.
Garlic & Shots	14 Frith St	020 7734 9505	££££	1 am	Garlic, garlic and more garlic. No-go zone for vampires.
Gay Hussar	2 Greek St	020 7437 0973	££	10.45 pm	Everything from strudel to cherry soup at this old-school Hungarian.
Haozhan	8 Gerrard St	020 7434 3838	£££	11 pm	Can't pick? This is the one.
Kettners	29 Romilly St	020 7734 6112	£££££	12 am	Sit and sup with the champagne set.
La Porchetta Pollo Bar	20 Old Compton St	020 7494 9368	££	12 am	Cheap and cheerful Italian. In the West End? Well, exactly.
Le Beaujolais	25 Litchfield St	020 7836 2277	££	10 pm	Get insulted by a Frenchman here in London—Mai oui!
Maison Bertaux	27 Greek St	056 0115 1584	££*	5 pm	Heavenly cakes, art gallery, boutique downstairs, what's not to like?
Malaysia Kopi Tiam	67 Charing Cross Rd	020 7287 1113	£	11 pm	A beef rendang-infused oasis away from the West End's clatter.
New World	1 Gerrard Pl	020 7734 0396	£	11.45 pm	Crispy duck, Dim Sum, custard dumplings... bring it on!
Stockpot	18 Old Compton St	020 7287 1066	££*	12 am	Fantastically cheap stodge.
Taro	10 Old Compton St	020 7439 2275	££	10.30 pm	Like Taro Brewer Street. But gayer, obviously.

Map 13 · Covent Garden

Battersea Pie Station	Covent Garden Piazza	020 7240 9566	£	6 pm	Who ate all the pies?
Café Mode	57 Endell St	020 7240 8085	££	11.30 pm	Pizza, pasta, salad. No fuss.
Belgo Central	29 Shelton St	020 7813 2233	££	11pm	Thoroughly enjoyable moules et frites. And beer... mmm... beer.
Candy Cakes	36 Monmouth St	020 7497 8979	£	8 pm	Cupcakes almost too beautiful to eat. But eat them anyway.
Food for Thought	31 Neal St	020 7836 9072	£	8.30 pm	Queues this long mean they've got cheap, veg food right.
Great Queen Street	32 Great Queen St	020 7242 0622	£££	11 pm	Affordable, and might be London's best gastropub.
Kulu Kulu	51 Shelton St	020 7240 5687	££	10 pm	Tiny conveyor belt sushi joint. Bang on the money.
Mon Plaisir	21 Monmouth St	020 7836 7243	£££	11.15 pm	Not up to typical Paris standards, but still tres bon!
The Punjab	80 Neal St	020 7836 9787	££	11.30 pm	Relive the days of the Raj in this old-school curry house.
Rock & Sole Plaice	47 Endell St	020 7836 3785	££	11 pm	London's oldest chippie. Est. 1871. On-street, fairy-lit picnic benches. Huge portions.
Rossopomodoro	50 Monmouth Street	020 7240 9095	£	12am	Chain Italian with very tasty pies. Cutlery prohibited!
Sarastro	126 Drury Ln	020 7836 0101	££	11.30 pm	Hilarious over-the-top decor; includes fornicating cherubs.
Souk Medina	1 Shorts Gardens	020 7240 1796	££	11 pm	Atmospheric Moroccan joint. Free refills on mouthwatering £20 set menu.

Arts & Entertainment • **Restaurants**

Key: £: Under £10 / ££: £10–£20 / £££: £20–£30 / ££££: £30–£40 / £££££: £40+
*: Does not accept credit cards. / †: Accepts only American Express / ††: Accepts only Visa and Mastercard
Time listed refers to kitchen closing time on weekend nights

Map 14 • Holborn / Temple

Asadal	227 High Holborn	020 7430 9005	£££	10.30 pm	Go on—venture down those stairs—it's worth it.
Indigo @ OneAldwych	1 Aldwych	020 7300 0400	£££	11 pm	Sunday brunch and a movie—all in the same place!

Map 15 • Blackfriars / Farringdon

Beppe's	23 West Smithfield	020 7236 7822	££	3 pm	As classically Italian as oversized sunglasses. Only much, much better.
The Bleeding Heart	Bleeding Heart Yard, off Greville St	020 7242 2056	£££	10.30 pm	Historic, hard to find, eccentric beauty.
Cafe du Marche	22 Charterhouse Sq	020 7608 1609	£££	11 pm	Wonderful French cuisine in delightful venue. Tucked away in Charterhouse Square.
Gaucho Smithfield	93 Charterhouse St	020 7490 1676	££	11 pm	Where cows would choose to be eaten.
Hix Oyster And Chop House	36 Cowcross St	020 7017 1930	£££	10.45 pm	Never tried beef and oyster pie?
Kurz + Lang	1 St John St	020 7993 2923	£	11.30 pm	Ze German Bratwurst sausage at its zizzling best.
The Larder	91 St John St	020 7608 1558	£££	10.30 pm	Fresh, seasonal food, good breakfast menu and takeaway sarnies.
Pho	86 St John St	020 7253 7624	£	10.30 pm	Steaming bowlfuls for hungry Clerkenwell workers. Specialises in street food.
Portal	88 St John St	020 7253 6950	££££	10.15 pm	Astoundingly good Portuguese. Swanky but not stuffy.
Smiths of Smithfield	67 Charterhouse St	020 7251 7950	£££	10.45 pm	Overflowing with yuppies and trendy types; pricey but tasty.
St Germain	89 Turnmill St	020 7336 0949	£££	11 pm	Sleek, chic. Bon Appetit.
St John's Smithfield	26 St John St	020 7251 0848	£££	11 pm	This place is ALL about the offal.
Tinseltown	44 St. John St	020 7689 2424	£	24 hrs	Funky diner serving great late-night milkshakes.
Vivat Bacchus	47 Farringdon St	020 7353 2648	£££	9.30 pm	Three wine cellars and a cheeseroom. A ROOM of cheese.
Yo! Sushi	5 St Paul's	020 7248 8726	£	11 pm	Sushi in Paul's shadow.

Map 16 • Square Mile (West)

Sweetings	39 Queen Victoria St	020 7248 3062	£££	4 pm	Old fashioned institution for nostalgia trips. Lunch only.

Map 17 • Square Mile (East)

Gaucho City	1 Bell Inn Yard	020 7626 5180	££££	11 pm	The best steakhouse in the city. Located in former gold vaults.
The Mercer	34 Threadneedle St	020 7628 0001	££	9.30 pm	Proper British grub in a light contemporary atmosphere.
Nusa Kitchen	2 Adams Ct	020 7628 1149	£	4 pm	Fresh soup made daily.
Rhodes 24	25 Old Broad St	020 7877 7703	£££££	8.30 pm	Anyone for Gherkin (building) with your Michelin star?
Wasabi	52 Old Broad St	020 7374 8337	£*	10 pm	Delicious sushi and bento for those in a rush.

Map 18 • Tower Hill / Aldgate

Jeff's Café	14 Brune St	020 7375 2230	£*	10 pm	Cheap as chips (which they serve here, incidentally).
S & M Café	48 Brushfield St	020 7247 2252	££	10 pm	Not what you think it is, perverts. Sausages and mash!

Map 19 • Belgravia

Amaya	Halkin Arcade, Motcomb St	020 7823 1166	££££	11.30 pm	Where the trendies go for their curry fix.
Boisdale, Victoria	15 Eccleston St	020 7730 6922	£££££	11 pm	Posh Scottish nosh. No deep-fried Mars Bars, sadly.
Noura	12 William St	020 7235 5900	££	11 pm	Frequently orgiastic Lebanese pig-outs, habibi.
One-O-One	101 Knightsbridge	020 7290 7101	££££	10 pm	One man's fish is another man's pleasure.
Yo! Sushi	102 Knightsbridge	020 7235 5000	££	10 pm	A London institution—we dream in sashimi on conveyor belts.

Arts & Entertainment · **Restaurants**

Map 20 · Victoria / Pimlico (West)

Grumbles	35 Churton St	020 7834 0149	££	11 pm	Unfashionably unfussy Brit/French home-cooking. Gorgeous pies, no grumbles.

Map 21 · Pimlico (East)

The Regency Café	17 Regency St	020 7821 6596	£*	7 pm	Proper British fry-ups and atmosphere in this 1940's café.
Vincent Rooms	76 Vincent Sq	020 7802 8391	£££	7 pm	Brilliant food served by awkward catering students.

Map 23 · St. James's

Inn The Park	St James' Park	020 7451 9999	££££	7.30 pm	Watch the ducks watching you as you eat.
Stockpot	38 Panton St	020 7839 5142	££*	10.45 pm	Treacle pud & custard. Bish bash bosh.
The Wolsey	160 Piccadilly	020 7499 6996	££	12 am	Step back in time for an elegant afternoon tea for under 20 quid.

Map 24 · Trafalgar Square / The Strand

Bistro 1	33 Southampton St	020 7379 7585	££	11.30 pm	Posh kebabs etc at bargain prices.
Cafe in the Crypt	6 St Martin's Pl	020 7839 4342	££	10 pm	Spooky sandwiches and fruit crumble.
Covent Garden Market Café	Covent Garden	020 7240 4844	£*	10 pm	Cheap egg 'n' chips in heart of tourist London.
Farmer Brown	4 New Row	020 7240 0230	££*	8 pm	Cheap and very cheerful. Great lunches.
Gourmet Burger Kitchen	13 Maiden Ln	020 7240 9617	££	11 pm	Go for the Kiwiburger. Don't question the ingredients. Trust us.
India Club	143 Strand (Second floor, Strand Continental Hotel)	020 7836 0650	£	11 pm	Quirky run-down BYOB eaterie; more character than Brick Lane equivalents.
J Sheekey	28 St Martin's Ct	020 7240 2565	££££	11 pm	Old-fashioned seafood haven that the celebs still love.
RS Hispaniola	Victoria Embankment	020 7839 3011	££	10 pm	Feel the bloat, on a boat.
Rules	35 Maiden Ln	020 7836 5314	£££££	10.30 pm	London's oldest restaurant with old-fashioned comfort food to match.
Scott's Sandwich Bar	10 New Row	020 7240 0340	£	4 pm	Gets very busy at lunch mainly for the salt beef.
Thai Pot	1 Bedfordbury	020 7379 4580	££	11 pm	Busy but fast with fresh and generous helpings. Delicious Massaman curry.
Wahaca	66 Chandos Pl	020 7240 1883	£££	11 pm	Tasty Mexican market food/tapas. Always busy.

Map 25 · Kensal Town

Santo	299 Portobello Rd	020 8968 4590	££	11.30 pm	Fresh, frisky Mexican. Too bad about the resentful waiters.
Thai Rice	303 Portobello Rd	020 8968 2001	££	10.30 pm	Jaw-dropping food in sterile, bland environment.

Map 29 · Notting Hill Gate

Beach Blanket Babylon	45 Ledbury Rd	020 7229 2907	££££	12 am	Maze of baroque nooks and crannies where celebs nibble discreetly.
Cafe Diana	5 Wellington Terrace	020 7792 9606	£	10.30 pm	Creepy, kitsch shrine to Princess Diana with so-so food.
Costas	14 Hillgate St	020 7229 3794	££	10.30 pm	Heavenly, Cypriot-run fish and chips. Hellish Notting Hill prices.
Crazy Homies	125 Westbourne Park Rd	020 7727 6771	££	10.15 pm	Avoid first date awkwardness over quality Mexican at this lively get-up.
The Electric Brasserie	191 Portobello Rd	020 7908 9696	££	10 pm	Uber-trendy, worth a visit for the eggs benedict alone.
Eve's Market Cafe	222 Portobello Rd	020 7221 2633	£		Traditional greasy caff with vintage nicotine stains.
Geales	2 Farmer St	020 7727 7528	£££	10.30 pm	Feels ever-so-slightly like a front to appease visiting Americans.
Lucky 7	127 Westbourne Park Rd	020 7727 6771	£££	10.30 pm	Atmospheric diner for wistful yuppies.
Manzara	24 Pembridge Rd	020 7727 3062	£	11 pm	Burek Obama for president! Arf.
Negozio Classica	283 Westbourne Grove	020 7034 0005			Half bar, half store selling high-end Italian kitchen goods.
Osteria Basilico	29 Kensington Park Rd	020 7727 9372	£££	11.30 pm	Quaint, buzzing and full of Italian rustic charm. A local hot spot.
Ruby & Sequoia	6 All Saints' Rd	0207 243 6363	££££	12am	On the razzle at the Ruby.
Taqueria	139 Westbourne Grove	020 7229 4734	££	11 pm	Wash down these fresh mini-tacos with a good tequila.

525

Arts & Entertainment · **Restaurants**

Map 30 · Bayswater

Berdees Coffee Shop	84 Bishop's Bridge Rd	020 7727 0033	£*	9 pm	Hubbly Bubbly Jubbly. Chubbly?
The Cow	89 Westbourne Park Rd	020 7221 0021	£££	9.45pm	Top end bar food. Smart restaurant upstairs.
Kiasu	48 Queensway	020 7727 8810	£	11 pm	The best budget Indonesian/Malaysian cuisine. Mmmm.... Char Kway Teow...
Royal China	13 Queensway	020 7221 2535	£££	11.15 pm	Keep the Cantonese dim sum comin'!
Tiroler Hut	27 Westbourne Grove	020 7727 3981	££££	12 am	Dementedly kitsch Austrian madhouse with lederhosen-clad waiters.

Map 31 · Paddington

Bonne Bouche	129 Praed St	020 7724 5784	£	4.30 pm	Deli counter is popular with local workers for sandwiches.
Comptoir Libanais	26 London St	020 7262 1111	£	1 am	For Lebanese on the run or sit-down tagines
Mandalay	444 Edgware Rd	020 7258 3696	£	10.30 pm	Cheap treats await, despite the God awful. situation.

Map 32 · Shepherd's Bush (West)

Abu Zaad	29 Uxbridge Rd	020 8749 5107	£	11 pm	A colourful Syrian welcome. Posh Kebabs.
Esarn Kheaw	314 Uxbridge Road	020 8743 8930	£	11.30 pm	Outstanding Thai. Transport your taste buds to Bangkok.
Vine Leaves Taverna	71 Uxbridge Rd	020 8749 0325	£	1 am	Friendly staff, traditional grub, huge portions.

Map 33 · Shepherd's Bush

Jasmine	16 Goldhawk Rd	020 8743 7920	££	11 pm	Awesome Thai.
Jumbucks	24 Shepherd's Bush Green	020 8811 8111	£	1 am	Proper Aussie pies and heaps of Cherry Ripes served by smily peeps.Streuth!
Le Cinnamon	158 Shepherd's Bush Rd	020 7602 8899	££	11.30 pm	Great for dates. Intimate and a biryani to win over any girl (or guy!).
Popeseye	108 Blythe Rd	020 7610 4578	££££	10.30 pm	London's ONLY member of the Aberdeen Angus Society.

Map 34 · West Kensington / Olympia

The Belvedere Restaurant	Abbotsbury Road	020 7602 1238	£££	11 pm	Sublime setting—the same cannot always be said for the service.

Map 35 · Kensington

Byron	222 Kensington High St	020 7361 1717	££	10 pm	London's best burger? Locals in the know say so.
Clarke's	124 Kensington Church St	020 7221 9225	££	10 pm	Elegant, English fine dining. Perfect brunch spot if feeling refined.
Kensington Roof Gardens	99 Kensington High St	020 7937 7994	££££	1 am	Truly spectacular roof gardens and devine restaurant 100 foot above HS Ken.
Maggie Jones's	6 Old Court Pl	020 7937 6462	£££	10.30 pm	A British culinary time warp, but we like it anyway.
Zaika	1 Kensington High St	020 7795 6533	££	10.45 pm	If you can afford to treat yourself this is the place. Starters at £12.95!

Map 36 · South Kensington / Gloucester Rd

Cafe Creperie	2 Exhibition Rd	020 7589 8947	£	11.30 pm	Parisian crepe haven a stones throw from the museums.
Caffe Forum	146 Gloucester Rd	020 7259 2322	£*	11 pm	Strange proverbs about cows on the wall and £3.75 pizza. Student digs.
Da Mario	15 Gloucester Rd	020 7584 9078	£££	11.30 pm	Apparently Princess Di's local Italian Pizzeria. Affordable and A+ pizza.
Jacobs	20 Gloucester Rd	020 7581 9292	££	10 pm	Brave the slow service for delicious veggie dishes and fresh juices.
The Kensington Creperie	2 Exhibition Rd	020 7589 8947	£*	11 pm	The best sweet and savoury crepes in London.
Little Japan	32 Thurloe St	020 7591 0207	£*	11.30 pm	Wowzers: bento for a fiver? Suspicious and delicious.
Oddonno's	14 Bute St	020 7052 0732	£	11 pm	Gelato fix for homesick Italians and ice-cream freaks alike.
Pasha	1 Gloucester Rd	020 7589 7969	££££	11.30 pm	Cozy, intimate cubby holes, A+ service and delicious, yet pricey, set menus.

Arts & Entertainment · **Restaurants**

Map 37 · Knightsbridge

Zuma	5 Raphael St	020 7584 1010	£££	12 am	If your gal likes sushi, ideal for a romantic night out.

Map 38 · Chiswick

Boys Authentic Thai	95 Chiswick High Rd	020 8995 7991	££	10.30 pm	The staff are as funky and fresh as the food.
Chris' Fish and Chips	19 Turnham Green Terrace	020 8995 2367	£*	12 am	It's all British-ness wrapped in warm, greasy paper.
The Devonshire	126 Devonshire Rd	020 7592 7962	££	11 pm	A more affordable version of Ramsay.
Fish Hook	6 Elliot Rd	020 8742 0766	££	10.30 pm	Get hooked on seafood.
Foubert's	2 Turnham Green Terrace	020 8994 5202	£	11 pm	Little Italian owned cafe. Excellent ice cream and gelato.
Franco Manca	144 Chiswick High Rd	020 8747 4822	££	10 pm	London's best pizza with longer opening hours.
High Road Brasserie	162 Chiswick High Rd	020 8742 7474	££	11 pm	As good as it looks. The continent comes to the High Road.
Kalamari	4 Chiswick High Rd	020 8994 4727	££	12 am	For those with a feta fetish.
La Trompette	5 Devonshire Rd	020 8747 1836	£££	10.30 pm	Unpretentious French restaurant with excellent service and set menus.
Maison Blanc	26 Turnham Green Terrace	020 8995 7220	£		The cupcakes look devine from the window. Just wait until you get inside.
Turnham Green Cafe	57 Turnham Green Terrace	020 8994 3839	££		Looks can be deceiving. Serves up good thai in a small space.
Zizzi	231 Chiswick High Rd	020 8747 9400	££	11.30 pm	Skip the mains—cut straight to the heavenly Apple Crumble.

Map 39 · Stamford Brook

Carpenter's Arms	89 Black Lion Ln	020 8741 8386	£££	11 pm	As gastropub as it gets.
Tosa	332 King St	020 8748 0002	£	10 pm	Low-key authentic yakitori (fried skewered meat) joint. Easy on the wallet.

Map 40 · Goldhawk Rd / Ravenscourt Park

Blah Blah Blah	78 Goldhawk Rd	020 8746 1337	££*	10.30 pm	Eccentric, worldly vegetarian. Kinda like your ex, only cooler.
Lowiczanka Polish Cultural Centre	238 King Street	020 8741 3225	££	10 pm	Stodgy grub, hard drink, concrete block. So Polish you'll need a passport.
Mahdi	215 King St	020 8563 7007	££	12 am	Truly authentic, unpretentious Iranian place -menu in Arabic 'n all. Tasty!
Sagar	157 King St	020 8741 8563	££	11 pm	Yummy South Indian veggie food at a great price.

Map 41 · Hammersmith

The Gate	51 Queen Caroline St	020 8748 6932	££££	10 pm	Light and airy by day, cosy at night. Lovely food.

Map 42 · Baron's Court

Best Mangal	104 N End Rd	020 7610 1050	££	1 am	Proper good kebabs with heeeaps of nosh. Can sit in too - a rarity.
Bombay Bicycle Club	352 North End Rd	08454788205	£££	11pm	Lighter, brighter, more expensive, less authentic Indian restaurant. Still yum.
Ta Krai	100 North End Rd	020 7386 5375	££	10 pm	Decent, cheap food. Interior as tacky as its name suggests.

Map 43 · West Brompton / Fulham Broadway / Earls Court

The Blue Elephant	4 Fulham Broadway	020 7385 6595	££££	11.30 pm	Disney's version of Bangkok—grandiose, expensive, but oh, so good.
Bodean's	4 Broadway Chambers	020 7610 0440	£££	11 pm	Stuff yourself on BBQ pulled-pork sandwiches. Yee haw!
Chutney Mary	535 King's Rd	020 7351 3113	££££	11.30 pm	Get coddled over a curry (at a price).
Pizza@Home	350 Old Brompton Rd	020 7244 8080	£*	10 pm	Maybe London's most authentic Italian pizza. Fast and cheap as chips!!
Vingt Quatre	325 Fulham Rd	020 7376 7224	£	24-hrs	24 hour booze! Incidentally, the food is very good.
Yo! Sushi	Fulham Road	020 7385 6077	££	11 pm	Japanese conveyor belt sushi for beginners.

Arts & Entertainment · **Restaurants**

Key: £ : Under £10 : ££ : £10–£20 : £££ : £20–£30 : ££££ : £30–£40 : £££££ : £40+
* : Does not accept credit cards / † : Accepts only American Express / †† : Accepts only Visa and Mastercard
Time listed refers to kitchen closing time on weekend nights

Map 44 · Chelsea

Aubergine	11 Park Walk	020 7352 3449	££££	11 pm	Foie gras, lobster and truffles. Need we say more?
The Bluebird	350 King's Rd	020 7559 1000	£££	10.30 pm	So it seems you can get a bacon butty and look cool on the Kings Road.
Eight Over Eight	392 King's Rd	020 7349 9934	££££	11 pm	Exotic and dripping with celebs.

Map 45 · Chelsea (East)

Chelsea Kitchen	451 Fulham Rd	020 3055 0088	£	11 pm	New place, same affordable stodge. A Winner.
Four o nine	409 Clapham Rd	020 7737 0722	££££	10.30 pm	Inviting and intimate, it's nice.
Le Columbier	145 Dovehouse St	020 7351 1155	£££	11 pm	Vive le Bistro!
Made In Italy	249 King's Rd	020 7352 1880	££	11 pm	"Food Mama used to Make." Unless you're not Italian, obviously.
My Old Dutch Pancake House	221 King's Rd	020 7376 5650	£	11.30 pm	Sweet or savory pancakey goodness in the heart of Chelsea.
The Pig's Ear	35 Old Church St	020 7352 2908	££	10pm	Quirky, restored boozer. Deep fried pigs ear anyone? Seriously.
Sushinho	312 King's Rd	020 7349 7496	£££	10.30 pm	Sushi pizza anyone? They have it here.
Tom's Kitchen	27 Cale St	020 7349 0202	££££	11 pm	Crush-worthy (maybe just us?) Tom Aiken's British brasserie masterpiece.
Tom's Place	1 Cale St	020 7351 1806	£££	11 pm	Posh chippie.

Map 46 · Sloane Square

The Admiral Codrington	17 Mossop St	020 7581 0005	£££	10.30 pm	Go for simplicity here. Even the chips they get exactly right.
Bibendum Restaurant & Oyster Bar	81 Fulham Rd	020 7581 5817	£££££	11 pm	French institution with a cool (literally) oyster bar.
Blushes Cafe	52 King's Rd	020 7589 6640	£	1.30 am	Always reliable, always packed. C'est La Vie.
Foxtrot Oscar	79 Royal Hospital Rd	020 7352 4448	££	10 pm	Tango Alpha Sierra Tango Yankee.
Le Cercle	1 Wilbraham Pl	020 7901 9999	£££	12 am	Tapas-sized French yumminess. Pears with caramel popcorn, anyone?
Tom Aikens	43 Elystan St	020 7584 2003	£££££	11 pm	Artistic approach to just about everything.
Restaurant Gordon Ramsay	68 Royal Hospital Rd	020 7352 4441	£££££	11 pm	Mmmmmm... debt...

Map 47 · Fulham (West)

The River Café	Thames Wharf, Rainville Rd	020 7386 4200	£££	11 pm	Fine dining by the Thames for champagne socialists.

Map 48 · Fulham

Drawing Room Cafe	Bishop's Ave	020 7736 3233	£	5 pm	A historical and elegant spot for a cup of Earl Grey and a scone.
Fisher's Chips	19 Fulham High St	020 7610 9808	£	10 pm	Quality chips AND quality punning. It's why Britain's Great.

Map 49 · Parson's Green

De Cecco	189 New King's Rd	020 7736 1145	££	11 pm	Belissimo! Spaghetti a'll Aragosta is the signature dish and it's goood!
Ghillies	271 New King's Rd	020 7610 9675	££	10.30pm	Chic, relaxed continental eatery.
Kebab Kid	90 New Kings Road	020 7731 0427	£*	10 pm	Kebabs so impressive you could bring your gran here.
Mao Tai	58 New King's Rd	020 7731 2520	££	1 am	Modern, chic and pricey-but-delectable Pan-Asian menu in Parsons Green.
Tendido Cuatro	108 New King's Rd	020 7371 5147	£££		Perfecto! Mouth watering iberico jamon, buzzing and friendly Spanish staff.

Map 50 · Sand's End

Deep	The Boulevard, Imperial Wharf	020 7736 3337	££££	11 pm	Set for Gordon Ramsay's F-word. F-ing good itself.
Sands End	135 Stephendale Rd	020 7731 7823	£££		Hearty, rustic Irish fare. Nowt much else around but makes the grade.

Map 51 · Highgate

The Bull	13 North Hill Ave	0845 456 5033	£££	12 am	Chic eatery with perfectly positioned front terrace.
Cafe Rouge	6 South Grove	020 8342 9797	££	11 pm	Decent French restaurant and cafe chain
Papa Del's	347 Archway Rd	020 8347 9797	££	11 pm	Nice place. Good cookies. £3 pizzas after 9pm!
Red Lion And Sun	25 N Rd	020 8340 1780	££££	10 pm	Excellent Sunday roasts.

Map 52 · Archway (North)

Bengal Berties	172 Archway Rd	020 8348 1648	££	11 pm	Spit and sawdust venue with excellent nosh.
Dean & Hudson	249 Archway Rd	020 8340 1698	£		Amazing cakes and sweets for twee sugar junkies.
Fahrenheit	230 Archway Rd	020 8347 0333	££	11 pm	Corking Caribbean food with a broad smile.
The Lighthouse	179 Archway Rd	020 8348 3121	££	11 pm	Outstanding fresh fish joint flies beneath radar.

Map 53 · Crouch End

Arocaria	48 The Broadway	020 8340 0580	£££		Uber cute and relaxed Greek place.
Banners	21 Park Rd	020 8348 2930	££££	11.30 pm	Notoriously child-friendly but the breakfasts make up for that.
Hot Pepper Jelly	11 Broadway Parade	020 8340 4318	££*	5 pm	Pepperphobes probably shouldn't come to this culinary wonder.
Milou's on the Hill	83 Hazellville Rd	020 7272 1188	£*	9 pm	Go there for the hilltop terrace and homemade smoothies.
Piya Cafe	59 The Broadway	020 8347 8861	££	12 am	Great cheap and friendly Mediterranean grub.
Thaitanic	66 Crouch End Hill	020 8341 6100	££	11 pm	Groanworthy name, moanworthy food!

Map 54 · Hornsey

Ridge Cafe	97 Tottenham Ln	£££	£		Good place for quick lunch or just a caffeine boost.

Map 55 · Harringay

Muna's	599 Green Lanes	020 8340 8411	£££	1 am	Extremely slow service, but at least the food is good.
The Village	421 Green Lanes	077 8518 7715	££	2 am	Mountains of lovely, stodgy food.

Map 56 · Hampstead Village

Bacchus Greek Taverna	37 Heath St	020 7435 1855	£	11 pm	Lovely little place that has been here an age.
Carluccio's	34 Rosslyn Hill	020 7794 2184	£££	11 pm	Deli by day, diner by night.
La Creperie De Hampstead	77 Hampstead High St	020 7372 0081	£*	11 pm	No crap crepes at this sublime French street stall.
The Louis Patisserie	32 Heath St	020 7435 9908	£	6 pm	Tea and gorgeous cakes beloved of elderly Eastern European gentlemen.
Tinseltown	104 Heath St	020 7435 2396	£	3 am	Welcome to milkshake heaven!

Map 57 · Hamstead Heath

Hampstead Tea Rooms	9 S End Rd	020 7435 9563	£££	6.30 pm	Slooooooooow service...but the breakfast is worth the wait.
Osteria Emilia	85 Fleet Rd	020 7433 3317	££££	11.30 pm	Sure, it's pricey but the locals can afford it.
Paradise	49 S End Rd	020 7794 6314	£££		Excellent Indian with a modern twist.
Polly's	55 S End Rd	020 7431 7947	£	5 pm	Sometimes you just fancy a sarnie and a cuppa.

Map 58 · Parliament Hill / Dartmouth Park

Al Parco	2 Highgate West Hill	020 8340 5900	£	10 pm	Probably the best pizza in London.
Bistro Laz	1 Highgate West Hill	020 8342 8355	£	11 pm	Lovely meze. Or order if next door's full.
Cafe Mozart	17 Swain's Ln	020 8348 1384	££	10 pm	Great place for lunch on a sunny day.
The Carob Tree	15 Highgate Rd	020 7267 9880	£££	11 pm	Swanky Greek place with nice terrace in summer.
Indian Spice Lounge	13 Swain's Ln	020 8340 7818	££	11 pm	Curry and cocktails. No really.
Kalendar	15 Swains Lane	020 8348 8300	££	11 pm	Pre-Heath brekkie, mid-Heath lunch or post-Heath dinner. All good!
Stingray Cafe	135 Fortess Rd	020 7482 4855	£	11 pm	Another reason why Tufnell Park rocks: great place!

Key: £ : Under £10 / ££ : £10–£20 / £££ : £20–£30 / ££££ : £30–£40 / £££££ : £40+
* : Does not accept credit cards./ † : Accepts only American Express / †† : Accepts only Visa and Mastercard
Time listed refers to kitchen closing time on weekend nights

Map 59 · Tufnell Park

Charuwan	110 Junction Rd	020 7263 1410	£££	10 pm	Friendly, quiet, tasty, cheap. Yup, it's pretty awesome.
Rustique Cafe	142 Fortess Rd	020 7692 5590	££	8 pm	Damn those tasty tasty cookies for being so small.
Spaghetti House	169 Fortess Rd	020 7485 7984	££	10 pm	Just like mama used to make it.
The Spice	161 Fortess Rd	020 7482 2700	££	11.30 pm	Top-notch curries

Map 60 · Archway

Archgate Café	5 Junction Rd	020 7272 2575	£	10 pm	Lovely English breakfasts face-off against equally ace Turkish food.
Iceland Fish Bar	11 Archway Rd	020 7272 6606	£	10 pm	Proper old-school chippie.
Junction Café	61 Junction Rd	020 7263 2036	£*	10 pm	Greasy. Spoon.
La Voute	10 Archway Rd	020 7281 7314	£	4.30 pm	Ace brekkies and lunches in this snazzy caff.
Mosaic Café	24 Junction Rd	020 7272 3509	£	10.30 pm	Head for the back garden sun-trap in Summer.
Nid Ting	533 Holloway Rd	020 7263 0506	£££	11.15 pm	Bigger, meatier portions than most Thai Restaurants.
RRC Thai Cafe	36 Highgate Hill	020 7561 0421	£	10.30 pm	Cheap, tasty and beautifully presented Thai food.
St Johns	91 Junction Rd	020 7272 1587	££££	11 pm	Gastro pub oasis stranded among the pound-shops of Archway.
The Toll Gate	6 Archway Close	020 7687 2066	££	11 pm	On with the pince-nez for slightly self-satisfied veggie venue.

Map 61 · Holloway (North)

The Landseer	37 Landseer Rd	020 7263 4658	££	9.30 pm	Gastropub extraordinaire.
Orexi	236 Hornsey Rd	020 7607 7098	££		Amazing: unchanged since elderly couple opened 30 yrs ago.
Tagine D'Or	92 Seven Sisters Rd	020 7700 7666	£		Tiny, weird and criminally cheap. Like the NFT!

Map 62 · Finsbury Park

Fassika	152 Seven Sisters Rd	020 7272 7572	££	12 am	Intimate with lovely food. Distinctly flirty waitresses though...
Le Rif	172 Seven Sisters Rd	020 7263 1891	£*	10 pm	Essential for all your banter and microwaved Tagine needs.
Petek	96 Stroud Green Rd	020 7619 3933	£	10.45 pm	Classy but cheap Turkish.

Map 63 · Manor House

Il Bacio	178 Blackstock Rd	020 7226 3339	££	11 pm	Friendly, reliable and huge portions.
New River Cafe	271 Stoke Newington Church St	020 7923 9842	£	11 pm	Steamy windows and top hangover cure fry-ups.

Map 64 · Stoke Newington

Alistair's Brasserie	35 Stoke Newington Church St	020 7249 2782	££££	10 pm	Luxurious food with gobshite, luddite customers. Mmmmm.
Anglo Asian	60 Stoke Newington Church St	020 7254 3633	££	11.30 pm	Classic curry house right down to the free sherry.
Blue Legume	101 Stoke Newington Church St	020 7923 1303	£	11 pm	Dreamy eggs benedict, served under a giant aubergine.
Fifty Six	56 Newington Green	020 7359 6377	££	11.30 pm	Bring a date.
Rasa N16	55 Stoke Newington Church St	020 7249 0344	££	11.30 pm	Vegetarian-style Indian cooking at its mouth-watering best.
Sariyer Balik	56 Green Lanes	020 7275 7681	£££	12 am	Turkish Seafood.
Yum Yum	187 Stoke Newington High St	020 7254 6751	£££	11 pm	Tasty tasty, Thai Thai. Go for the Kang Massuman.

Map 65 · West Hampstead

The Green Room	182 Broadhurst Gardens	020 7372 8188	££	11 pm	West Hampstead's newest joint brimming with charm. Nice risotto.
Small & Beautiful	351 Kilburn High Rd	020 7328 2637	£		Small and beautiful indeed, as is the bill.

Map 66 · Finchley Road / Swiss Cottage

Bradleys	25 Winchester Rd	020 7722 3457	£££	11 pm	Your friendly face in the neighbourhood that loves wine.
Camden Arts Centre	Arkwright Rd	020 7472 5500	£	6 pm	Excellent food in buzzing artistic setting.
Singapore Garden	83 Fairfax Rd	020 7328 5314	££	11 pm	Surprising flavours make a welcome alternative on a night out.

Map 67 · Belsize Park

Artigiano	12 Belsize Terrace	020 7794 4288	£££	11 pm	Fancy some fancy pasta?
Brasserie Gerard	215 Haverstock Hill	020 7431 8101	£££	11 pm	Bon jour. Une burger with fromage, merci please.
Curry Manjil	34 England's Ln	020 7722 9101	££	12 am	Local fave still going strong after 40 years.
Paradiso	36 England's Ln	020 7586 9001	££	11.30 pm	For those on a carbs, cheese and cream diet.
Retsina	48 Belsize Ln	020 7431 5855	££	11 pm	Lively Greek - grilled meat galore!
Violette Cafe	2 England's Ln	020 7586 4326	££	6.30 pm	Cakey goodness.

Map 68 · Kilburn High Road / Abbey Road

Little Bay	228 Belsize Rd	020 7372 4699	££*	11 pm	Crazy cheap. Crazy cute!

Map 69 · St. John's Wood

Tupelo Honey	27 Parkway, Camden	020 7284 2989	££	11 pm	A coffee-shop, wine bar and restaurant combined.

Map 70 · Primrose Hill

Cafe Seventy Nine	79 Regents Park Rd	020 7586 8012	£	6 pm	Excellent veggie fare, though you might have to wait.
The Hill Bar	94 Haverstock Hill	020 7267 0033	£££	11 pm	The Hill is an ideal place to meet friends before heading off to a show.
J Restaurant	148 Regents Park Rd	020 7586 9100	££	11 pm	Excellent food, especially brunch. Tempestuous service.
Legal Cafe	81 Haverstock Hill	020 7586 7412	£	6 pm	Great coffee, good food and wifi: a pleasant working environment.
Lemonia	89 Regents Park Rd	020 7586 7454	£££	11.30 pm	Fancy a real Greek meal?
Manna	4 Erskine Rd	020 7722 8028	££	11.30 pm	Aesthetically gorgeous veggie restaurant, serving scrumptious food.
Melrose and Morgan	42 Gloucester Ave	020 7722 0011	£	8 pm	Scrumptious food and coffee. Good for solo snacks.
Odette's	130 Regents Park Rd	020 7586 8569	£££	1 am	Delectably dainty restaurant, high-class service.
Primrose Bakery	69 Gloucester Ave	020 7483 4222	£	6 pm	A delectably dinky bakery. These cakes can't be missed.
Trojka	101 Regents Park Rd	020 7483 3765	££	10 pm	Authentically spartan but colourful decor. Nice 'n' quirky.
Two Brothers	297 Regents Park Rd	020 8346 0469	££	10 pm	Middle class fish & chips.

Map 71 · Camden Town / Chalk Farm / Kentish Town (West)

Andy's Taverna	81 Bayham St	020 7485 9718	££	11 pm	Big Greek restaurant with a garden.
Bar Gansa	2 Inverness St	020 7267 8909	££	12 am	More buzzing and pleasurable than a rampant rabbit.
Bar Solo	20 Inverness St	020 7482 4611	££	1 am	Where'd they find the waitresses? On the set of Clueless?
Bento Café	9 Parkway	020 7482 3990	££	11pm	Exquisite Japanese food at very reasonable prices.
Camden Bar and Kitchen	102 Camden High St	020 7485 2744	££	11 pm	Great burgers at this bohemian gem; sorry, McDonald's!
Cotton's	55 Chalk Farm Rd	020 7485 8388	££	10 pm	No hustle and bustle, just chill Jamaican-style.
Gilgamesh	The Stables Market, Chalk Farm Rd	020 7428 4922	£££*	12 am	Awesome surroundings will confuse the hell out of future archaeologists.
The Green Note	106 Parkway	020 7485 9899	££	11 pm	Excellent veggie tapas with a side of bongo drums.
Haché	24 Inverness St	020 7485 9100	££	10.30 pm	Burger heaven for both vegetarians and carnivores.
Kim's Vietnamese Food Hut some	Unit D, Camden Lock Palace	N/A	£*	11 pm	Once you pass the Spanish Inquisition, excellent slop.
Limani	154 Regents Park Rd	020 7483 4492	£££	11 pm	Greek-Cypriot fare in a sophisticated environment. Friendly service.

Marathon Cafe	87 Chalk Farm Rd	020 7485 3814	£*	4 am	Legendary late-night venue serving kebabs, chips and beer.
Marine Ices	8 Haverstock Hill	020 7482 9003	£	11 pm	Fantastic ice cream restaurant with '70s decor and autographed photos.
Market	438 Parkway	020 7267 9700	£££	11 pm	The only restaurant in Camden deserving of the name.
Muang Thai	71 Chalk Farm Rd	020 7916 0653	£	11 pm	Quiet vibe, tinkly music, reliably decent food.
My Village	37 Chalk Farm Rd	020 7485 4996	£	9pm	Cute vibrant organic shop serving food, tea and coffee.
Thanh Binh	14 Chalk Farm Rd	020 7267 9820	£	10 pm	Excellent Vietnamese with very friendly and chatty staff.
Viet-anh Cafe	41 Parkway	020 7284 4082	£	11 pm	Surly service, cheap plentiful food. Would it hurt to smile?
Woody Grill	1 Camden Rd	020 7485 7774	£*	12 am	Late night post-alcohol food without salmonella poisoning.
Yumchaa Tea Space	91 Upper Walkway, West Yard, Camden Lock Market	020 7209 9641	£*	6 pm	The carrot cake... oh mama!
Zorya Imperial Vodka Room	48 Chalk Farm Rd	020 7485 8484	££	12 am	Vodka, vodka and more vodka. Oh... and gorgeous food too.

Map 72 · Kentish Town

Bintang Cafe	93 Kentish Town Rd	020 7813 3393	££	11 pm	Good for eating copiously in a gaudy shack.
The Bengal Lancer	253 Kentish Town Rd	020 7485 6688	£££		The best (and priciest) indian in the area.
Eatzone	18 Fortess Rd	020 7485 0152	£*	11 pm	Quick and delicious, with roughly 1 gazillion choices. Addictive.
Le Petit Prince	5 Holmes Rd	020 7267 3789	££	11 pm	Adorable homage to French cartoon character with excellent merguez.
Mario's Cafe	6 Kelly St	020 7284 2066	£*	10 pm	Saint Etienne's local greasy spoon.
The Oxford	256 Kentish Town Rd	020 7485 3521	££	9.45 pm	Smug comfort eating.
Pane Vino	323 Kentish Town Rd	020 7267 3879	££	10.30 pm	Start as Italian. Food can be fantastic.
Phoenicia - Mediterranean Food Hall	186 Kentish Town Rd	020 7267 1267	£	11 pm	Coffee n' baclava, falafel, meze. All a steal.

Map 74 · Holloway Road / Arsenal

Dastarkhan	203 Holloway Rd	075 4521 1010	££	2 am	Frankly bizarre Khazak place. Entertaining, but so no nosh.
Morgan M	489 Liverpool Rd	020 7609 3560	£££££	11 pm	Divine Frenchie. Mais zut alors! £1200 bottles of wine!
Tbilisi	91 Holloway Rd	020 7607 2536	££££	11 pm	Get your Georgian on.

Map 75 · Highbury

San Daniele Del Friuli	72 Highbury Park	020 7226 1609	£££	12 am	Like mama used to make—well someone had to say it.
Ustun	107 Green Lanes		£	10 pm	Very nice lamachun.

Map 76 · Edgeware Road / Marylebone (North)

Sea Shell Of Lisson Grove	49 Lisson Grove	020 7224 9000	££	10.30 pm	Pescatarians will love this place—sorry, carnivores!

Map 77 · Mornington Crescent / Regent's Park

Chutneys	124 Drummond St	020 7388 0604	££	11.30 pm	Flavoursome, no-frills, fill-yer-boots affair. Bargainous buffet colossal.
Diwana Bhelpoori	121 Drummond St	020 7387 5556	££	11 pm	South-Indian veggie with tasty dosai and puris.
Mestizo	103 Hampstead Rd	020 7387 4064	£££	11 pm	Great. The margarita is made by the devil himself.
York & Albany	127 Parkway	020 7388 3344	£££	11 pm	Gordo on a budget.

Map 78 · Euston

Asakusa	265 Eversholt St	020 7388 8399	£££	11.30 pm	Authentic Japanese.
Banger Bros.	Euston Station	020 7387 6958	£	7.30 pm	Sing it: It's a small world (of sausages) after all!
Camino	3 Varnisher's Yard	020 7841 7331	£££	12 am	Sophisticated Spanish restaurant in Kings Cross. Seems wrong, somehow.

Chop Chop Noodle Bar	1 Euston Rd	020 7833 1773	£	11 pm	Great for a quick and cheap meal. Massive portions.
El Parador	245 Eversholt St	020 7387 2789	££	11 pm	Great tapas. A little ray of sunshine in your mouth.
Great Nepalese	48 Eversholt St	020 7388 6737	££	11 pm	Really the only option in the area.
Kitchin	8 Caledonia St	020 7713 8777	££	11 pm	Round-the-world all-you-can-eat. Vile and great.
Rodon Live	7 Pratt St	020 7267 8088	££	11 pm	Friendly rotund owner masks just above average food.
The Somerstown Coffee House	60 Chalton St	020 7691 9136	££	10 pm	Bistro food in grade II listed pub. Excellent set menu.
Tony's Natural Foods	10 Caledonian Rd	020 7837 5223	£	11 pm	Vegan salad bar with peaceout garden, man.

Map 79 • King's Cross

Addis	42 Caledonian Rd	020 7278 0679	££	11 pm	Lovely food with convivial sloth-like service.
Dallas Burger Bar	257 Caledonian Rd	020 7278 4955	£*	9 pm	JR smiles down as you destroy your arteries. Hilarious.
Euro Café	299 Caledonian Rd	020 7607 5362	£	10 pm	Loveable caff with some unusual specials.
Marathon	196 Caledonian Rd	020 7837 4499	££	12 am	Raw meat, ritualistic coffee and crazed dancing.
Menelik	277 Caledonian Rd	020 7700 7774	££	12 am	If only more places let you eat with your hands.
The New Didar	347 Caledonian Rd	020 7700 3496	£	12 am	Friendly staff willing to strike deals. Haggling gets you everywhere.
Oz	53 Caledonian Rd	020 7278 9650	£*	10 pm	Unusually well-kept greasy spoon.
Yum Yum	48 Caledonian Rd	020 7278 4737	£	11 pm	Super-cheap Chinese that may even remain in your stomach.

Map 80 • Angel / Upper St

Afghan Kitchen	35 Islington Green	020 7359 8019	£££*	10.45 pm	Only a few tables; Islington's smallest—and biggest— Afghan place.
The Albion	10 Thornhill Rd	020 7607 7450	££	10 pm	How many places offer whole suckling pigs? Not enough.
Alpino	97 Chapel Market	020 7837 8330	£	4 pm	This, guv'nor, is a proper tea'n'two slices caff. Alright?
The Breakfast Club	31 Camden Passage	020 7226 5454	££	9.30 pm	Not just breakfast, not a club. But just so gooood.
Candid Café	3 Torrens St	020 7837 4237	£	10 pm	Laid-back, arty cafe for dreamy types. Candle-lit. Perfect for lingering.
Desperados	127 Upper St	020 7226 3222	££	11.30 pm	Garish. More like the Mexico of MTV than the real world.
Elk in the Woods	39 Camden Passage	020 7226 3535	££	10.30 pm	Laid-back, hunting-themed eatery.
Fig and Olive	151 Upper St	020 7354 2605	££	11 pm	Incredibly busy at weekends which can affect service and quality.
Fine Burger Co	330 Upper St	020 7359 3026	£	10 pm	For when you've grown out of McDonalds.
Fredericks	Camden Passage	020 7359 2888	££		Swanky Euro-flash bistro.
Gem	265 Upper St	020 7359 0405	£££	11 pm	A good vibe is precious.
House	63 Canonbury Rd	020 7704 7410	££	10.30 pm	Gastro bar-restaurant where seasonal food's served with flair. For those feeling flush.
Indian Veg Bhelpoori House	93 Chapel Market	020 7833 1167	£	10 pm	Honest all-you-can-eat Indian. Veggie propaganda on walls.
Isarn	119 Upper St	020 7424 5153	££	11 pm	Pretty, flower-adorned food, green curry cooked to perfection. Candle-lit courtyard.
Itsuka	54 Islington Park St	020 7354 5717	£	12 am	Cheap set menus and heartfelt J-Pop.
La Forchetta	73 Upper St	020 7226 6879	££	11.30 pm	Unpretentious, cheap pizza. Eat fast, then leg it.
La Porchetta	141 Upper St	020 7288 2488	££	11 pm	This little pig says yes to good cheap pizza.
Le Mercury	140 Upper St	020 7354 4088	££	1 am	This place will seduce you AND your mother.
Masala Zone	80 Upper St	020 7359 3399	££	11 pm	Cheap, good thalis served on metal trays.
Mem & Laz	8 Theberton St	020 7704 9089	££	11 pm	Mediterranean chaos by candlelight.
Metrogusto	13 Theberton St	020 7226 9400	££	10.30 pm	Try not to let the menacing art put you off the amazing pasta.
Olive Grill	61 Upper St	020 7226 9002	£*	10 pm	The falafels are so good you may quit kebabs. Forever.
Ottolenghi	287 Upper St	020 7288 1454	££	11 pm	Staff you'll want to take home to meet your mum.
Pizzeria Oregano	19 St Alban's Pl	020 7288 1123	££	11 pm	Great pizza and lentil soup. Delicious odd couple.
Pomegranate	139 Upper St	020 7704 1002	££	12 am	Bright. And not in a clever way.
Rodizo Rico	77 Upper St	020 7354 1076	£££	11 pm	Meat. And lots of it.

533

Key: £ : Under £10 / ££ : £10–£20 / £££ : £20–£30 / ££££ : £30–£40 / £££££ : £40+
* : Does not accept credit cards / † : Accepts only American Express / †† : Accepts only Visa and Mastercard
Time listed refers to kitchen closing time on weekend nights

Tortilla	13 Islington High St	020 7833 3103	££	10 pm	Damn good burritos!
Vigata Ristorante	70 Liverpool Rd	020 7226 1475	££	10 pm	Sardonic shape of Sicilian? This lobster linguine will soon fix that.
Zaffrani	47 Cross St	020 7226 5522	££	11 pm	Thinking man's curry.

Map 81 · Canonbury

Angel Cafe	100 Essex Rd	020 7704 6866	£	11 pm	Blue collar fusion cuisine: Brit greasy spoon serving Turkish boreks.
Raab's Bakery	136 Essex Rd	020 7226 2830	£	6 pm	Use your loaf sunshine.
Sabor	108 Essex Rd	020 7226 5551	££££	11 pm	Latin American; even the tables are tropical.
Zigni House	330 Essex Rd	020 7226 7418	£	12 am	Hearty East African eatery with boho, raffish charm.

Map 82 · De Beauvoir Town / Kingsland

Casaba	162 Essex Rd	020 7288 1223	££	7 pm	Fresh spin on Turkish meze and shisha bar.
Huong Viet	12 Englefield Rd	020 7249 0877	££	11 pm	A crumbling old bath house? Look again.
Puji Puji	122 Balls Pond Rd	020 7923 2112	££	10 pm	Malaysian Malaysian.

Map 83 · Angel (East) / City Rd (North)

The Charles Lamb	16 Elia St	020 7837 5040	££	9.30pm	Chilled-out Sunday lunch perfection.
Shepherdess Cafe	221 City Rd	020 7253 2463	£	5pm	Cafe offering no-frills traditional English fare
William IV	7 Shepherdess Walk	020 3119 3010	££	12am	Lovely gastropub, off the beaten track and with delicious food.

Map 84 · Hoxton

The Bean	126 Curtain Rd	020 7739 7829	£*	8 pm	Decent coffee! It's hard to find, you know.
The Diner	128 Curtain Rd	020 7729 4452	£££	10.30 pm	Door-stopper burgers that should come with health warnings.
F.Cooke	150 Hoxton St	020 7729 7718	££	8 pm	Pies, Liquor, Eels... British culinary retardation at it's finest.
Fifteen	15 Westland Pl	020 3375 1515	£££££	10 pm	Lots of Jamie Oliver. Lots of great, expensive food.
Shish	313 Old Street	020 7749 0990	££	10 pm	Great kebabs in surroundings devoid of authenticity.
Yelo	8 Hoxton Sq	020 7729 4626	£	11 pm	Suspiciously quick service, but cheap and tasty so who cares?

Map 85 · Stoke Newington (East)

19 Numara Bos Cirrik	34 Stoke Newington Rd	020 7249 0400	££	10 pm	Meat, meat, meat—oh and onion, pomegranate and turnip salad.
Bagel House	2 Stoke Newington High St	020 7249 3908	£*	10 pm	Bagels to rival Brick Lane and without the queues.
Cafe Z Bar	58 Stoke Newington High St	020 7275 7523	£*	11 pm	Popular cheese-shop/hangover center for Stokey Lefties.
Testi	38 Stoke Newington High St	020 7249 7151	£££	12 am	Yes, it's named after bollocks. No, it's really not bollocks.
Thai Cafe	3 Northwold Rd	020 7249 2618	££	11 pm	Deceptively pokey, unimaginatively named, yet brilliant.
Three Crowns	175 Stoke Newington Church St	020 7241 5511	££	9.30 pm	Impressive Victorian pub that's undergone gastropubification.

Map 86 · Dalston / Kingsland

The Best Turkish Kebab	125 Stoke Newington Rd	020 7254 7642	£*	12 am	Feed your soul. Always buzzing.
Dalston Lane Café	170 Dalston Ln	020 7254 4704	£	5pm	French toast with bacon and maple: an alchemical combination of savoury and sweet.
Dem Cafe	18 Stoke Newington Rd	020 7254 6364	££	12 am	For when Zed Bar's too full.
El Panchos	176 Stoke Newington Rd	020 7923 9588	£	11 pm	Cheesoid mexican with decent cocktails.
Evin Bar and Cafe	115 Kingsland High St	020 7254 5634	££	11 pm	Fantastic Turkish place without the grease factor. Speciality is gozleme.
LMNT	316 Queensbridge Rd	020 7249 6727	£££	10.45 pm	Eat inside an urn or by a sphinx's paws.
Mangal 1	10 Arcola St	020 7275 8981	£*	12 am	May the grill's smoke guide you, meat-loving friends.

Mangal 2	4 Stoke Newington Rd	020 7254 7888	££	12 am	Gilbert & George aren't the only ones loving this one.
Peppers and Spice	20 Kingsland High St	020 7275 9818	£*	10.30 pm.	The real deal: jerk, oxtail, festival, plantain, ackee. Everyting irie.
Shanghai	41 Kingsland High St	020 7254 2878	££	10.30 pm	Tasty, good-value Chinese hiding behind the facade of a dingy old Kaff.
Somine	131 Kingsland High St	020 7254 7384	£*	24 hrs	Reanimating red lentil soup, Turkish style. Around the clock.
Stone Cave	111 Kingsland High St	020 7241 4911	££	12 am	Cave look and cave feel. Up-scale(ish) Turkish. And great.
The Tea Rooms	155 Stoke Newington Rd	020 7923 1870	£	10 pm	Stokey in a tea-cup. Pleasant...

Map 87 · Hackney Downs / Lower Clapton

Dunya	199 Lower Clapton Rd	020 8985 7989	£*	2 am	Cuz you can't diet all the time. Or any time.
India Gate	75 Lower Clapton Rd	020 8986 0505	£*	11 pm	Very, very cheap, pretty cheerful and a little rank.
Mess Café	38 Amhurst Rd	020 8985 3194	£	5pm	All manner of breakfast all the time.
Parioli	90 Lower Clapton Rd	020 7502 3288	£	9 pm	Best food of any kind in Clapton.
Pogo Cafe	76 Clarence Rd	020 8533 1214	£*	9 pm	Vegan co-op community caff. Real food for thought.

Map 88 · Haggerston / Queensbridge Rd

Faulkner's	424 Kingsland Rd	020 7254 6152	£££	10 pm	Legendary and traditional with traditional opening times
That Vietnamese Place	134 Kingsland Rd	020 7729 4843	££	10 pm	Not as memorable as the name would have you believe.
Uludag	398 Kingsland Rd	020 7241 1923	£		Great falafels and a bit of a nutter hub to boot.
Usha	428 Kingsland Rd	020 7241 0836	£	11 pm	One of few curry houses in the area. Consistently good.
Viet Hoa Café	70 Kingsland Rd	020 7729 8293	£	11.30 pm	Bland looking cafe hides gorgeous delicacies.

Map 89 · London Fields / Hackney Central

Buen Ayre	50 Broadway Market	020 7275 9900	££££	10.30 pm	Vegetarians take note—run for the hills.
Cafe Bohemia	2 Bohemia Pl	020 8986 4352	£	11 pm	Feeling Bohemian? Quirky cafe with live blues/jazz/world Saturday nights.
Cat and Mutton	76 Broadway Market	020 7254 5599	££	10 pm	Gastropub without the gastropub nastiness.
Corner Deli	121 Mare St	020 8986 0031	£	9 pm	Nice spot for brunch away from the bustle of Broadway Market.
Hai Ha	206 Mare St	020 8985 5388	££*	11 pm	Amazing BYO Vietnamese cafe.
R Cooke and Sons	9 Broadway Market	020 7254 6458	£*	8 pm	Lor' love a duck! Pie n' mash shop—liquor an' all!
The Spurstowe Arms	68 Greenwood Rd	020 7254 4316	££	11 pm	Suntrap beer garden, good wine selection and gamey menu. Marvellous.

Map 90 · Homerton / Victoria Park North

The Empress of India	130 Lauriston Rd	020 8533 5123	£££	10 pm	Spiffy menu from brekkie through to dinner in Hackney Village.
The Fish House	126 Lauriston Rd	020 8533 3327	££	9.45 pm	Not as cheap as chips but still very good.

Map 91 · Shoreditch / Brick Lane / Spitalfields

Beigel Shop	155 Brick Lane	020 7729 0826	£*	24 hrs	For 3am cravings; salted beef bagel from the Beigel Shop.
Brick Lane Clipper Restaurant	104 Brick Ln	020 7377 0022	££	12 am	For less spice-oriented connoisseurs, Bengali Clipper's exceptional lamb korma.
Boundary	2 Boundary St	020 7729 1051	£££	10.30 pm	Warehouse conversion, great view, some major boxes being ticked here.
Cafe Bangla	128 Brick Lane	020 7247 7885	££	12 am	Popular Bangladeshi adorned with psychedelic and surreal fantasy art.
Drunken Monkey	222 Shoreditch High St	020 7392 9606	££	12 am	Debauched, dimly-lit dim-sum drinking hole. Chinese lanterns and lethal mojitos.
Ethiopian Food Stall	Sunday Upmarket, Truman's Brewery, Brick Lane	N/A	£*	N/A	One of many great food stalls, get Brazilian dessert after!
Gourmet San	261 Bethnal Green Rd	020 7729 8388	£	11pm	Whole crabs and minimal English.
Green & Red	51 Bethnal Green Rd	020 7749 9670	£	11 pm	Foot-tappin' Mexican cantina for fab tacos and proper guacamole. Ole!
Hackney City Farm	1 Goldsmiths Row	020 7729 6381	££	4.30 pm	Animals! In Hackney! And some overpriced fry-up.

Key: £ : Under £10 / ££ : £10–£20 / £££ : £20–£30 / ££££ : £30–£40 / £££££ : £40+
* : Does not accept credit cards./ † : Accepts only American Express / †† : Accepts only Visa and Mastercard
Time listed refers to kitchen closing time on weekend nights

Hanoi Cafe	98 Kingsland Rd	020 7729 5610	££	11 pm	Cosy Viet joint, where the whole family's around.
Hawksmoor	157 Commercial St	020 7247 7392	£££	10.30 pm	France and America forget their differences for some serious steakage.
Jones Dairy Café	23 Ezra St	020 7739 5372	£*	3 pm	Sit back and watch the world go by at Columbia Road.
Les Trois Garcons	1 Club Row	020 7613 1924	££££	11 pm	Kitch décor/slick service/fantastic grub.
Noodle King	185 Bethnal Green Rd	020 7613 3050	£*	11.30 pm	Half the normal price; double the normal portions. Come hungry.
Ping Pong	3 Steward St	020 7422 7650	££	11 pm	Serviceable dim sum in a frantic shitstorm.
The Premises	209 Hackney Rd	020 7684 2230	££	11 pm	Bistro swarming with musicians thanks to next door's recording studio.
Que Viet	102 Kingsland Rd	020 7033 0588	££	11 pm	So du jour—even Marc Jacobs munches noodles here.
Rootmaster	Elys Yard	079 1238 9314	££	10 pm	Eat on a bus without looking homeless.
Rosa's	12 Hanbury St	020 7247 1093	££		Quirky, warm little Thai place.
Song Que	134 Kingsland Rd	020 7613 3222	££	11 pm	Still Little Vietnam's queen. An authentic, no-nonsense affair.
St John Bread and Wine	94 Commercial St	020 7251 0848	£££	11 pm	Minimalist and meaty. Anyone for deep-fried pig's head?
Story Deli	91 Brick Ln	020 7247 3137	£	9 pm	Lo-tech pizza joint. Think hipster Pizza Express.
Tay Do	60 Kingsland Rd	020 7739 0966	£	11 pm	Squish 'em in, feed 'em quick variety of cheap & filling Vietnamese cuisine.
Tay Do Cafe	65 Kingsland Rd	020 7729 7223	£££	12 am	Hectic and noisy. Just like Vietnam, then.
Viet Grill	58 Kingsland Rd	020 7739 6686	££	11 pm	Eccentric but tasty. Non-edible tropical fish as decor...

Map 92 · Bethnal Green

Bistrotheque	23 Wadeson St	020 8983 7900	££	11 pm	Brunch, burlesque and pianist playing Smells Like Teen Spirit. Fabulous.
E Pellicci	332 Bethnal Green Rd	020 7739 4873	£	4.30 pm	Challenge your hangover to survive their fry-ups.
Little Georgia	87 Goldsmiths Row	020 7739 8154	££	10 pm	Hearty fayre from the former Soviet State. No drinks licence.
Wild Cherry	241 Globe Rd	020 8980 6678	££	4 pm	Buddhist staff serve yummy breakfasts to hungover partiers. Instant karma.

Map 93 · Globe Town / Mile End (North)

Matsu	558 Mile End Rd	020 8983 3528	££	11 pm	Japanese food? In Mile End? You're 'avin a giraffe aintcha?
The Morgan Arms	43 Morgan St	020 8980 6389	£££	12 am	Which joker invented the term "gastropub"? This is one of them.

Map 94 · Bow

Chicchi	516 Roman Rd	020 8141 4190	£*	7 pm	The Italians reclaim Roman Road.
G.Kelly Pie & Mash shop	526 Roman Rd	020 8980 3165	£	7 pm	Servin' 'ot 'ome-made pies, jellied eels 'n mash since 1937.
The Roman Tandoori	432 Roman Road	020 8980 1390	££	10 pm	If you can't stand eels, 'ave a curry instead.

Map 95 · Whitechapel (West) / St Katharine's Dock

Cafe Spice Namaste	16 Prescot St	020 7488 9242	££	10.30 pm	Open-minded Indian that strays far from run of the mill.
The Empress	141 Leman St	020 7265 0745	£	11.45 pm	Forget Brick Lane. This is where it's at.

Map 96 · Whitechapel (East) / Shadwell (West) / Wapping

Il Bordello	81 Wapping High St	020 7481 9950	£££	10 pm	Upscale neighbourhood Italian.
Tayyabs	83 Fieldgate St	020 7247 6400	£	12 am	Lipsmacking seekh kebabs alone are worth the queues.

Map 97 · Stepney / Shadwell (East)

Wapping Food	Wapping Wall	020 7680 2080	£££	11 pm	Stunning dining in 100 year old powerstation/ art gallery. Go!

Map 98 • Mile End (South) / Limehouse

La Figa	45 Narrow St	020 7790 0077	££	11 pm	Tasty Italian in courtyard setting.
The Narrow	44 Narrow St	020 7592 7950	££	11 pm	Gordon Ramsay's nod to gastropubs—cracking views.
Orange Room Cafe	63 Burdett Rd	020 8980 7336	£££	11.30 pm	Tasty, fresh Lebanese food in a wasteland of stodgy takeaways.

Map 100 • Poplar (West) / Canary Wharf (West)

1802 Bar	Hertsmere Rd	020 7538 2702	££	11 pm	Dine inside the warehouse built by Napoleonic prisoners.
Browns	Hertsmere Rd	020 7987 9777	£££	11 pm	Always reliable.
Nicolas	480 One Canada Sq	020 7512 9092	££	10.30 pm	Micro French restaurant and vintners in one.
Plateau	Canada Pl	020 7715 7100	££££	10.30 pm	Striking views and truffle gnocchi.
Tiffin Bites	22 Jubilee Place	020 7719 0333	££	10 pm	Eat curry, watch Bollywood films.

Map 101 • Poplar (East) / Canary Wharf (East)

Gun	27 Coldharbour	020 7515 5222	£££	11 pm	Enjoyed by 18th century dockers and city workers alike.
Jamie's Italian	2 Churchill Pl	020 3002 5252	£££	11 pm	Bang-on Jamie O on the cheap.

Map 103 • Cubitt Town / Mudchute

Mudchute Kitchen	Pier St	020 7515 5901	££	5 pm	Food companion to the farm bit. Chi chi children.

Map 104 • South Bank / Waterloo / Lambeth North

Anchor & Hope	36 The Cut	020 7928 9898	££££	10.30 pm	A British gastro-pub obsession, long waits though.
Canteen	Royal Festival Hall, Belvedere Rd	084 5686 1122	££	10.30 pm	A menu that sums up the best of British food with aplomb.
Concrete	Southbank Centre	020 7928 4123	£	1 am	Restaurant/bar features Russian beer, food, absinthe.
The Cut Bar	66 The Cut	020 7928 4400	£££	11 pm	Brilliant chips. A cut above the rest.
Enis's Cafe	79 Waterloo Rd	N/A	£	11 pm	You wouldn't believe me if I told you. Just go.
Giraffe	Riverside Level 1	020 7928 2004	££	10.45pm	Good crowd pleaser. Though too much world music and balloons.
Livebait	45 The Cut	020 7928 7211	£££	11 pm	Very fishy, in a very good way.
Marie's Café	90 Lower Marsh	020 7928 1050	£	10.30 pm	Greasy spoon by day, a no-frills, super-yum BYO Thai by night.
Oxo Tower Wharf	Barge House St	020 7803 3888	££££	11 pm	You might have to rob a bank, but the view's amazing.
RSJ	33 Coin St	0207 928 4554	££	11 pm	Forget about those crappy South Bank chains. Go here.
Skylon	Belvedere Rd	020 7654 7800	££££	10.45 pm	Expensive, but staffs' uniforms and view make up for it.
Studio 6	56 Upper Ground	020 7928 6243	££	11 pm	Service with a reluctant grunt doesn't stop the crowds.
Tas Cut	33 The Cut	020 7928 2111	££	11.30 pm	Blink and you'll miss it. Buzzing Turkish cafe—best hummous in London.

Map 105 • Southwark / Bankside (West)

Baltic	74 Blackfriars Rd	020 7928 1111	££££	10.30 pm	Try Polish Hunter's stew: made with real Polish Hunters. Probably.
Blackfriars Cafe	169 Blackfriars Rd	020 7928 4034	£*	10 pm	Old-school, family-run greasy spoon; amazing fry-ups.
El Vergel	132 Webber St	020 7401 2308	£*	10 pm	Its Latin breakfast: Oh. My. God. Soooooo good.
Laughing Gravy	154 Blackfriars Rd	020 7721 7055	££	12 am	Ropey exterior. Sounds odd. Bugger to get to.
The Table	83 Southwark St	020 7401 2760	£*	10.30 pm	Go and find out why we're all obsessed.
Tate Modern Restaurant	Bankside	020 7887 8888	££	6 pm	Stunning views, crap food, clueless staff.

Map 106 • Bankside (East) / Borough / Newington

Amano	Clink St	020 7234 0000	££	10 pm	Trust Amano for stone-baked pizza and freshly-made flatbreads. We do.
Boot and Flogger	10 Redcross Way	020 7407 1184	££	8 pm	Splendidly gentleman's club-esque—all savile row suits and chesterfield sofas.

Arts & Entertainment · **Restaurants**

Brew Wharf	Brew Wharf Yard, Stoney St	020 7378 6601	££	11 pm	Unusual comfort food and tasty home brews.
Cantina Vinopolis	1 Bank End	087 0899 8856	££££	10.30 pm	Gourmet food and wine at a bad museum? Believe it.
Champor-Champor	62 Weston St	020 7403 4600	£££	10.15pm	Jaw-droppingly inspired high-end Malaysian. Totally impressive.
Feng Sushi	13 Stoney St	020 7407 8744	££	10 pm	The best sushi in London and available to takeaway. Dangerous!
Fish!	Cathedral St	020 7407 3803	££	10.30 pm	Great fish. Simple. Let it have its exclamation mark.
Hing Loong	159 Borough High St	020 7378 8100	£	11 pm	Stupidly cheap. Very cheerful. The duck rocks.
Nando's	215 Clink St	020 7357 8662	££	11 pm	Peri-peri madness underneath the arches.
Roast	The Floral Hall, Stoney St	084 5034 7300	££	9.30 pm	Meat, glorious meat. High-end food. Fab location.
Silka	Southwark St	020 7378 6161	£££	11.30 pm	Curry house that won't damage your arse in the morning.
Tapas Brindisa	18 Southwark St	020 7357 8880	££	11 pm	If you can bear the crowds, lovely market-bordering eaterie.
Tas Borough High Street	72 Borough High St	020 7403 7200	££	11 pm	Reduce your carbon footprint: come here and feel 1000 miles away.
Wright Bros Oyster Bar	11 Stoney St	020 7403 9554	£££	10.30 pm	Tastebuds say no, but libido says YES.

Map 107 · Shad Thames

Butlers Wharf Chop House	36 Shad Thames	020 7403 3403	£££	11 pm	What better place for British best than under Tower Bridge?
Delfina	50 Bermondsey St	020 7357 0244	££££	11 pm	Gallery/restaurant offering works of art on your plate.
Le Pont de la Tour	36 Shad Thames	020 7403 8403	£££££	11 pm	Blair & Clinton's rendezvous. Posh but gosh!
M Manze Pie and Mash	87 Tower Bridge Rd	020 7407 2985	£	2.30 pm	As English as it gets. Try it once.
Magdalen	152 Tooley St	020 7403 1342	££££	10.30 pm	Forever fascinating Franco-Spanish cuisine.
Village East	171 Bermondsey St	020 7357 6082	£££	11 pm	Superior food. Slick surroundings.

Map 108 · Bermondsey

| Poppy Hana | 169 Jamaica Rd | 020 7237 9416 | £ | 11 pm | Cute as a button Japanese. Don't be put off by the food sculptures. |

Map 109 · Southwark Park

| Mayflower | 117 Rotherhithe St | 020 7237 4088 | £££ | 9.30 pm | The pub Sunday Lunch was invented for. |

Map 110 · Park Rotherhithe (West) / Canada Water

Simplicity	1 Tunnel Rd	020 7232 5174	££	10.30 pm	Boldly goes where no restaurant has gone before: Rotherhithe.
Café Silka	30 Albion St	020 7237 2122	££		Wishes it were somewhere else, but nicely done.
The Rainbow	33 Brunel Rd	020 7231 0028	£££	11 pm	Will make you happily plump.

Map 111 · Rotherhithe (East) Surrey Quays

| Café Nabo | Surrey Docks Farm, Rotherhithe St | 020 7231 1010 | ££ | 10 pm | Rid the toxins with a healthy farmyard lunch. |

Map 112 · Kennington / Elephant and Castle

| Dragon Castle | 114 Walworth Rd | 020 7277 3300 | ££ | 11 pm | Odd locale for such a curious pocket of culinary authenticity. |
| Lobster Pot | 3 Kennington Ln | 020 7582 5556 | £££ | 10.30 pm | Dine to a soundtrack of seagull caws. We don't kid. |

Map 113 · Walworth

| La Luna | 380 Walworth Rd | 020 7277 1991 | ££ | 11 pm | Ignore exterior. It's the garlic bread inside that counts. |

Map 115 · Old Kent Road (East)

| Roma Café | 21 Peckham Park Rd | 020 7639 7730 | £ | 10 pm | Escape Peckham and enjoy a good fry-up here. |

Map 117 · Deptford (West)

| Yellow House | 37 Plough Way | 020 7231 8777 | £££ | 10.30 pm | The food stands out as much as the yellow building. |

Arts & Entertainment · **Restaurants**

Map 119 · Deptford (East)

Kaya House	37 Deptford Broadway	020 8692 1749	££	10.45 pm	Tiny but excellent. Toilet is in the kitchen!

Map 120 · Greenwich

Goddard's Pie Shop Booth	Fountain Court (off Greenwich Church Street)	080 0862 0400	£	6pm	Pie n' mash n' eels. Only at the weekend.
Greenwich Park Bar & Grill	1 King William Walk	020 8853 7860	£££	10 pm	Kobe steak burgers. Nuff said.
The Hill	89 Royal Hill	020 8691 3626	£££	10 pm	Bistro food. Local favourite.
Inside	19 Greenwich South St	020 8265 5060	£££	11 pm	Surprisingly sophisticated worldly foods for a modest local.
Piano Restaurant	131 Greenwich High Rd	020 8853 3020	£££££	2 am	Fish swim in the chandeliers. Get the idea?
Rivington Grill	178 Greenwich High Rd	020 8293 9270	£££	11 pm	Good for brekkie or dinner before a Picturehouse movie

Map 121 · Camberwell (West)

Kazakh Kyrgyz Restaurant	158 Camberwell Rd	020 7277 2228	££	1 am	Unsuspectingly tantalising Central Asian cuisine—belly dancer included.
New Dewaniam	225 Camberwell New Rd	020 7703 9318	£	12 am	Mouth-watering Indian takeaway for a tenner.
Su-Thai	16 Coldharbour Ln	020 7738 5585	££	10 pm	Reassuringly delicious Massaman curry & corn fritters.

Map 122 · Camberwell (East)

Angels & Gypsies	29 Camberwell Church St	020 7703 5984			Like some kind of Dali-Almodovar fantasy
Garavaggio's	47 Camberwell Church St	020 7207 1612	£	11 pm	Cheap Italian with impressive fare. Stands out from the rest.

Map 123 · Peckham

Bellenden Brasserie	168 Bellenden Rd	020 7252 9424	£££	11 pm	Too classy for us. We're too busy sniggering at "bell-end".

Map 124 · Peckham East (Queen's Road)

805 Bar Restaurant	805 Old Kent Rd	020 7639 0808	£££	12 am	West African oasis. In Peckham.

Map 126 · New Cross

Manzes	204 Deptford High St	020 8692 2375	£	5 pm	Who ate all the pies? You'll certainly want to.

Map 127 · Coldharbour Lane / Herne Hill (West)

Café Prov	2 Half Moon Ln	020 7978 9228	£££	10 pm	Local art (for sale) decorates this relaxed restaurant/bar/ cafe.
Ichiban Sushi	58 Atlantic Rd	020 7738 7006	£	11 pm	The bee's knees.
The Lounge	56 Atlantic Rd	020 7733 5229	£	10 pm	A local favourite for breakfast, recovery and hanging on weekends.
New Fujiyama	5 Vining St	020 7737 6583	£	10.30 pm	This place blows Wagamama's out of the water.

Map 128 · Denmark Hill / Herne Hill (East)

Lombok	17 Half Moon Ln	020 7733 7131	£££	10.30 pm	From Stir-fries to curries, a no-fuss pan-Asian standby.
Number 22	22 Half Moon Ln	020 7095 9922	££££	10.30 pm	Gorge yourself on Spanish wine, sherry and loads of brilliant tapas.

Map 129 · East Dulwich

The Palmerston	91 Lordship Ln	020 8693 1629	££££	10 pm	Gastropub that's a lot more gastro than pub.
Sea Cow	37 Lordship Ln	020 8693 3111	££	11 pm	Fishmonger meets chip shop with Billingsgate beauties.

Map 130 · Peckham Rye

The Rye	31 Peckham Rye	020 7639 5397	££	10 pm	A pocket of delicious East Dulwich swank Peckham side.
Thai Corner Cafe	44 Northcross Rd	020 8299 4041	££*	11 pm	Tiny, laidback neighbourhood cafe.

Arts & Entertainment · **Restaurants**

Map 131 · Vauxhall / Albert Embankment

Thai Pavillion East	78 Kennington Rd	020 7582 6333	££££	12 am	Thai food you will crave in retro round room.

Map 132 · Battersea (West)

The Greyhound	136 Battersea High St	020 7978 7021	£££	12 am	Quietly excellent gastro-pub. Worth seeking out.
Ransom's Dock	35 Parkgate Rd	020 7223 1611	£££	11 pm	Friendly, stylish, likes wine and children.

Map 134 · South Lambeth

Bar Estrella	115 Old South Lambeth Rd	020 7793 1051	£	12 am	Football on telly, tapas in tummy. The heart of Little Portugal.
Canton Arms	177 S Lambeth Rd	020 7582 0965	£££		Recently acquired by Anchor & Hope folks. Bring on the yuppies.
Hot Stuff	19 Wilcox Rd	020 7720 1480	£	10 pm	Hard to find. Slightly dingy. Mental Staff. Amazing food.

Map 135 · Oval

Adulis	44 Brixton Rd	020 7587 0055	£	11 pm	C'mon, it's yummmy and cheap. And we can't cook Eritrean.
The Bonnington Café	11 Vauxhall Grove	019 3257 1323	£*	10.30 pm	Cute as a vegan button.
Kebab and Hamburger Bar	32 Clapham Rd	020 7820 8846	£*	10 pm	Fancy a doner kebab? Go nowhere else.

Map 136 · Putney

Chakalaka	136 Upper Richmond Rd	020 8789 5696	££	10.30 pm	A truly zebra-fied exterior but fantastically authentic South African food.
La Mancha	32 Putney High St	020 8780 1022	££	11 pm	Awesome lobster.
Ma Goa	242 Upper Richmond Rd	020 8780 1767	££	11 pm	Amazing regional Goan cuisine.
Moomba Bar & Kitchen	5 Lacy Rd	020 8785 9151	£££	12 am	Messiah of brunch.
Olé Restaurant and Bar	240 Upper Richmond Rd	020 8788 8009	££	11.30 pm	Paella fanatics get in line.
Talad Thai	320 Upper Richmond Rd	020 8789 8084	££	10.30 pm	Thai-ny, family-run restaurant with Thai supermarket, cooking classes and Thai regulars.
Wallace & Co	146 Upper Richmond Rd	020 8780 0052	££	11 pm	Ethics on a plate from TV's Gregg Wallace.

Map 137 · Wandsworth (West)

Miraj	123 Putney Bridge Rd	020 8875 0799	£	10 pm	Curry in a hurry? Cheap, tasty take away joint.
Yia Mas	40 Upper Richmond Rd	020 8871 4671	££	11 pm	Cosy, welcoming Greek/Cypriot place. No plate smashing.

Map 138 · Wandsworth (Central)

Brady's	513 Old York Rd	020 8877 9599	££	11 pm	Up-market fish and chip cafe and take-away.
Kathmandu Valley	5 West Hill	020 8871 0240	££	11.45 pm	Nepalese is the new black (read: curry).

Map 139 · Wandsworth (East)

The Fish Club	189 St John's Hill	020 7978 7115	££	10 pm	The thinking man's chippie.
Steam	55 E Hill	020 8704 4680	£££	10.30 pm	Walks past the bar and find yourself in bistro heaven.

Map 140 · Clapham Junction / Northcote Rd

Cafe Parisienne	225 Lavender Hill	020 7924 5523	£	5 pm	Massive sarnies and baked potatoes
I Sapori di Stefano Cavallini	146 Northcote Rd	020 7228 2017	££	11 pm	Totally authentic. Pasta made on site daily.

Map 141 · Battersea (South)

The Lavender	171 Lavender Hill	020 7978 5242	££	11 pm	Rustic European eclectic—stellar cassoulets

Map 142 · Clapham Old Town

Benny's	30 North St	020 7622 5868	£*	11.30pm	Marvel at Benny's chest hair, chat and fish and chips.
Mooli	36 Old Town	020 7627 1166	££	11 pm	Good twist on the Italian local.
Tom Ilic	123 Queenstown Rd	020 7622 0555	£££	10.30 pm	British fare that's the business—a result of hard-earned talent.
Trinity	4 The Polygon	020 7622 1199	£££	10.30 pm	How to do local dining really quite fantastically well.

Map 143 • Clapham High Street

Alba Pizzeria	3 Bedford Rd	020 7733 3636	££	11.30 pm	A necessary pit stop before a Clapham night out.
Café Wanda	153 Clapham High St	020 7738 8760	££	10.30 pm	Back away from the fantastic dessert counter, real slow.
The Fish Club	57 Clapham High St	020 7720 5853	££	10 pm	Posh fish and chips, worth the extra clams.
Gastro	67 Venn St	020 7627 0222	££	12 am	Low-lit gallic bistro extraordinaire
The Pepper Tree	19 Clapham Common South Side	020 7622 1758	£*	11 pm	Speedy Thai with soul.
The Rapscallion	75 Venn St	020 7787 6555	££££	10 pm	Good fall-back. Wee bit dear.
San Marco Pizzeria	126 Clapham High St	020 7622 0452	££†	11.30 pm	Arguably the best pizza outside Italy—take that New York!
Tsunami	5 Voltaire Rd	020 7978 1610	££££	10.30 pm	The new Nobu. Unbelievable. Unfortunate name.

Map 144 • Stockwell / Brixton (West)

Franco Manca	4 Electric Lane	020 7738 3021	££	5 pm	Organic pizza perfection for around a fiver. Worth any wait.
Speedy Noodle	506 Brixton Rd	020 7326 4888	£*	1 am	Prime location and the cheapest, worst food in Brixton.
SW9 Bar Cafe	11 Dorrell Pl	020 7738 3116	£	9 pm	Great hangover curing breakfasts (and hangover causing booze).

Map 146 • Earlsfield

Carluccio's	537 Garratt Ln	020 8947 4651	££	11:30 pm	Sensational pasta dishes and optional curbside setting.

Map 147 • Balham (West)

The Bombay Bicycle Club	95 Nightingale Lane	020 8673 6217	££	10 pm	Award winning curries.
Chez Bruce	2 Bellevue Rd	020 8672 0114	££££	10.30 pm	Worth its fancy-pants (read Michelin) star.

Map 148 • Balham (East)

Dish Dash	11 Bedford Hill	020 8673 5555	££	11 pm	Tasty food. Tiny portions. Laid back vibe.
The Exhibit	12 Balham Station Rd	020 8772 6556	££	10pm	Cool, up-market venue. Friendly, laid back vibe.
Harrison's	15 Bedford Hill	020 8675 6900	££	10.30 pm	Great food if you can tolerate the 'look at me!' crowd.

Map 150 • Brixton

Asmara	386 Coldharbour Ln	020 7737 4144	££	11.15 pm	Disconcerting but delicious curry with pancakes to mop it up.
Franco Manca	4 Market Row	020 8747 4822	££		London's best pizza? Eclectic concoctions of sour dough goodness comes west.
Khan's	24 Brixton Water Lane	020 7326 4460	££	11 pm	Great curry, and BYO to boot. Have it!
The Lounge	56 Atlantic Rd	020 7733 5229	£	10pm	A local favourite for breakfast, recovery and hanging on weekends.
Negril	132 Brixton Hill	020 8674 8798	£	10 pm	Tasty Carribean with veg options (which are joy).
Opus Café	89 Acre Ln	0207 737 1414	£	6 pm	Cakes and coffee. Niceness.
Upstairs Bar and Restaurant	89 Acre Ln	020 7733 8855	££££	10.30 pm	A real find. Getting discovered. Sshhh.

Map 151 • Tooting Bec

Al Mirage	215 Upper Tooting Rd	020 8772 4422	£	10.30 pm	Better than Mirch Masala? We think so.
Masaledar Kitchen	121 Upper Tooting Rd	020 8767 7676	££	11 pm	Last word in top-notch Indian cuisine
Mirch Masala	213 Upper Tooting Rd	020 8672 7500	£	12 am	Cheap, no frills, award-winning curries. Sublime.
Spice Village	32 Upper Tooting Rd	020 8672 0710	£	11 pm	Go for grilled

Map 152 • Tooting Broadway

Jaffna House	90 Tooting High St	020 8672 7786	££	12 am	Mediocre curry fare beneath flourescent bulbs.
Radha Krishna Bhavan	86 Tooting High St	020 8682 0969	££	11.30 pm	Busy, buzzing, bhavan of South Indian curry.
Rick's Cafe	122 Mitcham Rd	020 8767 5219	£££	11 pm	Tooting's best culinary secret.
Sette Bello	8 Amen Corner	020 8767 5225	££	11 pm	A kiss on each cheek for every diner. Homely Italian.
Urban Coffee	74 Tooting High St	020 8682 9479	£*	10 pm	Nifty WiFi caff in the bowels of Tooting.

Yeah, okay, so we know the deal—don't mention the Recession. When it comes to retail, people will always spend whether money or no (that's how we got in this fine mess remember Stanley?), it's just that with little of the stuff about, people are more discerning about what they spend their hard-earned cash/State Benefits on. And of course if we didn't spend we would never collectively crawl out of this endless dirge of gloom. As the well observed slogan on the reusable eco-shopping bag from Modern Toss (available at **Magma, Map 12**) says, "Buy More Shit Or We're All Fucked". Indeed. But if the economic crisis is teaching us anything it's to be more picky about what we purchase and for retailers not just to deliver the goods but also all the extras that we as polite English people so foolishly see as just "extras". Primarily what we mean is, that intangible thing that contributes to a satisfying shopping experience and brings a customer back to the same store again and again: excellent service—helpfulness, genuine smiles and interest in the product and the customer. Beautiful packaging, loyalty cards, discounts, samples, invites to in-store events all help too. In an adverse way, consumers have never had more power than now to demand what they want or—as important—don't want.

One noticeable trend is a leaning towards handmade items and crafts which support local designers and artisans—Columbia Road and Cheshire Street are hotspots for this kind of thing. Yes there are a lot of these shops cropping up that purely sell "beautiful things" like **Shelf (Map 91)**, **Constructive Lives (Map 25)**, **Of Cabbages And Kings (Map 64)** and, (if it's a beauty of a decaying kind you're looking for) **Viktor Wynd's Shop of Horrors (Map 87)** to name a few (and we like them). But when it comes to fashion we also like to know that a little bit of love has been sprinkled into the making of an item. Special mention here must go to Amy Anderson of **Comfort Station (Map 91)** who produces the most thoughtful and whimsical pieces of jewellery and **Vivien of Holloway (Map 74)** who has built a real niche following but whose fabulous 1950s tailoring would make any gal feel like a doll. Both have gorgeous, well-fitted, unique shop spaces too. For blokes, **Folk (Map 5)** are renowned for their limited collections, particularly shoes which are hand-stitched (hence the price tag).

Part of this trend is Pop-Up Shops which are installed for a few months at a time sometimes displaying the work of a single designer/company or else a co-operative of independent designers. Not only is this a thrifty way of setting up shop in these uncertain times it also provides a showcase for new young things so always worth a look out—these tend to appear around Carnaby Street and Spitalfields, especially in the summer.

The Big Boys

When it comes to department stores, **Selfridges (Map 2)** is without a doubt the daddy—arguably, (and the emphasis is on that word depending on your budget) you can just get everything you need from here. **Harvey Nics (Map 37)** and **Harrods (Map 37)** are very much for ladies who lunch, and the Knightsbridge set use them like corner shops—that's not to say they don't have their uses. For a more personal touch, **Fenwick (Map 2)** and **Liberty (Map 10)** are wonderful British institutions which take you far from the madding crowd. If all these close-quarters encounters get up your nose head to **Whiteleys (Map 30)** or the Behemoth that is **Westfield Shopping Centre (Map 33)**.

Haute Et High Street

For flexing that plastic, Bond Street has always been the place to spend but Bruton Street, which branches off the main drag, is setting quite a precedent with **Matthew Williamson (Map 9)**, **Stella McCartney (Map 9)** and **Diane Von Furstenberg (Map 9)** all in residence. Always one to mix things up and throw us off track, **Marc Jacobs' (Map 9)** London store is to be found on Mount Street—check out the Marc for Marc Jacobs range for affordable designer garb—by which we mean £3 and upwards. Yes, really. If you want to feel like Alice down the rabbit hole, make a trip to **Dover Street Market (Map 9)**, owned by Rei Kawakubo of Comme Des Garçons—a real experience even if you're not buying. For those of us in the real world, **Topshop (Map 3)** is the grand kahuna of high street shopping—seventh heaven on three floors for fashionistas. For super-slick, sharp ready-to-wear you can't beat Spanish stores, **Zara (Map 2)** and **Mango (Map 3)** who both do high street with an edge and turnover is pretty quick to ensure their stock remains covetable. New contenders for higher end high-street include **Cos (Map 10)** and **Hoss Intropia (Map 10)**, and let's not forget our Stateside cousins who have sent ripples of excitement through the fash pack by opening flagship stores of **Anthropologie**, **Banana Republic** and **Abercrombie & Fitch** all **(Map 10)** in the Big Smoke. There are also little shopping oases to be found in the capital. St Christopher's Place is hidden behind the hustle and bustle of Oxford Street and houses cool European brands like **Marimekko (Map 2)** and **Noa Noa (Map 2)** alongside more familiar fare. Kingly Court (behind Carnaby Street—itself a great shopping spot for trend-led labels) has some nice boutiques in **The Black Pearl (Map 10)** and **Twinkled (Map 10)**. The area around Seven Dials in Covent Garden is eclectic with high-end boutiques like **Orla Kiely (Map 13)** and **Miss Lala's Boudoir (Map 13)** on Monmouth and skatewear at **Slam City Skates (Map 13)** and **Superdry (Map 13)** on Earlham. Edgy fashion abounds in Hoxton: head to **Good Hood (Map 84)** to start your shopping crawl or **No One (Map 91)** where they've got everything we want before we even know we want it.

Back To The Future

Man, we invented vintage. Us lovers of the mothball have been burrowing through rags in the far reaches of the city for decades. Some of the best-known, best-loved shops include **Rellik (Map 25)** in Portobello, **Annie's (Map 80)** in Islington (a favourite of La Moss), **Beyond Retro (Map 91)** in Shoreditch and **Absolute Vintage (Map 91)** (famous hunting ground for stylists). If you want to hear what the young, stylish and clueless get up to head to **Rokit (Map 71)** and eavesdrop on the staff's mindnumbing conversations. For genuine thrift, the turnover of goods in our charity shops is mind-boggling. **Oxfam Dalston (Map 86)** is renowned for being a good rummage: it's hit and miss but then that's the nature of the thrifting beast. Most hardy shoppers will happily tread the city twice over for good charity shop finds but if you want some certainty of finding designer threads you

can't beat the **British Red Cross** in both Victoria **(Map 19)** and Chelsea **(Map 45)** where you will discover the likes of Ralph Lauren, Armani and pairs of Manolos amongst the usual flotsam and jetsam. **The Notting Hill Housing Trust (Map 35)** is also a reliable source of local celebrities' cast-offs from like, yesterday. For all you true vintage fashion fiends who want to mingle with like-minded souls and find genuine vintage togs (i.e. pre-1980s) the **Frock Me! Vintage Fashion Fair (Map 45)** is unequalled for choice and variety. Wake up and smell the mould.

Keep On Running, Cycling, Skating Etc.

Lillywhite's (Map 10) is the obvious place to go for cheap sportswear—it has earned a bit of a bargain basement tag where once it was prestigious (the Lillywhites were instrumental in the game of cricket during the 19th century) but it doesn't stop the shoppers pouring in, and tourists buying their favourite London team football shirts. **Sweatshop (Map 17)** is a chain of stores but the original Teddington shop is frequented by world-class athletes as well as Sunday joggers. The staff really know their stuff (why is this so rare!?). An equally good indie chain is **Runners Need (Map 20)**. If it's sweatshop-made stuff you're after head to **Niketown (Map 2)**, which is as scary as the name suggests. Though we're no Amsterdam, the economic shitstorm has inspired many Londoners to don skintight clothes and take to two wheels. **Bobbin Bicycles (Map 6)** in Clerkenwell embraces that fun with a range of beautiful vintage and special edition bikes. Their website proclaims "We're more like a boutique than a bikeshop,"—to keep over-heads down there is no store but an appointment-only service at Bobbin's workshop, giving a real personal touch. If you're after a battered old charmer of a bike, **Recycling (Map 112)** does a fab job at selling second-hand wheels. If you've had your designer bike nicked, head down to Brick Lane and buy it off some dodgy geezer. **Slam City Skates (Map 13)** is the only dedicated place for Southbank skaters to get their duds.

Home Sweet Home

John Lewis (Map 2) is a British standard (read: very sensible) and has been the store of choice for middle-class couples' wedding lists for decades. Their maxim is "never knowingly undersold", with fantastic staff (who all get a share of the profits), and MOR but well-made stuff. **Twentyoneone (Map 80)** is a designer's wet dream selling originals as well as new items. So impressive is their collection that they often lend out furniture to film companies who want the authentic look of an era on set. The wonderfully named **Timorous Beasties (Map 6)** make wickedly amusing wallpapers—their most famous being a toile de jouy design for modern days (spot the alcopop-drinking chavs and the Gherkin in the background). For a no-nonsense approach to home furnishing visit the grimey **Second Time Around (Map 87)**. **Labour and Wait (Map 91)** does the retro home stuff better than most. If you want personable, "Where can I find one of these?" type of service try **Russell's Hardware & DIY (Map 151)** in Tooting or **KTS The Corner (Map 88)** in Dalston.

Electricity For You And Me

Traditionally, Tottenham Court Road is the hideout for the anally retentive Hi-Fi nut and the nerdoid pirate radio enthusiast a-like. The area positively thrums with electricity and in all cases it's best to shop around, play prices against each other and barter until you get the lowest price—often cash payment will get you well below the RRP. **Computer Exchange (Map 3)** is the one-stop shop for gaming, DVDs, computing and phones, which—as the name suggests—will part-exchange and knock money off for cash transactions. For audiovisual, **Richer Sounds (Map 106)** is a trusted chain, and if we're talking electronics in the purist sense, **Maplin (Map 3)** is geek central. Whether you'll get anyone who knows what they're talking about is another matter. Photography enthusiasts should check out the **London Camera Exchange (Map 24)** for old-school SLRs and digital cameras. They specialise in Pentax, Nikon and of course, Leica.

Food Glorious Food

We're a piggish race, us Londoners. Whether it's forcing down jellied eels or overpriced mushroom sandwiches down **Broadway Market (Map 89)**, our bellies is never empty, guvna. While we're at it, we'll have an ostrich burger and some raclette down **Borough Market (Map 106)**. We have New York (and in particular, the Magnolia Bakery) to thank for the invasion of cupcake stores but the original and best is the **Hummingbird Bakery (Map 29)** which makes Red Velvet cupcakes that taste like little pieces of baked orgasm. Just try and restrain yourself from licking the last morsels of frosting from the paper. Nostalgia for old style sweetie shops can be bought at **Mrs. Kibble's Olde Sweet Shop (Map 10)** whether your fetish is for cola cubes, sherbet flying saucers or Wham bars. Numerous Italian delis can be found around the city selling cured meats, buffalo mozzarella, biscotti and everything else that Mama used to make—**I Camisa & Son (Map 11)** is small but crammed full of delicacies. Organic freaks can bypass the rather average Whole Foods chain and head to local independent places like **The Grocery (Map 91)** or **Mother Earth (Map 75)**. For the cheapest and best coffee-to-go in Soho try the Algerian Coffee Stores. Looking for Unicum? Look no further than **Gerry's Spirits Shop (Map 11)** where you can find obscure liquors like Zubrowka Bison Grass Vodka and good quality Cachaça.

Art And Craft Supplies

Crafty types and closet Van Goghs can pick up supplies at **Cass Art (Map 80)** three-storey flagship store in Islington. There's everything here for aspiring Manga cartoonists and weekend watercolourists alike, and lots of fun bits and pieces for school holiday/rainy day projects in the basement. Much of the high quality stock can be found at cut-price throughout the year—stock up on Moleskine note and sketchbooks which are frequently marked down. **The London Graphic Centre (Map 13)** has more design-led stock as well as fine art material attracting architects and graphic designers. Known for its greeting cards and stationery, **Paperchase (Map 3)** on Tottenham Court Road also has—true to its name—an astonishing array of handmade papers on its top floor—from flocked designs to fibrous papers made with dried flowers. You've got to love **Blade Rubber (Map 4)** just for its name, and for keeping sketches, photos, and memories intact. **Wyvern Bindery (Map**

6) is one of few of its kind to offer book-making services.

Axes, Saxes, Drums, Strums...

Traditionally, Tin Pan Alley (real name: Denmark Street) has always been the hub of musical creativity in the city. Back in the day when rents were affordable, a community grew up around this little side street which went on to see Jimi Hendrix and The Beatles record in the basements, and a young Elton John sitting on the rooftops penning "Your Song". Nowadays you may spot Jack White trying out a Digitech Whammy or Jonny Greenwood looking for some new toy to replace his Marshall Shred Master. If we had to choose a couple, we'd bag Macaris for cheapness and **Wunjos (Map 12)** for friendliness. There are plenty of independent music stores to be found in London's boroughs, and often they are specialists, happy to have a natter about what exactly it is that you're looking for and what the weather's like. Try **Top Wind (Map 104)** for all your flute needs, **Duke of Uke (Map 91)** for banjo and ukulele-lovers, though the staff are a little arsey, and **Phil Parker (Map 1)** for all you jazz cats needing a hand with your brass. For the medieval troubadour in your life, **Hobgoblin (Map 3)** has its own luthier who makes lutes. Try **Ray Man (Map 71)** in Camden for unusual ethnic instruments and curious boxes. For the largest collection of sheet music in Europe, **Chappell of Bond Street (Map 11)** (now on Wardour Street but they've kept the name) is your destination. One thing though, will you instrument shop assistants please stop jamming when you're talking to us?

Music Non Stop

The slow, painful death of the CD can be seen in almost every indie music store in London, and it coincides with the financial doom and gloom that has befallen Virgin Records, Zavvi and Sanctuary (thankfully we still have one branch of **Fopp (Map 12)** left). Bizarrely, the death march of the traditional record shop has become a moonwalk: more and more boutique record shops are springing up selling new and used wax. The Berwick Street vinyl epicenter may have been drained of late, but other parts of London have become haunts for us of

haunched posture and good taste. **Sister Ray (Map 11)** is forever teetering on the edge, while **Revival Records (Map 11)** is the long gone Reckless Records' offspring. If you find yourself on the Essex Road, have a gander at **Flashback (Map 83)** and **Haggle Vinyl (Map 83)**: you're sure to find something to please and appeal in the former and appall in the latter. **The Music & Video Exchange (Map 29, 71)** in Notting Hill was way ahead of its time and has been the swapshop of choice for years—it's still the king as far as we're concerned. When south of the river, do as Camberwellians do and drop in at **Rat Records (Map 121)**. To guarantee a withering look from a record shop lifer go and discuss the use of naivety in Legowelt's output at **Phonica (Map 10)** in Soho. Catch some indie schmucks at **Pure Groove (Map 15)** in Holloway, and many a muso's all-round fave, **Sounds of the Universe (Map 11)** is owned by the Soul Jazz label.

Antiques And Bric-A-Brac, Flea Markets And Stalls

There may have been a time, dear reader, when Markets sold fleas. And Brics and bracs. Perhaps we used to know what these elusive words meant. Frankly, we numbskulls at NFT don't care about etymology unless it's second hand and collectable. First stop on many shoppers' lists—both serious collectors and weekend browsers—are **Alfie's Antique Market (Map 76)** and **Gray's Antique Market (Map 2)**. Here you'll find art, antiques, jewellery, vintage clothing and rare books all housed under one roof.

Once the centre of the Britpop phenomenon in the '90s and a thriving mini-metropolis for vintage and antique stalls, Camden is going through something of an identity crisis with parts of the old Stables market and the Arches being shut down and redevelopment looming: what used to be a hotchpotch high street full of character is fast becoming an identikit of any other shopping street in England. Much of the area was damaged by a fire in 2009, which thankfully gutted the Hawley Arms but unfortunately not all the tat that has come to be sold in abundance round here. **Proud Gallery (Map 71)** has taken over the listed Horse Hospital building and packs of German and French kids on school trips puzzlingly rifle through the emo and goth gear that overfloweth. There is some gold to be found though in shops like **Episode (Map 71)** and **Rokit (Map 71)**, and **Aldo Liquidation (Map 71)** is good for a bargain (or practising your rugby tackle). Certainly the place still has atmosphere.

Well-known to scavengers, **Camden Passage (Map 80)** in Angel, rather confusingly, is a welcome retreat from the mallrat-filled N1 centre across the road in Islington. The Mall and also Pierrepoint Arcade (tucked away behind the passage) offer a cornucopia of clothing, jewelry, military paraphernalia, homewares, prints, and a host of other bits and bobs. On Saturdays, market stalls set up in the street and surprises like original Givenchy earrings from 1978 (4 quid!) can be salvaged from amongst the knick-knacks. This is another brilliant little vintage bazaar continually threatened by chains and redevelopment. Go protest by buying any old crap.

Brick Lane (Map 91) also opens up on Sunday and in the summer there is a real carnival feel with fruit and veg, plumbing and DIY bits and pieces, electricals, toilet ries, furniture (dentist's chair anyone?), clothes, DVDs lining the lane and spiling into Sclater Street. Watch your bags and all the silly haircuts. All manner of weirdness can be observed from performance art to people

seemingly emptying out the contents of their bedrooms onto tarpaulins and sheets looking for enthusiastic buyers. Who wants to buy Tron on video? Somebody does. Brick Lane also has the added advantage of having many a watering hole and curry house where you can stop and people-watch if it all makes you want to go all 'Falling Down' on their asses. If that's not your thing, **(Up)Market** is held in the **Truman Brewery (Map 91)** every Sunday and showcases new designers as well as housing some vinyl, vintage and gourmet street food. It's got to be said that all this is superior to the now sanitized **Spitalfields Market (Map 91)**.

Roman Road Market (Map 94) is proper gorblimey, lor' love a duck cockerney territory and there's lots to be had from fruit and veg, bed linen, factory seconds and branded clothing with the labels cut out. If Lady Luck is stroking your inner thigh you get some great bargains at **Deptford Market (Map 119)**.

Though certainly not as bountiful in treasure as the car boot sales of other parts of the country, London does have some. The best in Zone 2 is definitely the **Battersea Car Boot Sale (Map 141)**, a sprawling mess that kicks of around midday in a godsend to all us alcoholics and narcoleptics..

Map 1 · Marylebone (West)

Green Valley	36 Upper Berkeley St	020 7402 7385	Essential Lebanese supermarket: get the manoushe.
Maroush Deli	45 Edgware Rd	020 7723 0773	Lebanese food emporium—fresh coffee, ice-creams and best houmous in town.
Phil Parker	106 Crawford St	020 7486 8206	Brass-o-rama.
Primark	499 Oxford St	020 7495 0420	Enter the scrum.
Spymaster	3 Portman Sq	020 7486 3885	Stab-proof vests, in house P.I., you know, the usual.
Totally Swedish	32 Crawford St	020 7224 9300	Salt liquorice and Plopp bars for scandiphiles.

Map 2 · Marylebone (East)

Browns South Molton Street	24 S Molton St	020 7514 0016	Sleep with someone rich, then bring them here.
The Button Queen	76 Marylebone Ln	020 7935 1505	Antique buttons galore for budding fashionistas.
Content Beauty/Wellbeing	14 Bulstrode Street	020 3075 1006	Exceptional selection of organic beauty products.
Daunt Books	83 Marylebone High St	020 7224 2295	Almost intimidatingly beautiful book shop.
Divertimenti	33 Marylebone High St	020 7935 0689	Go and pretend you need a £500 coffee machine.
Duffer of St George	268 Oxford St	020 7836 3722	Rude tees.
Fenwick	63 New Bond St	020 7629 9161	A welcome escape from Oxford Street for those in the know.
French Sole	61 Marylebone Ln	020 7486 0021	Spendy but these pumps can withstand London's terrible pavements.
Gray's Antique Market	58 Davies St	020 7629 7034	A world of bygone beauty a skip away from Bond Street.
John Lewis	278 Oxford St	020 7629 7711	Where John Betjeman would have gone if the world exploded.
La Fromagerie	2 Moxon St	020 7935 0341	Blow your inheritance on some Abbaye De Trois Vaux
Marimekko	16 St Christopher's Pl	020 7486 6454	Retro prints from Jackie Kennedy's favourite Finn.
Monocle	2 George St	020 7486 8770	From the folks who brought us the magazine with the same name, a store geared towards travel
Niketown	236 Oxford St	020 7612 0800	Like a real town! Owned by Nike! But without sweatshops.
Noa Noa	14 Gees Ct	020 7495 8777	Desirable Boho Danish label.
Paul Smith	38 Marylebone High St	020 7935 5384	Kitsch and dolls from the fashion designer. Don't ask why.

Paul Smith Sale Shop	23 Avery Row	020 7493 1287	Cheap designer suits. Sweet.
Romanian Charity Shop	Lamb's Conduit St	020 8761 2277	Good quality clothes, good cause, warm feeling inside.
Selfridges & Co	400 Oxford St	080 0123 400	A Mecca for the shopping elite who want everything.
Skandium	86 Marylebone High St	020 7935 2077	Ikea for grown-ups.
VV Rouleaux	102 Marylebone Ln	020 7224 5179	Trimmings and ribbons like you've never seen.
The Widescreen Center	47 Dorset St	020 7935 2580	Telescopes, binoculars, projectors, screens, film cameras & virtual reality.
Zara	242 Oxford St	020 7318 2700	Spiffy suits and cute casualwear from the Balearic brand.

Map 3 • Fitzrovia

Beard Papa	143 Oxford St	020 7494 9020	Cream puffs for Japanophiles.
British Museum shop	Great Russell St	020 7323 1234	Have you lost your Elgin Marbles?
Chess & Bridge	369 Euston Rd	020 7388 2404	Chess fetishists won't be able to control themselves here.
Computer Exchange	32 Rathbone Pl	084 5345 1664	Good selection of secondhand DVDs, games and gadgets.
Harmony	103 Oxford St	020 7734 5969	Also known as Butt Plugs R Us.
Hobgoblin Shop	24 Rathbone Pl	020 7323 9040	Folky paradise; impressive/amusing collection of alternative instruments.
Mango	225 Oxford St	020 7434 3694	Let's go Mango!
Maplin	218 Tottenham Ct Rd	020 7323 4411	A whole world of technical geekery to immerse yourself in.
Paperchase	213 Tottenham Ct Rd	020 7467 6200	More than meets the eye to this high street card shop.
R.D. Franks	5 Winsley St	020 7636 1244	Fashion book and magazine emporium.
Scandinavian Kitchen	61 Great Titchfield St	020 7580 7161	Smorgasbord!
Stargreen Box Office	20 Argyll St	020 7734 8932	Try here for tickets to sold-out gigs.
Topshop	216 Oxford St	020 7636 7700	Kate Moss still loves it. We do too.
Topshop	36 Great Castle Street	084 4848 7487	Clothing for the New Generation.
Urban Outfitters	200 Oxford St	020 7907 0800	Heaps of streetwear and crazy things for your house.

Map 4 • Bloomsbury (West)

Blade Rubber Stamps Ltd	12 Bury Pl	0845 873 7005	Scrapbooking materials plus traditional and made-to-order rubber stamps.
Cinema Bookshop	13 Great Russel St	020 7637 0206	Shrine to literary study of the moving image.
Gosh! Comics	39 Great Russell St	020 7636 1011	A Japanese school boy's wet dream. Comics galore!
James Smith & Sons	53 New Oxford St	020 7836 4731	Umbrella shop - because you might just need one.
London Review Bookshop	14 Bury Pl	020 7269 9030	Big books, big name personal appearances; and cake!
Maplin	218 Tottenham Ct Rd	020 7323 4411	A whole world of technical geekery to immerse yourself in.
Paperchase	213 Tottenham Ct Rd	020 7467 6200	More than meets the eye to this high street card shop.
Shepherds Bookbinders	76 Southampton Row	020 7831 1151	Like a Continental papeterie; beautiful specialty paper and bookbinding.
York Cameras	18 Bury Pl	020 7242 7182	New and second hand, specializing in Canon.

Map 5 • Bloomsbury (East)

Antoni & Alison	43 Rosebery Ave	020 7833 2002	Home of "bonkers" fashion duo.
Bibas Hair & Beauty	72 Marchmont St	020 7837 9555	Lovely, friendly hair salon, excellent prices, 15% student discount.
Brunswick Center	Hunter St	020 7883 6066	Brutalist shopping centre pushing the utopian/dystopian envelope.
The Flash Centre	68 Marchmont St	020 7837 5649	Studio lighting specialists.
Folk	49 Lamb's Conduit St	020 7404 6458	Great clothes, even better shoes.
International Magic	89 Clerkenwell Rd	020 7405 7324	When you need some tricks up your sleeve.
Joy	Brunswick Centre	020 7833 3307	Funky Urban Outfitters type stuff, but cheaper.
Magma Concept Store	117 Clerkenwell Rd	020 7242 9503	Funky book & novelty shop.
Something	58 Lamb's Conduit St	020 7430 1516	For when you're looking for a little sumthin-sumthin

Map 6 • Clerkenwell

The Black Tulip	28 Exmouth Market	020 7689 0068	Think all florists are the same?
Bobbin Bicycles	397 St John St	020 7837 3370	Making commuting fun - London's nicest cycling enthusiast.
Brindisa Retail	Borough Market Floral Hall	020 7713 1600	Chorizo, salchichon, Serrano ham—famed importers Brindisa have it all.The Family Business.
Covet	21 Arlington Way	020 7713 8453	Unique fashions from local designers.
EC One Jewellery	41 Exmouth Market	020 7713 6185	Gorgeous sparkly fings.
London Tattoo	332 Goswell Rd	020 7833 5996	Was on the telly. Caused quite a buzz.
M and R Meats	399 St John St	020 7837 1781	So meat-savvy they'll even know the best cut on you.
Metro Imagining	32 Great Sutton St	020 7865 0000	Photo processing.
Tattoo Shop	58 Exmouth Market	020 7278 9526	Tatts for all the family.
Timorous Beasties	46 Amwell St	020 7833 5010	Outlandish prints for the daringly tasteless home.
Wyvern Bindery	56 Clerkenwell Rd	020 7490 7899	Book binding for theses, portfolios and presentations. Repairs and restoration.

Map 7 • Barbican / City Road (South)

Bread & Honey	205 Whitecross St	020 7253 4455	Streetwear for discerning Hoxtonites.

Arts & Entertainment · **Shopping**

Map 9 · Mayfair / Green Park

APC	35 Dover St	020 7409 0121	Not cheap but so, so chic.
Diane Von Furstenberg	25 Bruton St	020 7499 0886	Forget the LBD, every girl needs a DVF.
Dover Street Market	17 Dover St	020 7518 0680	Serious designer wear for people with serious money.
Marc Jacobs	24 Mount St	020 7399 1690	Never out of fashion.
Matthew Williamson	28 Bruton St	020 7629 6200	The boy who knows how to dress real girls.
Stella McCartney	30 Bruton St	020 7518 3100	Stella's star keeps rising despite initial doubts in Fahionland.

Map 10 · Piccadilly / Soho (West)

Abercrombie & Fitch	7 Burlington Gardens	084 4412 5750	Like GAP but more expensive.
American Apparel	3 Carnaby St	020 7297 9400	25% off all sexual harrassment lawsuits.
Anthropologie	158 Regent St	020 7529 9800	Go check out the innovative window dressing if nothing else.
Apple Store	235 Regent St	020 7153 9000	Get your hardware here so you can buy NFT apps.
Arigato	48 Brewer St	020 7287 1722	Japanese food store and sushi bar. Lychee jelly sweets, anyone?
b store	24 Savile Row	020 7734 6846	Tell the bank you'll look REALLY cool in these shoes.
Banana Republic	224 Regent St	020 7758 3550	Your Stateside buddies don't need to ship over your clothes anymore.
Behave	48 Lexington Sreet	020 7734 6876	Hipster clothes.
Beyond Retro Soho	58 Great Marlborough St	020 7434 1406	Biggest, original, live-bands-on-Saturday vintage.
The Black Pearl	10 Kingly Ct	020 7439 0702	Because your earrings should rock as hard as you do.
Burlington Arcade	Burlington Arcade & Piccadilly		Welcoming shoppers since 1819.
Cos	222 Regent St	020 7478 0400	COS you can. See what I did there?
The European Bookshop	5 Warwick St	020 7734 5259	For when you get sick of English.
Fortnum And Mason	181 Piccadilly	020 7734 8040	The world's poshest marmalades.
Freggo	27 Swallow St	020 7287 9506	Argentinean ice cream for insomniacs. About freakin' time.
Georgina Goodman	44 Old Bond St	020 7493 7673	The only shoe worth having since that Mellon woman bought Jimmy Choo.
Hamley's	188 Regent St	087 1704 1977	World's biggest toy store. Terrifying just before Christmas.
Hatchard's	187 Piccadilly	020 7439 9921	Still musty, floors still creak, despite being owned by The Man.
Hoss Intropia	211 Regent St	020 7287 3569	High-end high street.
Lazy Oaf	19 Fouberts Place	020 7033 4291	Rockin good little design shop with the emphasis on illustration
Liberty	214 Regent St	020 7734 1234	Splendid wood-panelled department store. Beautiful and obscure scents and perfumes.
Lillywhites	24 Lower Regent St	087 0333 9600	Good if you know exactly what you're looking for.
Mrs Kibble's Olde Sweet Shoppe	57 Brewer St	020 7734 6633	Tooth-rottingly good sweet shop. Who needs incisors, anyway?
Muji	41 Carnaby St	020 7287 7323	Japanese chain hits London—simple, minimalist goods but great quality.
Phonica	51 Poland St	020 7025 6070	Cutting edge vinyl/CD shop; alas, no Michael Bolton in stock.
Playlounge	19 Beak St	020 7287 7073	Toys for adults, no not those types of toys.
Richard James	29 Savile Row	020 7434 0605	Bespoke contemporary Savile Row tailoring.
Rigby & Peller	22 Conduit St	084 5076 5545	Furnishers of the Queen's basement.
SKK (Lighting)	34 Lexington St	020 7434 4095	Change your bedroom ambience, light up your love life.
Stella McCartney	30 Bruton St	020 7518 3100	Stella's star keeps rising despite initial doubts in Fahionland.
Twinkled	1 Kingly Ct	020 7734 1978	Awesome selection of vintage clothes and accessories.
Twosee	21 Fouberts St	020 7494 3813	Many exclusives at this quirky boutique, for those that care.
The Vintage Magazine Shop	39 Brewer St	020 7439 8525	Yellowing magazines and a million student classic posters.
Whole Foods Market	69 Brewer St	020 7434 3179	Overwhelming selection of organic exotica.

Map 11 · Soho (Central)

Algerian Coffee Store	52 Old Compton St	020 7437 2480	Pick up some Blue Mountain beans and a 95p cappu-to-go.
American Retro	35 Old Compton St	020 7734 3477	Random hipster Americano junk. Recommended.
Bang Bang	9 Berwick St	020 7494 2042	Intimate secondhand clothes shop.
Calumet Trading	175 Wardour St	020 7434 1848	Cameras and accessories.
Chappell of Bond Street	152 Wardour St	020 7432 4400	...Which is actually on Wardour Street.
Cheapo Cheapo Records	53 Rupert St	020 7437 8272	The name's no lie - Cheapo records and DVDs.
Cowling & Wilcox	26 Broadwick St	020 7734 9556	Good arts supplies shop to spend your Monet in (groan!).
Gerry's	74 Old Compton St	020 7734 2053	A veritable alcoholic's Utopia.
I Camisa & Son	61 Old Compton St	020 7437 7610	The best Italian deli out of Italy.
Paradiso Boudoir	60 Dean St	020 7287 6913	Sexier than most sex shops.
Revival Records	30 Berwick St	020 7437 4271	Sickly phoenix risen from the ashes of Reckless Records.
Sister Ray	34 Berwick St	020 7734 3297	Alternative vinyl, CDs and DVDs.
Snog	9 Brewer St	020 7494 3301	Healthy dessert!
Sounds of the Universe	7 Broadwick St	020 7734 3430	Blow your friends' minds with obscure African vinyl.
Vinyl Junkies	94 Berwick St	020 7439 2923	Get your fix, you grubby vinyl fiend.

Map 12 · Soho (East)

Angels	119 Shaftesbury Ave	020 7836 5678	Chock full of fancy dress outfits.
Fopp	1 Earlham St	020 7845 9770	May Fopp never, ever die again. Long live the music bargain!
Forbidden Planet	179 Shaftesbury Ave	020 7420 3666	Cult/film/TV memorabilia shop that will leave Star Wars fans salivating.
Harmony	167 Charing Cross Rd	020 7734 5969	Also known as Butt Plugs R Us.

Julienne & Porselli	9 West St	020 7836 2862	Before American Apparel...when only dancers wore dancewear...
Kokon to Zai	57 Greek St	020 7434 1316	Mad fashion laboratory providing competition for The Pineal Eye.
Macaris	92 Charing Cross Rd	020 7836 2856	Family-run instrument shop with historic roots.
Magma	16 Earlham St	020 7240 7571	Super-cool housewares and knick-knacks from the Magma gods.
Magma	8 Earlham St	020 7240 8498	The high priest of f'ing cool books.
Maison Bertaux	27 Greek St	056 0115 1584	Secret basement boutique run by the girl-in-the-know, Pippa Brooks.
Ray's Jazz	113 Charing Cross Rd	020 7437 5660	Convivial Shop/Cafe. Essential for Americana and, uh, jazz!
Rockers	5 Denmark St	020 7240 2610	Quiffs, picks, riffs and licks. Sick.
Turnkey	114 Charing Cross Rd	020 7419 9999	Every musical gadget you need for your next glitchtronica symphony.
Wunjo Guitars	20 Denmark St	020 7379 0737	Mind-bendingly friendly Scot selling lovely vintage gear...

Map 13 · Covent Garden

Artbox	29 Earlham St	020 7240 0097	Hello Kitty overload.
The Astrology Shop	78 Neal St	020 7497 1001	For people who believe that shit - and people who don't.
The Bead Shop	21 Tower St	020 7240 0931	Great resource for amateur beaders and professional designers
Ben's Cookies	13 The Piazza	020 7240 6123	Cookie chain good. Chips in dough yum.
Blackout II	51 Endell St	020 7240 5006	Vintage heaven.
Cath Kidston	28 Shelton St	020 7836 4803	Kitsch at its most chic, and vice-versa.
Coco de Mer	23 Monmouth St	020 7836 8882	High-class, kinky fun.
Cybercandy	3 Garrick St	084 5838 0958	For when a plain old Mars bar just won't cut it.
David and Goliath	4 The Market Pl	020 7240 3640	Droll, funky t-shirts and other fun stuff.
Hope and Greenwood	1 Russell St	020 7240 3314	Old style sweets.
Kiehls	29 Monmouth St	020 7240 2411	Kiehls UK Flagship store of New Yorks' famous apothecarists.
Libidex at Liberation	49 Shelton St	020 7836 5894	Caters for all your kinks. Yes, even that one.
The Loft	35 Monmouth St	020 7240 3807	Designer jumble sale.
London Graphic Centre	16 Shelton St	020 7759 4500	One stop shop for graphics geeks.
Miss Lala's Boudoir	18 Monmouth St	020 7836 6670	Dangerously hot underwear. Visit only if your purse is full.
Neal's Yard Dairy	17 Shorts Gardens	020 7240 5700	Follow your nose to very fine cheeses.
Nigel Hall	18 Floral St	020 7379 3600	Where to get business casualed well.
Octopus	54 Neal St	020 7836 2911	Makes the everyday so much more fun.
Orla Kiely	31 Monmouth St	020 7240 4022	Trademark cutesy prints from the Irish designer.
Pop Boutique	6 Monmouth St	020 7497 5262	Retrotastic!
Rokit	42 Shelton St	020 7836 6547	Vast array of vintage clothing.
Scoop	40 Shorts Gardens	020 7240 7086	Queues out the door for freshly made gelato. Fragola rocks.
Screenface	48 Monmouth St	020 7836 3955	Professional theatre make-up which can withstand the sweat of clubbing.
Slam City Skates	16 Neal's Yard	020 7240 0928	Rambunctious skate shop.
Stanford's	12 Long Acre	020 7836 1321	Treasure trove of maps, travel books and accessories.
Superdry	24 Earlham St (Thomas Neal Centre)	020 7240 9437	Super funky pseudo-Japanese urban wear. Friendly staff.
Tabio	66 Neal St	020 7836 3713	Only the Japanese could create such an array of socks.
Urban Outfitters	42 Earlham St	020 7759 6390	Heaps of streetwear and crazy things for your house.

Map 14 · Holborn / Temple

| Konditor & Cook | 46 Gray's Inn Rd | 020 7404 6300 | Unusual location to find K&C's famous Magic Cakes.. |
| Topshop | 60 The Strand | 020 7839 4144 | Clothing for the New Generation. |

Map 15 · Blackfriars / Farringdon

| Pure Groove Records | 6 West Smithfield | 020 7778 9278 | Cool instore gigs/events and great selection of new indie releases. |

Map 16 · Square Mile (West)

Church's Shoes	90 Cheapside	020 7606 1587	An English shoe institution.
Manucci	5 Cheapside	020 7248 1459	Feeling out of place? Get a suit here.
Space NK Apothecary	145 Cheapside	020 7726 2060	Skin care heaven.

Map 17 · Square Mile (East)

| Paul A Young Fine Chocolates | 20 Royal Exchange | 020 7929 7007 | "Everytime you go away..." you take a piece of chocolate. |
| Sweatshop (City branch at Cannon's Gym) | Cousin Lane | 020 7626 4324 | Ickle version of the athletes' favourite frequented by suits. |

Map 18 · Tower Hill / Aldgate

| A. Gold | 42 Brushfield St | 020 7247 2487 | Perfect for impressive picnic supplies. But smells like a sock. |
| Montezuma's | 51 Brushfield St | 020 7539 9208 | Chocolate you'd leave your boyfriend for. |

Petticoat Lane Market	Middlesex St	N/A	No petticoats here love, but look for the FCUK stall
Precious	16 Artillery Passage	020 7377 6668	One of few independent boutiques left standing.
Sweaty Betty	5 Rood Lane	020 7929 1790	Clothes for you to stretch in, Gretchen...

Map 19 · Belgravia

British Red Cross Victoria	85 Ebury St	020 7730 2235	Green welly-brigade territory. Good range of mens' suits.
Moyses Flowers	Peter Jones - Sloane Sq	020 7881 6425	Tastefully delicate posies to enchant your beloved.
Mungo & Maud	79 Elizabeth St	020 7952 4570	Real dogs don't wear clothes! Chihuahuas do though... and pugs...

Map 20 · Victoria / Pimlico (West)

Grays of Westminster	40 Churton St	020 7828 4925	Charming period shop specializing in Nikon.
La Bella Sicilia	23 Warwick Way	020 7630 5914	Old-skool deli with cheery old owners and pasta aplenty.
Rippon Cheese Stores	26 Upper Tachbrook St	020 7931 0628	A world of cheese.
Runners Need	24 Palace Street	020 7630 5056	Place for all you joggers "who go round and round"
Topshop	18 Victoria St	020 7828 6139	Clothing for the New Generation.

Map 21 · Pimlico (East)

Black Rose	112 Belgrave Rd	020 8279 2014	Gothic. Very, very gothic.

Map 22 · Westminster

Haelen Centre	41 Broadway	020 8340 4258	All your hippy, wholemeal, organic needs under one roof.
National Map Centre	Caxton St	020 7222 2466	Nope, still can't find it.

Map 23 · St. James's

Richard Caplan	25 Bury St	020 7807 9990	New and used equipment specializing in Leica.

Map 24 · Trafalgar Square / The Strand

Austin Kaye	425 The Strand	020 7240 1888	Vintage watches. Don't expect e-bay prices.
Australia Shop	27 Maiden Ln	020 7836 2292	Relive the holiday (minus the sun. Or Brad the dive-instructor).
Gelato Mio	45 Villiers St	020 7930 5961	You scream, I scream, yeah, we get it.
The Italian Bookshop	5 Cecil Ct	020 7240 1634	"Of course, there is only one way to read Dante..."
London Camera Exchange	98 Strand	020 7379 0200	My lens is longer than yours.
Motor Books	13 Cecil Ct	020 7836 5376	The ultimate Dad shop.
Rohan	10 Henrietta St	020 7831 1059	Super-friendly fleece-clad staff wielding waterproofs.
Stanley Gibbons	399 Strand	020 7836 8444	World's leading stamp dealer attracts collectors, investors and the curious.

Map 25 · Kensal Town

Constructive Lives	312 Portobello Rd	020 8969 1399	Get your Trellick Tower mug here!
Honest Jon's	278 Portobello Rd	020 8969 9822	Obscure and rare Jazz, Funk, Reggae and Hip-Hop.
Rellik	8 Golborne Rd	020 8962 0089	Opposite the Trellik Tower - geddit? Specialises in Queen Viv (Westwood).
What Katie Did	281 Portobello Rd	0845 430 8743	Fabulous 1940s-inspired boudoir boutique for rib-crushing corsets, stockings and pointy bras.

Map 28 · Ladbroke Grove / Notting Hill (West)

Cowshed	119 Portland Rd	020 7078 1944	Express mani-pedis for women who have places to go etc.
The Cross	141 Portland Rd	020 7727 6760	The original London boutique...still going...
Gelato Mio	138 Holland Park Ave	020 7727 4117	Get ice-cream, head to park.
Jeroboams	96 Holland Park Ave	020 7727 9359	London's largest independent wine merchant.
Virginia	98 Portland Road	020 7727 9908	If money is no object, what you want is here.

Map 29 · Notting Hill Gate

& Clarke's Bread	124 Kensington Church St	020 7229 2190	All-butter brioche and honey loaves for Harvey Nics, Selfridges, and you.
Bodas	38 Ledbury Rd	020 7229 4464	Everyday underwear that gives M&S a run for its money.
The Grocer on Elgin	6 Elgin Crescent	020 7221 3844	Restaurant standard ready meals for lazy people.
The Hummingbird Bakery	133 Portobello Rd	020 7229 6446	Takeaway cupcakes reminiscent of New York's Magnolia Bakery.
James Knight of Mayfair	67 Notting Hill Gate	020 7221 6177	The Queen's fish at the Queen's prices.
Melt	59 Ledbury Rd	020 7727 5030	Posh chocs made before your bulging eyes.
Mr Christian's Delicatessen	11 Elgin Crescent	020 7229 0501	Great little deli with non-Portobello Rd prices.
Music & Video Exchange	38 Notting Hill Gate	020 7243 8574	Invented second hand record shops. Best in London.
Negozio Classica	283 Westbourne Grove	020 7034 0005	Half bar, half store selling high-end Italian kitchen goods.
Diane von Furstenberg	83 Ledbury Rd	020 7221 1120	High end wear for those who can afford it.
Portobello Road Market	223 Portobello Rd	n/a	Antiques, clothes, food, and more. A London institution.
R Garcia and Sons	248 Portobello Rd	020 7221 6119	Overwhelming selection of Spanish groceries.
Retro Man	34 Pembridge Rd	020 7792 1715	Vintage fixes for modern men. And men only.

Retro Woman	32 Pembridge Rd	020 7598 2233	Exclusive vintage ware that's worth it.
Rough Trade West	130 Talbot Rd	020 7229 8541	More character and better records than the soulless East Branch.
Travel Bookshop	13 Blenheim Cresent	020 7229 5260	I DARE you to ask them about Hugh Grant.

Map 30 · Bayswater

Al Saqi Books	26 Westbourne Grove	020 7229 8543	Specialist book shop for anything and everything Middle Eastern.
Planet Organic	42 Westbourne Grove	020 7727 2227	Organic heaven.
Porchester Gate Spa	Queensway & Porchester Rd	020 7793 3980	Proper old school art deco Turkish baths and spa for less than £25!
Whiteleys Shopping Centre	Queensway	020 7229 8844	Slightly more soulful than Smithfields.

Map 32 · Shepherd's Bush (West)

Nut Case	352 Uxbridge Rd	020 8743 0336	About time nuts got some respect.

Map 33 · Shepherd's Bush

Westfield Centre	Ariel Way	020 3371 2300	Very likable shopping center. Really.
Whole Foods Market	63 Kensington High St	020 7368 4500	Overwhelming selection of organic exotica.

Map 35 · Kensington

Ben's Cookies	12 Kensington High St	020 7376 0559	Chunky cookies in wonderous flavours. Hidden in High Street Ken Station.
Buttercup Cake Shop	16 St Albans Grove	020 7937 1473	No other pleasure on earth comes close to these cupcakes.
Homebase	195 Warwick Rd	084 5640 7062	So much stuff that you never knew you needed.
Notting Hill Housing Trust	57 Kensington Church St	020 7937 5274	There's gold in that 'Hill.
Trailfinders	194 Kensington High St	020 7938 3939	Personable one stop shop for travel bookings, advice and services.
Urban Outfitters	36 Kensington High St	020 7761 1001	Heaps of streetwear and crazy things for your house.
Whole Foods Market	63 Kensington High St	020 7368 4500	Overshelming selection of organic exotica.

Map 36 · South Kensington/Gloucester Rd

Partridges Deli	17 Gloucester Rd	020 7581 0535	Family run mega-deli to the queen.
Snog	32 Thurloe Pl	020 7584 4926	Crazy frozen yoghurt joint with interior mad enough to be in Tokyo.

Map 37 · Knightsbridge

Burberry	2 Brompton Road	020 3367 3000	Flagship store of the classic British brand.
Divertimenti	227 Brompton Rd	020 7581 8065	Go and pretend you need a £500 coffee machine.
Harrods	87 Brompton Rd	020 7730 1234	Arch conspiracy theorist Mr Al-Fayed's still classy department store.
Harvey Nichols	109 Knightsbridge	020 7235 5000	More 1999 than 2009, but still a great department store.
Rigby & Peller	2 Hans Rd	084 5076 5545	Sexy lingerie fit for a queen...for THE Queen?
Skandium	247 Brompton Rd	020 7584 2066	For lottery winners who can't shake their love of Ikea.
Space NK Apothecary	307 Brompton Rd	020 7589 8250	Skin care heaven.

Map 38 · Chiswick

As Nature Intended	201 Chiswick High Rd	020 8742 8838	Main store from orgainc food company. Pricey but worth the trek.
The Bread Shop	296 Chiswick HIgh Rd	020 8747 8443	Bloomin' marvellous bread! Great selection and they even do spelt loaves.
Mortimer & Bennett	33 Turnham Green Terrace	020 8995 4145	Gourmet deli that is guaranteed to get you excited about pickled asparagus.
Eco-Age	213 Chiswick High Rd	020 8995 7611	Colin Firth's eco-friendly homeware store with recycled chairs and eco-paint.
Outsider Tart	83 Chiswick High Rd	020 7096 1609	Amazing cupcake selection to lure you away from Red Velvet.
Oxfam Books	90 Turnham Green Terrace	020 8995 6059	Fantastic fiction selection - the rich read too!
Something Nice	40 Turnham Green Terrace	020 8742 7135	Gifts you didn't even know you wanted. Great if you're stumped for pressies.
Theobroma Cacao	43 Turnham Green Terrace	020 8996 0431	Which translates as "Chocolate Thrombosis". Choccy penises? Leave it out!
Wheelers Garden Centre	Turnham Green Terrace	020 8747 9505	Last chance station for forgotten occasions next to Turnham Green tube.

Map 39 · Stamford Brook

Mac's Cameras	262 King St	020 8846 9853	Used and hard-to-find gear. Heaven for photography nerds.
Thai Smile	287 King St	020 8846 9960	Heaven for those who love Asian cooking. For the rest it's just intriguing.

Arts & Entertainment · **Shopping**

Map 40 · Goldhawk Rd / Ravenscourt Park

Bushwacker Wholefoods	132 King St	020 8748 2061	Small and friendly organic and health food shop. Booja, Booja Ice-cream!!

Map 42 · Baron's Court

Curious Science	319 Lillie Road	020 7610 1175	Stock up on stuffed mutant cow heads and cases of eyeballs.

Map 43 · West Brompton / Fulham Broadway / Earls Court

Fulham Broadway Centre	Fulham Road	020 7385 6965	Shopping, cinema, reurants and tube station all in one place.

Map 44 · Chelsea

Furniture Cave	533 Kings Rd	020 7352 2046	Swanky. Huge. Quintessentially Kings Road.
Richer Sounds	258 Fulham Rd	033 3900 0027	Chain selling all things electronic, technologic, an so forth.
The Shop At Bluebird	350 King's Rd	020 7351 3873	Spend a fortune here and become an "edgy" individual.

Map 45 · Chelsea (East)

British Red Cross Chelsea	69 Old Church St	084 5054 7101	Known locally as La Croix Rouge Boutique.
Frock Me! Vintage Fashion Fair	Chelsea Town Hall, Kings Rd	020 7254 4054	Held every couple of months, "pre-war" tearoom refreshes shopping casualties.
The Hummingbird Bakery	47 Old Brompton Rd	020 7584 0055	Notting Hill's big brother with seating to devour Red Velvets and lattes.
Kate Kuba	24 Duke of York Sq	020 7259 0011	What more could a woman want?! Shoes, shoes, shoes...
Nomad Books	781 Fulham Rd	020 7689 9988	Glorious little place with added coffee shop.
Sweaty Betty	125 King's Rd	020 7349 7597	Clothes for you to stretch in, Gretchen...

Map 46 · Sloane Square

Fresh Line	55 King's Rd	020 7881 0900	Home made cosmetics—fresh!
Patridges Deli	2 Duke of York St	020 7730 0651	Family run mega-deli to the queen.
Peter Jones	Sloan Sq	020 7730 3434	Upmarket department store. Argos of the 'daharlings' with cash to splash.
Rigby & Peller	13 Kings Rd	084 5076 5545	Sexy lingerie fit for a queen...the queen?
Space NK Apothecary	307 King's Rd	020 7351 7209	The Superdrug for the Sloane Square ladies who lunch.

Map 48 · Fulham

Hurlingham Books	91 Fulham High St	020 7736 4363	More stacked than Arnie was in the 70s.

Map 51 · Highgate

The Corner Shop	88 Highgate High St	020 8340 1118	Locals' favourite fending off the advance of Tesco's.
Dragonfly Wholefoods	24 Highgate High St	020 8347 6087	Great little organic food shop and juice bar.
Highgate Butchers	76 Highgate High St	020 8340 9817	Reassuringly expensive meat. Them cows must have lived like kings.
Hop N Pops	389 Archway Rd	020 8348 0624	Great selection for all budgets.
Le Chocolatier	78 Highgate High St	020 8348 1110	Essential at Easter—not just eggs but whole chocolate chickens.
Mind	329 Archway Rd	020 8341 1188	Great selection for skint book worms.
Oxfam	80 Highgate High St	020 8340 3888	Musty bookstore with some cracking titles.
Second Layer Records	323 Archway Rd	078 7805 1726	I was into Avant Rock before you were etc. etc.
Walter Castellazzo Design	84 Highgate High St	020 8340 3001	A lot of cool and ridiculously pricey things.
Wild Guitar	393 Archway Rd	020 8340 7766	Get your retro gear in this brilliant guitar shop.

Map 52 · Archway (North)

Archway Cycles	183 Archway Rd	020 8340 9696	Because tube fares will just keep going up.
Archway Video	220 Archway Rd	020 8340 2986	Local favourite with videos/DVDs for sale and rent.
The Green Room	192 Archway Rd	020 8340 7759	Amazing selection of weird things you probably don't need.
Pax Guns	166 Archway Rd	020 8340 3039	Errm... "best" gun shop in the area?
Wine of Course	216 Archway Rd	020 8347 9006	Impress the guests at your next dinner party.

Map 53 · Crouch End

Walter Purkis And Sons	17 The Broadway	020 8340 6281	Proof fish don't need their tasty batter skins.

Map 57 · Hampstead Heath

Daunt Books	51 S End Rd	020 7794 8206	A right daunty little shop.
Giocobazzi's Delicatessen	150 Fleet Rd	020 7267 7222	The taste of posh Italy.

Map 58 · Parliament Hill / Dartmouth Park

BABA	11 Swain's Ln	020 8442 9111	Quirky kitchenware and gifts.
Corks	9 Swain's Ln	020 8340 4781	Superb selection of interesting wines and beers.
Forks	7 Swain's Ln	020 8340 1695	Friendly, well-stocked deli. Fresh crepes in summer!

Map 59 · Tufnell Park

The Blue Carbuncle	130 Junction Rd	020 7272 6691	Uber-cool vintage clothes, cameras and collectibles.
The Hornsey Trust Charity Shop	124 Fortess Rd	020 7267 2338	Eccentric staff? Check. Affluent, moth-eaten cast offs? Check.
North London Adoption Centre	135 Junction Rd	020 7272 6048	Need a cat? Of course you do! Miau!

Map 60 · Archway

Second Chance	7 St John's Way	020 7281 5449	Heaps of rubbish and the occasional incredible find.
Super Persia	621 Holloway Rd	020 7272 2665	Very proud little shop specializing in Iranian sweets.

Map 61 · Holloway (North)

Michael's Fruiterers	56 7 Sisters Rd	020 7700 1334	Fruit n veg fest. Nowhere's fresher.

Map 62 · Finsbury Park

The Happening Bagel Bakery	284 Seven Sisters Rd	020 8809 1519	Another Haringey gem, with some delicious pastries too!

Map 64 · Stoke Newington

Ark	161 Stoke Newington High St	020 7275 9311	Cute little interiors and gift shop.
The Beaucatcher Salon	44 Stoke Newington Church St	020 7923 2522	Hairdressers and community hub.
Belle Epoque Boulangerie	37 Newington Green	020 7249 2222	Fancy schmancy, delicious pastries.
Bridgewood & Neitzert	146 Stoke Newington Church St	020 7249 9398	Renowned string section repair, exchange and sales.
Church Street Bookshop	142 Stoke Newington Church St	020 7241 5411	Great shack with out of print books and shite records.
Metal Crumble	13 Stoke Newington Church St	020 7249 0487	Affordable, flippin' gorgeous, jewellery made on site.
Mind	11 Stoke Newington Church St	020 7812 9210	Great little chazza benefiting from middle-class donors.
Of Cabbages & Kings	34 Kersley Rd	020 7254 0060	Another of those crafty little shops that keep popping up.
Ribbons and Taylor	157 Stoke Newington Church St	020 7254 4735	Long-standing vintage clothes shop—Stokey original.
Rosa Lingerie	3 Church Walk	020 7254 3467	The oldest knickers in Stokey.
Route 73 Kids	92 Stoke Newington Church St	020 7923 7873	Bus inspired toy shop.
S'graffiti	172 Stoke Newington Church St	020 7254 7961	You've been framed.
Sacred Art	148 Albion Rd	020 7254 2223	(Needles + Ink + Skin) x Pain = Art.
The Spence Bakery	161 Stoke Newington Church St	020 7249 4927	Bread elevated to an art form.
Stoke Newington Farmers Market	Stoke Newington Church St & Stoke Newington High St	020 7502 7588	Overpriced, organic, natural, Hea…Zzzzzzzzz.

Map 65 · West Hampstead

Party Party	206 Kilburn High Rd	020 7624 4295	Party Party Stuff Stuff!
Primark	54 Kilburn High Rd	020 7624 4664	Enter the scrum.

Map 67 · Belsize Park

Belsize Village Delicatessen	39 Belsize Ln	020 7794 4258	For a truly international picnic basket.
Lotus and Frog	32 England's Ln	020 7586 3931	Quirky gifts for young and old.

Map 70 · Primrose Hill

Judith Michael & Daughter	73 Regents Park Rd	020 7722 9000	Gorgeous vintage to help you lighten your purse.
Nicolas (off licence)	67 Regents Park Rd	020 7722 8576	A wide range of wines, including some cheap ones.
Press	3 Erskine Rd	020 7449 0081	Impressive array of brands for a boutique. Good sales.
Primrose Hill Books	134 Regents Park Rd	020 7586 2022	Fabulously curated selection of new books.
Primrose Newsagent	91 Regents Park Rd	020 7722 0402	Newsagent, stationers, post office, drycleaners and internet cafe.
Richard Dare	93 Regent's Park Rd	020 7722 9428	Quite lovely kitchen/cooking products.

Shepherd Foods	59 Regents Park Rd	020 7586 4592	Highly priced but quaint local deli.
Shikasuki	67 Gloucester Ave	020 7722 4442	Affordable vintage and modern design.
Sweet Pea	77 Gloucester Ave	020 7449 9292	Unusual handmade jewelry.
Tann Rokka	123 Regents Park Rd	020 7722 3999	Wildly expensive "lifestyle store" in old Primrose hill train station.
Yeomans Grocers	152 Regent's Park Rd	020 7722 4281	Greengrocer that sells flowers and has a great juicebar.

Map 71 • Camden Town / Chalk Farm / Kentish Town (West)

Acumedic	101 Camden High St	020 7388 6704	Chinese medicine centre offering acupuncture AKA polite masochism.
Arckiv Vintage Eyewear	Chalk Farm Rd and Castlehaven Rd	077 9010 2204	Those film kids get their vintage eyewear here.
Aldo Sale Shop	231 Camden High St	020 7284 1982	If you find shoes that fit they're free. Not really.
Cyberdog	The Stables Market, Chalk Farm Rd	020 7482 2842	Enormous sci-fi set displaying PVC, neon, and leather clubbing wear.
Episode	26 Chalk Farm Rd	020 7485 9927	Unusual vintage store with comparatively low ringworm risk.
Escapade	45 Chalk Farm Rd	020 7485 7384	Dress up as Wonder Woman! Also caters for females.
Eye Contacts	10 Chalk Farm Rd	020 7482 1701	Opticians that sells uber-trendy spectacles.
Fresh & Wild, Camden	49 Parkway	020 7428 7575	Organic and wholefood oasis with eat-in possibilities.
Graham and Green	164 Regents Park Rd	020 7586 2960	Wonderfully dinky yet scarily pricey shop.
Metal Militia	258 Camden High St	020 7734 5720	Screeeeammm for me Camden High Street!!
Music & Video Exchange	208 Camden High St	020 7267 0123	Great secondhand music shop, seemingly staffed by grouches on Mogadon.
Proud Camden	Chalk Farm Rd	020 7482 3867	Stock up on contemporary photography.
Ray Man Music	54 Chalk Farm Rd	020 7692 6261	Wonderful shop full of exotic instruments. Bavarian noseflute, anyone?
Rokit	225 Camden High St	020 7267 3046	Second hand, sorry, vintage clothing store to the stars.
Sounds That Swing	46 Inverness St	020 7267 4682	"It ain't worth a thing..." rockabilly, psych and doo-wop.
Traid	154 Camden High St	020 7485 5253	Characterful recycled clothes. Touch of wank, but still we like.
Up The Video Junction	Middle Yard, Camden Lock Pl	077 9266 1294	Rare, out-of-print, cult DVDs.
Village Games	65 The West Yard	020 7485 0653	Huge selection of boardgames.
Whole Foods Market	49 Parkway	020 7428 7575	Overwhelming selection of organic exotica.

Map 72 • Kentish Town

Blustons	213 Kentish Town Rd	020 7485 3508	Clothes for grannies. Those under 70 need not enter.
Dots	132 St Pancras Way	020 7482 5424	Friendly music shop with free hash cakes...OK, just cookies.
Fish	161 Kentish Town Rd	020 7267 0139	Gift shop run by actress Sophie Thompson.
Phoenicia - Mediterranean Food Hall	186 Kentish Town Rd	020 7267 1267	Olives, just-roasted nuts, baclava, ice-cream bar. Meze heaven. Ditch Sainsburys.
Pro Percussion	205 Kentish Town Rd	020 7485 4434	BANG! BOOM! CRASH! For drummers young and old.

Map 73 • Holloway

| Bumblebee Natural Foods | 33 Brecknock Rd | 020 7284 1314 | Hot veggie lunches, lush cakes. Organic fruitopia over the road. |
| DOC Records | 5 Cardwell Terrace, Cardwell Rd | 020 7700 0081 | Probably full of contagious diseases. Worth a rummage. |

Map 74 • Holloway Road / Arsenal

21st Century Retro	162 Holloway Rd	020 7700 2354	Mothballs and tweed in this retro paradise.
Fettered Pleasures	90 Holloway Rd	020 7619 9333	Treat your man to something nice.
House of Harlot	90 Holloway Rd	020 7700 1441	Funky fetish fashion.

Map 75 • Highbury

Cabbies Delight Auto Parts	9 Green Lanes	020 7226 1692	21,000 car parts and 21 years experience.
La Fromagerie	30 Highbury Park	020 7359 7440	Blow your inheritance on some Abbaye De Trois Vaux.
Mother Earth	282 St Paul's Rd	020 7354 9897	Unfortunate New Age name, decent little shop.
Vivien of Holloway	294 Holloway Rd	020 7609 8754	Want to dress like Joan from Mad Men?

Map 76 • Edgeware Road / Marylebone (North)

Alfie's Antique Market	25 Church St	020 7723 6066	Kitsch oddball sanctuary for vintage treats.
Archive Secondhand Books & Music	83 Bell St	020 7402 8212	Old and unusual books.
Elvisly Yours	233 Baker St	020 7486 2005	With stalkers like these, it's no wonder Elvis is hiding.
London Beatles Store	231 Baker St	020 7935 4464	All you need is love, and no taste.
Lord's Cricket Shop	Lord's Cricket Ground, Lisson Grove	020 7616 8570	They won't even ask why you want a cricket bat.

Map 77 • Mornington Crescent / Regent's Park

| Calumet Trading | 93 Drummond St | 020 7380 1144 | Cameras and accessories. |
| Greens and Beans | 131 Drummond St | 020 7380 0857 | Wheat grass, supplements and tofu. |

Arts & Entertainment · **Shopping**

Map 78 · Euston

All Ages Records	27 Pratt St	020 7267 0303	Truly independent punk & hardcore record shop. F*** the system!
Housmans Bookshop	5 Caledonian Rd	020 7837 4473	Bookshop for progressive peaceniks and radical revolutionaries.
Peyton & Byrne	Pancras Rd	020 7278 6707	Cupcake perfection.
Transformation	52 Eversholt St	020 7388 0627	The world's largest shop for transvestites and transsexuals. Seriously.
Wills-Moody Jumble Sale	21 Phoenix Rd	020 7419 6891	Monthly indie-themed bric-a-brac. Cool moustaches everywhere.

Map 79 · King's Cross

Cosmo Cornelio	182 Caledonian Rd	020 7278 3947	Old-skool, moustache trimming Italian barbers.
King's Cross Continental Stores	26 Caledonian Rd	020 7837 0201	1960s Italian deli still run by original Italian owners. Fab.

Map 80 · Angel / Upper St

A Ferrari Deli	48 Cross St	020 7226 1951	Yes, Mr Ferrari's grumpy. But he is 102.
After Noah	121 Upper St	020 7359 4281	Stuff your Nintendo Wiis—these are proper toys, retro-style.
Annie's Vintage Costume and Textiles	12 Camden Passage	020 7359 0796	Proper vintage—1900s to 1940s.
Camden Passage	Camden Passage	020 7359 0190	Thingamebobs, whatsits and doodahs aplenty.
Cass Art	66 Colebrooke Row	020 7354 2999	Large, neat-as-a-pin, extremely pleasing art supply shop.
Gill Wing Kitchen Shop	194 Upper St	020 7226 5392	Splendid array of kitchen gadgetry to keep foodies amused.
Monte's Deli	23 Canonbury Ln	020 7354 4335	Tasty, but look elsewhere if you need a hearty meal.
Palette London	21 Canonbury Ln	020 7288 7428	Islington's eclectic vintage shop—clothes, books, homeware.
Paul A Young Fine Chocolates	33 Camden Passage	020 7424 5750	"Everytime you go away..." you take a piece of chocolate.
Raymond Roe Fishmonger	35 Chapel Market	020 7833 8656	Market stall with a sea's worth of fish.
Twentytwentyone	274 Upper St	020 7288 1996	Bauhaus to Boontje and beyond.

Map 81 · Canonbury

Get Stuffed	105 Essex Rd	020 7226 1364	Polar bear for the living room, anyone? Taxidermy emporium.
HG Lockey & Sons	8 Halton Cross St	020 7226 7044	For all your, er, coal and smokeless fuel needs.
Handmade and Found	109 Essex Rd	020 7359 3898	For something totally unique.
James Elliot Master Butcher	96 Essex Rd	020 7226 3658	So much choice they'd probably stock human if they could.
Planet Organic	64 Essex Rd	020 7288 9460	Organic heaven.
Raab's The Baker's	136 Essex Rd	020 7226 2830	Crusty white bloomers, chelsea buns. No paninis.
Sew Fantastic	107 Essex Rd	020 7226 2725	If you'd thought it up, you'd have opened it too.

Map 82 · De Beauvoir Town / Kingsland

2&4 Gallery	4 Southgate Rd	020 7254 5202	Independent shop selling furniture but coffee too.
North One Garden Centre	25 Englefield Rd	020 7923 3553	Dinky little garden centre catering for dinky little London gardens.

Map 83 · Angel (East) / City Rd (North)

Flashback	50 Essex Rd	020 7354 9356	Don't come in whistling Barbie Girl.
Haggle Vinyl	114 Essex Rd	020 7704 3101	Record shop that reminds you how little you know about music.
Past Caring	54 Essex Rd	N/A	Oddball collection of furniture, pictures and, if you're lucky, mannequins.

Map 84 · Hoxton

Favela Shop	12 Hoxton St	020 3222 0042	Brazilian bikinis for, er, when the sun shines.
Good Hood	41 Coronet St	020 7729 3600	Like American Apparel before it got shit.
Sh!	57 Hoxton Sq	084 5868 9599	Dildo-tastic! Guys must come (ahem) accompanied by a galpal.

Map 85 · Stoke Newington (East)

Bargain Bookshop	153 Stoke Newington High St	020 7249 8983	Books! Bargains! AH!
Hamdys	167 Stoke Newington High St	020 7254 0681	Porn-free newsagents run by stubborn maverick.
Rouge	158 Stoke Newington High St	020 7275 0887	Cool Chinese housewares. Via Belgium of course.
Stoke Newington Bookshop	159 Stoke Newington High Street	020 7249 2808	Long-standing local stellar indie bookshop.

Map 86 · Dalston / Kingsland

Centre Supermarket	588 Kingsland Rd	N/A	Beers from all corners of the globe.
Dalston Mill Fabrics	69 Ridley Rd	020 7249 4129	Veritable treasure trove for budding Vivienne Westwoods and John Gallianos.
Oxfam	514 Kingsland Rd	020 7254 5318	Flagship charity shop. Go find treasures!
Party Party	9 Ridley Rd	020 7254 5168	Fancy dress and party supplies plus an outstanding cake decorating department.
Ridley Road Market	51 Ridley Rd	084 4357 4634	Absolutely mental market... bush meat, wonky haircuts you name it.
Sound 323 @ Cafe Oto	18 Ashwin St	077 0735 2638	Blisteringly avant-garde record shack.
St Vincent's	484 Kingsland Rd	020 7249 3511	Christian charity shop. Jesus galore.
Turkish Food Centre	89 Ridley Rd	020 7254 6754	Olives and feta galore, bakery onsite, plus other fresh groceries.

Map 87 · Hackney Downs / Lower Clapton

Palm 2	152 Lower Clapton Rd	020 8533 1787	Legendarily friendly corner shop beloved of bloggers.
The Pet Shop	40 Amhurst Rd	020 8986 6862	Brillant local pet shop.
Salvation Army Clapton	122 Lower Clapton Rd	020 8985 3902	Come all ye unfaithful...
Second Time Around	60 Lower Clapton Rd	020 985 5536	Buy back the old shit that got stolen last week.
Umit & Son	35 Lower Clapton Rd	020 8985 1766	Crazed film buff selling vintage porn, super 8 and crisps?!?
Viktor Wynd's Shop of Horrors	11 Mare St	020 7998 3617	Macabre and marvellous shop and gallery

Map 88 · Haggerston / Queensbridge Rd

KTS The Corner	415 Kingsland Road	020 7249 3199	Helpful DIY store if you can't do it yourself.

Map 89 · London Fields / Hackney Central

Artvinyl	13 Broadway Market	020 7241 4129	The best vinyl and CD covers, printed on canvas.
Broadway Market	Broadway Market	N/A	Yummy mummies and Guardian-reading couples peruse.
Burberry Factory Shop	29 Chatham Pl	020 8985 3344	Ever wondered how Burberry became associated with chavs?
Candle Factory	184 Mare St	020 8986 6356	Well-made, well-priced candles.
L'eau a la Bouche	49 Broadway Market	020 7923 0600	Cute French delicatessen shop.
Lazy Days	21 Mare St	078 1632 3848	Not far from Hackney Road where you'll find more furniture.

Map 90 · Homerton / Victoria Park North

Cheech Miller	227 Victoria Park Rd	020 8985 9900	Everything you need for the park: kites, frisbees, skateboards, unicycles.
The Ginger Pig	99 Lauriston Rd	020 8986 6911	Brilliant butcher bequeathing beef to the Borough.
Sublime	225 Victoria Park Rd	020 8986 7243	Boudoir-like boutique selling select and independent labels.
Work Shop	77 Lauriston Rd	020 8986 9585	Beautiful handmade pottery for home and kitchen by Caroline Bousfield Gregory.

Map 91 · Shoreditch / Brick Lane / Spitalfields

A Butcher of Distinction	91 Brick Ln	020 7770 6111	Distinct indeed, impeccable collection of preppy, fresh n' clean stylings.
Absolute Vintage	15 Hanbury St	020 7247 3883	If Imelda Marcos ran a misanthropic clothes shop.
Bangla City	86 Brick Ln	020 7456 1000	Breaks the rule saying you should avoid smelly supermarkets.
Bernstock Speirs	234 Brick Ln	020 7739 7385	Look no further if you're searching for a signature titfer.
Beyond Retro	112 Cheshire St	020 7613 3636	The Daddy of all jumble sales.
Blackmans	44 Cheshire St	020 8 5088 3505	Are plimsolls still cool on Brick Lane? Help!
Brick Lane	Brick Ln	N/A	Nathan Barleys still pissed off their face from the night before.
Brick Lane Market	91 Brick Ln	020 7770 6028	Great Sunday market with lots of food and cool clothes.
Caravan	3 Redchurch St	020 7033 3532	Quirky interiors shop with items new and old on offer.
A Child of The Jago	10 Great Eastern St	020 7377 8694	Slapdash assortment of otherworldly vintage.
Comfort Station	22 Cheshire St	020 7033 9099	Quirky and comforting collection of handmade jewellery.
Columbia Road Market	Columbia Rd	N/A	Get there early, nab outside tables for brekkie then shop.
Columbia Road Flower Market	Columbia Rd	N/A	A Sunday morning hot spot for plant lovers. After 2pm is prime bargain time.
Duke of Uke	22 Hanbury St	020 7247 7924	For all your many ukelele and banjo needs.
FairyGothMother	15 Lamb St	020 7377 0370	Not entirely "Goth" - a Dita Von Teese of a shop...
The Grocery	54 Kingsland Rd	020 7729 6855	Selling the good life to lower Kingsland Road.
Hurwundeki	98 Commercial St	020 7392 9194	Boutique-y empire slowly creeping across London.
Junky Styling	91 Brick Ln	020 7247 1883	Bespoke tailoring from old rags. But posher.
Labour And Wait	18 Cheshire St	020 7729 6253	Brilliant wee shop selling old and old looking goods.
The Laden Showrooms	103 Brick Ln	020 7247 2431	Eclectic bazaar of small labels scavenged by stylists and starlets.
Lapin & Me	14 Ezra Street	020 7739 4384	Cute shop selling toys for big kids and little kids.
Luna and Curious	198 Brick Ln	020 7033 4111	Curiouser and curiouser...lovely local artists' and designers' co-operative.
No One	1 Kingsland Rd	020 7613 5314	Sporty designer wear. Killer shades.
Nudge Records	20 Hanbury St	020 7655 4823	Notorious little shack owned by the Brothers Collishaw. Reggae/dub.
Prick Your Finger	260 Bethnal Green Rd	020 8981 2560	Haberdashery brought to you by whimsical St Martin's grads.

Present	140 Shoreditch High St	020 7033 0500	Fashionable designer menswear shop with a coffee bar.
Rough Trade East	91 Brick Ln	020 7392 7788	East London outpost of the absurdly cool Rough Trade Records.
Ryantown	126 Columbia Road	020 7613 1510	Home of the ever popular paper cutter Rob Ryan.
Second Tread	261 Hackney Rd	020 7033 9862	In every fashionista's little black book: seconds and ex-model shoes.
Shelf	40 Cheshire Street	020 7739 9444	Neat selection of craftsty stuff you don't need but want
Taj Stores	112 Brick Ln	020 7377 0061	Weird and wonderful Eastern food.
Tatty Devine	236 Brick Ln	020 7739 9191	Bonkers jewellery loved by celebs, fashionistas and hipsters.
Taylor Taylor	12 Cheshire St	020 7033 0330	Salon for the indulgent customer.
Taylor Taylor	137 Commercial St	020 7377 2737	French boudoir-style hairdressers with free cocktail bar. Feel like a princess.
Treacle	110 Columbia Rd	020 7729 0538	Dreamy cupcakes. Don't ask for coffee - this is a TEAshop!

Map 92 · Bethnal Green

AP Fitzpatrick	142 Cambridge Heath Rd	020 7790 0884	Art supplies and expert advice.
Paul Mark Hatton	65 Roman Rd	020 8981 7110	Pocket ashtray anyone? Fans include Jack Nicholson and Liv Tyler.

Map 94 · Bow

Pure	430 Roman Rd	020 7364 1717	The place to spend your wedge in E3.
Roman Road Market	Roman Rd	020 7377 8963	Big, colourful, cheap as chips—bargain tat hawked by lively east-end traders.
Sew Amazing	80 St Stephens Rd	020 8980 8898	Long established sewing machine shop. Repairs and recycling service provided.
South Molton Drugstore	583 Roman Rd	020 8981 5040	Branded cosmetics and toiletries at knock-down prices.

Map 97 · Stepney / Shadwell (East)

East End Thrift Store	Assembly Passage	020 7423 9700	Come on Thursday nights for the in-store parties.
John Lester Wigmakers	32 Globe Rd	020 7790 2278	Need a syrup?

Map 104 · South Bank / Waterloo / Lambeth North

The Bookshop Theatre	51 The Cut	020 7633 0599	Thesp-oriented but charming, including a tiny stage for performances.
Calder Bookshop - The Bookshop Theater	51 The Cut	020 76202900	Enduringly fashionable hub for the unfashionably literate.
I Knit London	106 Lower Marsh	020 7261 1338	The UK's only knitting shop with a licensed bar. Wool is cool.
Konditor & Cook	22 Cornwall Rd	020 7261 0456	Yummy scrummy choccies and cake.
Oasis	84 Lower Marsh	020 7401 7074	Friendly independent salon for massages, waxing, facials and fab pedicures.
Radio Days	87 Lower Marsh	020 7928 0800	Cave of vintage wonders.
ScooterCaffe	132 Lower Marsh	020 7620 1421	Scooter shop has superb coffee. Word spreads. Becomes café too.
Silverprint	12 Valentine Pl	020 7620 0844	Specialist dealer in photographic consumables.
Southbank Book Market	Under Waterloo Bridge	0871 663 2501	Fun little scribe's market in brilliant surroundings.
Top Wind	2 Lower Marsh	020 7401 8787	Serious flute worship.
Waterloo Camping	37 The Cut	020 7928 4110	Eccentric army surplus/camping store, run by two friendly brothers.
What The Butler Wore	131 Lower Marsh	020 7261 1353	'60s, '70s vintage boutique—retro-glam party garments plus resident moggy, Binky.

Map 105 · Southwark / Bankside (West)

Elephant & Castle Market	Elephant & Castle	N/A	An anti-Portobello Road Market...slightly dodgy but dirt-cheap.

Map 106 · Bankside (East) / Borough / Newington

Borough Market	8 Southwark St	020 7407 1002	Go on an empty stomach and feast on samples.
Brindisa Retail	32 Exmouth Market	020 7713 1600	Chorizo, salchichon, Serrano ham—famed importers Brindisa have it all.The Family Business.
Elephant & Castle Market	Elephant & Castle	020 7703 5678	An anti-Portobello Road Market...slightly dodgy but dirt-cheap.
German Deli	8 Southwark St	020 7378 0000	Sauerkraut and sausages if you like that kinda stuff.
Paul Smith	13 Park St	020 7403 1678	Kitsch and dolls from the fashion designer. Don't ask why.
Richer Sounds	2 London Bridge Walk	033 3900 0021	The original store of this small chain offering low prices.
Vinopolis	1 Bank End	020 7940 8300	Wine tasting and buying megastore. Spitting optional.

Map 107 · Shad Thames

The Design Museum Shop	28 Shad Thames	020 7940 8754	Stuff you wish you'd thought of.
Fine Foods	218 Long Lane	020 7403 7513	Little, local Italian deli to coo over.
Long Lane Deli	218 Long Ln	020 7403 7513	A popular Italian delicatessen.
United Nude	124 Bermondsey St	020 7407 3758	Nope, we don't understand these shoes At All.

Map 111 · Rotherhithe (East) Surrey Quays

Decathlon	Surrey Quays Rd	020 7394 2000	The Daddy of sports & outdoors shops.

Map 112 · Kennington / Elephant and Castle

Pricebusters Hardware	311 Elephant & Castle Shopping Centre	020 7703 8244	Impressively cheap, friendly staff and an amusing collection of bric-a-brac.
Recycling	110 Elephant Rd	020 7703 7001	They sell'em bikes, they fix'em bikes. Second hand.

Map 113 · Walworth

Mixed Blessings Caribbean Bakery	12 Camberwell Rd	020 7703 9433	Bread that's so good you'll need to queue.

Map 114 · Old Kent Road (West) / Burgess Park

Old Kent Road Food Centre	252 Old Kent Rd	020 7277 4368	Your basic nice grocery store.

Map 119 · Deptford (East)

Deptford Market	Deptford High St	N/A	Cheap, busy, eclectic: Proof that there IS life in Deptford.

Map 120 · Greenwich

Belle	20 College Approach	020 8465 5777	Plush retail experience with attentive staff.
Bullfrogs	22 Greenwich Church St	020 8305 2404	Strange name, decent shop. Independent boutique.
Cheeseboard	26 Royal Hill	020 8305 0401	Buy your cheese then head to Theatre of Wine...
Compendia	10 The Market	020 8293 6616	No, not bored games, good old fashioned board games
Emma Nissim	10 Greenwich Market	020 8853 3139	Eclectic collection of t-shirt designs, and silk scarves and ties.
Meet Bernard	23 Nelson Rd	020 8858 4047	Dapper gents outfitters.
Mr Humbug	Greenwich Market	020 7871 4944	Infinitesimal old-fashioned sweets to relive your childhood sugar buzzes.

Map 121 · Camberwell (West)

Butterfly Walk Shopping Centre	Denmark Hill	N/A	The usual attractions.
Rat Records	348 New Camberwell Rd	077 9542 4575	Ramshackle and friendly. There's bargains if you've got superhuman patience.

Map 123 · Peckham

Curious Science	5 Commercial Way	020 8961 3113	Stock up on stuffed mutant cow heads and cases of eyeballs.
Persepolis	30 Peckham High St	020 7639 8007	Can a deli change your life? Yes. Yes, it can.
Primark	51 Rye Ln	020 7639 9655	More of a chance of scoring that 'it' item at this branch.

Map 127 · Coldharbour Lane / Herne Hill (West)

Blackbird Bakery	208 Railton Rd	020 7095 8800	London needs more lovely independent bakeries (like this).

Map 128 · Denmark Hill / Herne Hill (East)

Tales on Moon Lane	25 Half Moon Ln	020 7274 5759	Cute children's bookshop (as if there were any other kind!).

Map 129 · East Dulwich

The Cheeseblock	69 Lordship Ln	020 8299 3636	Best cheese south of the river.

Map 130 · Peckham Rye

Hope And Greenwood	20 North Cross Rd	020 8613 1777	Twee but tasty old-style sweets.

Map 133 · Battersea (East)

London Recumbents	Battersea Park	020 7498 6543	Much more fun in theory than in practice.

Map 134 · South Lambeth

Lassco House & Garden	30 Wandsworth Rd	020 7394 2100	Homebase for the unique, antique, or eccentric.
New Covent Garden Market	New Covent Garden Market	020 7720 2211	Known as London's Larder. Nowhere near Covent Garden

Map 139 · Wandsworth (East)

Cake Boy	2 Kingfisher House, Battersea Reach	020 7978 5555	Cookery school and cake emporium extraordinaire.

Map 140 · Clapham Junction / Northcote Rd

Anita's Vintage Fashion Fair	Battersea Arts Centre, Lavender Hill	020 8325 5789	Hardcore collectors, designers, and students find inspiration amongst the rails.
Dub Vendor	274 Lavender Hill	020 7223 3757	Dub, reggae, ska, rocksteady, roots, dancehall record specialist.
EF Russ	101 Battersea Rise	020 7228 6319	Model specialist—trains, boats, planes and more.
Huttons	29 Northcote Rd	020 7223 5523	Eclectic mix of unusual clothes, furniture and gifts.
Kiehls	20 Northcote Rd	020 7350 2997	Can't beat face masks with algae extracts or pear-flavoured lipbalm.
QT Toys and Games	90 Northcote Rd	020 7223 8637	Toys for big and small kids. Cool gifts.
Party Superstores	268 Lavender Hill	020 7924 3210	The queues on Halloween will scare you to death.
Space NK Apothecary	46 Northcote Rd	020 7228 7563	Skin care heaven.
Sweaty Betty	136 Northcote Rd	020 7978 5444	Look like a total Betty, like, even when you're sweaty.
TK Maxx	St John's Rd & Barnard Rd	020 7228 8072	The best bargains in town.
Traid	28 St John's Rd	020 7924 3065	Characterful recycled clothes. Touch of wank, but still we like.
Vintage Market Place	Battersea Arts Centre	020 8325 5789	Hardcore collectors, designers, and students find inspiration amongst the rails.
Whole Foods Market	305 Lavender Hill	020 7585 1488	Overwhelming selection of organic exotica.

Map 141 · Battersea (South)

Avalon Comics	143 Lavender Hill	020 7924 3609	Proper geeky indie comic shop. Marvel-lous.
Battersea Car Boot Sale	401 Battersea Park Rd	079 4138 3588	Yeah! A huge, tumultuous boot sale that starts mid afternoon!
Comet Miniatures	44 Lavender Hill	020 7228 3702	Get your Airfix fix. Model shop and sci-fi.

Map 142 · Clapham Old Town

Puppet Planet	787 Wandsworth Rd	020 7627 0111	Not great if you're pupaphobic but otherwise rather charming.

Map 143 · Clapham High Street

Apex Cycles	40 Clapham High St	020 7622 1334	Bikes fixed, bikes sold.
Esca	160 Clapham High St	020 7622 2288	Your Clapham Common picnic starts here.
M. Moen & Sons	24 The Pavement	020 7622 1624	Butcher for the bourgeoisie, incredibly good, massively expensive.
Paws	62 Clapham High St	020 7720 9962	Attendant, napping canines remind shoppers where the takings will go.
Today's Living Health Store	92 Clapham High St	020 7622 1772	Health foods, herbal remedies and other jiggery pokery.

Map 144 · Stockwell / Brixton (West)

A&C Co Continental Grocers	3 Atlantic Rd	020 7733 3766	Portuguese-owned institution, famous for pestos, chorizo and mamma's tortilla.
Lisa Stickley London	74 Landor Rd	020 7737 8067	Dotty 1940s-inspired handbags to tea-towels. Cath Kidston but better.
The Old Post Office Bakery	76 Landor Rd	020 7326 4408	Disused P.O turned artisan baker's. Local loaf? The Brixton Rye.

Map 146 · Earlsfield

The Earlsfield Bookshop	513 Garratt Ln	020 8946 3744	Dusty old secondhand book haven.

Map 147 · Balham (West)

Bon Vivant	59 Nightingale Ln	020 8675 6314	Great local deli.

Map 148 · Balham (East)

Moxon's	Westbury Parade	020 8675 2468	Fresh fish for foodies with deep pockets. Knowledgeable staff.

Map 149 · Clapham Park

MacFarlanes	48 Abbeville Rd	020 8673 5373	Gourmet goodness galore.

Map 150 · Brixton

Traid	2 Acre Ln	020 7326 4330	Characterful recycled clothes. Touch of wank, but still we like.

Map 151 · Tooting Bec

Russell's Hardware & DIY	46 Upper Tooting Rd	020 8767 7555	DIY treasure chest. Friendly, helpful owners.
Wandsworth Oasis HIV/AIDs Charity Shop	40 Trinity Rd	020 8767 7555	Thrift store treasure trove.

Map 152 · Tooting Broadway

Tooting Market	21 Tooting High St	020 8672 4760	Quaint indoor labyrinth worth nosing about.

to rebuild or re-map your city transport?

we've Quickmapped England's largest city and Scotland's too

we've also MapMovie'd England's largest sports venue Wembley, the largest shopping complex Meadowhall Sheffield and greatest street festival Notting Hill carnival.

commission us to MapMovie your opportunity

Street Index

Street Index

Aspen Way	100	A2	Avarn Road	152	A2	Baildon Street	119	B1
	101	A2	Ave Maria Lane	15	B2	Bailey Mews	127	B1
Aspenlea Road	47	A1	Avebury Street	84	A1	Bainbridge Street	4	B1
Aspern Grove	57	B1	Aveline Street	131	B2	Baird Street	7	A2
Aspinden Road	109	B1	Avenell Road	62	B2	Baker Street	1	A2
Apsley Road	138	B2		74	A2		76	B2
Assam Street	95	A1		75	A1	Baker's Mews	2	B1
Assata Mews	75	B1	The Avenue	38	A2	Baker's Rents	91	A1
Assembly Passage	97	A2		120	A2	Baker's Row	5	B2
Astbury Road	124	A2		140	A2/B2		6	B1
Aste Street	103	A1		141	B1	Bakers Field	73	A2
Astell Street	45	A2/B2		147	A2	Bakers Hall Court	18	B1
Astle Street	141	A2		148	A2	Bakery Close	135	B1
Aston Street	98	A1	Avenue Close	69	B2	Bakery Place	140	A1
Astoria Walk	145	B1	Avenue Road	52	A2	Balaclava Road	108	B1
Astrop Mews	40	A2		53	A1	Balcombe Street	76	B2
Astrop Terrace	40	A2		66	B2	Balcorne Street	90	B1
Astwood Mews	36	B1		69	A1/B1	Balderton Street	2	B1
Asylum Road	116	B1	Averill Street	47	A2	Baldwin Crescent	121	A1
	124	A1	Avery Farm Row	19	B2	Baldwin Street	7	A2
Atalanta Street	47	A2	Avery Row	2	B2	Baldwin Terrace	83	B1
Atheldene Road	146	B1	Avis Square	97	B2	Baldwin's Gardens	14	A2
Athelstane Grove	94	B1	Avoca Road	151	A2/B2	Bale Road	98	A1
Athelstane Mews	62	B1	Avocet Close	115	A1	Balfe Street	79	B1
Atherden Road	87	A2	Avondale Park Gardens	28	B1	Balfern Grove	38	B2
Atherfold Road	143	A2	Avondale Park Road	28	B1	Balfern Street	132	B2
Atherstone Mews	36	B1	Avondale Rise	129	A2	Balfour Mews	9	A1
Atherton Street	132	B2	Avondale Square	115	A1	Balfour Place	9	A1
Athlone Close	87	B2	Avonley Road	125	A1/B1	Balfour Road	75	A2
Athlone Street	71	A2	Avonmore Place	34	B1	Balfour Street	113	A1/A2
Atkins Road	148	A2	Avonmore Road	34	B1/B2	Balham Grove	148	A1/B1
	149	B1/B2	Avonmouth Street	106	B1	Balham High Road	147	B2
	150	B1	Axminster Road	61	B1/B2		148	A2/B1
Atlantic Road	127	A1/B1	Aybrook Street	2	A1		151	A1/A2
	144	A1	Aylesbury Road	113	B2	Balham Hill	148	A2
Atlas Mews	74	A2	Aylesbury Street	6	B1/B2	Balham New Road	148	B1
	86	B1	Aylesford Street	21	B1/B2	Balham Park Road	147	B1/B2
Atney Road	136	A2	Aylward Street	97	A1/A2	Balham Station Road	148	B1
Atterbury Road	55	B1	Aynhoe Road	41	A2	Balladier Walk	99	B2
Atterbury Street	21	A2	Ayres Street	106	A1	Ballance Road	90	A2
Attneave Street	6	B1	Ayrsome Road	64	A2	Ballantine Street	138	A2
Atwood Road	40	B2	Ayrton Road	36	A2	Ballast Quay	103	B2
Aubert Park	74	A2	Aytoun Place	145	A1	Ballater Road	144	B1
	75	A1	Aytoun Road	145	A1	Ballingdon Road	147	A2
Aubert Road	75	A1	Azania Mews	71	A2	Balls Pond Place	82	A1
Aubrey Place	68	B1	Azenby Road	122	B2	Balls Pond Road	82	A1/A2
Aubrey Road	29	B1	Azof Street	103	B2	Balmer Road	94	B1
	54	B1				Balmes Road	82	B1/B2
Aubrey Walk	29	B1	**B**			Balmoral Grove	73	B2
Auburn Close	125	B2				Balmore Street	59	A1
Auckland Road	140	A1	Baalbec Road	75	B1	Balniel Gate	21	B2
Auckland Street	131	A2	Babmaes Street	23	A2	Baltic Court	110	A2
Auden Place	70	B1	Baches Street	84	B1	Baltic Place	82	B2
Audley Close	141	B2	Back Church Lane	95	A1/A2/B2	Baltic Street East	7	A2/B2
Audley Square	9	A1	Back Hill	5	A1	Baltic Street West	7	B1/B2
Audrey Street	88	B2	Back Lane	53	A2	Balvaird Place	21	B2
Augusta Street	99	B2		56	B1	Bamber Road	123	A1
Augustine Road	33	B2	Backhouse Place	114	A1	Bamborough Gardens	33	B1
	41	A2	Bacon Grove	107	B2	Banbury Road	90	B1/B2
Augustus Close	40	A2	Bacon Street	91	A1/A2	Banbury Street	132	B2
Augustus Street	77	A2	Bacons Lane	51	B1	Bancroft Road	92	B2
Auriga Mews	64	B1	Bacton Street	93	A1		93	B1
Auriol Road	34	B1	Baden Place	106	A2	Banfield Road	130	A2
Austin Friars	17	A2	Badminton Road	147	A2	Banim Street	40	A2/B2
Austin Friars Passage	17	A2	Badsworth Road	121	A2	Banister Mews	65	B2
Austin Road	141	A2	Baffin Way	101	A2	The Bank	51	B2
Austin Street	91	A1	Bagley's Lane	49	A2	Bank End	106	A1
Austral Street	104	B2		50	A1	Bank Street	100	B2
Avalon Road	49	A2	Bagshot Street	114	A1/B1	Bankside	105	A2

Street Index

Street Index

Street Index

Street Index

Street Index

Street Index

Street Index

Street Index

Street Index

Street Index

Street Index

Street Index

Street Index

Street Index

Street Index

Street Index

Street Index

Street Index

Street Index

Street Index

Street Index

Street Index

Street Index

Street Index

Street Index

Street Index